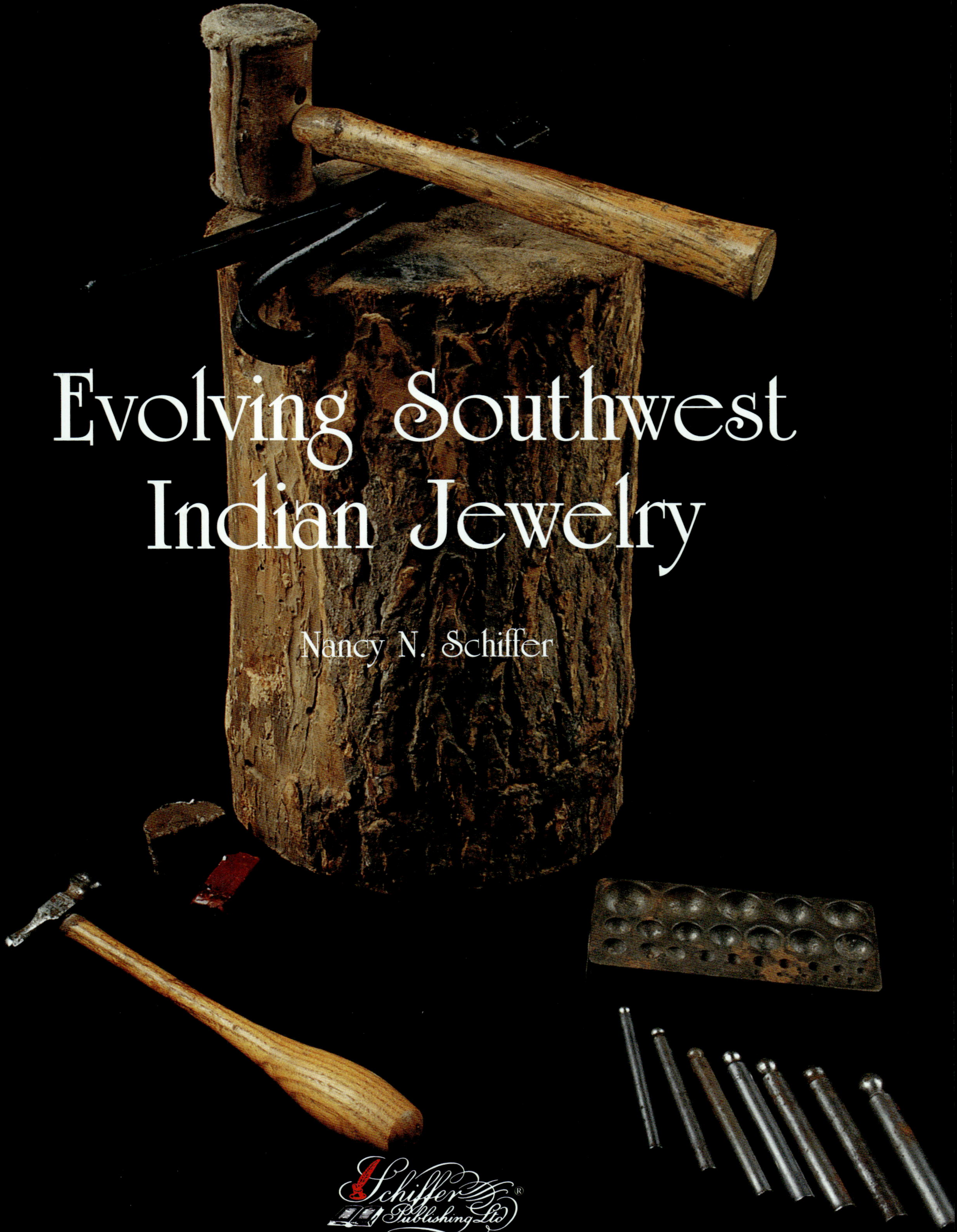

Evolving Southwest Indian Jewelry

Nancy N. Schiffer

Schiffer Publishing Ltd®
4880 Lower Valley Road, Atglen, PA 19310 USA

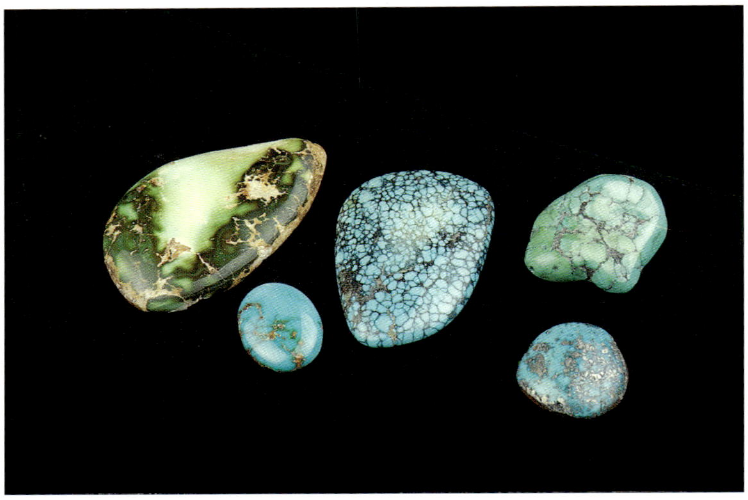

Turquoise cabochons. *Courtesy Lynn D. Trusdell, Crown & Eagle Antiques.*

Library of Congress Control Number: 2003100148

Designed by Bonnie M. Hensley
Cover design by Bruce Waters
Type set in UnivrstyRoman Bd BT/Zurich BT

ISBN: 0-7643-1723-7
Printed in China
1 2 3 4

Published by Schiffer Publishing Ltd.
4880 Lower Valley Road
Atglen, PA 19310
Phone: (610) 593-1777; Fax: (610) 593-2002
E-mail: Schifferbk@aol.com
Please visit our web site catalog at **www.schifferbooks.com**
We are always looking for people to write books on new and related subjects. If you have an idea for a book, please contact us at the above address.

This book may be purchased from the publisher.
Include $3.95 for shipping. Please try your bookstore first.
You may write for a free catalog.

In Europe, Schiffer books are distributed by
Bushwood Books
6 Marksbury Ave. Kew Gardens
Surrey TW9 4JF England
Phone: 44 (0)20 8392-8585; Fax: 44 (0)20 8392-9876
E-mail: Bushwd@aol.com
Free postage in the UK. Europe: air mail at cost.
Please try your bookstore first.

Current Market Values are included for contemporary jewelry where they were available. Vintage and antique jewelry is unique, their values depending entirely on a subjective market; therefore, they are not evaluated here.

Acknowledgments

My gratitude is extended to the many people who have contributed to this book by sharing their knowledge and collections with me, and thereby with the readers. It is upon their shoulders, and the shoulders of the authors cited in the bibliography, that this project began.

I especially thank Lynn D. Trusdell, a specialist in old silver jewelry at Crown and Eagle Antiques, Inc., New Hope, Pennsylvania. Particular thanks also must be given to Indian trader Walter Kennedy, who shared the jewelry in his Dennehotso collection, which he gathered over many years of work in the remote northern sections of the Navajo reservation. And I especially acknowledge a wonderful private collector who has chosen to remain anonymous.

Sincere appreciation goes to:

Al Anthony, Adobe Gallery, Albuquerque and Santa Fe
Diana and Guy Berger, Palms Trading Company, Albuquerque
Eilene and Eric Bromberg
Margerete and Fred Chase, Enchanted Mesa Indian Arts, Albuquerque
Elizabeth B. Collar, Albuquerque
Bing Crosby, Bing Crosby's Indian Art, Inc., Albuquerque
Donna Davies, Gerald Peters Gallery, Santa Fe
Caroline Foreback, Indian Post, Allentown, Pennsylvania
Tommy Elkins, Willa and Tom Bastien, Indian Traders West, Santa Fe
Ed and Jeff Foutz, Shiprock Trading Company, Shiprock
Kay and Bill Foutz, Foutz Trading Company, Shiprock
Cathren and Mary Harris, Turquoise Lady, Albuquerque
Ed Houters, Tandy Brands Accessories Company, Fort Worth
Harold L. James
Beverly McGee, McGee's Indian Arts, Holbrook
Bruce and Ron McGee, McGee's Indian Art Gallery, Keams Canyon
Nancy Peake
Lisa and Timothy Pitt
Leonard D. Prins, Prins and Volkhardt Jewelers, Strafford, Pennsylvania.
Marian Rodee, curator, Maxwell Museum, University of New Mexico, Albuquerque
Bert and Peter Schiffer, for their help with the photographs
Tim Scott, for his help with the manuscript and his wonderful pictures
Jim Silva, Bernalillo
Sarah and Bill Turnbaugh, University of Rhode Island
Peter Waidler, Dewey Gallery, Santa Fe
Bruce M. Waters for his fine photography
Tom Woodard, Santa Fe
Margaret and Barton Wright
Fern Yung, Crow's Nest Art Gallery, La Porte, Texas
and those who prefer to remain anonymous. Thank you all.

Title page: Pounding block and silversmithing tools in use since the early 20th century. *Courtesy of Tom Z.*

Contents

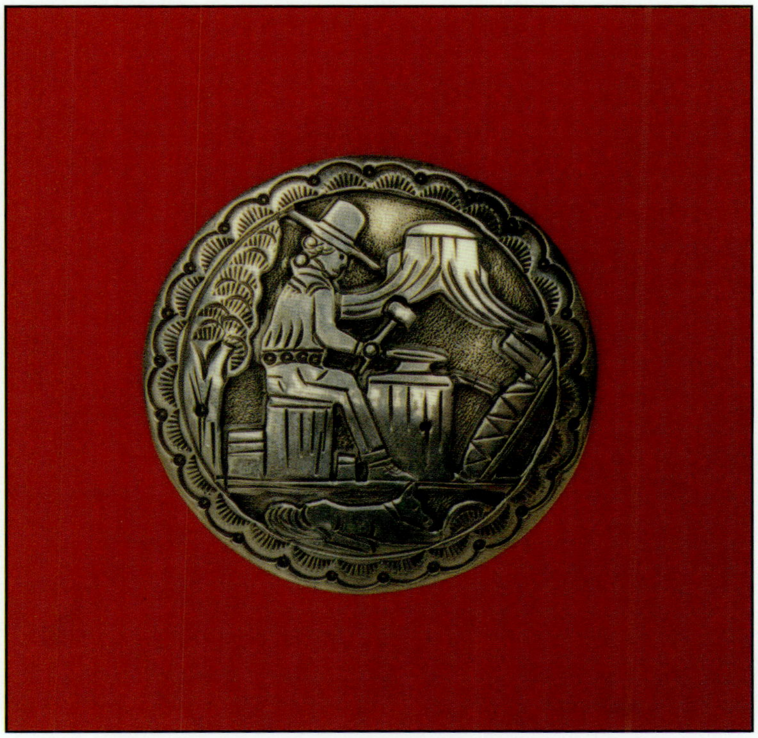

Sterling silver pin depicting a Navajo silversmith at his work-bench with a high mesa in the background. Signed JD

Traders Among the Silversmiths

The beginnings of Southwest Indian silversmithing extend back into the mid-nineteenth century when various influences converged. Arthur Woodward gives a convincing argument for the antecedents in eastern woodland Indian cultures and their trade with white trappers.[1] As these Indians were pushed westward to the Great Plains, the silver ornament tradition was modified but was carried along. Trade and hostile relations among Plains and Southwest tribes introduced silver to the Navajos. Coupled to this are stories of itinerant Spanish/Mexican silversmiths working among the Rio Grande Pueblos and Navajo in the early decades of the nineteenth century. They undoubtedly provided silver items to the Indians and taught their trade as well. Then came the Long March to Bosque Redondo (1863), at Fort Defiance, Arizona, where the Navajo witnessed much of white man's culture. Here, Indians who knew blacksmithing saw modern techniques of that trade. The step to Indians silversmithing was not far behind. John Adair presents a good discussion of the probable first Indian silversmiths and their forges, primitive but effective as they were.[2] The progression of influences is fascinating research and recommended to the readers of this work. For this study, though, we are not so much concerned with how the Southwest Indians learned silversmithing as what they did with it once learned. It is the evolution of design concepts that interests this author. Therefore we accept that silversmithing was learned, and hope to examine the evolution of forms that has subsequently taken place.

Enough cannot be said about the influences non-Indian traders have had on the development of jewelry styles in the American Southwest. Since the beginning of the reservation system in 1868, many traders have taken up the challenge to make a life among the Indians profitable and pleasant. McNitt goes to great effort in his thorough book *Indian Traders* to accurately document the lives of some of the earliest generations of these entrepreneurs. "In the Southwest, traders...most fully realized their effectiveness as an influence for the Indians' good. While the agent often had his own interests to serve—financial, religious, or political—traders have helped to better the lot of the Indian."[3]

"To better the lot" is a judgmental statement, made in retrospect, and with all the cultural differences in the world hanging in the balance. It is not in the scope of this work, either, to confront the issues, which come up each time, a person of one culture passes judgment on the work of a person of another culture. Instead, those issues are kept apart from this study of the jewelry as a continually developing art form. Therefore, we will try to point out some examples of influences traders have had on the evolving jewelry designs.

The influences are seen to be both direct and indirect. Sometimes the economic situation warranted drastic changes in the jewelry business so that it would benefit both the trader and the jewelers. Or, traders would make available certain materials or tools or instruction which the jewelers could utilize in their designs. Other times incentives were imposed on the communities from the outside: world wars, rationed materials, or consumer demand were powerful influences. Working together, Indian craftsmen and white traders helped each other while they were involved in the daily business of making, using and selling jewelry.

Among the earliest and most influential white traders among the southwest Indians were the Spanish language interpreters, friends and later business competitors Thomas Keam and Juan Lorenzo Hubbell.

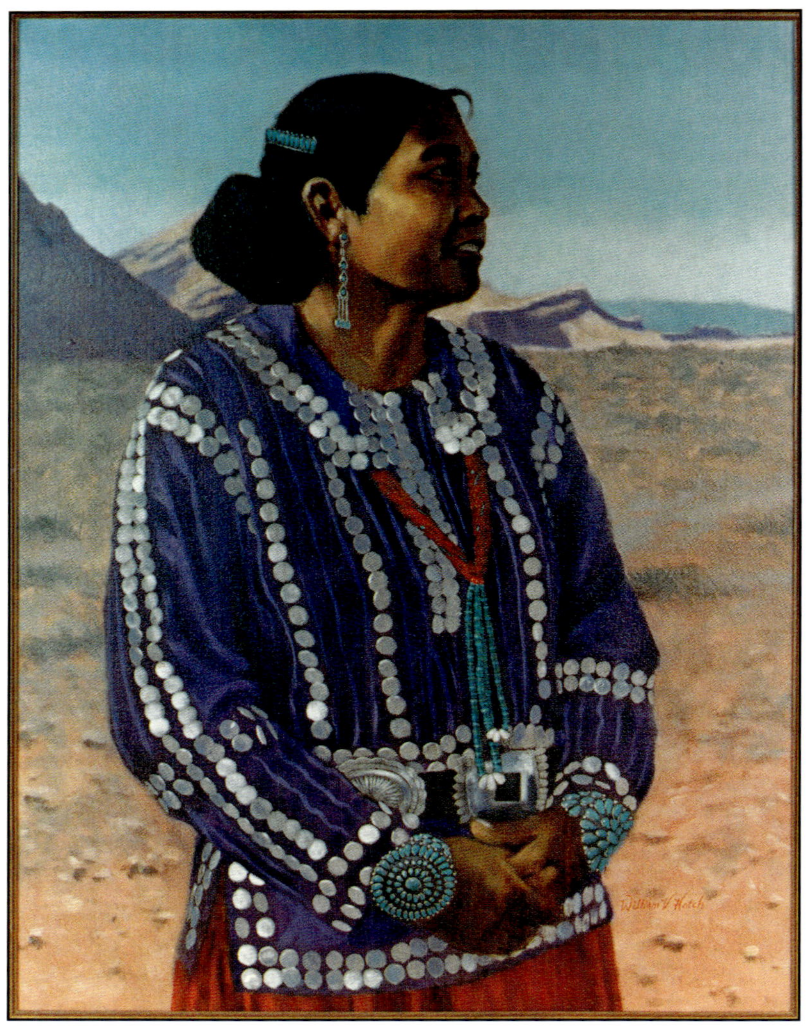

Oil painting of a Navajo woman wearing a velvet blouse decorated with silver buttons and a selection of Navajo jewelry. Painted by William V. Hatch, 1980s. *Dennehotso collection*.

Thomas Keam

Thomas Keam was an immigrant Englishman who had been a successful interpreter to the U.S. agent at Fort Defiance in 1869. After political jockeying for appointment as licensed traders, which went on for years,[4] Keam settled in a canyon at the edge of the Hopi homeland, which has come to bear his name. Keams Canyon was a desolate and hostile region in 1875 when Thomas and his brother, William Keam, were licensed to trade with the Navajo and Hopi Indians. Keam maintained a respectful attitude toward the local inhabitants, learned their languages and customs, and gained their trust. These abilities to relate to the Indians have been shared by all the successful traders. Keam very likely had contact with silver prospectors passing through his region.[5] "His pawn room glittered with a treasure of Navajo silver and turquoise."[6] In a letter of 1886 to Indian Commissioner J.D.C. Atkins, Keam discussed his offer to house a school for Hopi and Navajos and described the local Indians as "willing to work, and several have grown rich by their trades of silversmith, blacksmith, or saddler, which they have acquired from their contact with the few whites near them."[7] A petition signed by twenty Hopi governors or clan priests at the same time (1886) read in part:

> We are also greatly concerned for our children. We pray that they may follow in their fathers' footsteps and grow up—good of heart and pure of breath. Yet we can see that things are changing around us, and many Americans are coming in this region. We would like our children to learn Americans' tongue and their ways of work.
>
> We pray you to cause a school to be opened in our country, and we will gladly send our children."[8]

The school opened in the fall of 1887.

In 1901 Keam is known to have shown some interest in a copper mining venture on the Navajo reservation in an area still known as Keam's District which has been successfully mined in the decades hence. He undoubtedly encouraged the local people to help themselves, and learning jewelry making was one way they could do that.

Thomas Keam sold his trading post to Lorenzo Hubbell, Jr. in 1902, and went to his family home in England where he died in 1904. The McGee family owns the post presently.

J. L. Hubbell

New Mexico native Juan Lorenzo Hubbell began a trading business at Fort Defiance, Arizona, in about 1871 or 1872. His knowledge of the Spanish language and terrain made him useful to the U.S. Army there on numerous occasions to help them deal with the local people. Through the Indian agency at Fort Defiance in 1874, he and fellow translator Thomas Keam were asked to help work out some difficult political border problems[9] with Navajo leader Ganado Mucho and other Indian leaders. Later, in 1878, Hubbell bought the Pueblo Colorado trading post from William B. Leonard, which had been started by Charles Crary in 1871. It is probably no coincidence that a neighbor of the Pueblo Colorado site was Navajo leader Ganado Mucho whom Hubbell had known by then for several years. This leader encouraged his people to trade with Hubbell then and even after he became chief of all the Navajos, and out of respect for their friendship, Hubbell named his trading post "Ganado," a name by which the place has continued to be known. Ganado Mucho was buried at a small hill overlooking Hubbell's store.

Hubbell's business flourished under these conditions, for he could supply his Indian customers with food, tobacco and farming supplies in exchange for their blankets, crops and wool. From this location, Hubbell, like all traders before 1880, sent teams of oxen with trade goods to Albuquerque, New Mexico, and on to Fort Dodge, Kansas, by way of the Rio Grande valley and over the Santa Fe trail. On the return trip they brought back supplies from the East for their trading posts. In 1880 Hubbell opened a second trading post at Navajo leader Manuelito's vicinity east of Fort Defiance, but he held it only one year. This was the first of Hubbell's expansion posts, which eventually dotted Arizona and gave him a commanding strength in the trading business. Also in 1880-1881, the Atlantic & Pacific Railroad was completed through Albuquerque and continued west, so supplies became easier for him to obtain at depots close to Ganado.

Navajos near the post were influenced by M. Hubbell's fascination for design. His rug business was increased significantly after he instituted colors and designs from Turkish rugs.[10] Jewelry makers of the region used some of the same designs in their work and were able to get the Persian turquoise he imported from 1890 inward.

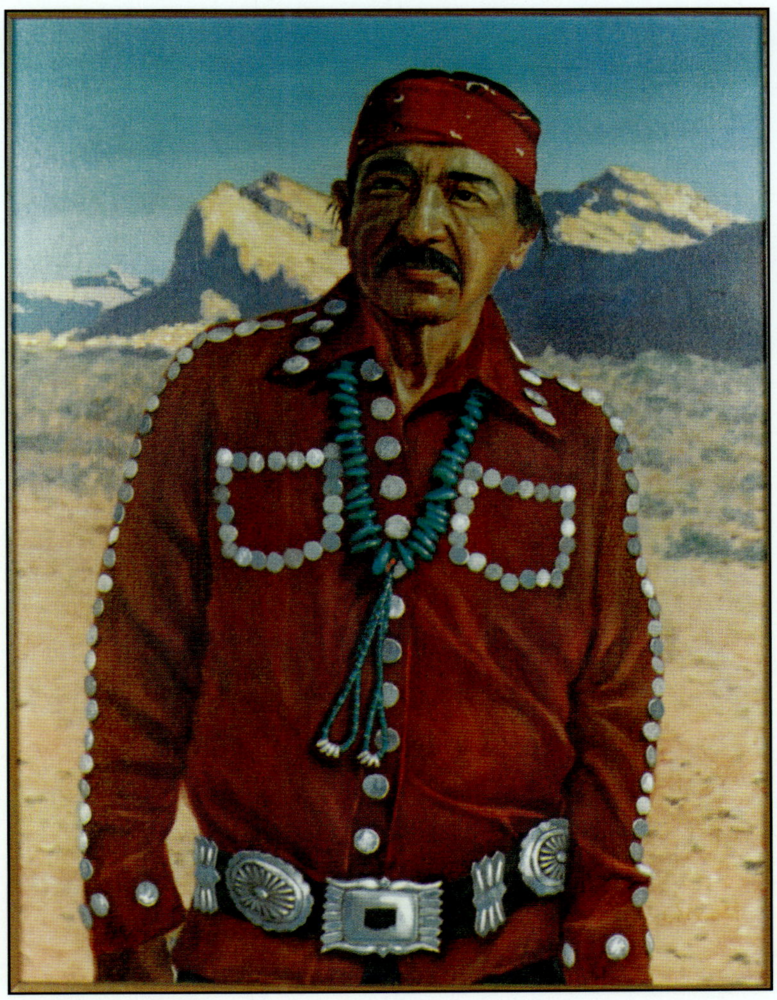

Oil painting of a Navajo man wearing an assortment of Navajo jewelry and a shirt ornamented with silver buttons. Painted by William V. Hatch, 1980s. *Dennehotso collection*.

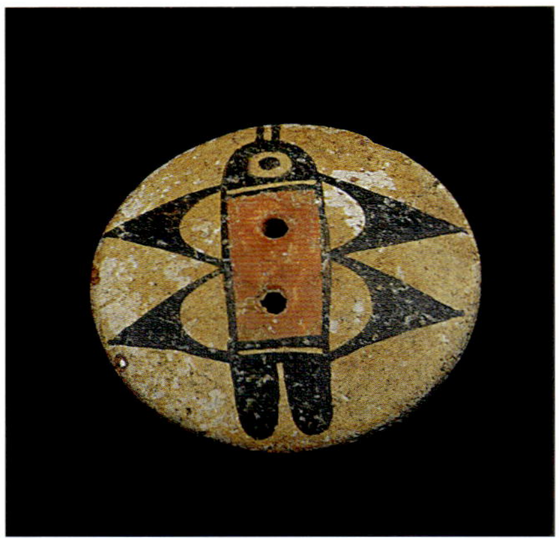

Early 20th century ceramic button made by Fanny Nampeyo, Hopi. The stylized dragonfly design appears on a button probably made for a woman's shawl. *Courtesy Lynn D. Trusdell, Crown & Eagle Antiques.*

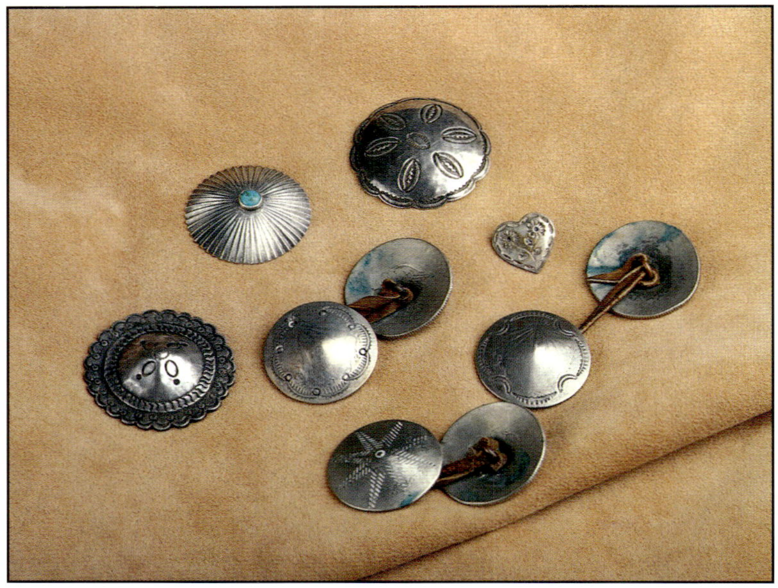

Navajo silver buttons of the type often used on women's bull hide and buck skin boots. *Courtesy Lynn D. Trusdell, Crown & Eagle Antiques.*

After 1900, when more tourists came, many of the old Indian mines known since ancient times were opened up to make local turquoise available again.

The trading post was kept under Hubbell family control until 1967, when it became part of the U.S. National Park system. Today the post is kept operating by trader Bill Malone.

Tools

While stationed at Fort Wingate as surgeon to the U.S. Army, Washington Matthews wrote and article, *"Navajo Silversmiths"*, which was published in 1880-1881 in the Second Report of the Bureau of Ethnology. Herein he states that, besides the raw silver bars to make the jewelry,

Doubtless the tools obtained from American and Mexican traders have influenced their art. Ordinary scissors, purchased from the whites, are used for cutting their metal after it is wrought into thin plates...Their iron pliers, hammers, and files they purchase from the whites... Awls...are sometimes purchased and sometimes made by the Indians... Their borax is purchased from the whites, and from the same source is derived the fine wire with which they bind together the parts to be soldered... For polishing, they have sandpaper and emery-paper purchased from the whites.[11]

Traders, then and subsequently also provided decorative punches. Leather stampers also used early punches, and the designs on late nineteenth-century jewelry bear this out. The simple star and crescent punches were used to create designs that continue to dominate much of the jewelry of a traditional nature. In the 1880s, four traders got commercially made dies with designs of their own choosing which had no meaning to the Indians. They were merely decorative. Unfortunately, some designs were presumed by other white people to be of Indian origin when they were not.

Pawn

At the trading posts, the early traders bought and sold goods and many conducted a barter system which developed in a land practically devoid of hard cash. An Indian's jewelry was an important feature of the barter system, called pawn, for in place of cash the jewelry could be held as credit by a trader as collateral on the next season's wool, sheep, or crop. In 1885, the son of a Navajo named Tymolti came into the store [at Ganado] and requested to see a silver belt he had left there in pawn. He had pawned the belt so he could pay a bet. When [the trader] Cotton laid the belt on the counter for the brave to see it, he grabbed it, ran off, mounted his horse and raced away. Cotton requested the Indian Agent to recover the belt for him; to no avail.[12]

C. N. Cotton

In 1881, 22-year old Clinton Neal Cotton from Ohio rode the new railroad west to Albuquerque to seek his fortune. He had helped to support his family since he was eleven, when his father died, by working as an apprentice telegraph operator. Once in Albuquerque, he obtained a job with the Atlantic & Pacific Railroad at their most western post. As the track building progressed, Cotton moved with it and reached Fort Wingate that year. Here in the midst of Navajo territory, Cotton was an important link with the rest of the world. He transferred orders for supplies and livestock and composed all the communications for the out-going messages. Cotton learned everything about the business transactions in that area. He became acquainted with important Navajo chiefs as well as white traders, and those friendships lasted his lifetime.

During this period, Cotton made the acquaintance of Juan Lorenzo Hubbell. As Hubbell's trading empire was growing, his service was also needed in the community settling disputes between the Indians and the U. S. government. That meant he needed a trustworthy partner to run his business while he dealt with politics. Cotton apparently impressed Hubbell favorably, for Cotton bought half interest in Hubbell's Ganado trading post in 1884. While Hubbell cultivated his political interests, Cotton ran the business. In fact, in June of 1885, Cotton bought out Hubbell's half interest in Ganado. Because of boundary disputes at Ganado itself between 1887 and 1900, Cotton was the licensed trader there, and Hubbell was designated the clerk.

In late 1888, Cotton moved his wife and two children from Ganado to Gallup, New Mexico, where, because of the coal deposits nearby, a decent sized town was growing next to the railroad tracks. He continued to run the business at Ganado, but he also built in Gallup a two-story warehouse measuring 25 X 60 feet. By then "he must have concluded the only way to get ahead would be to develop a wholesale business, selling to traders but especially buying wool, blankets and jewelry and to establish this business at a point favorably located for transportation."[13]

Cotton also was one of the first traders to recognize potential for a commercial market for Navajo silver.

At the time there was no outside demand for Navajo silverwork, but Cotton was planning for the years ahead. Prior to 1900 most Navajo silverwork was made just for the Navajo themselves. He discussed it with Hubbell, then brought in from Cubero, New Mexico a Mexican silversmith named Naakaii Daadil, which means *thick-lipped Mexican*. Cotton introduced him at Ganado in 1884, and with Benedito and other silversmiths from Mexico, Naakaii Daadil started teaching the craft to the men in Ganado. Cotton wrote later that in 1898 he shipped a mass of early Navajo silverware to the Denver mint as bullion and received for it the sum of $800.[14]

From these early years of contact, the traders were providing some of the necessary ingredients for the growth of jewelry production. But the success of the industry would only be measured if the jewelry would sell.

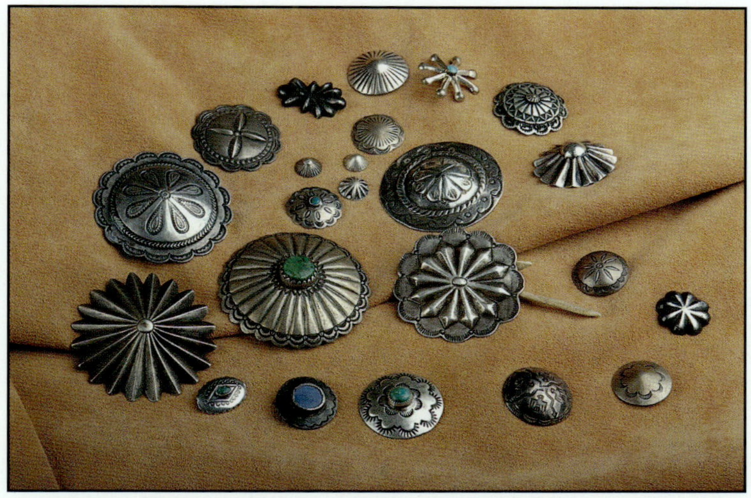

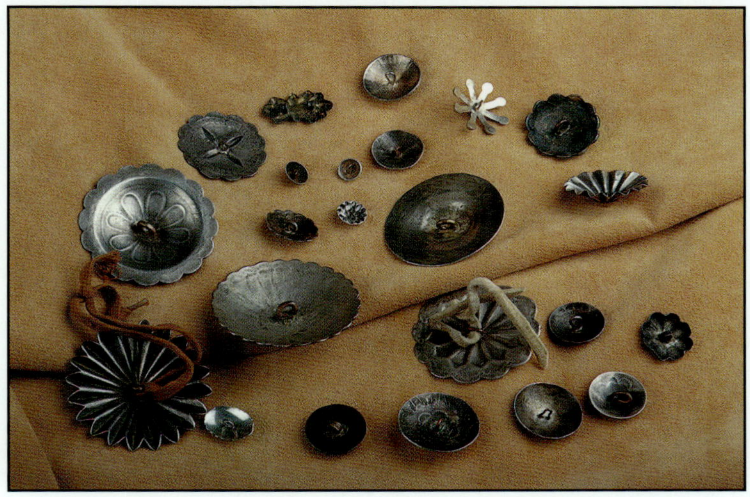

Early silver Navajo buttons with fine chisel work and embossing decoration. The back view shows copper loops to secure the buttons to clothing. *Courtesy Lynn D. Trusdell, Crown & Eagle Antiques.*

Fred Harvey Company

When Fred Harvey founded his company in 1876, he opened a lunchroom at the Santa Fe Railroad station in Topeka, Kansas. He built this restaurant with his experience as a dishwasher and restaurant worker for 25 years, which he acquired after he came to the United States from England at the age of 15.

From his vantage on the Topeka station platform, he foresaw opportunity, and convinced the president of the Santa Fe that he could provide better dining to the railway passengers. Twenty-five years later, he owned 26 restaurants along the train routes, 16 hotel / restaurants, 15 newsstands, and 20 dining cars.

When the railroad came to Albuquerque in 1880, representatives of the Fred Harvey Company arrived, too. They were gradually building rest stops dedicated to the comforts of the Eastern tourists for whom travel beyond the rail lines was adventure in itself. By 1889 when the trains went that far, tourists detrained and took horse and wagon pack trains north from Gallup to Ganado and on west to Keams Canyon to see the Indians. Gradually, the Fred Harvey Company provided not only food and shelter at the train stops, but gift shops as well with souvenirs from this exotic region. Company people bought trinkets, blankets, baskets, pottery and jewelry from the white traders on and near the reservations to resell in their own shops.

In 1899, a Harvey Company man named Herman Schweizer became the main organizer and buyer for the Fred Harvey Indian Department.

One of his earliest projects involved linking up with the commercial network built up by the traders, and thereby establishing contact with the Navajo producers. He needed such contact because he had some ideas about how Navajo jewelry might be modified to make it more marketable to Anglo customers. While the Navajo themselves liked their jewelry massive, large and bold, Anglo travelers and tourists favored jewelry that was lighter and a bit more delicate. Schweizer decided that he could increase his supply and demand at the same time by providing the Navajo silversmiths with materials like sheet silver and pre-cut stones through a number of trading posts. Commercially this plan proved a great success. The smiths began to make lighterweight jewelry at a good rate of production and the products sold readily in the Harvey Company outlets.[15]

Schweizer also brought Indian silversmiths into Albuquerque to demonstrate, and therefore heighten tourist's interest in, jewelry making.

The success of this venture did have an effect on the nature of Navajo jewelry. Many Navajo artisans began to produce lighter and cheaper jewelry specifically for this tourist market, and there is some truth to the charge that this commercial emphasis posed a threat to the vigor of native Navajo design. I am among those, on the other hand, who maintain that this commercial venture had more beneficial than detrimental effects in the long run. It exposed a very large number of non-Indian people to at least a taste of the satisfactions inherent in Navajo art, thereby helping significantly to build the grass-roots base of appreciation of the sort that nurtures any vital art form. And it allowed many more Navajo than might otherwise have done so to learn the basics of the craft and the design vocabulary. More top-rate artists are going to emerge from a large population of craftsmen than from a small group, other things being equal.[16]

Herman Schweizer continued in this capacity strengthening his influence on the silver industry and eagerly building a big business for the Company through the growth of the tourist trade in the 1920s. Harvey stores all along the railroad lines were supplied with Indian goods, including jewelry, in large quantities. Not only did he provide goods for the stores, but also serious private collectors and major museums came to him throughout the period to acquire Indian products for their collections. He also helped to create a large Company collection, which was distributed in the 1980s primarily to the Heard Museum in Phoenix and Museum of Northern Arizona in Flagstaff. His impact publicizing the Indian crafts throughout the country, coupled with the growing number of traders during the period, is fact. During the 1930s, as the Depression years gripped the country, Schweizer saw the business change. Tourism fell off, sales slackened, and by 1939 he "commented unhappily, 'People just simply are not looking for anything except modern products and mostly cheaper things.'[17]

Gallup

Mexican and Spanish traders dominated commercial trade with the Navajo south of Gallup, N. M. from the days of the Conquistadors in the 16th century through the middle of the 19th century. Trouble with Navajo Indians in the area was constant for the U.S. Army even after the new Fort Wingate was established nearby in 1868. When the railroad was built, on its way to California, many traders were attracted to the area and built posts all along its fringes. One of the early traders here was Hans Neumann at Guam, N. M. who supplied Herman Schweizer, at his request, with some of the first rugs with swastika designs.[18] Some jewelry of the early 1900s also has swastika designs as decoration. Later, in the 1930s, its association with Nazi Germany made it an illegal design, so it was not used again until very modern times (1980s) when it regained its Indian name, "whirling logs." Gallup's gradual growth commercially eventually eclipsed many of the outlying traders including Neumann by 1913.

Gallup has continued to be the major Navajo trading point, and many families besides Cotton grew here. The Woodards, Turpens, and others each had bench silversmiths who worked for them and took their suggestions for jewelry designs. For example, after a "thunderbird" petroglyph design was found during excavations in the 1920s, a stylized thunderbird appeared on jewelry for the tourist trade. It has no meaning in the Indian culture.

At Zuni, just south of Gallup, many traders came and went from the 1870s forward, including the Vanderwagens whose patriarch Andrew came from Holland in 1896 as a missionary for the Christian Reform church in Michigan. Finding little success in his work, he eventually stayed as a trader because he liked the people. In the 1920s, C.G. Wallace began to organize the jewelry business here with great success.

Concern for the promotion of Indian arts and crafts among the traders throughout the Southwest caused an organization to be formed in 1931 in Gallup called the United Indian Traders Association (see mark on page 217). The members were instrumental in providing guidelines for the quality of crafts and a system of marking them to insure to the public the purity of Indian-made claims for their origin.

C.G. Wallace/Zuni

In 1918 Charles Garrett Wallace, a 20-year-old from North Carolina, boldly followed a childhood fascination with Indian stories and culture, came to visit a friend in Gallup and stayed. He got a job with a trader at Zuni, and after a few years bought the post for himself. At the time, there were "five smiths in the village who were doing some silver work, primarily for their own people, and some for the Navajo."[19]

Wallace saw potential for all if their energy could be channeled to productivity, and he must have been persuasive for this is a success story in the end. "When I came to Zuni, they gambled, they played and they didn't do much work at all. I made up my mind that I'd have every man, woman and child working — and by the time I left [1970] just about all of them were."[20]

He obtained for Zuni craftsmen turquoise from a shop in Denver, and eventually from mines at Lone Mountain, Nevada; Villa Grove, Colorado; copper mines in Arizona, and the Last Chance mine in Arizona, which he owned. He encouraged jewelry making during the 1930s with turquoise inlay, particularly promoting channel inlay techniques. He urged Zuni silversmiths to stamp silver to make the jewelry more ornate and eventually worked with about 300 Zuni and Navajo smiths. He and his staff worked hard to sell the jewelry to Navajos, other traders, museums, and general customers all over the country. He encouraged them to "stay with tradition and do unique pieces... I didn't want their work to become too common. Individuality and authenticity are what made Indian jewelry valuable."[21] During the 1940s, when turquoise became hard to get, he introduced tortoise shell, petrified wood, and colored shell for inlay in channel settings.

Mr. Wallace became successful in his work by several accounts. His encouragement sponsored an artistic awakening among the Zuni, which has proven appealing to the buying public. Many families at Zuni now are supported by the jewelry business. His personal wealth was secured through his work and a large collection of Indian jewelry that was auctioned in 1975.

Other Traders

Many other traders also worked closely with Indian silversmiths and found new customers around the country. For example, Fred Chase worked for C.G. Wallace at Zuni for a number of years and later ran with his wife, Margarete, the Enchanted Mesa shop in Albuquerque. Many customers of all these traders have contributed to the success of the changing Indian jewelry designs. Albuquerque grew to become major distribution point for trade with the East, while Scottsdale, Arizona, developed into a resort and art town especially serving customers to the west.

In the northern reaches of the Navajo reservation, Mormon settlers seeking religious freedom came and several became traders. The Shiprock post was begun in 1903 by W.T. Shelton, who conducted craft fairs each October with prizes to encourage the natives. Others who came were H.B. Noel, the Hatch family, Bruce Bernard, Will Evans, Russell Foutz, and others. All of the families grew and many continue to trade today. (The Kennedy family came and worked inland at remote areas.) Their successes have helped to secure in the minds of the American people, if not the world at large, a prominent place for jewelry of the American southwest in folk art tradition.

Hopi

When Philadelphians from the University of Pennsylvania Dr. Harold S. and Mary-Russell Colton moved to Flagstaff, Arizona in 1926, they founded the Museum of Northern Arizona and worked to encourage and improve the quality of Hopi crafts. In 1930 they started an annual Hopi Craftsman Exhibit, and in 1931 the Junior Indian Art Show to encourage their work. By 1938, the Bureau of Indian Affairs' Indian Arts and Crafts Board was sponsoring projects to improve crafts. The Coltons saw this as an opportunity to get some support for their concerns for the Hopis.

Mrs. Colton developed some strong and far-sighted ideas, which she hoped, would benefit the craftsmen. In 1938 she wrote:

> There is only one way to make Hopi silversmithing worthwhile, it must be *different* from any other Indian silversmithing. They must produce *Hopi Silver*, not Navajo, Pueblo, or Zuni. It must be absolutely unique, and of course, the supply will always be limited. Therefore, if we can create a worthy product, using only *Hopi design*, and advertise it well, we might in time create a small worthwhile market.[22]

She gathered designs from Hopi baskets, pottery and textiles and planned with Virgil Hubert of the Museum staff how they could be used in silver appliqué techniques. Hopi silversmith Paul Saufkie was one of the first to try the designs and be successful. Others found they needed finer tools, different silver sources and solders. Gradually these problems were overcome, and by the end of 1941, several Hopi silversmiths were producing good results. But time and world events were not on their side. After the Japanese attack on Pearl Harbor in December of 1941, life changed dramatically. Not only were young men taken for national service, but also rationing curtailed many goods, especially metals and turquoise. The silver project at the museum was halted for five years.

After the war, the G.I. training program provided an opportunity for veterans to sponsor an 18-month silversmithing course for Hopi servicemen....The classes were started in February of 1947. Paul Saufkie was hired as the technical instructor and [another Hopi silversmith] Fred Kabotie, along with his job as an art teacher at Hopi High School in New Oraibi, was the design instructor.[23]

While the program taught many silver making techniques, one new one evolved which now is considered especially Hopi. The new technique, the *Hopi Silver*, came to be known as "overlay." Years later now, Hopi overlay is a solid part of the southwest Indian silver tradition, and smiths from other tribal backgrounds are incorporating it into their work. Overlay is a significant contribution to the continually evolving Indian style.

Later Developments

As the post-war economy in the 1950s improved, paved roads began to replace dirt in the reservation area. More travelers from Europe and America came to see the land and its people. By the early 1970s, Indian-made jewelry was entering a period of renewed popularity in America. In fact, by 1975, so great was the demand for Indian designs that experts feared for the future of the business because so much inferior jewelry was selling at prices that would have been gotten only for superior pieces five years previous. Not only were the Indians themselves falling into the habit of making lightweight silver with inferior stones, but foreign mass-produced jewelry was also found frequently available at shops throughout the country. A weakening in this trend occurred as the market became saturated and events in the Middle East drew the nation's interests to fuel economy rather than travel. By the early 1980s the rage for Indian silver jewelry subsided.

Artists, however, awakened perhaps by the boom years, continued to study and experiment, and built on the success of a few unusually talented makers. They helped to change jewelry design into its present state, combining more European styles and a wider range of materials so that traders have a wide range of choices to offer their customers.

Summary

Throughout the hundred year span of silver making in the Southwest, many of the innovations in jewelry design were instigated by traders to accommodate the tourist trade. Various non-Indians who foresaw progress to better the Indian's life style began innovation. "Navajo jewelry [is a product] of the interaction between a number of different cultures, and the rolls played by the Spanish and Anglos were just as vital and legitimate to the history of these art forms as was the role of the Navajo."[24] The evolution continues...

[1] Arthur Woodward, *Navajo Silver: A Brief History of Navajo Silversmithing* (Flagstaff, Ariz.: Northland Press, 1971), pp. 1-9.
[2] John Adair, *The Navajo and Pueblo Silversmiths* (Norman, Okla.: University of Oklahoma Press, 1975), pp 16ff.
[3] Frank McNitt, *The Indian Traders* (Norman, Okla.: University of Oklahoma Press, 1972), jacket summary.
[4] *Ibid*, p. 166ff.
[5] *Ibid*, p. 178.
[6] *Ibid*, p. 188.
[7] *Ibid*, p. 193.
[8] *Ibid*, p. 194.
[9] *Ibid*, pp. 146-153.
[10] Marian Rodee, *Weaving of the Southwest* (West Chester, Pa.: Schiffer Publishing Ltd., 1987), p.90.
[11] Washington Matthews, "Navajo Silversmiths," *Second Report of the Bureau of Ethnology; 1880-1881,* (Palmer Lake, Colo.: Filter Press, reprinted edition of 19680, pp. 25-32.
[12] Lester L. Williams, *C.N. Cotton and His Navajo Blankets* (Albuquerque: Avanyu Publishing Inc.), p. 19.
[13] *Ibid*, p. 29.
[14] *Ibid*, pp. 25-26.
[15] Byron Harvey III, E. W. Jernigan, and Gary Witherspoon, *White Metal Universe: Navajo Silver from the Fred Harvey Collection* (Phoenix: The Heard Museum, 1981), p. 11.
[16] *Ibid.*
[17] Byron Harvey III, *The Fred Harvey Fine Arts Collection, An Exhibition* (Phoenix: The Heard Museum, 1976), p.4.
[18] McNitt, *The Indian Traders*, p. 235.
[19] Mike Tharp, "You Can't Beat Something with Nothing," *Arizona Highways*, August 1974 (Phoenix: Arizona Department of Transportation), p. 37.
[20] *Ibid.*
[21] *Ibid*, p. 38.
[22] Margaret Nickelson Wright, *Hopi Silver, The History and Hallmarks of Hopi Silversmithing* (Flagstaff, Ariz.: Northland Press, 1989), p. 38.
[23] *Ibid*, pp. 47-48.
[24] Harvey, Jernigan, Witherspoon, *White Metal Universe*, p. 11.
[1] Dale Stuart King, *Indian Silverwork of the Southwest, Illustrated—Volume Two* (Tucson: Dale Stuart King, 1976), p. 61.

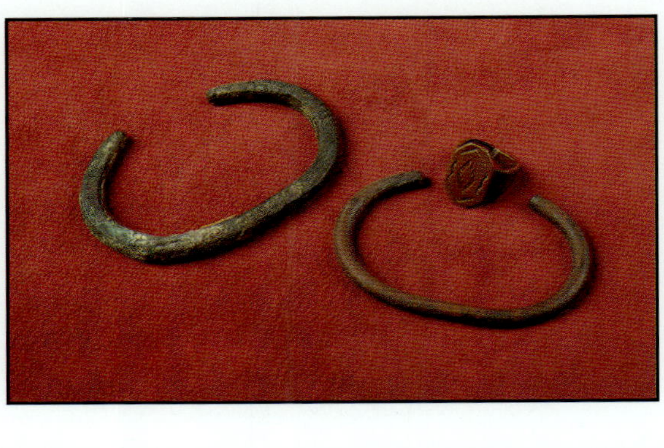

Two old copper wire bracelets and a finger ring of copper, Navajo, c.1900. *Courtesy Lynn D. Trusdell, Crown & Eagle Antiques.*

Traditional Jewelry-making Techniques

The Indian silversmiths brought to their work a love of colorful ornamentation and artistic abilities, which were tapped by the creative processes. Having learned the skills to make jewelry from Mexicans and whites, the tools used in the early years were also related to those cultures, not their own. Leather punches, awls, and files lent themselves to simple geometric designs in the hands of Indians. There are not symbolic designs on early jewelry that have any more meaning to the Indians than to the white traders who supplied the tools. (See Traders chapter.)

From at least 1863 onward, bars of raw metal, including brass and copper, were available in the East to traders. The J. Wharton Company of Philadelphia, for example, produced German silver to the trade, which actually contained no silver at all, but is an alloy of copper (three parts), nickel and zinc (one part each). This Navajos are known to have used in some of their earliest efforts.

Indians also utilized Mexican pesos and American dollars and smaller coins as raw materials. By 1890, the U. S. government discouraged their defacing money by using it for jewelry, but the practice continued, though lessened, until about 1940.

Traders in the late 1930s arranged to obtain 1-ounce silver slugs from smelters for Indian smiths to use. The use of sterling silver roughly dates from this period and grew more important as the decade advanced. When the Arts and Crafts Board was established in the 1930s, traders were able to demand better materials and tools for the Indians, and on into the 1940s able to get silver when metal rationing due to the war effort elsewhere restricted many of the jewelers. Therefore, Indian silver in limited quantities was still made into jewelry and available for sale in the 1940s.

Wrought Silver

Bars of silver were hammered by hand and worked at the forge to create wrought jewelry. Drawn silver wire was available for bending cold into bracelets. Then, decorations could be added with punches, awls and files. Traders provided dies from about 1880 onward, and flux to enable a smooth solder.

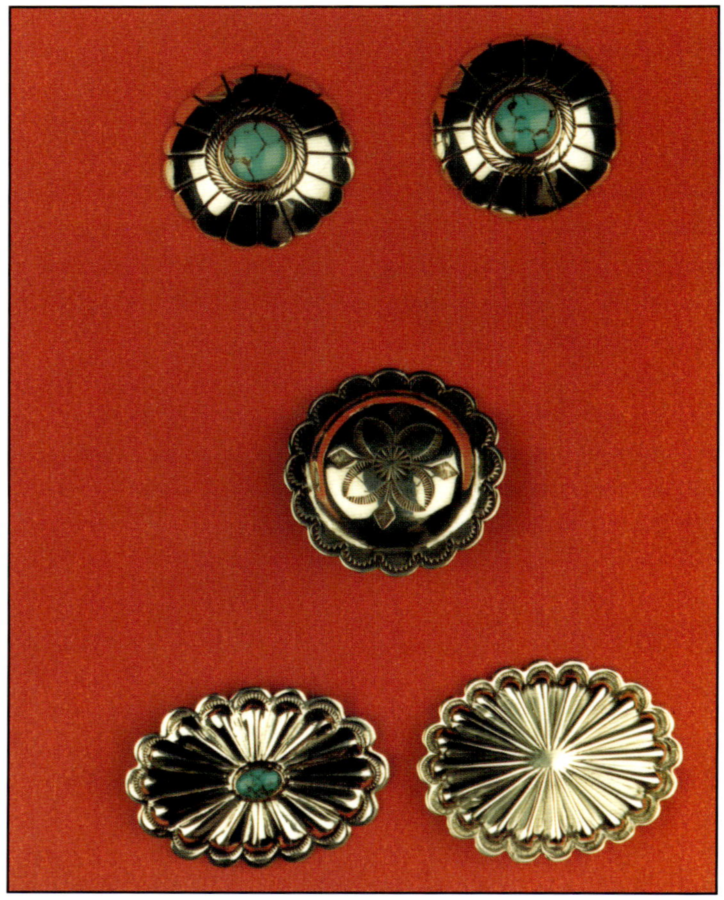

Oval buttons of wrought silver, one with turquoise, unmarked. / Silver scarf slide, unmarked. / Round buttons set with turquoise by Francis Jones, Navajo, made in the old style, circa 1970s.

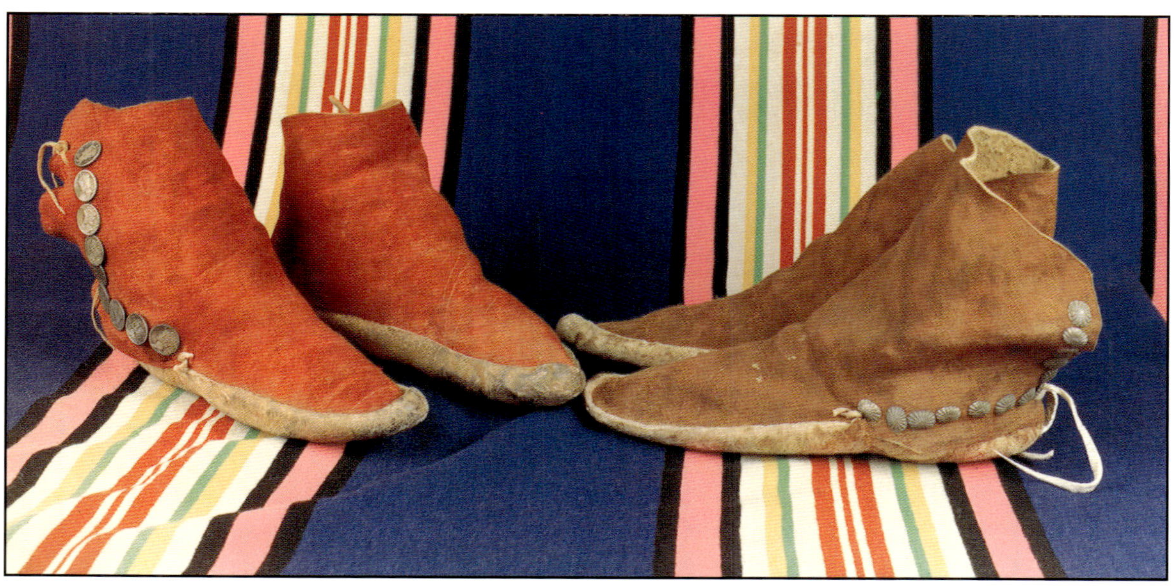

Moccasins made with bull hide bottoms, buckskin tops and coin silver buttons at the closures and for ornamentation.

In earlier times, Navajo men carried pouches since they did not have pockets in their pants. They carried tobacco and personal items in them. Today they are used as a dress-up item when attending "sings" and social events.

Special tobacco canteens, probably patterned after U.S. Army water canteens originally, were carried by Navajo men on ceremonial occasions, generally in their decorated pouch.

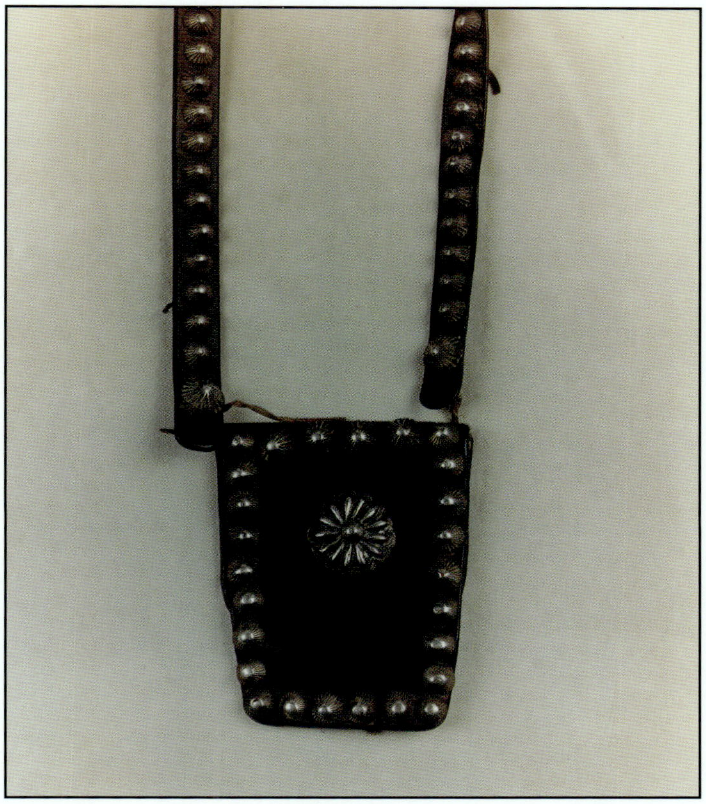

Man's pouch of leather decorated with embossed silver buttons, Navajo, circa 1900. *Crown & Eagle Antiques Inc.collection*

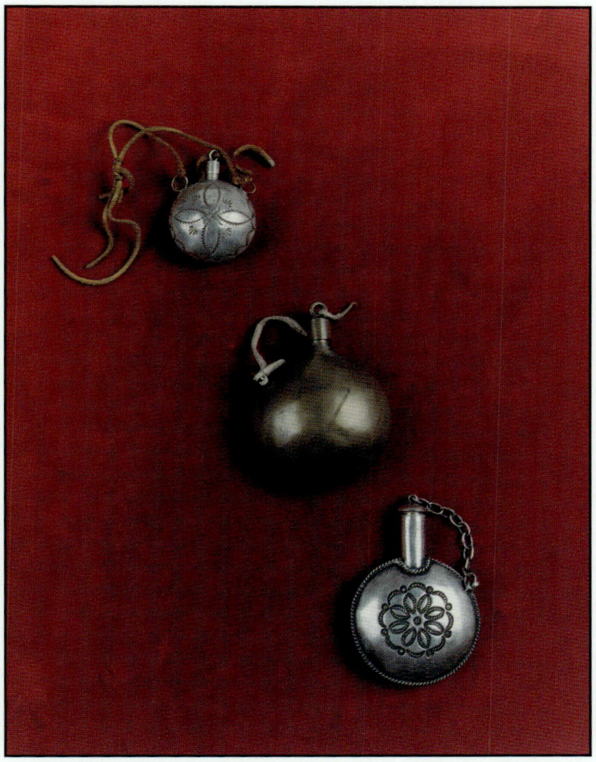

Made after 1868 in the image of a U.S. Army water canteen, tobacco canteens were made by Navajo silversmiths as very special objects, some say with the neck sized to measure out sufficient tobacco to fill a peace pipe bowl: at the top, a silver canteen from the 1920s. / Rare brass canteen circa 1900. / Silver canteen from the 1940s. *Lynn D. Trusdell collection*

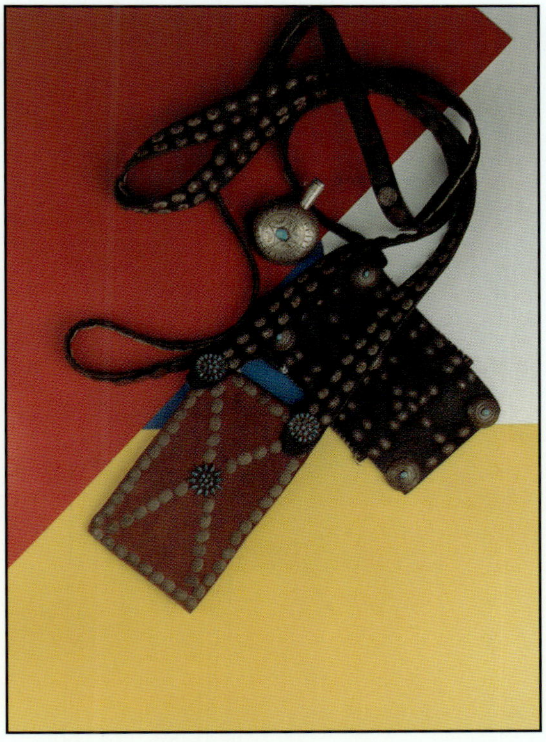

Man's leather pouch decorated with small silver buttons and three Zuni cluster pins. / Sterling silver tobacco canteen decorated with hand stamping and three Sleeping Beauty turquoise nuggets, circa 1940s. / Man's leather pouch with silver dimes on the shoulder strap, small silver buttons, and five round conchos, each set with a turquoise stone.

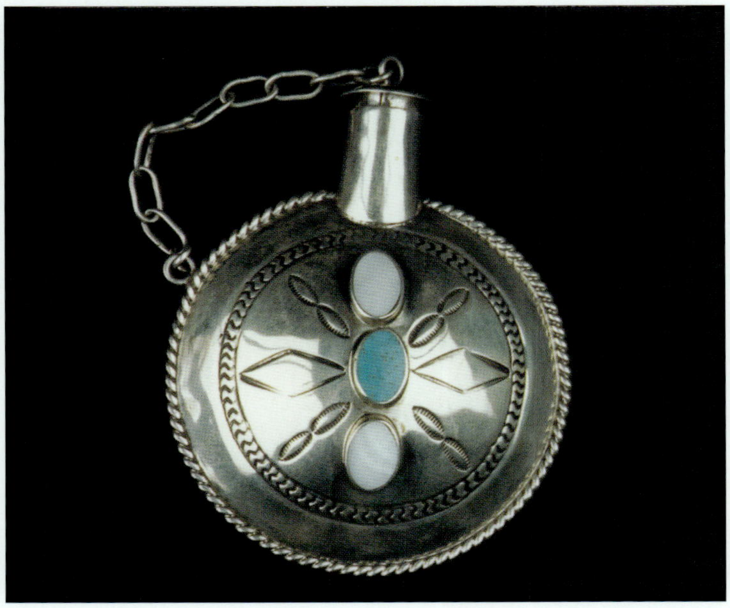

Silver canteen set with turquoise and shell, made by Kee Benally, Navajo, circa 1960s.

Stamped Decoration

The dies used for decorations presented a myriad of design possibilities. Here they have been used on silver hatbands, a truly Navajo creation.

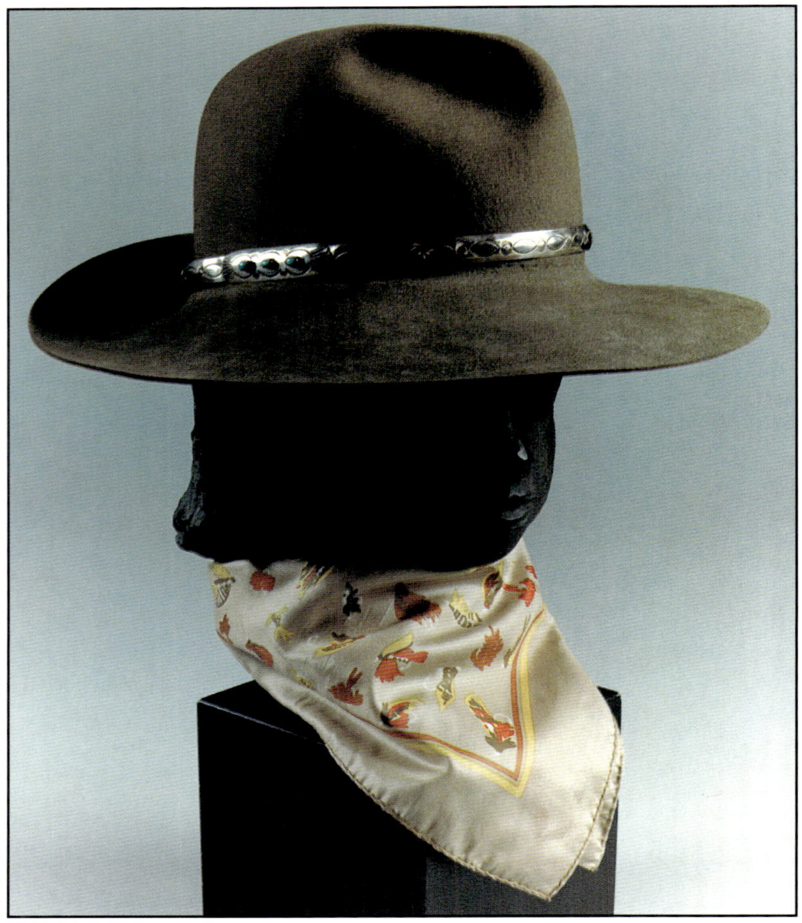

Navajo hat band of stamped silver set with turquoise, 1980s. *Leonard D. Prins collection*

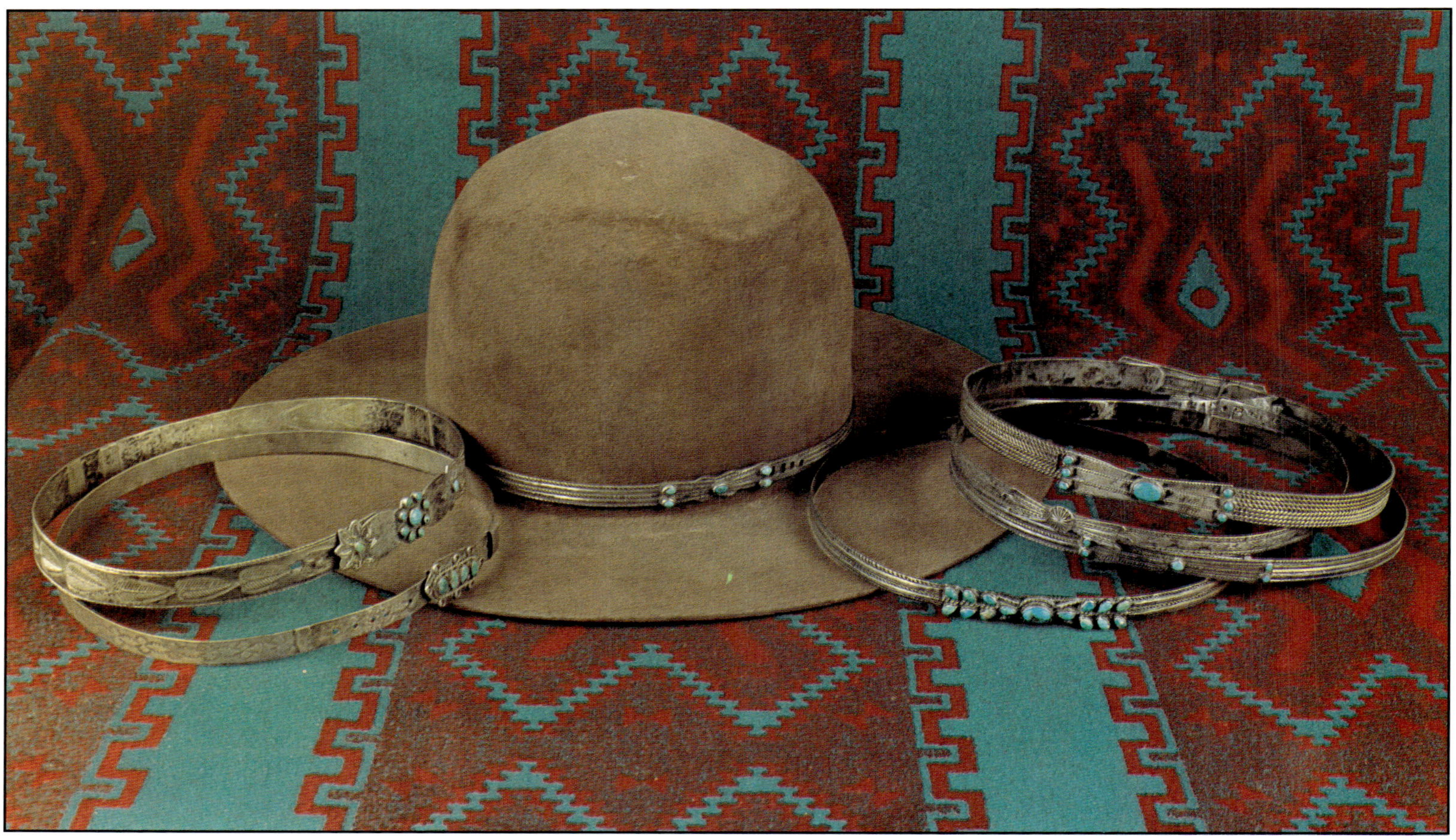

Group of stamped silver Navajo hatbands dating from the 1890s to 1920s and set with Morenci and Villa Grove turquoise.

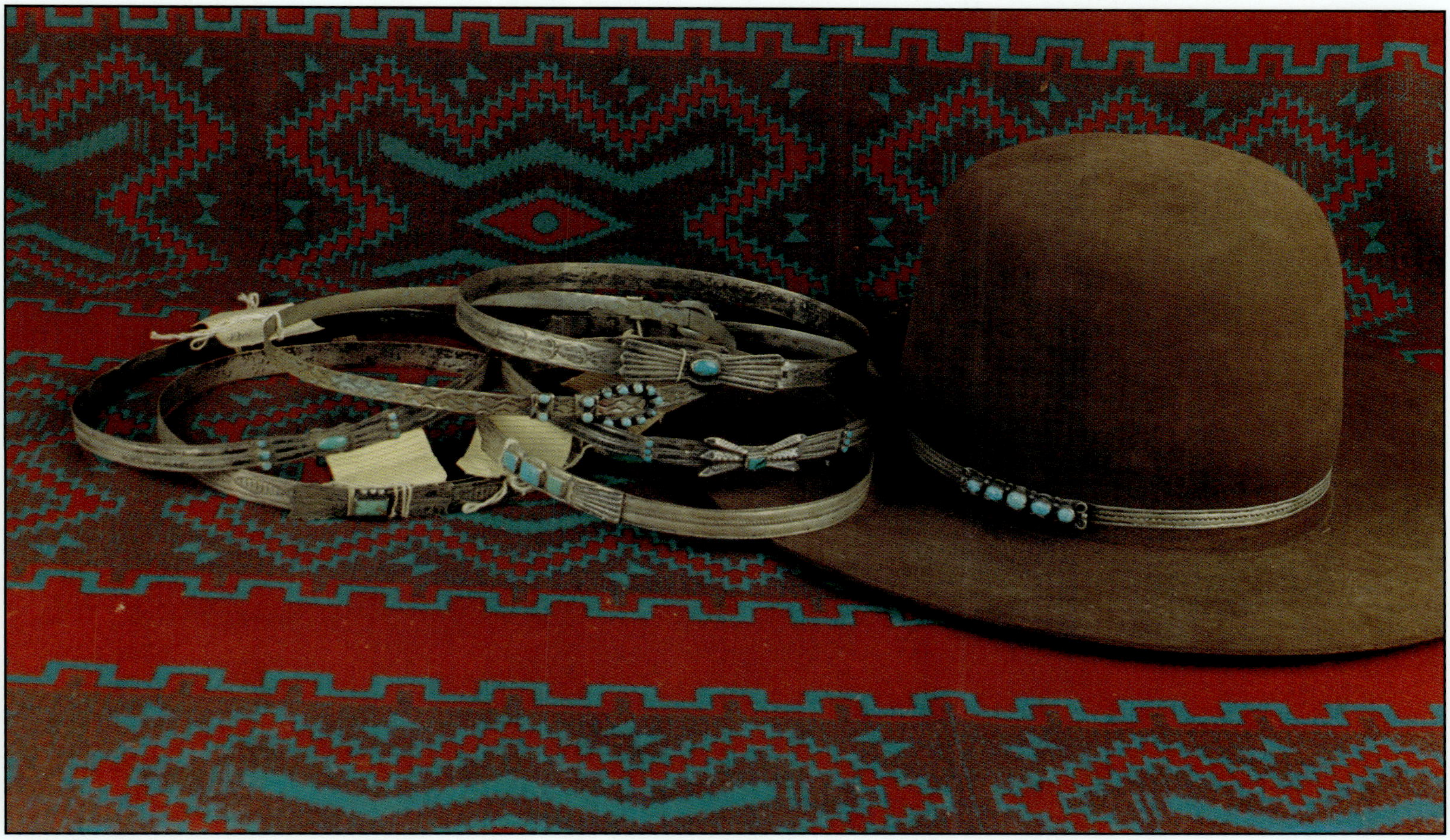

Old Navajo pawn hatbands of stamped sterling silver and Godber turquoise from the 1920s.

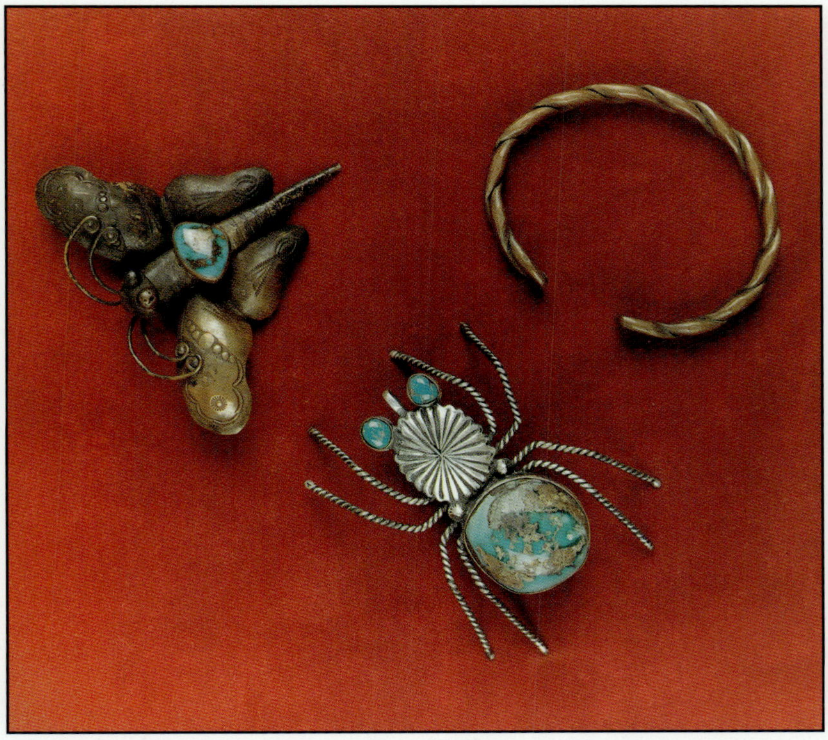

Copper butterfly pin set with turquoise dating from the late 1930s or early 1940s. / Bracelet of twisted copper wire from the 1920s. / Silver and turquoise pendant in the form of a spider, 1980s. *Lynn D. Trusdell collection*

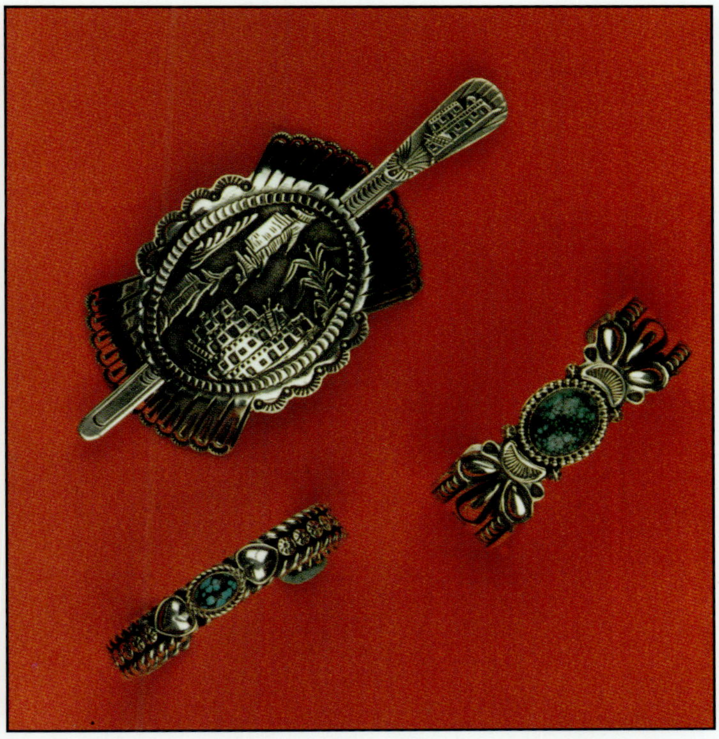

Hair ornament of wrought and overlay silver in a design depicting mesas and Pueblo style buildings, circa 1989 by Eugene Hele. / Two wrought silver bracelets set with turquoise, circa 1989 by D. Reeves. *Keams Canyon Arts and Crafts collectio.*

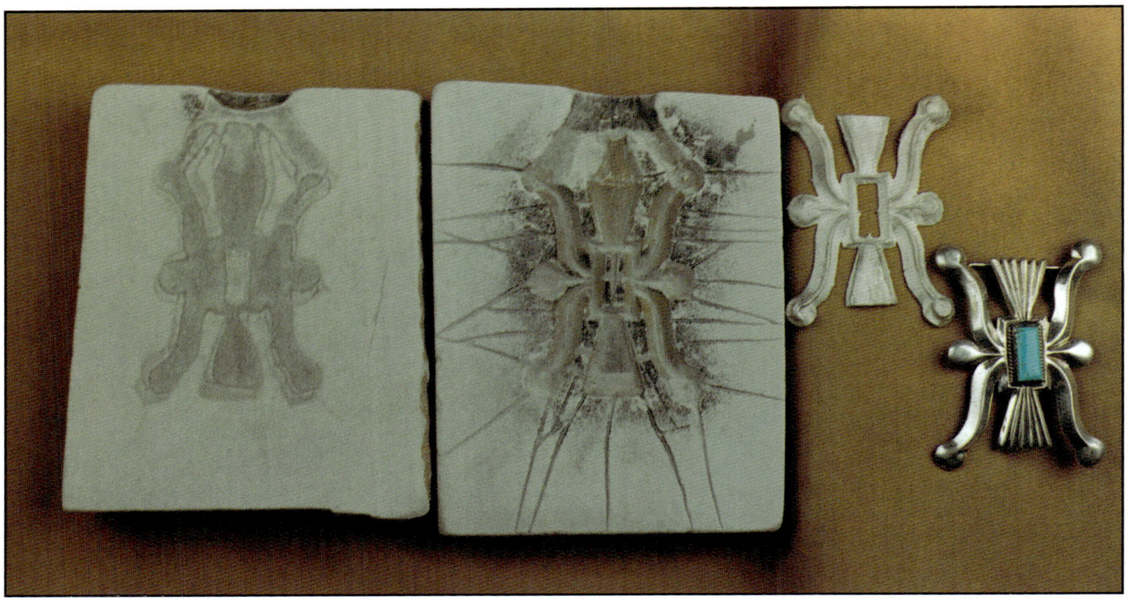

A sandstone 2-part mold with a the raw casting and finished buckle. Navajo. *Turquoise Lady collection*

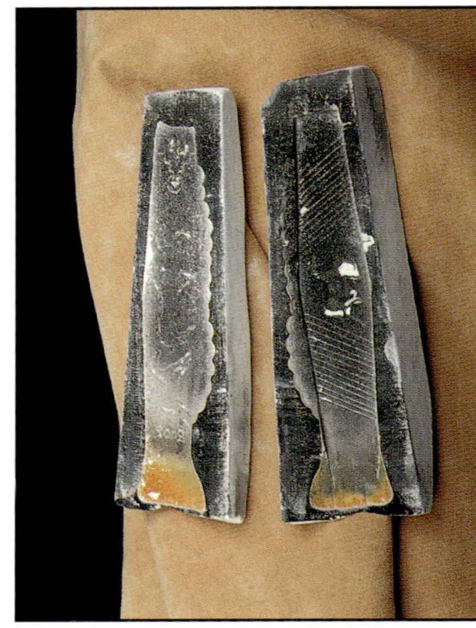

Tufa sandstone two-part mold for a bracelet design, by Anthony Lovato, Santo Domingo, 8-1/4" long x 2-5/8" wide, 2002. *Courtesy of Gerald Peters Gallery, Santa Fe, New Mexico*

Sand Casting

One of the oldest silver techniques achieved after the Indians began to work with hot metal at a forge, circa 1875, was the process of sand casting. The name derives from early times when images were made in the desert sand and molten metal was poured into the image. In modern times, this process is done with tufa (volcanic porous) stone, which is mined locally in the Southwest.

The stone is prepared for casting by cutting both the design and the overflow and air outlets into the surface of one stone. A second stone is cut out to the depth of the required design. When fastened together, molten silver is poured in from the top. When cool, the casting is released from the mold. Files and polishing clean up the casting. Chisels complete the design and, in this case, a turquoise stone was set into the center.

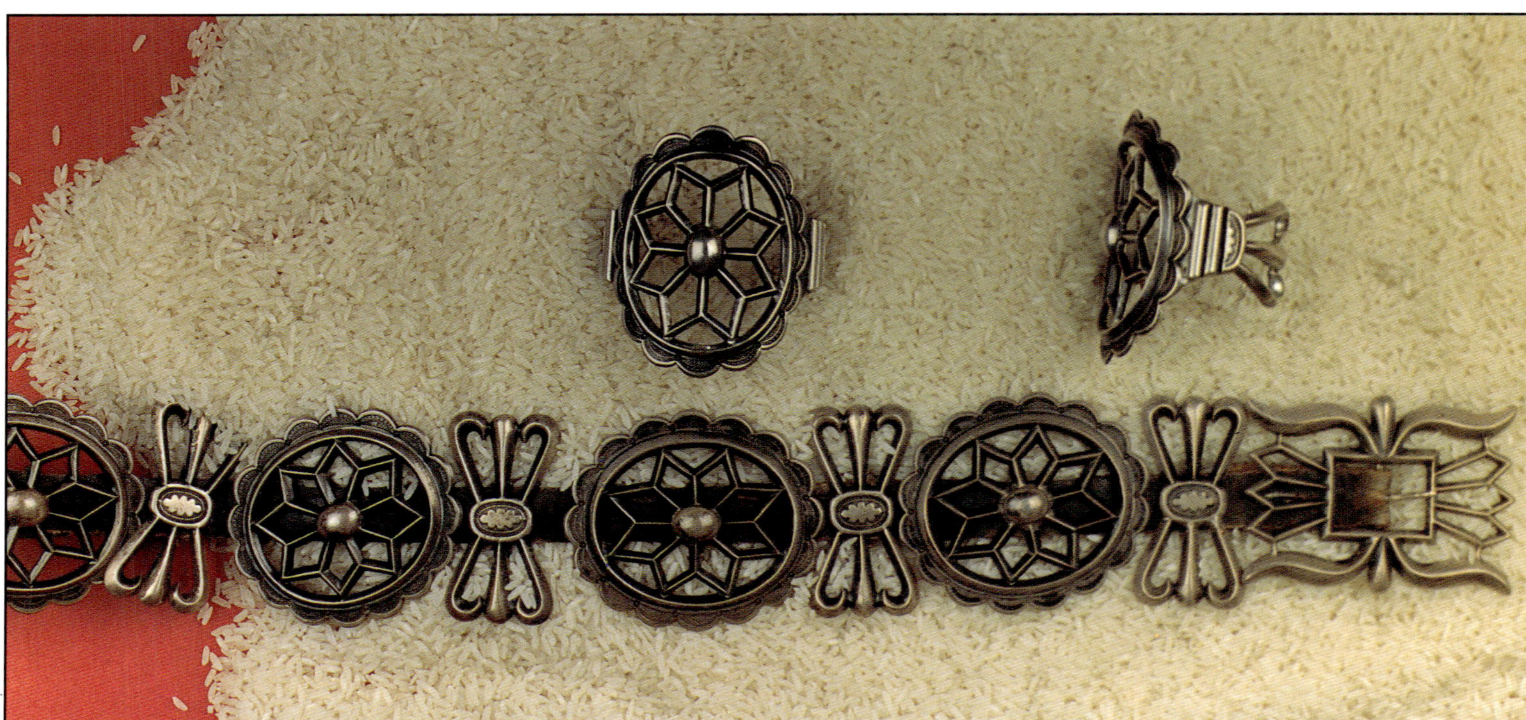

Navajo belt and two bracelets made from sand cast sections, 1970s. *Enchanted Mesa collection*

Inlay Decoration

The Zuni tradition of stone cutting has led this pueblo to produce some of the best lapidaries in the industry today. Since Zuni is close to the railroad lines, it was one of the first jewelry-making areas to get electricity, which was used to run stone cutting and polishing tools. Stone-to-stone and figurative stone inlays have become highly complicated designs in recent years at the hands of skilled artists.

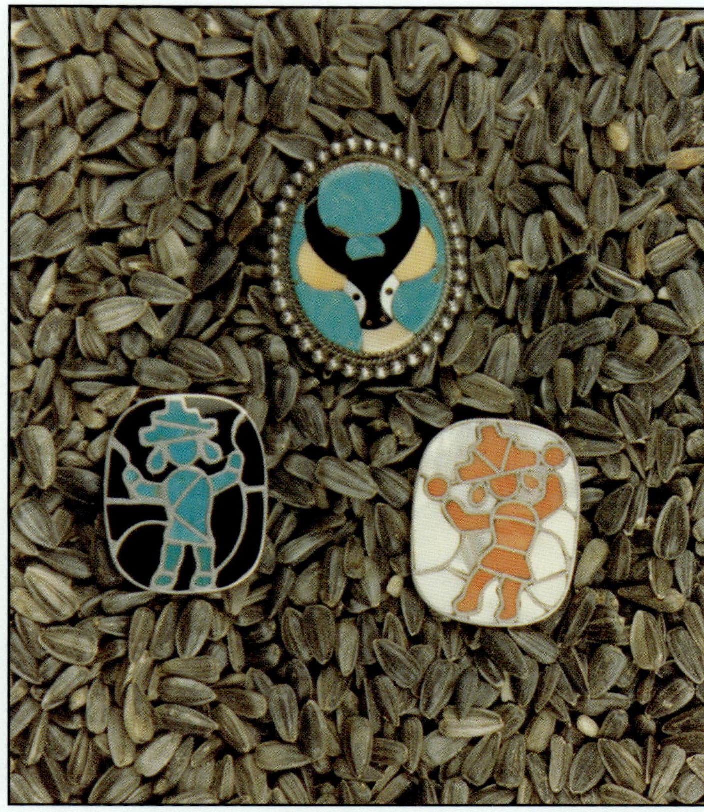

Trader C.G. Wallace developed these designs in the 1960s for Zuni stonecutters. *Enchanted Mesa collection*

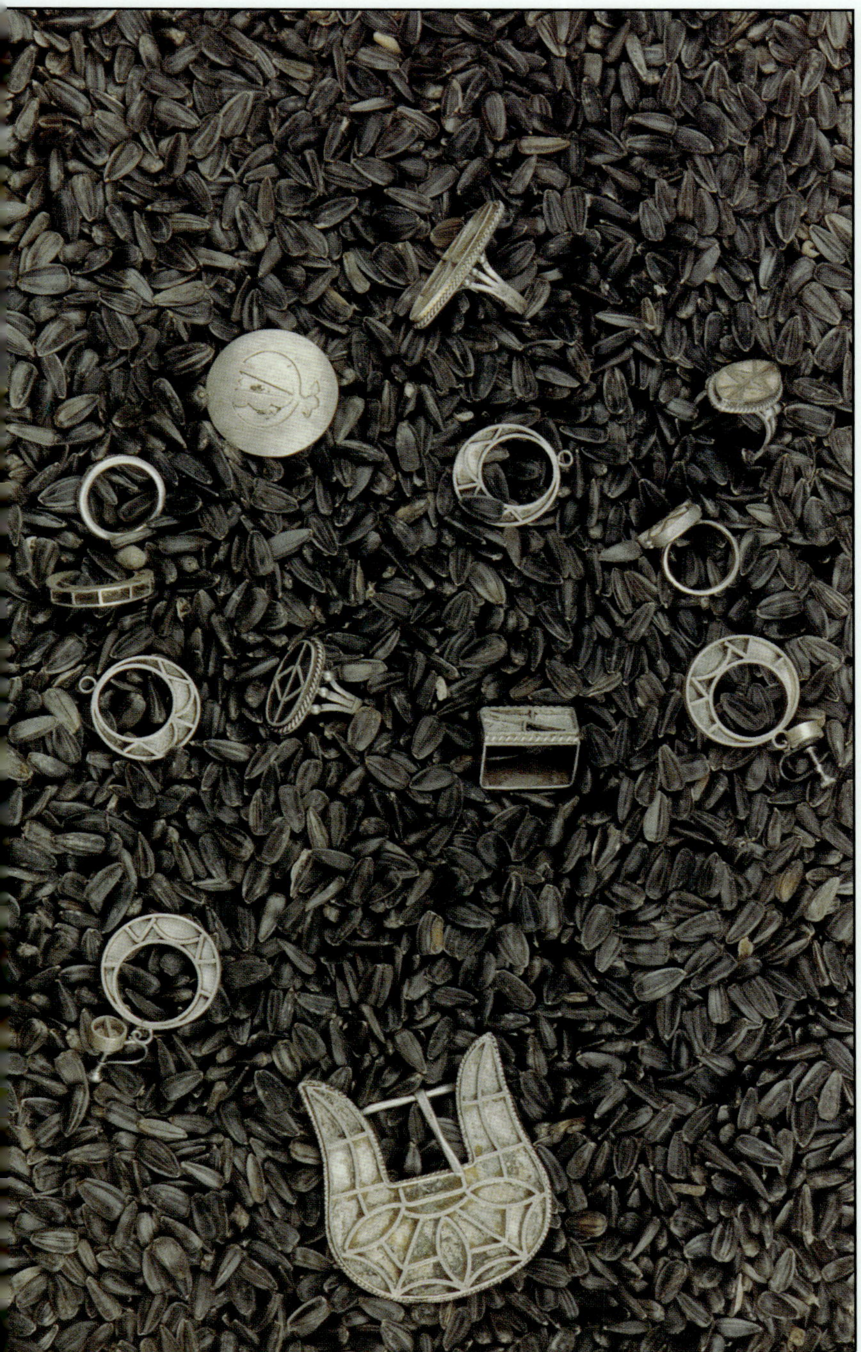

Fine channel inlay blanks made for Zuni jewelry, 1960s-1970s. *Enchanted Mesa collection*

Channel Inlay

Made popular by Zuni silversmiths and trader C.G. Wallace and company in the 1940s (see page 8), channel inlay has become a distinct jewelry style. Turquoise, shell, stone and wood can be inserted into wire compartments to form the designs. Blank settings for channel inlay are prepared separately, and the stones are cut to fill the openings.

Zuni lapidarists have developed and perfected the process of laying cut stones into pre-formed silver channels creating smooth surfaces. Many combinations of colored stones can be worked this way to create patterns from subtle to elaborate.

Overlay Decoration

The development of overlay decoration for jewelry occurred with Hopi silversmiths in the late 1930s as described on page 9. Its success was not unnoticed throughout the Southwest, and soon Navajo and Zuni silversmiths were also practicing overlay. The process is here illustrated:

The stages of constructing an overlay bracelet are demonstrated by this series by Kee Benally. The top silver bar (#1) is the unworked raw material. A second bar (#2) is cut through with the decorative pattern. The cut bar is laid over the solid bar and soldered to it. Stamped designs are added above and below the cut design. The incised areas are blackened and the bars are curved to form the bracelet.

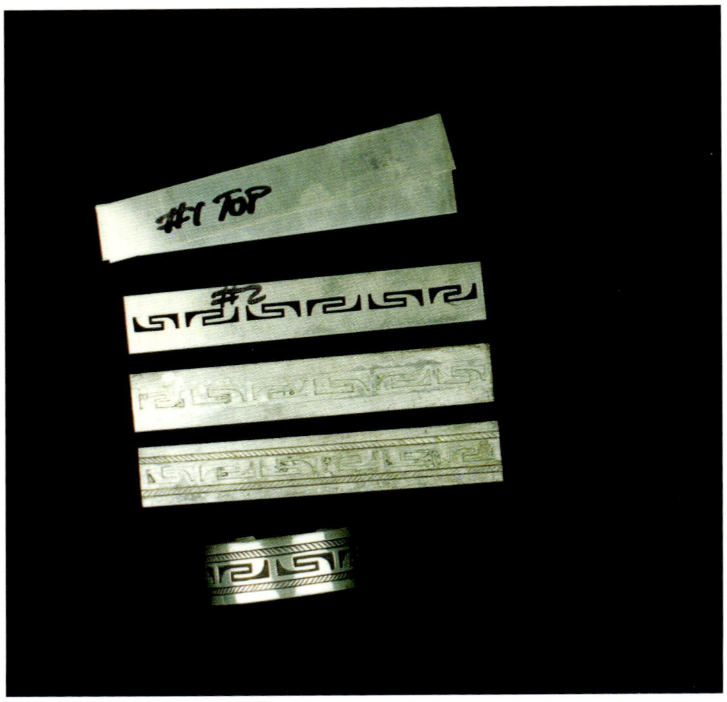

From the blank silver sheet to a finished bracelet in overlay technique.

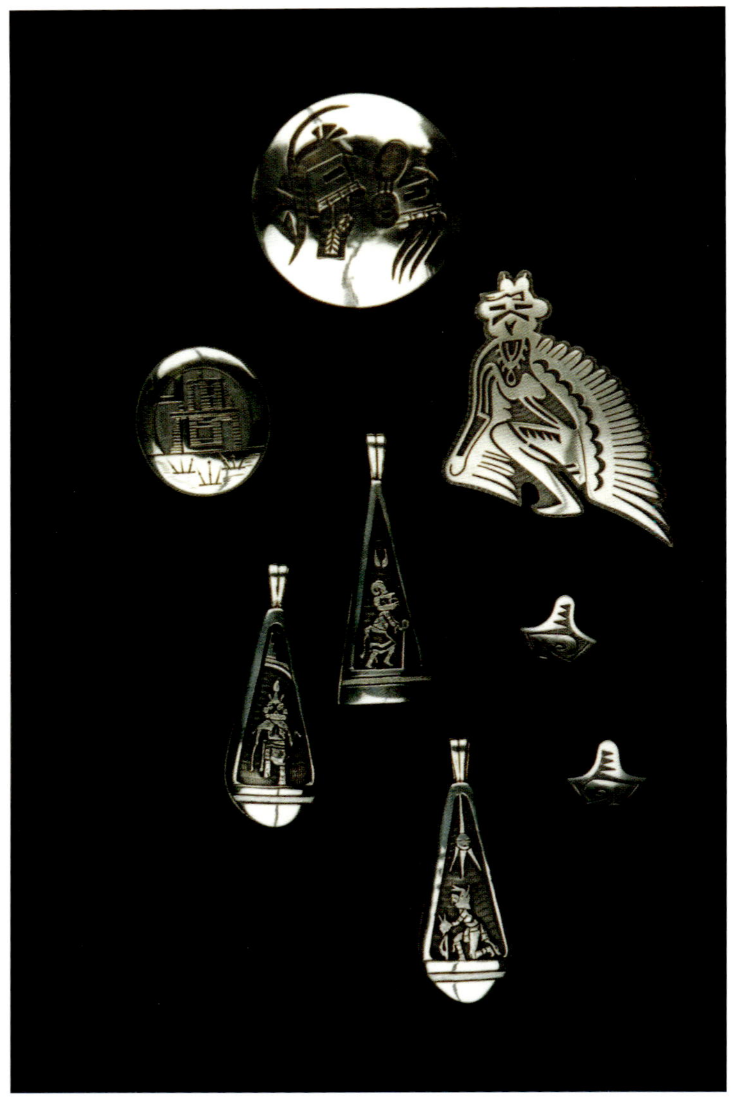

Group of overlay jewelry by Hopi artists in the late 1980s. Large round pendant by Richard Powiki. / Oval pin with buildings design by Ricky Euochwytewa.

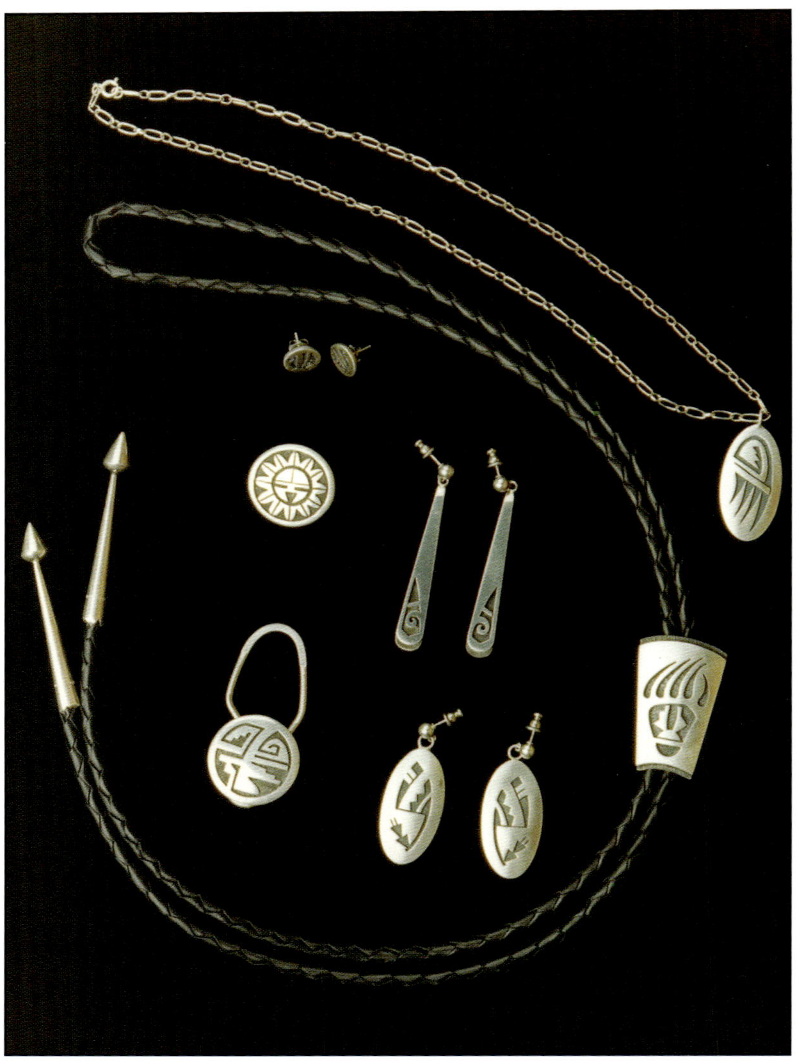

Hopi overlay jewelry including sunface, bear paw, and geometric designs, 1989. *Bing Crosby collection*

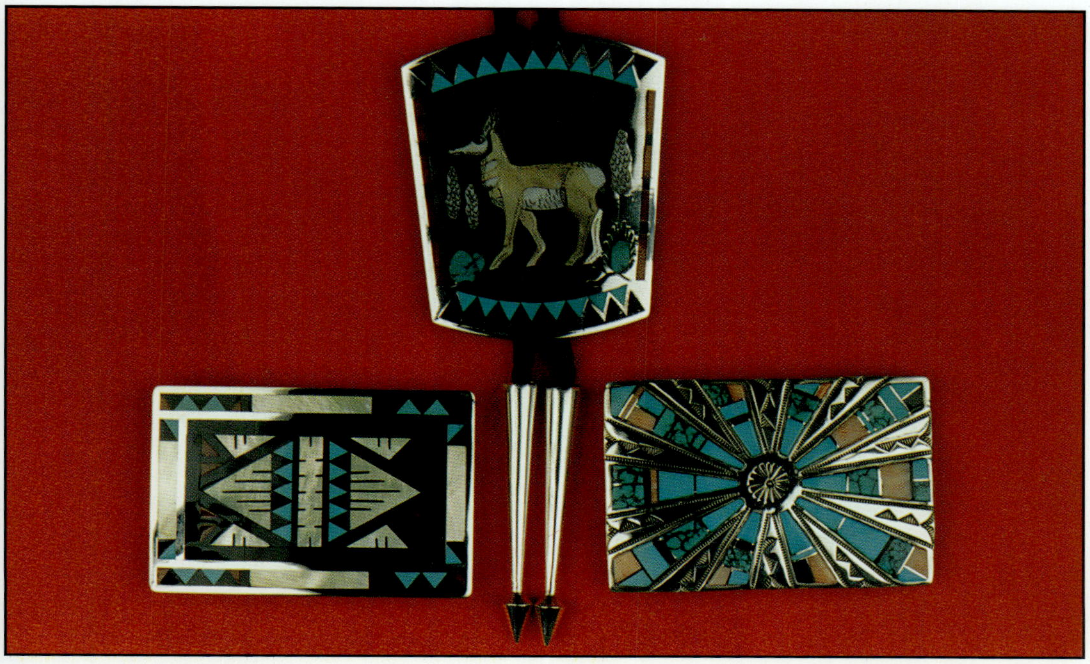

Bolo tie slide with scenic inlay of a buck in etched mosaic by Ruddell and Nancy Laconsello. / Flat inlaid buckle by Alex and Marylita Boone. / Buckle with radiating inlay and stamped work, unsigned, all 1980s. *Keams Canyon Arts and Crafts collection*

Gold Jewelry

The use of gold has come gradually to Indian artists beginning in the 1960s. Ten-, fourteen- and eighteen-karat gold has been used, but the most widely and successfully has been fourteen-karat. Gold wire in the forms of bracelets and earrings have been made, and lately far more elaborate designs in gold overlay and stamped work are being produced. More skill is required to control gold than silver, and gold's higher monetary value have limited its use to the better artists.

In the late 1980s, story-telling scenes representative of Navajo life and legends created a new style of ornamentation. Among the proficient artists who work in this style are contemporary Navajo jewelers Clarence Lee and Paul Arviso whose work is recognizably individualistic.

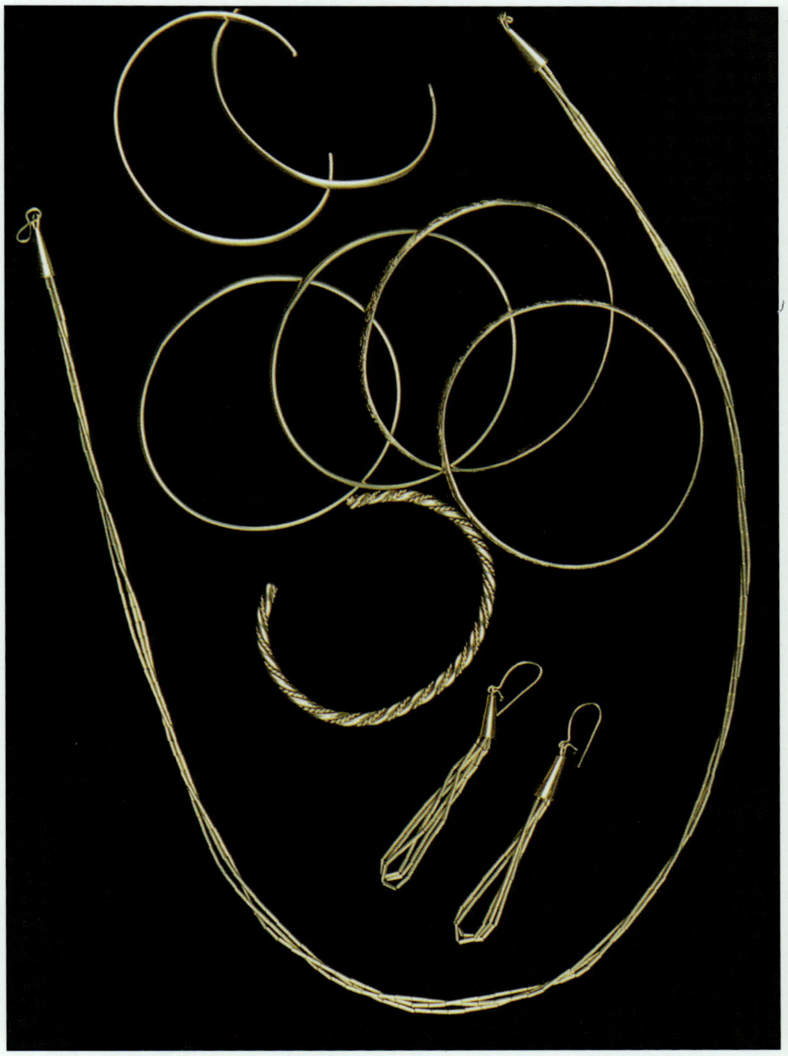

This group of gold jewelry from the 1980s is indicative of the gradual use of gold by Indian artists through the decade. Bracelets are left plain, are stamped and are twisted with wire. / Tiny gold heishi are strung as earrings and a necklace. None marked. *Turquoise Lady collection*

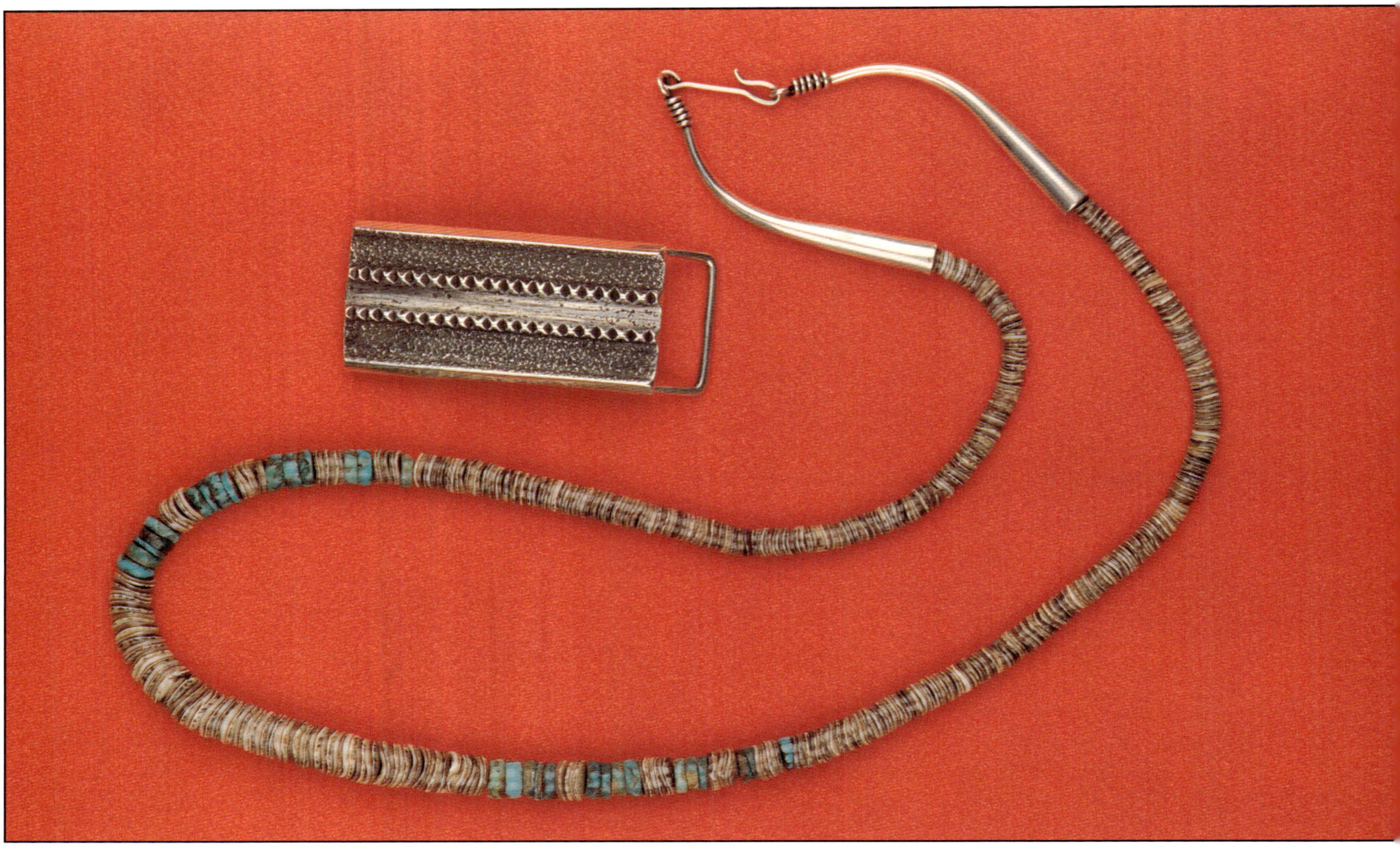

Buckle of cast and wrought silver. / Shell and turquoise bead (heishi) necklace, circa 1970s, both by Charles Loloma. *Dewey Gallery collection*

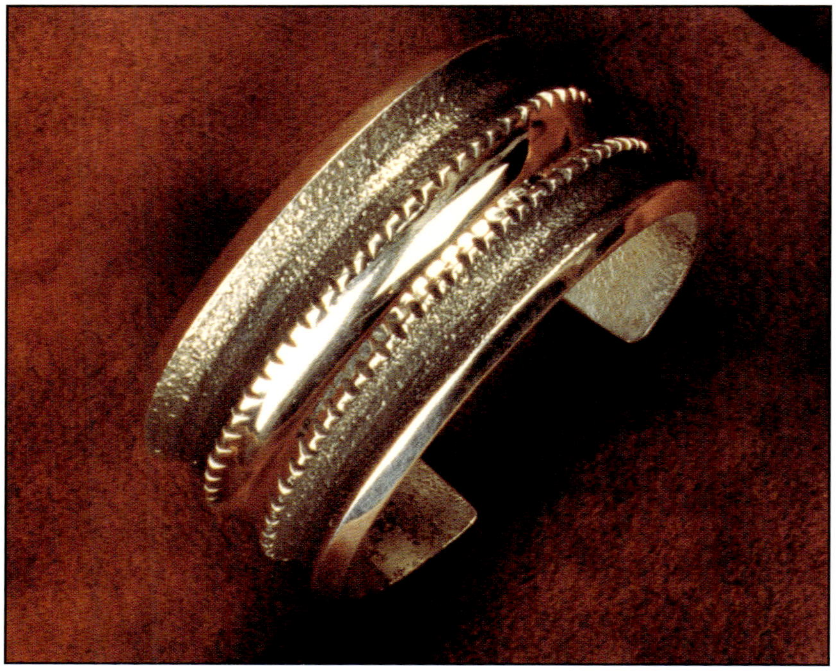

Bracelet of cast and wrought silver by Charles Loloma, early 1950s. *Brett W. Bastien collection*

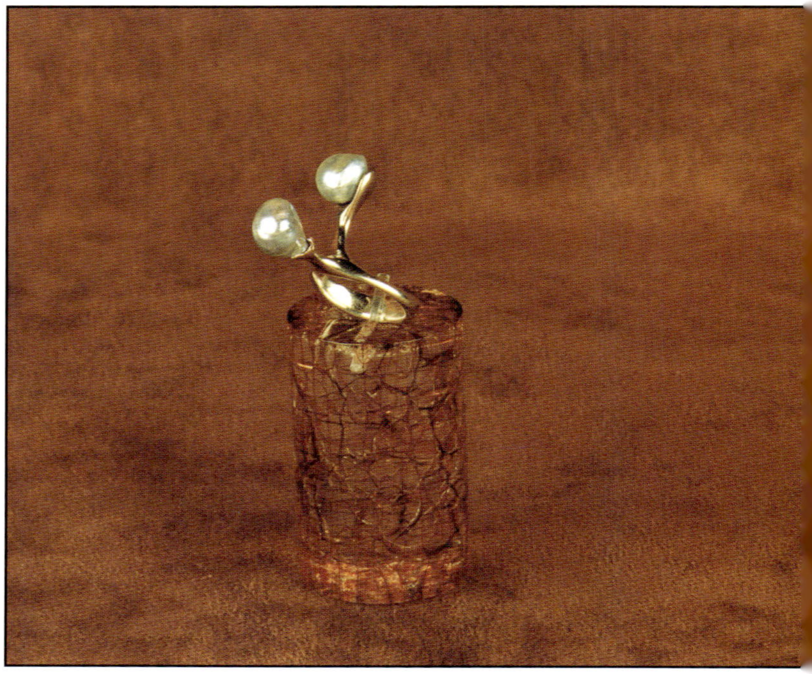

Lady's finger ring of gold and Baroque pearls, circa 1960s, by Charles Loloma. *Brett W. Bastien collection*

Jewelry Innovations

The primary methods of designing jewelry in the Southwest Indian tradition used wrought, overlay, sand cast or inlay techniques. In the 1950s a few young artists began to experiment with combinations of these techniques, and to launch out on new ideas of creative design for jewelry. French jeweler Pierre Touraine shared knowledge of European techniques with a few Southwest Indian jewelers at his Scottsdale, Arizona studio in the 1970s. Harvey Begay, Charles Supplee and Ted Charvese moved to Scottsdale to study with Touraine. He encouraged them to try new methods and adapt a positive philosophy about their work. They and others found new directions for their work and commercial success in the process.

Both on and off the reservations, jewelers were developing personal styles. Two of the most successful, and therefore influential to later designers, were Preston Monongye and Charles Loloma (Hopi). They were artists competent in several media whose attention was individually drawn to jewelry where the freedom to advance their creative ideas was challenged by the multiple techniques and materials available to them.

Charles Loloma's work in jewelry over forty years exemplifies in microcosm the evolution that continues in the field today. Beginning with wrought silver pieces in the 1950s, he carefully learned lapidary skills to a master craftsman's caliber, and moved on to work in gold. By the 1960s he was searching out knowledge of European jewelry making techniques and incorporating them in his work. He studied jewelry design in Europe. As his designs progressed, he attracted and was attracted to an ever-wider group of customers. While he benefited enormously from all the diverse influences, his designs maintained an unmistakable character of Indian design. His designs have since been reinterpreted by the legion of jewelers in his wake. His greatest success has come with the combination of lapidary and metal-smithing techniques to produce stone inlay forms in silver and gold bases. His experimentation coupled with carefully cultivated technical skill has produced jewelry, which has been awarded prizes on several continents. Now known worldwide as a superior designer and maker of fine jewelry, he has achieved recognition far beyond his Hopi mesa homeland. And he has been a stirring example to younger artists who strive for excellence in craftsmanship, create innovative designs, and hope for commercial success.

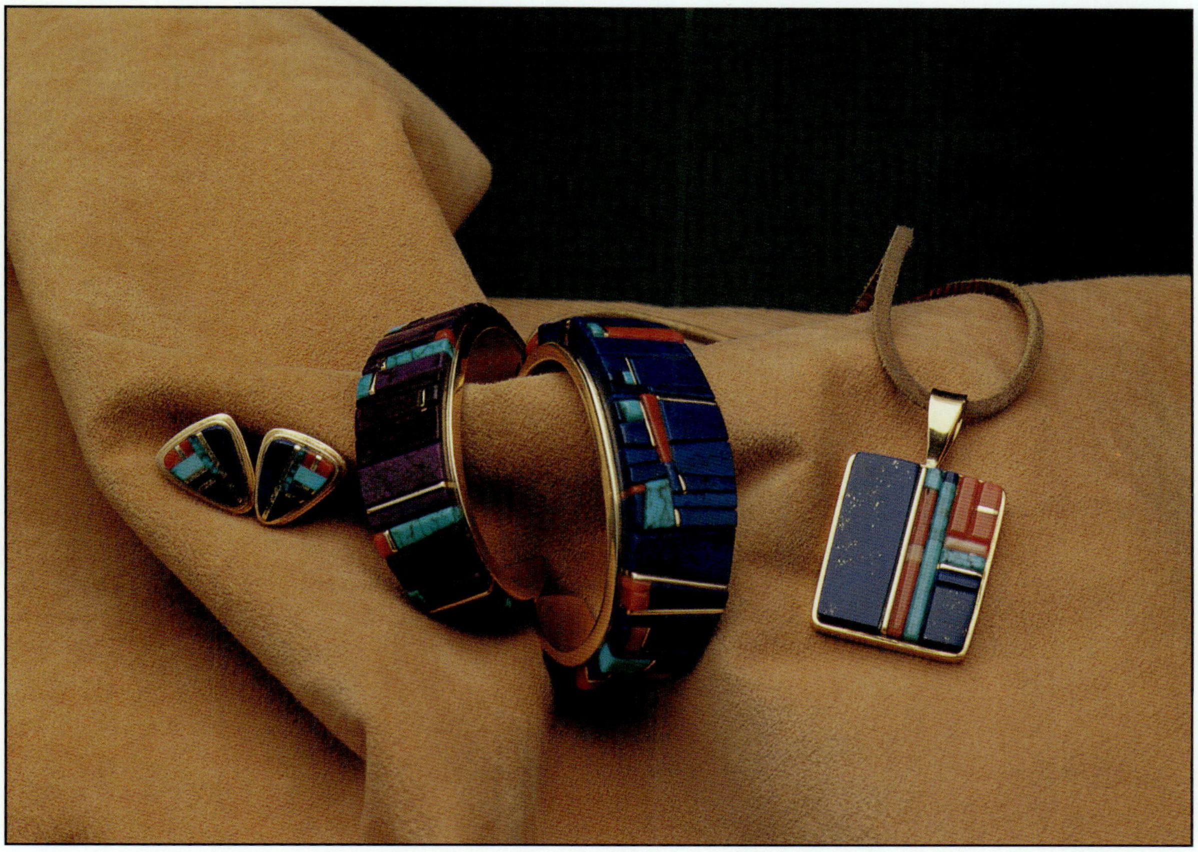

The technique of stone to stone inlay was advanced and made popular by Hopi artist Charles Loloma in the early 1960s. Since then it has been reinterpreted in many different combinations of stones by many jewelers. Two bracelets, c.1986, and a pendant of stone-to-stone inlaid technique by Charles Loloma. Matching earrings by his nieces, who use the name Son-Wai.

Preston Monongye has become established as one of the most innovative contemporary Indian silversmiths. His work displays more than a Hopi background because he dared to be different in his techniques. His bold designs incorporate large sand cast units and unusual stone inlays, both figurative and geometric in character. His work has been controversial for not falling into Hopi standards, but neither does it convey merely his Mexican and Mission background. He has made his work more than the sum of his various heritage parts.

Monongye's ability to teach younger talented artists including his son Jesse, and his success in competitions has caused his style to be copied, and built upon in subsequent years. Therefore, he now is seen as having provided some of the necessary stimulation to the evolving nature of jewelry design.

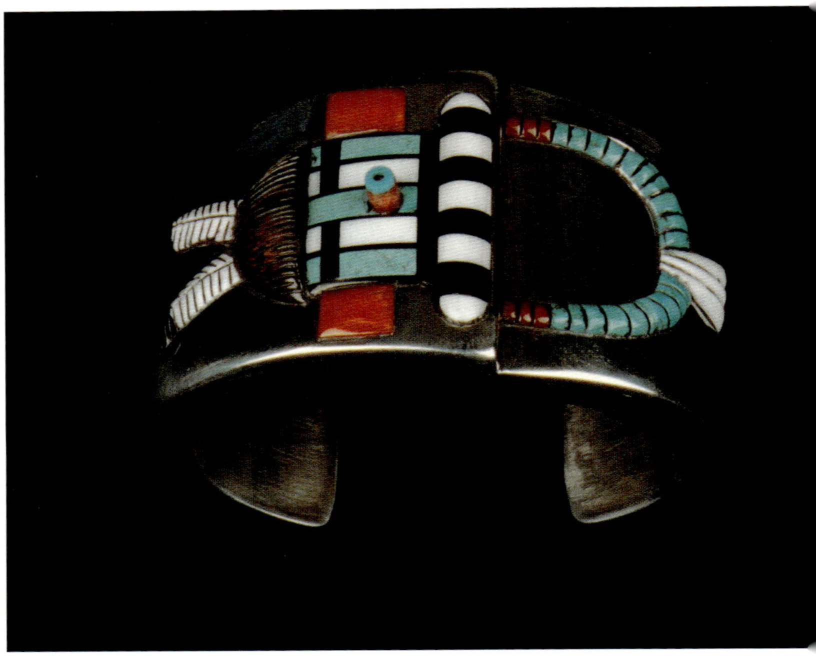

Silver cuff bracelet inlaid with shell, jet, turquoise and coral in a Corn Kachina design by Preston Monongye in 1974 when this piece won first prize in the July Fourth competition at the Museum of Northern Arizona, and second prize for best craftsman. *Dewey Gallery collection*

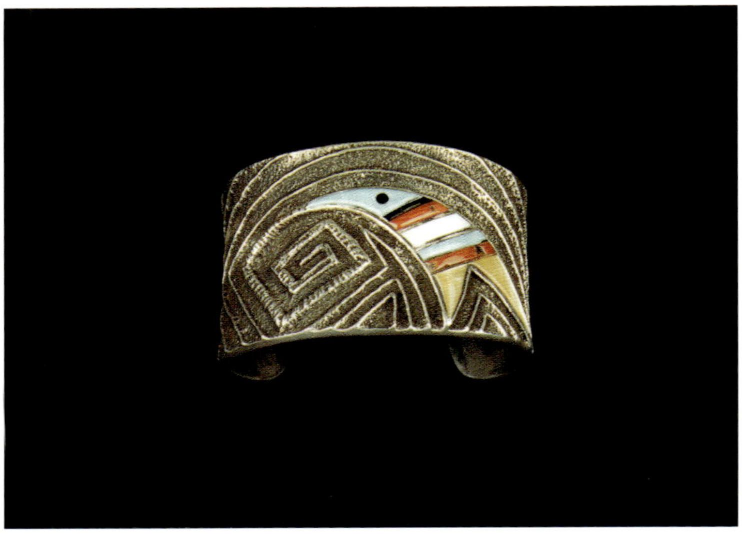

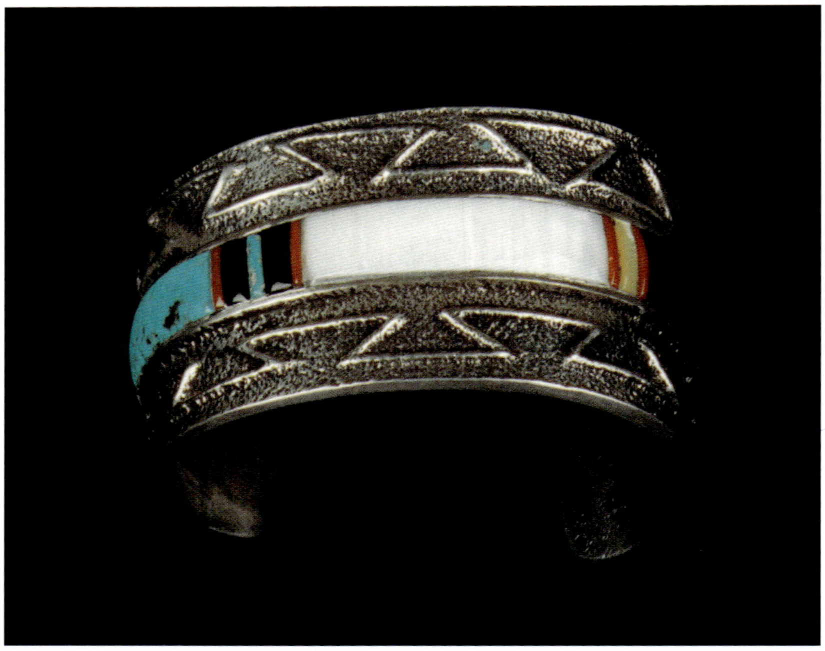

Two cuff bracelets of cast silver with inlaid turquoise, jet, coral and shell by Preston Monongye. *Dewey Gallery collection*

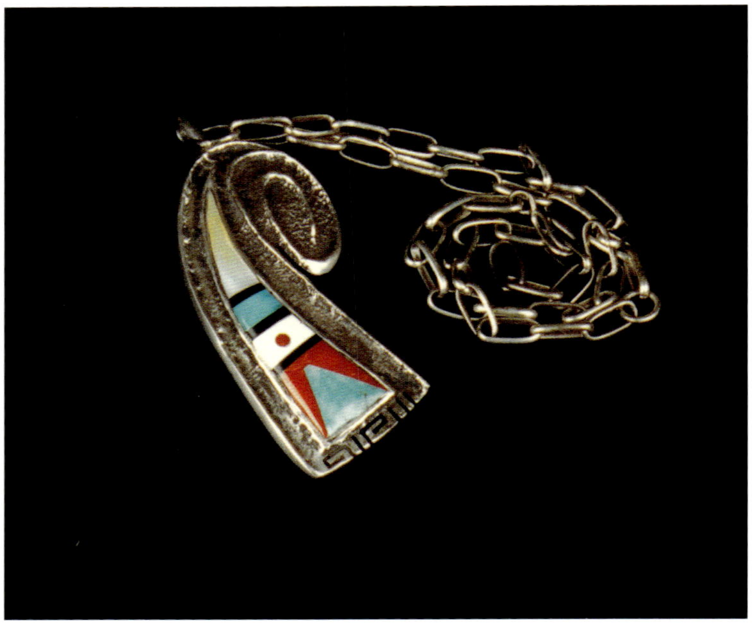

Cast and wrought silver pendant inlaid with shell, jet, turquoise and coral on a hand wrought silver chain, both by Preston Monongye. *Dewey Gallery collection*

As the use of gold became more accepted by customers, the further challenge of working gold was met by daring smiths. One of the leaders is Paul Arviso, a Navajo artist. His work is quite diversified, including fascinating stone inlay as well as gold overlay. He has also furthered the story telling style with deep significance to his designs. While not divulging the secrets of his people, he has communicated the presence of symbolism in his work. Personal thoughts for the owner of his jewelry are incorporated into special pieces.

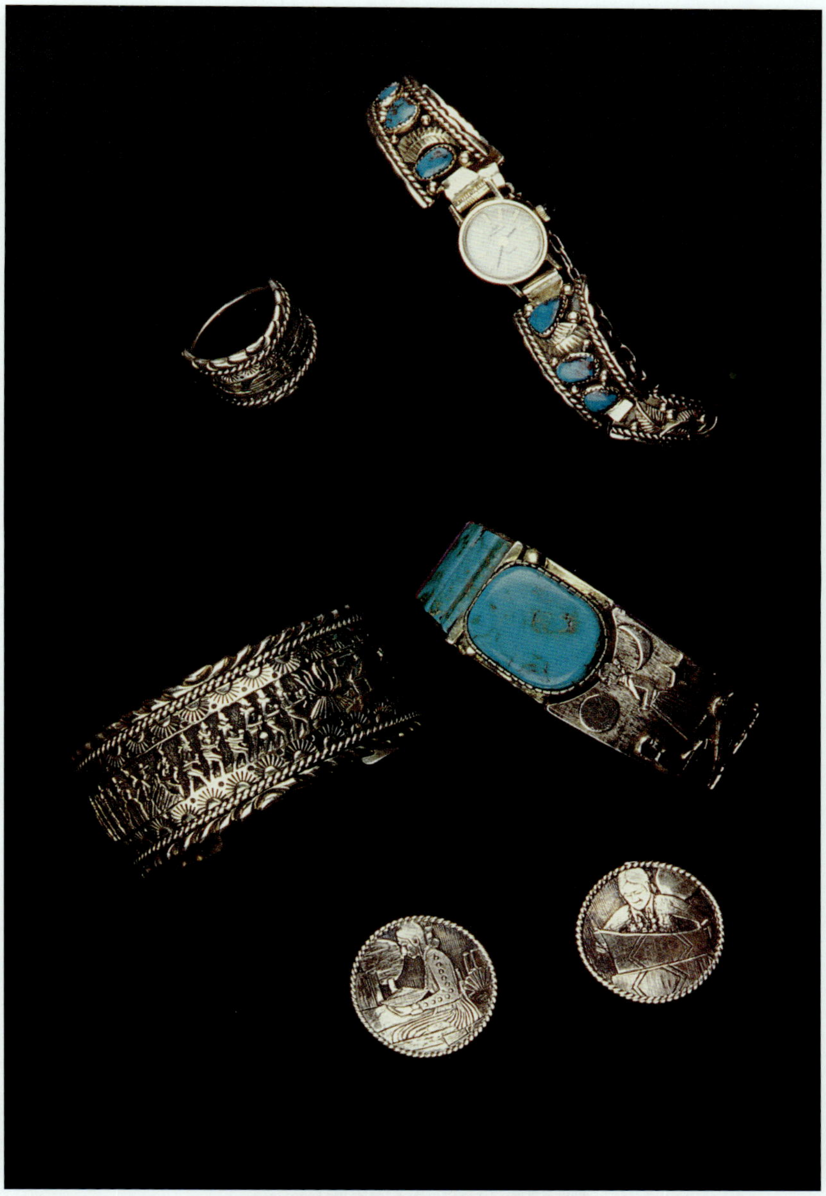

This group of jewelry from the 1980s, by Navajo Paul Arviso, shows the diversity he achieved. Gold watchband set with turquoise. / Finger ring and bracelet of gold overlay technique depicting stories of Navajo culture. See note below. / Bracelet combining gold overlay and lapidary skills in an original composition. / Pair of earrings in gold overlay technique depicting Navajo women's work. *Turquoise Lady collection*

Note: The owner of the storyteller bracelet has shared the artist's explanation of the design as contained in a letter from Mr. Arviso to the owner:

August, 1983
Dear (bracelet owner)

I finally finished the bracelet. It took me much longer than I had expected, because 14K gold is a much harder metal than silver, so the work went slowly. Also, the subject matter may have contributed to slowing me down, from a psychological standpoint, as the "Yei Bi Chai" is a winter ceremony.

I chose to do this because I think that it is a substantial part of the culture, and being of the Navajo people, and I may never have the opportunity to state it in gold again. So, even [though] I was greatly concerned about the results of stepping out of harmony with nature, I decided to do the "Yei Bi Chai" anyway. I want you to know that this is not done disrespectfully or as an attempt to sell my culture, but as a statement of an artist, about where he came from, before it is lost or forgotten, maybe something for my people in the future.

The top of the bracelet is a nine-day ceremony called the "Yei Bi Chai." It is for healing. The bracelet shows that last day of the ceremony when the dancers wear full dress and masks. With the bracelet facing you, you will see, on the right side, a picture of a butte or rock. I put this in to place you in Navajo land. Next, a hogan with smoke from its chimney. The Medicine Man makes his sand painting and sings inside. There is a huge fire, for it is cold during the winter nights. (Actually there should be more fires.) There are eight Yei dancers. The first is the Bi Chai (grandfather). The next are six Yei dancers, and the last Yei dancer is acting like a clown in the crowd.

The group of people are wrapped in blankets because of the cold. Some will watch the dancers and others have a chance to socialize.

The dance shows how the Yei Gods gave the Navajo people the healing chant long ago.

On the underside of the bracelet [inside surface] I put a sand painting. This painting is not the real thing, it is from me about the real sand painting.

I put First Man and First Woman as Yeis. The figure with the round head is the Male in the East, and the Female in the West. The center (water) is the point of origin where the Navajo people emerged from the underworld. There are four sacred mountains surrounding the figures in the center, which represent the things on the earth and in the sky for the benefit of the Dine' (Navajo). The sheep (animals), corn (plants), the eagle (things that fly), these are earth. The sky [is] represented by the star (night) and the sun (day). The Navajo people are protected by lightning arrows, which are held by the Yeis. For the Navajo people, these are things that are necessary for life. These things are the beginnings of the Navajo people, which evolve into ceremonies such as the "Yei Bi Chai."

I have been told if you know these things you will always be able to help yourself through life; if not, you can become lost.

Paul

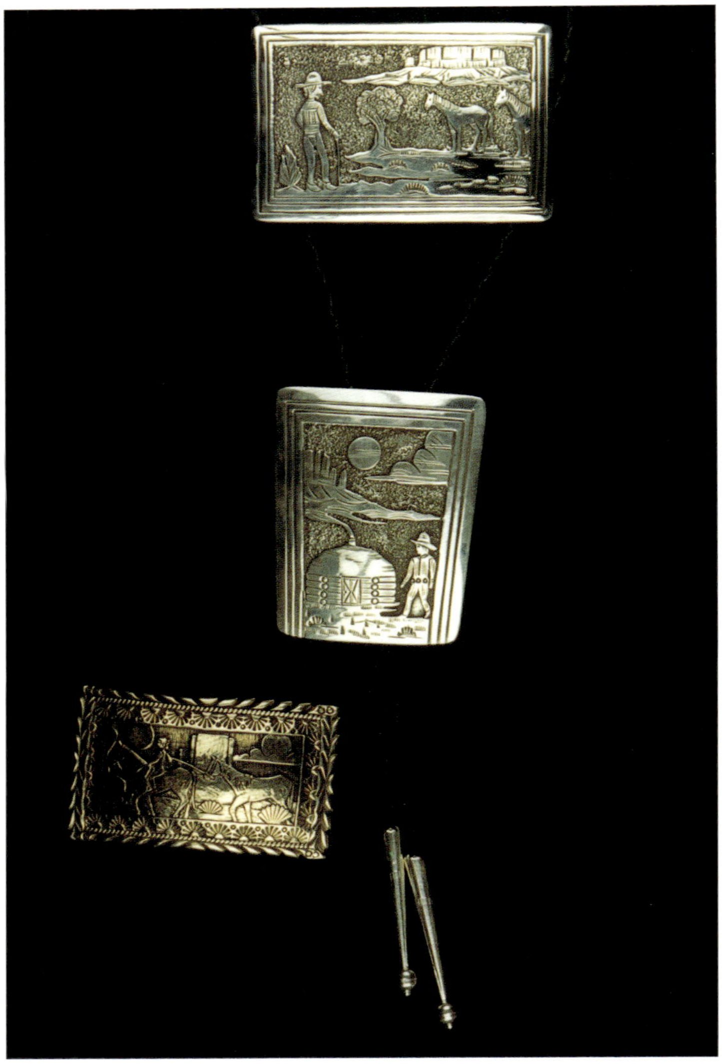

Experimentation with diverse materials led to the use of imported stones by many of the better silversmiths in the 1980s. Lapis lazuli (blue), lavulite (purple), malachite (green), opals, and diamonds are among the non-native materials used.

Silver buckle and matching bola tie show a man in a Southwest landscape with horses, and approaching his hogan home. / Gold buckle depicting two horses and rider by Paul Arviso, Navajo. *Turquoise Lady collection*

Andy Kirk, Navajo, forged silver into this set to hold lapis lazuli which has been polished into oval shapes, circa 1989. *Indian Post collection*

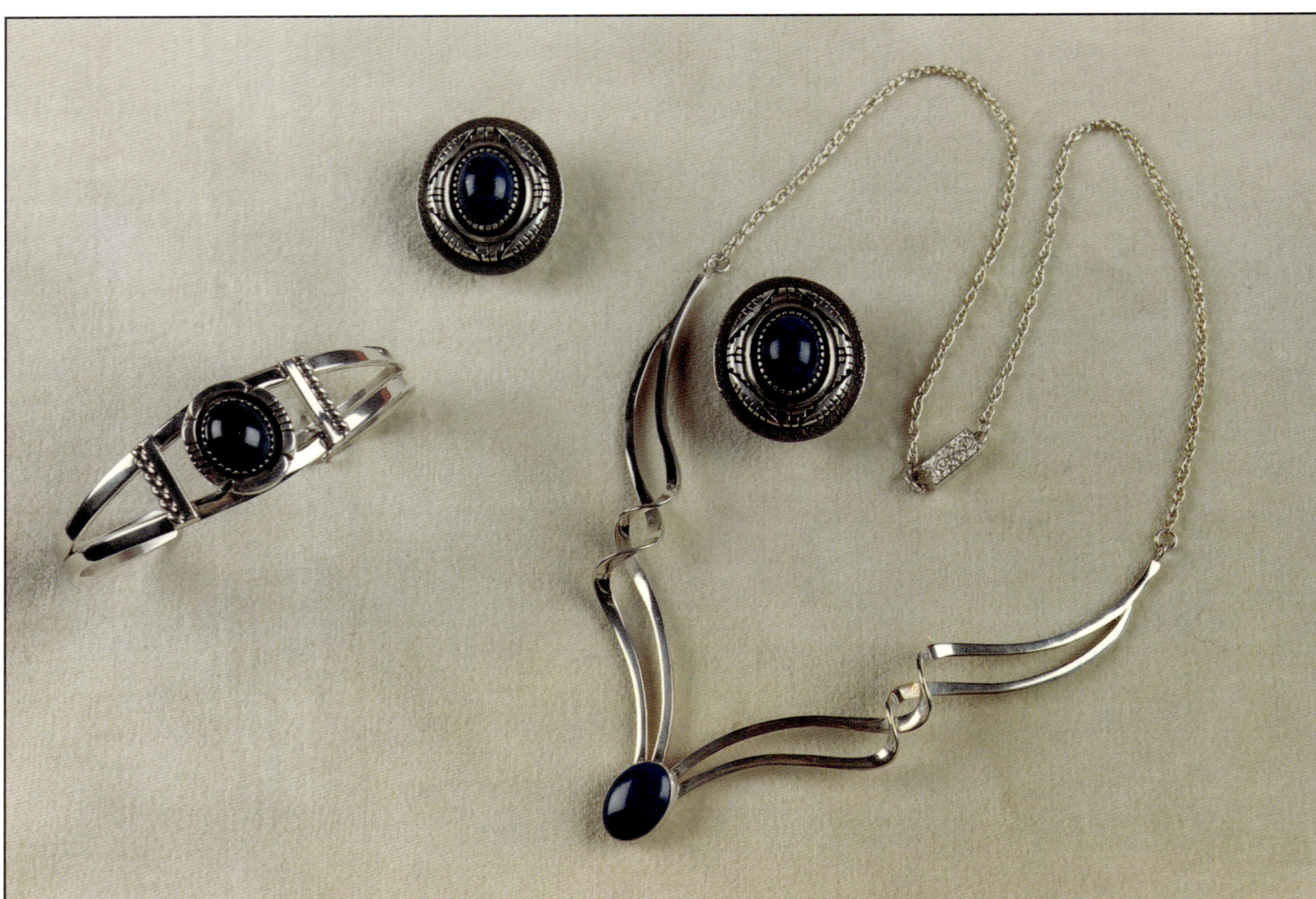

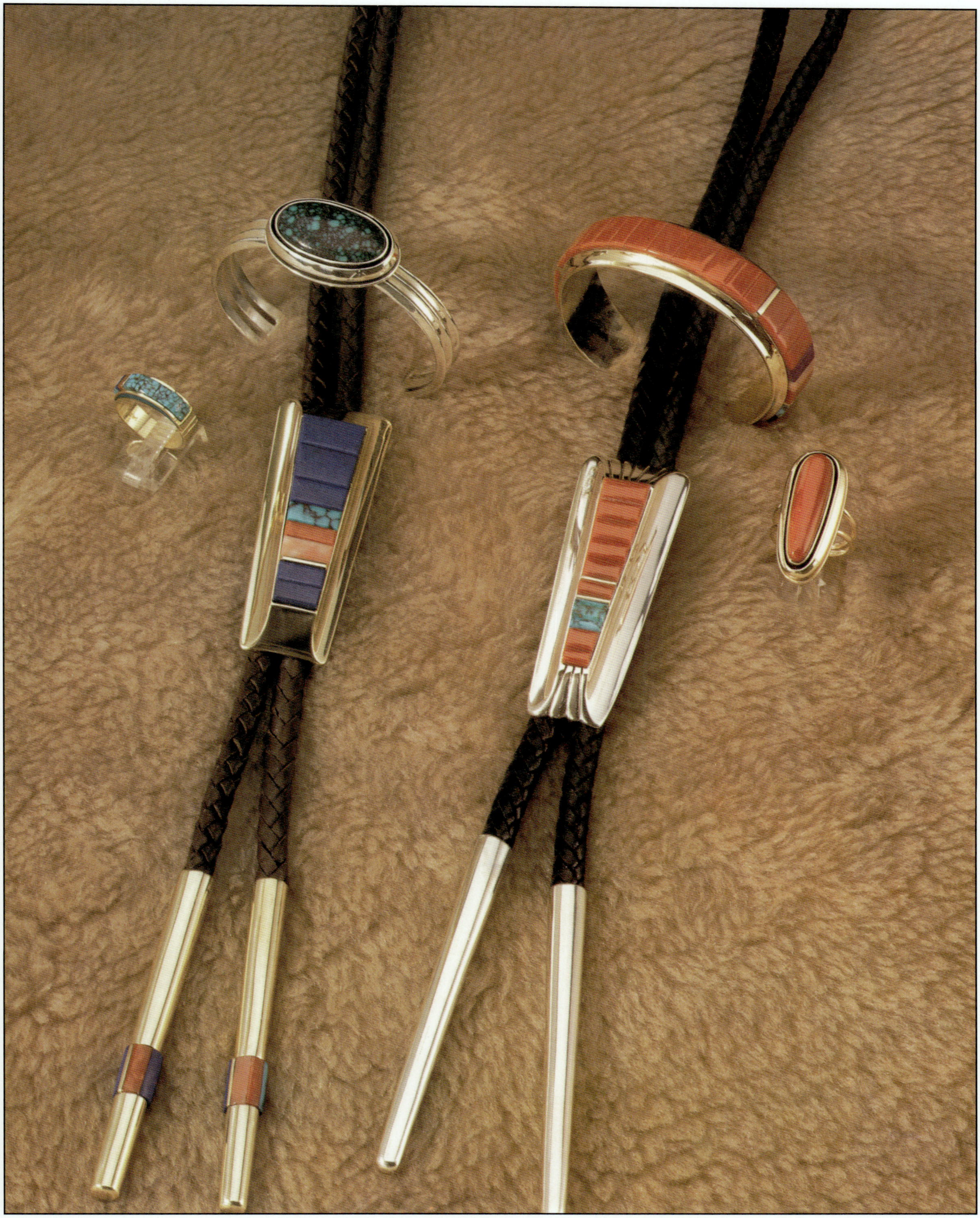

Victor Beck, Navajo, used turquoise, coral, lapis lazuli, sugalite and mother of pearl with silver and gold to create these ornaments for men and women in the 1980s. *Artist's collection*

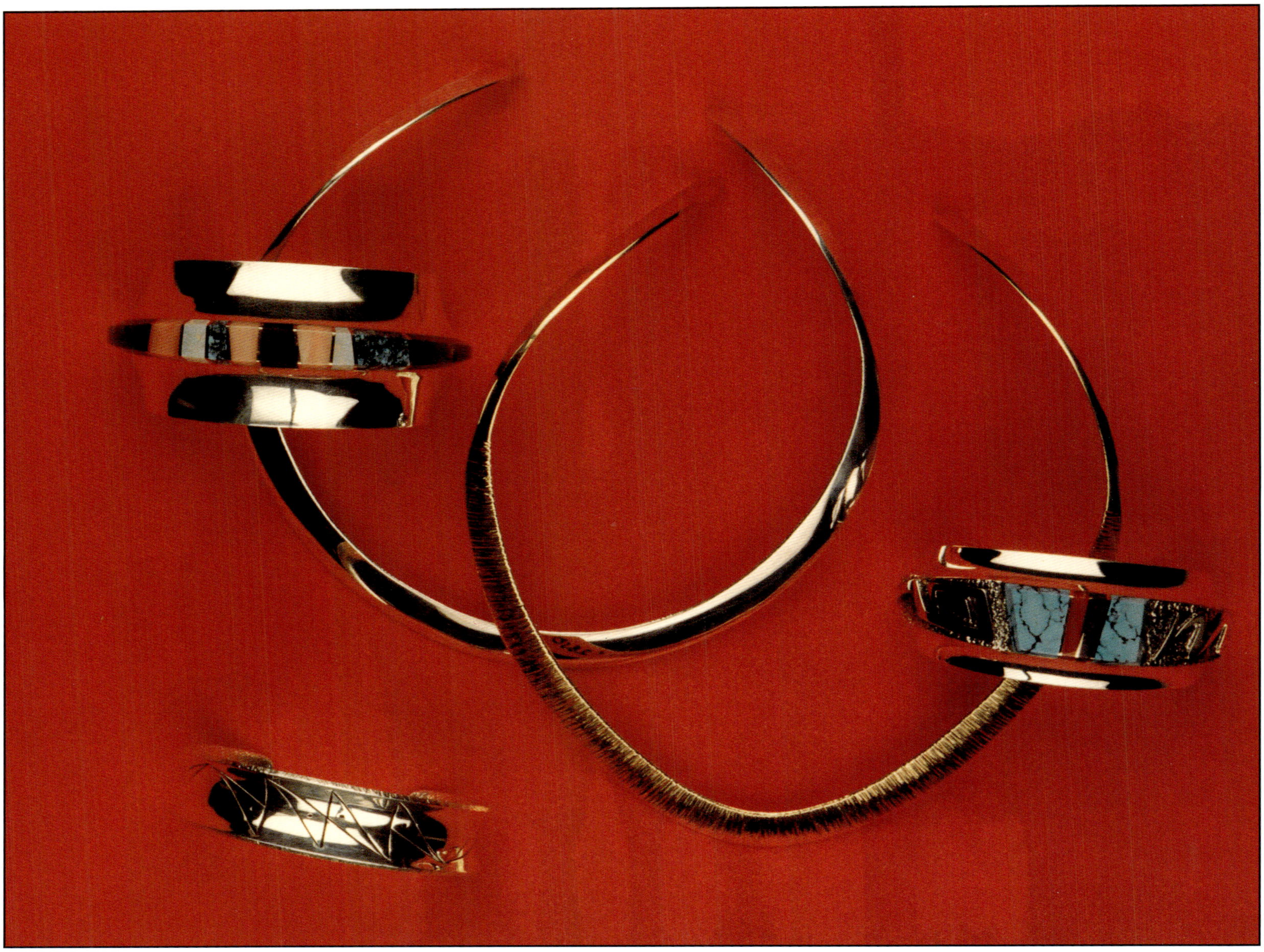

Using his skills to work silver and gold, Duane Maktima, Hopi, designed these bracelets and necklaces in the 1980s. The inlaid stones include lavulite, coral, turquoise and shell. *Dewey Gallery collection*

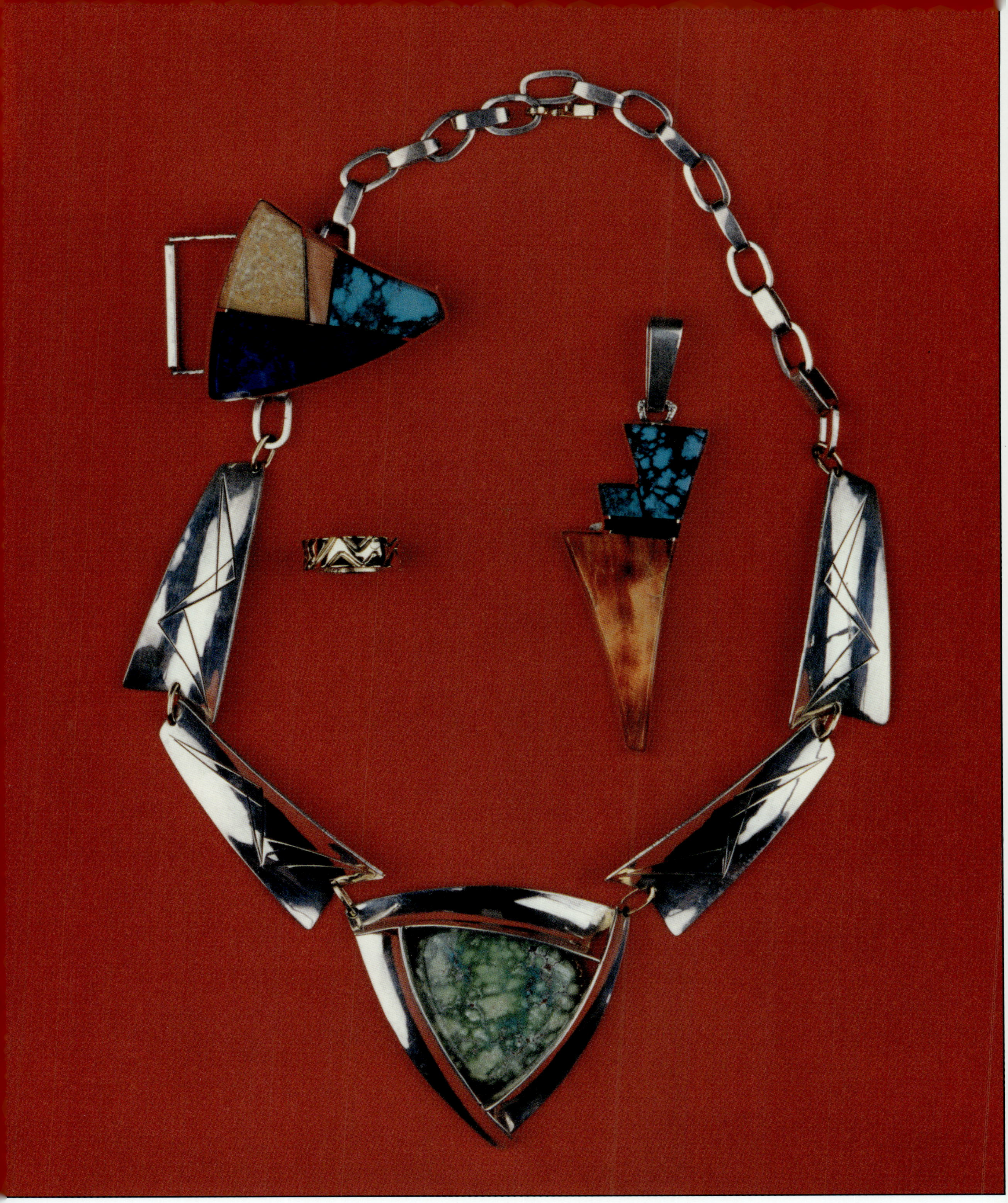

The inlaid stones form the colorful aspects of these interesting designs by Duane Maktima, Hopi. Buckle, pendant, gold ring and link necklace, 1980s. *Dewey Gallery collection*

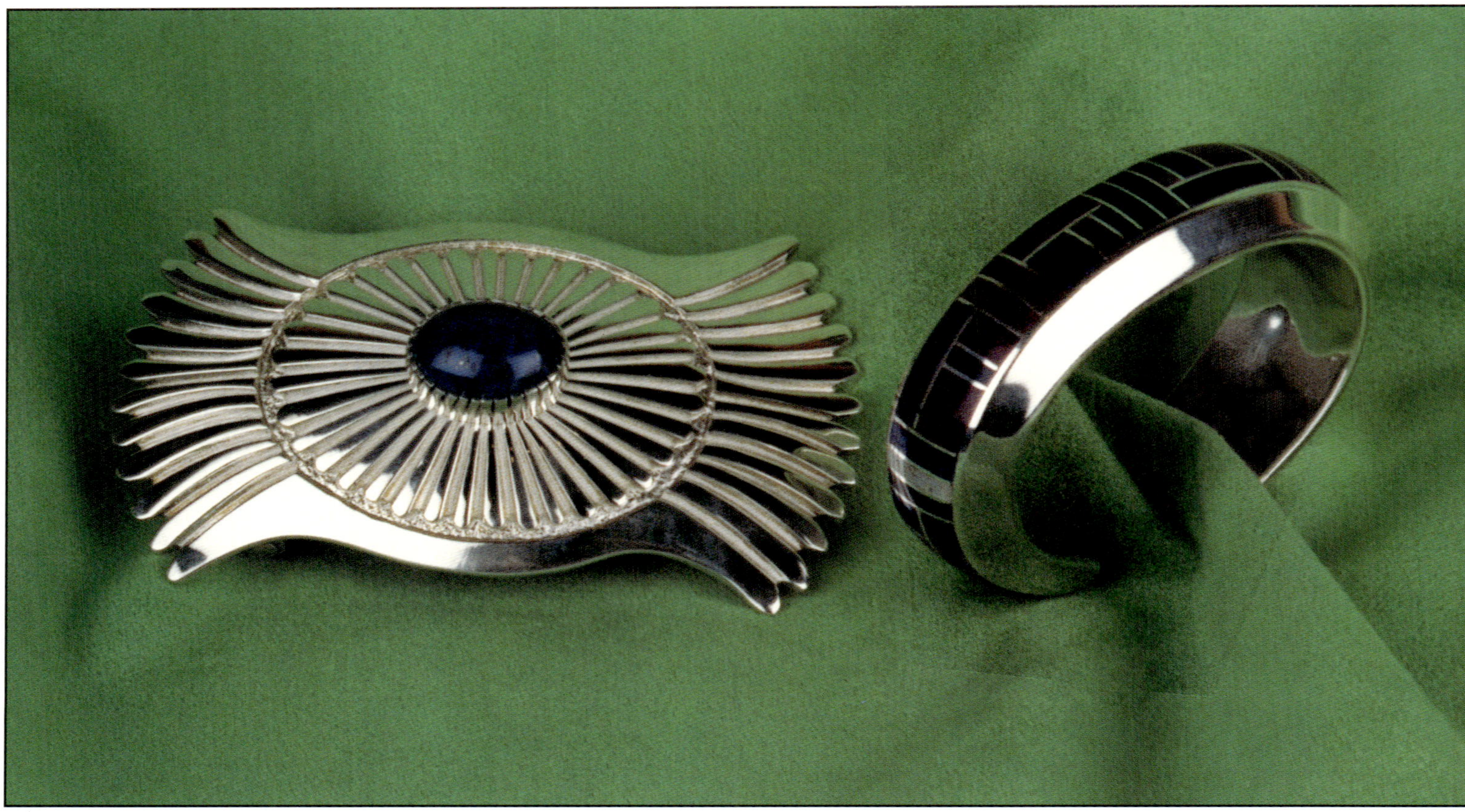

Tommy Jackson, Navajo, used lapis lazuli as the focal point of this striking silver buckle, and combined lapis lazuli with lavulite in a tight mosaic pattern in channel inlay on this silver bracelet, 1980s. *Indian Traders West collection.*

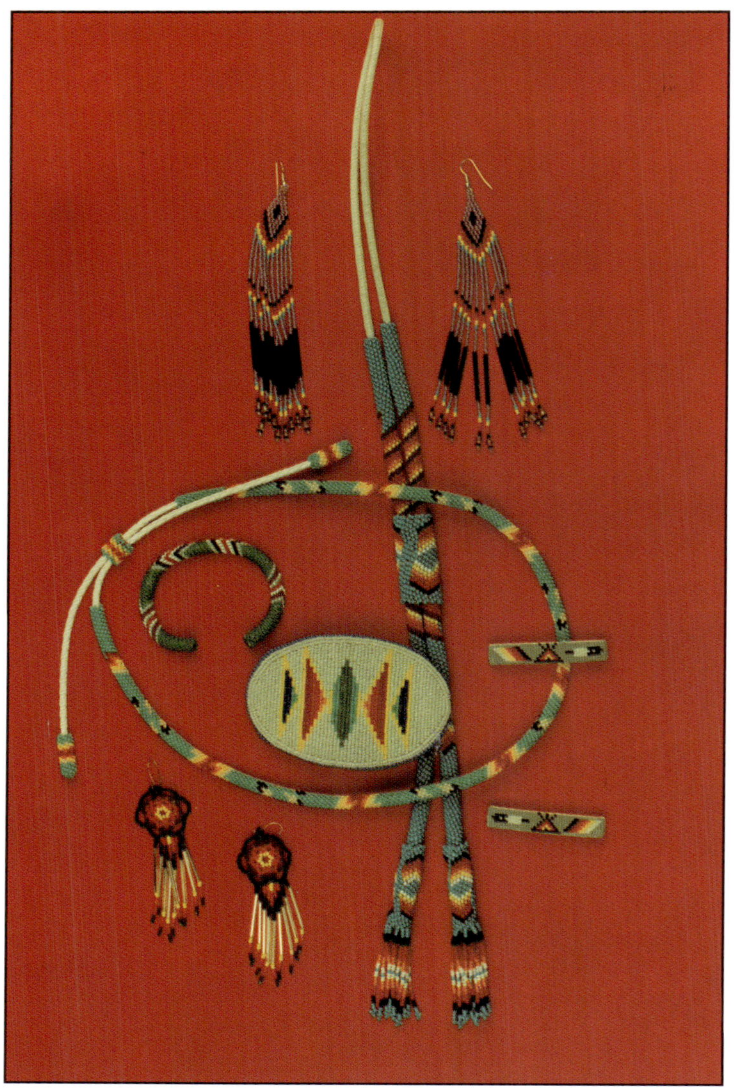

Prominent among the new generation of silversmiths are Navajo artists Nelson Howard, Earl Plummer, and Melvin Cleveland. Each has created his own style and developed techniques that set their work apart from the crowd. Nelson Howard has been working with silver and turquoise since 1972. He respects the materials as gifts from The Maker, and tries to show his respect by creating deeply significant designs.

Earl Plummer draws his inspiration from nature. The red rocks of the Arizona landsape, clouds, shapes of trees, and the line a wash makes coming out of the hills is all beautiful to him; these images inspire his jewelry designs.

Melvin Cleveland has worked in the old style since the age of nine with this step-father's help and encouragement. He studied with Tommy Yellowhorse. As his skills improved, he made most of his own tools. About eight years ago he began making pendants with black jet inlayed with intricate designs. He has developed his inlay further for many jewelry items, often including Yei figures for their healing powers.

As the decade of the 1980s closed, increasing amounts of Navajo beadwork were produced by young aspiring crafts people, no doubt inspired by the tradition of beadwork among their Plains neighbors. The beads were commercially obtained and combined in original designs. Long dangling earrings, bolo tie, hatband, bracelet, buckle, two barrettes, short dangle earrings, 1989. *Turquoise Lady collection*

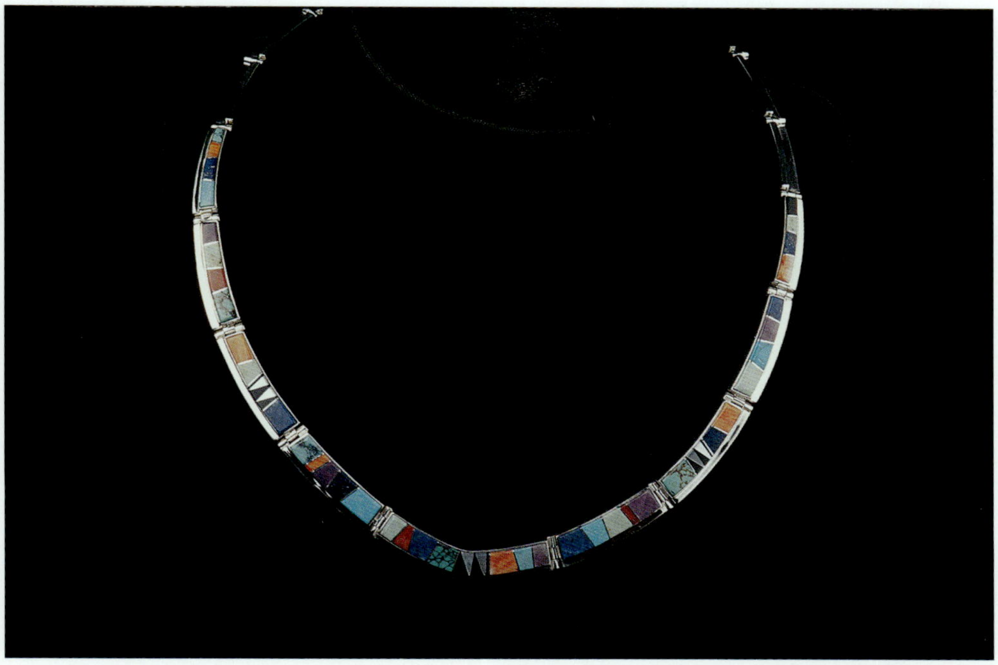

Silver and stone inlay necklace by Earl Plummer, Navajo. *Courtesy McGee's, Holbrook*

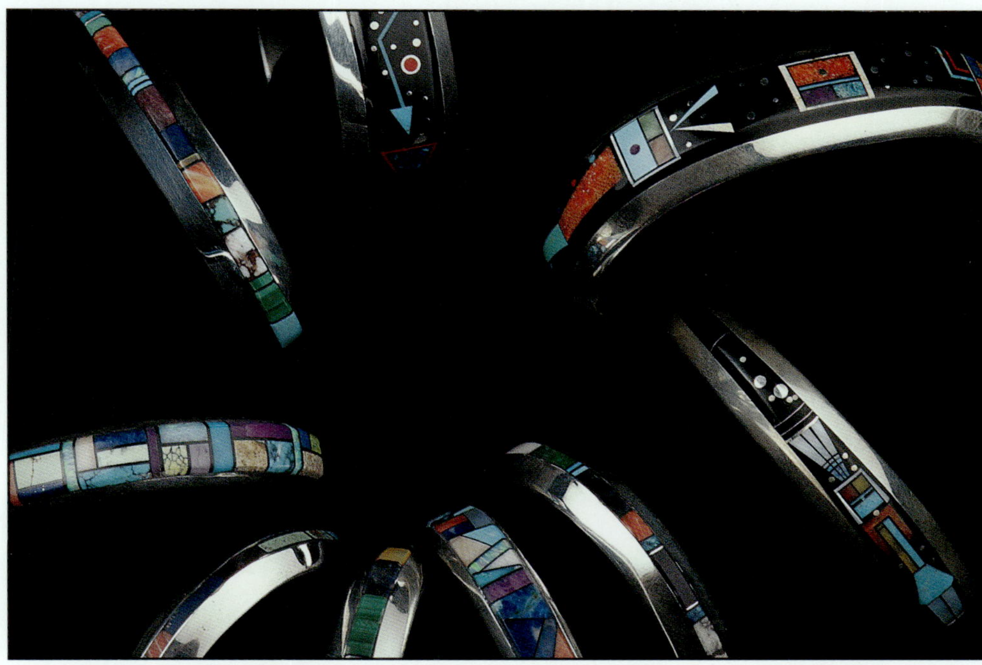

Bracelets with fine stone inlay in original designs for jewelry by Melvin Cleveland, Navajo. *Courtesy McGee's, Holbrook*

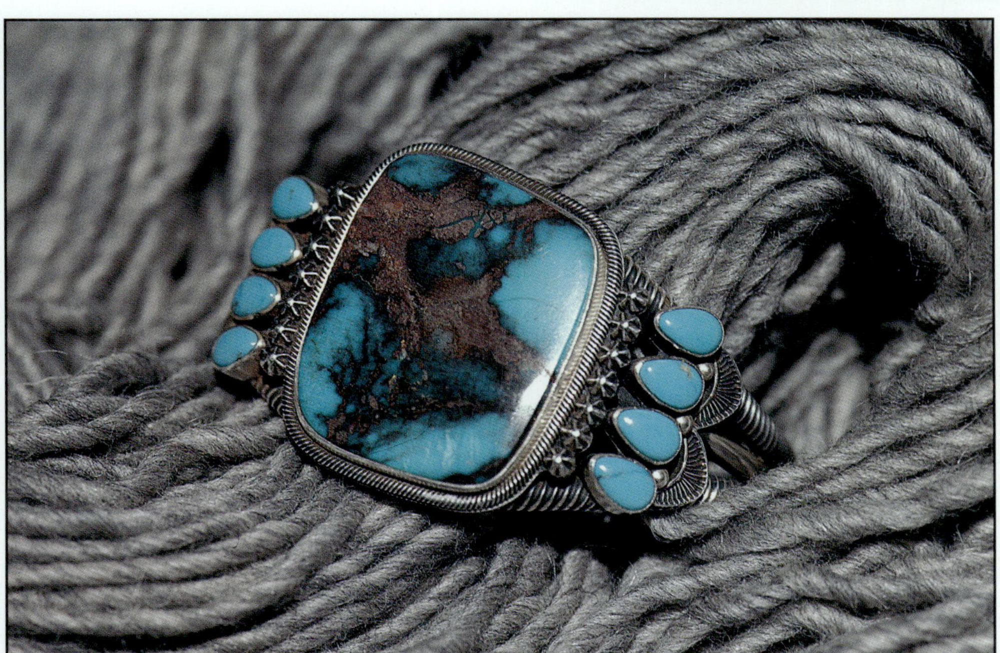

Silver cuff bracelet with a large, beautiful, and unusually markedBusbee turquoise stone made for his wife Millie Nelson by Howard Nelson, Navajo, 2001. *Courtesy McGee's, Holbrook*

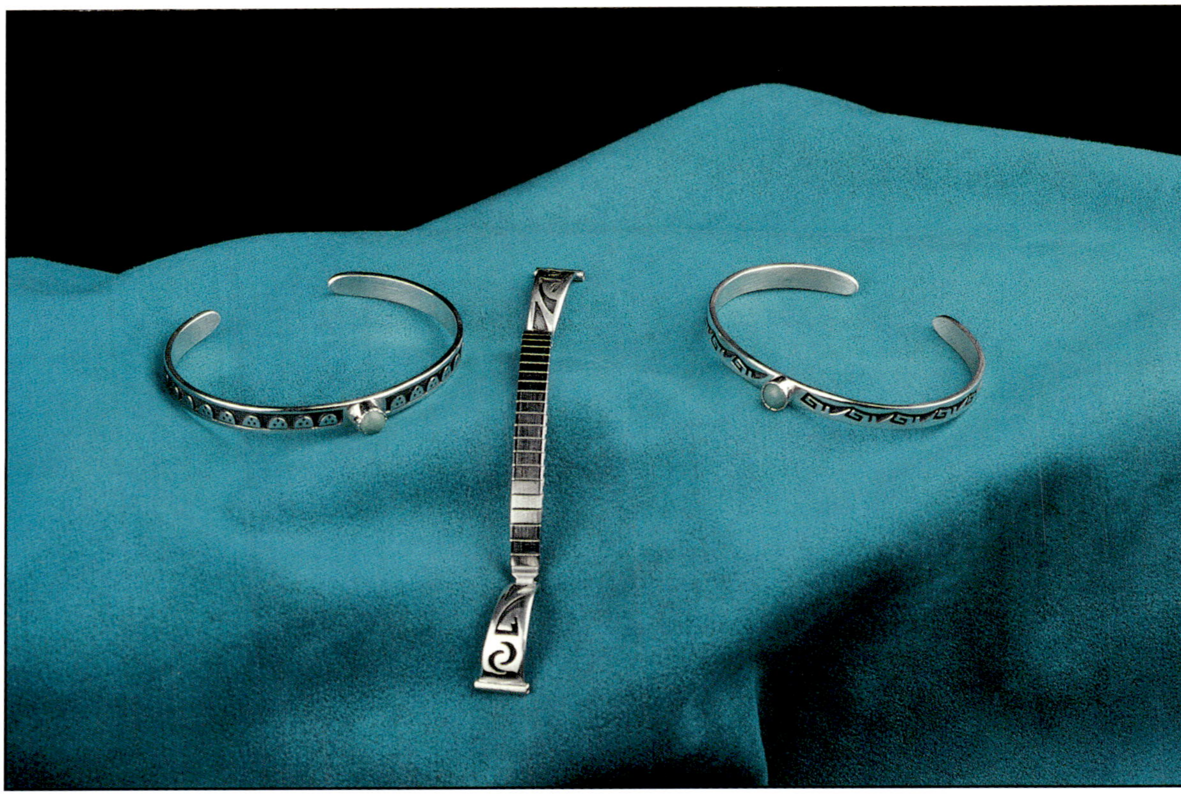

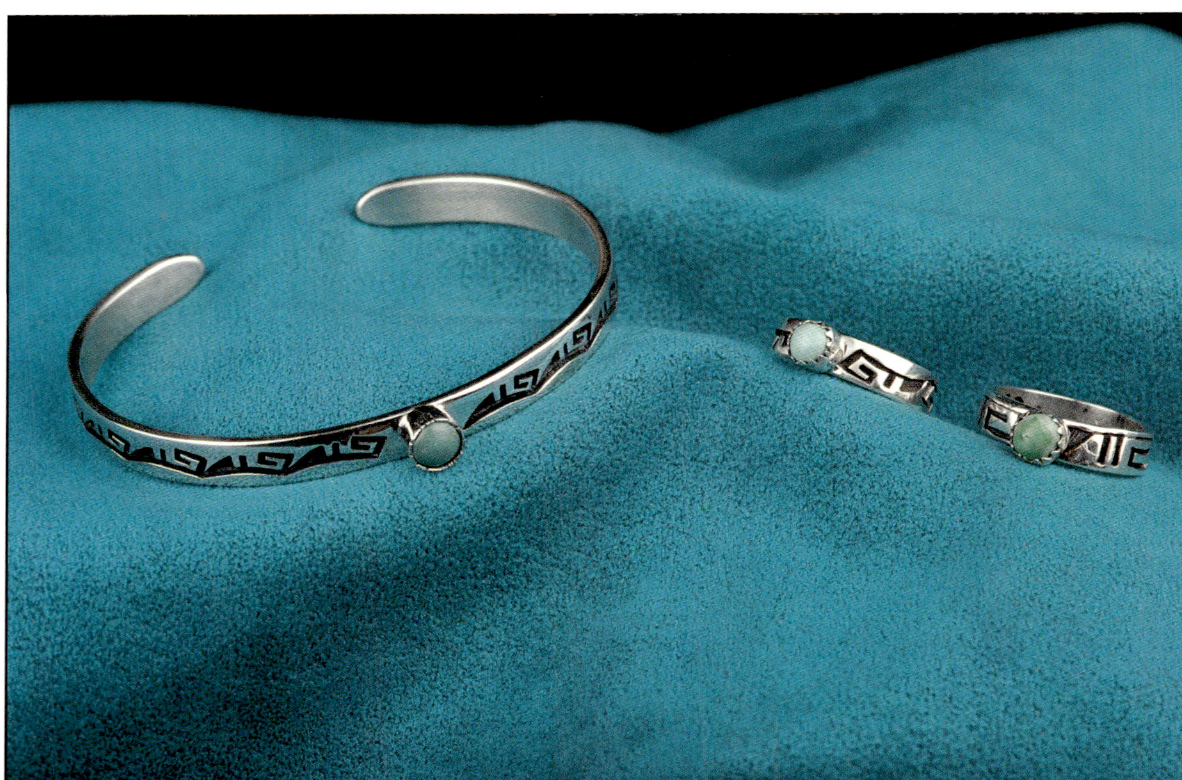

Two bracelets, a watchband, and a ring by a new woman silversmith, Elene Atokuku, Hopi, 2001. *Courtesy McGee's, Keams Canyon*

Anthony Lovato forms silver and gold jewelry by tufa casting. His meticulous craftsmanship and use of highly polished stones of subtle colors is harmonious with his symbolic designs. He carries on his Santo Domingo family's tradition of jewelry making, often including the corn symbols of his clan's traditional stories.

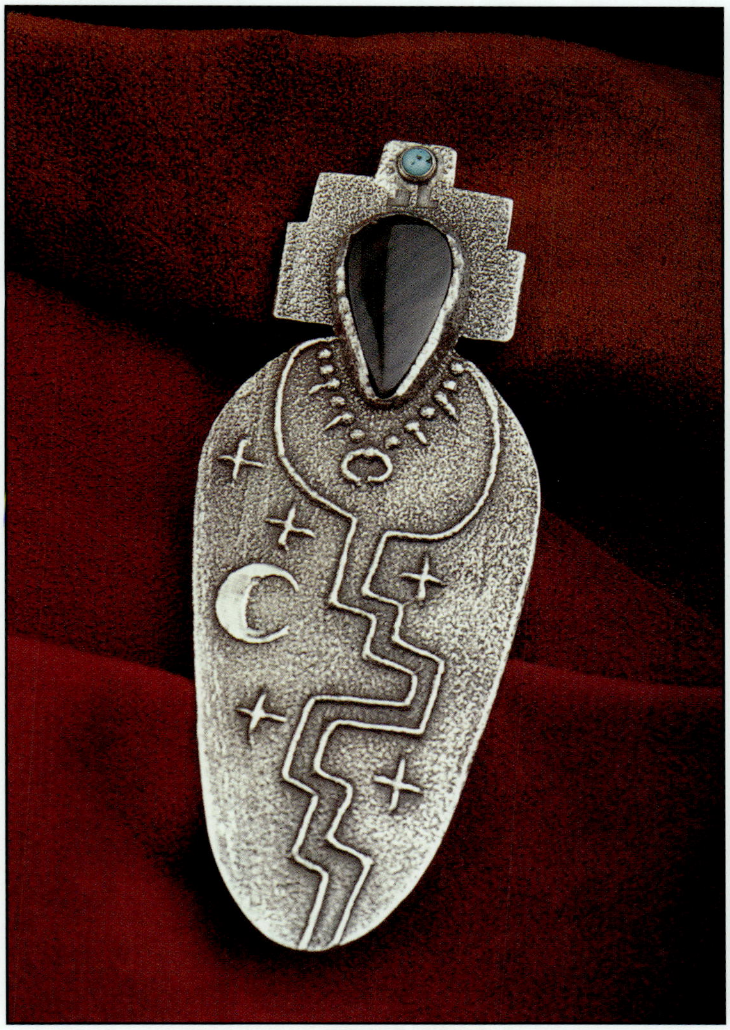

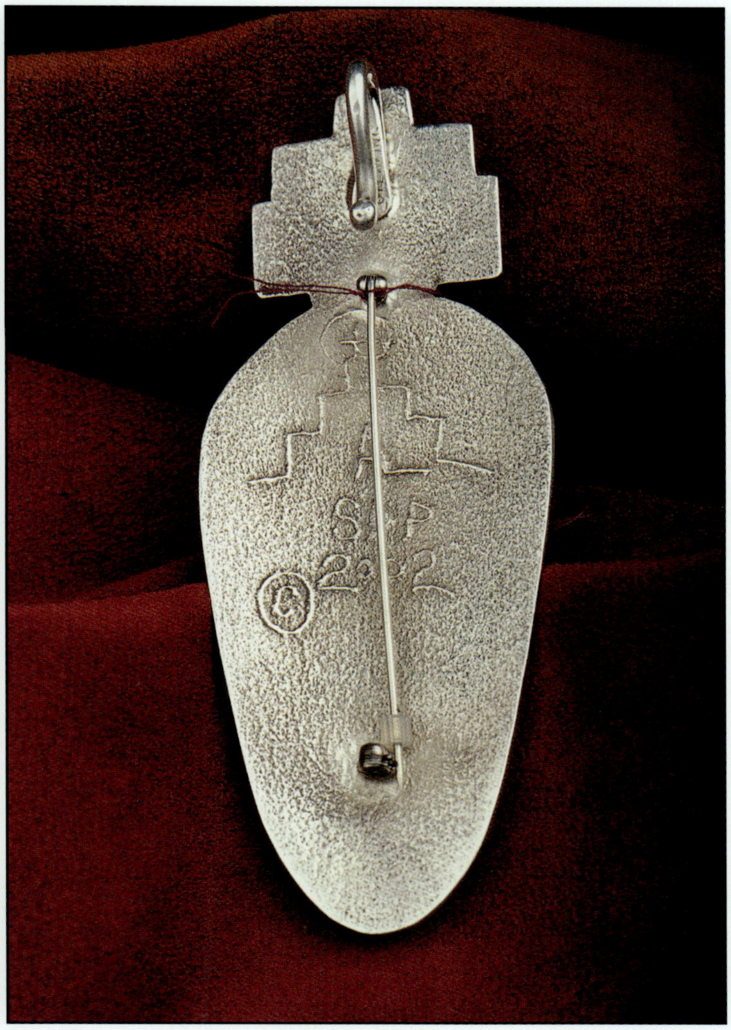

Sterling silver, turquoise, and peacock obsidian spirit pin/pendant of "Night Spirit" design by Anthony Lovato, Santo Domingo, 4" long, 2002. *Courtesy of Gerald Peters Gallery, Santa Fe, New Mexico* ($500)

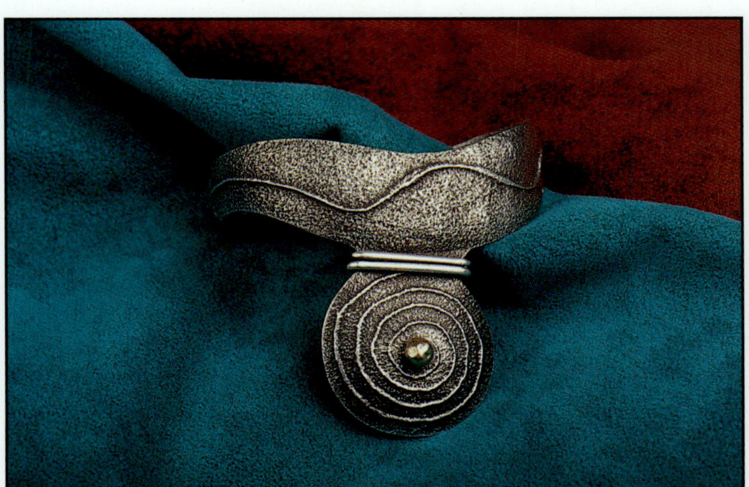

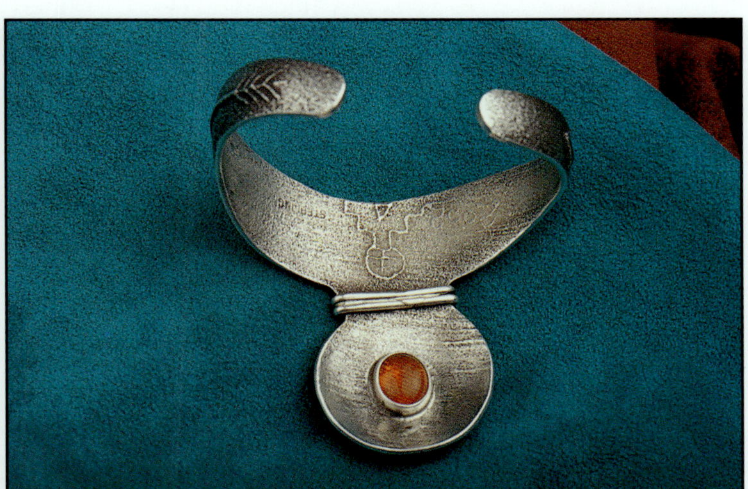

Sterling silver and Mexican opal arrow bracelet by Anthony Lovato, Santo Domingo, 3-1/2" long x 1-1/4" wide, 2002. *Courtesy of Gerald Peters Gallery, Santa Fe, New Mexico* ($350)

Belts

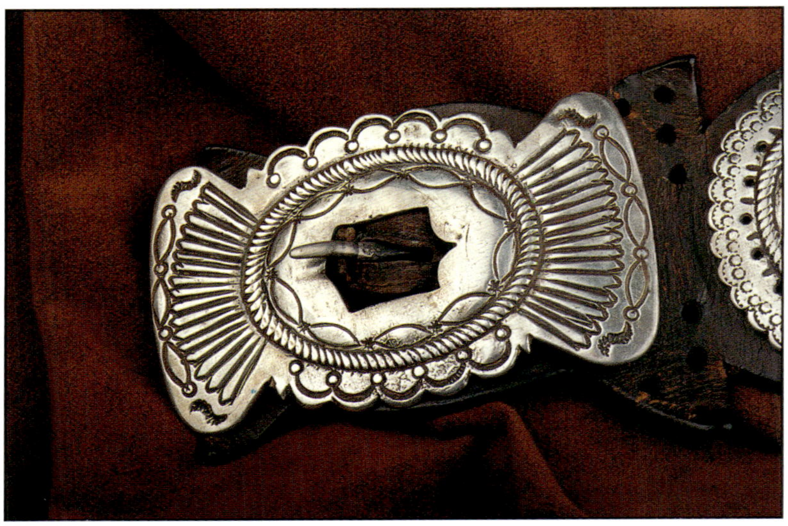

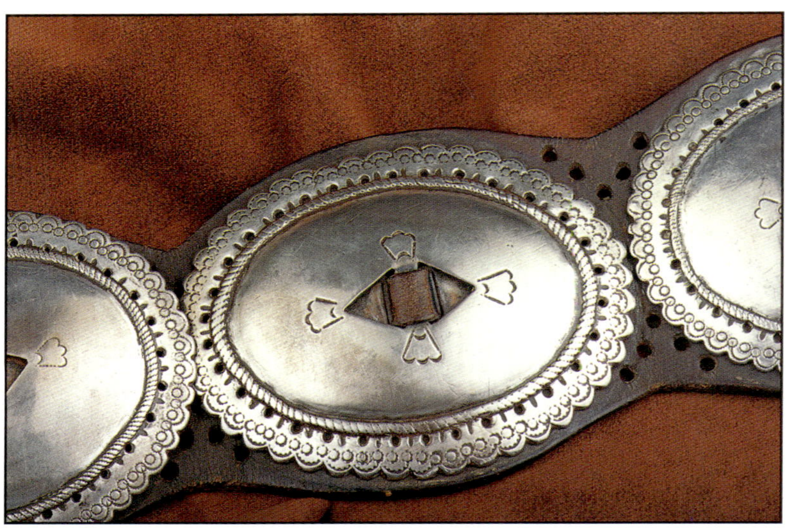

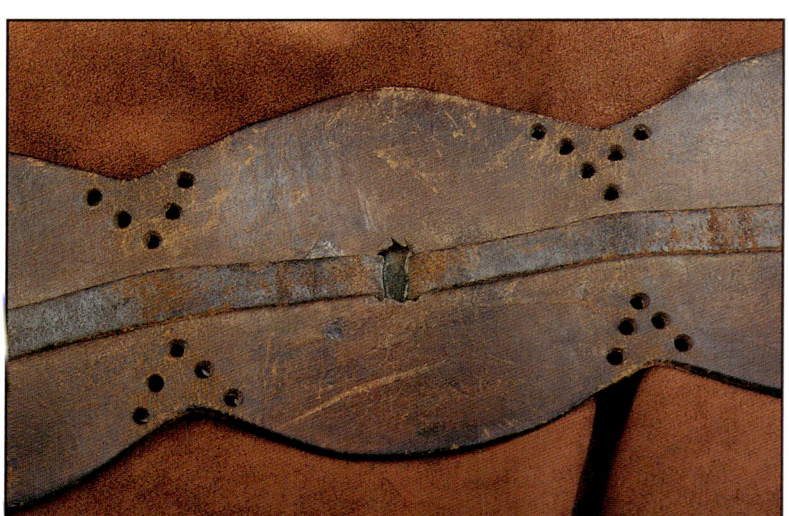

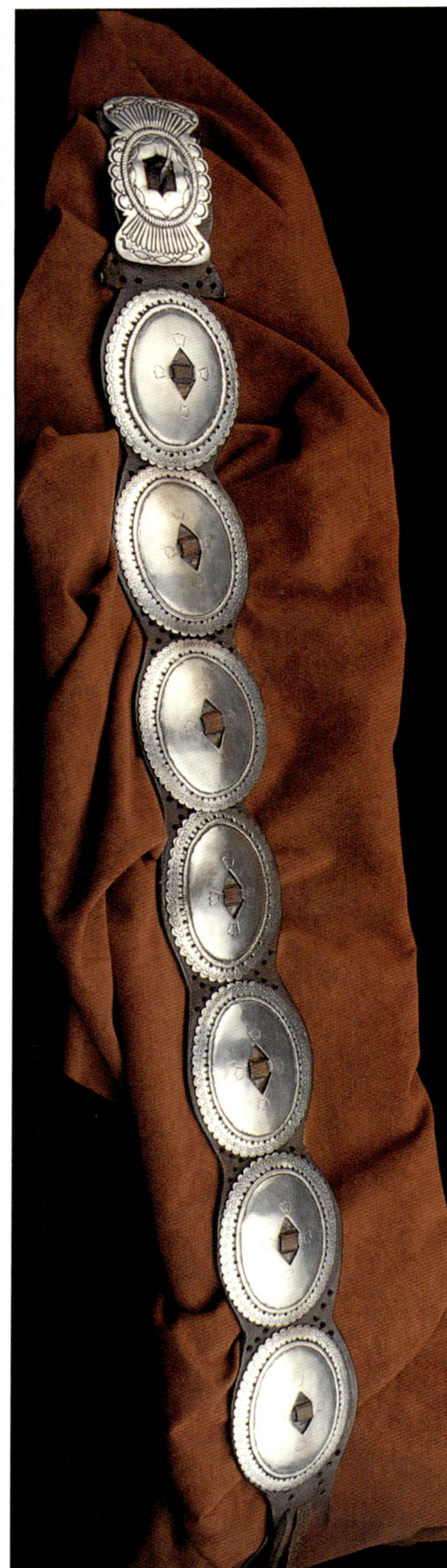

First phase Navajo silver concha belt with seven conchas open at the centers mounted on old leather. This belt displays the finest workmanship of the early period, probably that of Slender Maker of Silver, a legend in Navajo jewelry circles. The buckle is original. c.1880. *Lynn D. Trusdell, Crown & Eagle Antiques*

Derived from Plains Indian hair ornaments which were worn on leather straps and Spanish horse decorations, and very early (1870s) made an important ornament for a Navajo chief, concha belts evolved into a particular Navajo form of jewelry. The evolution from "first phase" conchas with a diamond-shaped opening through which the leather strap passed to "second phase" conchas with closed surfaces was made after Navajo silversmiths began using solder to fix a loop of wire to the back of the concha to hold the strap.

The use of minted coins by Southwest silversmiths in the fabrication of early pieces, belts in particular, is shown by the remaining milled ridges, which appear on the concha edges. The presence of these ridges assures the correct term "coin silver" to describe the material.

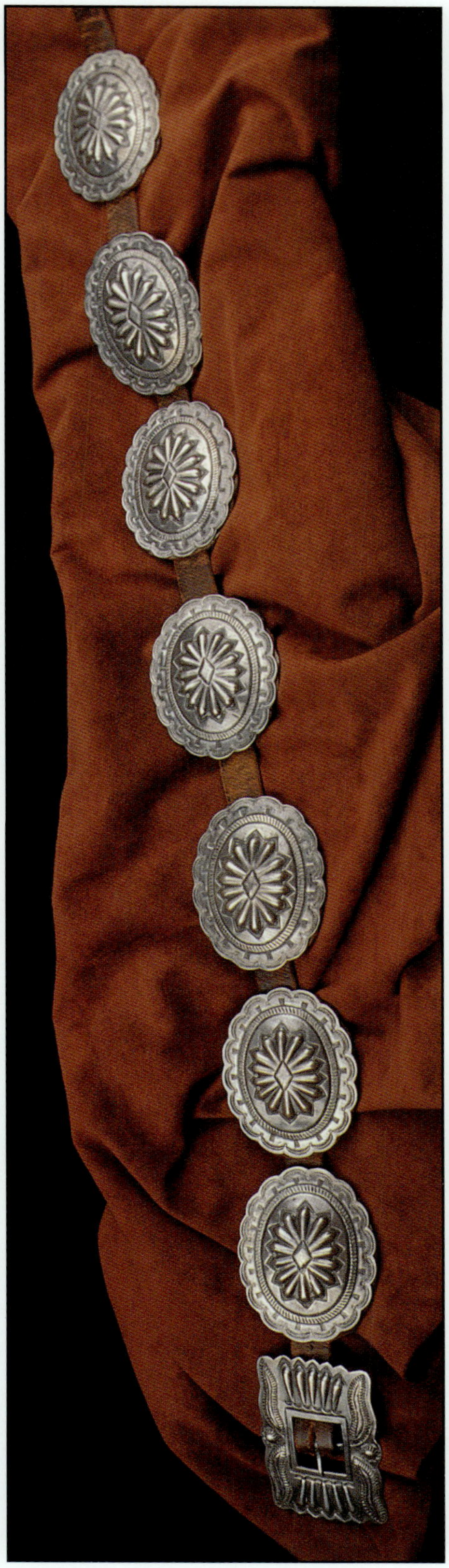

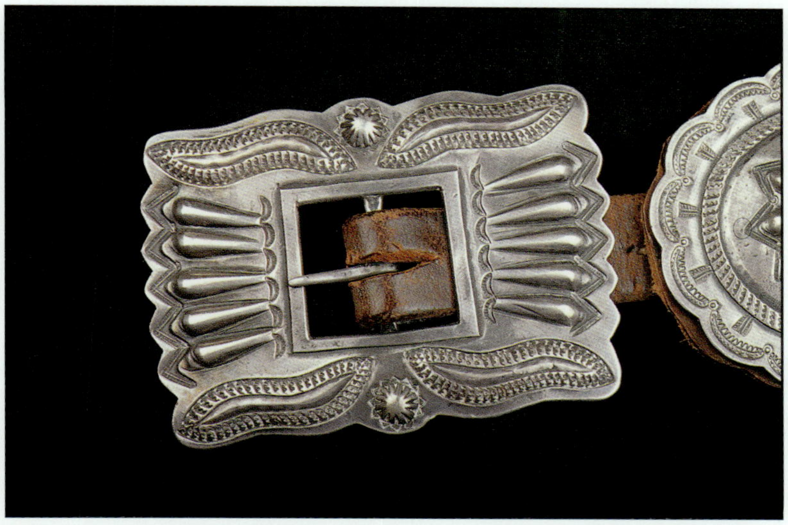

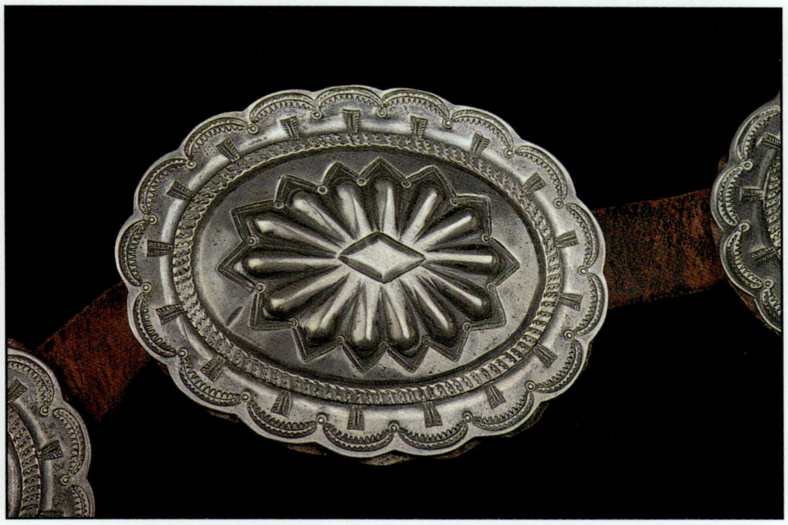

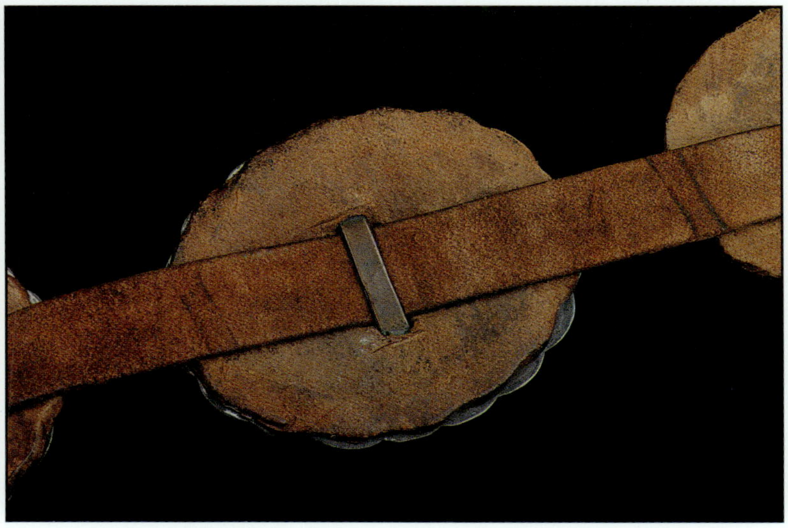

Second phase Navajo silver concha belt of seven conchas closed at the centers. Fine repoussé work appearson the buckle and conchas. c.1900-1910. *Lynn D. Trusdell, Crown & Eagle Antiques*

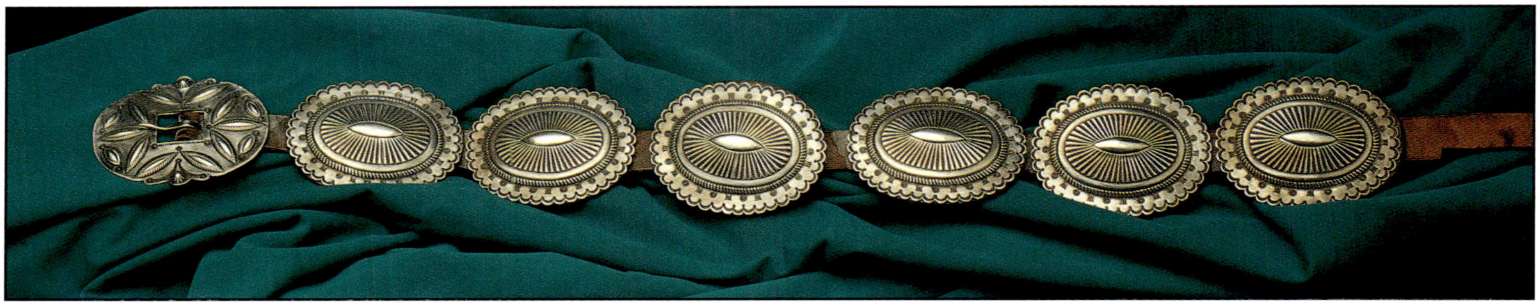

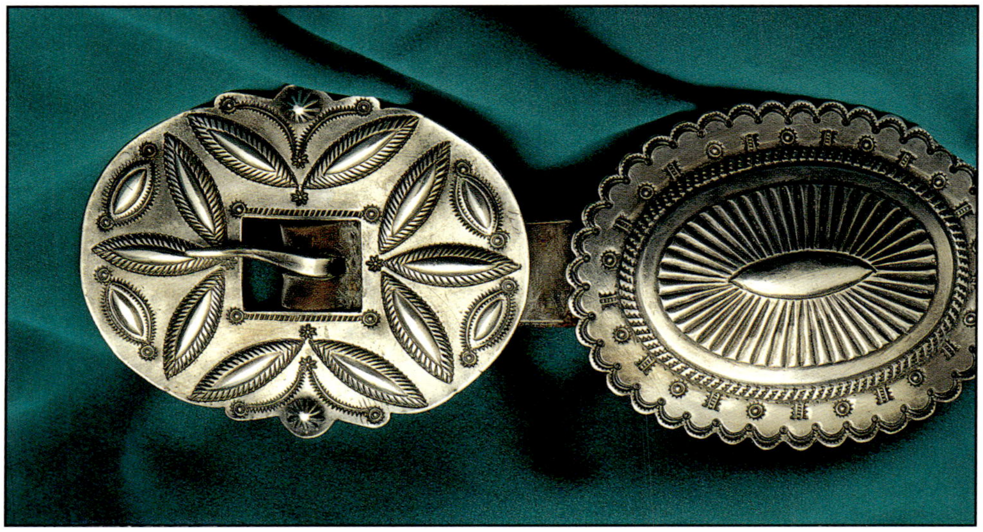

A fine second phase Navajo silver belt.

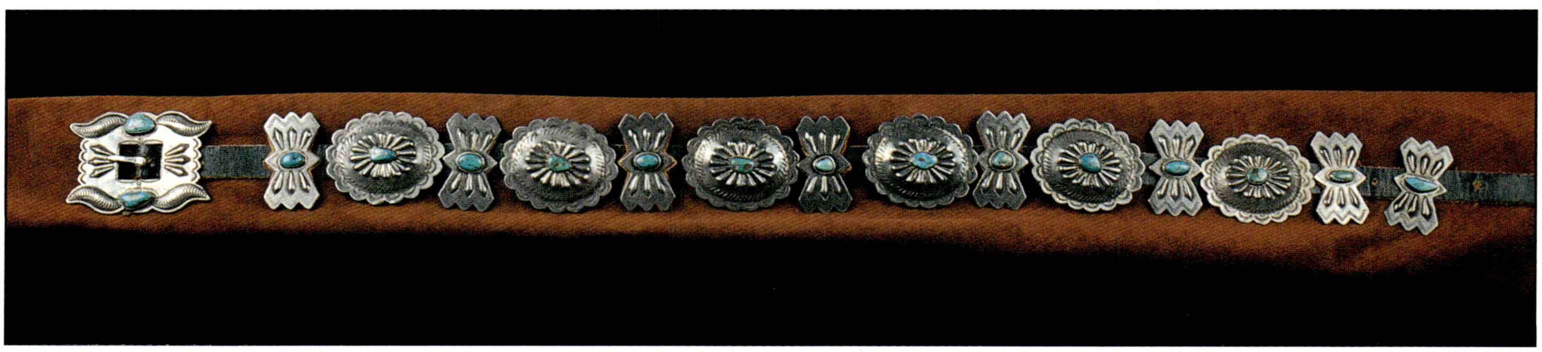

Third phase Navajo silver concha belt with butterfly-shaped silver spacers between the conchas and matching turquoise ornaments. The buckle is original. *Lynn D. Trusdell, Crown & Eagle Antiques*

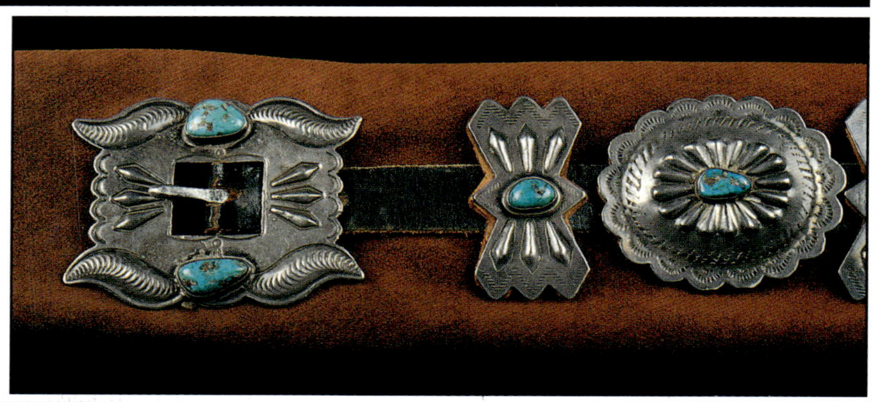

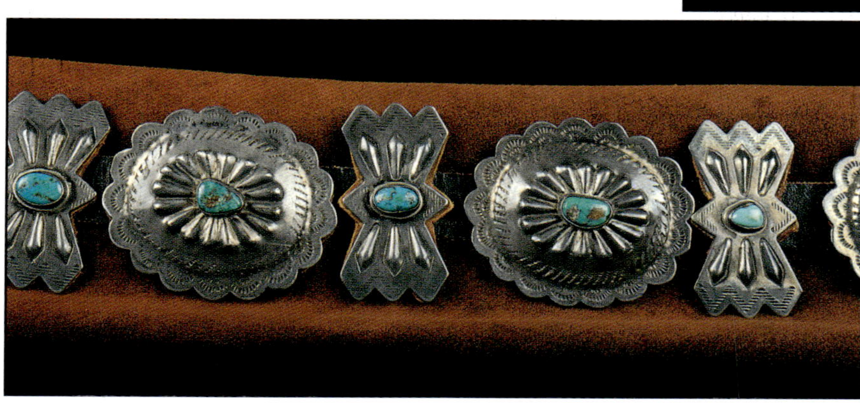

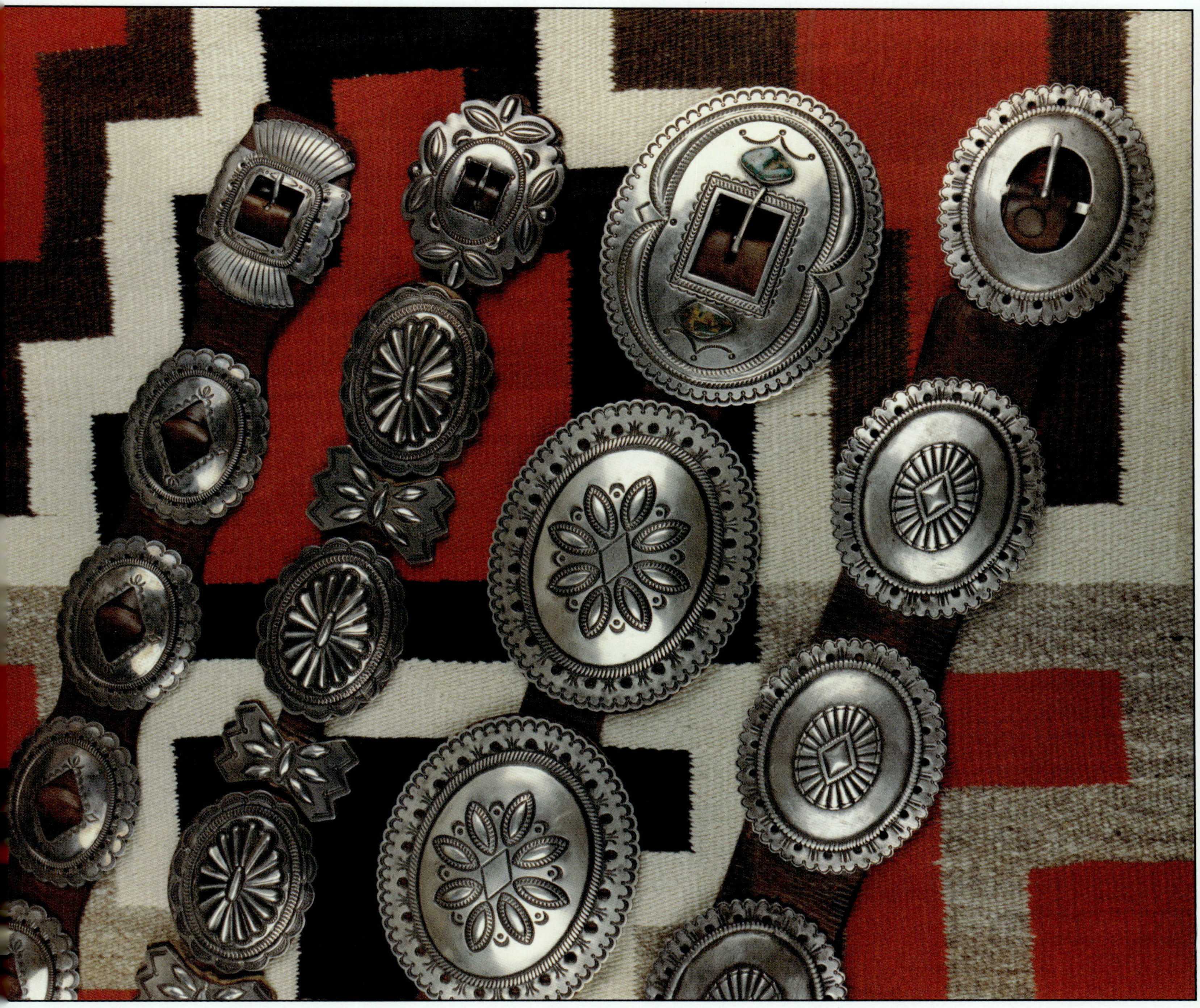

First phase revival concha belt, circa 1950, with punched designs on the silver. / Second phase concha belt, circa 1915-1920, with "butterfly" shaped silver spacers between the embossed concha. / Large and finely made concha belt by Roger Skeetz, Sr., 1938, representing the classical Navajo form. *Crown & Eagle Antiques, Inc.collection.* / Concha belt with matching buckle of heavy weight silver and excellent decoration, circa 1910. *Lynn D. Trusdell collection*

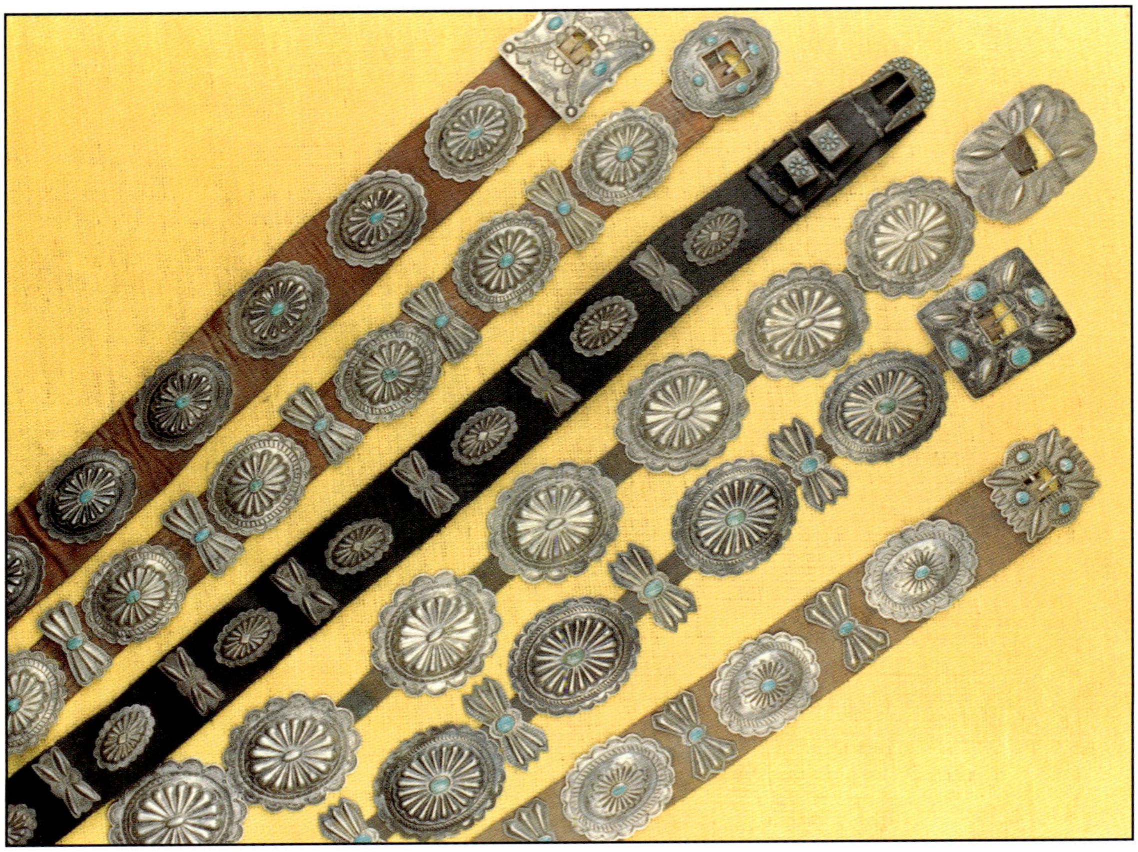

Navajo belt of ten coin silver conchas with very good quality stamp work and Villa Grove turquoise, circa 1920. / Silver Navajo belt with six conchas, six butterfly spacers and 16 Morenci turquoise stones, circa 1920. / Zuni ranger buckle on a Navajo belt with nine conchas, eight butterfly spacers and 66 small Morenci turquoise stones, circa 1950. / Coin silver buckle on a Navajo belt with seven conchas, circa 1920. / Early Navajo belt with seven conchas, six butterflies and 15 Morenci turquoise stones, circa 1900. / Coin silver Navajo belt with seven conchas, six butterfly spacers, and 17 Morenci turquoise stones, circa 1920. *Dennehotso collection*

Handmade dies were used to make this heavy hand rolled silver concha belt, circa 1915. / Early Navajo belt with five conchas and six butterflies of finely stamped coin silver and 15 turquoise stones from the Villa Grove, Morenci, and Royston mines, circa 1910. / Seven coin silver conchas and six butterfly spacers with early stamping die decoration are ornamented with 17 Morenci and Royston turquoise stones on this Navajo belt, circa 1910. / Navajo belt with seven coin silver conchas and nine Bisbee turquoise stones, circa 1940. / Sterling silver Navajo belt with seven conchas and seven butterfly spacers ornamented with 19 Morenci turquoise stones, circa 1920. *Dennehotso collection*

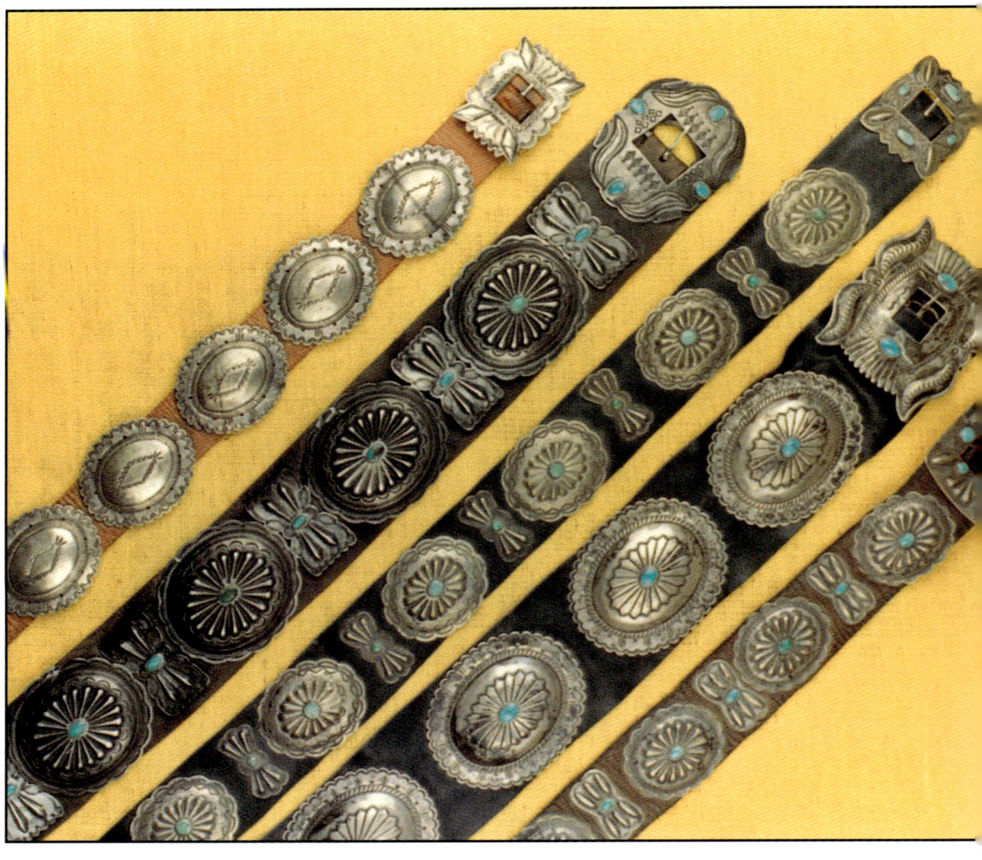

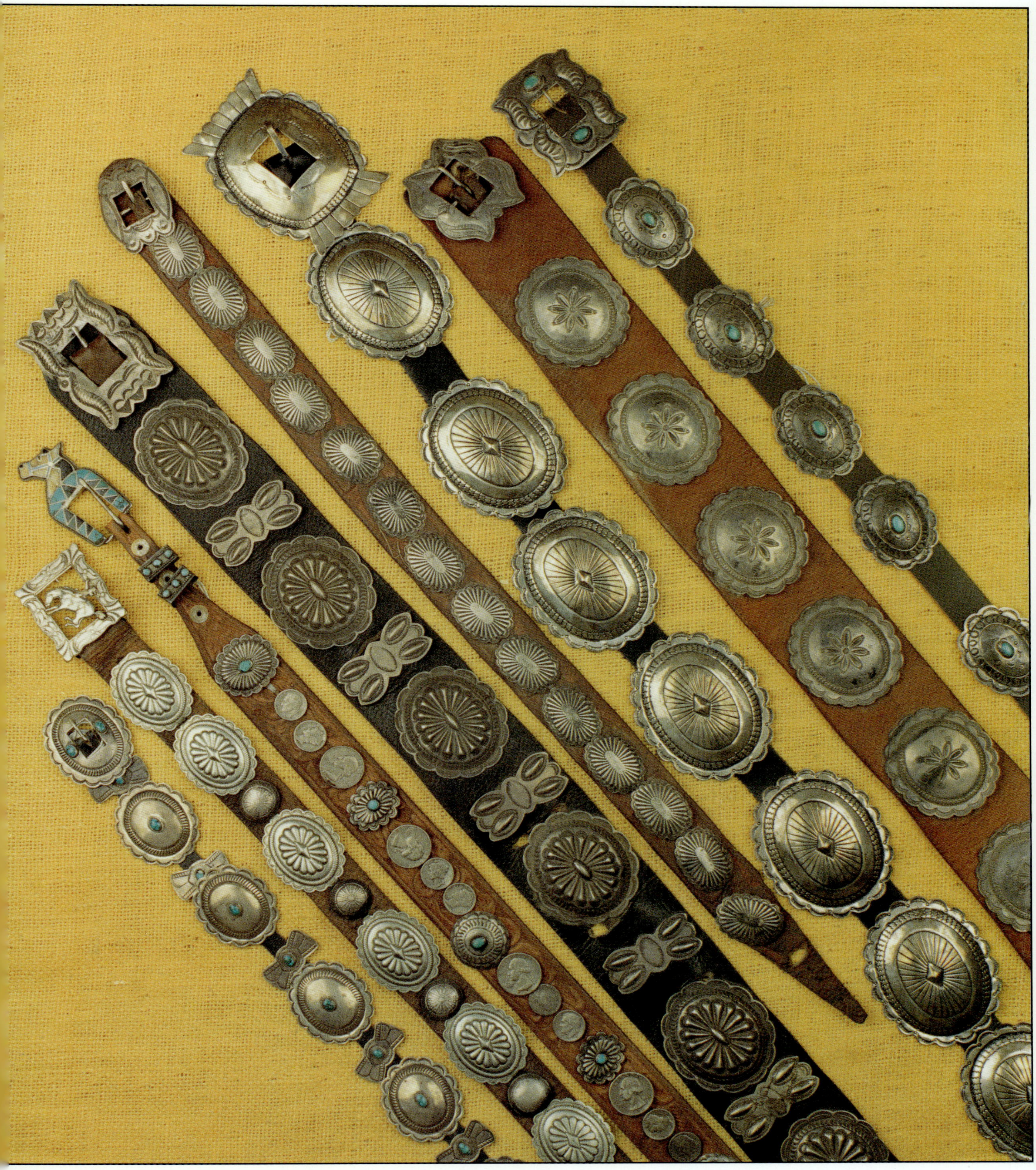

Made by a Navajo silversmith for the tourist trade through the Fred Harvey stores along the Santa Fe railway, this lightweight silver belt has 12 conchas and 12 butterfly spacers with 26 Bisbee turquoise stones, circa 1920. / Homemade Navajo belt and buckle with 12 nickel conchas and eight small concha buttons of sterling silver, one with a Snake Eye turquoise stone, circa 1950. / Homemade Navajo belt with seven unmatched conchas, six silver U. S. quarters and 12 dimes and a Zuni four-piece ranger buckle set, circa 1950s. / Navajo belt and buckle with seven deeply stamped rolled silver conchas, circa 1920s. / Coin silver Navajo concha belt (probably for a child), circa 1940. / Navajo belt of ten sterling silver conchas and a buckle, circa 1930s. / Navajo belt and buckle with 11 conchas ornamented with 13 Royal Blue turquoise stones, late 1940s. *Dennehotso collection*

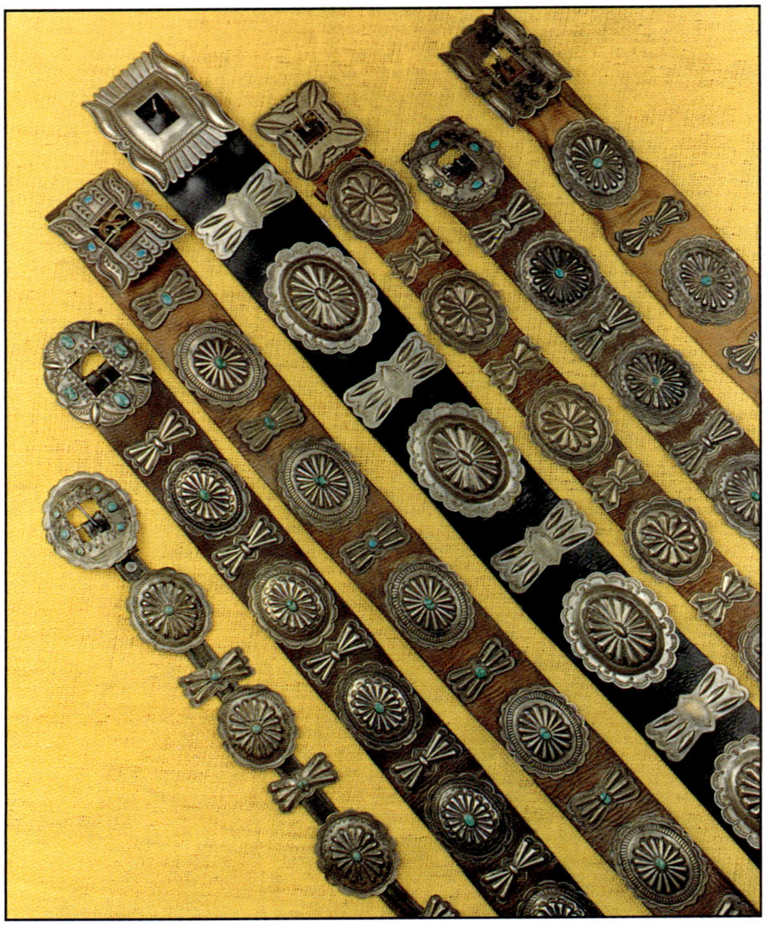

Rolled coin silver Navajo belt with six crudely stamped conchas and five butterfly spacers ornamented with 17 Morenci turquoise stones made in the early 1900s. / Navajo belt and buckle with seven sterling silver conchas, eight butterfly spacers and 11 Fox turquoise stones, circa 1920. / Sterling silver Navajo belt with five conchas, six butterfly spacers and 15 old Morenci turquoise stones, circa 1920. / Navajo belt from the 1960s with five conchas and five butterfly spacers. / Coin silver Navajo belt with seven conchas, six butterfly spacers and a buckle with deep stamping decoration, circa 1920. / Navajo coin silver belt and buckle with seven conchas and seven butterfly spacers, circa 1920. / Navajo sterling silver belt, circa 1915, with seven conchas, six butterfly spacers and a buckle ornamented with six turquoise stones from the Old Morenci mine. *Dennehotso collection*

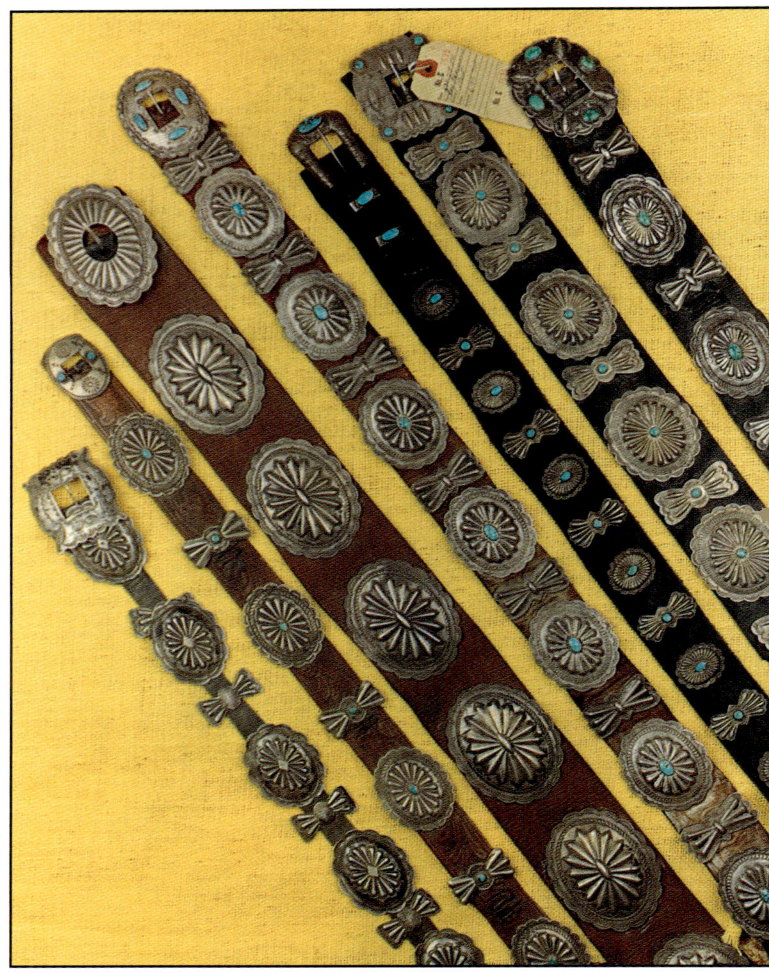

From the "boom period" of the early 1970s came this Navajo belt with ten conchas and spacers. / In contrast, a homemade Navajo belt and buckle with seven sterling silver conchas and five butterfly spacers ornamented with 14 Morenci turquoise stones, circa 1920s. / Old stamping techniques are apparent on the seven rolled silver conchas and butterfly spacers of this Navajo belt from the 1920s. / Seven coin silver conchas and seven butterfly spacers with 11 high grade Burnham turquoise stones ornament this Navajo belt from the 1920s. / A home-made belt from the 1950s includes two handmade conchos, seven machine-stamped conchos, eight machine-stamped butterfly spacers and a sterling silver Navajo ranger buckle set. / 13 stabilized Morenci turquoise stones ornament the sterling silver Navajo belt with four conchas and five butterfly spacers from the 1960s. / Classic Navajo design is presented by this sterling silver belt and buckle with six conchas, seven butterfly spacers and ten Ajax turquoise stones from the 1920s. *Dennehotso collection*

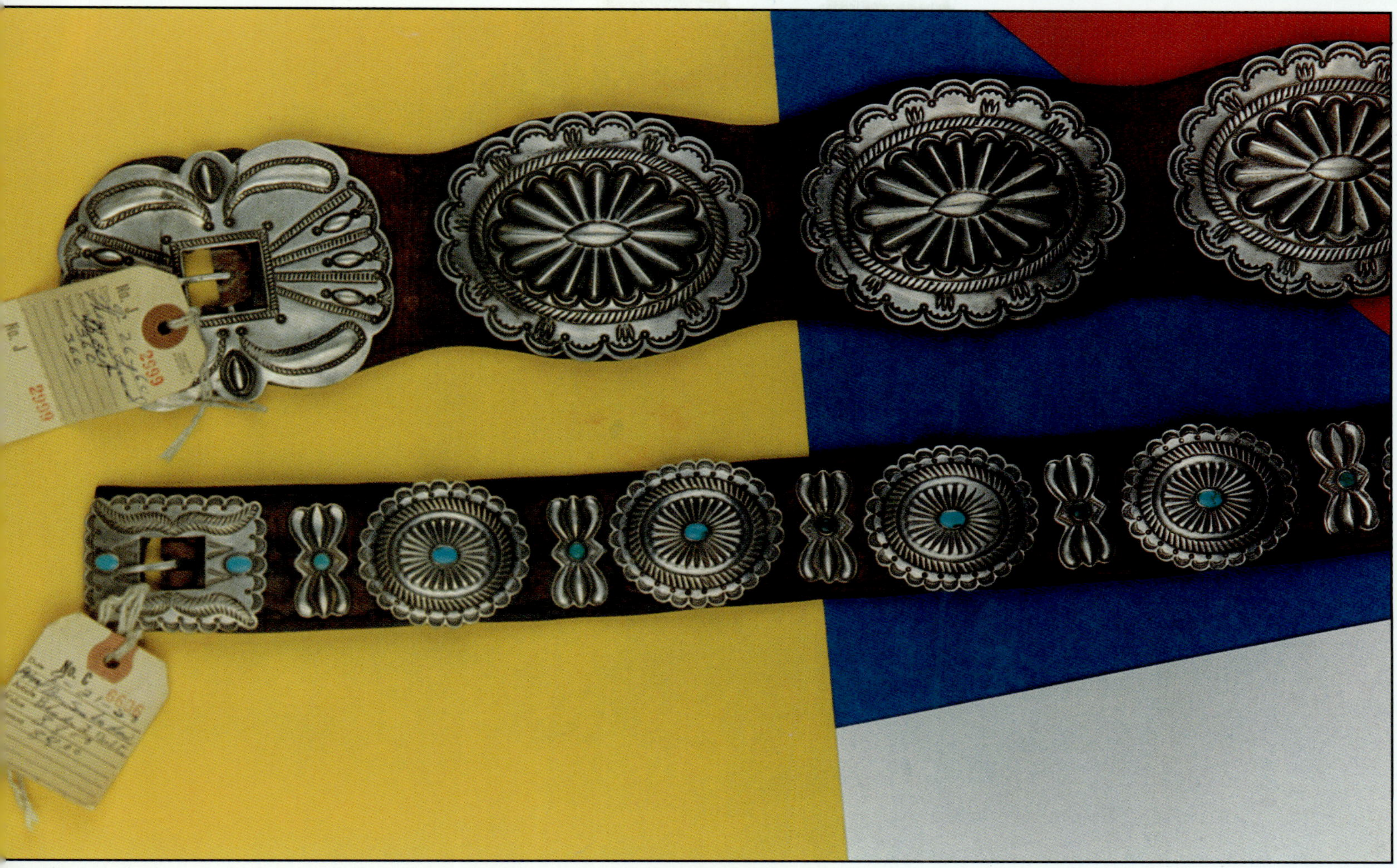

Using a system of trading goods with a professional trader on or off the reservation, a system known as "pawn", fine belts such as these have come into the hands of non-Indians. Put up by Indians as collateral against the future payment of goods needed at the time, valuable possessions sometimes lay with the trader for many years. If the debt was not paid, the pawned item became the property of the trader and could be sold. These belts still have their old pawn tickets intact. The large conchas are good examples of heavy, well-made conchas of the 1920s. The smaller belt, sometimes known as a "good luck" belt, has turquoise-set conchas and butterfly spacers, circa 1930s. *Dennehotso collection*

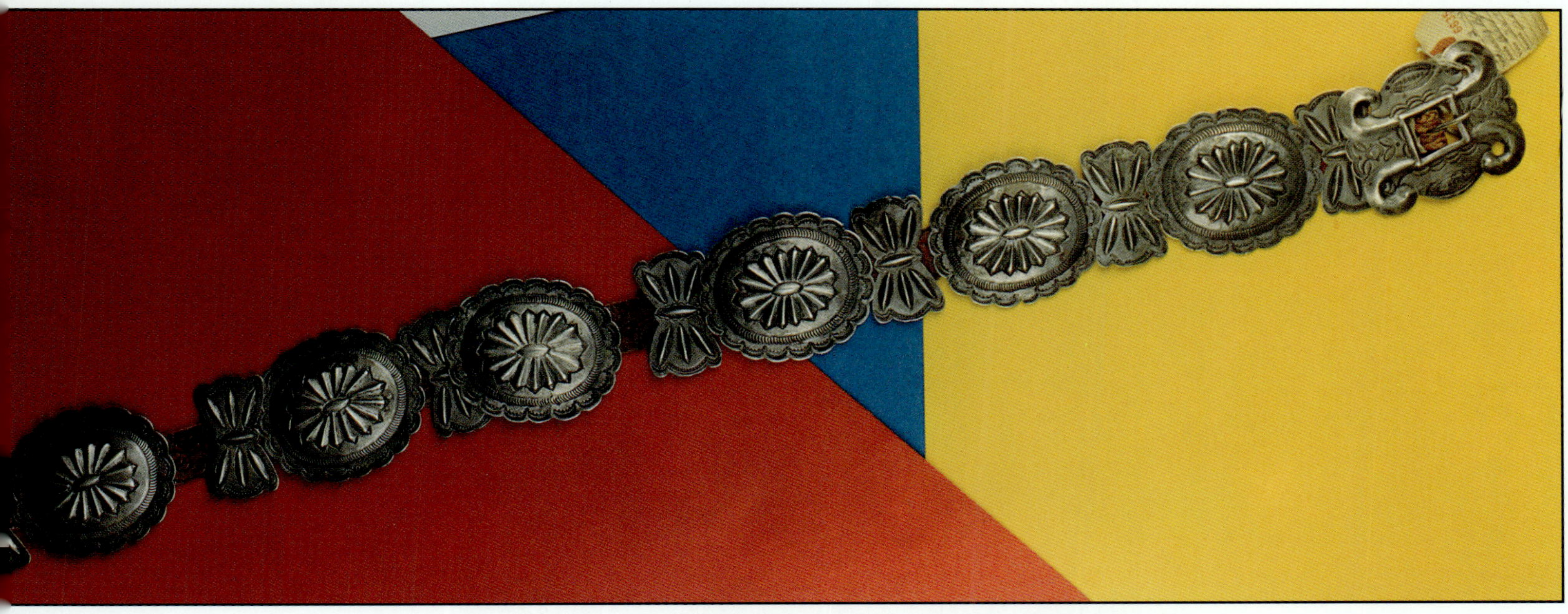

Coin silver concha belt of excellent technique, circa 1930, with a pawn ticket attached. *Dennehotso collection*

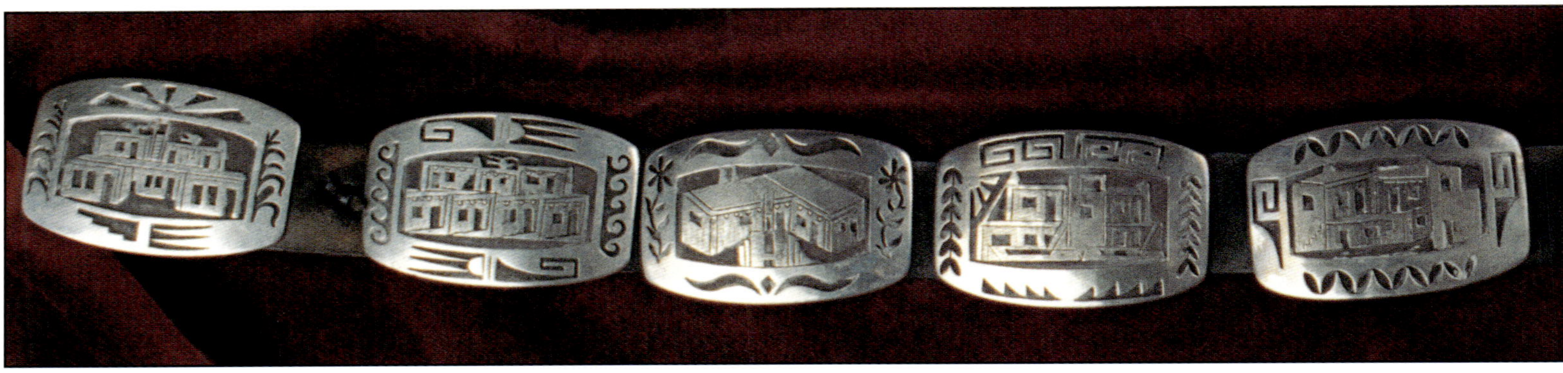

Hopi silver concha belt with a story design made in the 1970s at Shungopavi Village, but not signed.

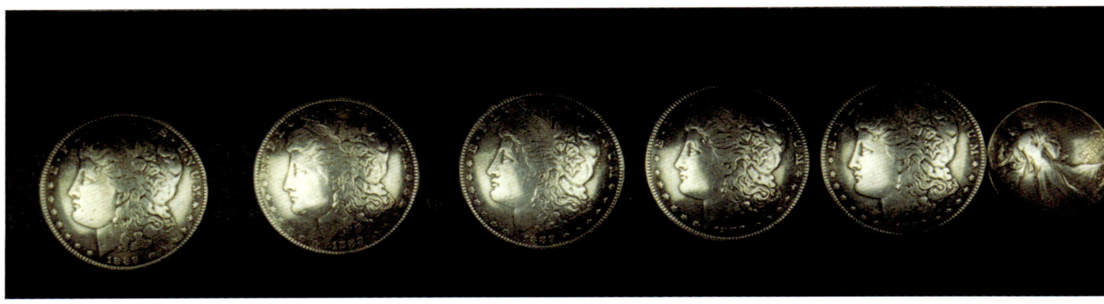

American silver dollars and quarters have been hammered into domed shape and strung together to form this belt. The latest dated coin is 1947. *Turquoise Lady collection*

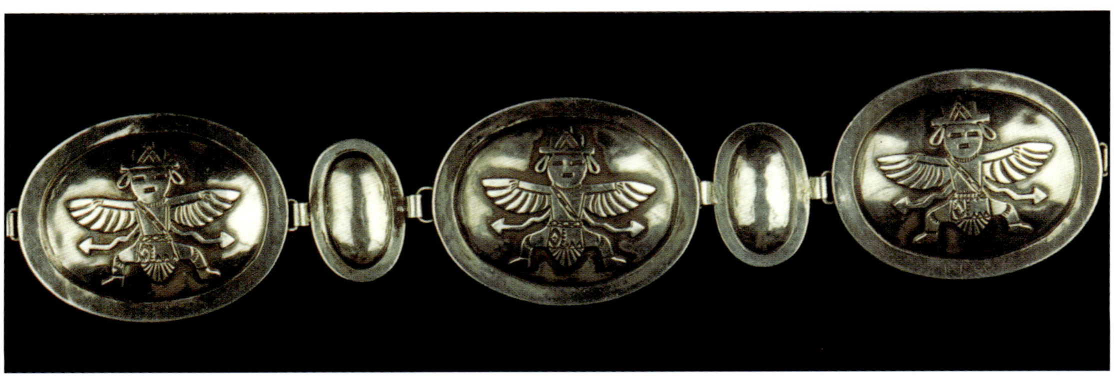

Navajo silver belt of linked medallions made in 1956 with repeating conchas decorated with a kachina figure and alternating with a plain oval spacer. *Turquoise Lady collection*

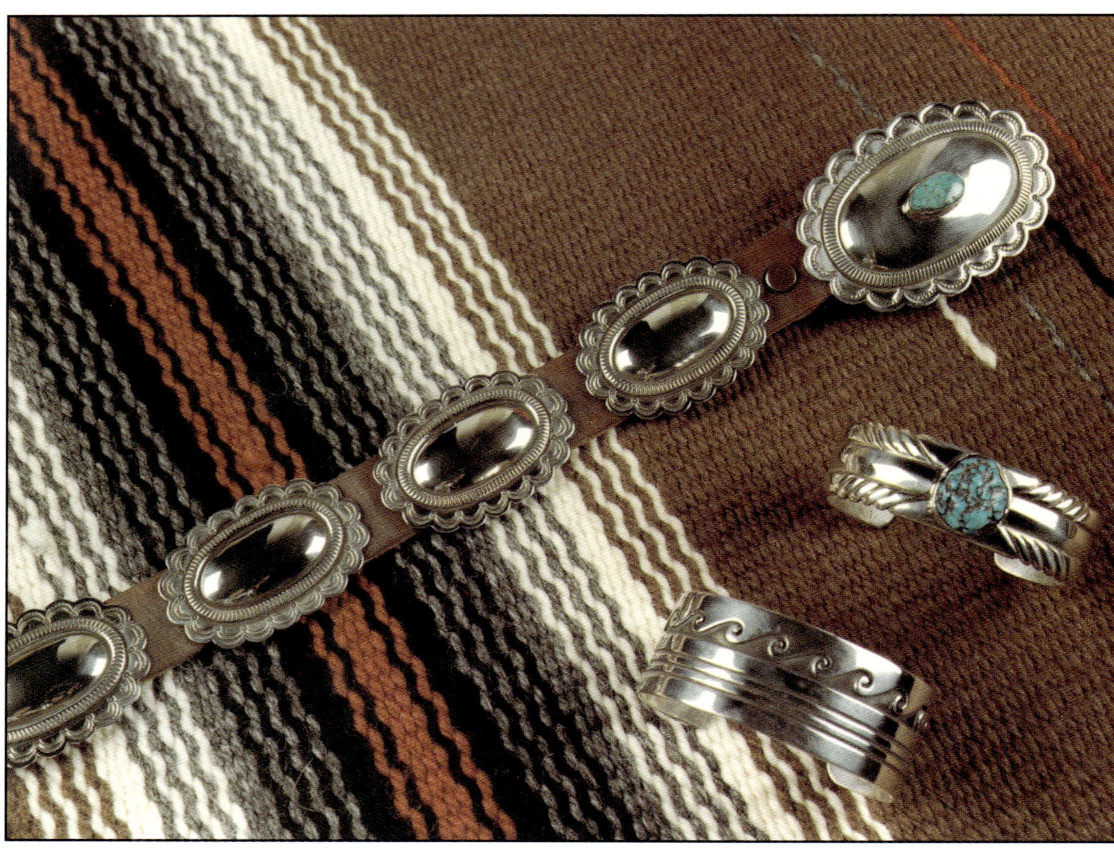

Belt of oval conchas outlined with beautiful stamped decoration and a matching larger buckle with a turquoise stone made in the 1970s. / Two bracelets, one of overlay decoration and one of stamped decoration with a single turquoise stone, all by Joe Quintana, Cochiti. *Indian Post collection*

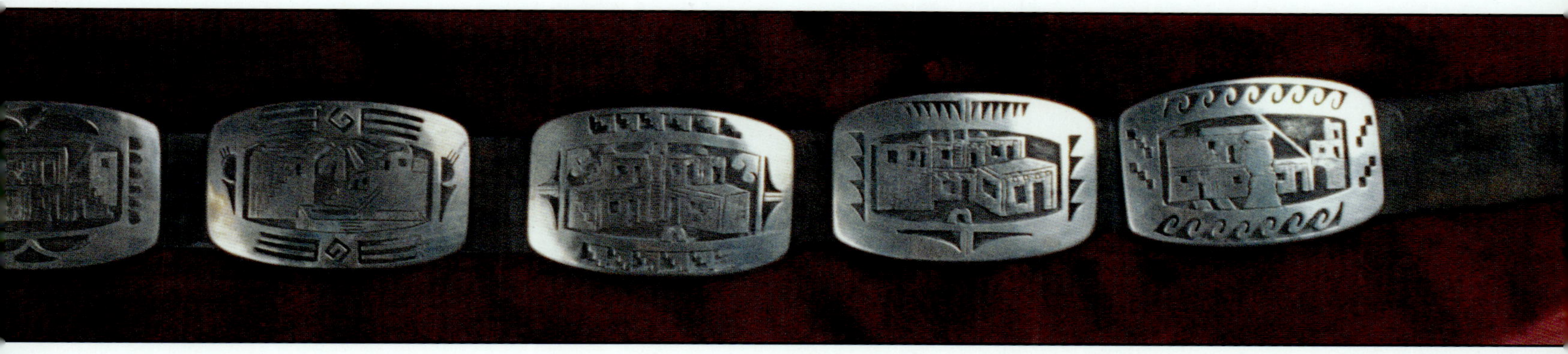

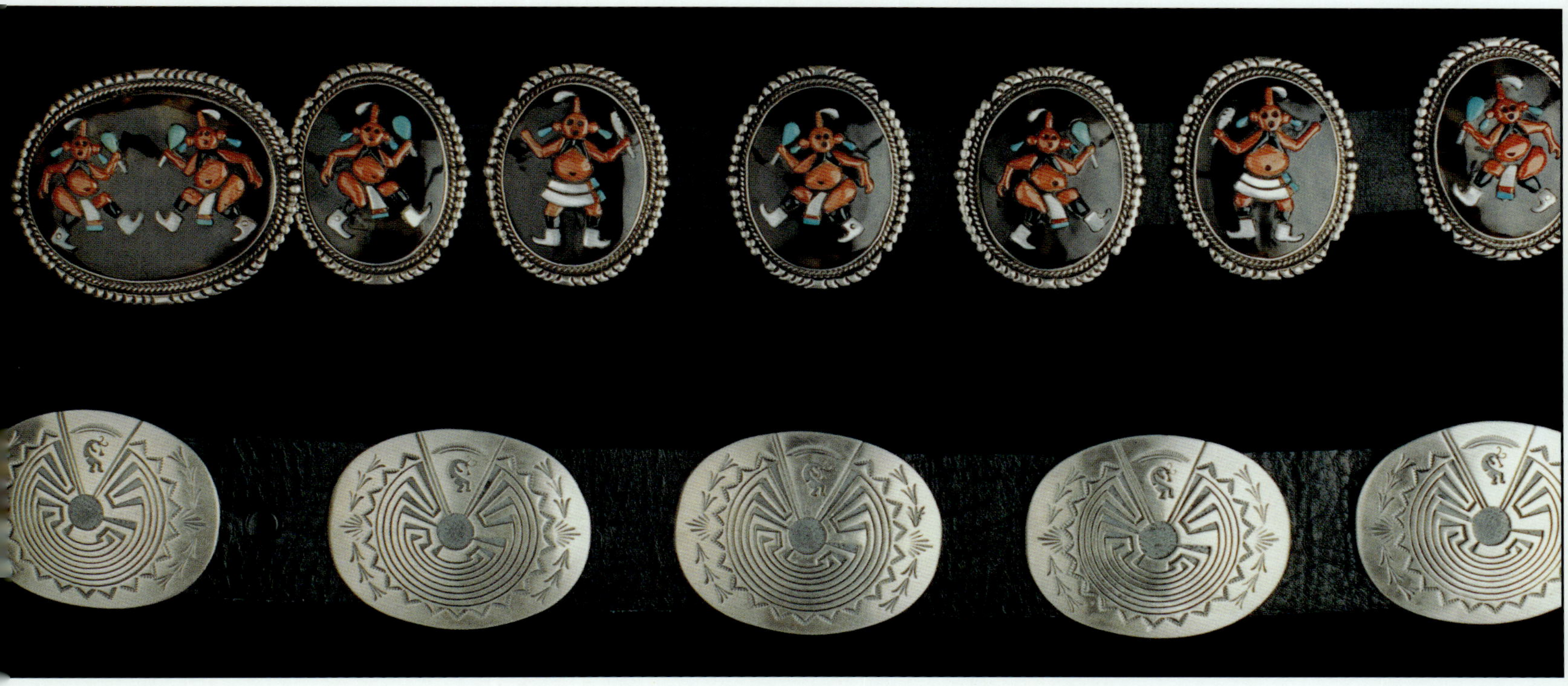

Concha style belt of tortoise shell inlaid with raised mosaic mudhead kachina designs, made by Augustine and Rosalie Pinto, Zuni, circa 1966. / Navajo concha belt with silver Man In The Maze design. *Bing Crosby collection*

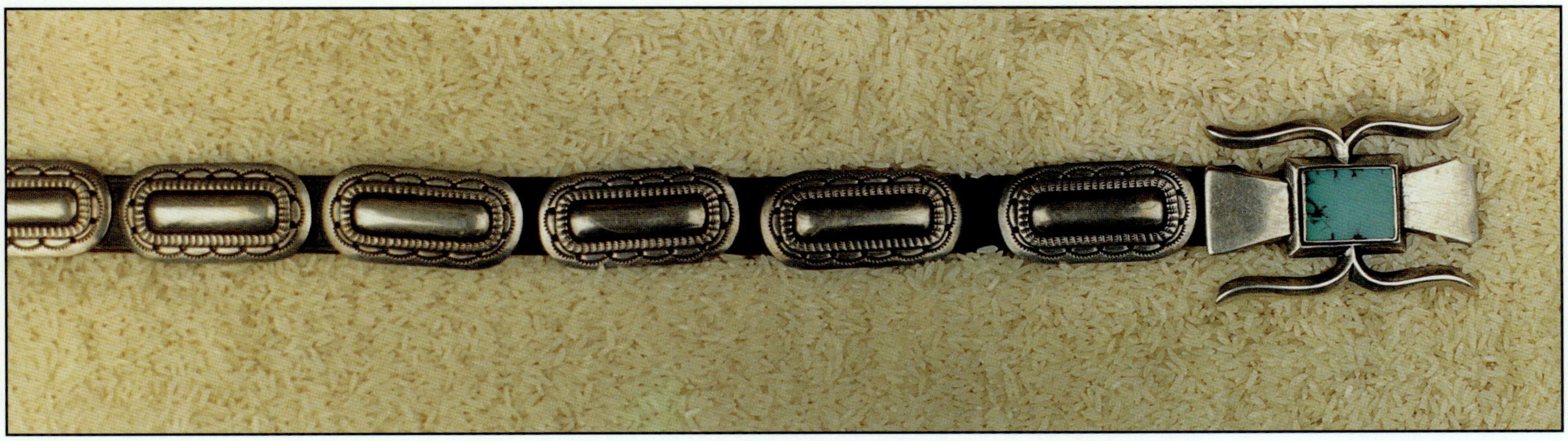

Beautifully stamped conchas and a dynamic buckle of ketoh design with turquoise make up a belt of Navajo origin from the 1970s or early 1980s. *Enchanted Mesa collection*

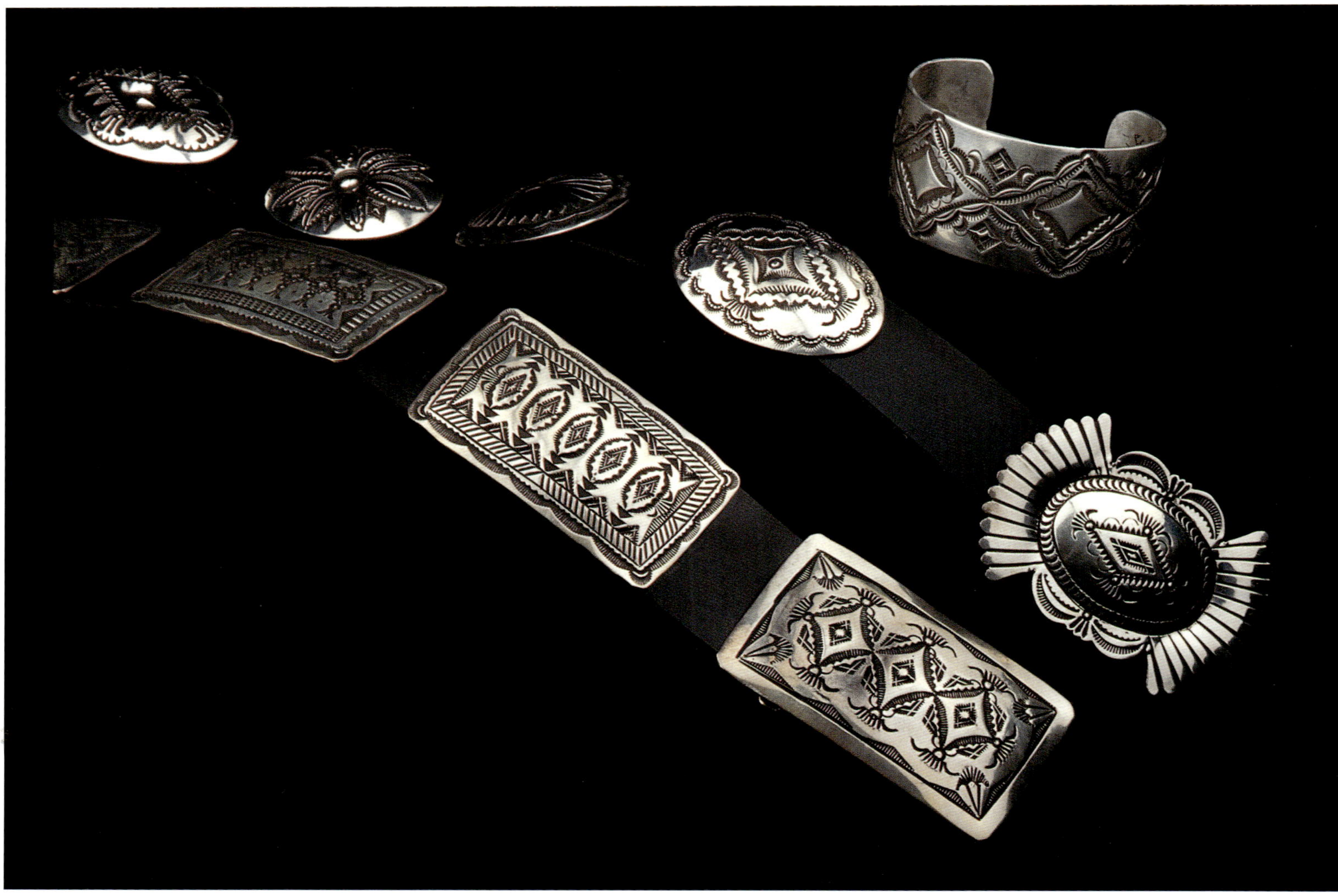

Two concho belts ($600 and $450) and cuff bracelet ($135) by Vincent Platero, Navajo. *Courtesy of Palms Trading Company*

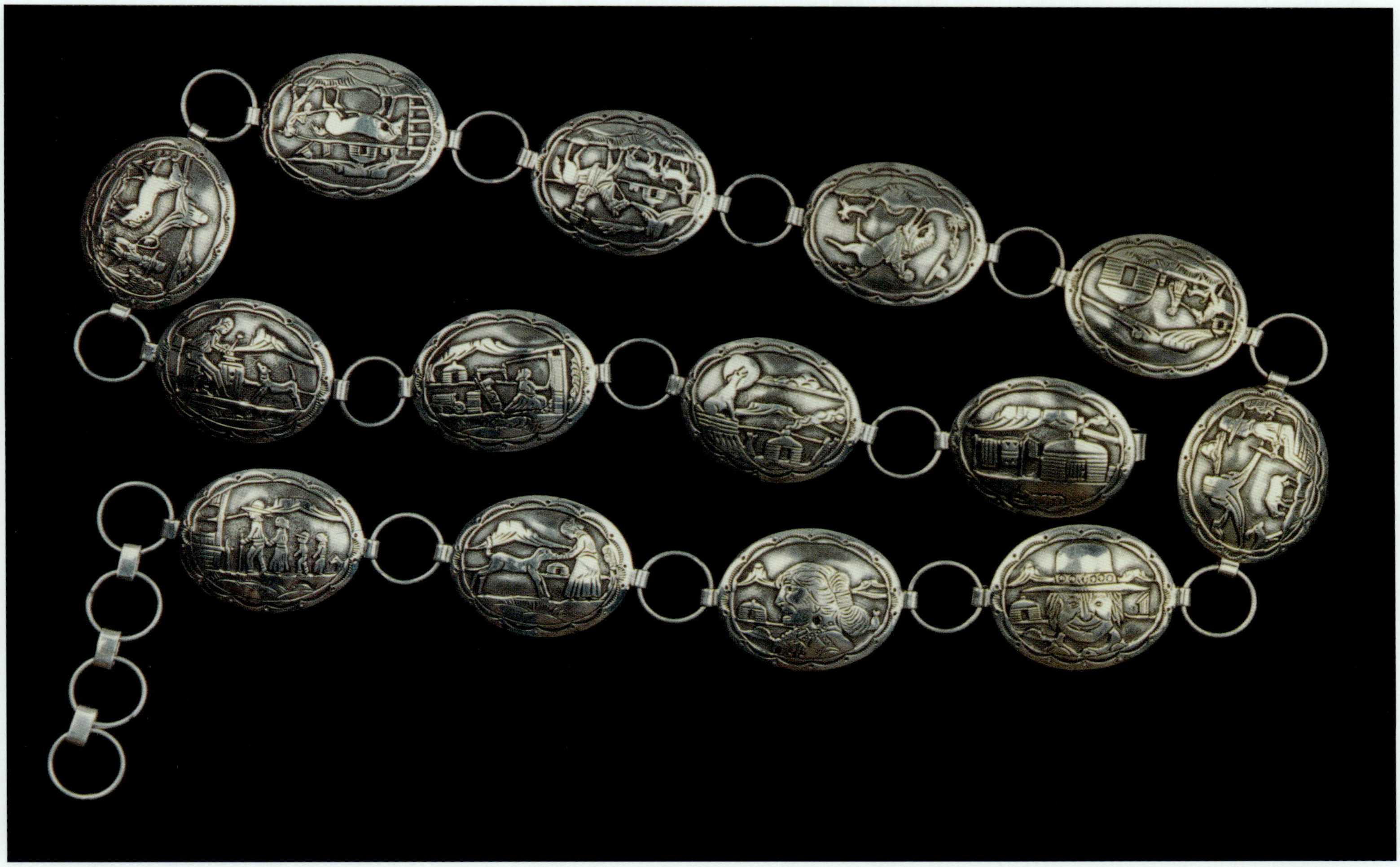

Navajo silver overlay linked belt designed to tell the stories of everyday life including traditional occupations of family members, made by Jones D., 1989. *Bing Crosby collection*

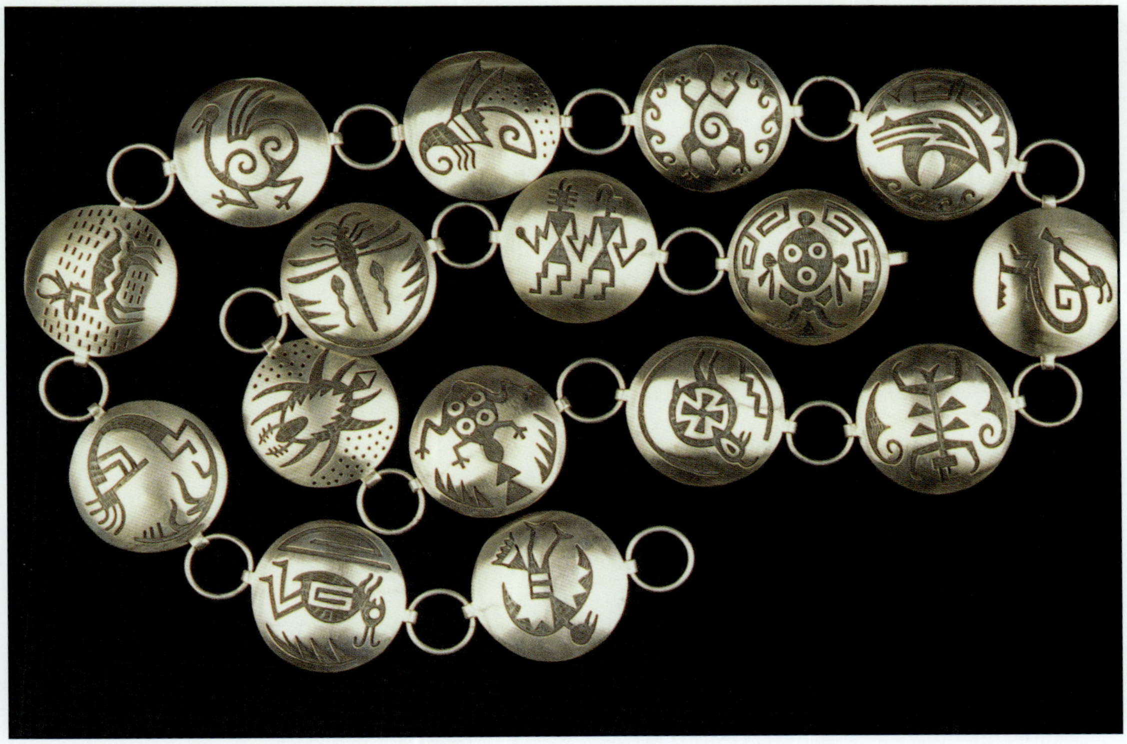

Hopi silver overlay link belt with symbolic designs made by Manuel Hoyungua, 1989. *Keams Canyon Arts & Crafts collection*

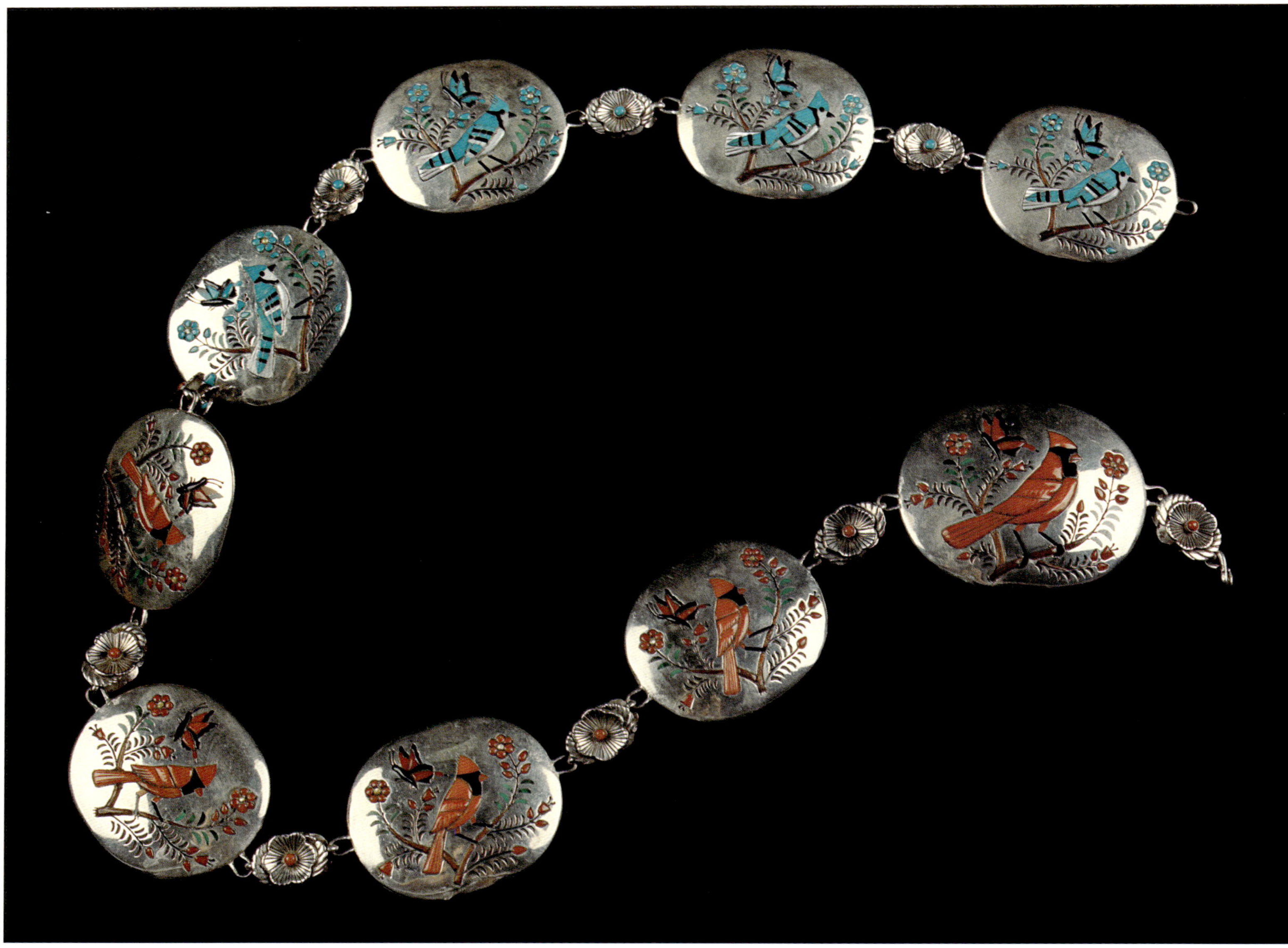

Reversible silver link belt inlaid with turquoise bird design on one side of the oval medallions and turquoise bird design on the reverse side of each, both sides detailed with inlaid jet, made in 1976 by Silas and Berdie Ohmsatte, Zuni. *Private collection on permanent loan to Ohio University*

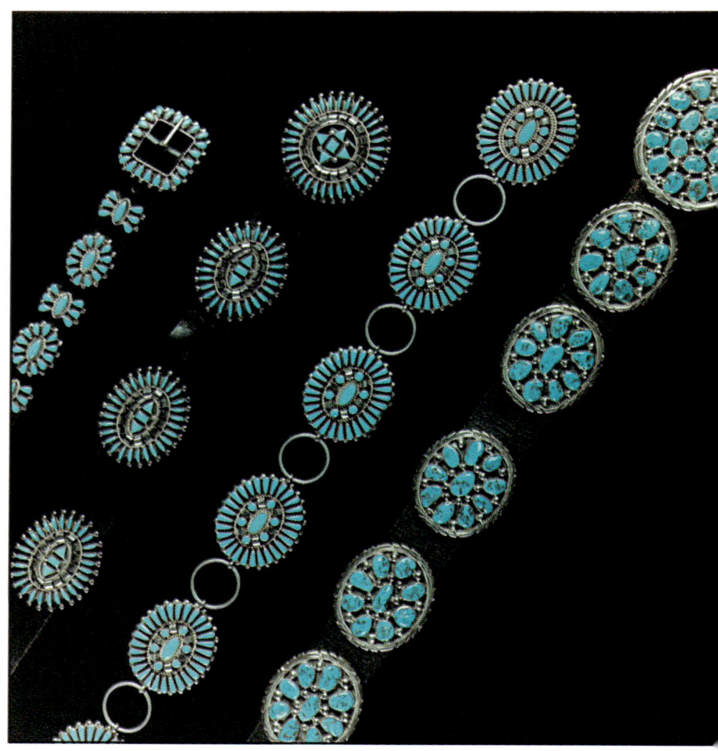

Small belt with turquoise-set conchas, butterfly-shaped spacers and buckle. / Belt with conchas and buckle set with needlepoint turquoise by Betty Etsate, Navajo, circa 1988. / Link belt with turquoise-set medallions by Andrew and V. Ned, Navajo, circa 1988. / Thick silver belt with turquoise-set conchas signed in illegible script. *Leonard D. Prins collection*

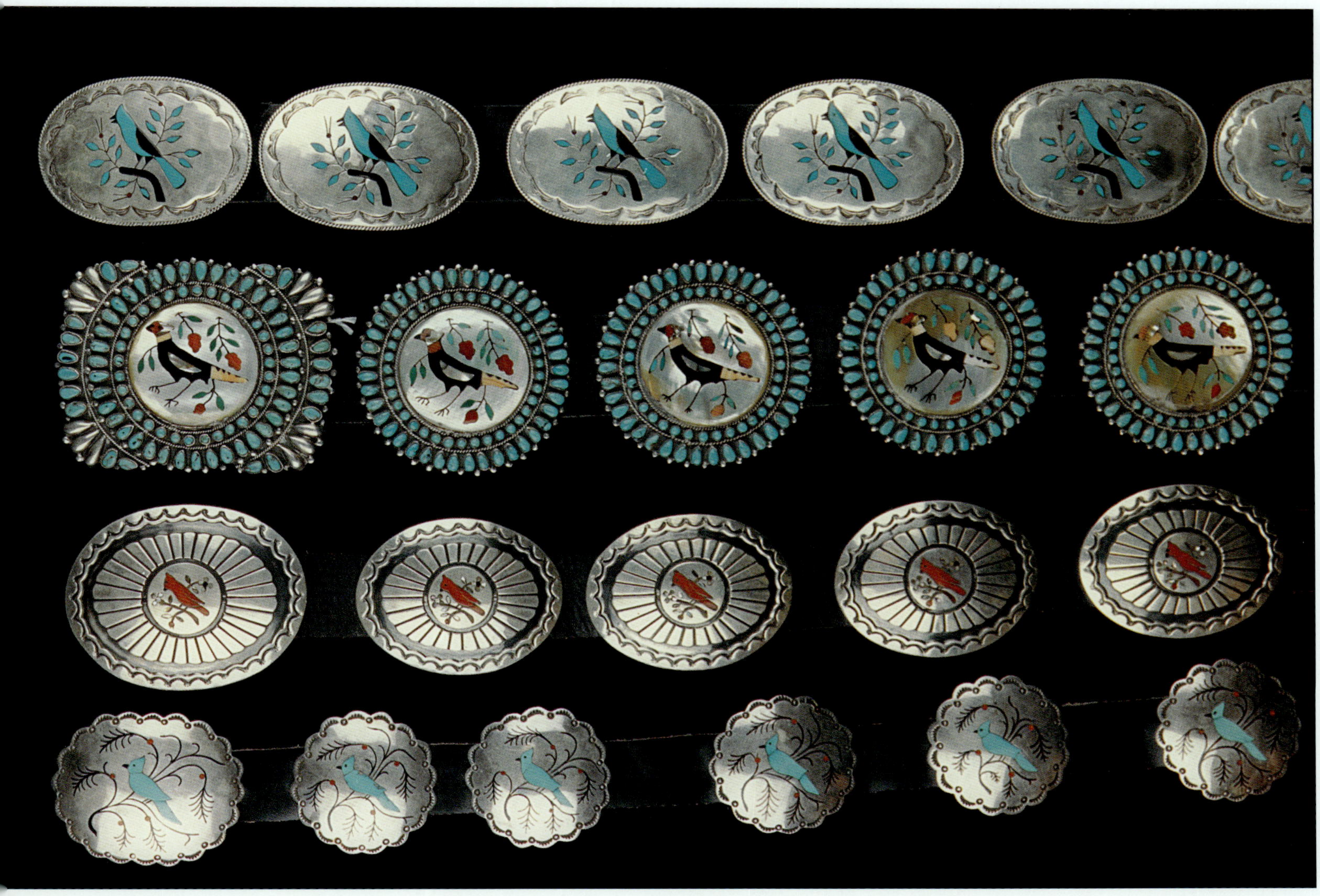

Concha belt of oval silver medallions inlaid with turquoise and jet in a bird design, marked by B. B., Zuni, 1980s. / Navajo silver concha belt and buckle with turquoise needlework set around circular shell medallions inlaid with turquoise, jet, and coral in a bird pattern, by Victor Moses Begay, 1980s. / Buckle and belt of oval silver conchas inlaid with coral in a bird design, by Charlie Mike Yazzie, Navajo, mid-1980s. / Belt and buckle of silver medallions inlaid with turquoise in a bird design, marked J L, probably Zuni, 1980s.

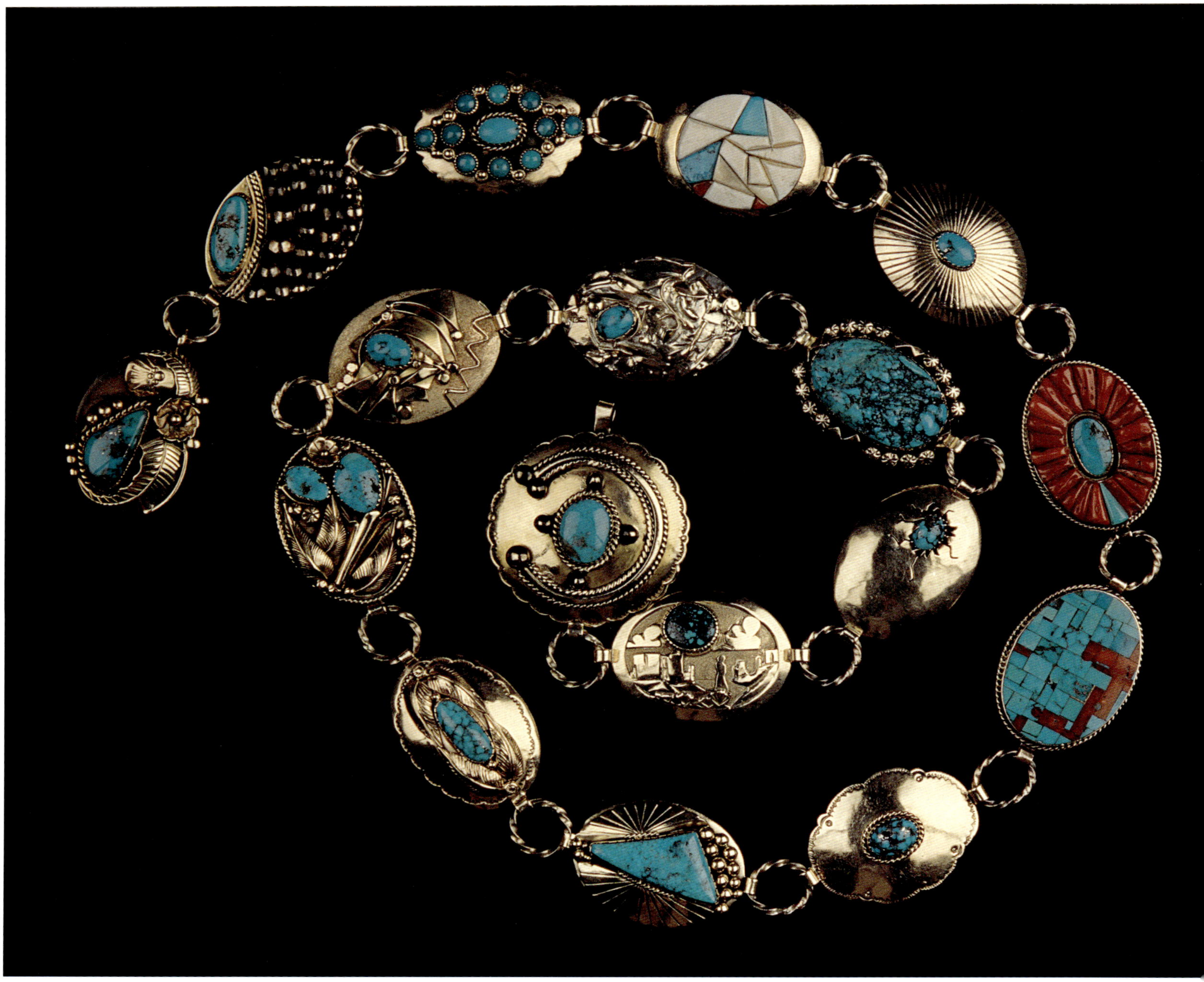

14-karat gold link storyteller belt made circa 1984 by Paul Arviso, who has commented on its creation:
Many times people ask me about the ideas I put into jewelry. They wonder how I dream up so many different ideas. I always have a standard answer, "I don't know!" It is just natural for me to make things. When [the belt's owner] asked me to make this belt for her, I told her that I would share with her the ideas that went into making this belt.
My grandfather and father both taught me that whenever you are going to do something that is special, something that is good, you have to do it with prayers. In Navajo Way there are a lot of ceremonies, stories and legends that I use to draw from to get ideas, and I put these ideas into my jewelry. When I make something that is special for myself or my mother, my grandmother or a close friend, I put good thoughts into it. I make the piece with prayer, and that is how I made this belt. I'm not saying that all jewelry is made like this. Some pieces are made for bread and butter. But special pieces have a lot of thought and a lot of work, and this belt took me over a year from start to finish.

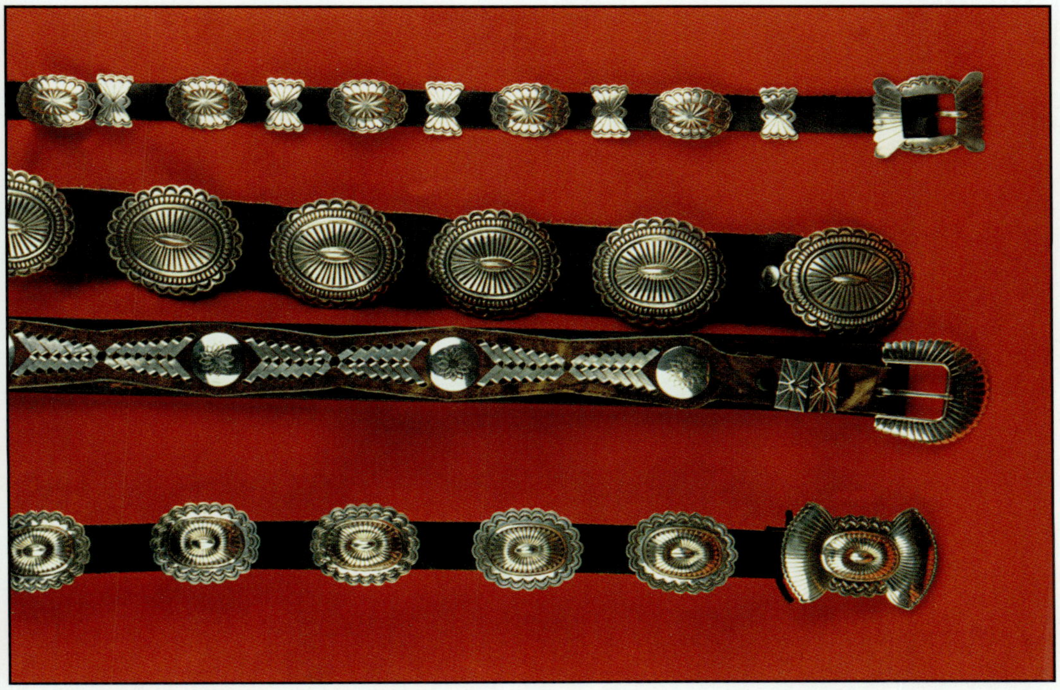

Belt of twelve oval silver conchas and twelve butterfly spacers with buckle by Susie Lee, Navajo, 1989. / Belt of eleven conchas nicely stamped, unmarked. / Western style belt and buckle with silver strips and medallions, by B. L.(?), 1980s. / Belt with ten sterling silver conchas, unmarked. *Foutz Trading Company collection*

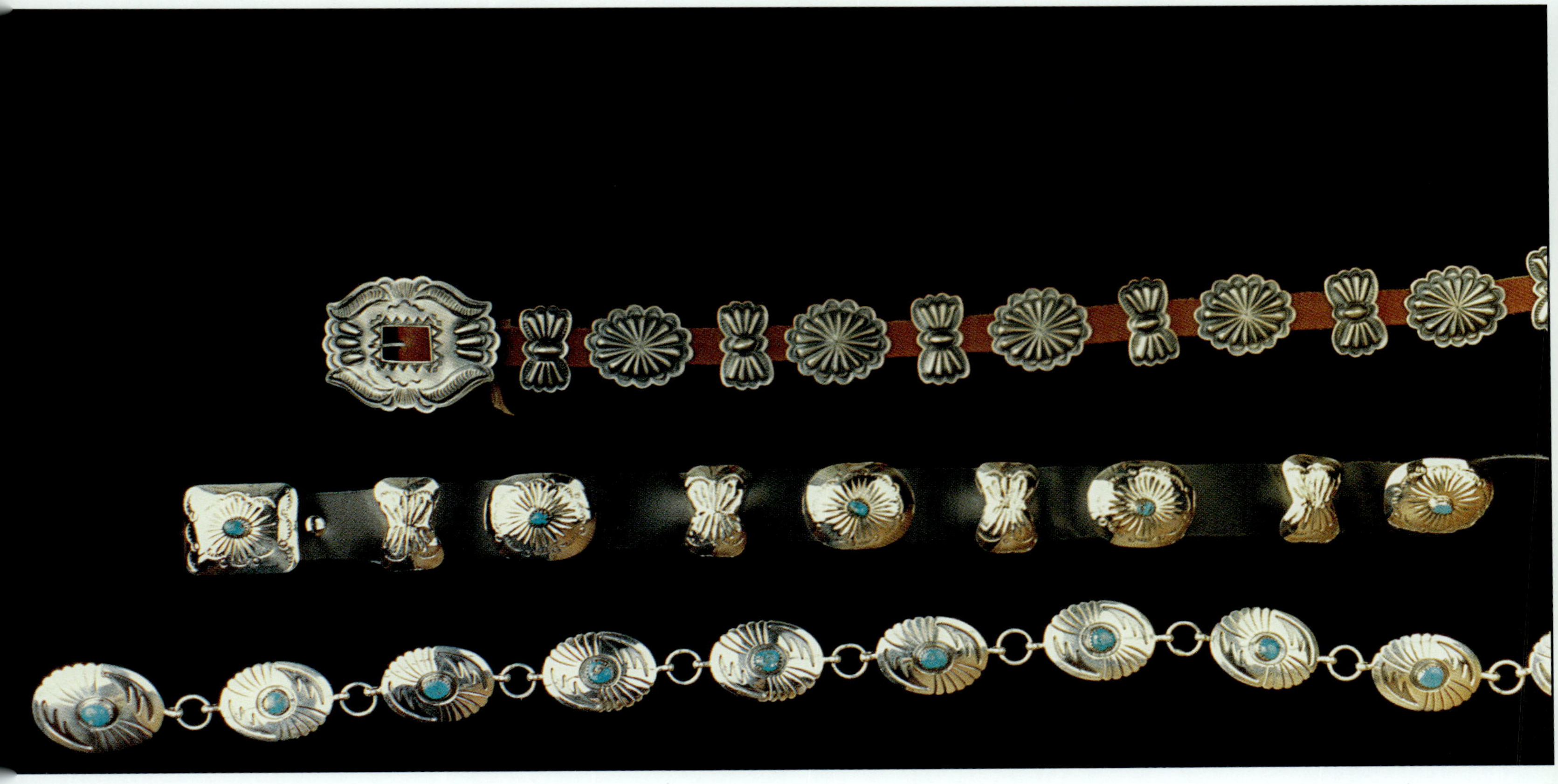

Concha belt and buckle with stamped silver conchas and butterfly spacers by H. Morgan, Navajo. / Concha belt and buckle with silver conchas set with turquoise and plain butterfly spacers, unmarked. / Link belt of silver medallions set with turquoise by Charlie Mike Yazzie, Navajo, 1989. *Bing Crosby collection*

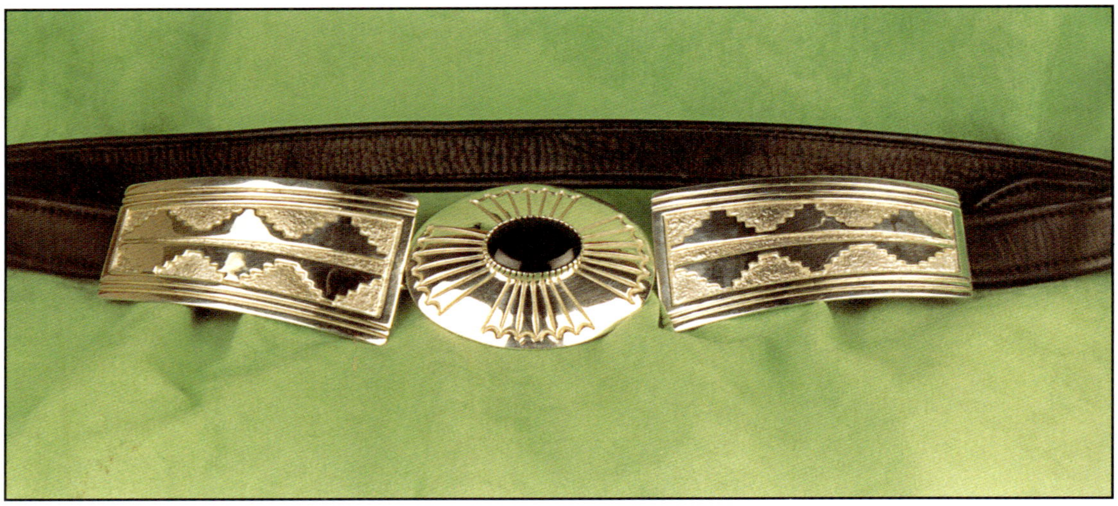

Leather belt with geometric-patterned silver ends and a buckle set with an oval jet inlay by Tommy Jackson, Navajo, 1989. *Indian Traders West collection.*

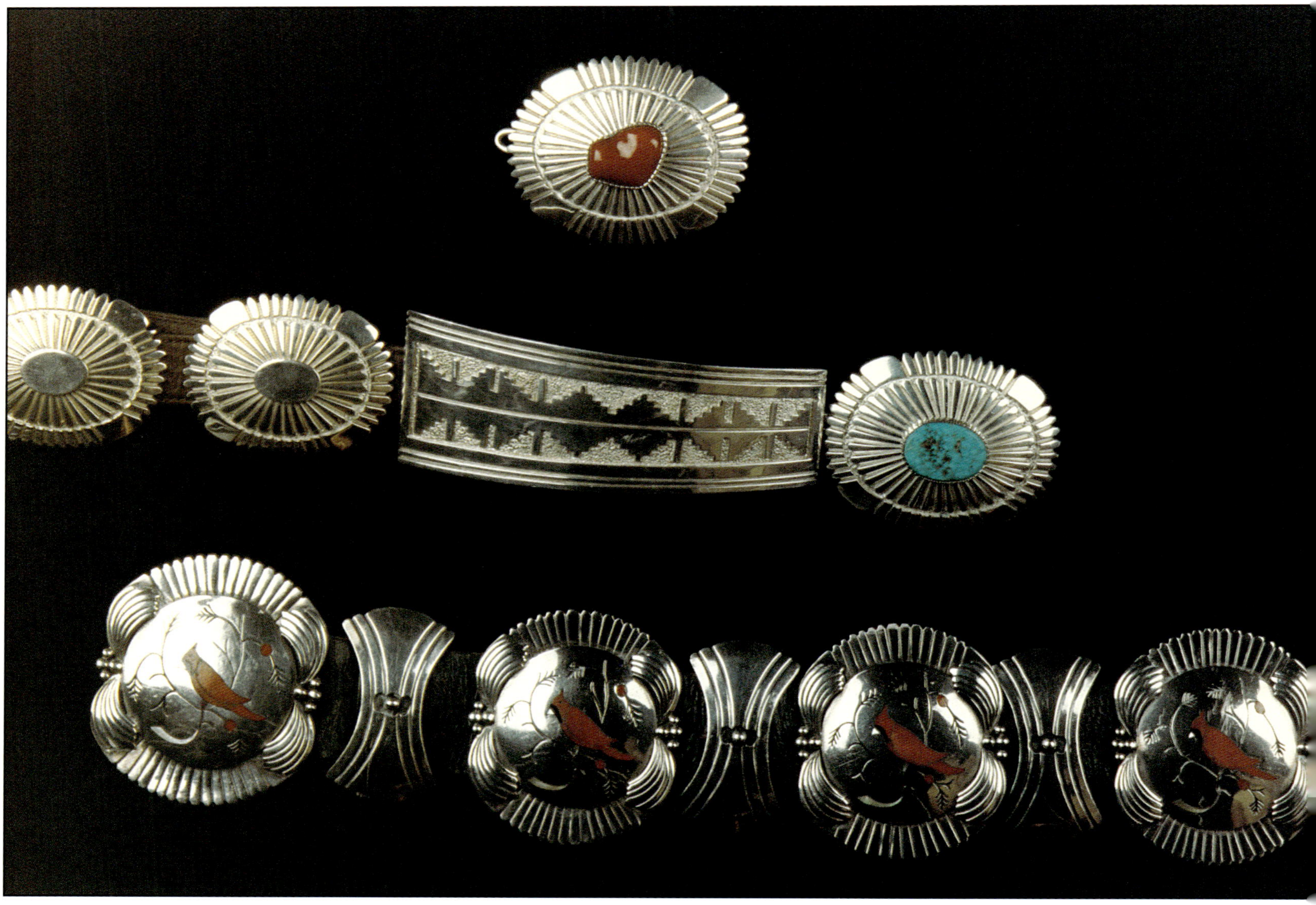

Two silver buckles and a concha belt of beautiful technique in an original design by Tommy Jackson, Navajo, 1985. The buckles are set with stones, one with coral and one with turquoise, and can be interchanged. / Silver belt of strong design with coral bird- pattern inlaid conchas and silver spacers by Charlie Mike Yazzie, Navajo, 1985.

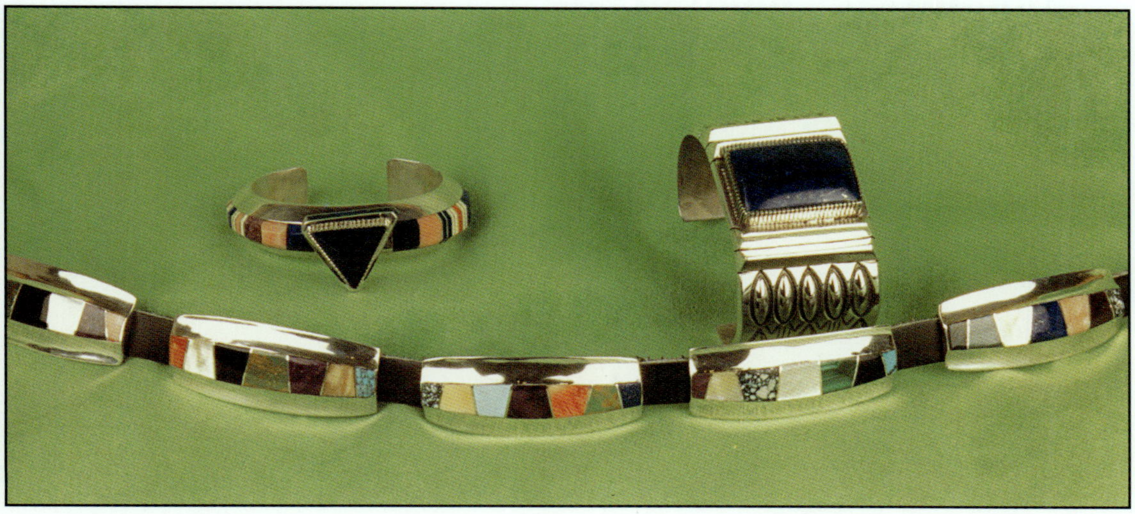

Two bracelets and a belt of bold designs in silver set with a variety of colored stones including lapis lazuli, turquoise, lavulite, shell and jet by Gibson Nez, Navajo, 1989. *Indian Traders West collection.*

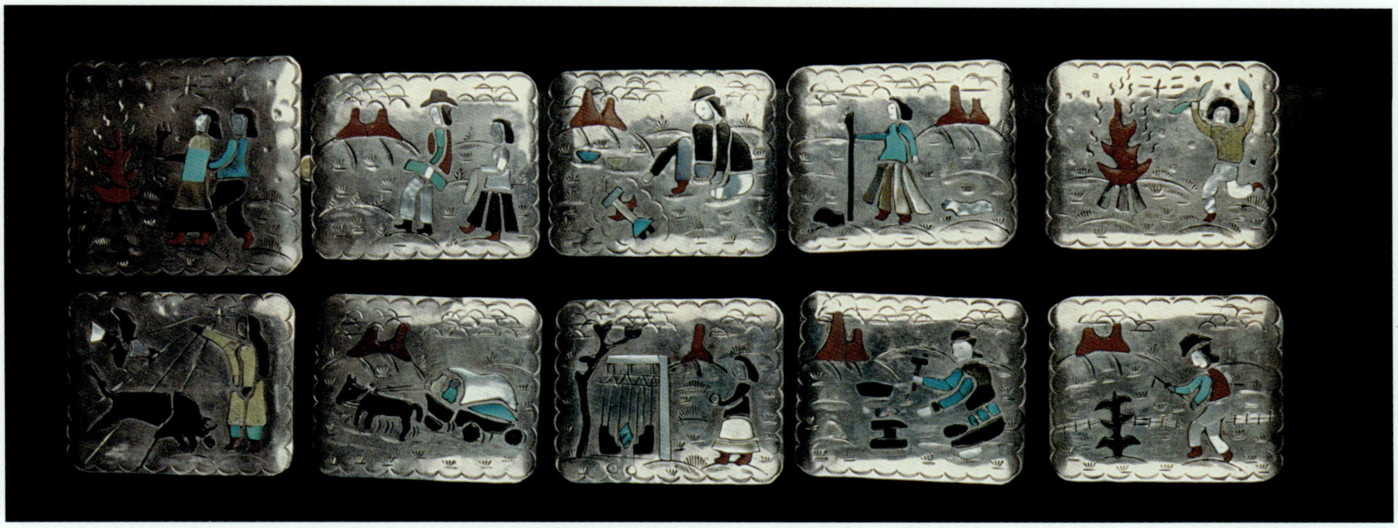

Highly unusual belt of ten silver plaques decorated with a narrative design including stamping and inlaid coral, turquoise, jet and shell. Each plaque depicts a different phase of the story. The maker is not known, 1980s.

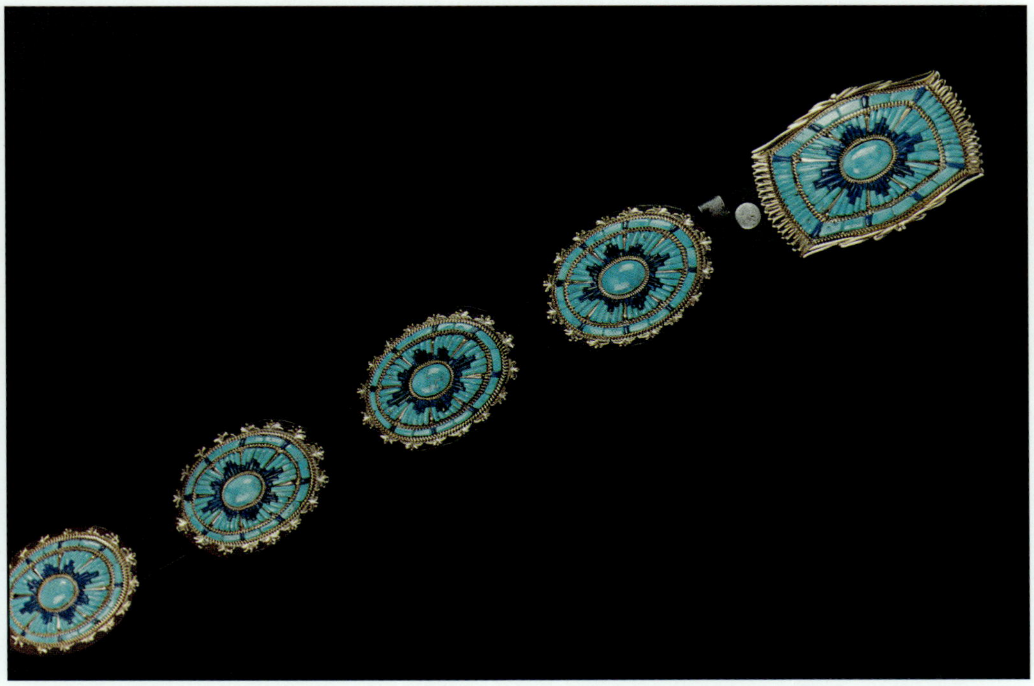

This remarkable belt is the achievement of several specialized jewelers who worked together for its creation. Jim Griffith of Albuquerque designed the eight oval gold conchas in 1979 with gem grade turquoise and lapis lazuli stones cut by La Vern Pino, Zia Pueblo, other work by Joseph Coriz, Santo Domingo Pueblo, and Mario and Ramon Marrufo. *Private collection*

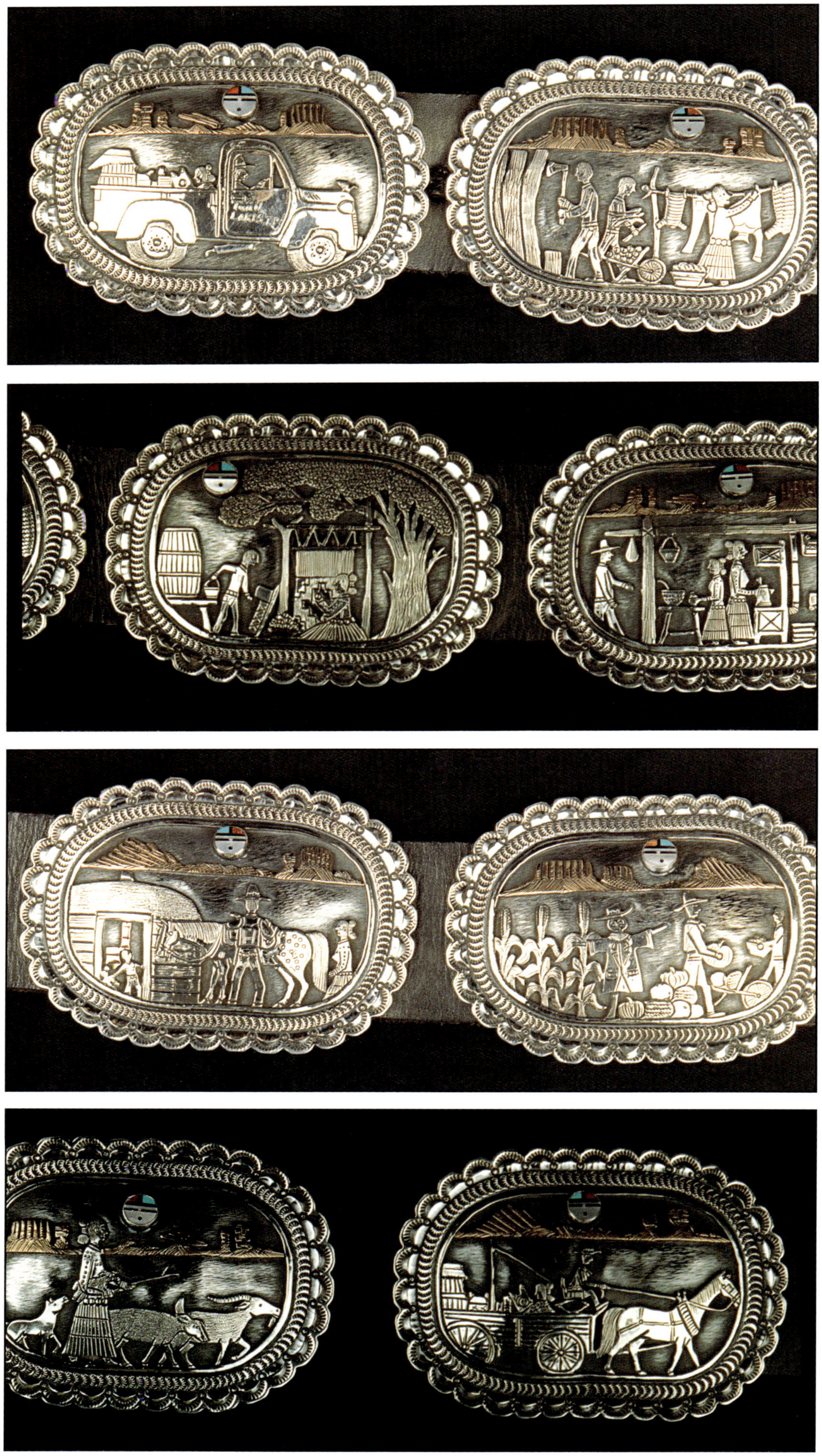

Wonderfully imaginative belt made by Clarence Lee, in 1989, from silver, copper, inlaid shell, coral, jet, and turquoise in a narrative design carried out continuously from one concha to the next. The buckle shows a pick-up truck (inspired, according to the maker, by a real person, Jimmy Jim, who drives a similar vehicle) hauling a family and goods to the Twin Lakes Trading Post. The seven conchas show scenes from a traditional Navajo lifestyle. 1- Chopping wood and laundry set out on a line to dry. 2- Man carrying a bucket of water, child on a cradleboard, and woman weaving under the shade of a tree. 3- Man entering the summer cooking arbor in the mountains with girl preparing a meal, woman at the stove, and boy bringing a box. 4- Family and horse at the winter residence, the hogan. 5- Fall harvest of corn and melons with a scarecrow, man and boy. 6- Woman and a dog tending the sheep and goats. 7- Old style trip to the trading post in a wagon with the horse. *Clarence Lee collection*

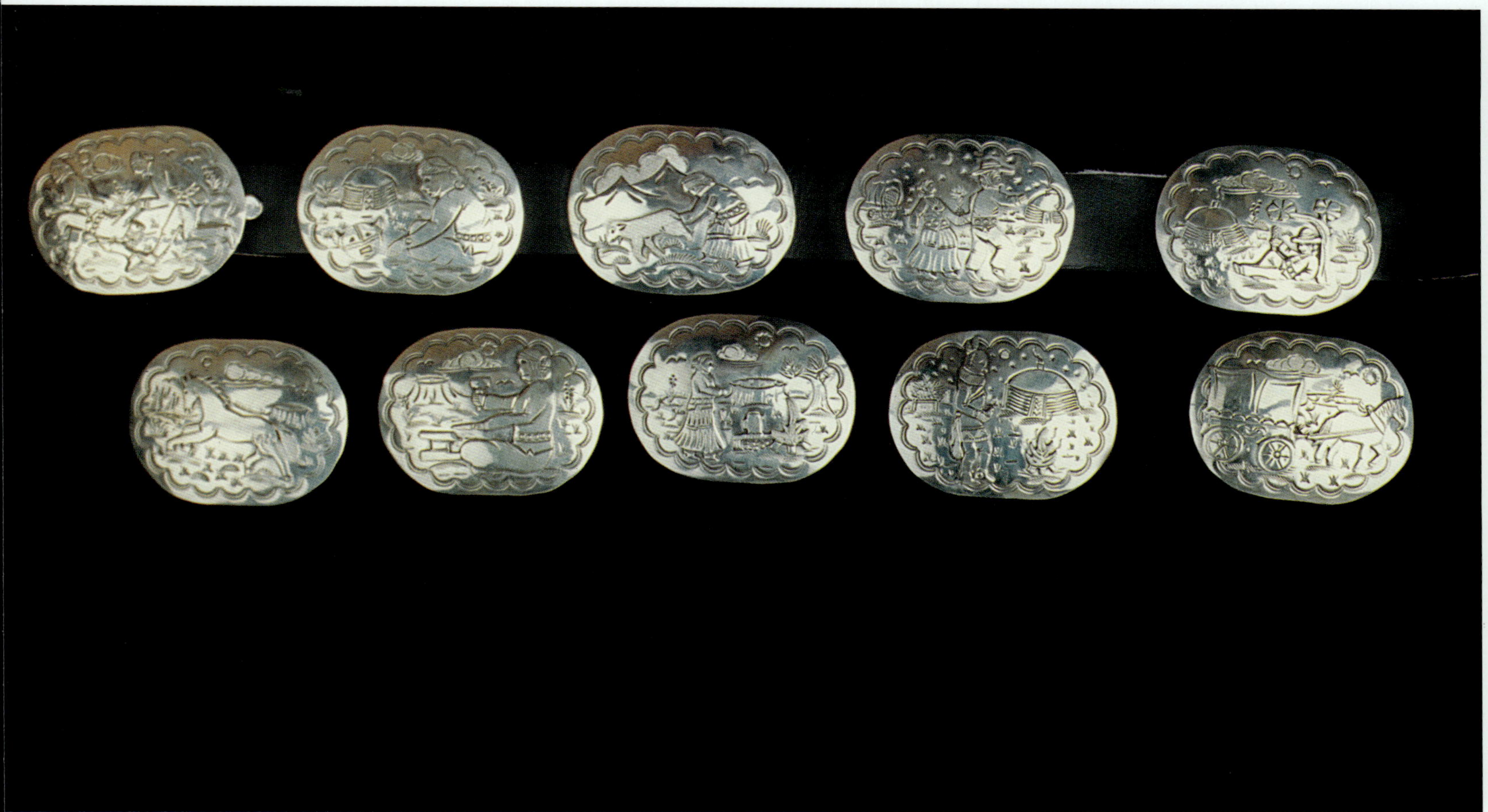

Silver concha belt with nine conchas and a buckle stamped and chiseled to relate a story, each plaque with a different phase of the tale, by B-C-T, 1989. *Bing Crosby collection*

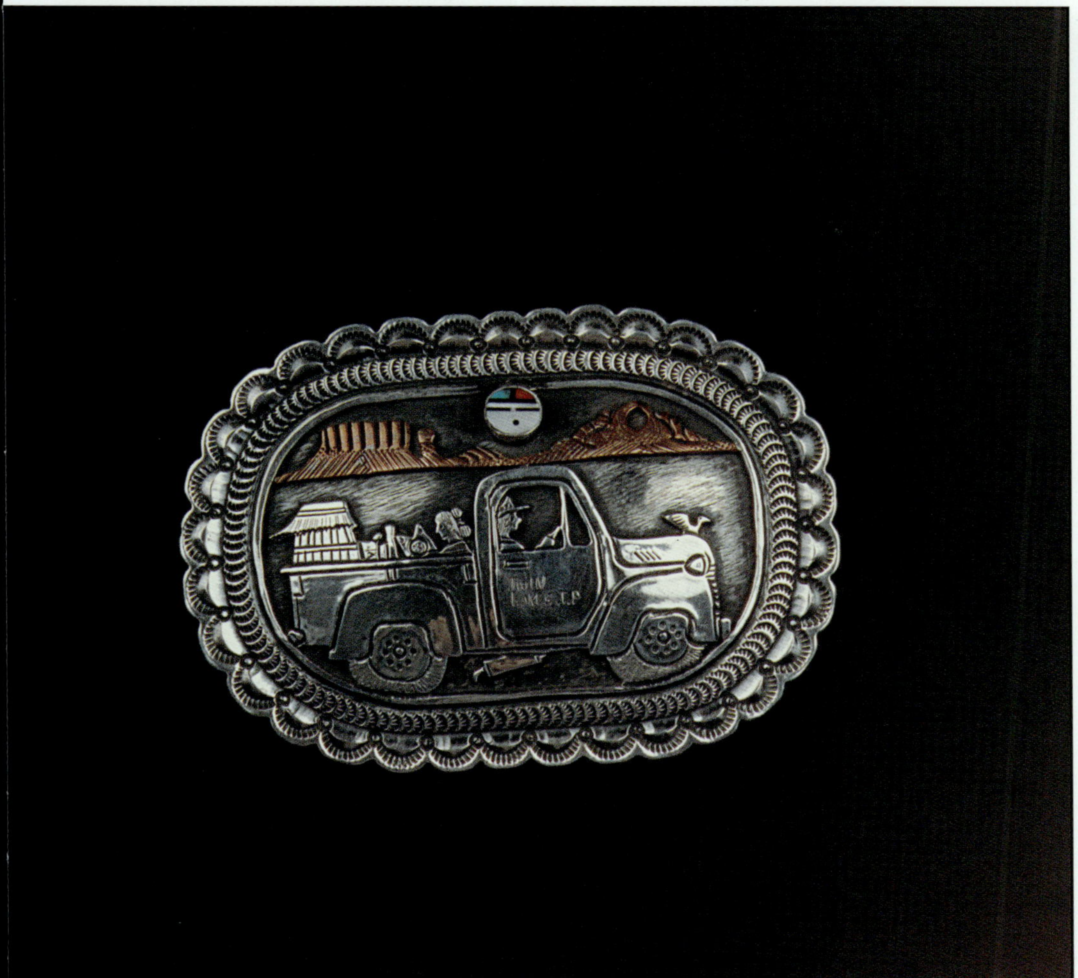

Buckle to the belt shown opposite by Clarence Lee.

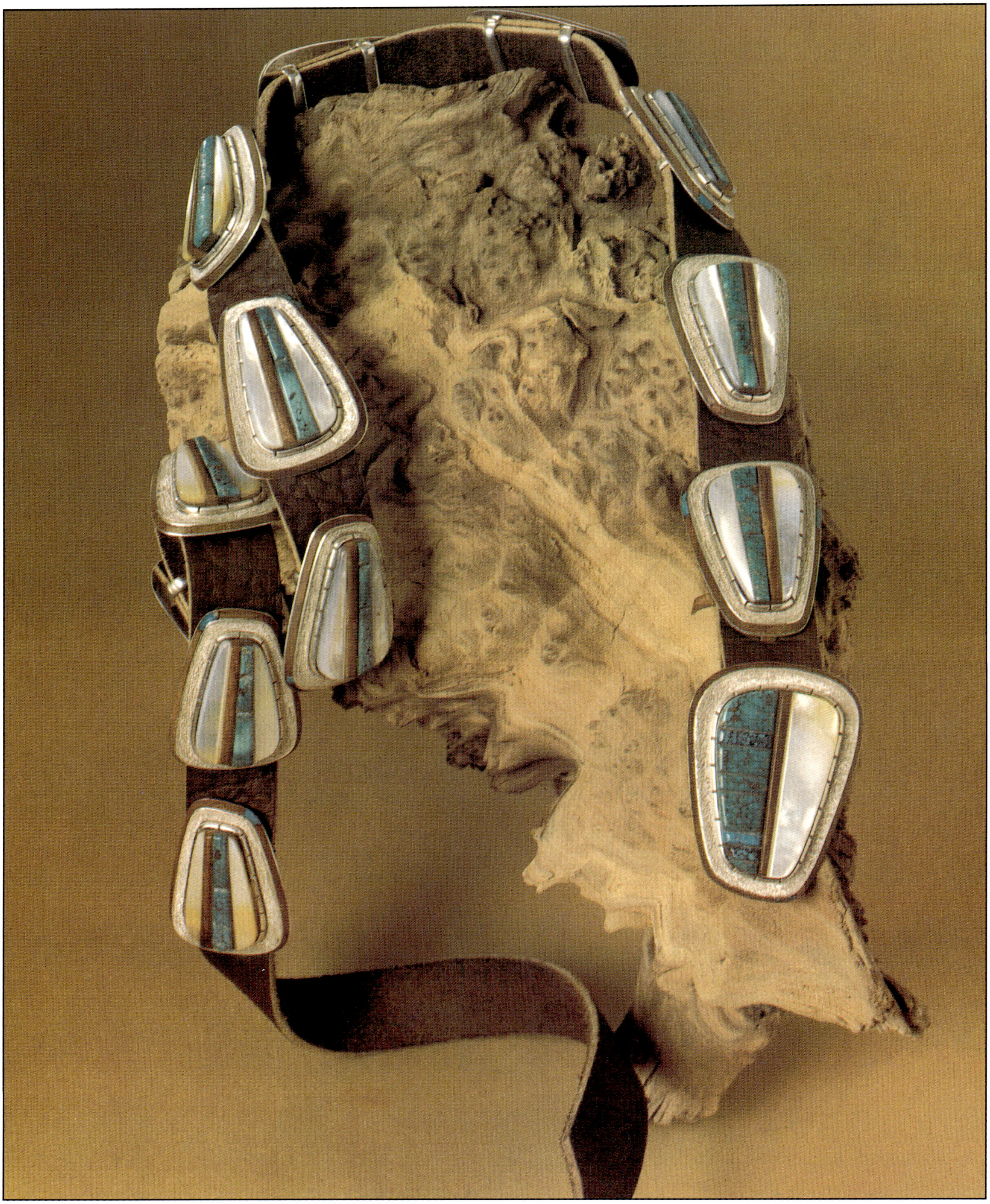

The daring use of new materials and designs by jewelers increased in the 1970s and 1980s to produce intriguing belts of great beauty. This is one of the best. Twelve conchas and a matching buckle form a belt of silver set with ironwood, mother of pearl and turquoise in a stylized geometric design by Victor Beck, Navajo, 1989, *Artist's collection*

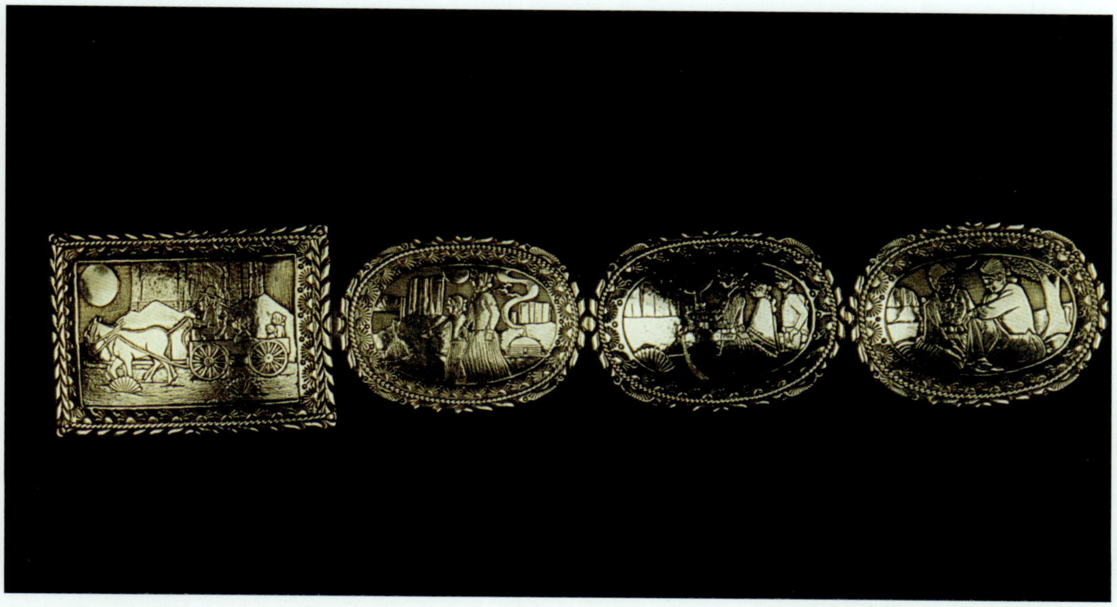

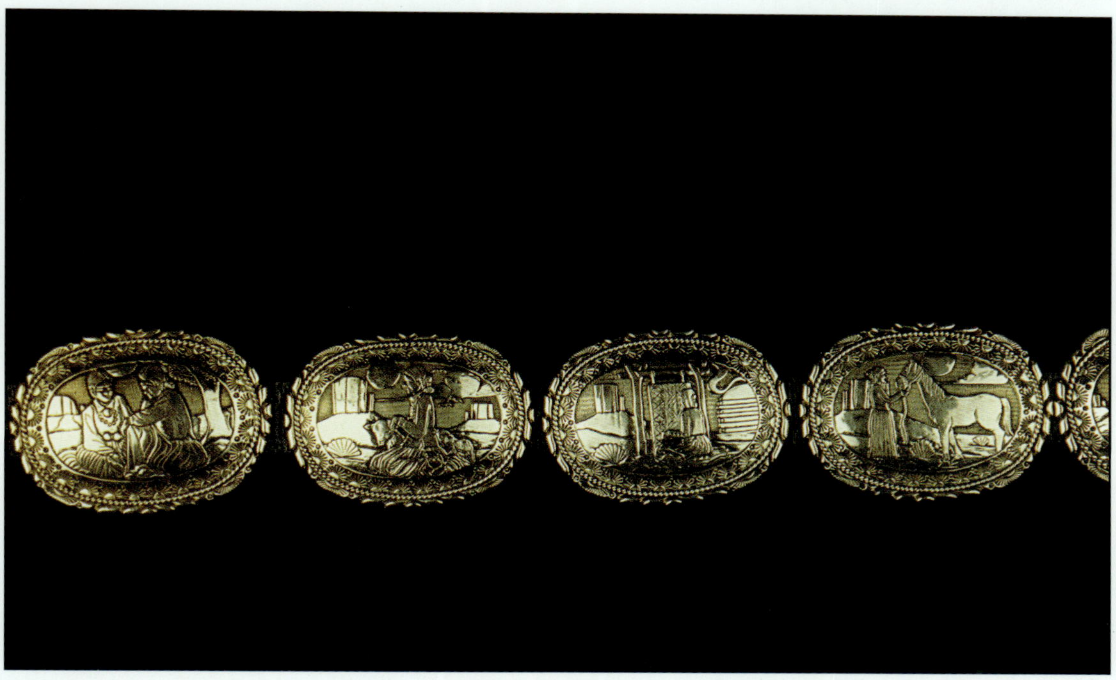

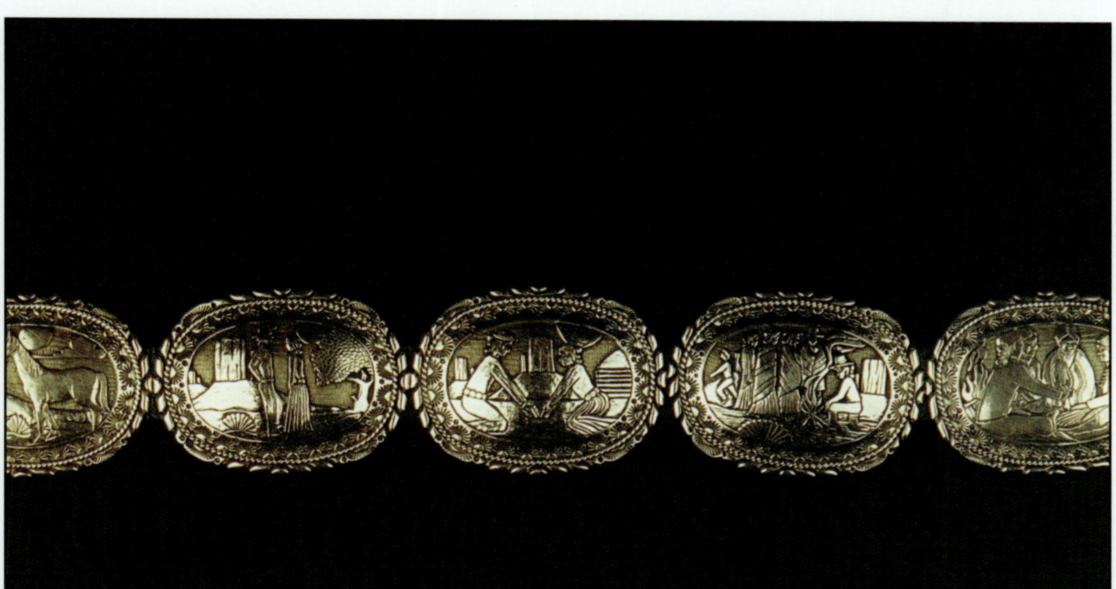

Gold narrative belt including a rectangular buckle and ten oval conchas, each depicting a different phase of traditional Navajo family life, worked in 14 karat gold overlay, texturing and stamping to create a dynamic composition of individual designs by Paul Arviso, Navajo, 1985. *Turquoise Lady collection*

Buckles

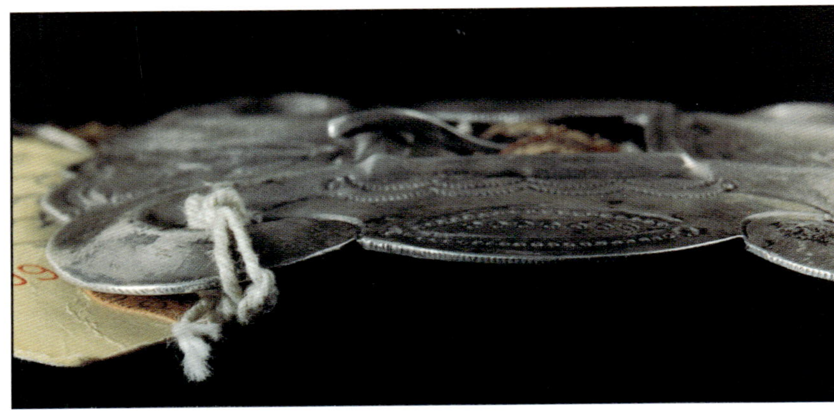

Old buckles may retain the milled edges of minted coins used as the silver source. The presence of these ridges verifies the use of the term "coin silver" to describe the material.

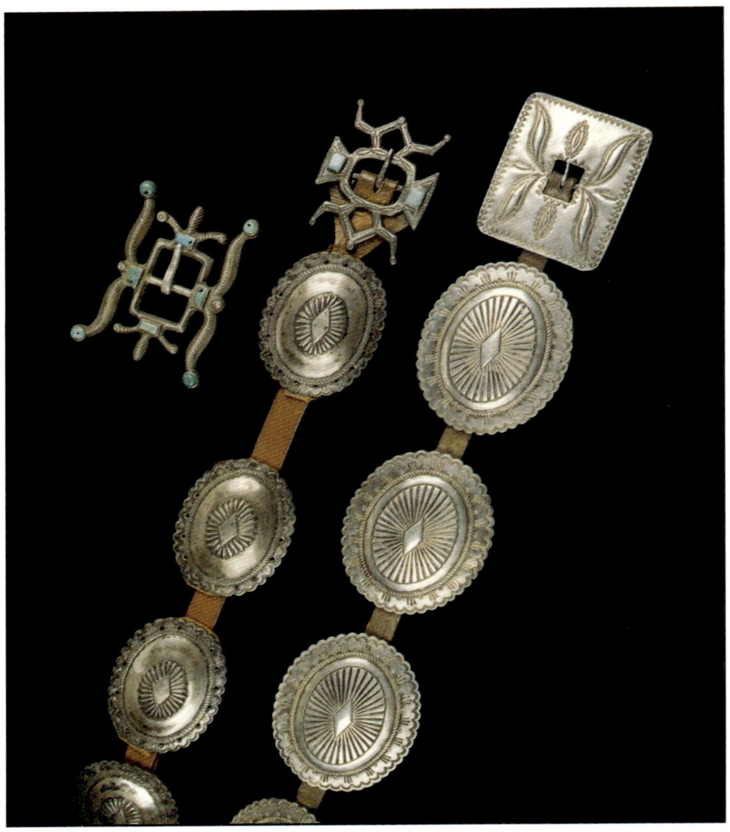

Navajo sand cast buckle, circa 1910, set with older turquoise beads, which are drilled for stringing. / Concha belt with original sand-cast stamped buckle set with two turquoise stones, circa 1890. / Large concha belt with wrought rectangular buckle decorated with stamped corn leaves design, circa 1890. *Lynn D. Trusdell collection*

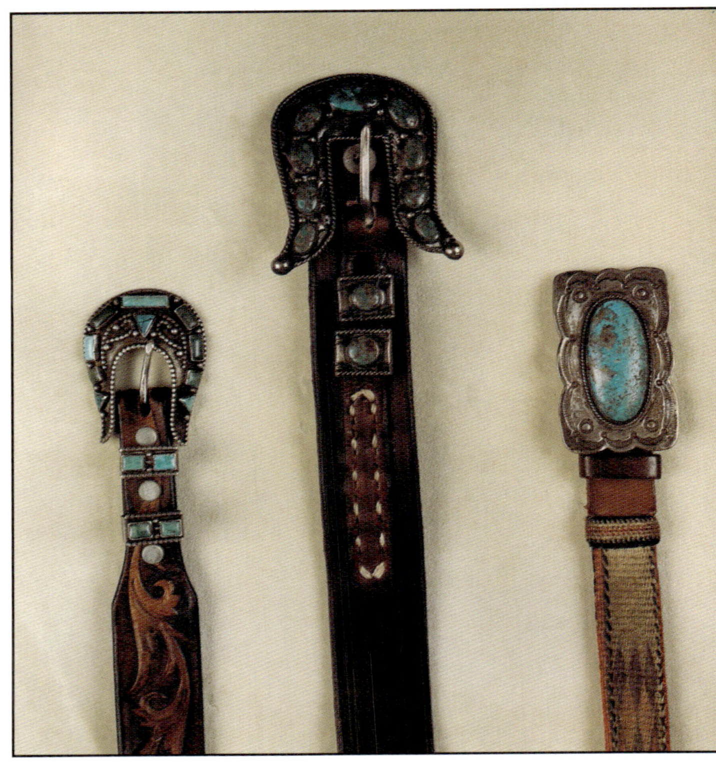

Ranger buckle of embossed silver and set turquoise on a tooled leather belt, circa 1930s, Navajo. / Ranger buckle of silver set with Blue gem turquoise on a leather belt, 1940s. / Large Blue gem turquoise set a in silver buckle on a fine Navajo horsehair belt, 1920s. *Lynn D. Trusdell collection*

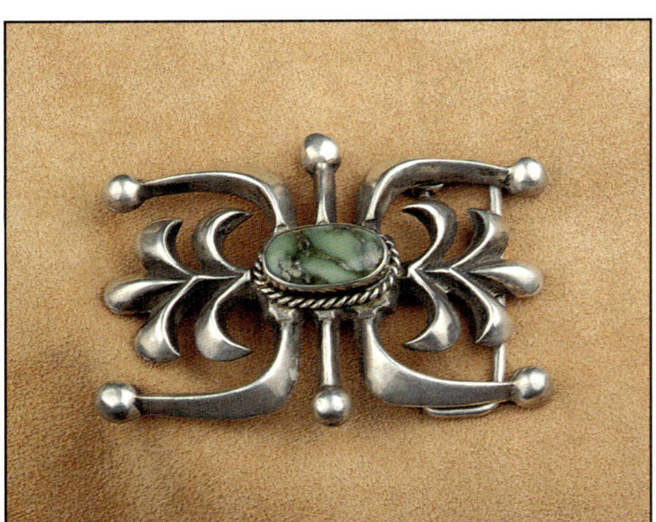

Navajo sand cast silver buckle with turquoise. *Lynn D. Trusdell, Crown & Eagle Antiques*

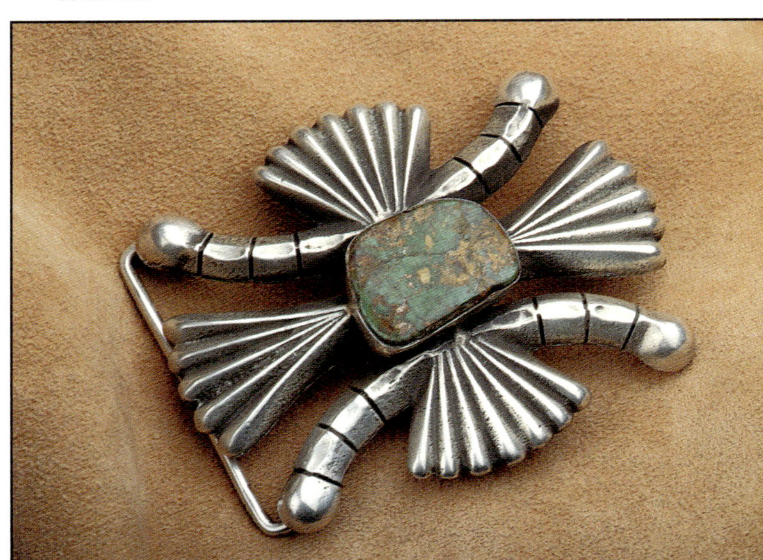

Contemporary Navajo silver and cast buckle. *Lynn D. Trusdell, Crown & Eagle Antiques*

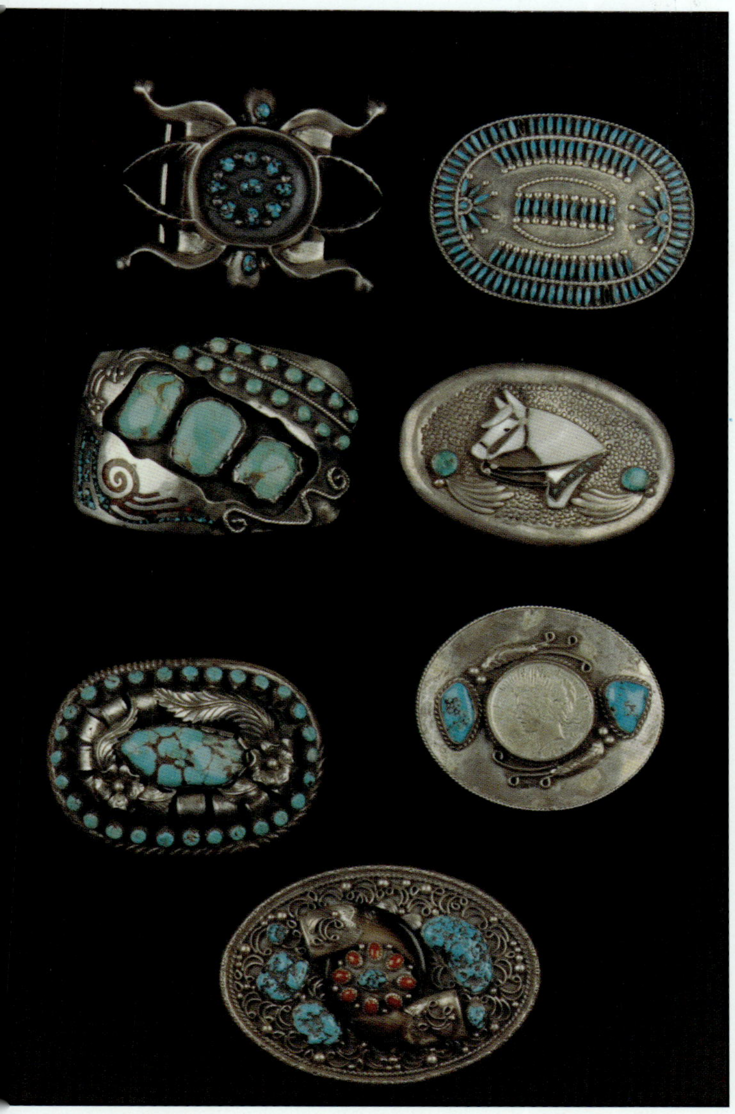

Navajo sand cast buckle set with Persian turquoise, circa 1960. / Oval buckle of silver and needlepoint treated Kingman turquoise, circa 1960. / Navajo rectangular nickel buckle set with Royston turquoise , circa 1970. / Zuni oval silver buckle with horse head design inlaid with white shell and Kingman turquoise, circa 1950. / Nickel silver buckle with treated Pilot Mountain turquoise, circa 1960s. / Navajo silver buckle set with a 1922 United States silver dollar and treated Kingman turquoise, circa 1950s. / Navajo buckle set with two bear's claws, Kingman turquoise and coral, circa 1950s. *Dennehotso collection*.

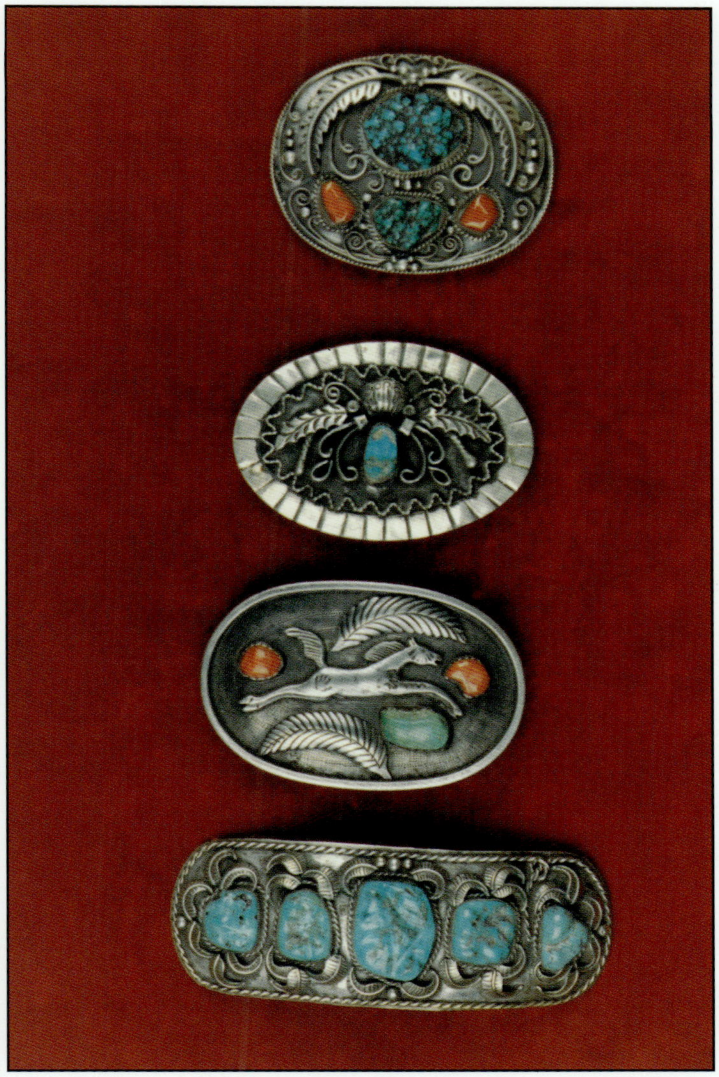

Old silver buckle decorated with wirework, two turquoise nuggets and two coral stones by K Z. / Old buckle of silverwork set with a turquoise stone. / Oval silver buckle with a horse and two leaves in overlay decoration ornamented with one turquoise and two coral stones, 1966. / Long silver buckle with five large turquoise nuggets, 1976. *Private collection on permanent loan to Ohio University*

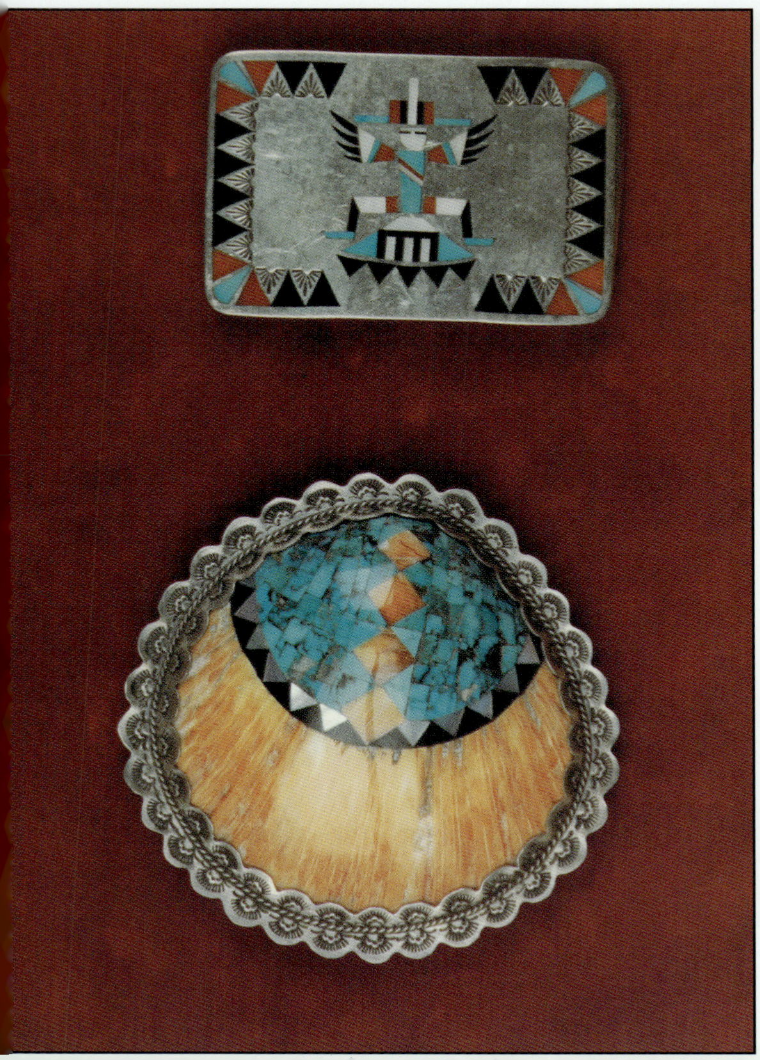

Silver rectangular buckle inlaid with a mosaic Knifewing god design in coral, jet, shell and turquoise by Fred and Lolita Natachu, Zuni, 1978. / Buckle of stamped silver and Spring oyster shell inlaid with jet, mother of pearl and turquoise, 1978. *Private collection on permanent loan to Ohio University*

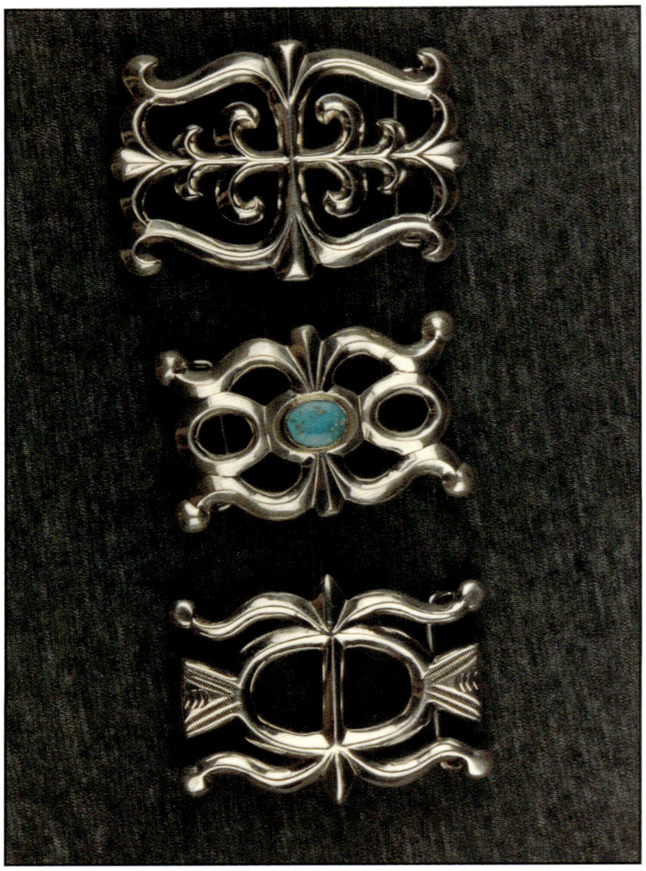

Three Navajo sand-cast buckles with different versions of the corn leaves design, none marked, 1980s. *Enchanted Mesa collection* .

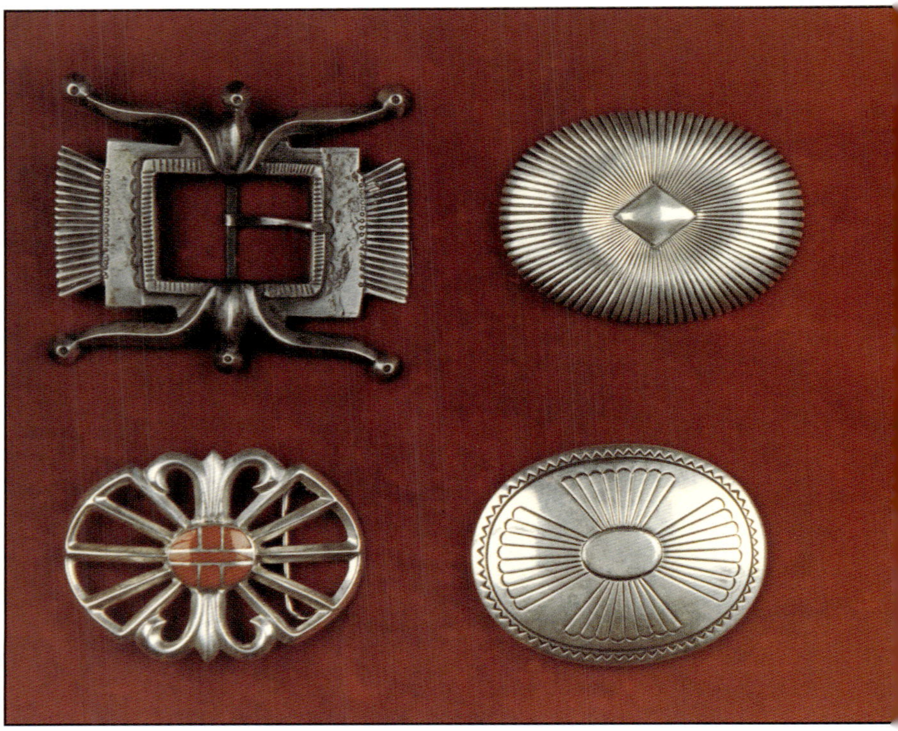

Old sand cast buckle made rectangular with corn leaves design. / Oval silver buckle with a sunburst design by Ivan Kee, Navajo, 1979. / Sand-cast oval buckle ornamented with a channel-set coral medallion. / Silver buckle with wrought and stamped four-rays design by Willie Shaw, circa 1980. *Private collection on permanent loan to Ohio University*

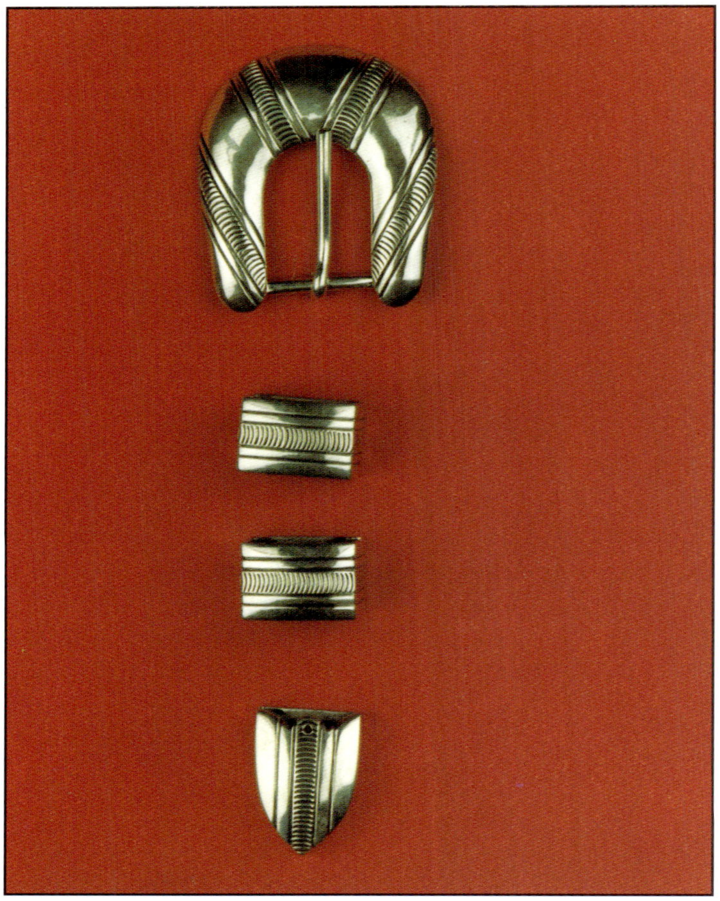

Wrought silver ranger buckle with rows of stamped border decoration by Joe D. Yazzie, Navajo, 1970s.

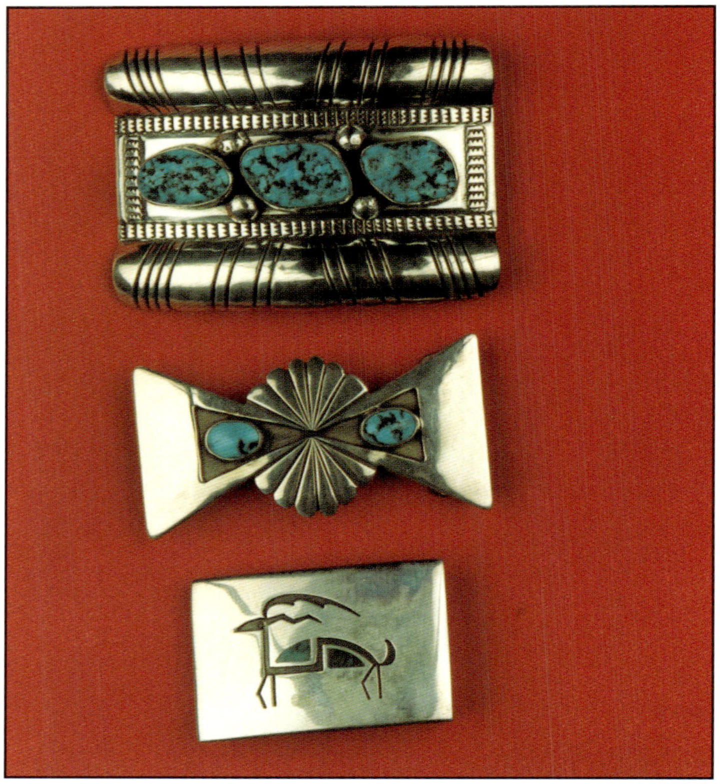

Strongly designed rectangular buckle set with three turquoise stones by Kee Joe Benally, Navajo, 1970s. / Bow-shaped silver overlay buckle set with two turquoise stones by Kee Joe Benally, 1970s. / Small rectangular buckle of overlay technique with deer design and two inlaid turquoise stones by Willie Yazzie, Navajo, 1970s.

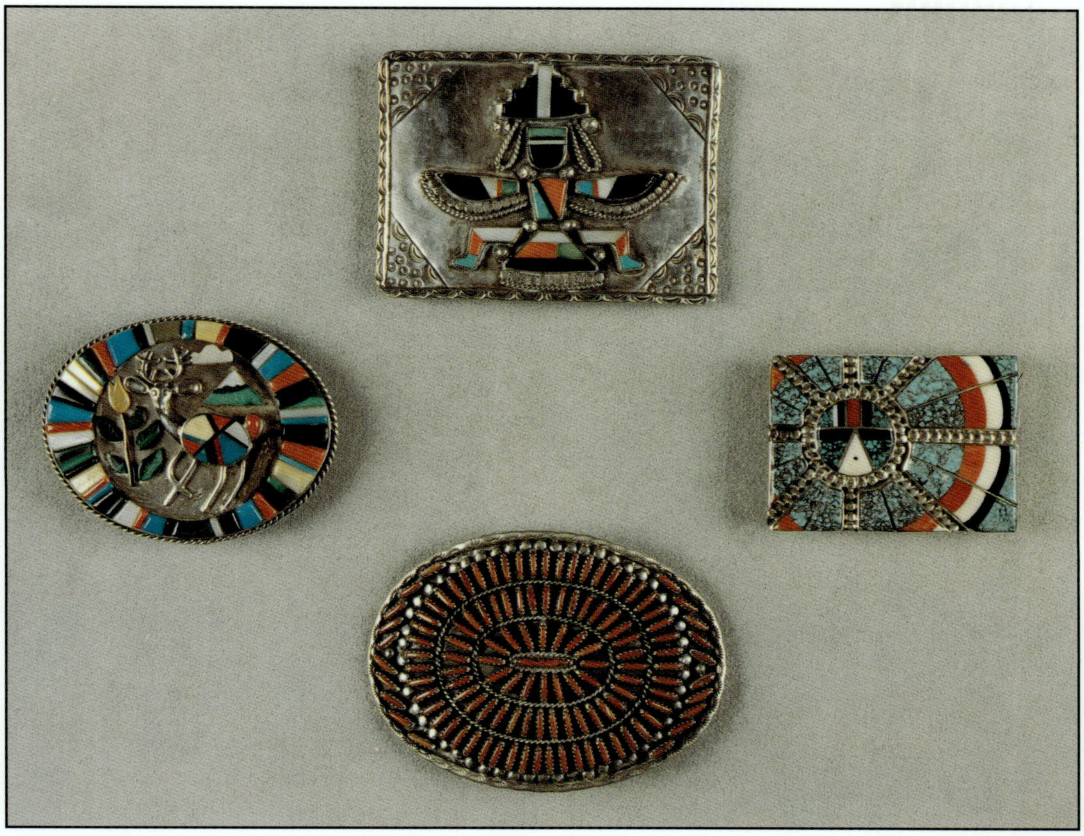

Silver rectangular buckle inlaid with an Eagle dancer design in jet, shell, turquoise and coral by Knifewing (Ray Tracey, Navajo), 1981. / Oval silver buckle with a mosaic inlaid design including a deer with shell, malachite, coral, turquoise, and jet by Raymond Boyd, Navajo. / Rectangular buckle of silver and mosaic inlay with sunface design in turquoise, shell, coral and jet by Oscar & Elexius, 1989. / Coral needlepoint and silver buckle by JY (scratched in), 1978. *Private collection on permanent loan to Ohio University*

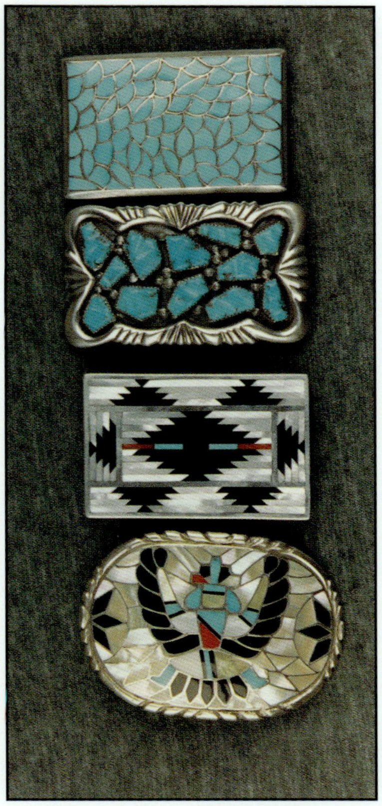

Rectangular buckle of channel inlaid turquoise in curvilinear design by Rodney and Georgeann Hughte, Zuni, 1980s. / Silver buckle with turquoise chunks carefully arranged by George and Lupeta Leekity, Zuni, 1980s. / Rectangular silver buckle covered with mosaic inlay in a geometric pattern of carefully arranged lines of mother of pearl, jet, turquoise and coral by Charlene Dishta, Zuni, 1980s. / Oval silver buckle with an all-over mosaic inlay of a bird design in mother of pearl, jet, turquoise and coral by Ralph and Lilly Kallestewa, Zuni, 1980s. *Enchanted Mesa collection*

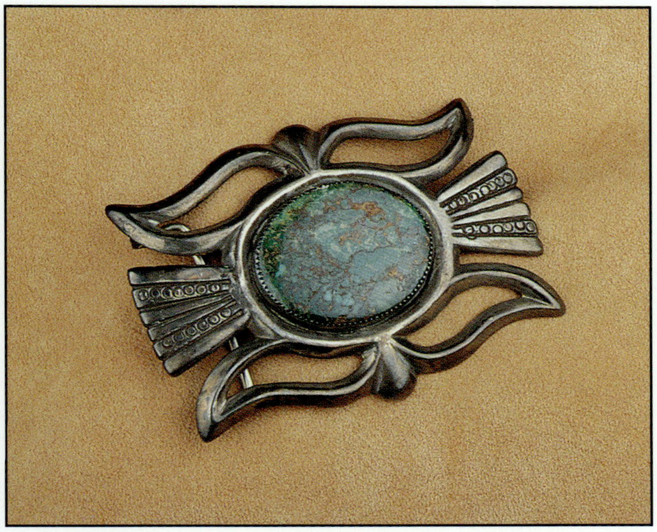

Navajo silver sand-cast buckle with turquoise. *Lynn D. Trusdell, Crown & Eagle Antiques*

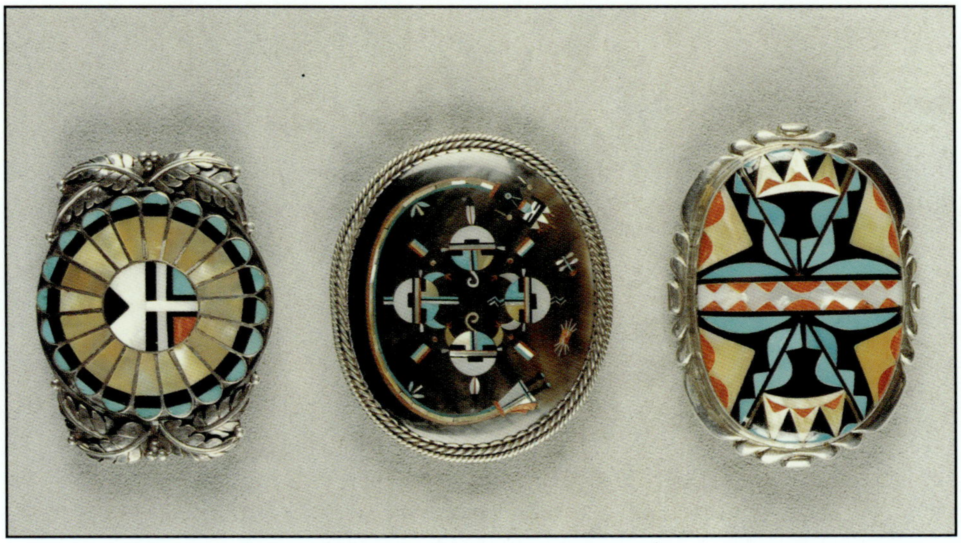

Left: Silver and channel inlaid buckle with a sunface design of mother of pearl, shell, jet, turquoise and coral, unmarked, 1980s. / Center: Beautiful and delicately detailed buckle of silver and tortoise shell inlaid with a sandpainting design, by Tom Z. / Right: Bold oval buckle of silver with mosaic inlay of geometric design including jet, mother of pearl, coral and turquoise by Wayne and Virginia Quam, Zuni, 1980s. *Private collection on permanent loan to Ohio University*

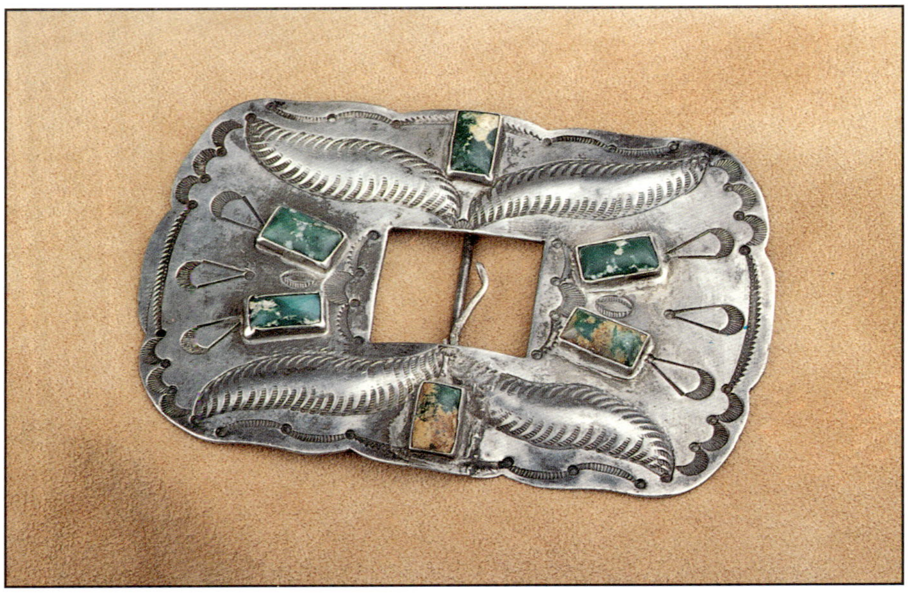

Navajo silver buckle with turquoise, unmarked. *Lynn D. Trusdell, Crown & Eagle Antiques*

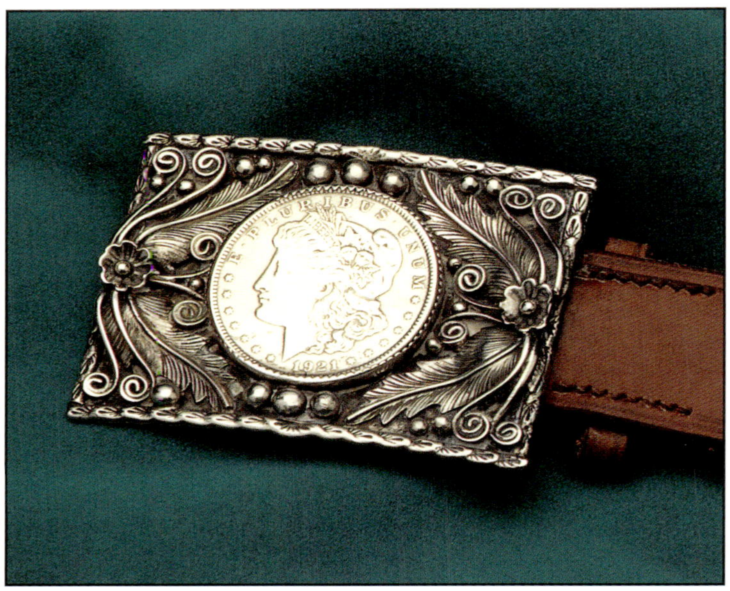

Navajo silver buckle with filigree decoration of wonderful detail and a mounted American silver dollar coin dated 1921.

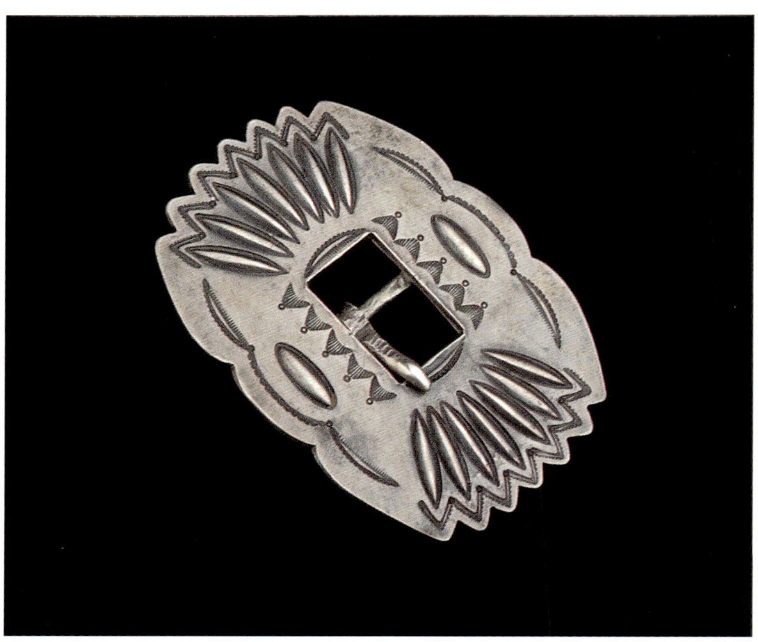

Navajo silver buckle. *Lynn D. Trusdell, Crown & Eagle Antiques*

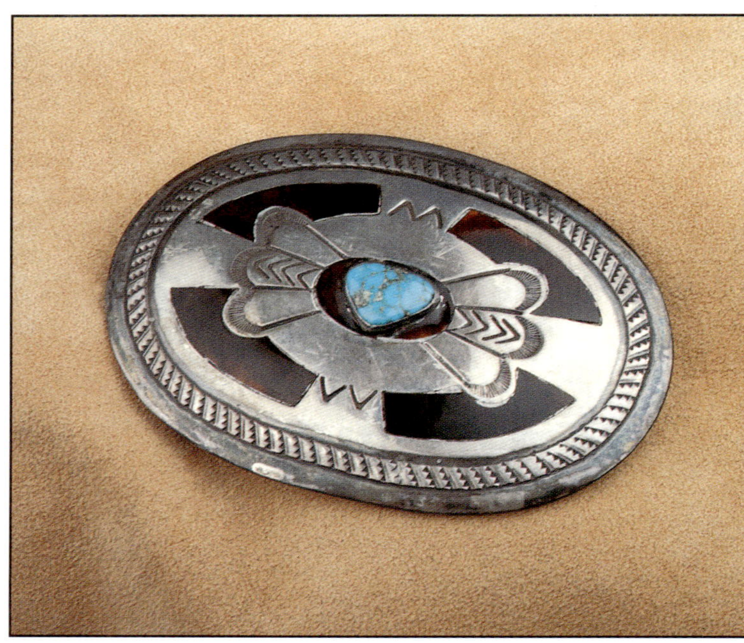

Navajo silver buckle with tortoise shell and turquoise inlayed. *Lynn D. Trusdell, Crown & Eagle Antiques*

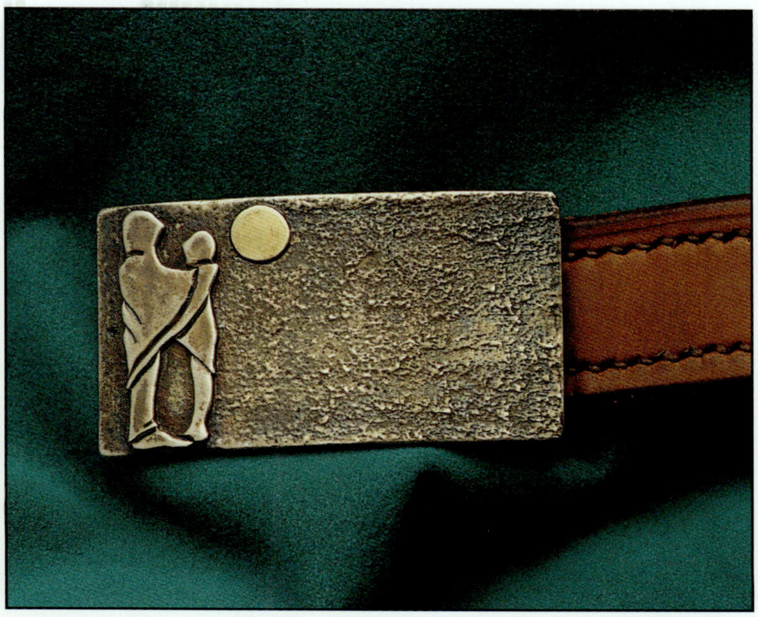

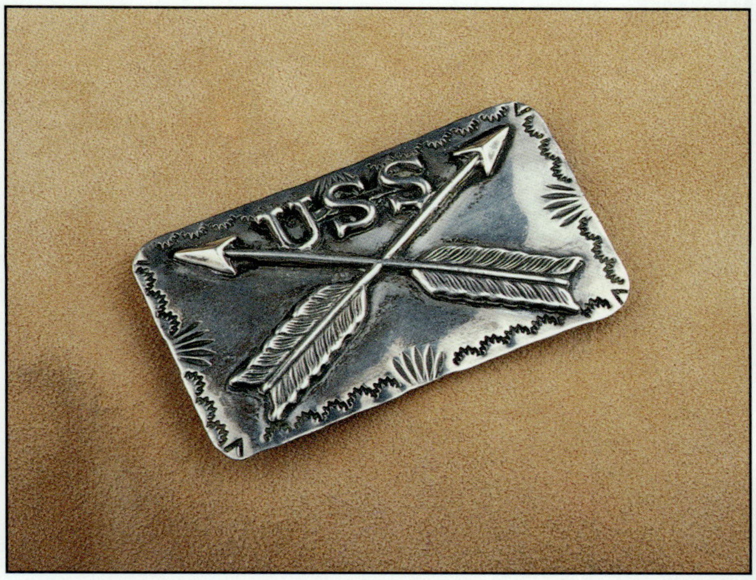

Navajo silver buckle with the image of an embracing couple under a gold full moon, by Paul Arviso, c.1995.

Navajo silver buckle with crossed arrows design and USS, stamped on the back 036-26-3545, 1940s. *Lynn D. Trusdell, Crown & Eagle Antiques*

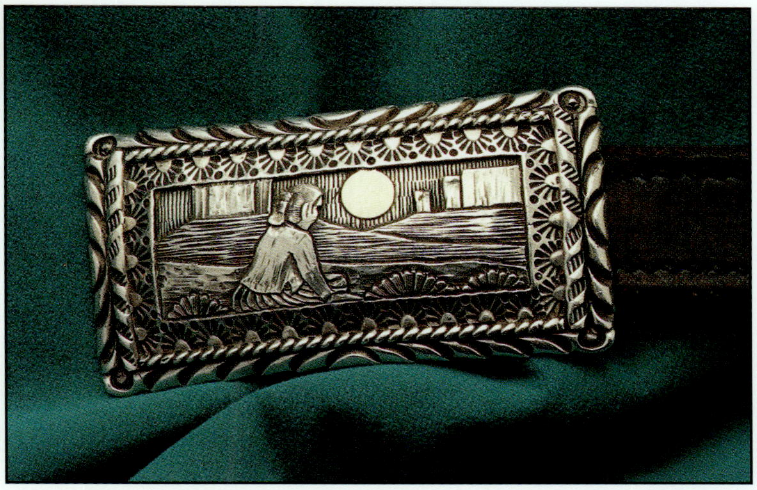

Navajo silver buckle with a pastoral scene showoing a woman and desert mesas under a full moon, by Paul Arviso, c.1995.

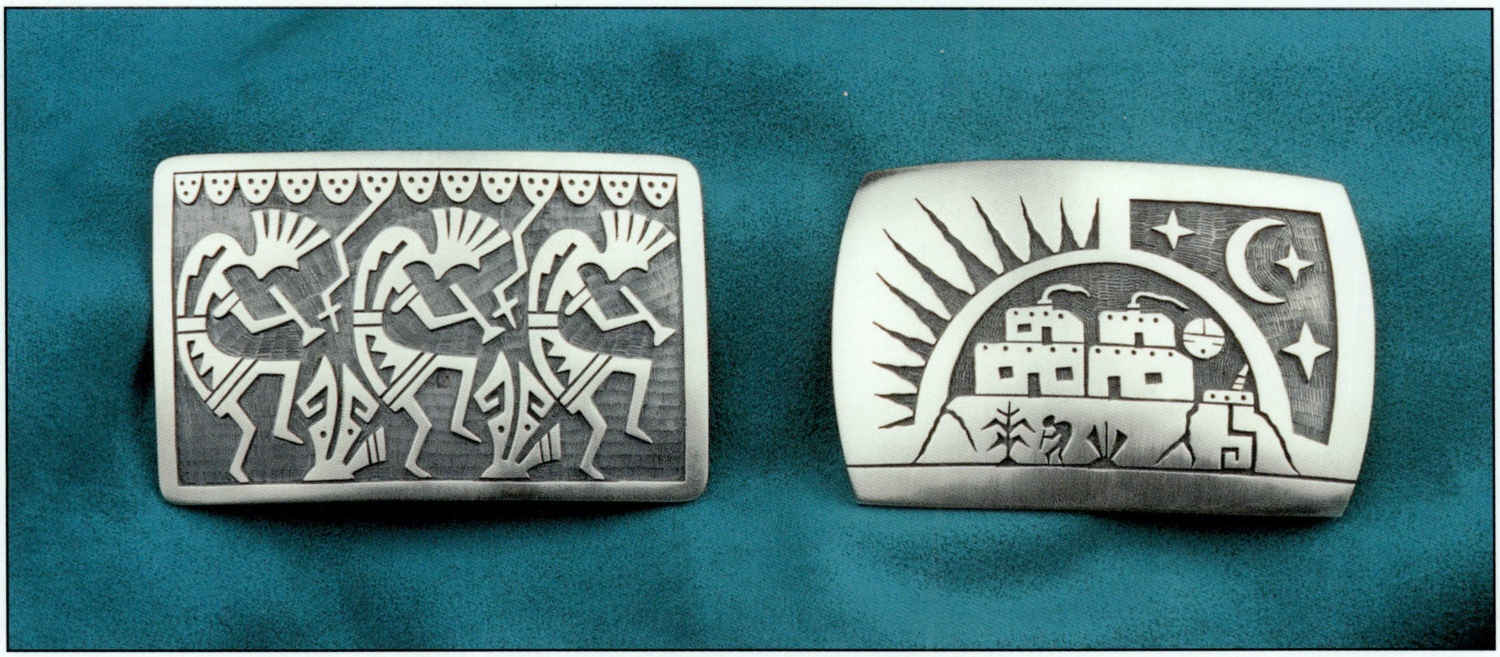

Left: Buckle by Petra Lamson with three Kokopeli in the design.
Right: Buckle with moon and star in design by Edward Lomahongva, Pueblo. *Courtesy McGee's, Keams Canyon*

Silver buckle appliquéd with silver, copper and a mosaic medallion with mother of pearl, jet, turquoise and coral. The design shows a shepherdess with a lamb, dog, sheep and goat all walking in a mountainous Southwest landscape by Clarence Lee, 1989. *Clarence Lee collection*

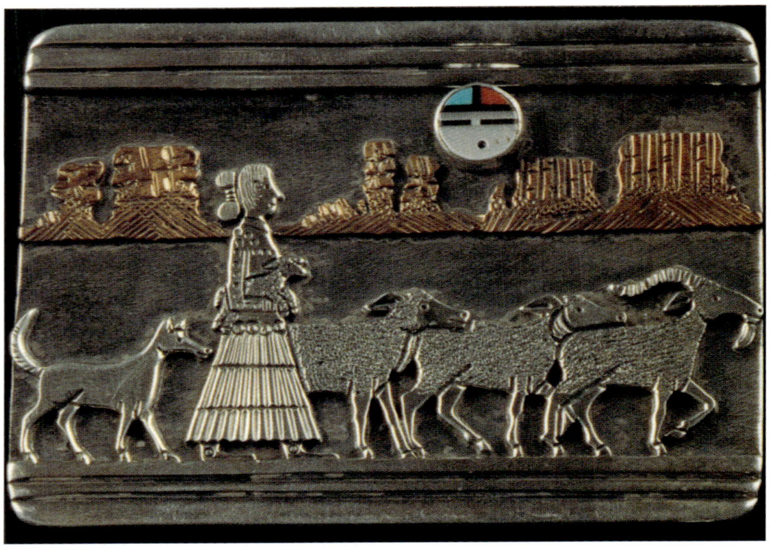

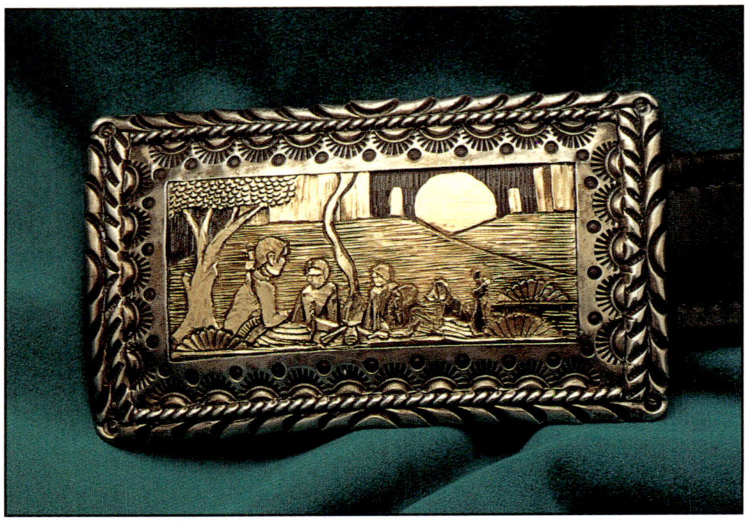

Navajo silver buckle with a gold narrative scene of people clustered around a campfire as a full moon is rising, by Paul Arviso, c.1997.

Navajo gold buckle with a narrative scene of people taking a meal next to a covered wagon, by Paul Arviso, c.2001.

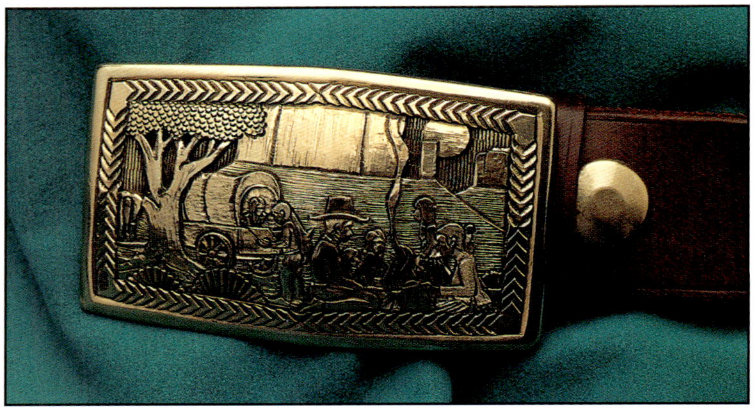

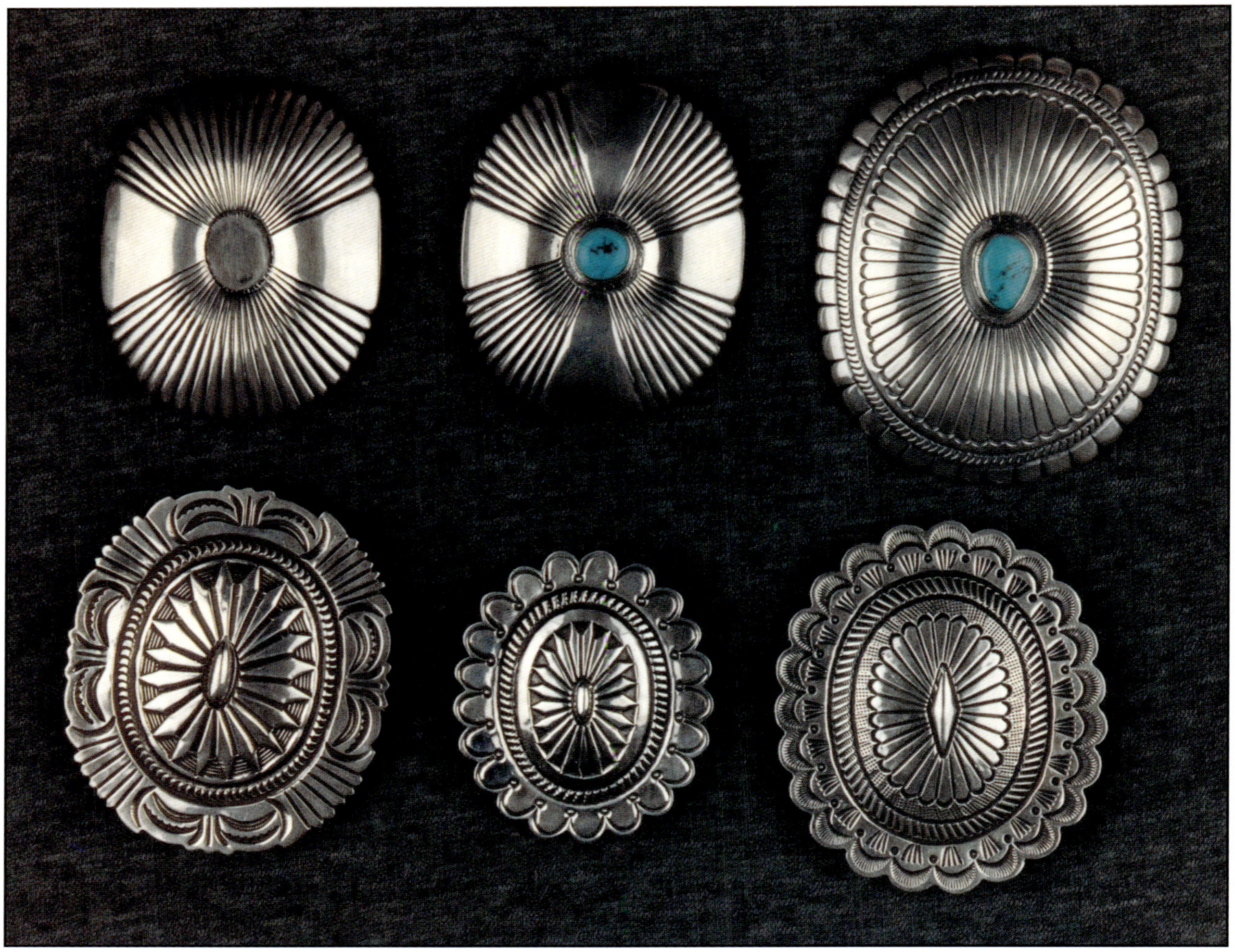

Silver buckle with wrought ray pattern by Willie Shaw, Navajo. / Oval silver buckle with center turquoise, unmarked. / Large oval silver buckle with ray design and turquoise by Willie Shaw, Navajo. / Two large oval silver concha buckles with beautiful stamped designs by Carson Blackgoat, Navajo. / Small silver concha buckle by P. Yellowhorse, Navajo. All from the 1980s. *Enchanted Mesa collection* .

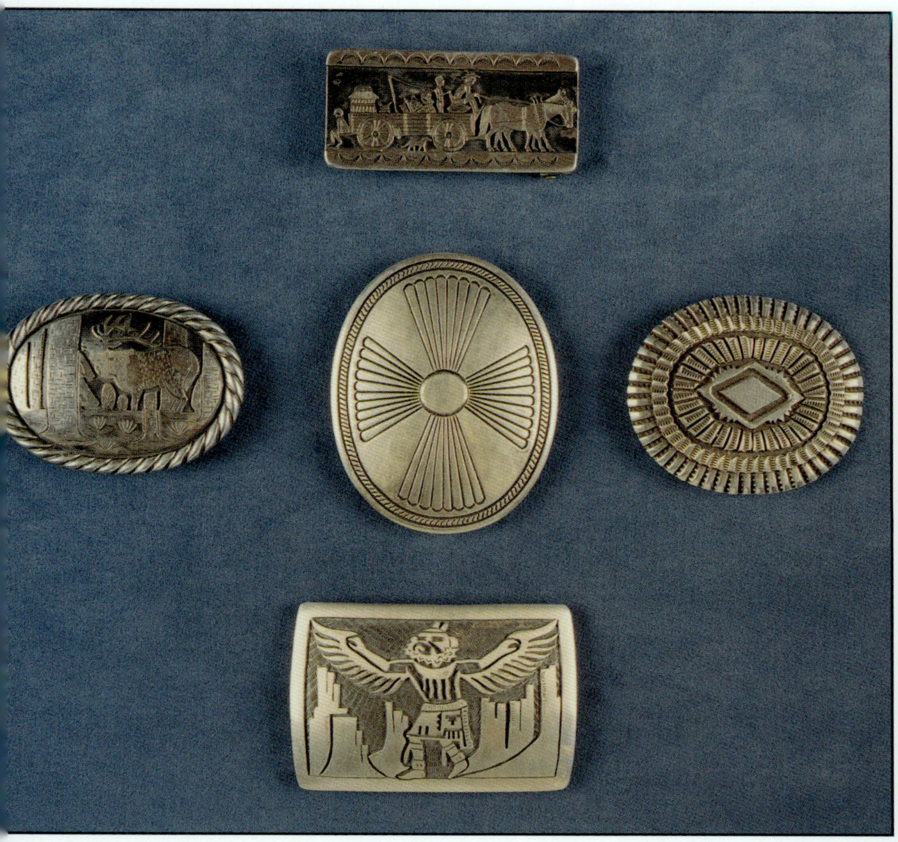

Rectangular silver buckle with appliqué decoration depicting a family and goods being transported in a horse-drawn wagon by Clarence Lee, Navajo, 1980. / Oval silver buckle depicting an elk in a landscape worked in overlay technique by Tom Bahe, 1979. / Oval concha style buckle with four rays design by Willie Shaw, Navajo, 1980. / Wrought silver buckle with a concha design boldly stamped, 1983. / Rectangular buckle designed with an eagle dancer in overlay technique by Watson Honanie, Hopi, 1979. *Private collection on permanent loan to Ohio University*

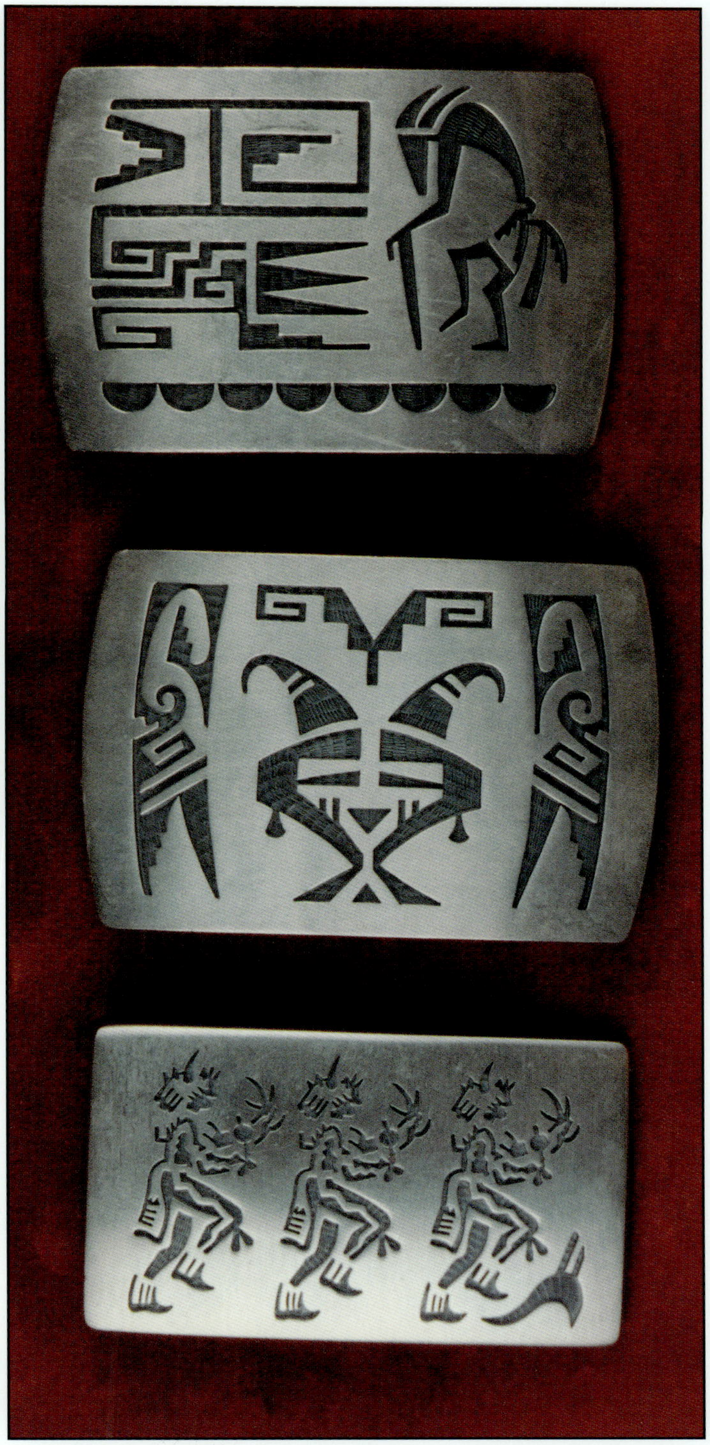

Three Hopi silver overlay buckles: two by Bobby Sekakuku with Humpback and Geometric designs. / one by Bradley Gashwazra with three dancers design. *Private collection*

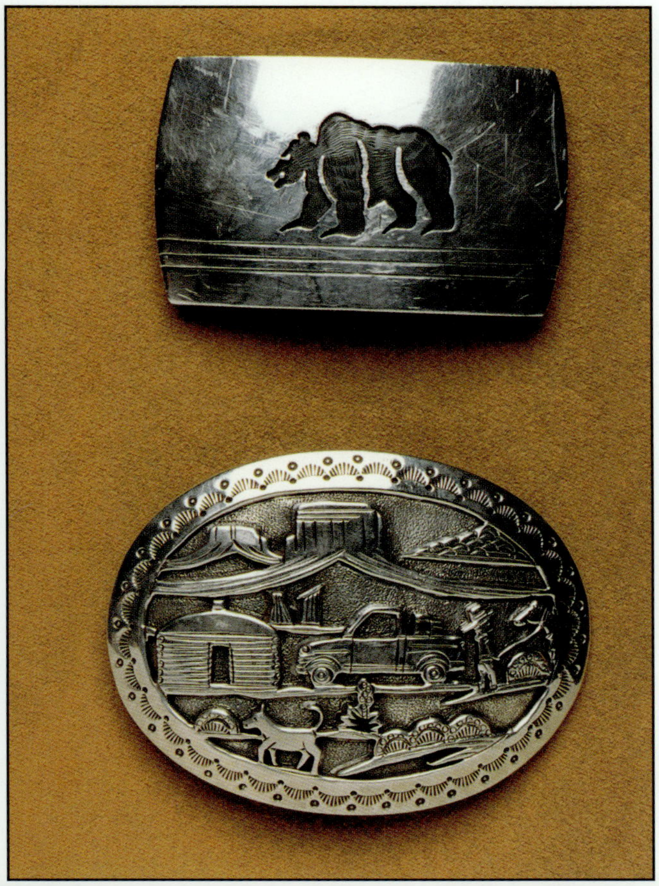

Hopi silver overlay buckle with bear design by Bobby Sekakuku, late 1980s. / Navajo silver storytelling buckle with landscape hogan, truck, man chopping wood and dog, by Jones D., late 1980s.

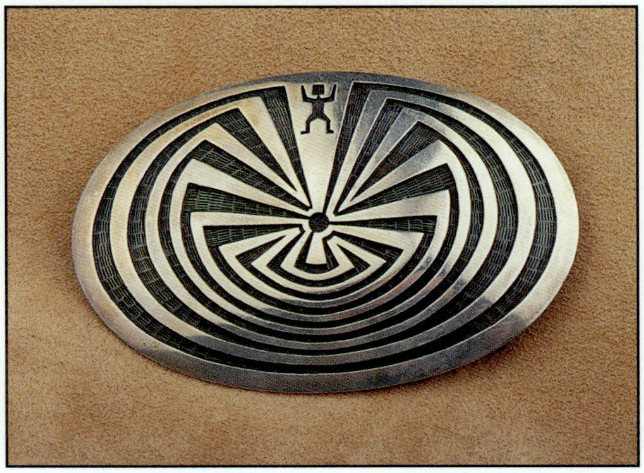

Oval Hopi silver overlay buckle with Man in a Maze design. *Lynn D. Trusdell, Crown & Eagle Antiques*

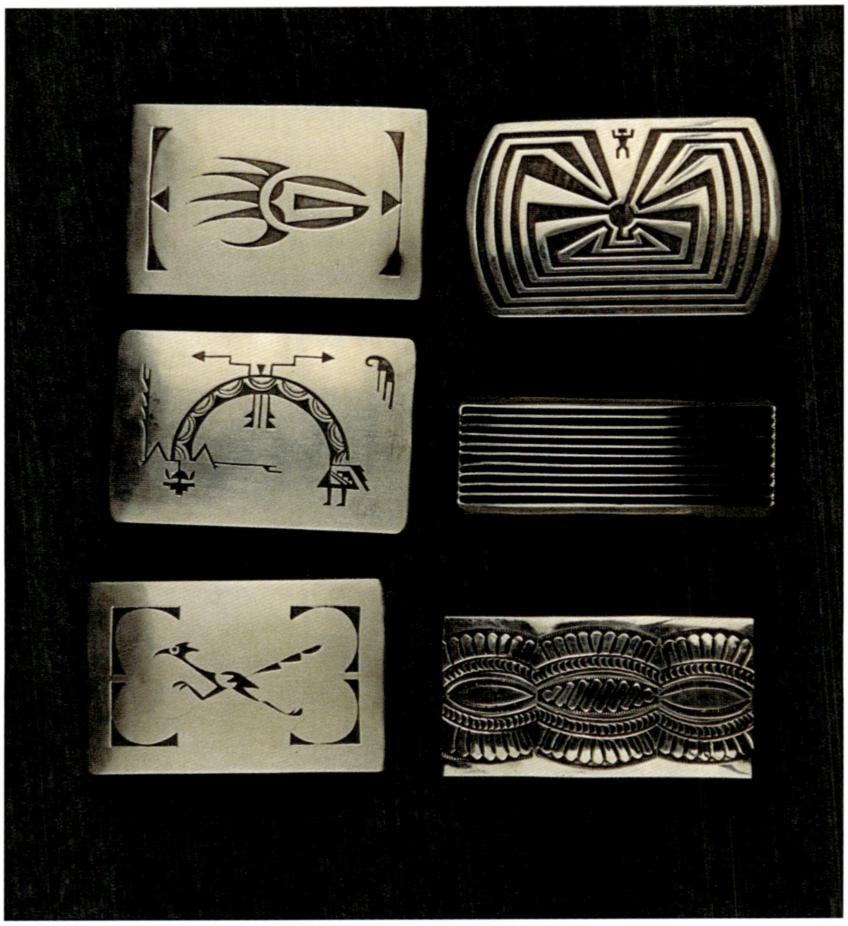

Six silver buckles from the 1980s: Bear paw design in overlay technique by Willie Yazzie, Navajo. / Man in a maze design in overlay by Mitchell Sockyma, Hopi. / Overlay Yei figure design, mark indistinct. / Wrought parallel lines by Tom Yazzie, Navajo. / Roadrunner design by Willie Yazzie, Navajo. / Stamped concha design by Carson Blackgoat, Navajo. *Enchanted Mesa collection*

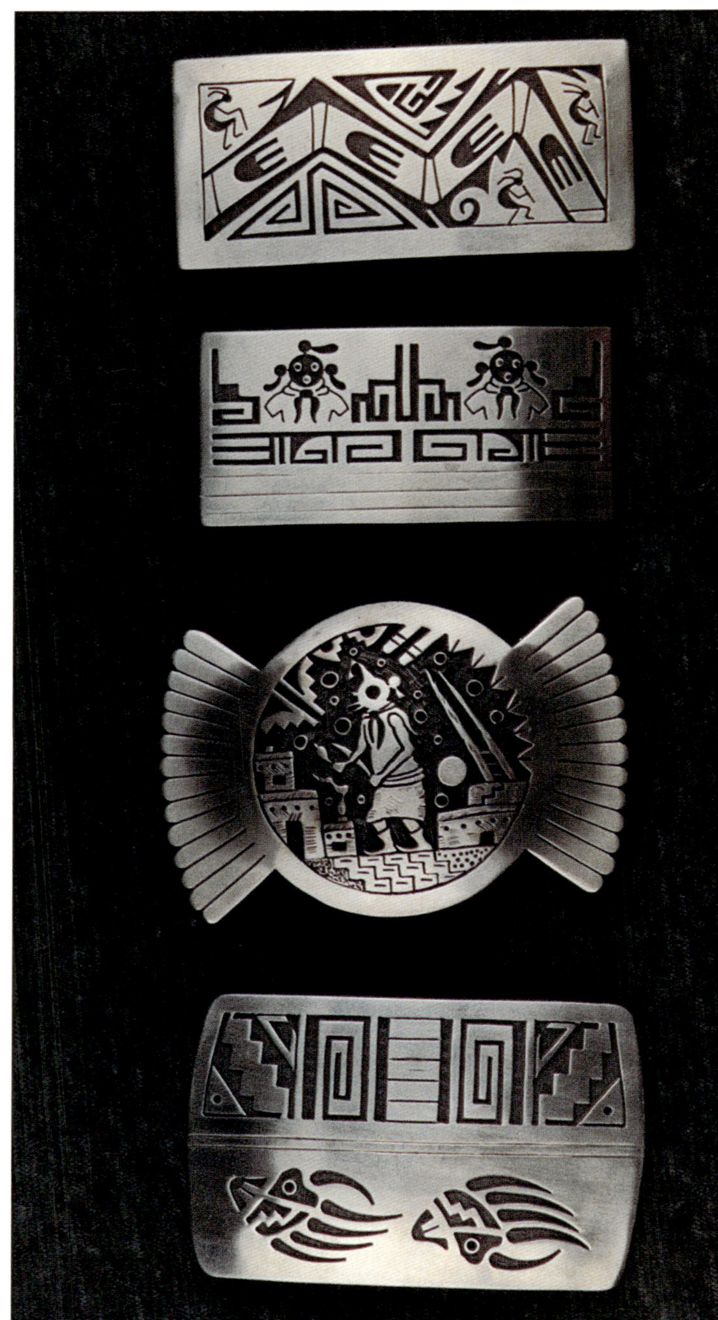

Four silver overlay buckles by Hopi silversmith Bobby Sekakuku made in the 1980s: Bearpath pattern / Two mudheads design / Mudhead and kiva design / Border with bearpaw design. *Enchanted Mesa collection*.

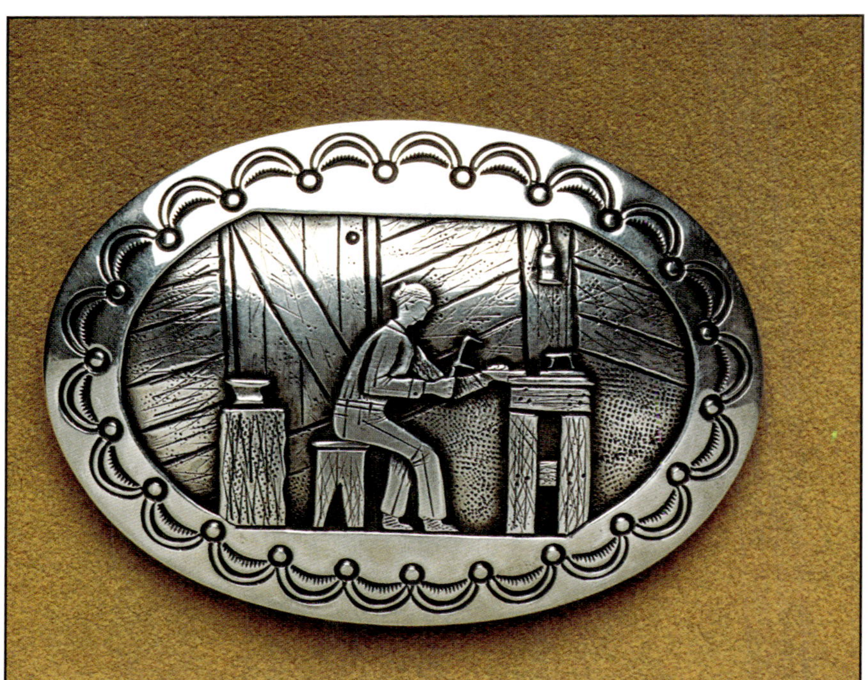

Silver wrought and overlay buckle showing a silversmith working at his bench, made by R.H. Begay, Navajo, 1980s.

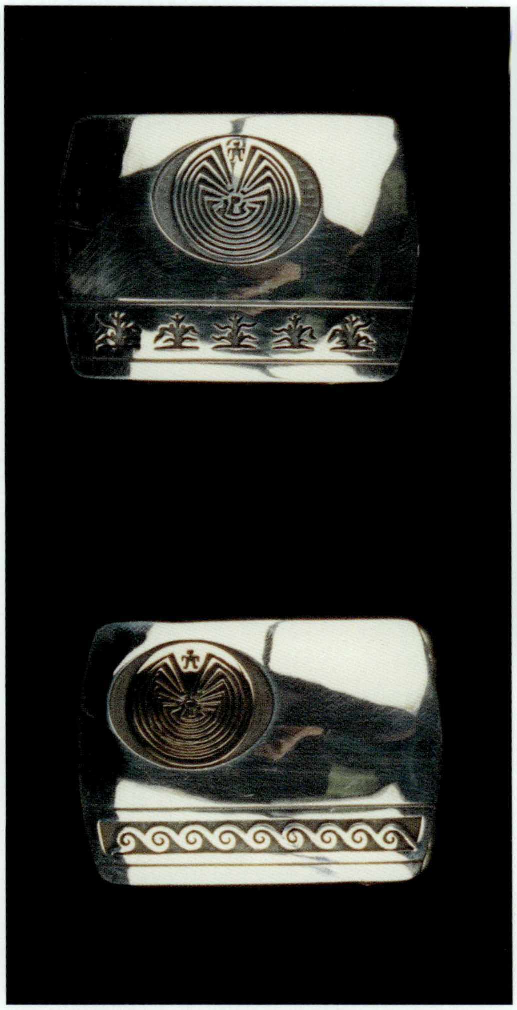

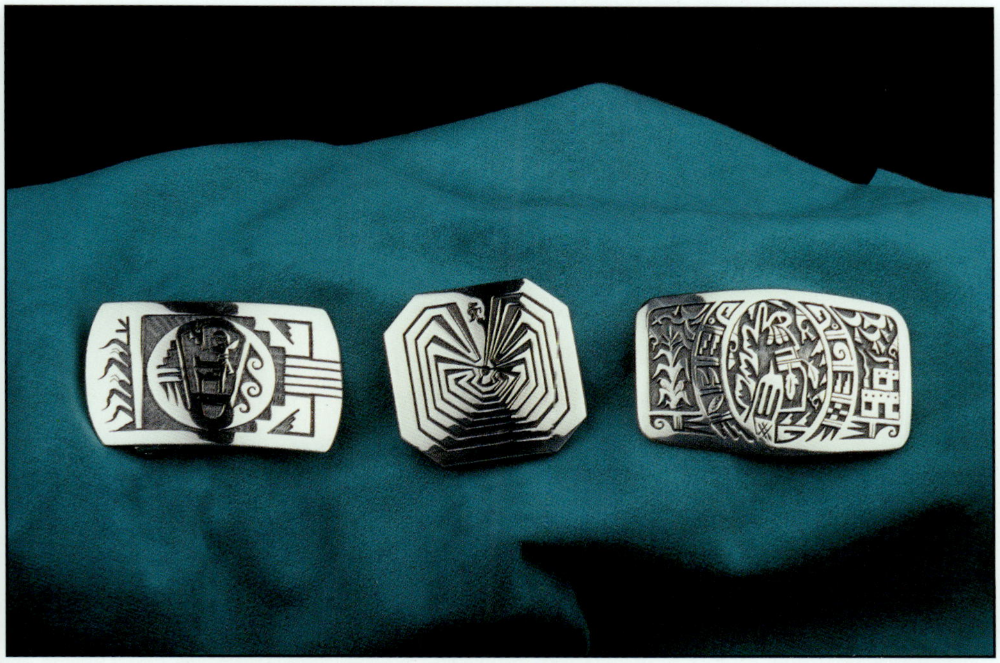

Left: Buckle with deeply cut designs by Timothy Mowa, Hopi.
Center: Round buckle with man in a maze design by Fernando Puhuhefvaya.
Right: Buckle with Longhair kachina, water waves, corn stalk, and village scene by Darren Silas, Hopi. *Courtesy McGee's, Keams Canyon*

Two silver buckles by Jason Takala, Hopi, with Man in the Maze design, one with corn plants border, / other with gold maze and scroll design border, 1980s. *Keams Canyon Arts & Crafts collection*

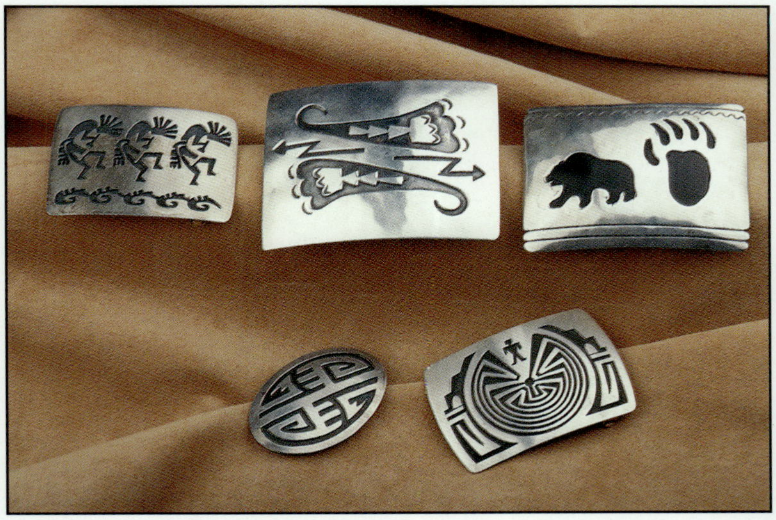

Five Hopi silver buckles with overlay design including: three Kokopeli, lightning and rain clouds, bear and bearpaw, geometric scroll, and man in a maze. *Lynn D. Trusdell, Crown & Eagle Antiques*

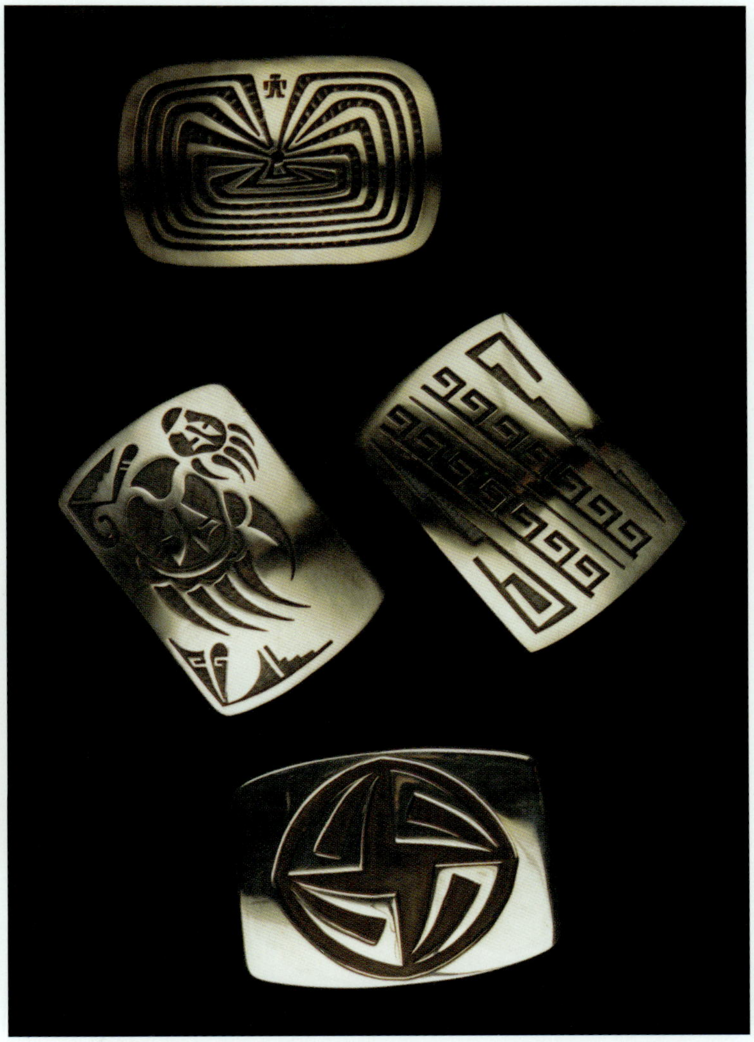

Four Hopi sterling silver buckles from the 1980s: Man in the maze design by Alvin Sesolde, Pima (learned from his brother-in-law Jason Takala, Hopi). / Bear paws design by Raymie Namingha. / Greek key design by Cleve Honyaktewa. / Star design by Wilmer Kavena, Sr.

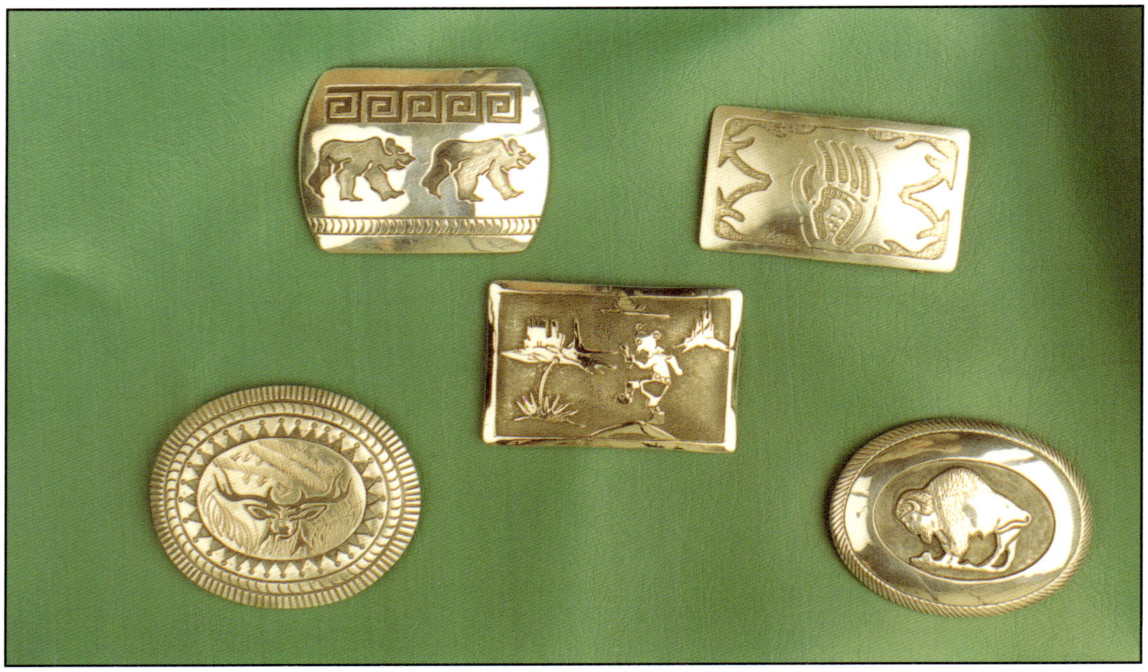

Five silver overlay buckles made in 1989: Two bears design by Rosco Scott, Navajo. / Bear paw design by Billy Slim, Navajo. / Interesting mudhead dancing in a landscape design, unmarked. / Oval with chiseled borders and buck's head by Herman Slinkey, Navajo. / Heavy medallion with buffalo in relief work by Tom Bahe. *Bing Crosby collection*

Buckle and earrings of silver decorated with an imaginative and romantic night sky theme mosaic inlay including turquoise, lapis lazuli, malachite, coral, shell and mother of pearl by Jessie Monongye, Navajo, 1980s. / Gold buckle with textured surface and turquoise inlay in a dynamic geometric design by Al Nez, Navajo.

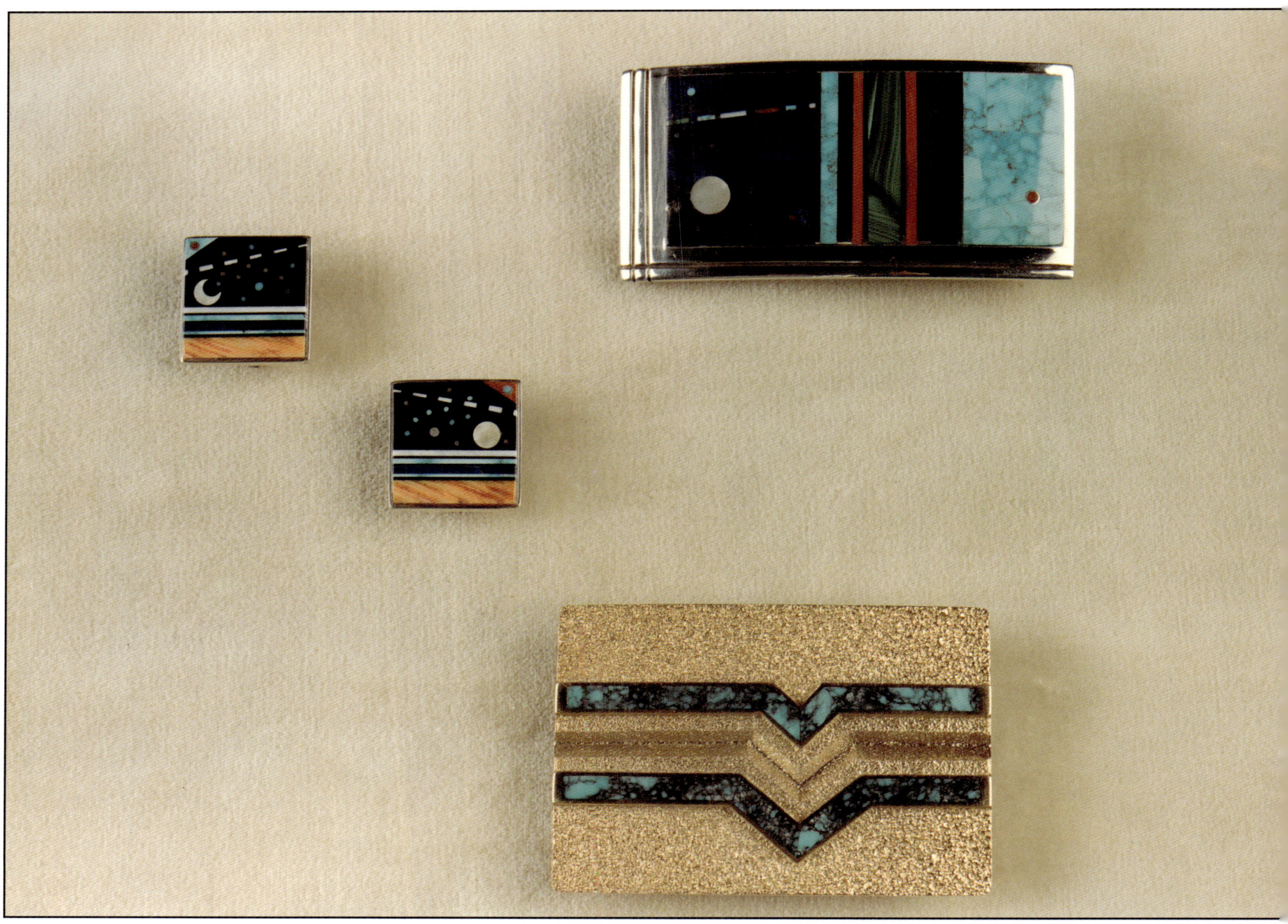

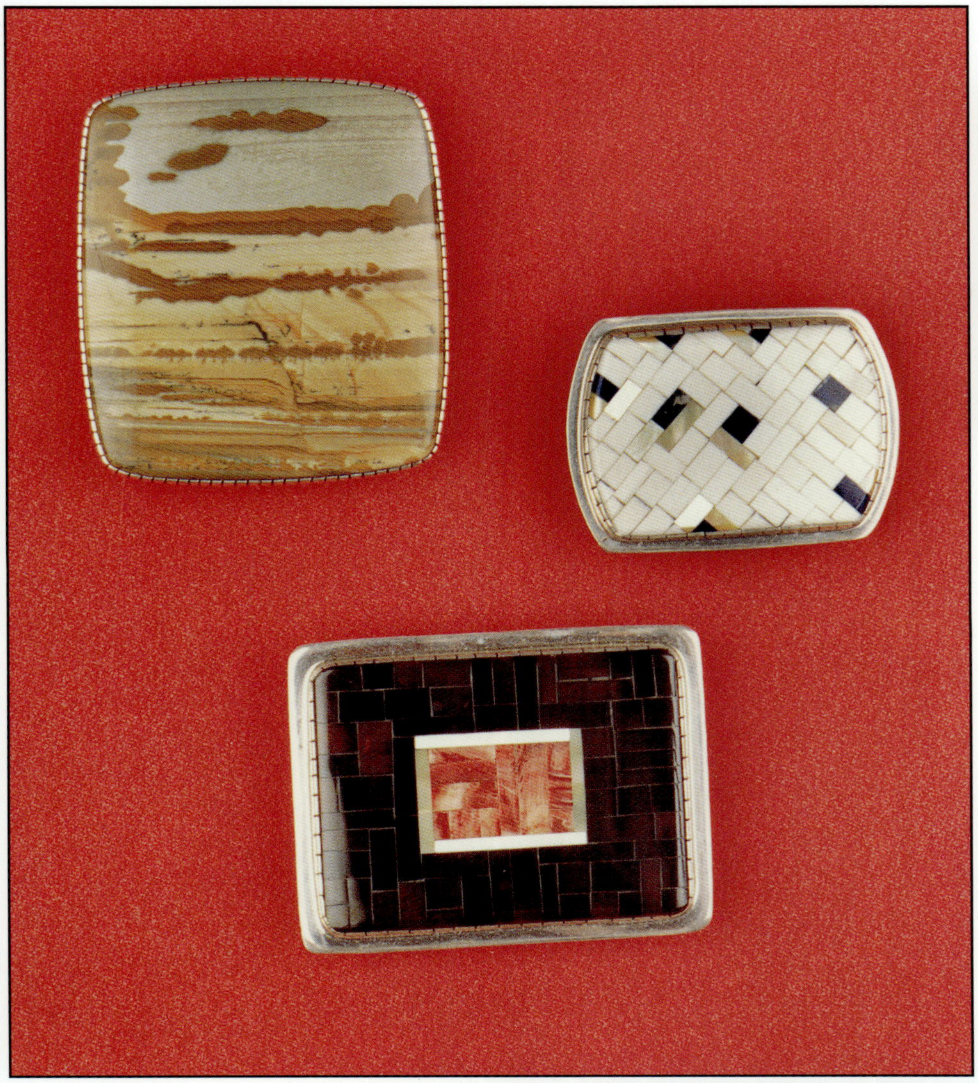

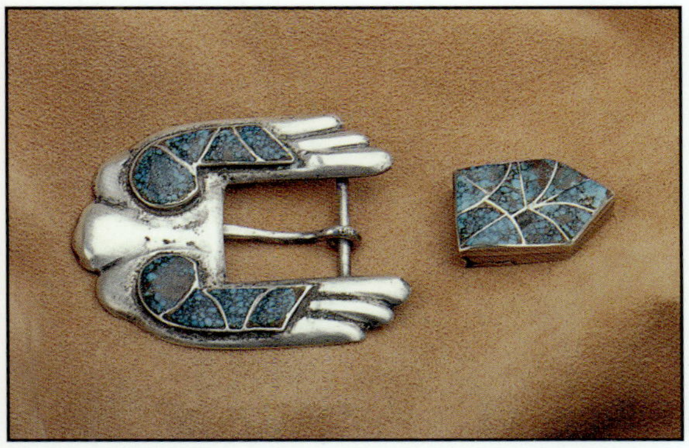

Ranger style Navajo silver buckle set with Berman spiderweb turquoise. *Lynn D. Trusdell, Crown & Eagle Antiques*

Silver buckle with single stone mounted on top, which has a pattern remarkably similar to a Southwest landscape, made by Gail Bird, Santo Domingo. / Two silver buckles with stone, mother of pearl and shell inlay in geometric designs by Charlie Bird, Santo Domingo, 1980s. *Dewey Gallery collection*

Ranger buckle set with inlayed stones by Jim Harrison. *Courtesy of Palms Trading Company* (825)

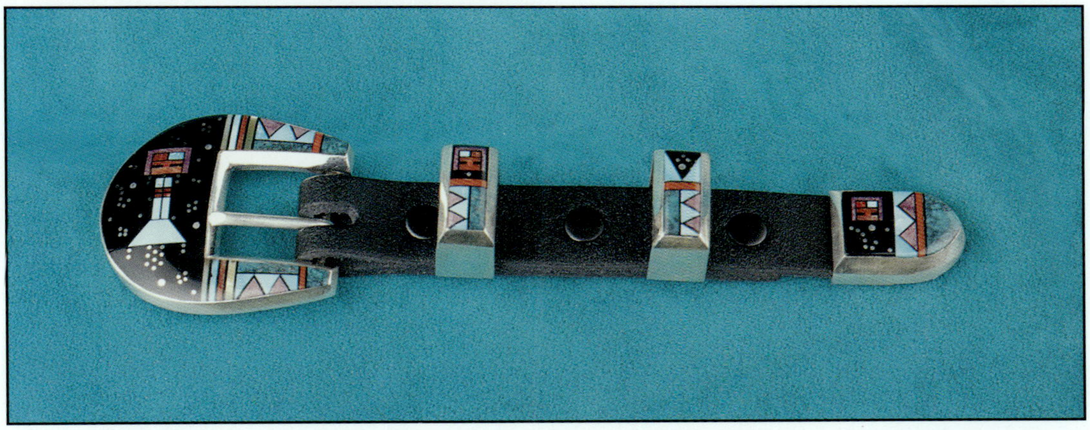

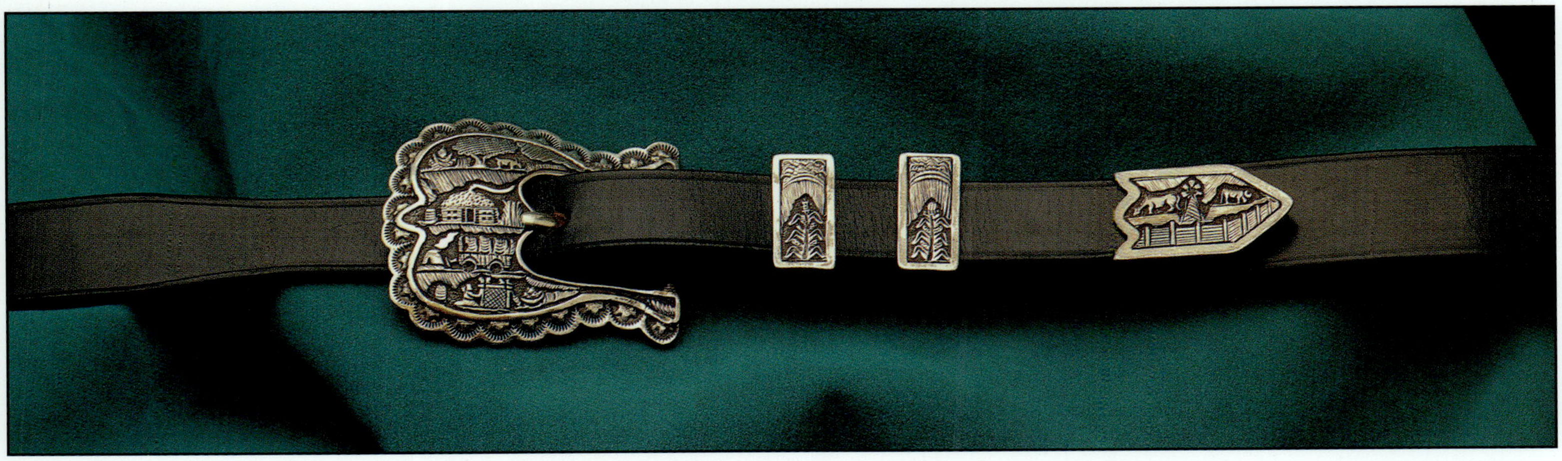

Navajo ranger buckle with narrative scene on the buckle of rural landscape with sheep, hogan, covered wagon, and a woman weaving at a loom. The two keepers have a corn design, and the belt tip has animals in a corral.

Bracelets

Bow Guards

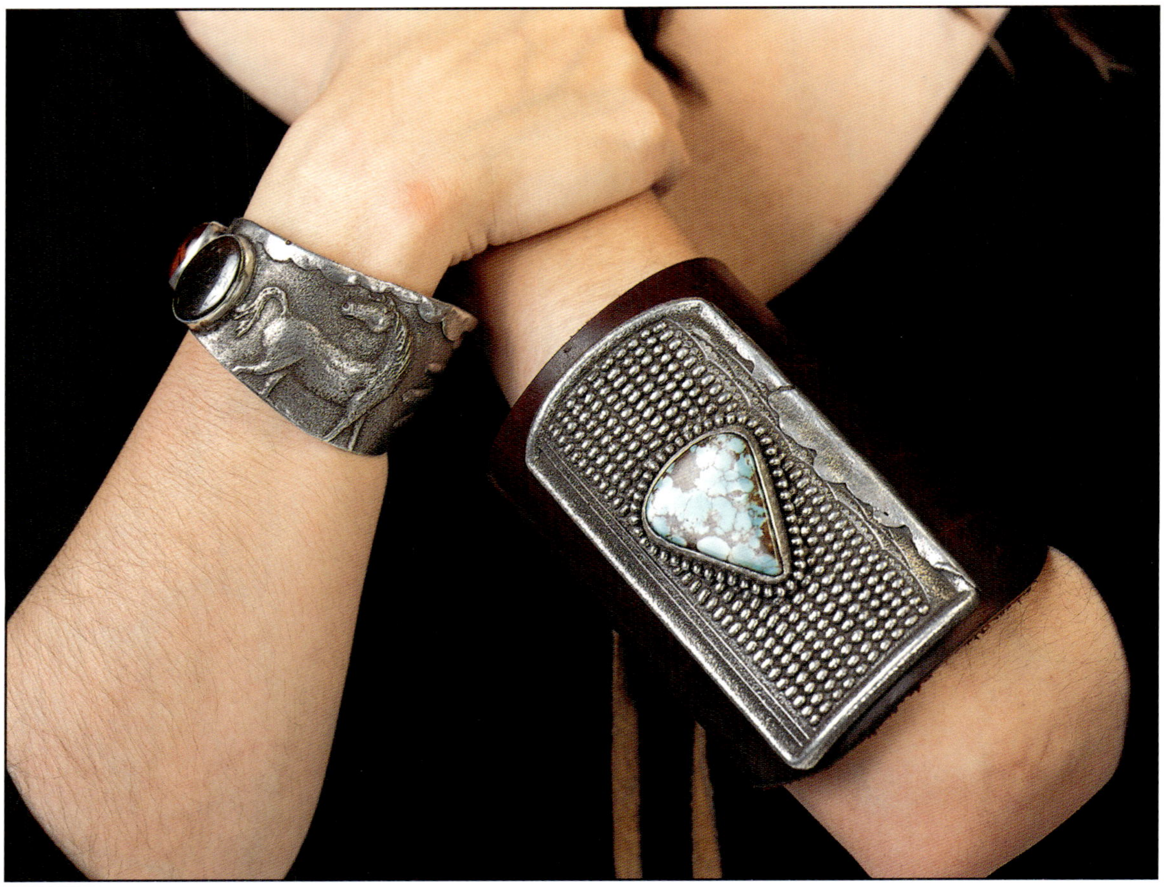

Sterling silver, Australian Boulder opal, and amber bracelet with horse design on the outside, by Anthony Lovato, Santo Domingo, 3-1/2" long x 1-1/4" wide. Leather bow guard with cast silver plaque in a corn row design with a triangular nugget of Pilot Mountain turquoise, by Anthony Lovato, Santo Domingo, 2002. *Courtesy of Gerald Peters Gallery, Santa Fe, New Mexico* ($900 and $1400)

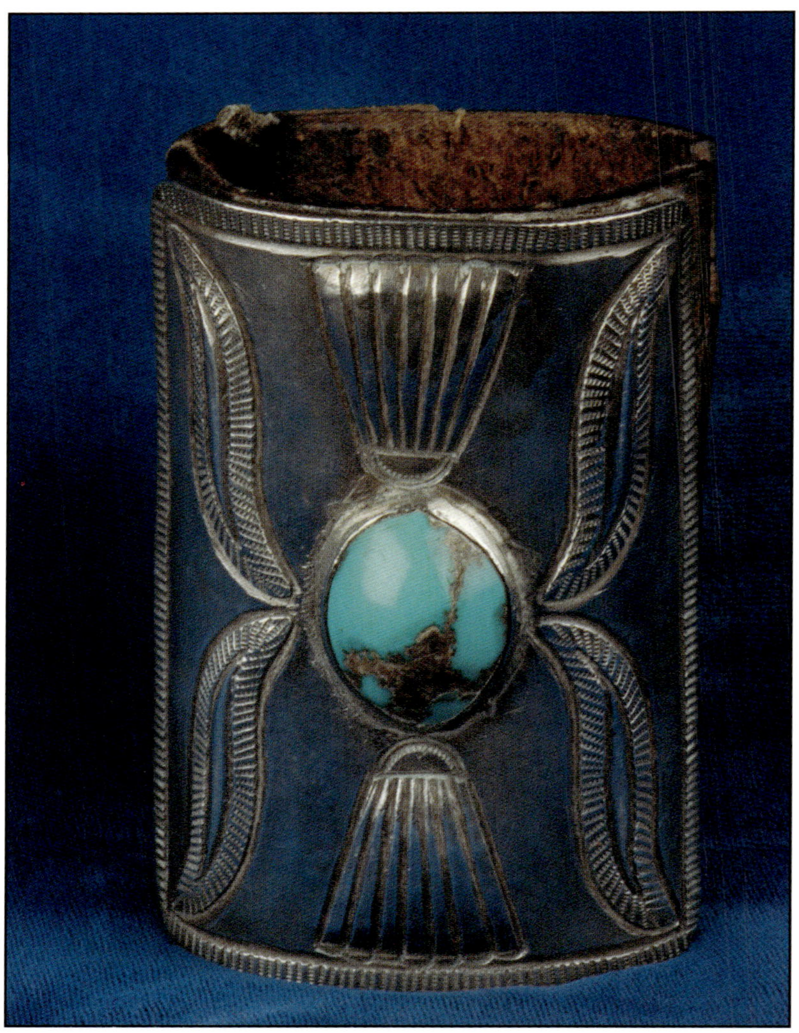

Old Navajo leather bow guard with silver stamped and repoussé design of rays and corn leaves and a single polished turquoise stone, circa 1930s. *Maxwell Museum collection*

Navajo leather bow guard with wrought silver plaque inlaid with coral in rays and corn leaves design by Kee Benally, 1970s. *Private collection*

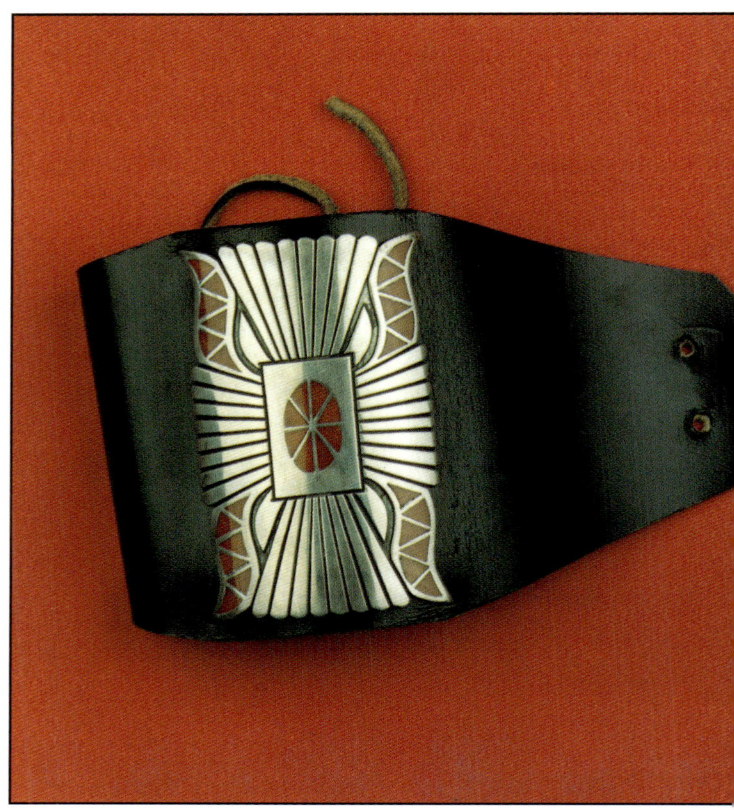

Early Bracelets

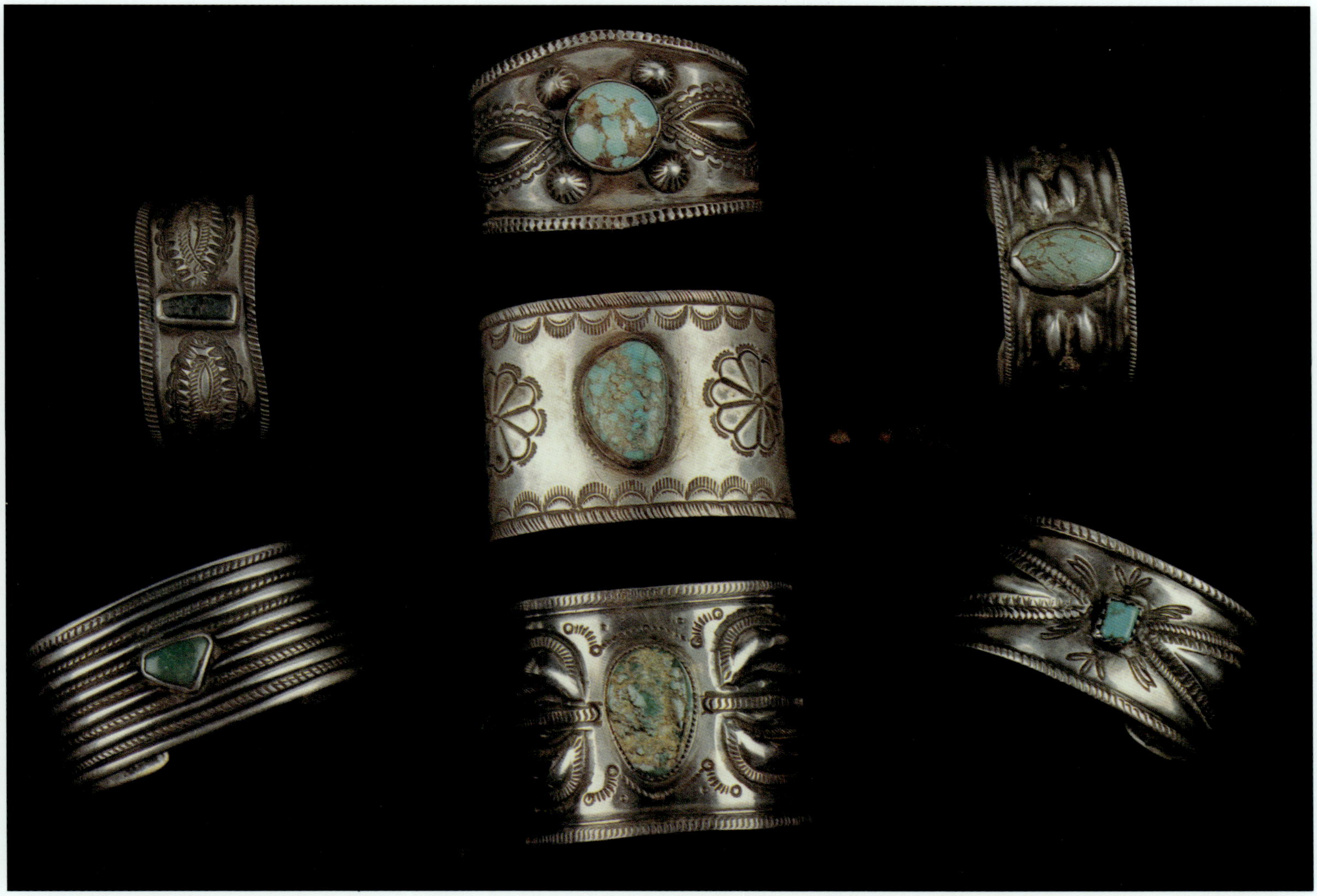

Navajo silver and turquoise bracelets: Left top - Stamped and filed work design and a folded silver bezel around Cerillos turquoise, circa 1890s. / Copy of an earlier design and set with a triangular turquoise, circa 1940s. / Center - Filed edges surround design made with button dies, circa 1900. / Heavy cuff with floral designs flanking turquoise, circa 1915-20. / Royston turquoise between stamped and repoussé wing design, circa 1920s. / Right - Repoussé flanking the turquoise and filed edges, circa 1890 - 1900. / Square Blue gem turquoise and raised work decoration, circa 1910. *Lynn D. Trusdell collection*

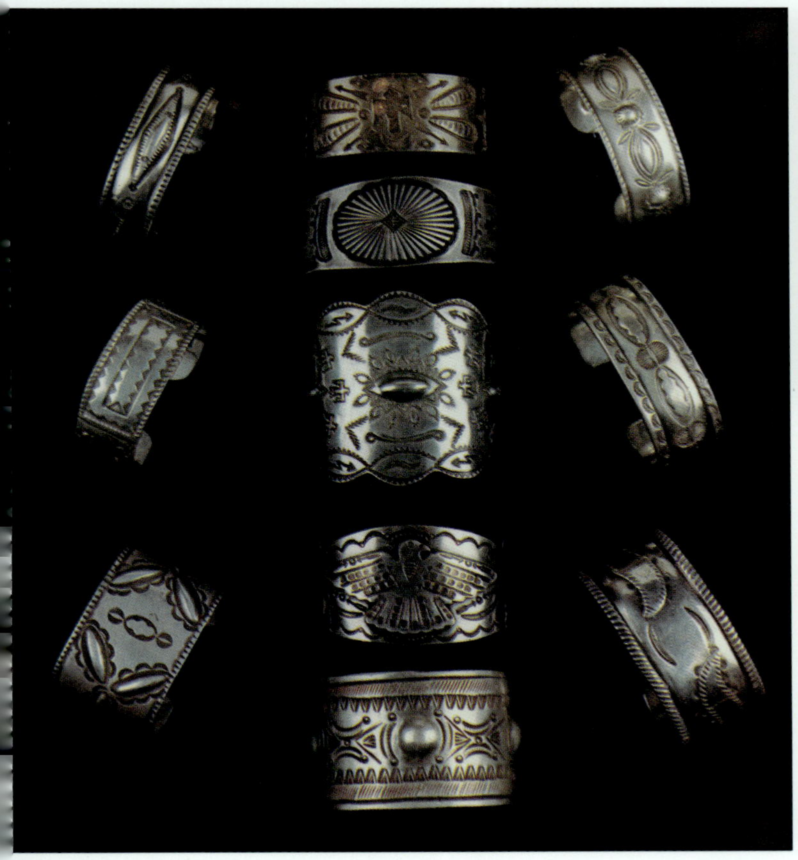

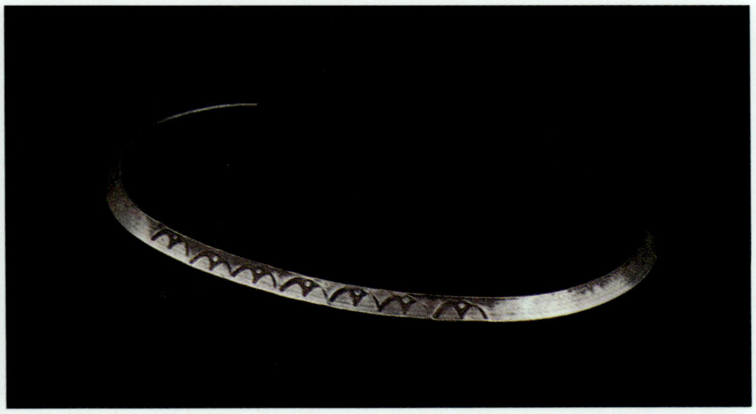

Child's single bar, stamped bracelet by Slender Maker of Silver, using his characteristic stamp design, c.1880. *Lynn D. Trusdell, Crown & Eagle Antiques*

All-silver Navajo stamped bracelets ranging from circa 1900 to circa 1930: Left top - Repoussé decoration, circa 1900. / Heavy coin silver with filed decoration, circa 1915-20. / Heavy coin silver cuff decorated with hand-made stamps, c.1910. / Center -Tourist style cuff with thunderbird design, 1940s. / Cuff with a button die design in the center, circa 1920s. / Tourist style cuff with stamped designs, 1930s. / Tourist style cuff with thunderbird design, 1940s. / Wide cuff with domed and stamped decoration, circa 1900. / Right - Stamped button die design, 1930s. / Domed and stamped, circa 1900. / Free-form stamped design with filed edges, 1930s. *Lynn D. Trusdell collection*

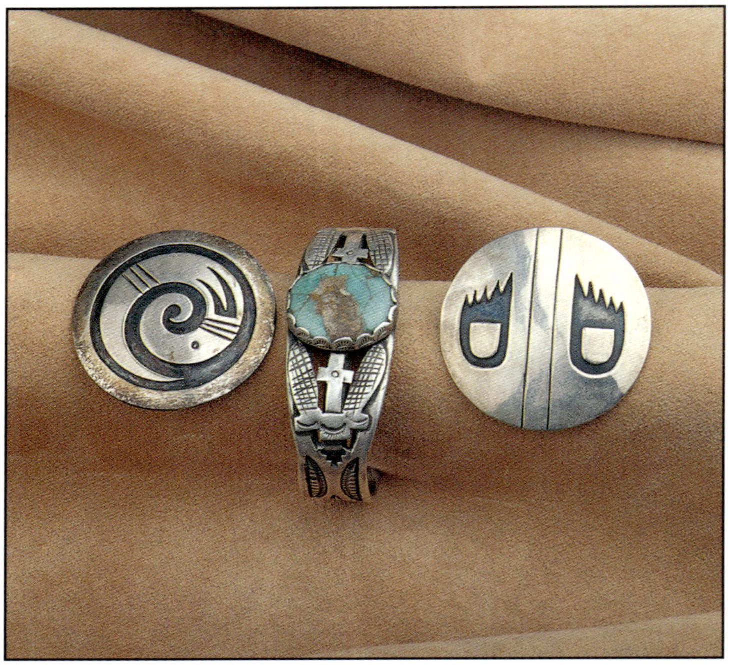

Two old Hopi pins, with swirl and bear paw designs respectively, and a bracelet with Christian crosses and two corn stalks in the design. *Lynn D. Trusdell, Crown & Eagle Antiques*

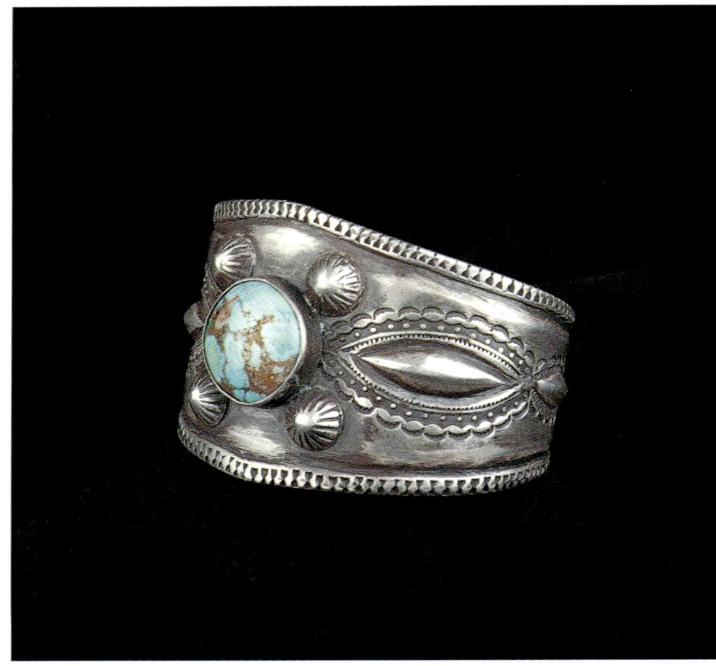

Navajo cuff bracelet displaying very good use of button stamp dies and raised sides around a single turquoise, 1930s. *Lynn D. Trusdell, Crown & Eagle Antiques*

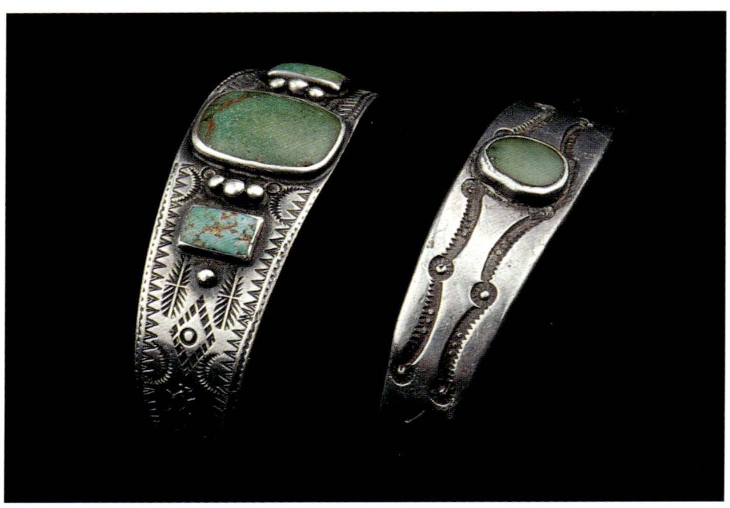

Left: Fred Harvey style Navajo tourist bracelet that is transitional from the earlier, three-stone style to the punch-decorated style, c.1920s.
Right: Navajo tourist bracelet with a single ingot of Cerillos turquoise on a silver bracelet with stamped decoration, 1930s. *Lynn D. Trusdell, Crown & Eagle Antiques*

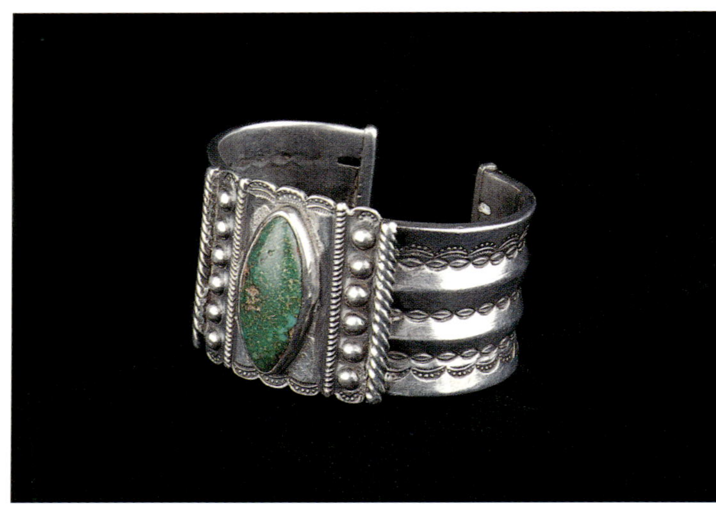

Heavy Navajo cuff bracelet with filed, ribbed, and stamped decoration and flattened edges; raindrops and twisted sides flanking a Cerillos turquoise stone, c.1910-15. *Lynn D. Trusdell, Crown & Eagle Antiques*

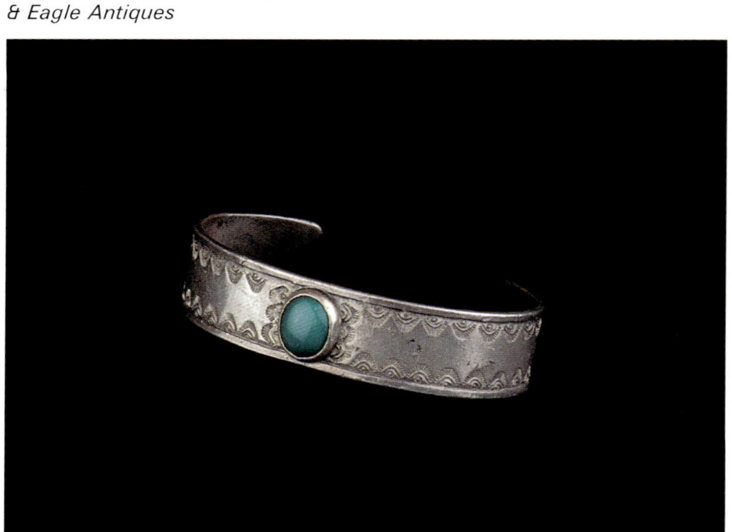

Flattened coin silver Navajo bracelet transitional in style from the early heavy type to almost the light tourist type with simple stampings, c.1920. *Lynn D. Trusdell, Crown & Eagle Antiques*

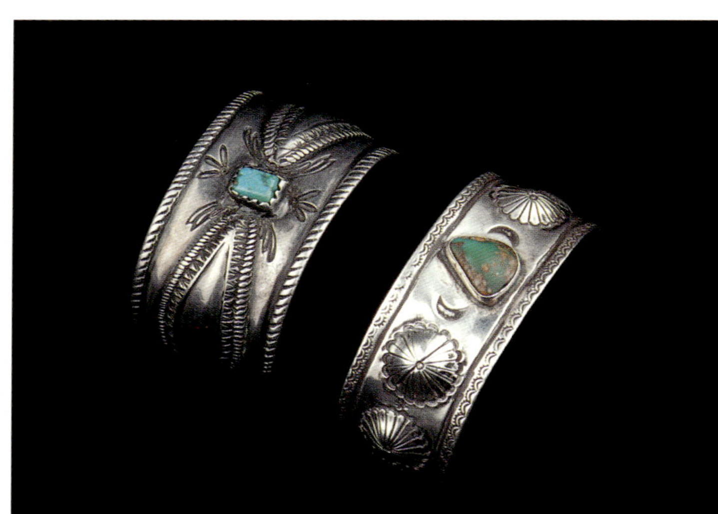

Two early Navajo cuff bracelets with fancy silver work and single turquoise stones, c.1920-30. *Lynn D. Trusdell, Crown & Eagle Antiques*

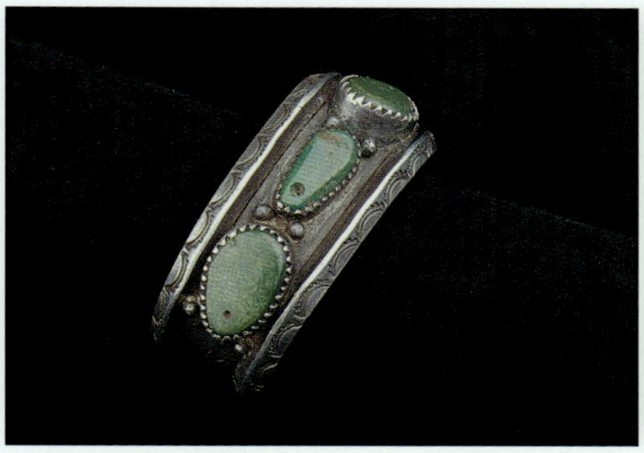

Fine early Navajo silver bracelet with three drilled stones (indicating they were old at the time they were put into the bracelet, perhaps being ear drops originally) and serrated bezels on ingot silver with two stamped triangular wires on the sides. *Lynn D. Trusdell, Crown & Eagle Antiques*

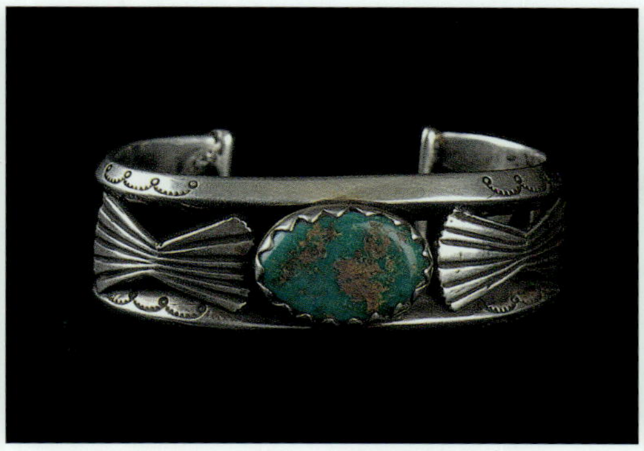

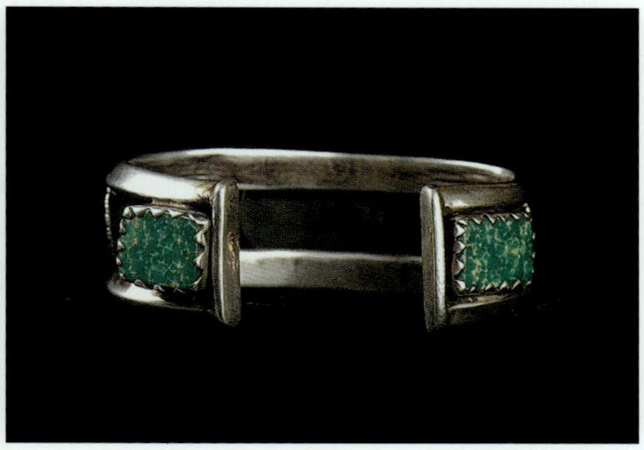

Large man's Navajo ingot silver bracelet with bow-tie designs that divide three Blue Gem turquoise stones in serrated bezels, mounted on stamped triangle wire, c.1900-1910. *Photographer Freddy Perojo. Courtesy The Pitt collection*

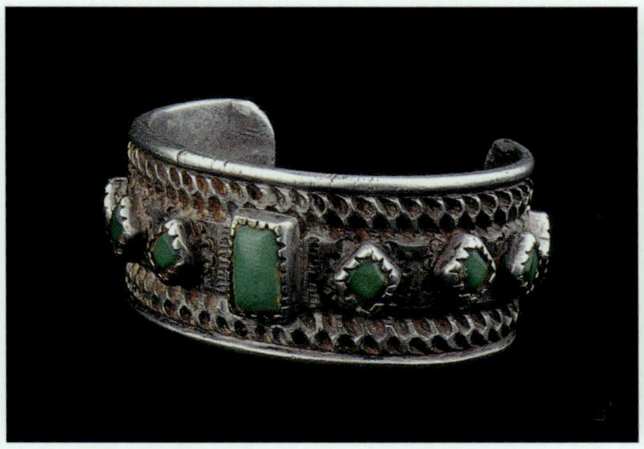

The earliest Fred Harvey tourist style Navajo cuff bracelet of ingot silver with nine turquoise stones: one square and eight of diamond shape, mounted in serrated bezels and with file decoration made with only two tools on the edges, c.1890. *Lynn D. Trusdell, Crown & Eagle Antiques*

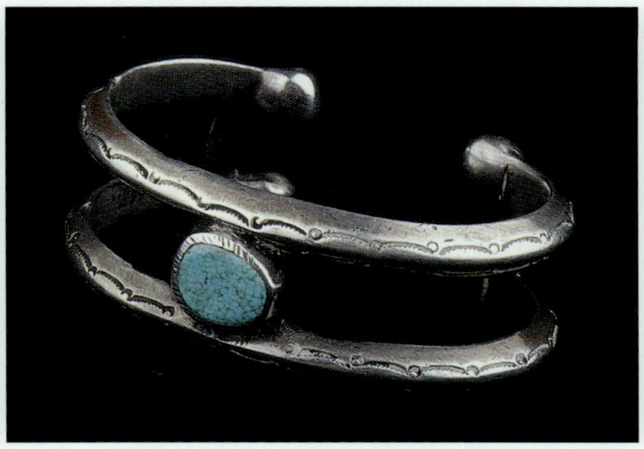

Large man's Navajo silver bracelet with a single #8 Spiderweb turquoise stone between two simply stamped triangular wires with silver ball terminals on each side. This bracelet was in the collection of Earl Horter, c.1910. *Lynn D. Trusdell, Crown & Eagle Antiques*

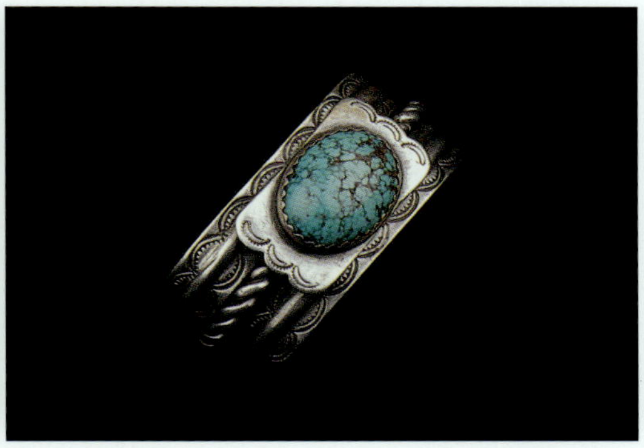

Large single Spiderweb turquoise stone on a flattened plate set with a hand-drawn sire at the center, unusual wire over the stamping, and a serrated bezel on the stone, late 1920s. *Lynn D. Trusdell, Crown & Eagle Antiques*

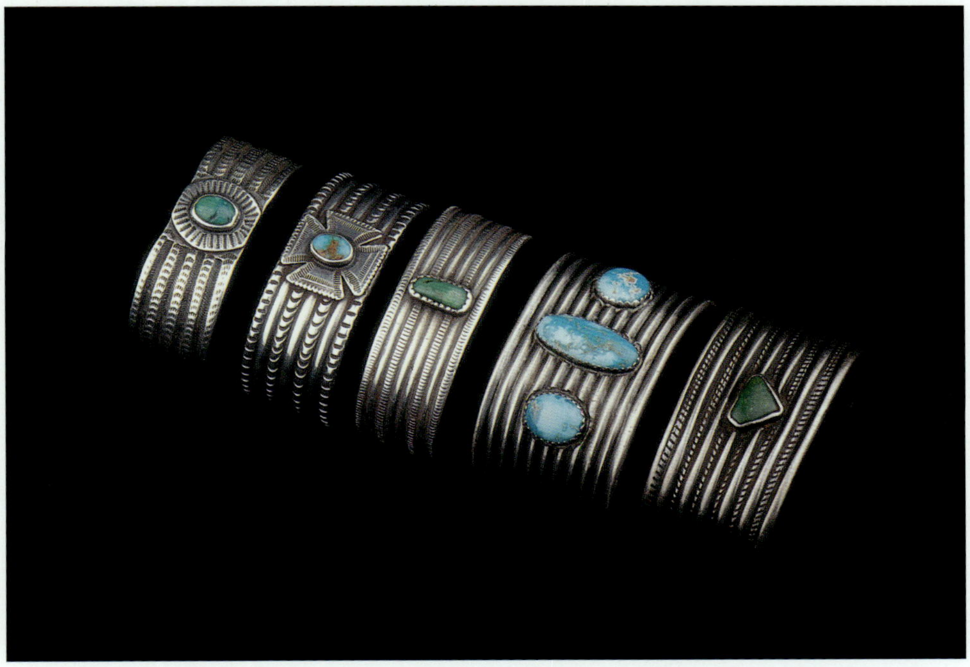

Group of five early Navajo cuff bracelets with small turquoise stones and file and chilsel work decoration, c.1920. *Lynn D. Trusdell, Crown & Eagle Antiques*

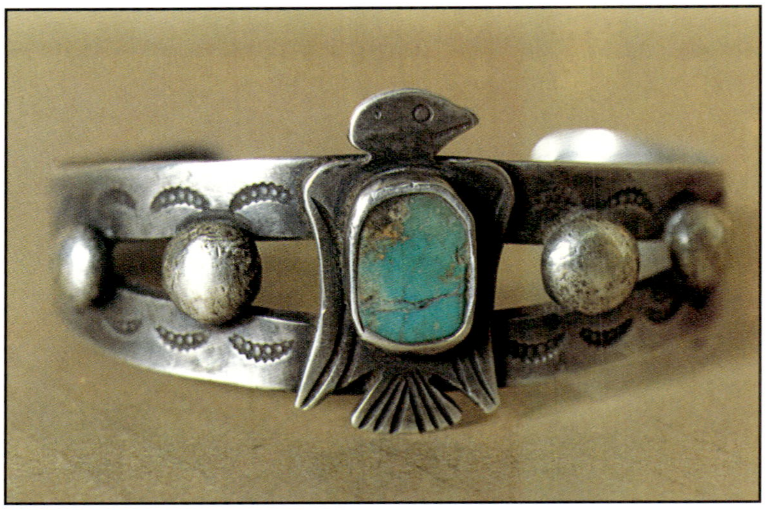

Wrought silver bracelet with two stamped bands joined by domed buttons and a bird design set with a turquoise stone, circa 1920s. *Adobe Gallery collection*

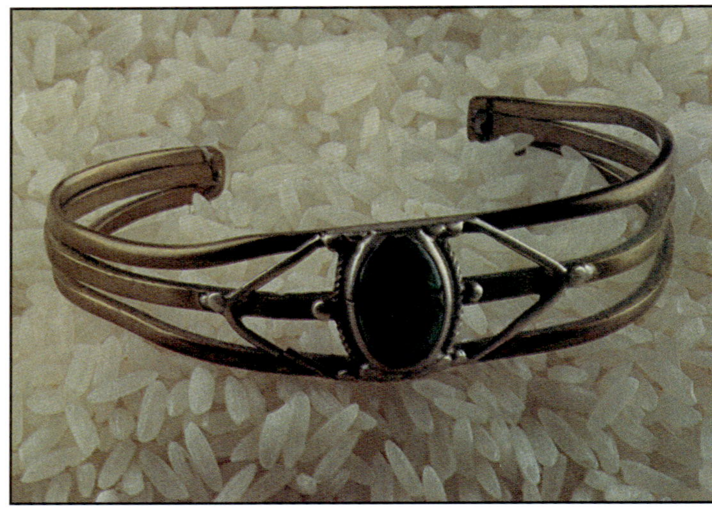

Silver and brass wires support the turquoise stone on this bracelet, circa 1912. *Enchanted Mesa collection*

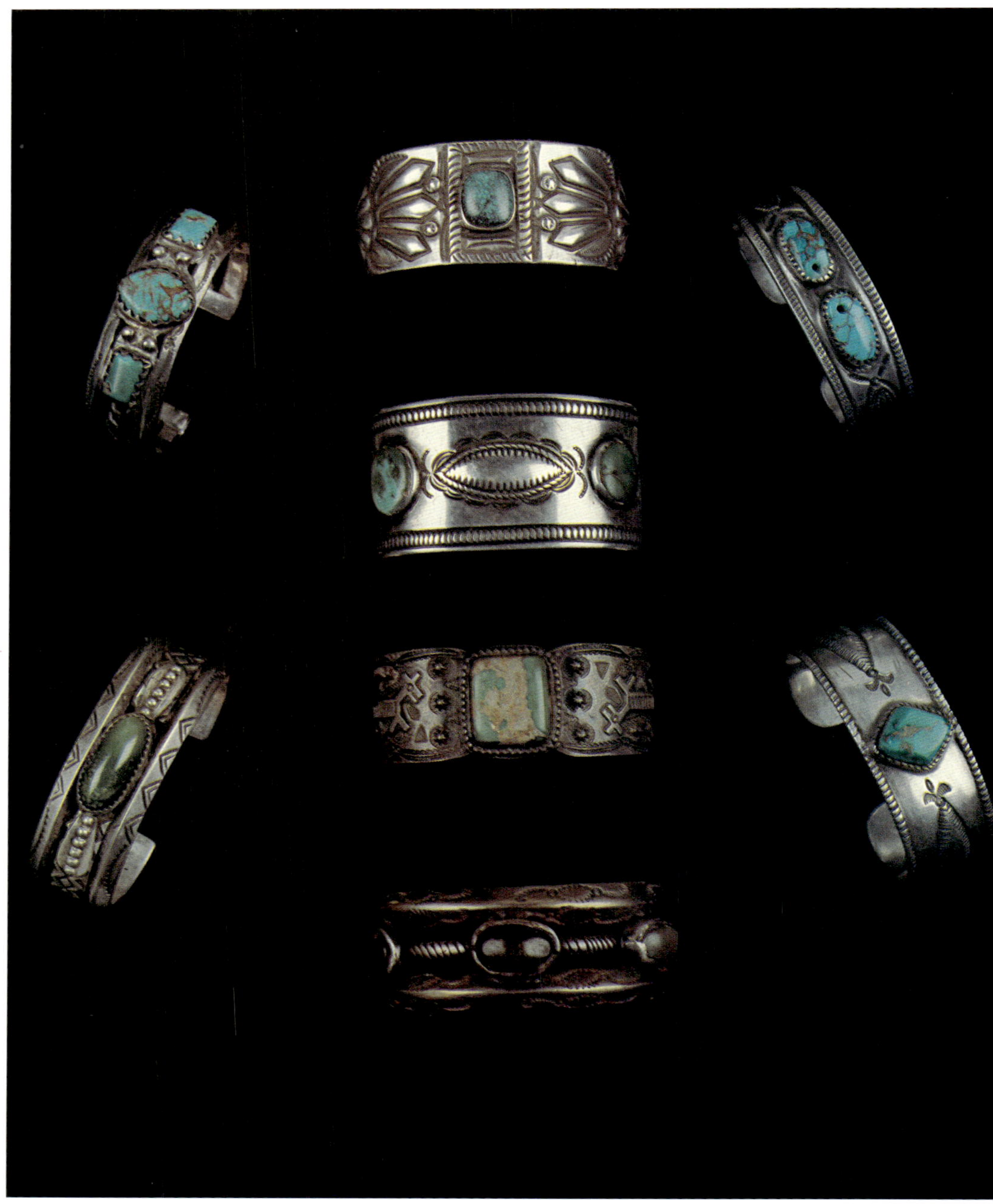

Navajo silver bracelets set with turquoise: Left Top: Blue gem turquoise and silver beads set between two side bars, circa 1910. /Bottom: Heavy and unusual bracelet with two side bars framing a Cerillos turquoise stone and silver raindrop beads, circa 1910. Center: Heavy cuff with wrought floral design and a single Burnham turquoise stone, circa 1910. / Cuff with two Blue gem turquoise stones divided and flanked by stamped water bug designs, circa 1920. / Tourist trade style with square Cerillos turquoise stone and silver overlaid design of dogs, circa 1930. / Two triangular stamped wires flank a central filed wire and stones set in folded bezels, circa 1900. Right: Two older drilled Blue gem turquoise ear bobs have been mounted on this bracelet with filed edges, circa 1910. / Diamond-shaped turquoise stone set in a serrated bezel on a cuff with stamped and filed design, circa 1900. *Lynn D. Trusdell collection*

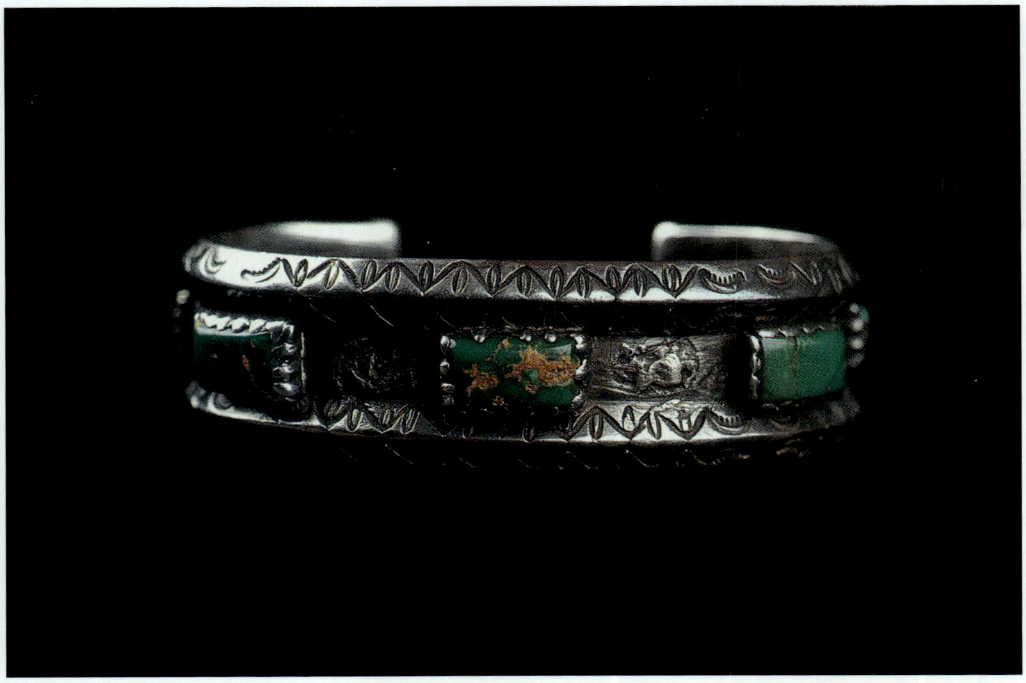

Three Cerillos turquoise stones mounted on an ingot silver plate between two stamped triangular wires, c.1910-15. *Photography by Freddy Perojo. Courtesy The Pitt collection*

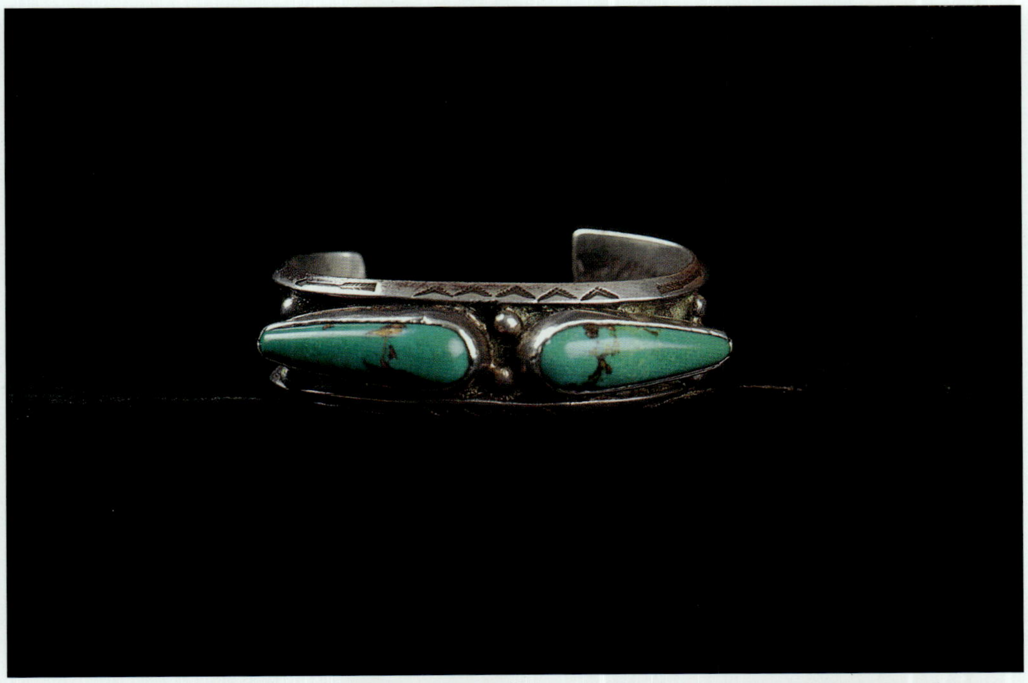

A Navajo silver bracelet with very unusual cuts of old Cerillos turquoise in a teardrop design. Coin silver stamped triangular wire are ingot silver, c.1915-20. *Photography by Freddy Perojo. Courtesy The Pitt collection*

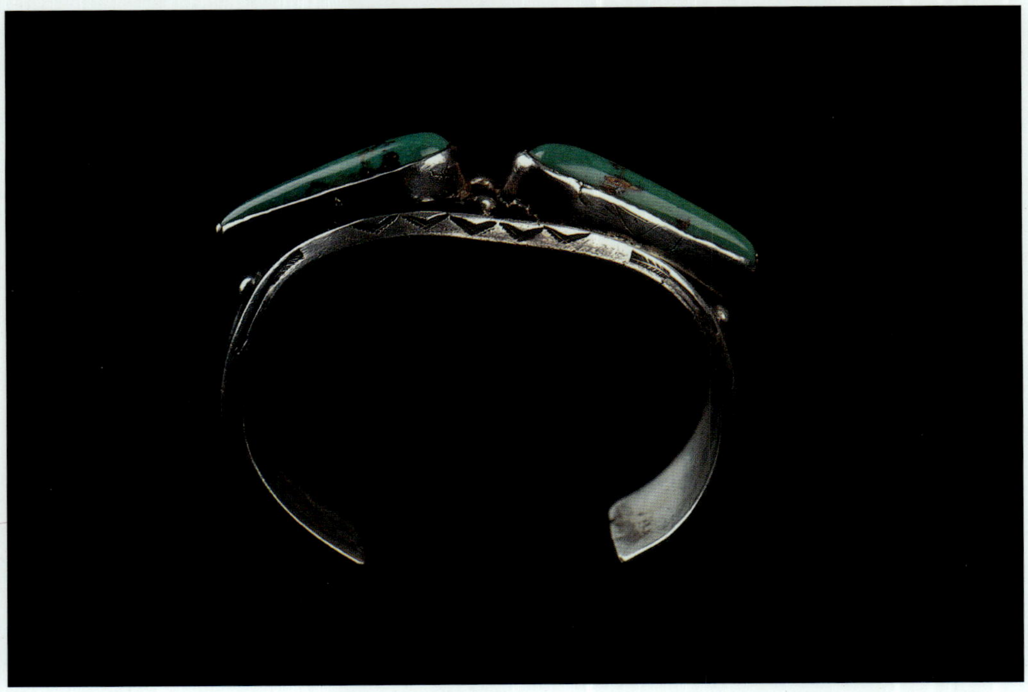

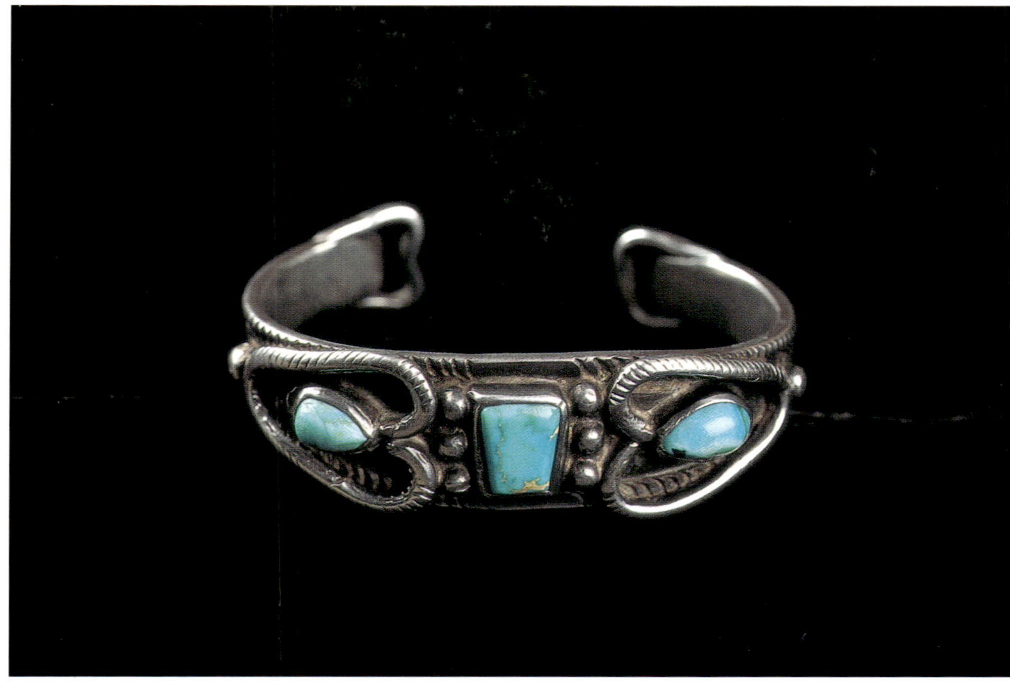

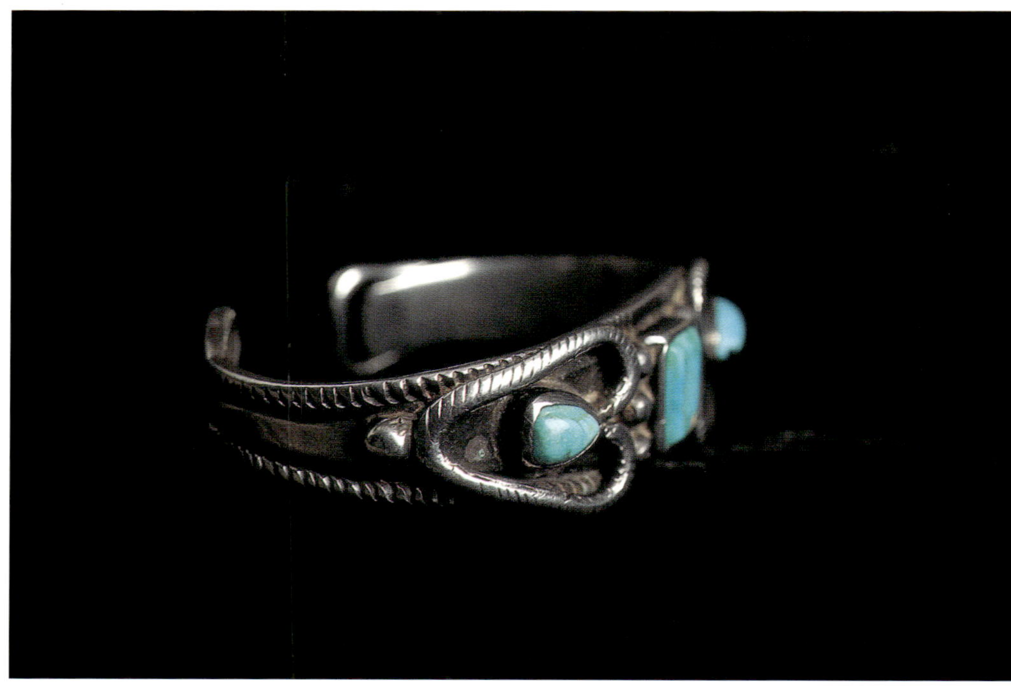

Classical Navajo silver bracelet of the 1920s with drawn round wire surrounding two tapering rounded Blue Gem turquoise stones and a central tapering square cut Blue Gem turquoise stone. The bracelet terminals are flaring flattened wire, c.1920. *Photography by Freddy Perojo. Courtesy The Pitt collection*

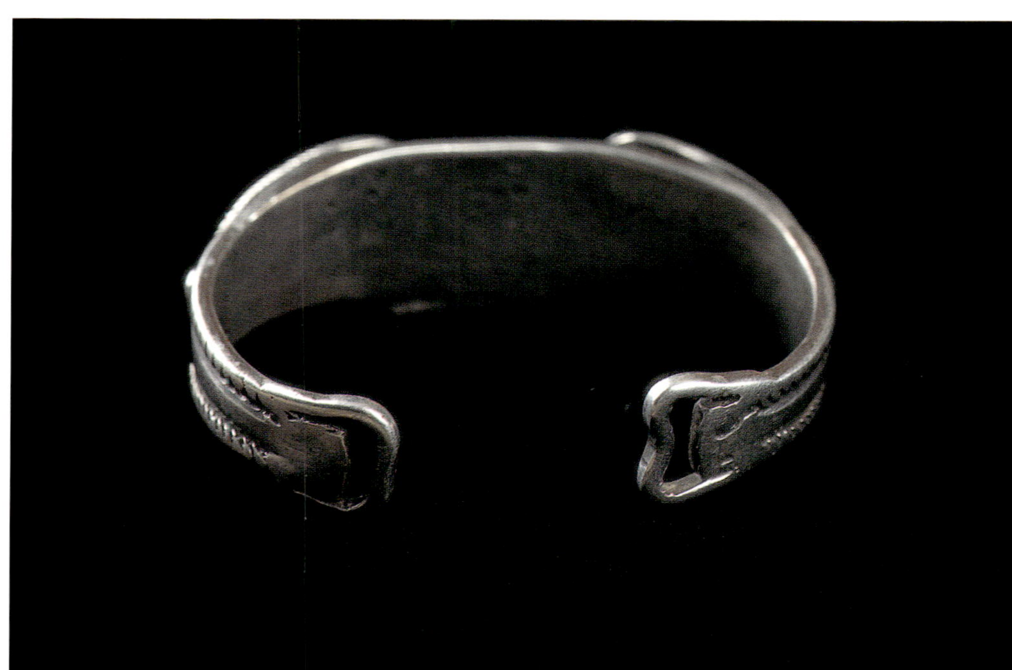

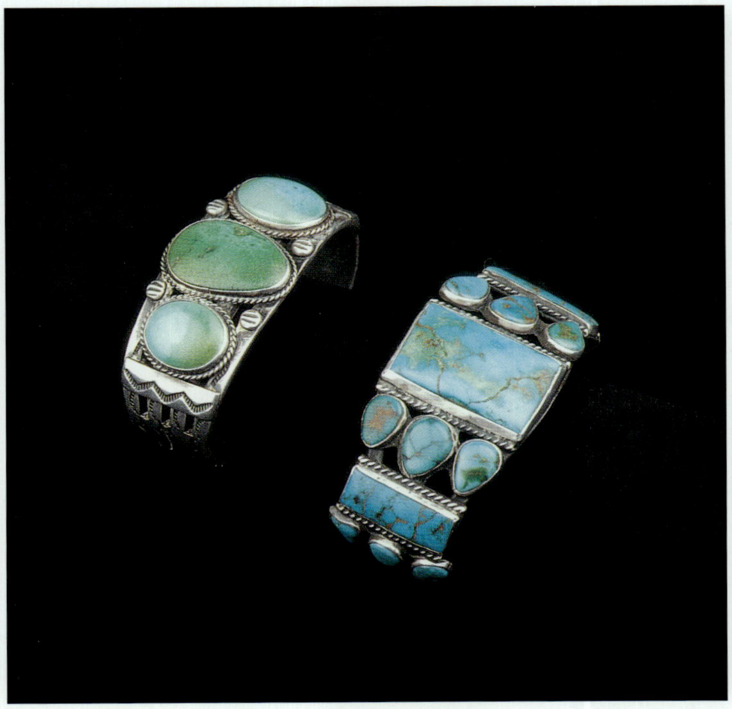

Left: Navajo silver cuff bracelet with three Fox turquoise stones, one a pear shape and two round. These are mounted on a heavy ingot silver flattened band, c.1920.
Right: Early Zuni cuff bracelet with alternating square and three teardrop probably Morenci turquoise stones, c.1920. *Lynn D. Trusdell, Crown & Eagle Antiques*

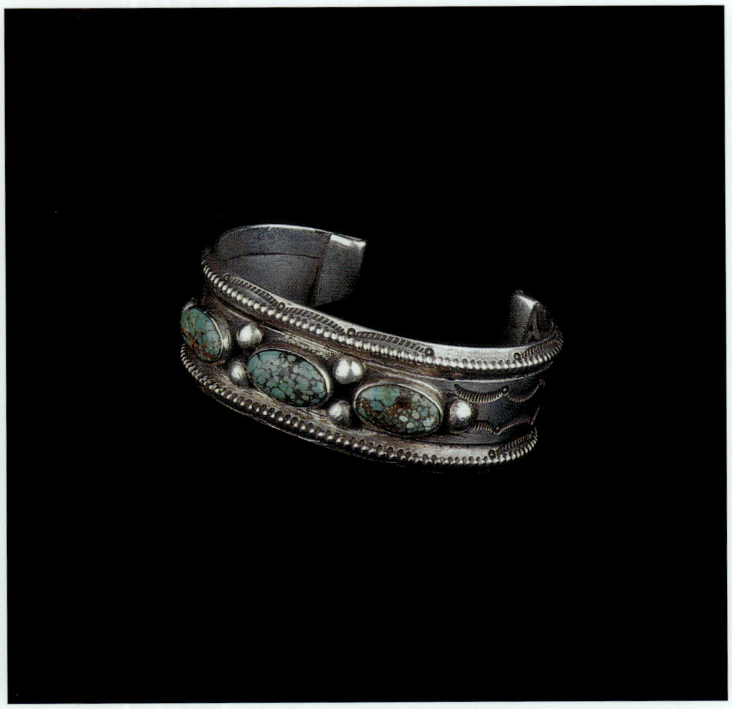

Navajo silver cuff bracelet with three turquoise stones mounted on a flattened and stamped ingot with two stamped swirls on each side. Rounded terminals are on the back. *Lynn D. Trusdell, Crown & Eagle Antiques*

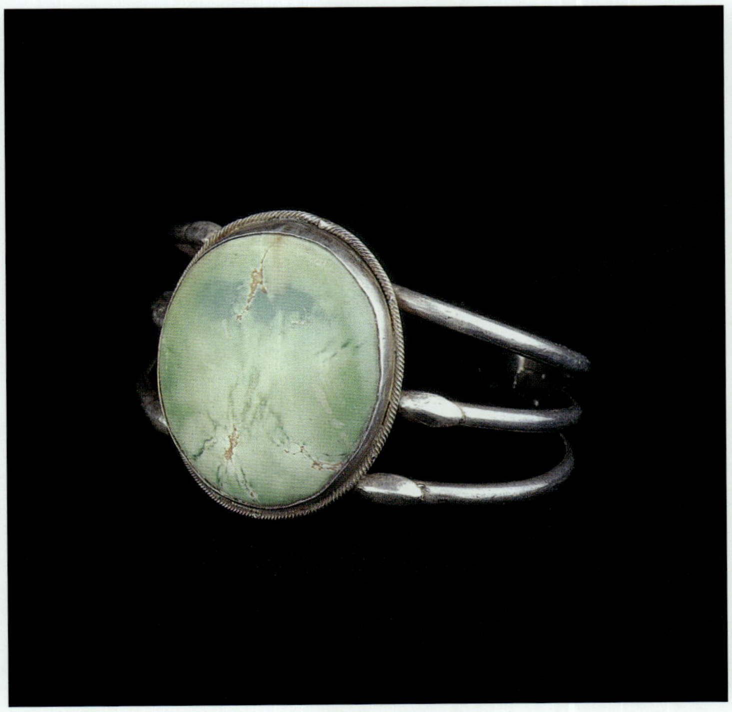

Navajo silver bracelet with a large Cerillos turquoise stone mounted on simple silver wires, collected in the 1920s Earl Horter collection. *Lynn D. Trusdell, Crown & Eagle Antiques*

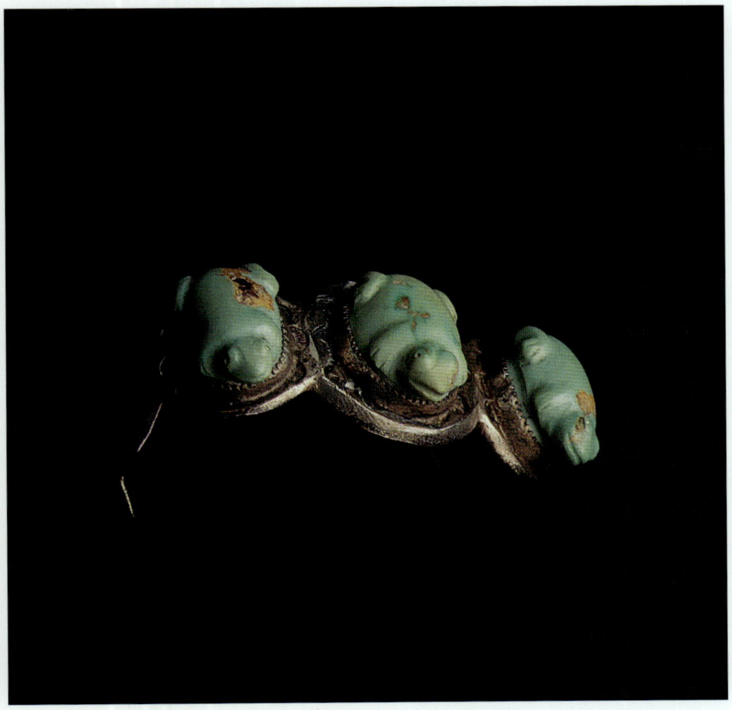

Zuni silver bracelet with three carved turquoise frogs mounted in plain bezels, made by Leekya Deysee.

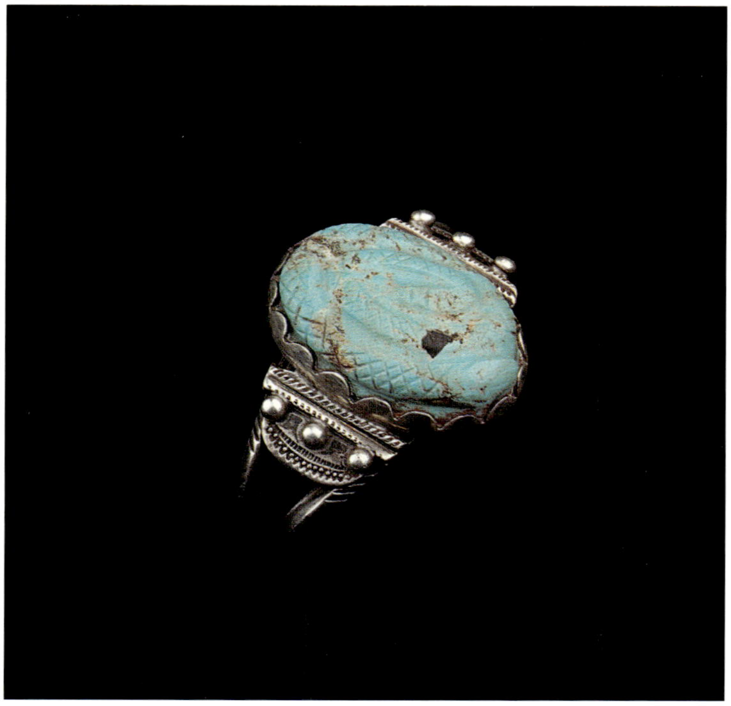

Early Zuni bracelet with a turquoise stone mounted in a serrated bezel carved in a snake design and mounted on triangular wires. The work is attributed to the renowned turquoise carver Leekya Deysee. *Lynn D. Trusdell, Crown & Eagle Antiques*

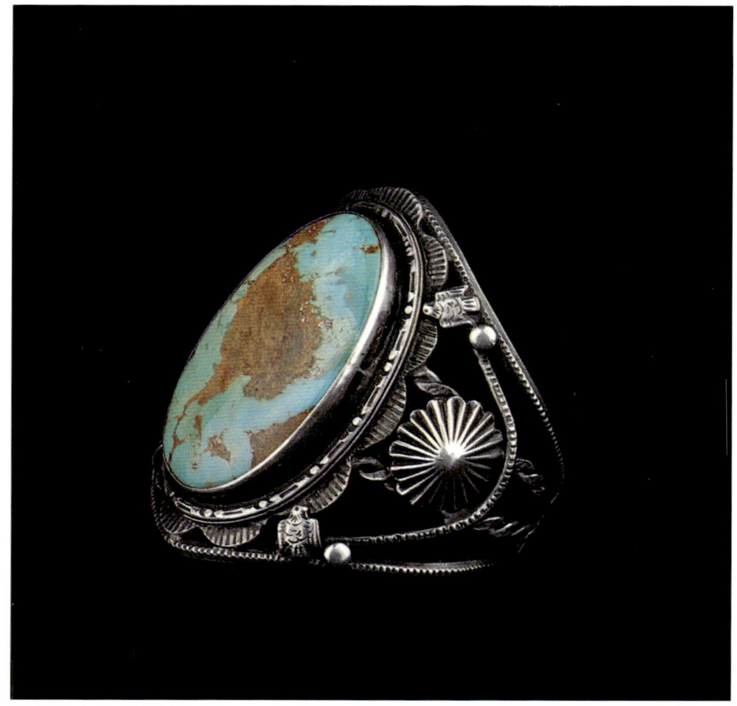

Beautiful and sophisticated Navajo silver bracelet with a large Blue Gem turquoise stone mounted in a plain bezel over reticulated work on thin drawn and twisted wires. Little thunderbird designs and button stamped ornaments are on the sides, c.1930s. *Lynn D. Trusdell, Crown & Eagle Antiques*

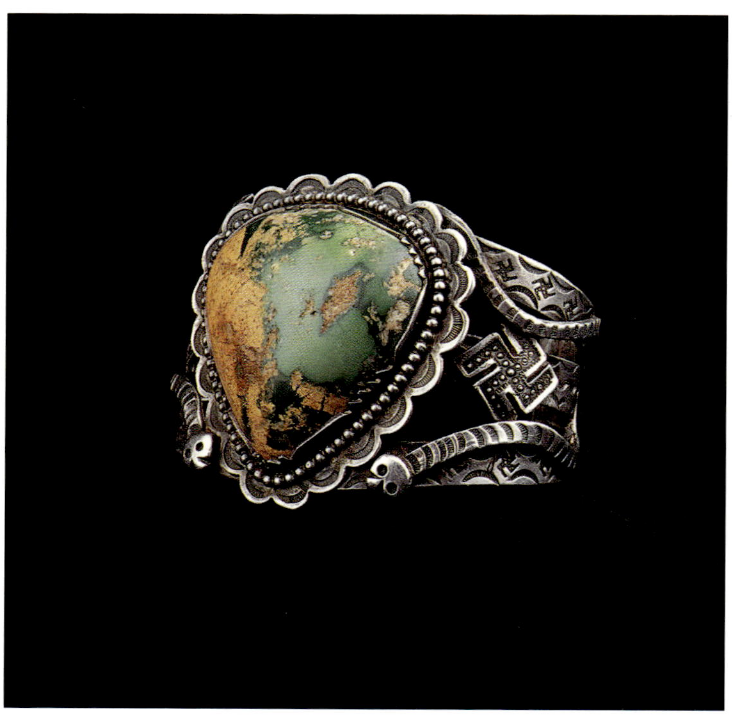

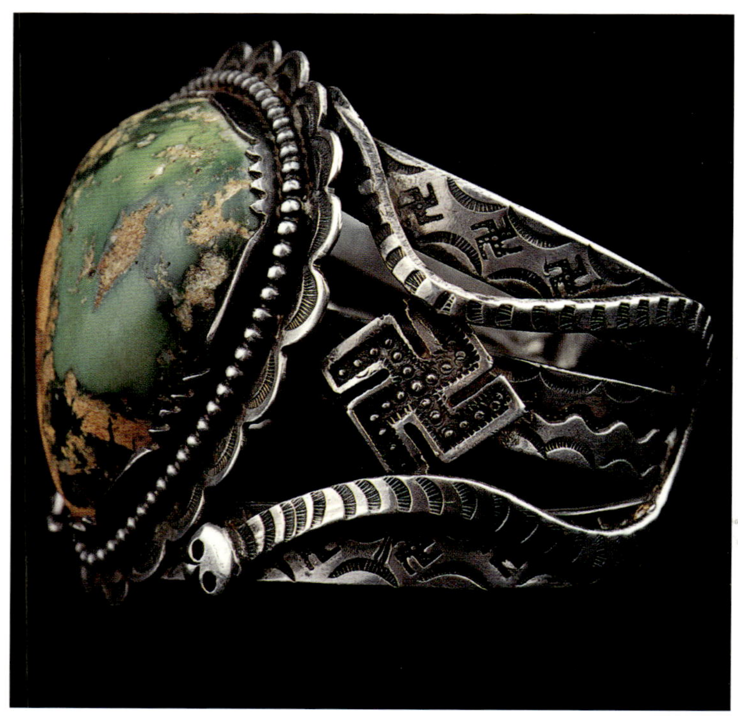

Large Man's Navajo silver bracelet with a rounded triangular Cerillos turquoise stone set on a flattened plate of ingot silver, with rattlesnakes and swastikas as applied decorations, c.1920s-30s. *Lynn D. Trusdell, Crown & Eagle Antiques*

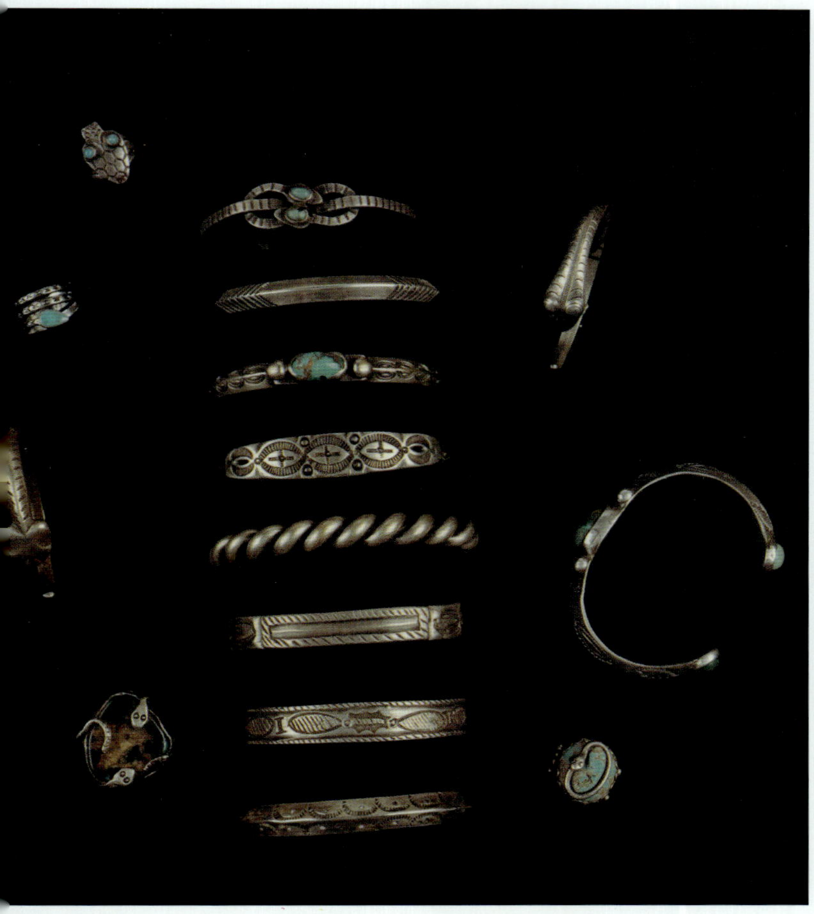

Rings and bracelets with a snake theme are included in this group of early Navajo jewelry. Left - Snake rings set with turquoise and a wrought silver bracelet stamped with a snake skin design, and a ring set with turquoise and bordered by two snake designs which is mounted on a hinged bezel that opens to reveal a small cavity, 1920s. / Center - bracelet of intertwining snakes design set with two turquoise stones, made for the tourist market, 1930s. / Filed triangular wire bracelet, circa 1920s. / Stamped triangular wire bracelet with Blue gem turquoise, circa 1930s. / Stamped flat tapering bracelet stamped with crosses in the design, 1920s. / Twisted wire bracelet, circa 1940s. / Flat stamped bracelet, 1930s. / Early flat stamped bracelet, circa 1910. / Stamped triangular wire bracelet from the 1920s. / Right- Simple snake designed bracelet , 1920s. / Very early triangular wire bracelet shown on its side to demonstrate the single oval polished turquoise set into the top and the two similar at the terminals, circa 1910. / Ring with turquoise set into the silver band. *Lynn D. Trusdell collection*

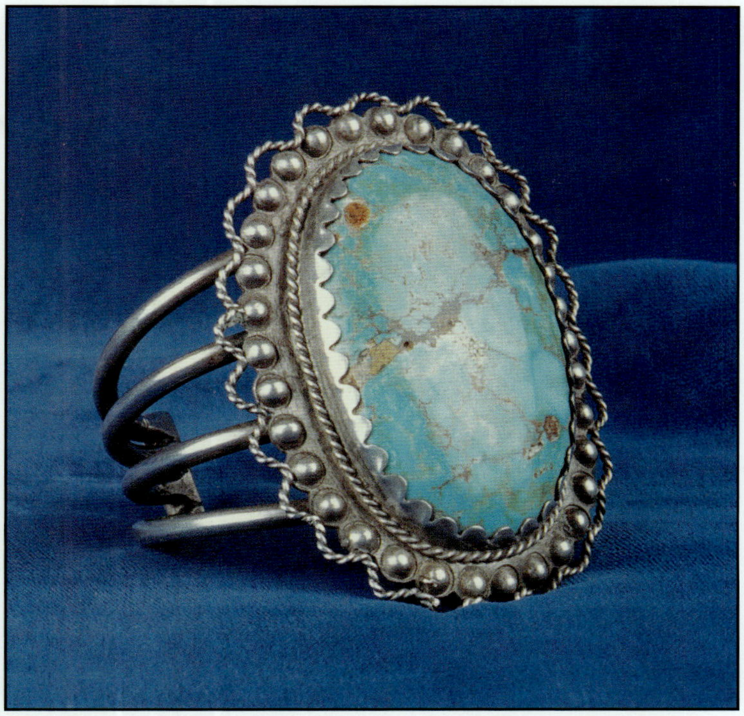

Four silver wires support a beautiful and large polished turquoise stone within a serrated bezel and carefully wrought frame of wires and beads, Navajo, circa 1930s. *Maxwell Museum collection*

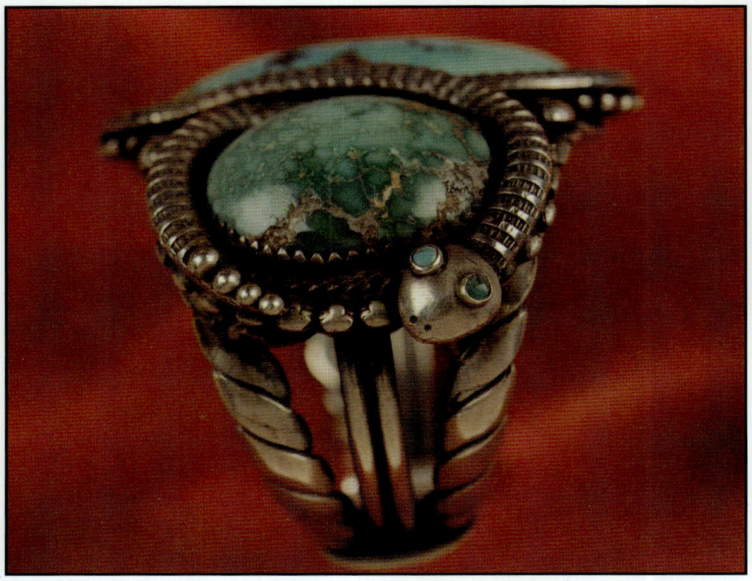

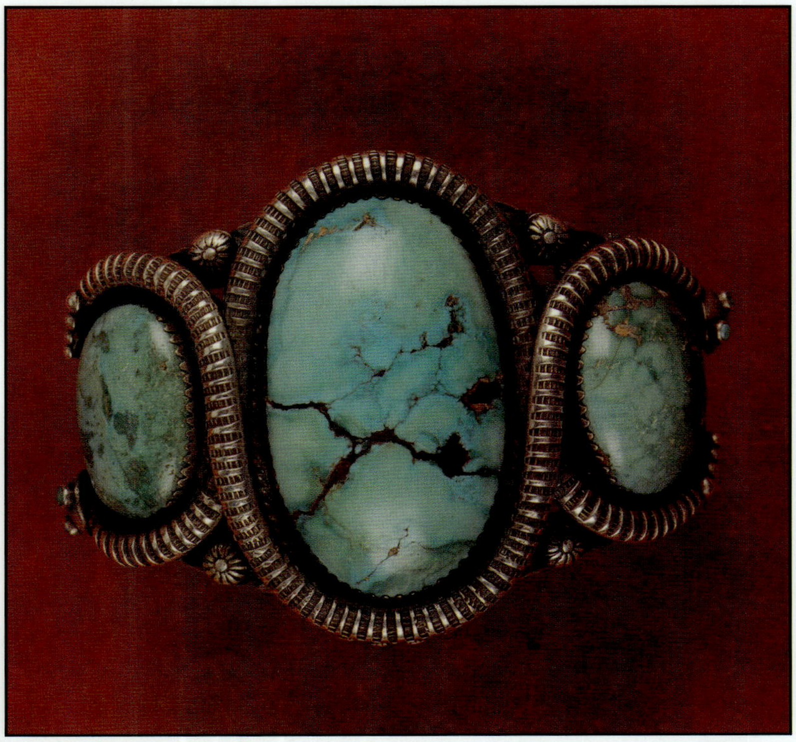

The silversmith demonstrated lots of personality in this bracelet where three polished turquoise stones are framed by two stamped silver snake figures, the heads set with turquoise eyes, and supported by three wrought silver bands, two of rope design, late 1920s or early 1930s. *Lynn D. Trusdell collection*

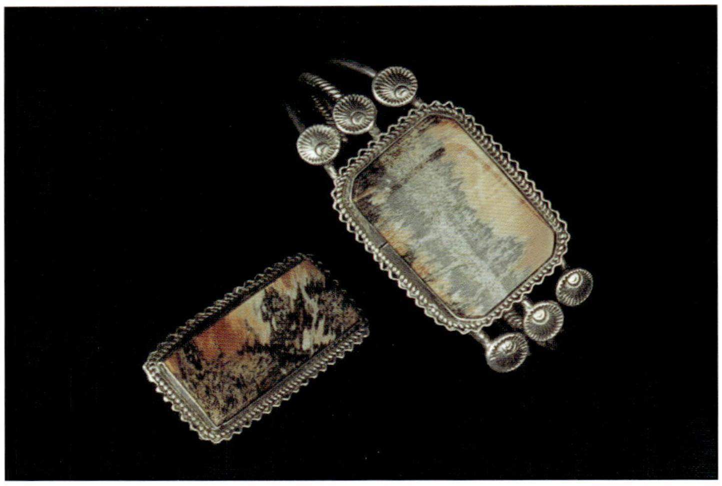

Navajo ring and bracelet with petrified wood set into wrought and stamped silver, 1935. *Turquoise Lady collection*.

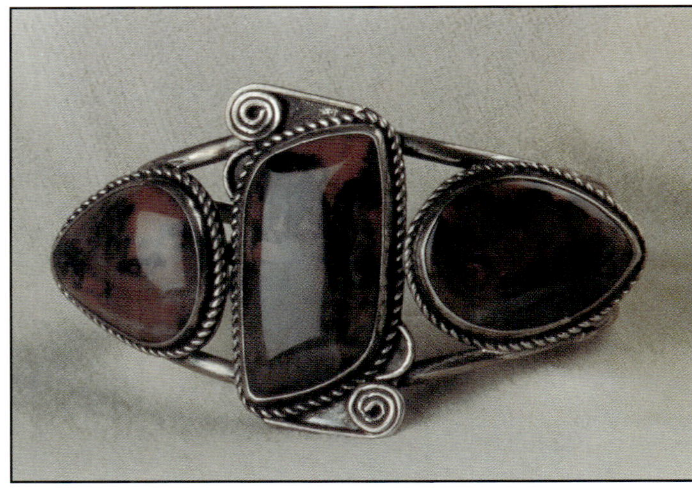

Bracelet of silver wire and bezels containing three polished pieces of petrified wood, Navajo. *Private collection on permanent loan to Ohio University*

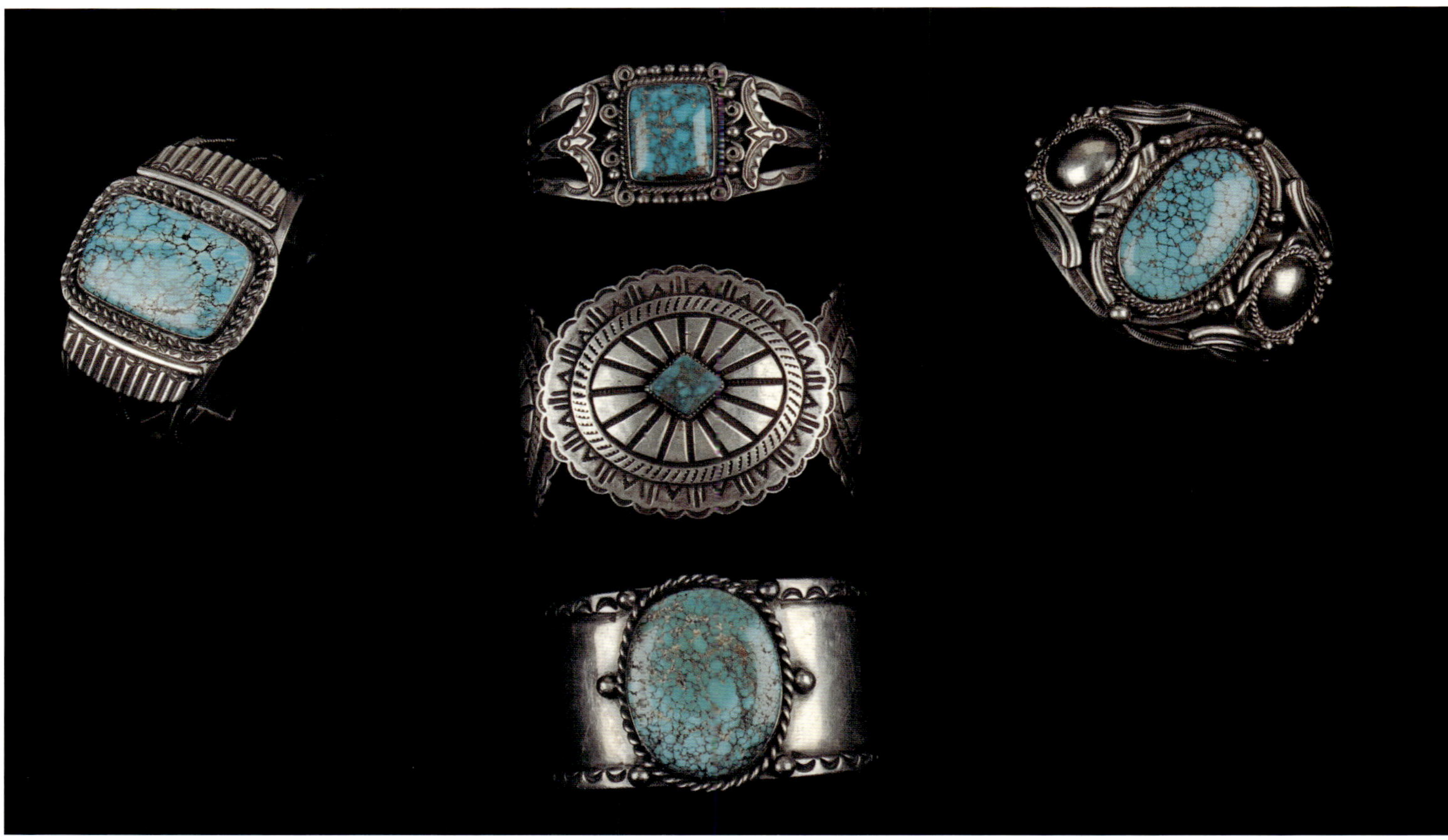

Turquoise-set Navajo bracelets: Left - A Lone Mountain spiderweb turquoise stone rests within a stamped bezel with scrolled applied silver decorations, 1930s. / Center - Tourist style stamped bracelet with a rectangular Burnham spiderweb turquoise, circa 1930. / Three silver conchas, one set with Burnham turquoise, are curved to make a bracelet, 1940s. / Wide cuff with # 8 spiderweb turquoise, 1920s. / Right - Wrought and appliqué silver work is combined with # 8 spiderweb turquoise, 1940s. *Lynn D. Trusdell collection*

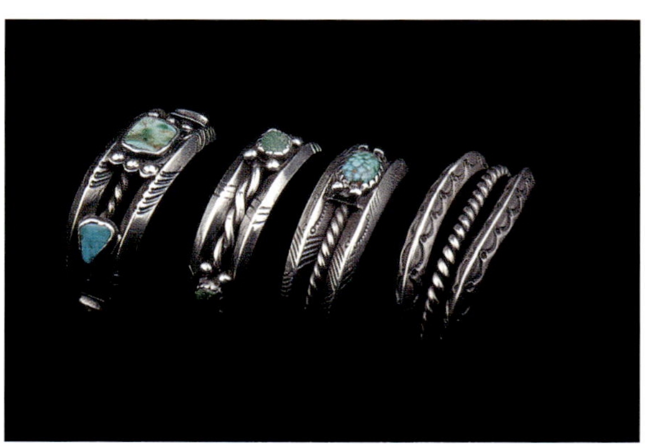

Four early Navajo silver bracelets, each with a different method of hand drawing wire. The second from the right has #8 Spiderweb turquoise, c.1920 from the Earl Horter collection. The bracelet at the far right is unusually elaborate for an all-silver bracelet. *Lynn D. Trusdell, Crown & Eagle Antiques*

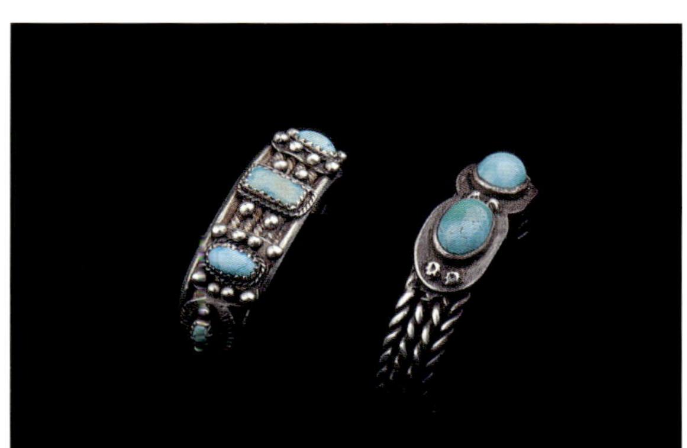

Left: Well designed Navajo silver bracelet with five turquoise stones in twisted wire and serrated bezels mounted on five sets of twisted wires on the band, c.1920s.
Right: Large Navajo silver bracelet with two oval turquoise stones in smooth bezels mounted on oval plates with raindrop ornaments on each side and four rows of hand-drawn twisted wire in the band, c.1915-20. *Lynn D. Trusdell, Crown & Eagle Antiques*

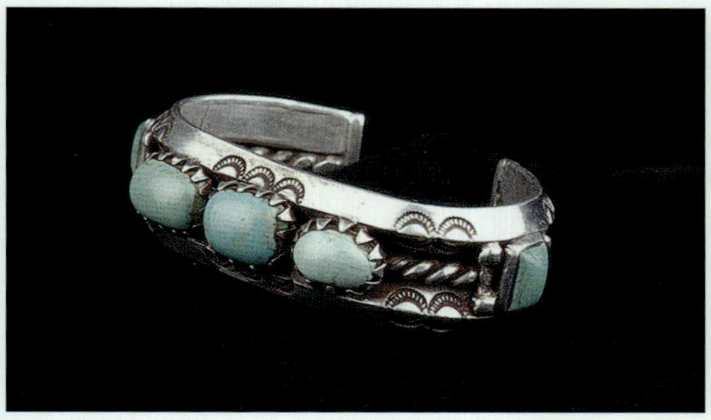

Navajo silver bracelet with an unusual arrangement of three oval turquoise stones flanked by two square turquoise stones in serrated bezels and mounted on twisted and triangular wires. *Lynn D. Trusdell, Crown & Eagle Antiques*

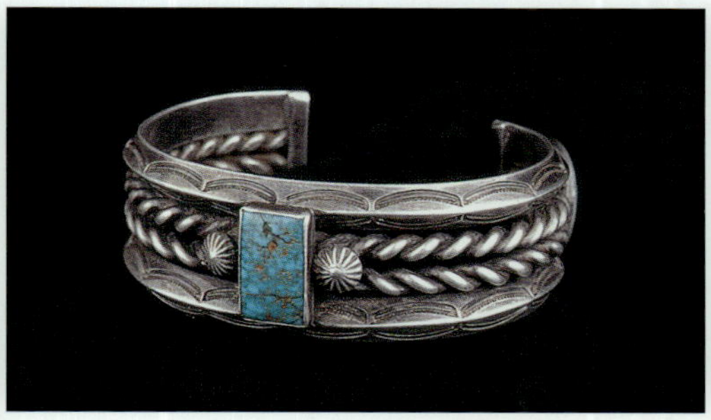

Navajo silver bracelet with two triangular stamped wires and two hand-drawn twisted wires supporting a single Lone Mountain turquoise rectangular stone with a button-stamp die on each side. *Lynn D. Trusdell, Crown & Eagle Antiques*

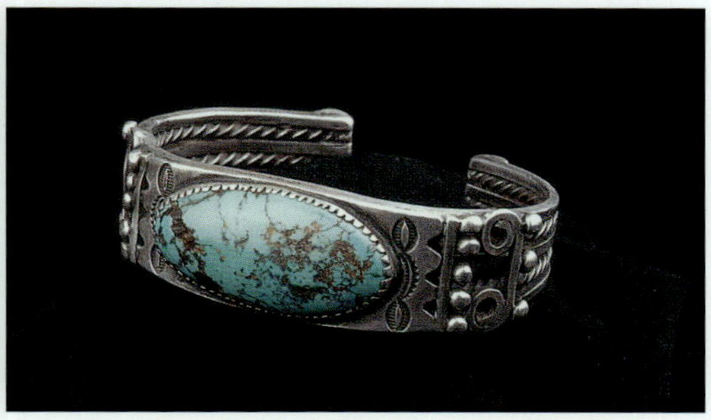

Large man's Navajo silver bracelet with an oval turquoise stone resting on a stamped flat plate with raindrops decoration. A band of twisted wires has flattened wires in between, c.1920s. *Lynn D. Trusdell, Crown & Eagle Antiques*

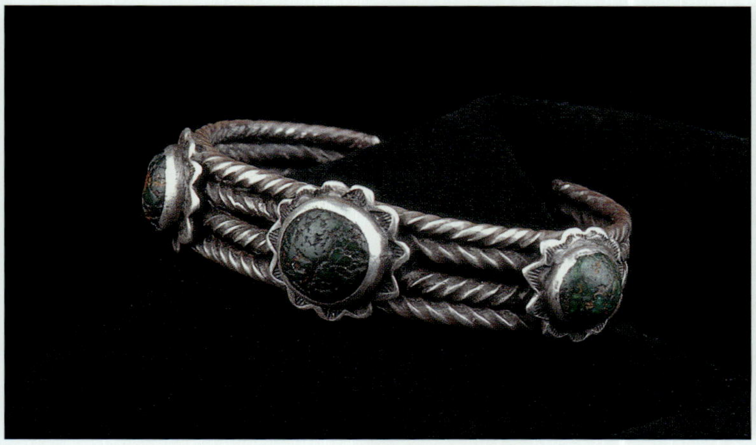

Three rows of hand-drawn wire with scalloped plates, each with Cerillos turquoise, c.1915-20. *Lynn D. Trusdell, Crown & Eagle Antiques*

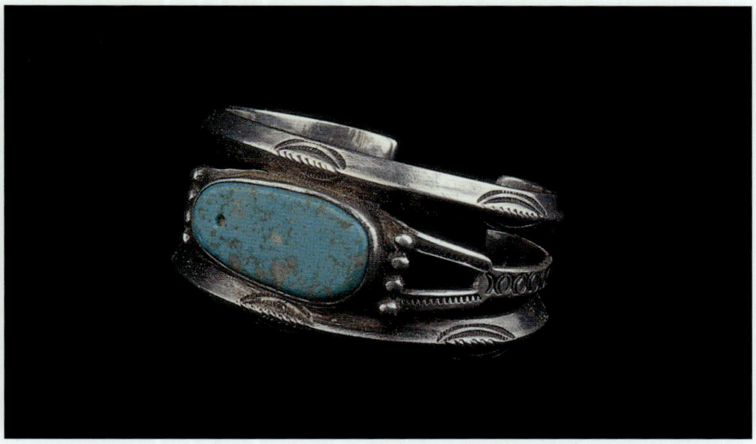

Navajo silver bracelet with a single drilled oval turquoise stone (originally from an older ear bob or necklace) mounted on heavy ingot silver including a flat central band instead of twisted wire and two triangular stamped rim wires, c.1920. *Lynn D. Trusdell, Crown & Eagle Antiques*

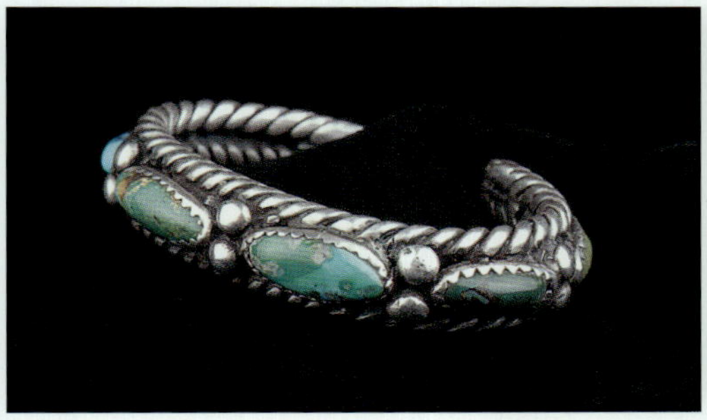

Old Navajo silver bracelet featuring three oval turquoise stones with rain-drop decorations mounted on twisted wire rims. Formerly in the collection of Robert Oppenheimer, c.1915-20. *Lynn D. Trusdell, Crown & Eagle Antiques*

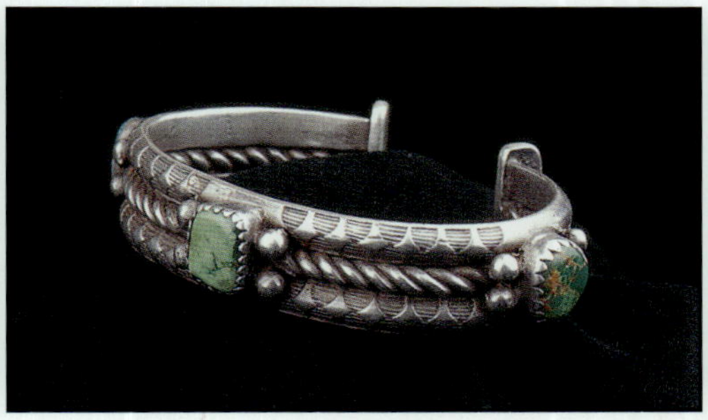

Large Navajo man's silver bracelet with three rectangular turquoise stones and raindrop ornaments on one twisted and two triangular wires with unusual stamped decoration. The turned-back terminals are particularly heavy, c.1910-20. *Lynn D. Trusdell, Crown & Eagle Antiques*

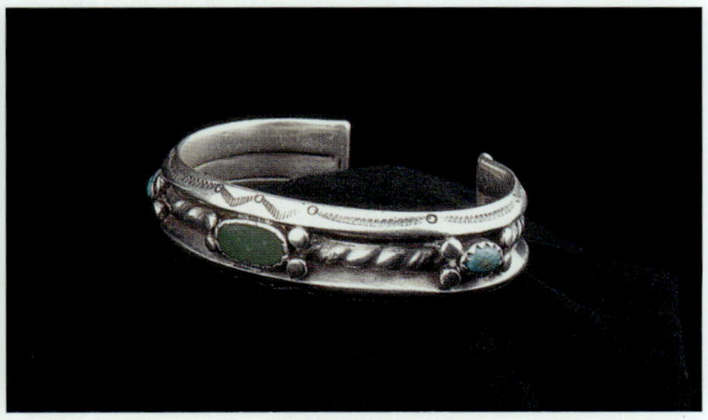

Rather simple Navajo silver bracelet with mixed oval turquoise stones on a single twisted and two triangular stamped wires, c.1910-20. *Lynn D. Trusdell, Crown & Eagle Antiques*

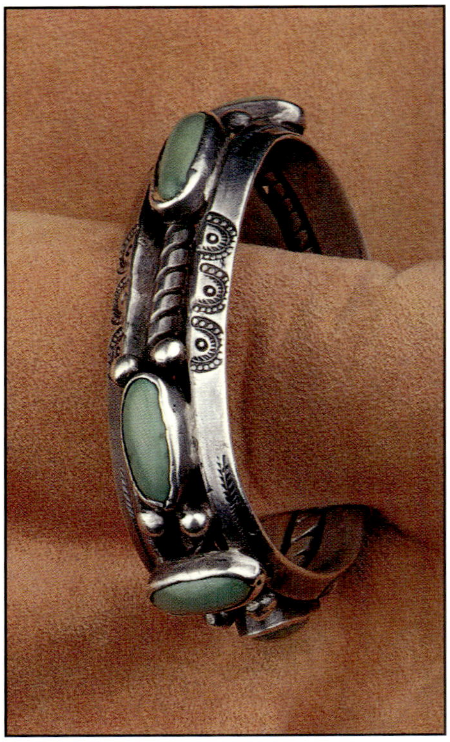

Heavy Navajo man's silver bracelet with six oval turquoise stones mounted both horizontally and vertically on twisted and unusually stamped triangular wires, c.1920. *Lynn D. Trusdell, Crown & Eagle Antiques*

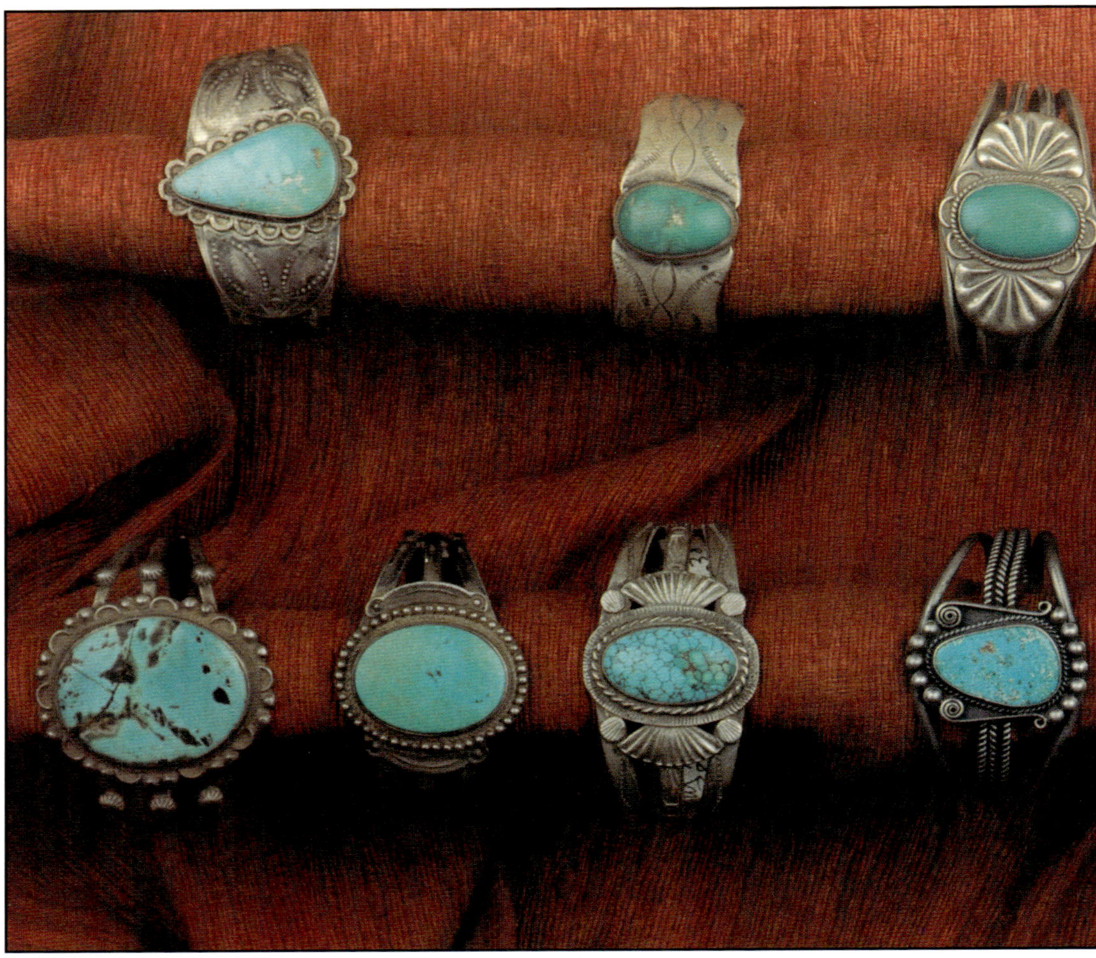

Navajo silver bracelets from the 1920s and 1930s set with turquoise from different mines: Kingman, Fox mine, Burnham spiderweb, Royal Blue, Old Morenci, McGinnis, and Leadville. *Dennehotso collection*.

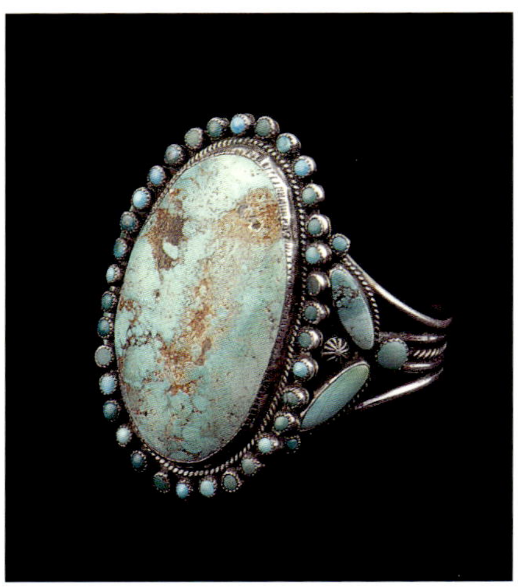

Zuni or Navajo silver bracelet with large oval turquoise stone as a flower design in a serrated bezel and twisted wire border inside a frame of small round turquoise mounted to a 6-strand round and twisted wire band with six small stones flanking the top, c.1920. *Lynn D. Trusdell, Crown & Eagle Antiques*

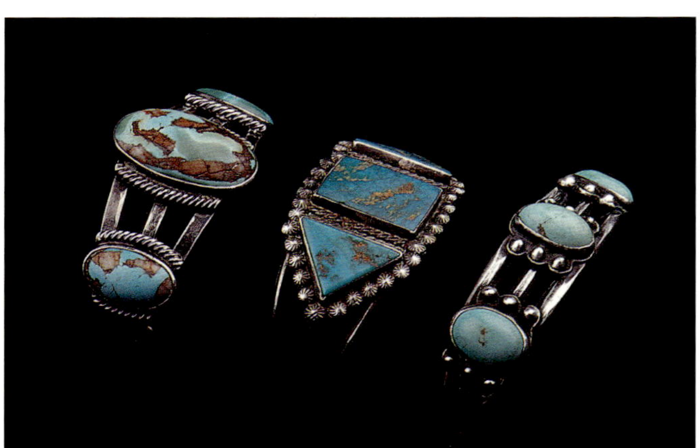

Left and right: Two Navajo silver bracelets with three turquoise stones each displaying sophisticated style in the split shank design.
Center: Rectangular and triangular Blue Gem turquoise set in raindrops decoration and twisted wire band, c.1930s, formerly in a collection of the Wheelwright Museum. *Lynn D. Trusdell, Crown & Eagle Antiques*

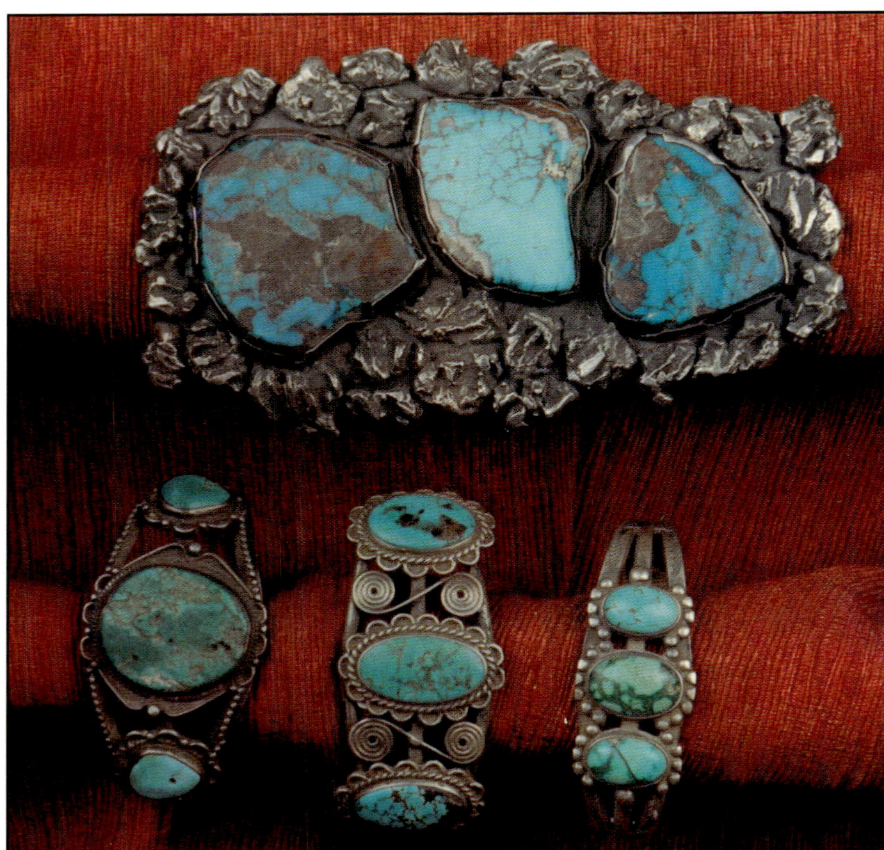

Large Navajo ceremonial bracelet of wrought silver with three enormous Bisbee turquoise stones, circa 1970s. / Bracelet of Navajo silver and three older turquoise stones each drilled for use in other jewelry, circa 1930s. / Navajo silver bracelet with wirework and turquoise from the Bisbee, McGinnis and Royal Blue mines, circa 1930. / Morenci and other turquoise mounted in a Navajo bracelet, circa 1920s. *Dennehotso collection*.

Line Bracelets

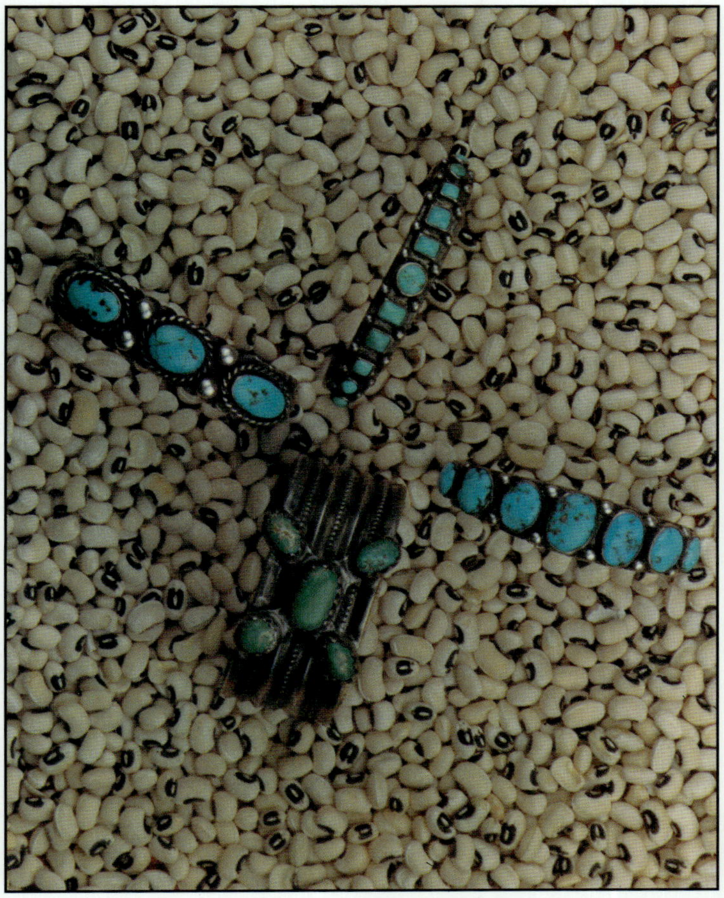

Four Navajo bracelets from the early days: Three turquoise stones set in a line on a silver band with twisted wire and dots, circa 1925. / Eleven graduated turquoise stones set in a line into silver, 1920s. / 7-stone line bracelet set in silver, circa 1927. / Five green turquoise stones on a silver ribbed cuff. *Enchanted Mesa collection*.

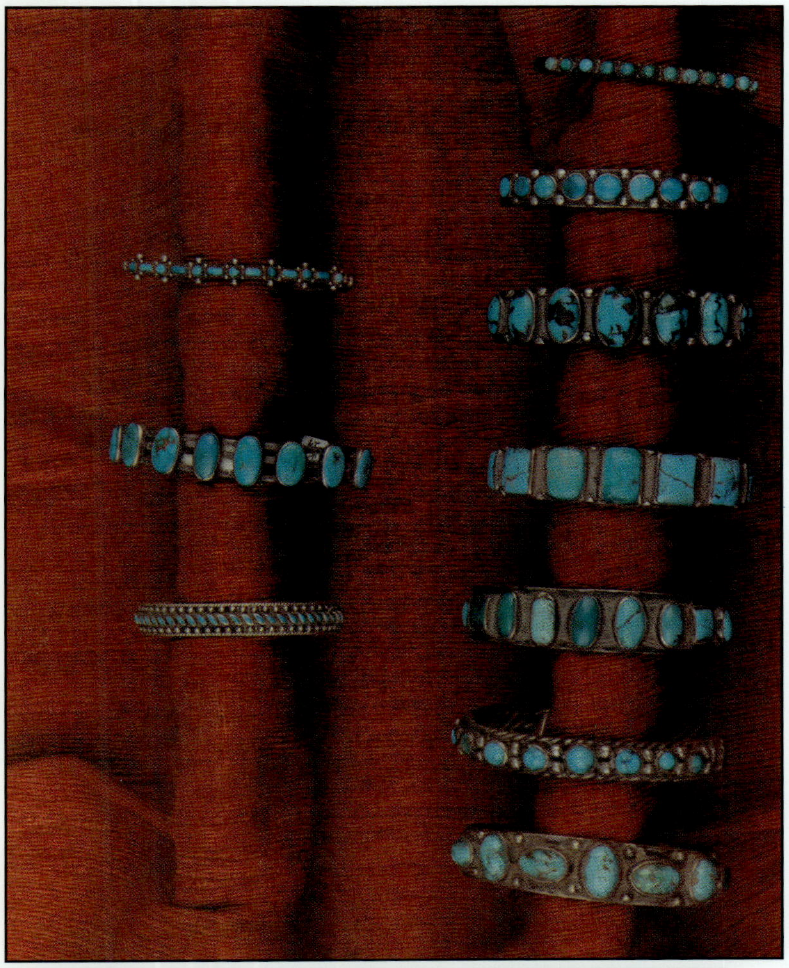

Ten Navajo single-row line bracelets of silver set with turquoise from various mines in Nevada and New Mexico, 1920s to 1940. *Dennehotso collection*.

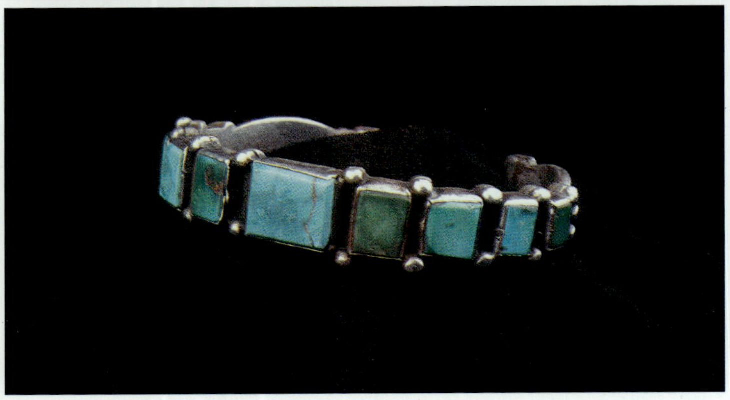

An especially beautiful Navajo line bracelet with rectangular turquoise stones from various mines mounted on a heavy ingot silver band with stamping on the terminals, c.1920. *Lynn D. Trusdell, Crown & Eagle Antiques*

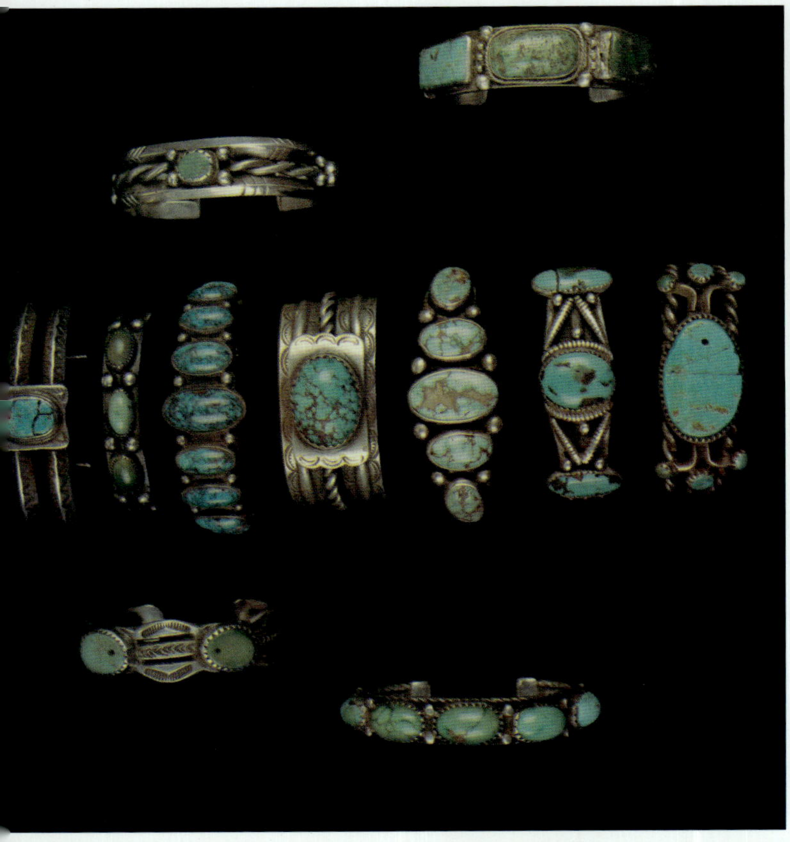

Early silver Navajo bracelets with single or row-set turquoise: from the top - three rectangular stones, 1930s. / Revival design with twisted wire from the 1920s. / Double stamped triangular wire bracelet with flat plate and solitary turquoise, circa 1910. / Line-set bracelet with serrated bezels, circa 1900-1910. / Oval graduated Burnham spiderweb turquoise bracelet from the 1940s. / Silver cuff with flat stamping and round wire, a flat plate and single turquoise from the 1920s. / Five oval Fox turquoise stones of light tone in a bracelet from the 1930s. / An interesting design has been formed by the setting of this bracelet from the first decade of the twentieth century. / Twisted wire and sand cast elements support an old turquoise stone that has been drilled for an ear bob, circa 1910. Bottom left - Two Cerillos turquoise stones in serrated bezels rest on a split stamped band, circa 1910. / Five Morenci turquoise stones rest between twisted wires in this bracelet from the 1920s. *Lynn D. Trusdell collection*

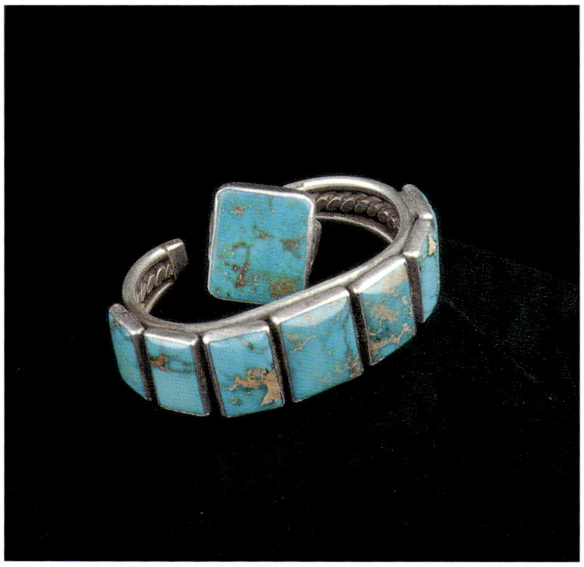

Particularly fine Blue Gem turquoise mounted as a simple line bracelet in silver with a matching finger ring, c.1920s. *Lynn D. Trusdell, Crown & Eagle Antiques*

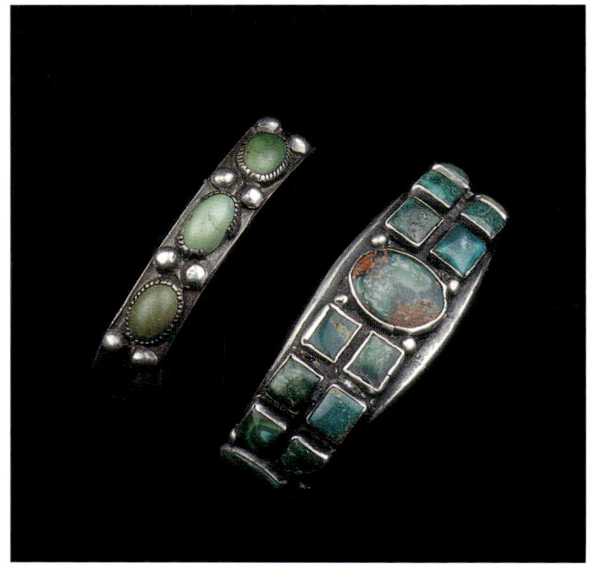

Left: Navajo silver line bracelet with three Cerillos turquoise stones mounted in serrated bezels, c.1915-20. Right: Dark green turquoise row bracelet with a large round stone flanked by parallel rows of square stones and round stones on the terminals (not visible), c.1915. *Lynn D. Trusdell, Crown & Eagle Antiques*

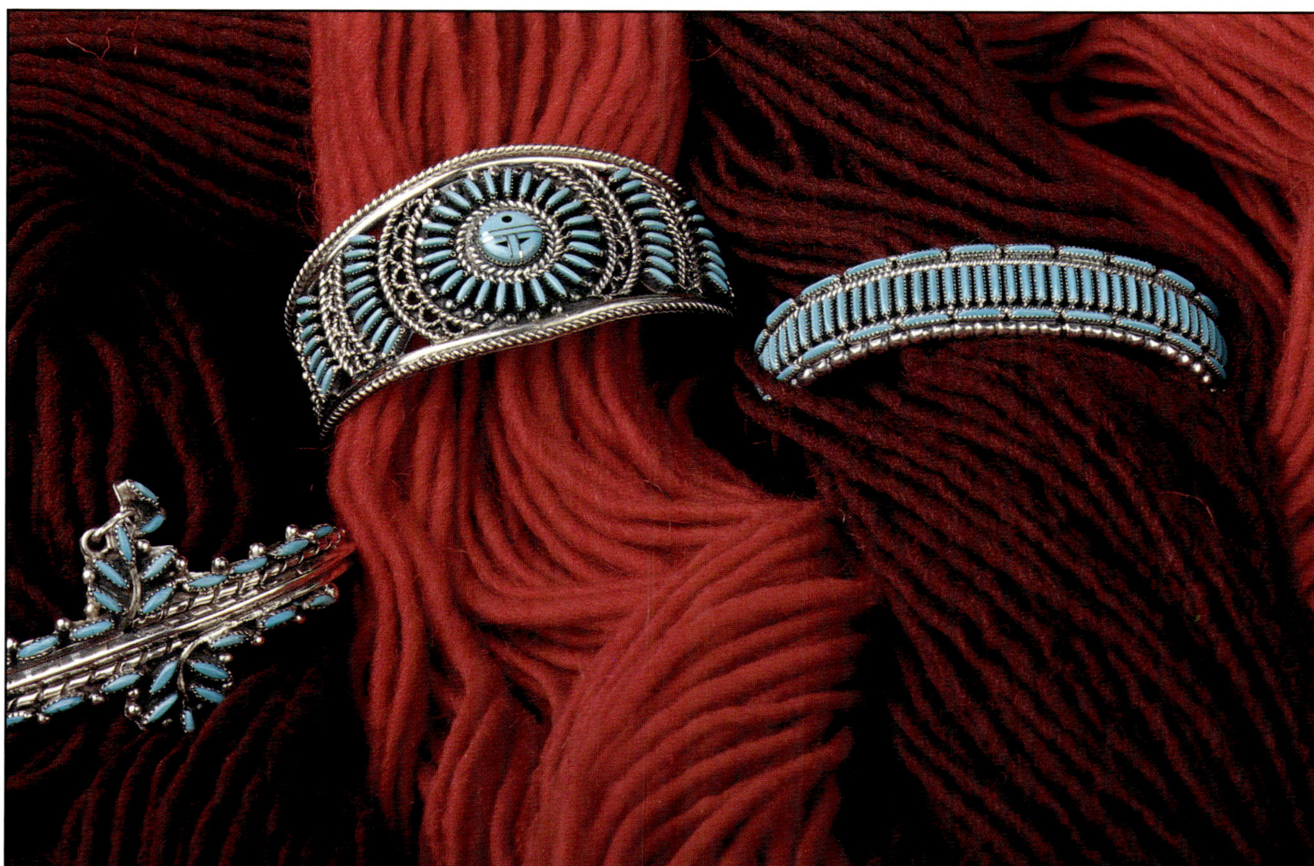

Three Zuni silver bracelets including needlepoint turquoise stones, each in a different design, 2001. *Courtesy McGee's, Holbrook*

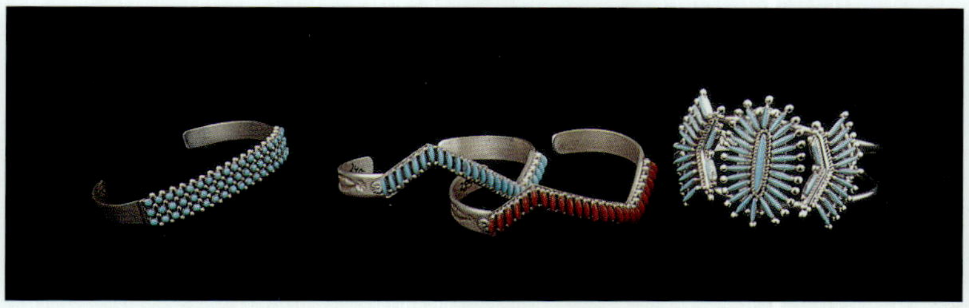

Petit-point style Zuni bracelets. A 3-row bracelet of round turquoise stones by T-A. H & - Bowekaty.($255) / Two single v-shape bracelets in coral and turquoise ($285). / A wide bracelet set with turquoise by Lance and Cordelia Waatsa ($255). *Courtesy of Palms Trading Company*

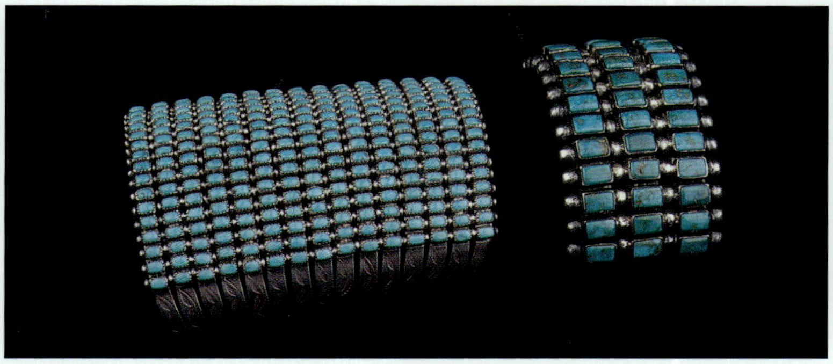

The finest Zuni lapidary work is apparent in these silver line bracelets. 15-rows of matching square-cut turquoise stones. / Three rows of rectangular-shaped turquoise stones separated by raindrops of silver. *Lynn D. Trusdell, Crown & Eagle Antiques*

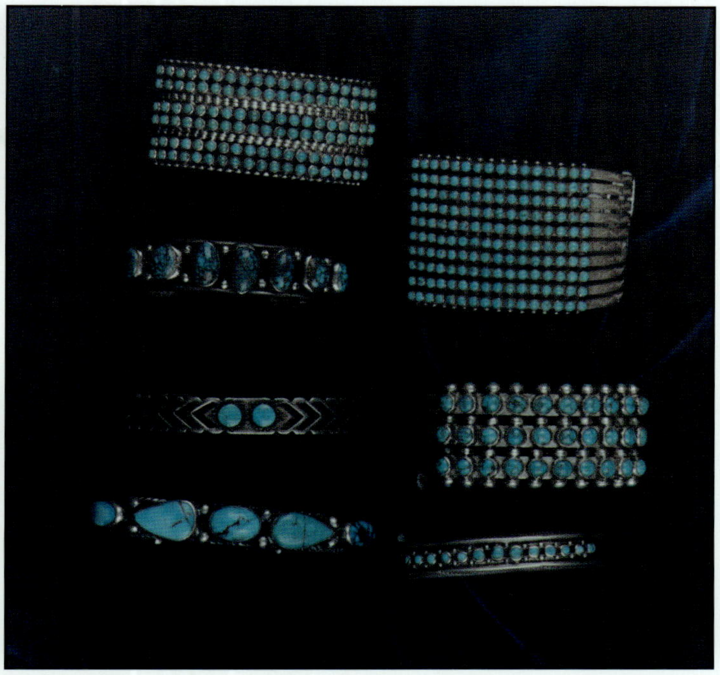

Line bracelets in a variety of designs from a single line to ten lines spanning the first four decades of this century. The immense popularity of line bracelets peaked in the 1940s. *Private collection on permanent loan to Ohio University*

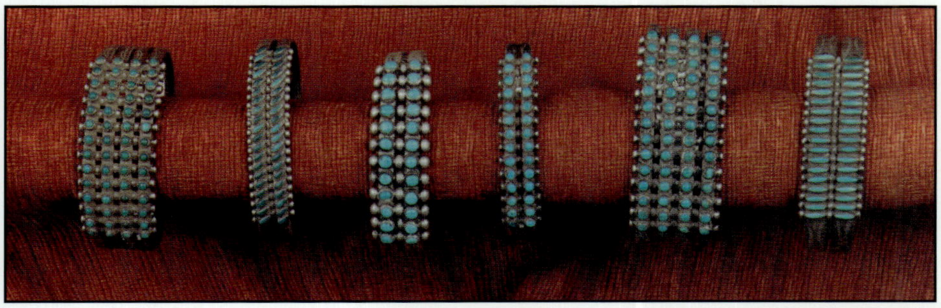

Group of Zuni bracelets from the 1930s: From the left, four-line bracelet set with Kingman "snake-eye" (small round) turquoise. / Two-line bracelet set with Morenci petit-point turquoise. / Bracelet of two lines of Morenci turquoise. / Two lines of Morenci "snake-eye" turquoise. / Four-line bracelet with 56 Old Morenci turquoise stones. / Needlepoint Morenci turquoise set in two lines with stamped decoration. *Dennehotso collection*.

This group of sand cast bracelets displays a range of designs through the first half of the 20th century: Left: a design with cast hearts on each side of the central group of Morenci turquoise stones, late 1910s. Center from the top: a very fine design and skilled workmanship including a serrated bezel and cast hearts on each side, circa 1915. / Heavy coin silver bracelet with three stones from the 1940s. / Solitary turquoise in a setting from the 1950s. Right: another design from the 1950s where the large central stone dominates the design. *Lynn D. Trusdell collection*

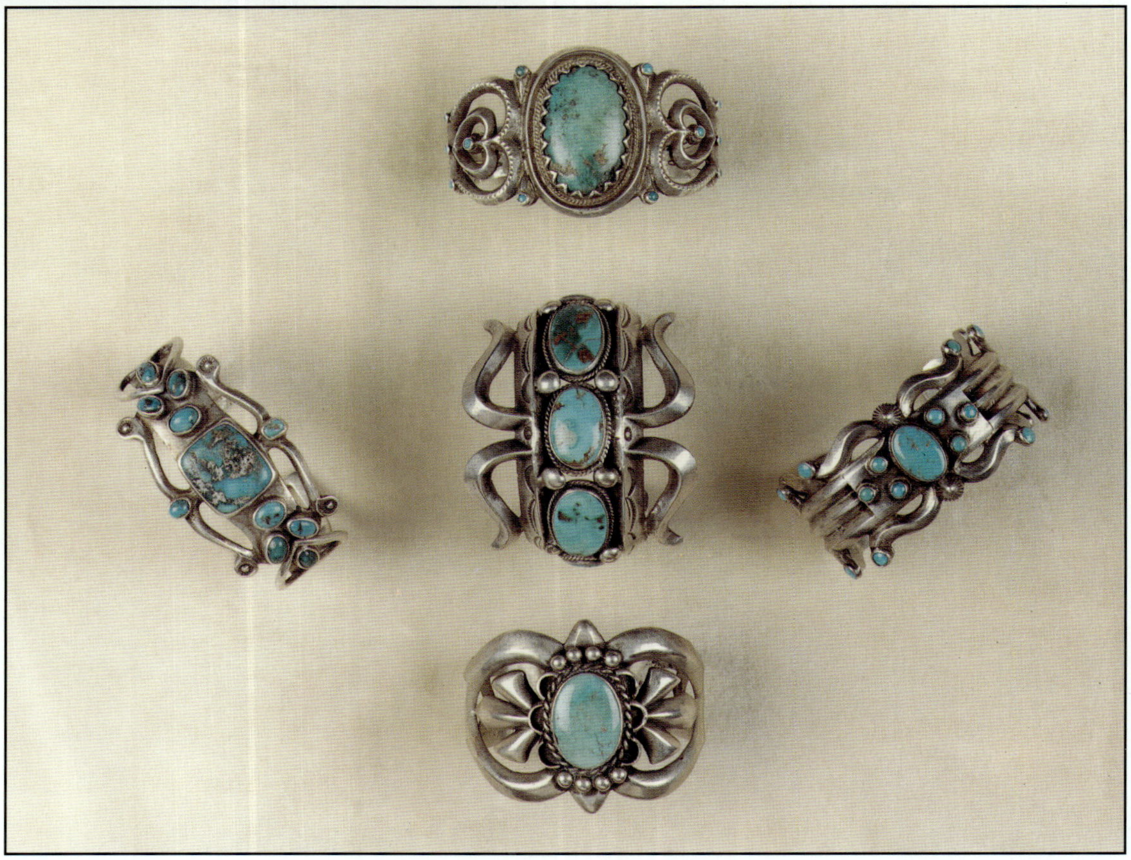

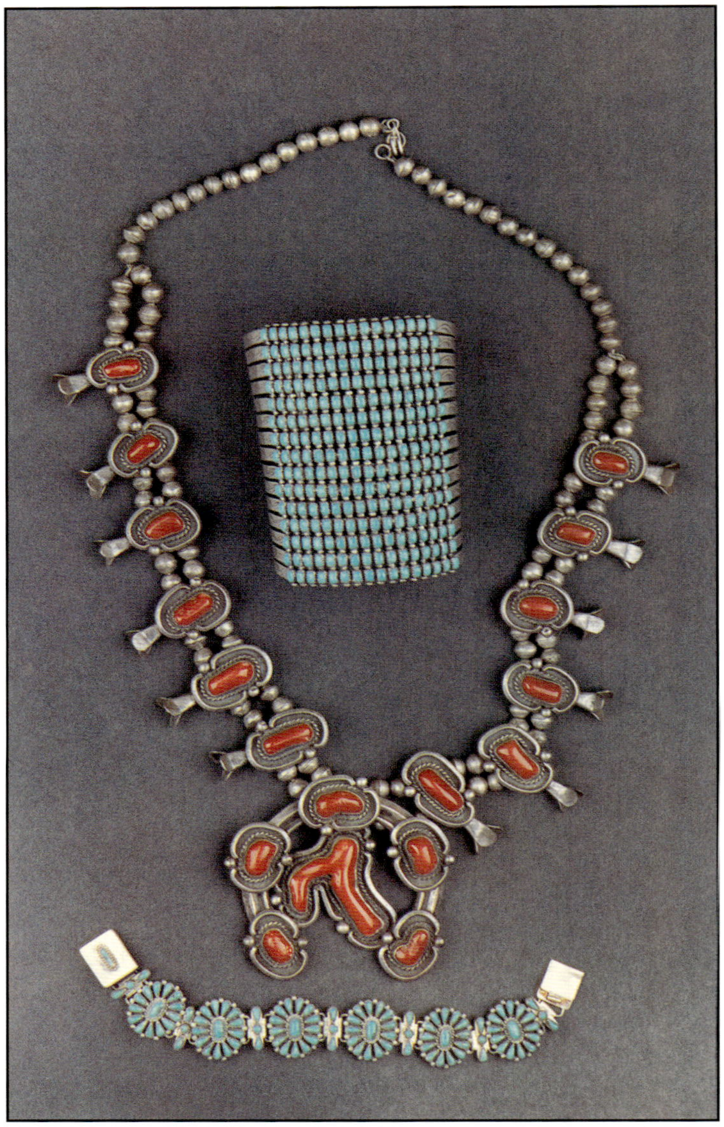

A 15-line Zuni tapered cuff bracelet from the 1940s makes a bold appearance. In contrast, the branch coral is set in a striking squash-blossom necklace. Below, a Zuni link bracelet set with turquoise makes a good comparison of different styles. The Zuni crafts people are skilled in diverse materials and designs. *Private collection*

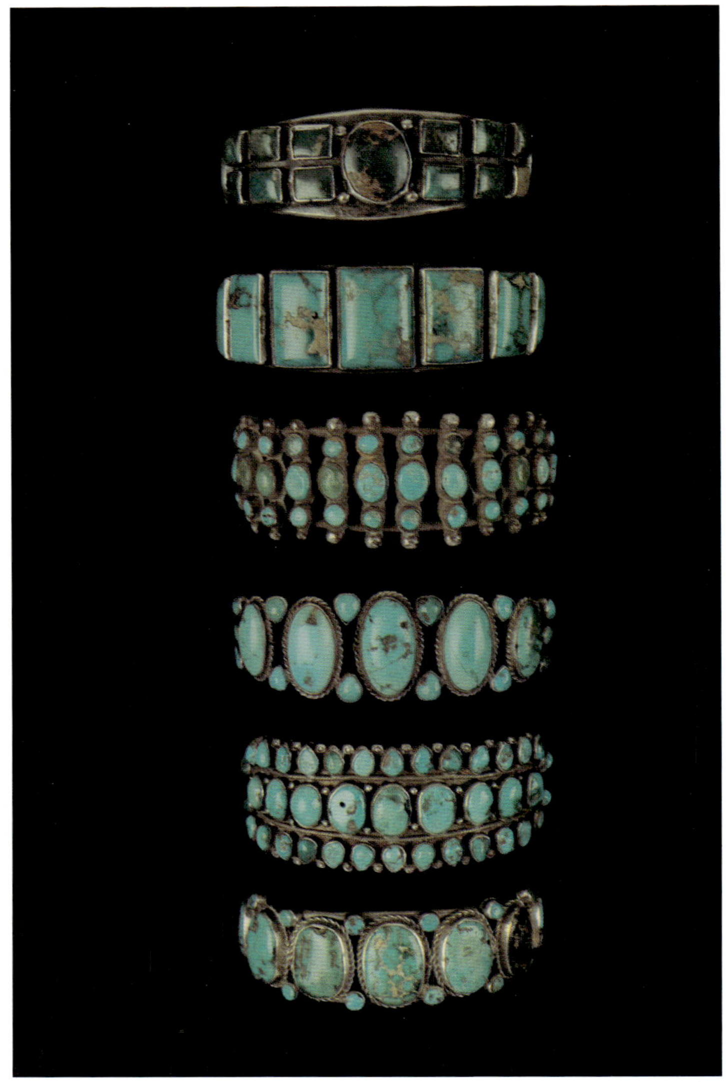

Variations of line-set design evolved to combine stones of different sizes and shapes, becoming the forerunners of cluster designs. From the top: dark green Blue Gem turquoise in a bracelet from circa 1915. / Square Blue Gem turquoise set as a single line bracelet, Zuni. / Triple rows of various round stones and round wire, 1930s. / Oval turquoise offset by turquoise dots and round wire, 1930s. / Fine Zuni lapidary skill is displayed in this bracelet of Morenci turquoise, 1930s. / Another bracelet of off-set stones and round wire construction, 1930s. *Lynn D. Trusdell collection*

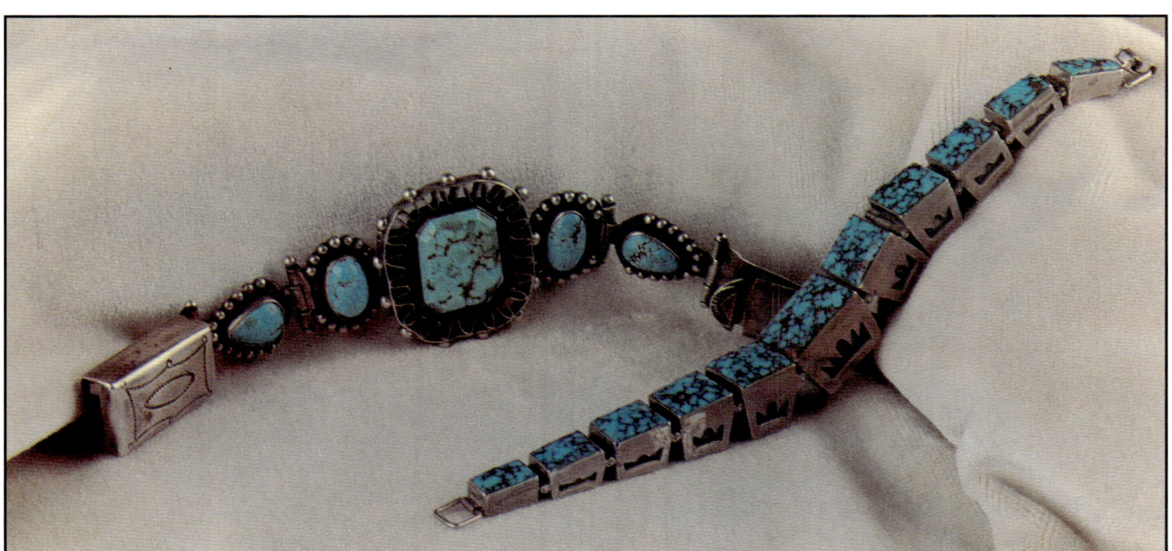

Link bracelets are relatively unusual in Southwest jewelry and these two make a nice contrast of styles. On the left, the links comprise single turquoise stones within flower-like wirework frames, circa 1920. / On the right, tapering box-like links hold square stones in a precision design from the 1950s. *Private collection on permanent loan to Ohio University*

Cluster Bracelets

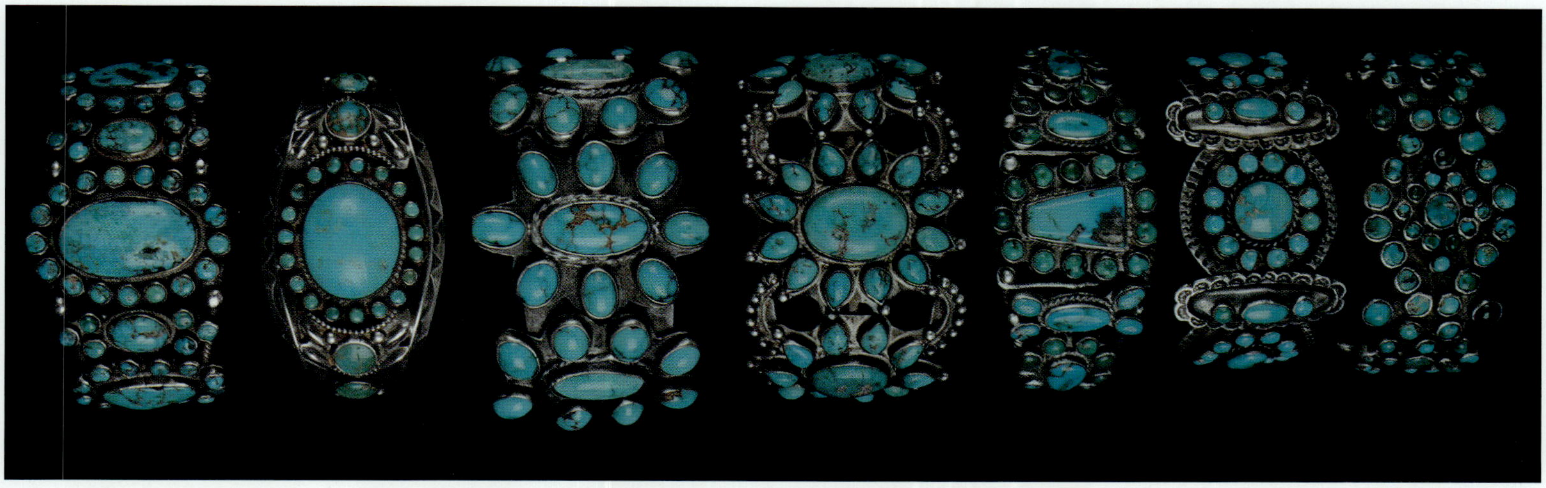

This marvelous group of Zuni cluster bracelets from the 1920s and 1930s displays the excellent stonecutting skill demonstrated by so many Zuni crafts people. *Lynn D. Trusdell collection*

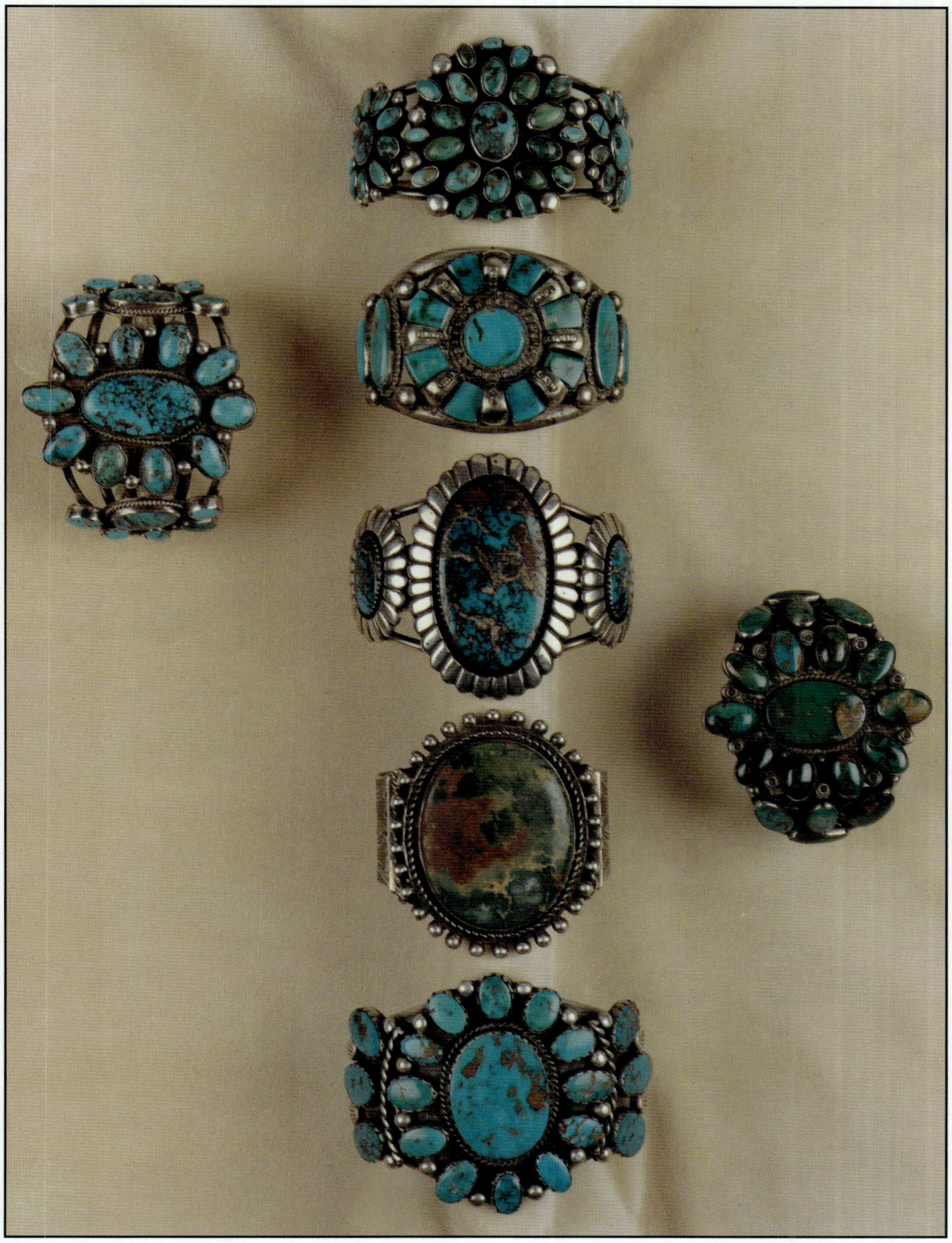

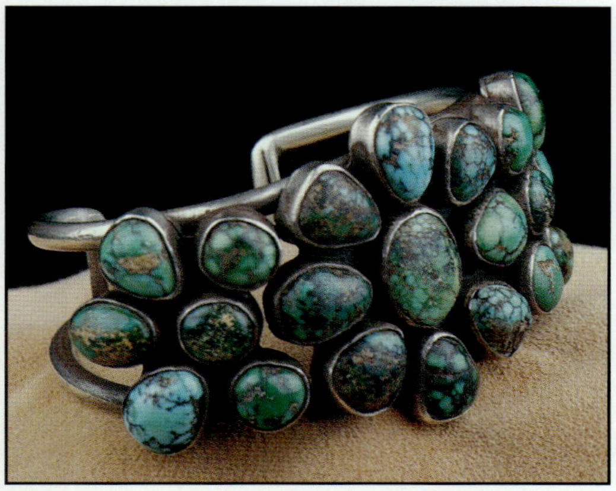

Large man's cluster bracelet with three groups of Spiderweb and other mines' turquoise stones which have matching matrixes, c.1920s. *Lynn D. Trusdell, Crown & Eagle Antiques*

Turquoise stones, which are carefully chosen and matched, create interesting jewelry beyond the makers' design as they display harmonious color tones. This group of cluster bracelets shows off the diversity of turquoise. Top, Burnham spiderweb turquoise in a cluster bracelet from the 1940s. / Left, Morenci turquoise with a copper matrix, 1930s. / Cerillos turquoise bracelet from the 1940s. / Large oval and two smaller Bisbee turquoise stones with pink quartz running through it; the bold silverwork suggests a Hopi origin from the 1940s. / Large single Morenci stone in a 1940s bracelet. / An early and good example of a Navajo cluster bracelet of the 1920s. / Bottom, Navajo bracelet from the 1930s with old Blue Gem turquoise of a green color. *Lynn D. Trusdell collection*

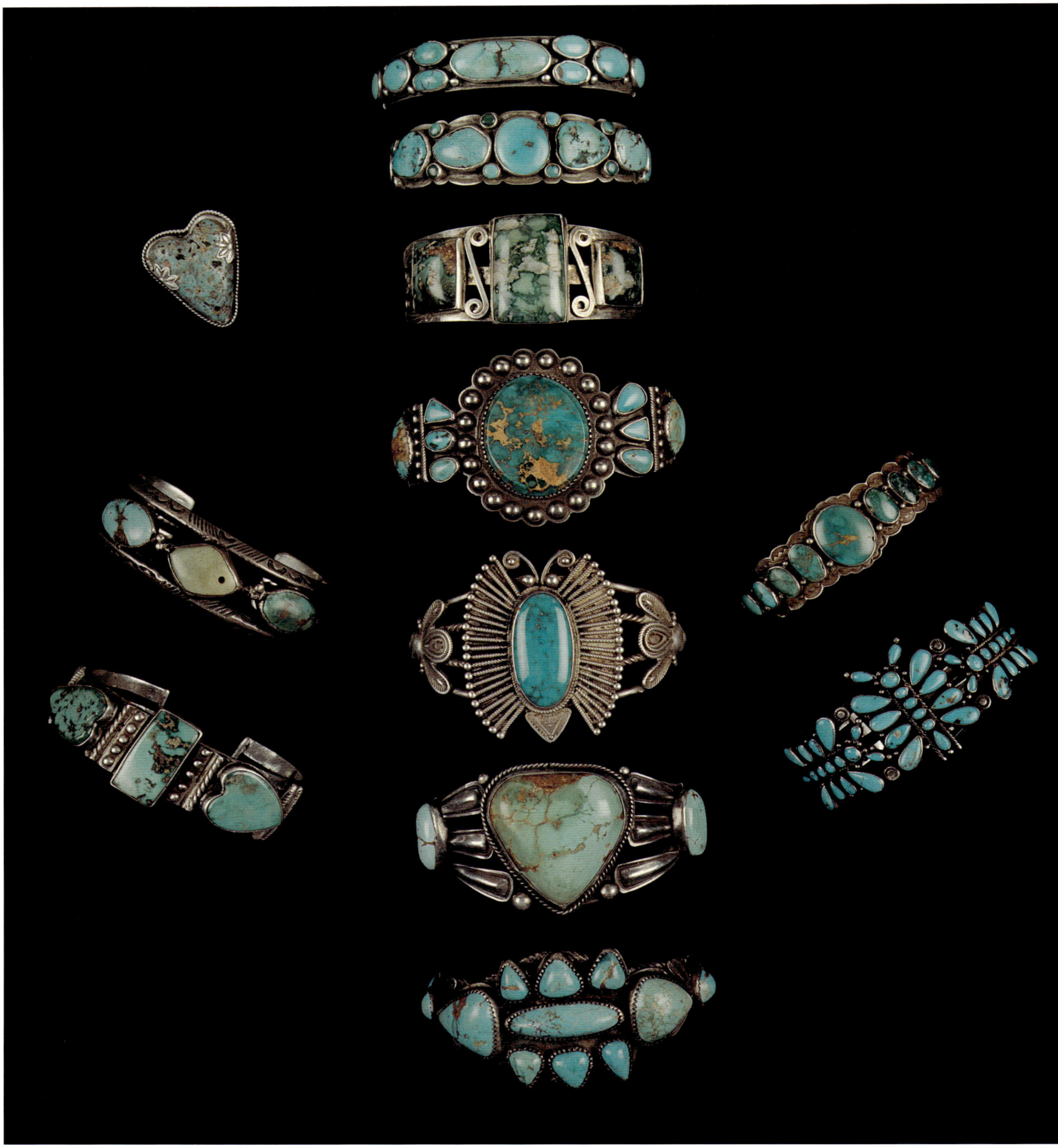

The diversity of cluster bracelets is challenging to a collector. Here are some unusual types: Left: heart-shaped ring and two early bracelets which show turquoise of various shapes and colors. / Center: Zuni row bracelet from the 1920s and 1930s period. / Zuni line bracelet from the 1940s. / Tourist trade wide bracelet from the 1940s. / Bracelet with unusual stones combined in an atypical setting with round wire, 1940s. / Hopi bracelet of butterfly design with a single Morenci spiderweb turquoise from the late 1940s or early 1950s. / Heart shaped Fox turquoise on a triple split silver band. / Twisted wire supports the turquoise of this bracelet from 1915-20. / Right: symmetrical graduated stones from the 1930s. / Hopi design with butterfly forms arranged both vertically and horizontally. *Lynn D. Trusdell collection*

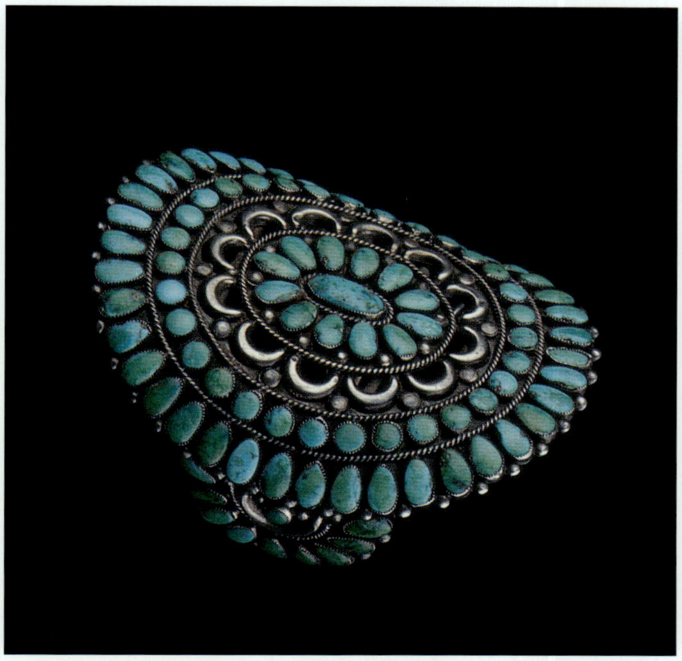

Large Zuni cluster bracelet with matching Blue Gem turquoise stones, 1940s. *Lynn D. Trusdell, Crown & Eagle Antiques*

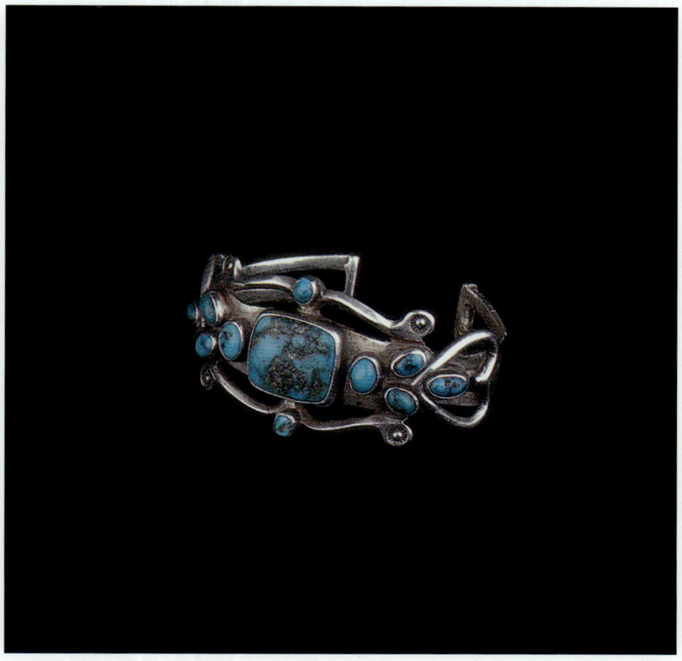

Early Navajo sand cast silver bracelet with Lone mountain turquoise, c.1920s. This bracelet was given to a Catholic priest on the Navajo reservation in the 1950s and was acquired from him. *Lynn D. Trusdell, Crown & Eagle Antiques*

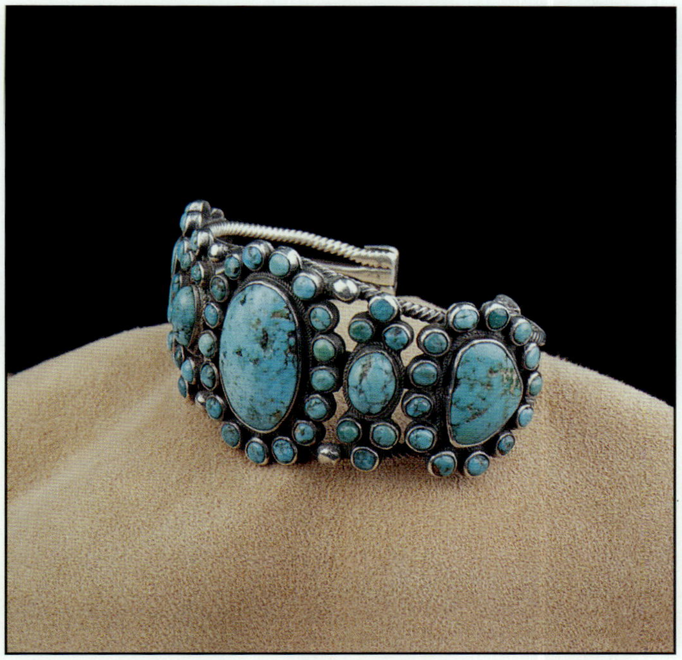

Multi-stone Zuni cluster bracelet with three large and two small clusters of turquoise set in silver, c.1930. *Lynn D. Trusdell, Crown & Eagle Antiques*

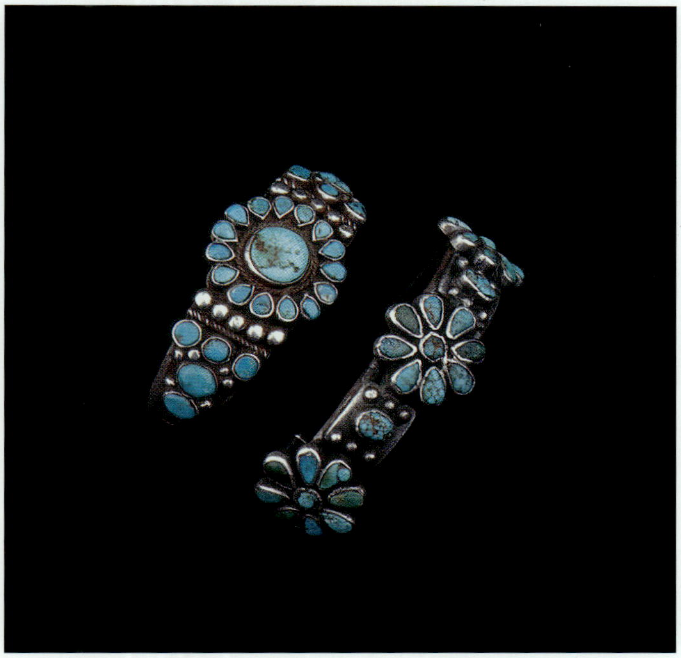

Two really fine Zuni cluster bracelets with different designs, c.1930. *Lynn D. Trusdell, Crown & Eagle Antiques*

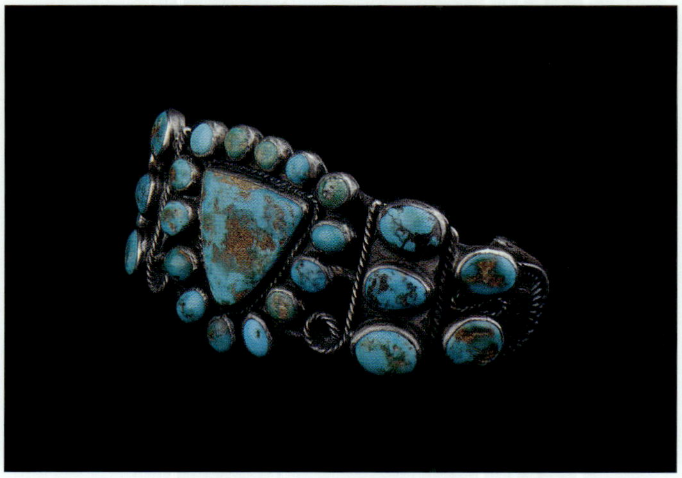

A fine Zuni cluster bracelet with a triangular Blue Gem turquoise stone surrounded with round and pear-shaped cuts mounted on twisted wire with terminals. Formerly in the Freulingheusen collection. *Lynn D. Trusdell, Crown & Eagle Antiques*

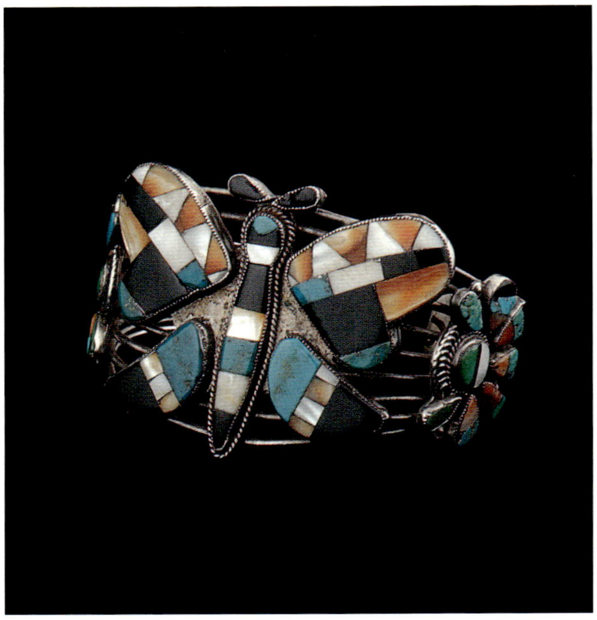

Zuni stone-to-stone cluster bracelet with a large spread-wing butterfly and two sunface designs mounted to silver wires, 1930s. *Lynn D. Trusdell, Crown & Eagle Antiques*

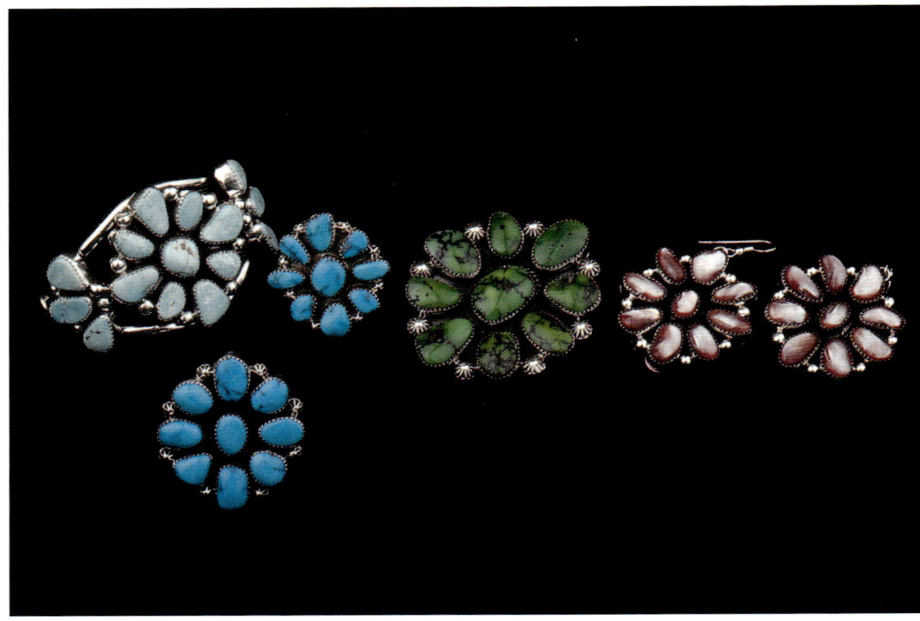

Group of jewelry set with large stones by Pat Platero, Navajo: bracelet ($240) and earrings ($135) with pale blue Dry Creek turquoise. / Buckle with green stabilized Skyhorse turquoise ($180). / Drop earrings with pink stones ($99). c.2000. *Courtesy of Palms Trading Company*

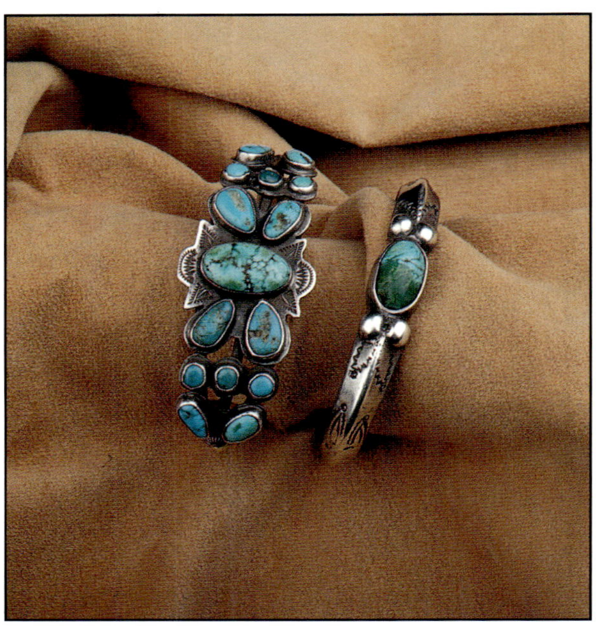

Left: A beautiful Zuni cluster turquoise stone bracelet with flat silver plates set on round wires, c.1920.
Right: An early stamped silver band with oval turquoise and round stones in the terminals (not shown), c. 1910.
Lynn D. Trusdell, Crown & Eagle Antiques

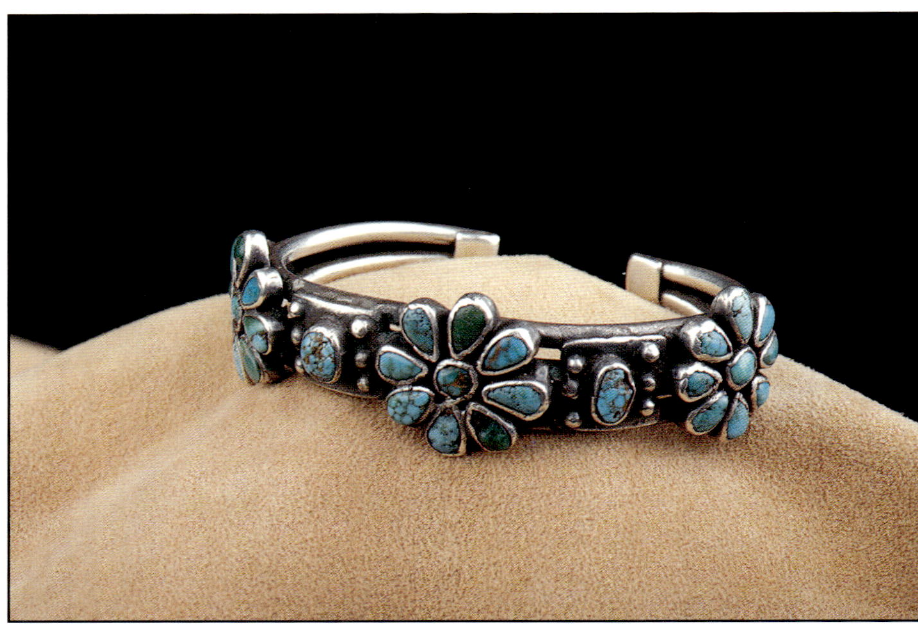

Large Zuni man's bracelet with turquoise stones (most #8 Spiderweb) clustered on simple round wire, each cluster on a separate plate, c.1915. *Lynn D. Trusdell, Crown & Eagle Antiques*

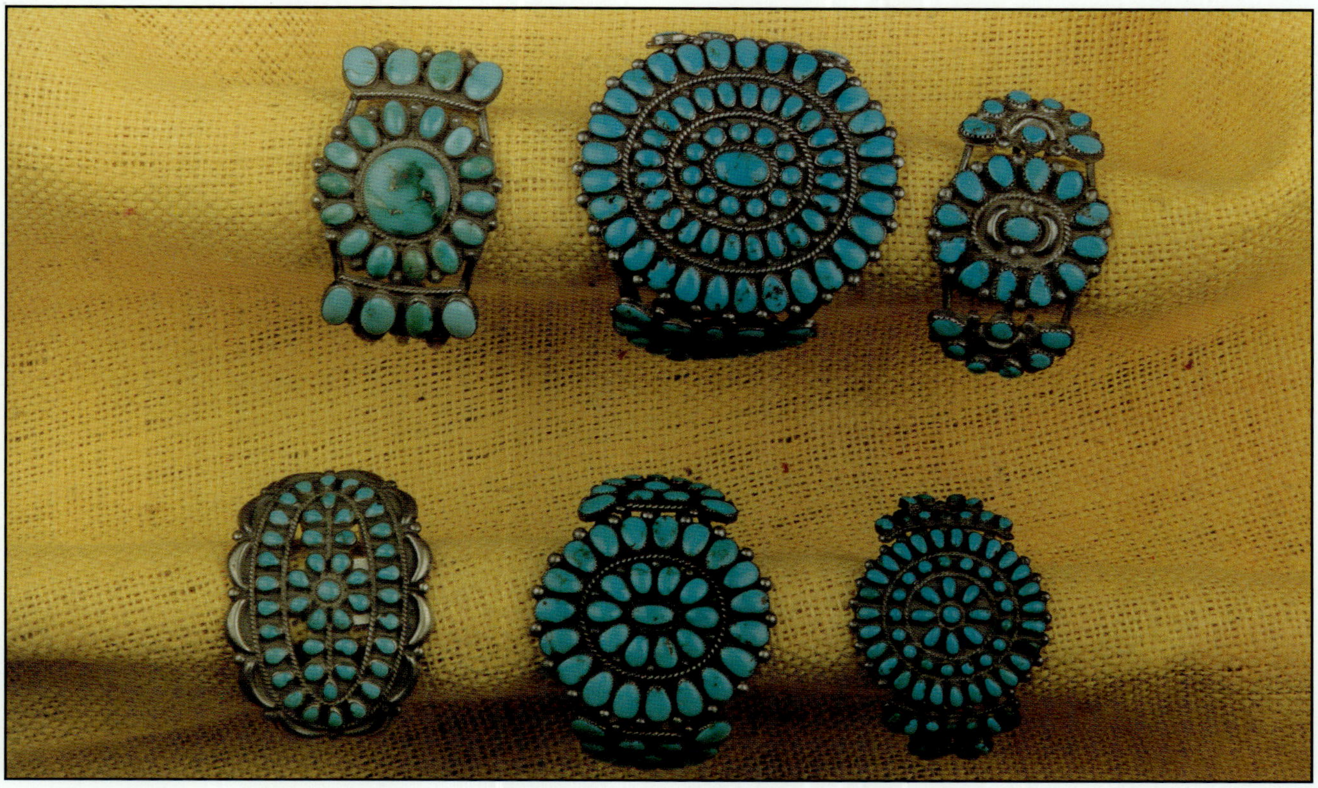

Six Zuni cluster bracelets of sterling silver and Morenci and Royal Blue turquoise stones from the 1940s and 1950s. *Dennehotso collection*

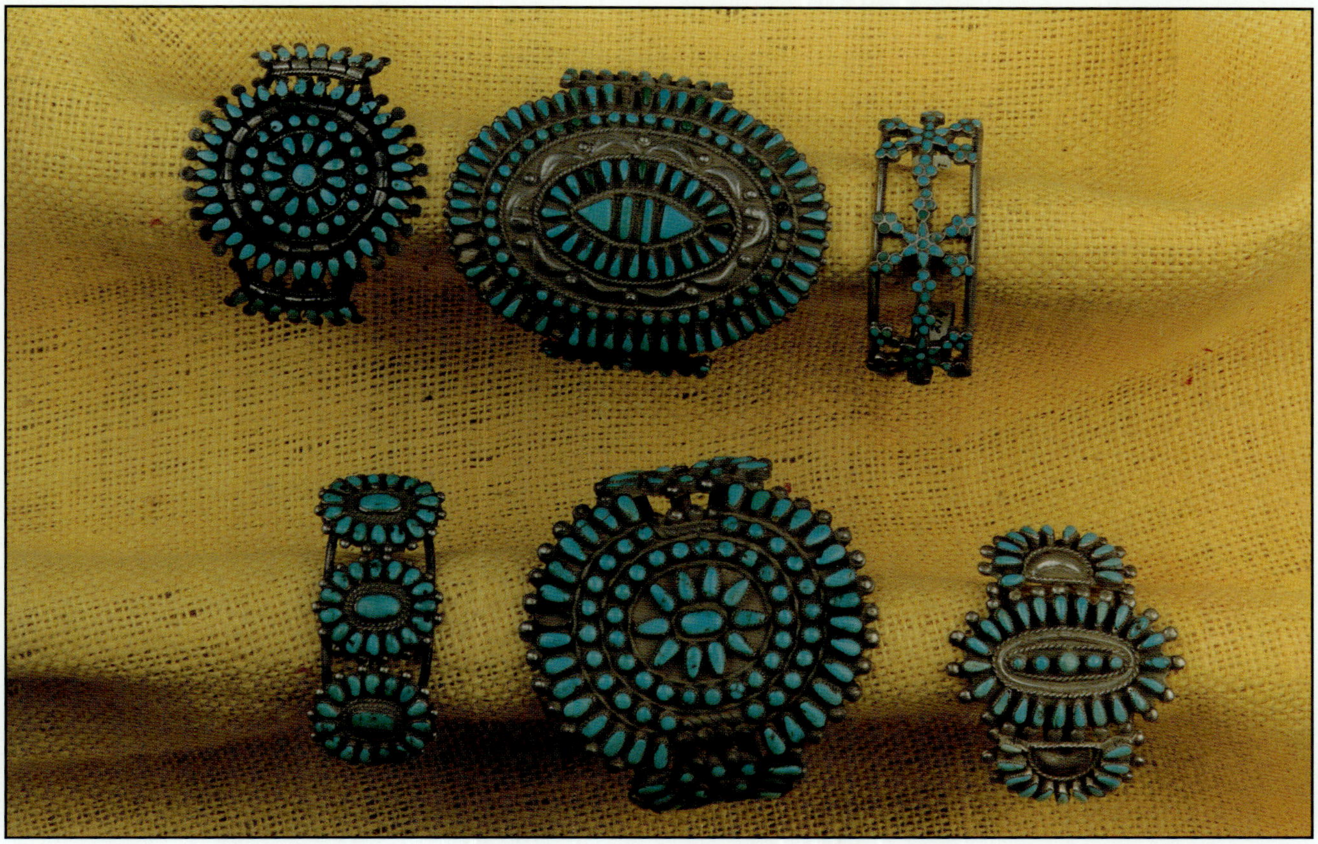

Six cluster bracelets set with Morenci turquoise: Top from left, bracelet by Navajo artist Victor Moses Begay in the Zuni style, circa 1960. All others of Zuni origin. / Large oval bracelet circa 1950. / Bracelet with snowflake design turquoise inlay, circa 1930. / Bottom, three clusters joined, circa 1950. / Large round cluster, circa 1950. / Small oval design, circa 1950. *Dennehotso collection*

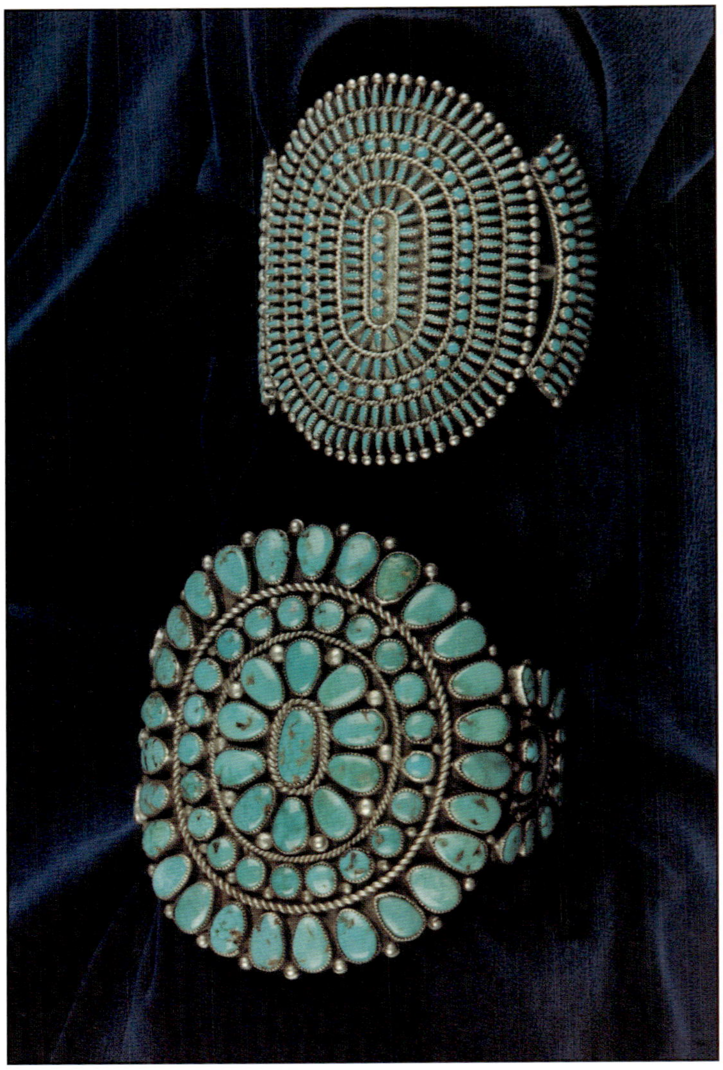

Above: Handsome Zuni petit-point turquoise bracelet by Rosemary G. Panteah.
Below: Large cluster bracelet of Lone Mountain turquoise signed by Florence James, July, 1956. *Private collection on permanent loan to Ohio University*

Six Navajo cluster bracelets from the 1920s and '30s with a variety of turquoise stones. *Dennehotso collection*

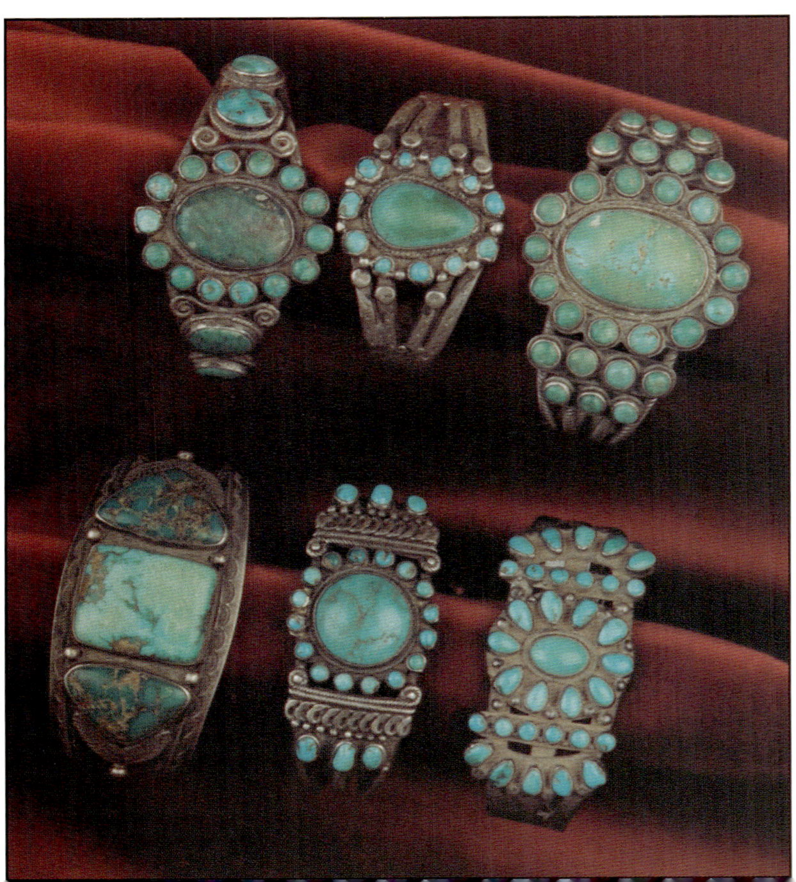

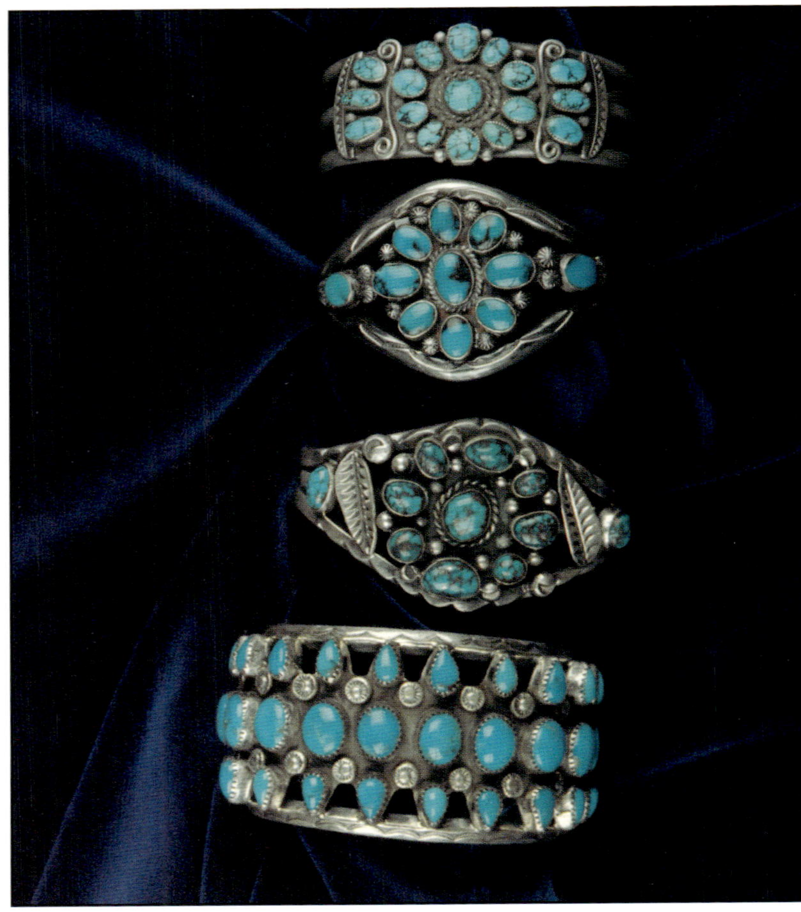

Group of Navajo bracelets of various designs: Large triple line bracelet with Kingman turquoise. / Unusual bracelet combining small turquoise stones with silver leaf appliqué. / Cluster bracelet of Lone Mountain turquoise. / Bisbee turquoise stones arranged in a cluster design. *Private collection on permanent loan to Ohio University*

Exceptionally large stones present special design opportunities to jewelers. These four examples display carefully made bracelets, which Indians would wear for special ceremonies. From the top: Ramon Platero set two large oval Morenci turquoise stones in an overlapping design with silver in 1958. / Three very large, non-uniform-shaped turquoise stones are mounted on four heavy silver hoops in the largest bracelet. / Two giant Fox turquoise stones are framed by a silver border with leaf decorations. / Three big irregularly shaped turquoise stones are set in a line on three silver hoops. *Private collection on permanent loan to Ohio University*

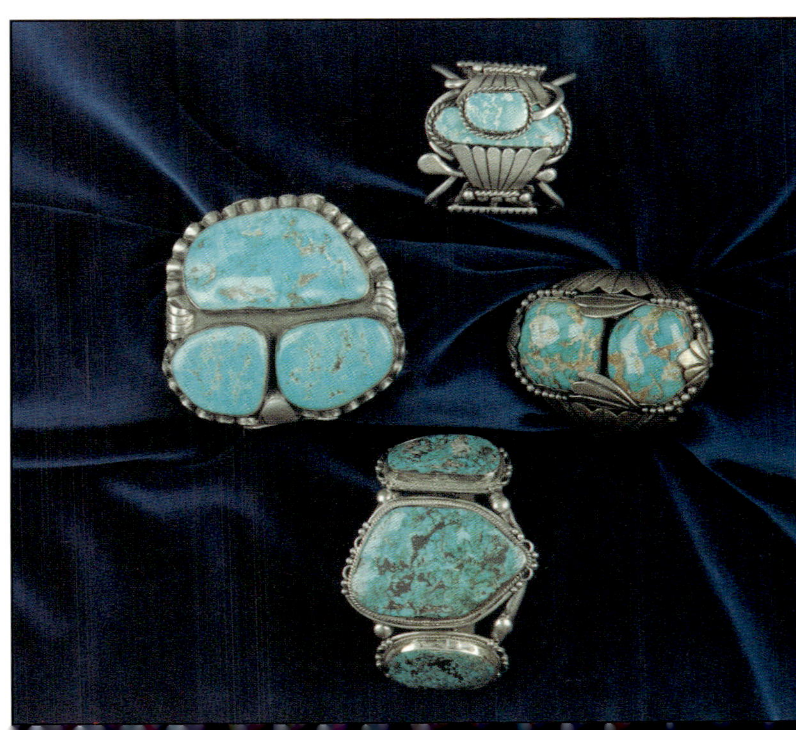

Metal Bracelets

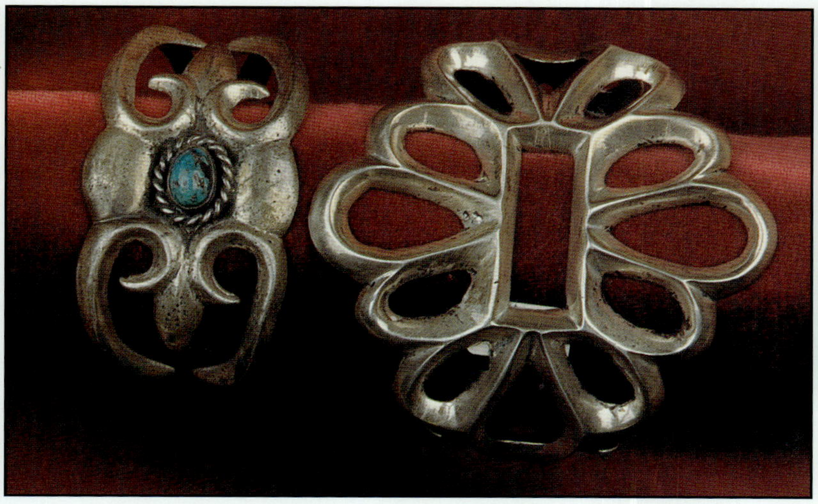

Two Navajo sand-cast sterling silver bracelets from the 1960s: Left: Bracelet set with Persian turquoise. / Right: Bracelet made by Betty Rose Billy of Manuelito Canyon, New Mexico. *Dennehotso collection*

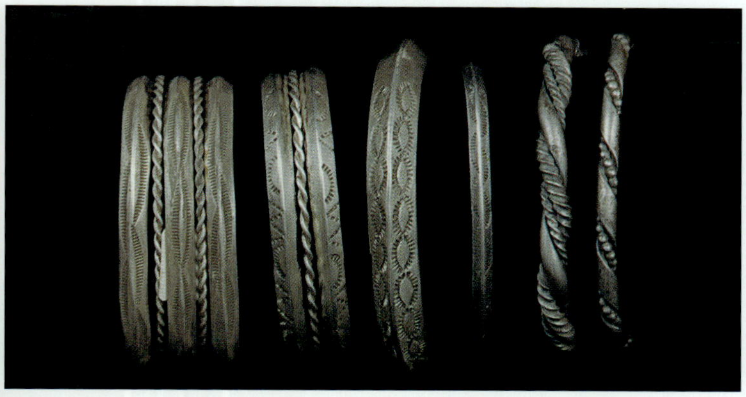

The general popularity of bangle bracelets in the 1950s encouraged Indian silversmiths into the production of many varieties. These were sometimes designs from the early 1900s brought back to use. This group demonstrates the uses of stamped triangular and twisted wires for bangle bracelets, 1948 to the 1960s. *Dennehotso collection*

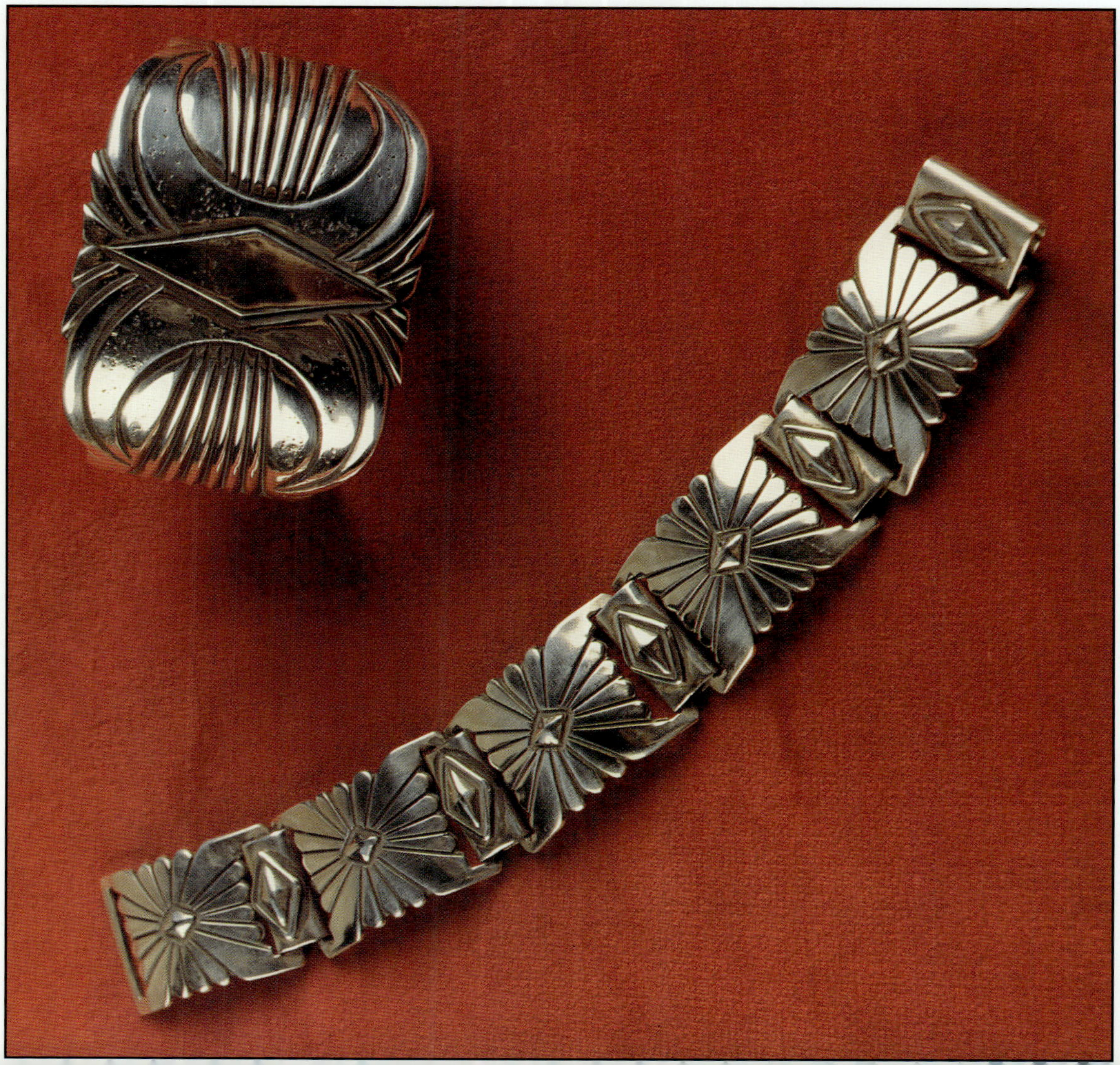

Sterling silver cuff and link bracelet by Navajo silversmith Wilson Jim, 1980s. *Indian Post collection*

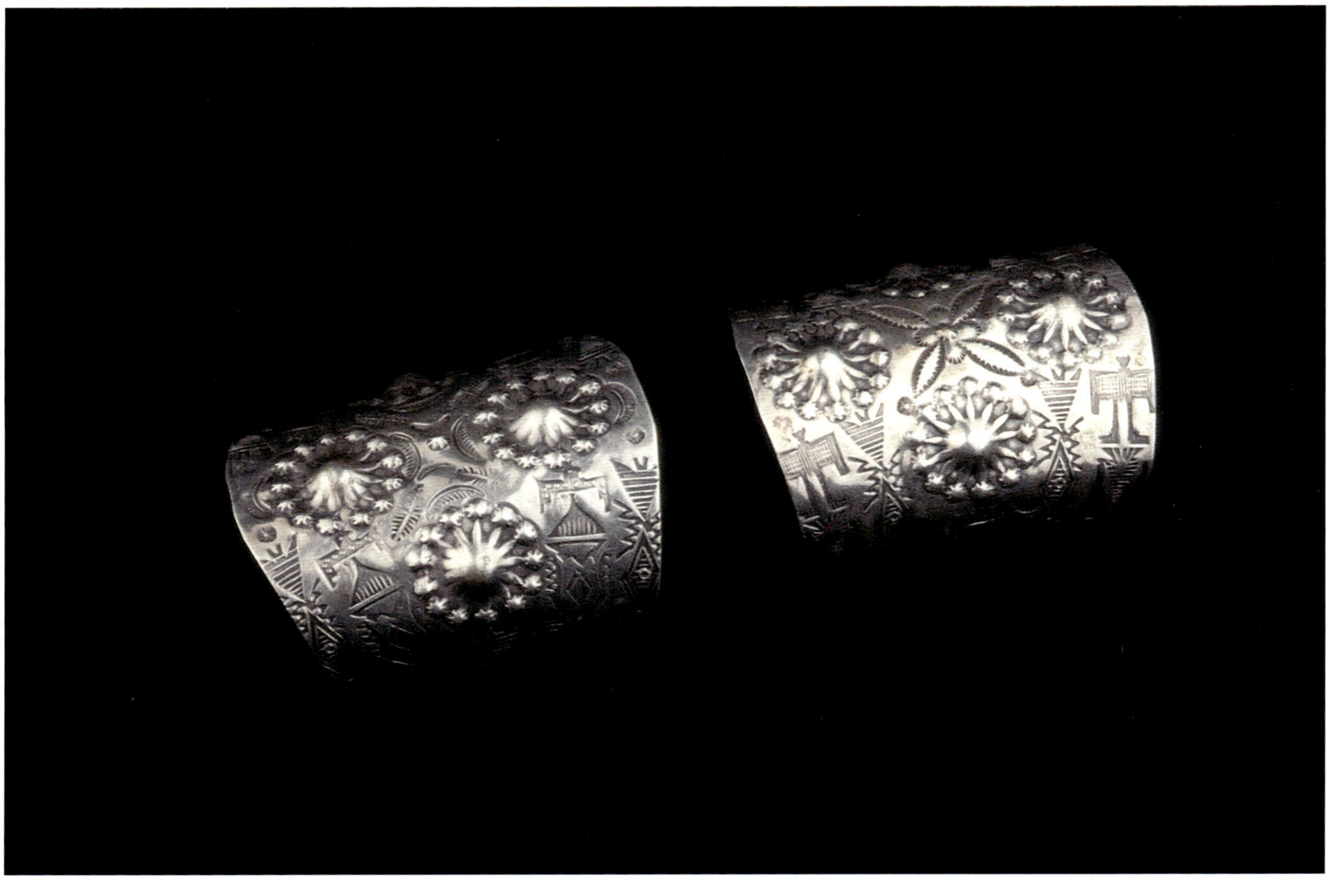

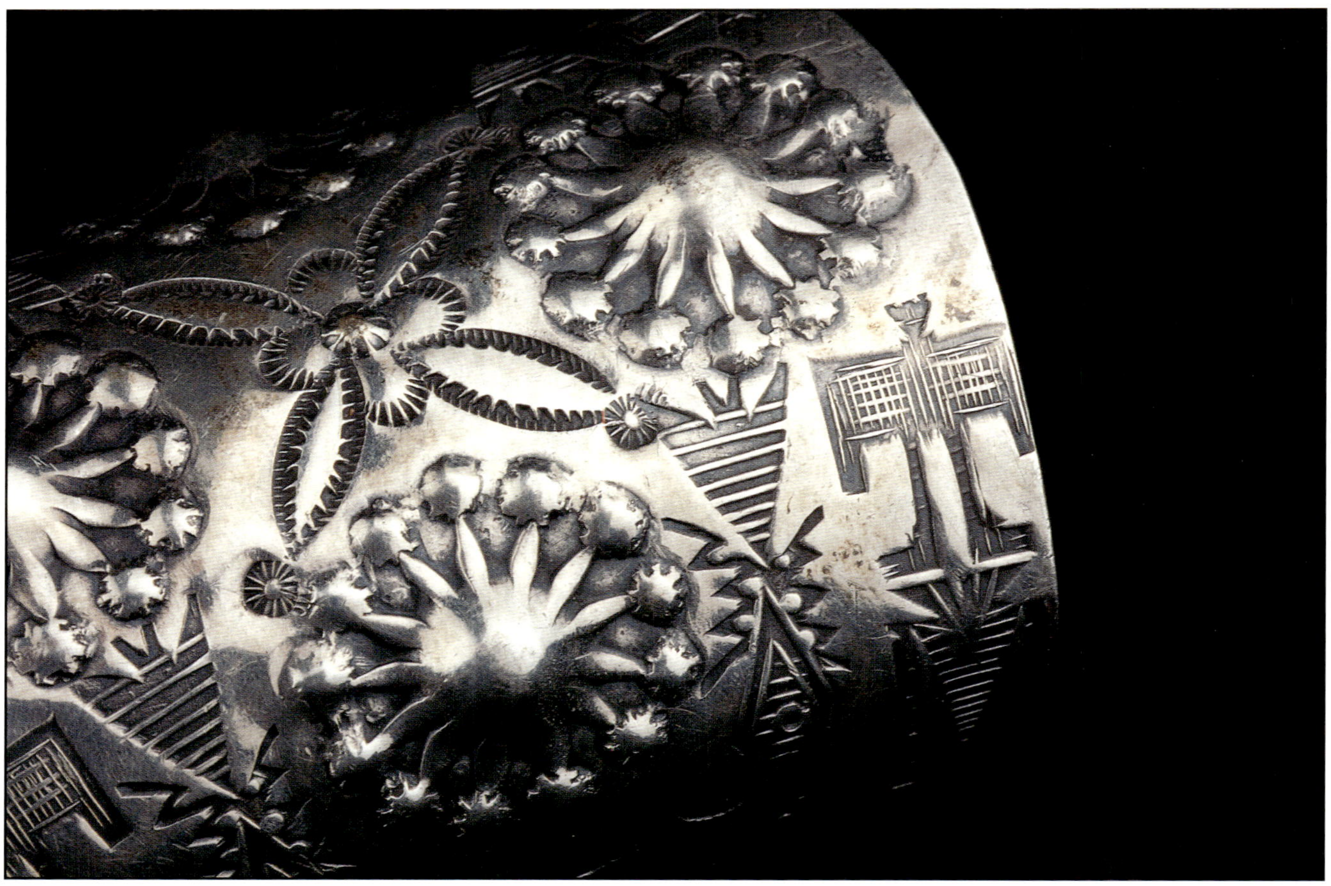

Unusual matching pair of Navajo silver cuff bracelets/gauntlets. The masterful silver work in repoussé button design is elaborately stamped, c.1930s. *Lynn D. Trusdell, Crown & Eagle Antiques*

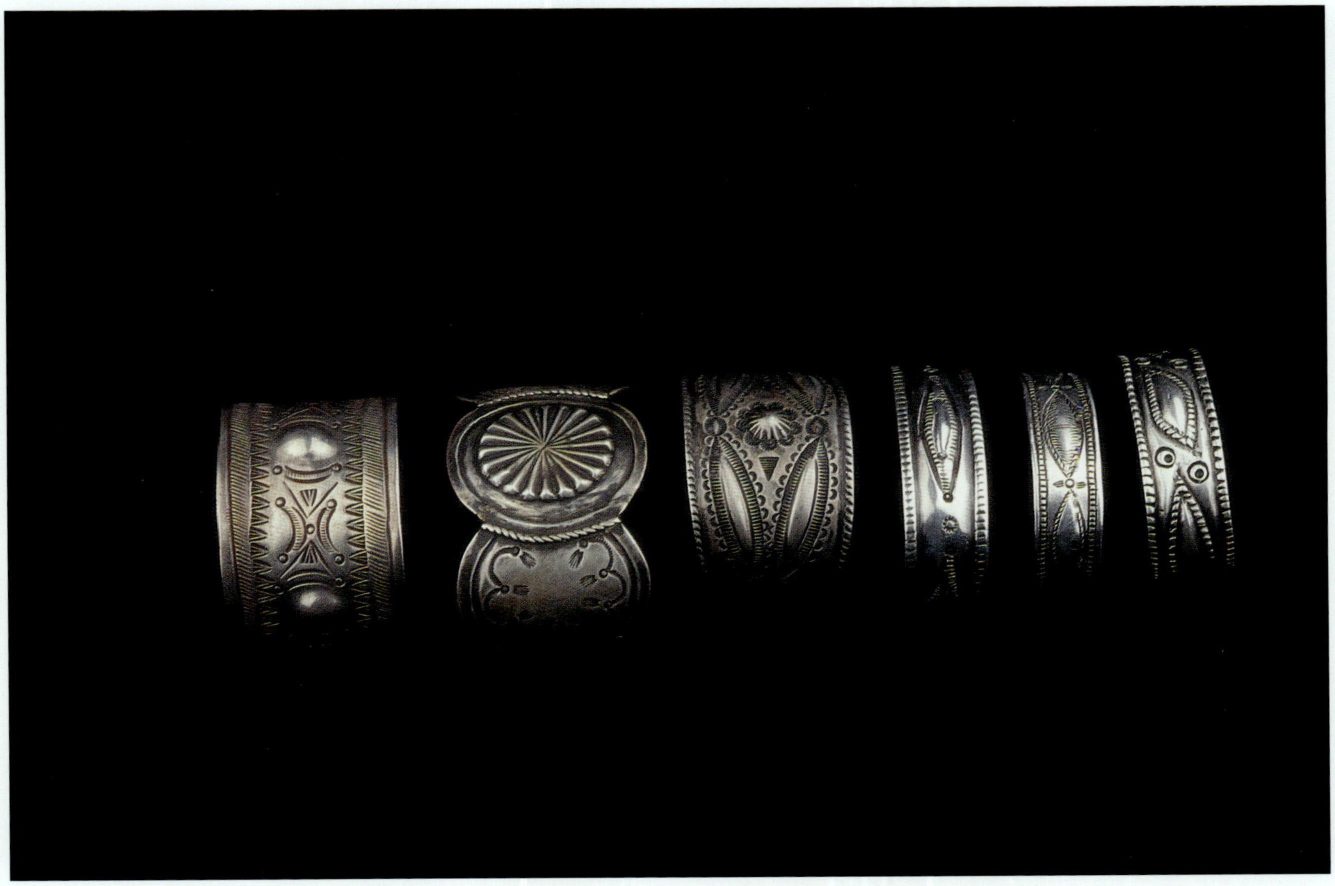

Fine quality group of early Navajo silver cuff bracelets, c.1920s. *Lynn D. Trusdell, Crown & Eagle Antiques*

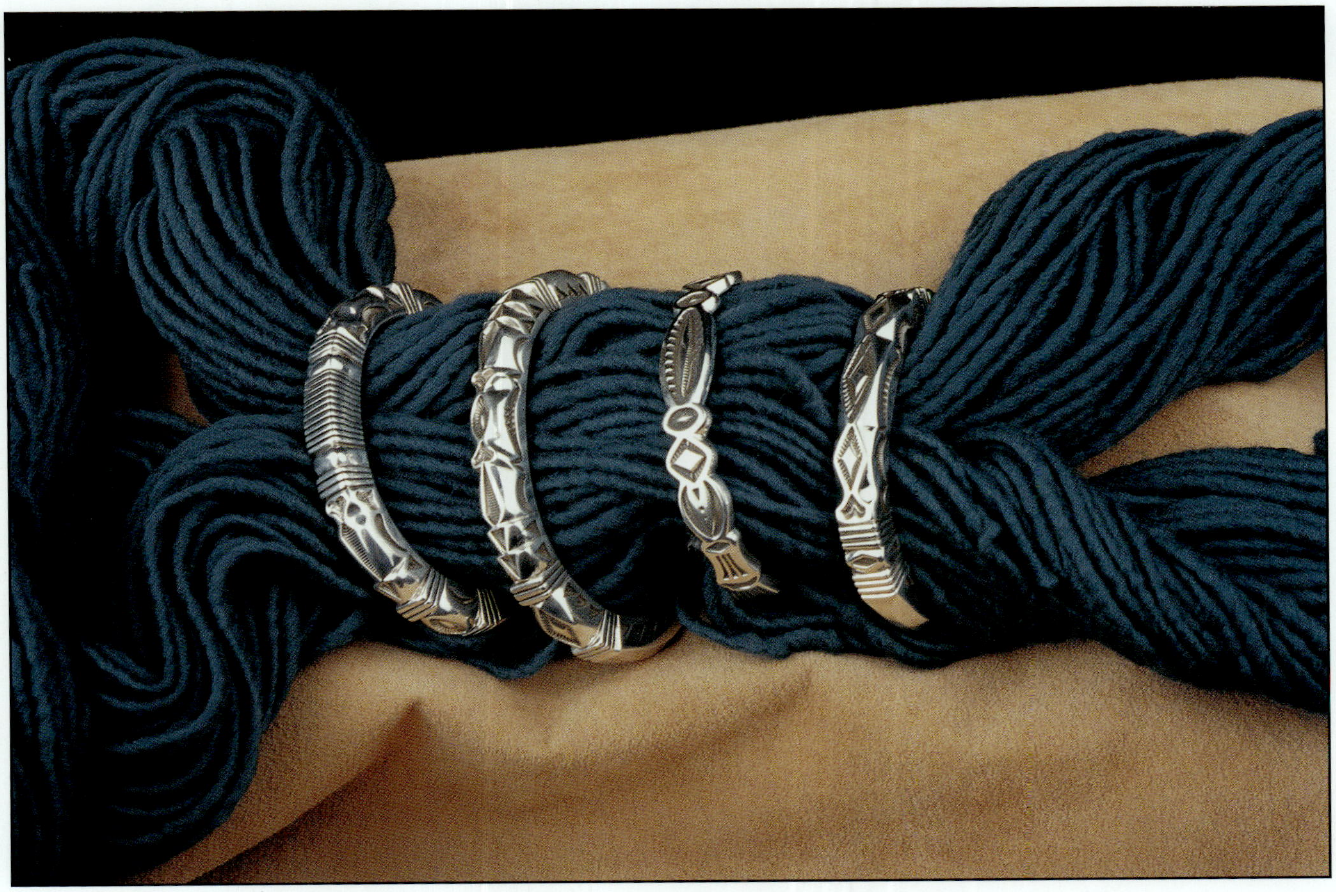

Four silver bracelets by Thomas Curtis, Navajo, 2001. *Courtesy McGee's, Keams Canyon*

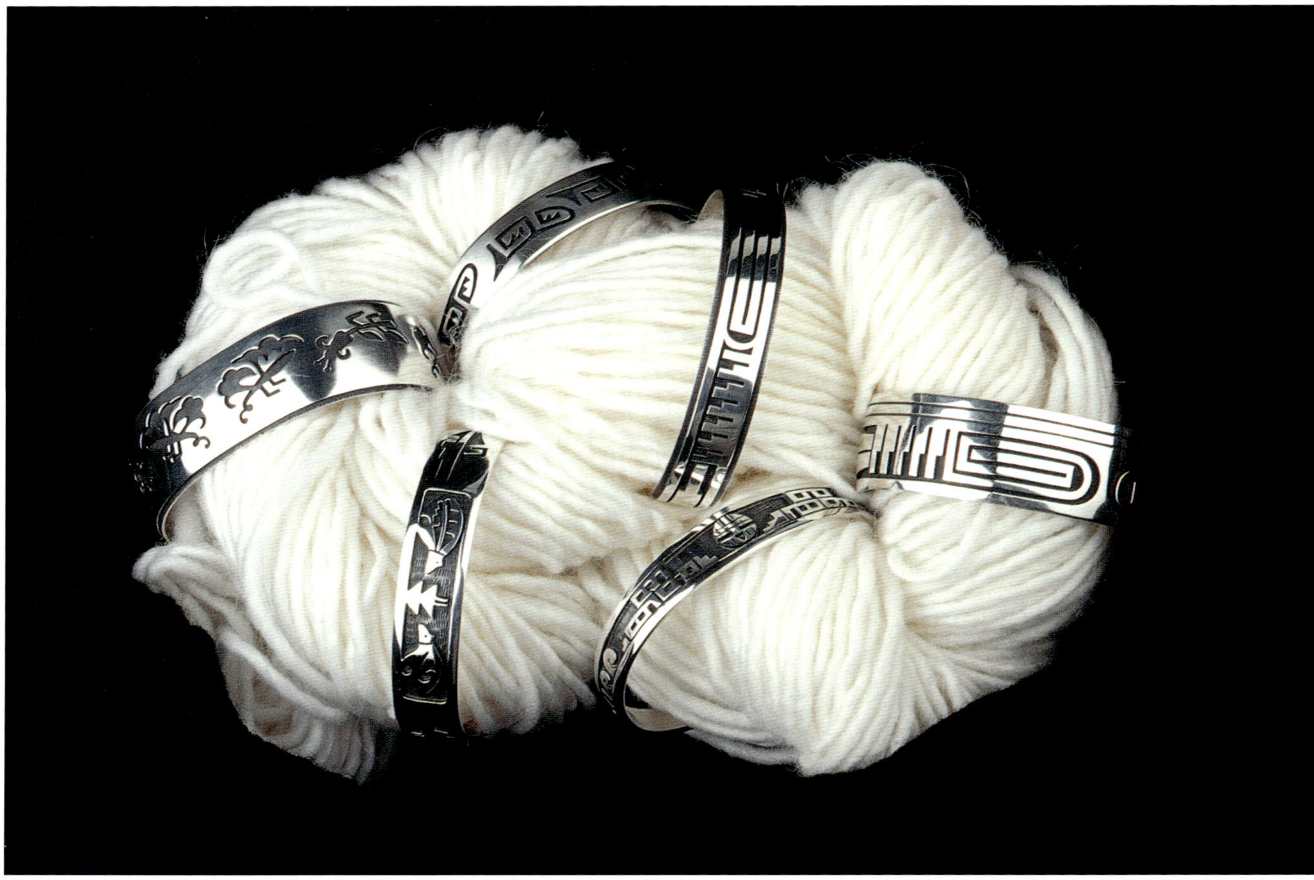

Six Hopi silver bracelets in overlay style, 2002. Wide band with blossoms design by NF ($240). / Bears design by T ($165). / Sunface and pueblos design by Puhuhefvaya ($120). / Three with geometric designs ($133, $165, and $240). *Courtesy McGee's, Holbrook*

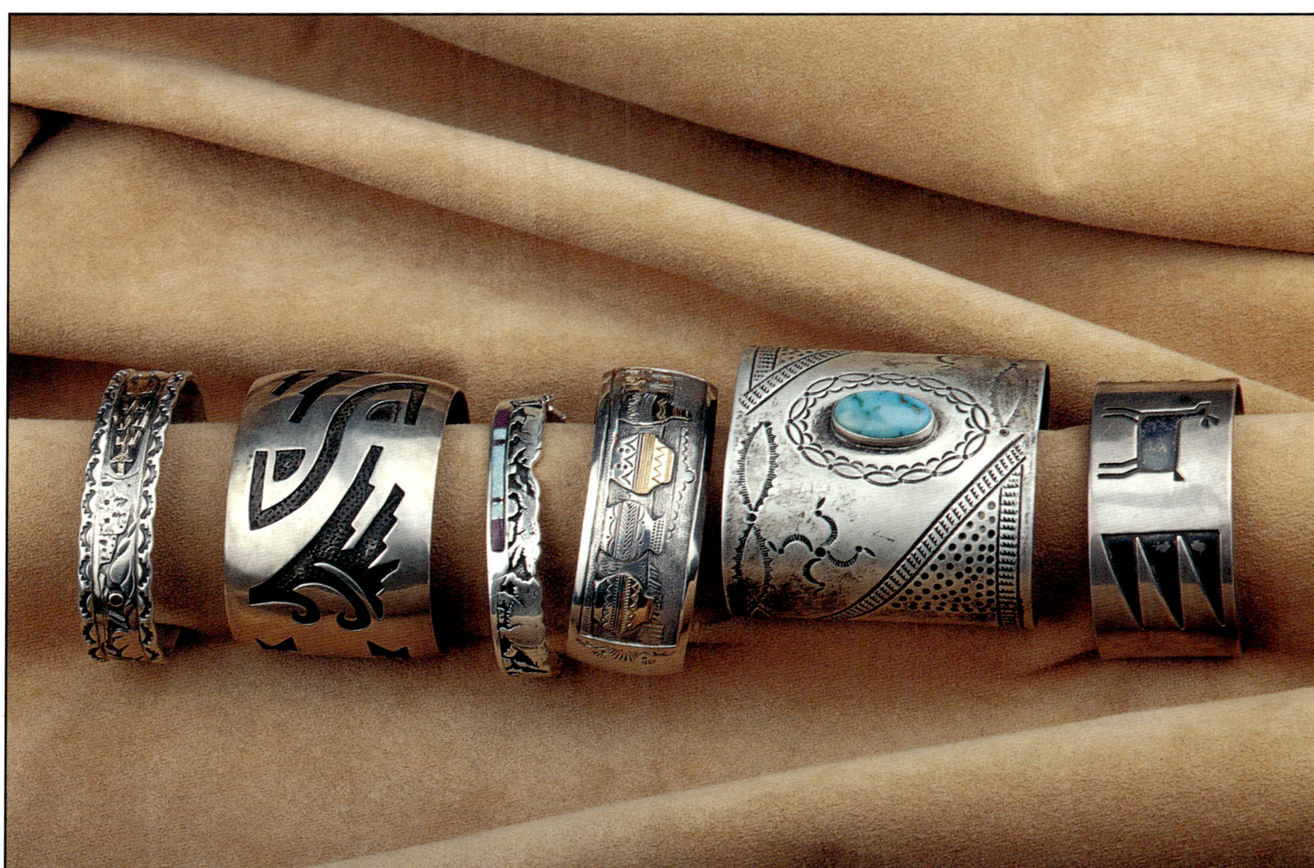

Group of six various Hopi overlay bracelets in silver and gold. The wide cuff set with a turquoise stone is punched decoration c.1940. *Lynn D. Trusdell, Crown & Eagle Antiques*

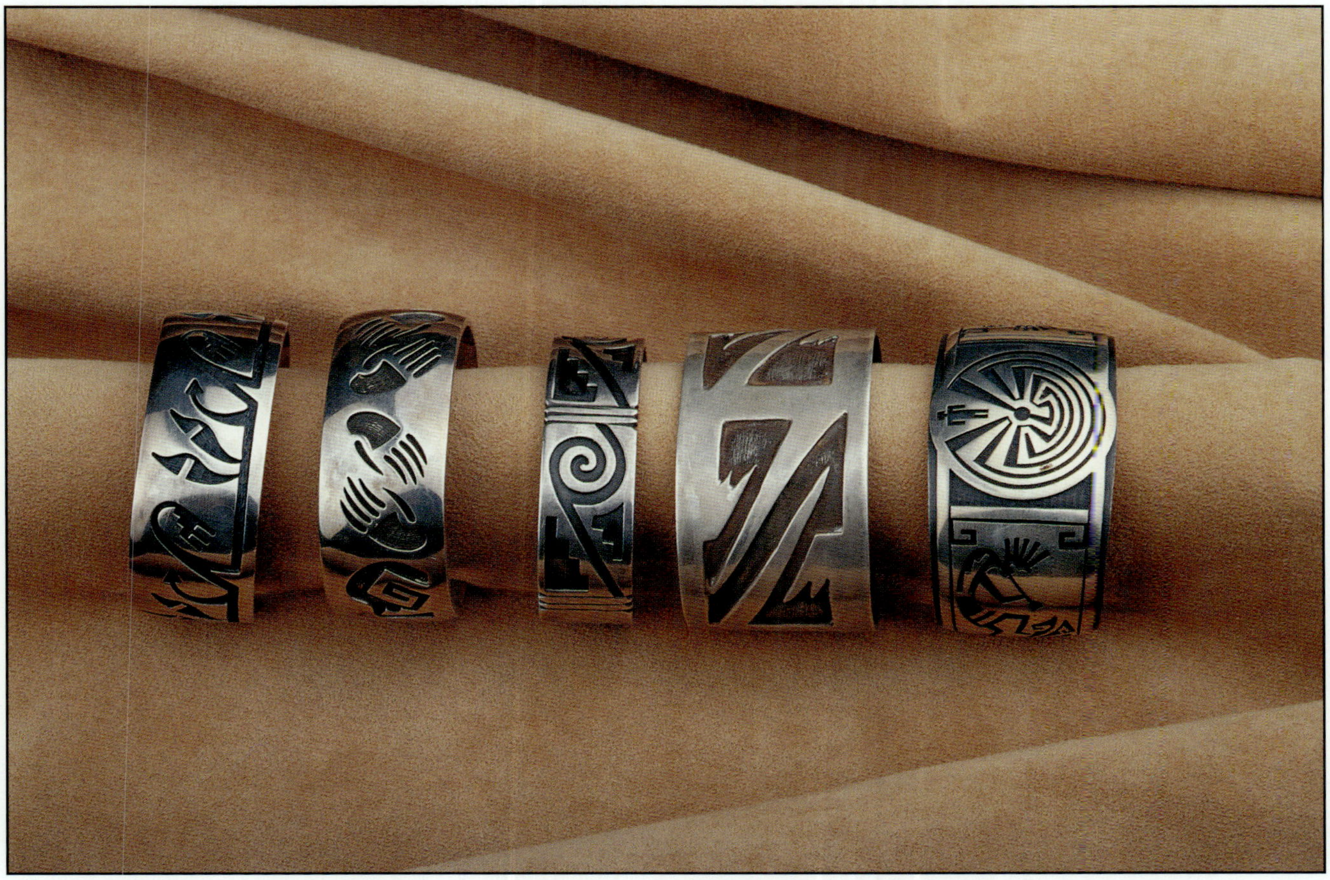

Group of five Hopi silver overlay bracelets with various designs. *Lynn D. Trusdell, Crown & Eagle Antiques*

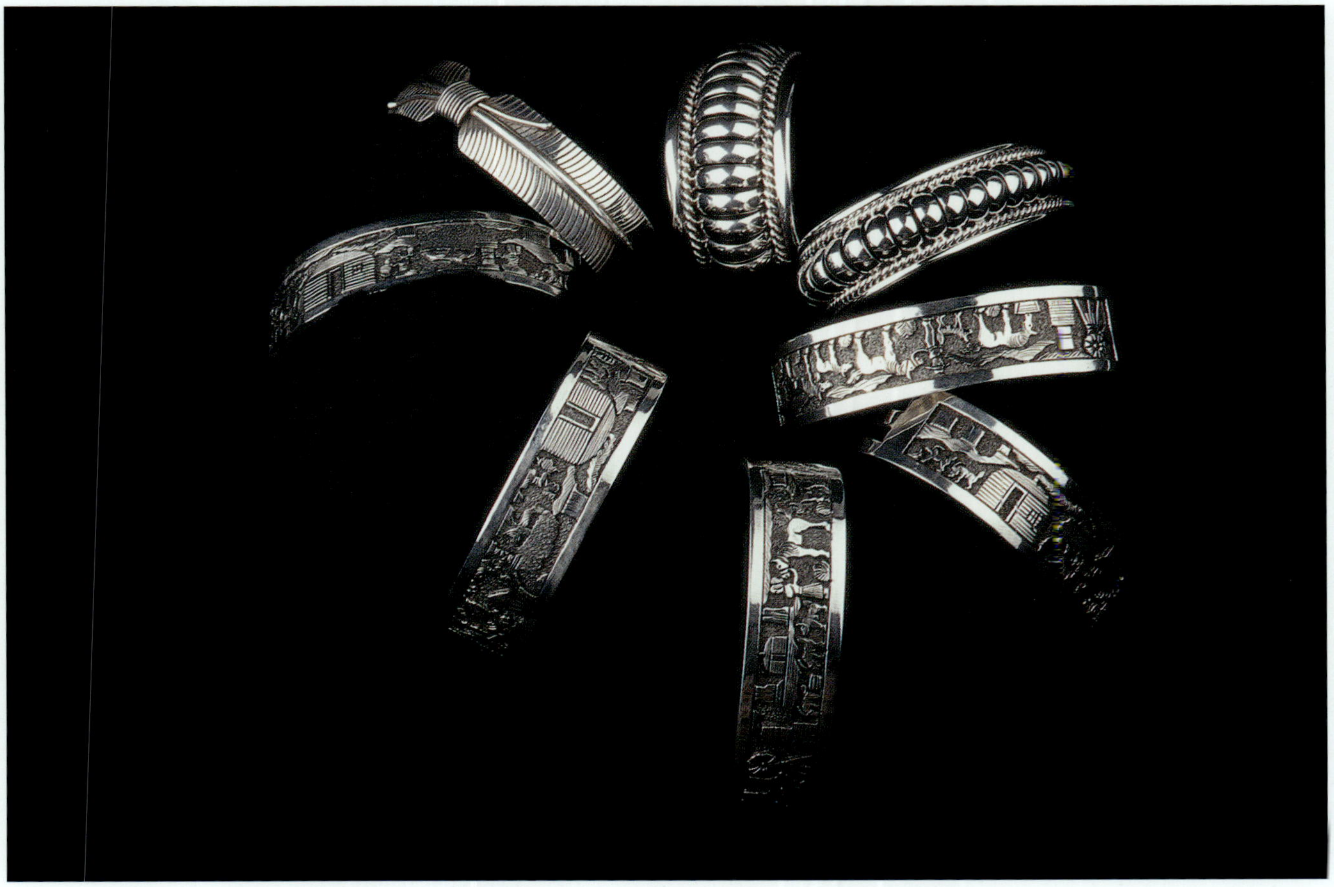

Group of Navajo silver bracelets, c. 2002. *Courtesy McGee's, Holbrook*

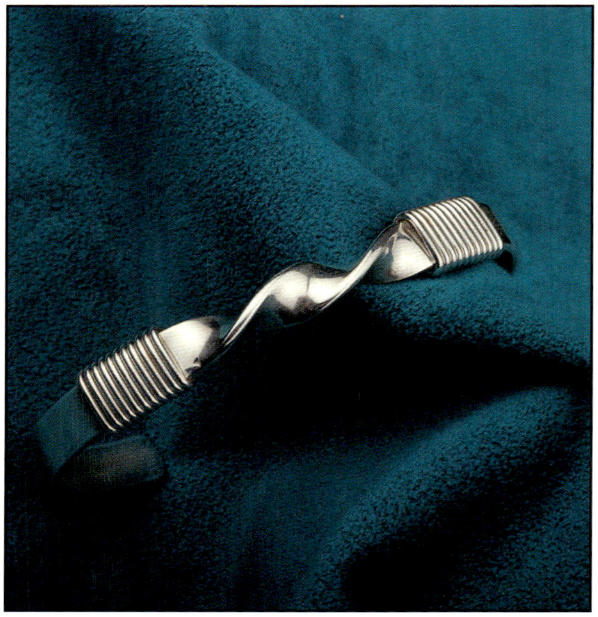

Silver bracelet with a double twist at the center, by Steve Arvizu, Navajo, 2002. *Courtesy of Palms Trading Company* ($30)

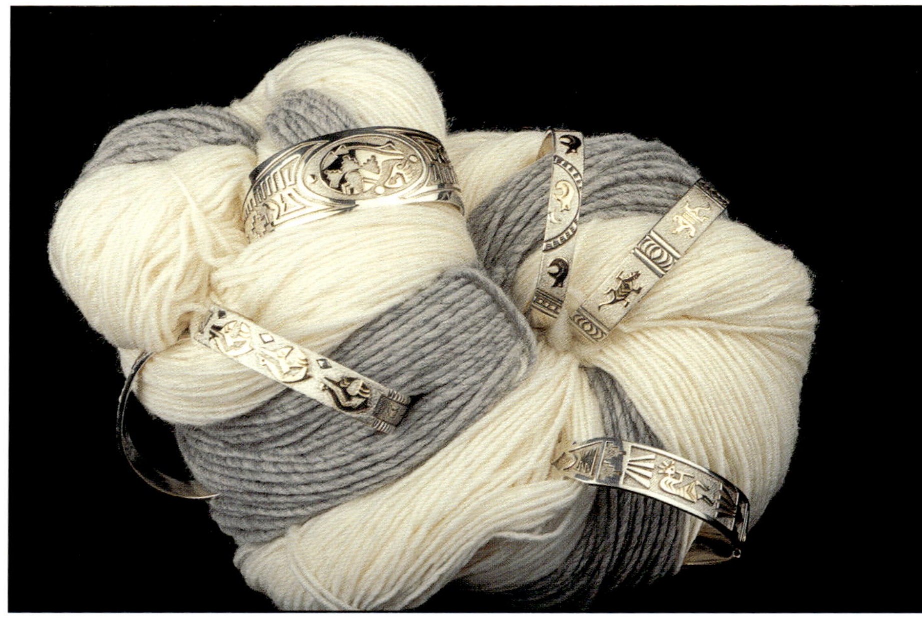

Six silver bracelets by Thomas Curtis, Navajo, 2002. Courtesy McGee's, Keams Canyon, Arizona

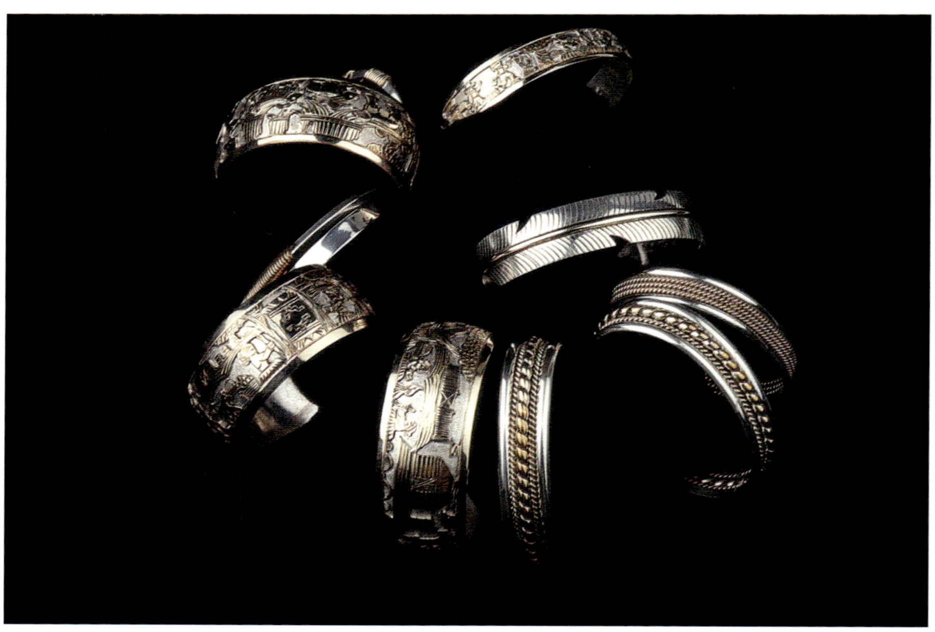

Group of eight Navajo silver and gold bracelets, 2002. *Courtesy McGee's, Holbrook*

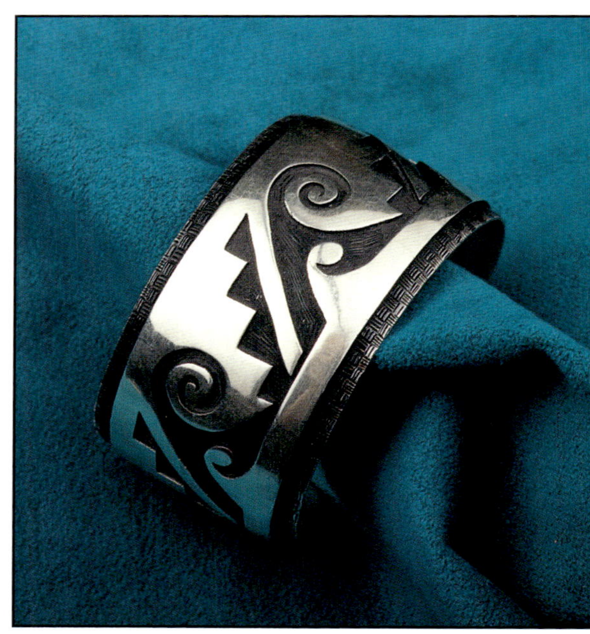

Silver overlay cuff bracelet by Joe Josytewa, Hopi, 2002. *Courtesy of Palms Trading Company* ($255)

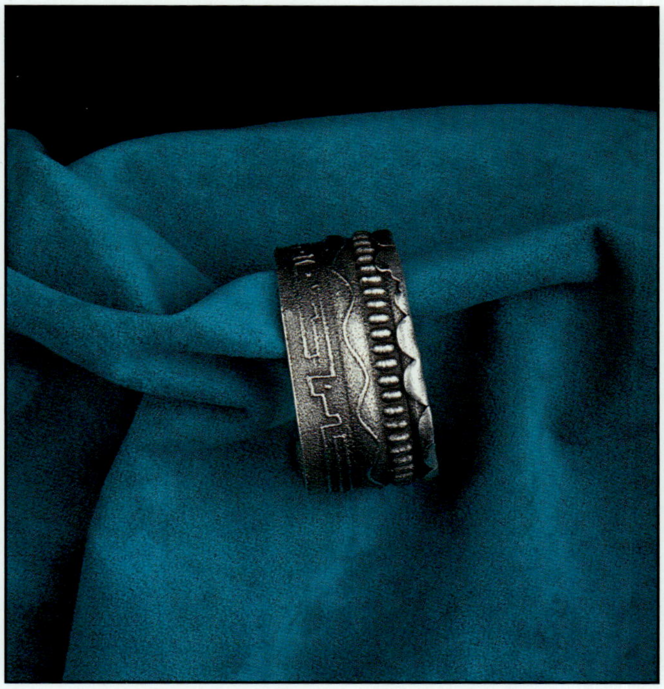

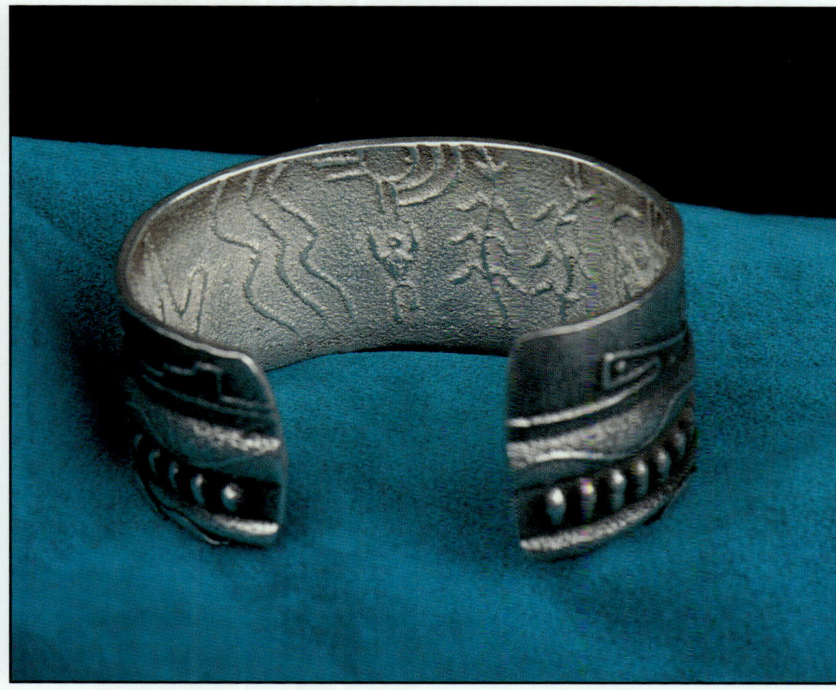

Sterling silver corn bracelet, by Anthony Lovato, Santo Domingo, 3-1/2" long x 1-1/4" wide, 2002. *Courtesy of Gerald Peters Gallery, Santa Fe, New Mexico* (500)

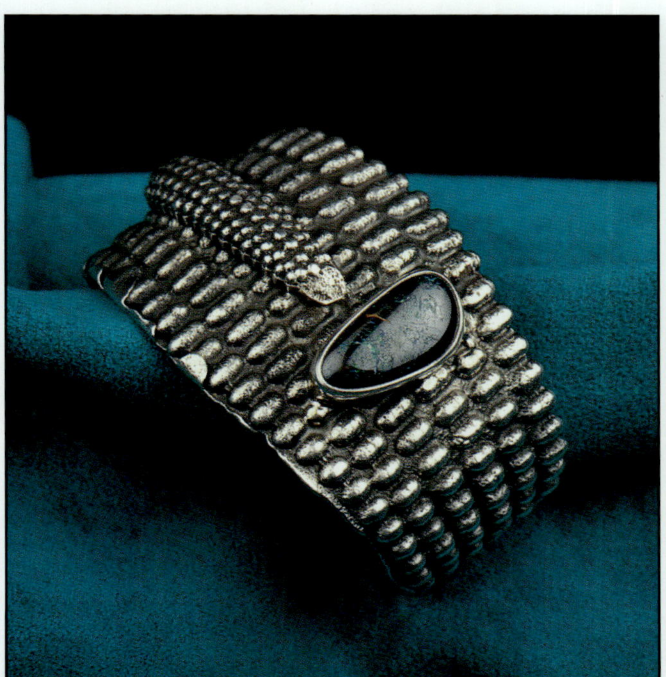

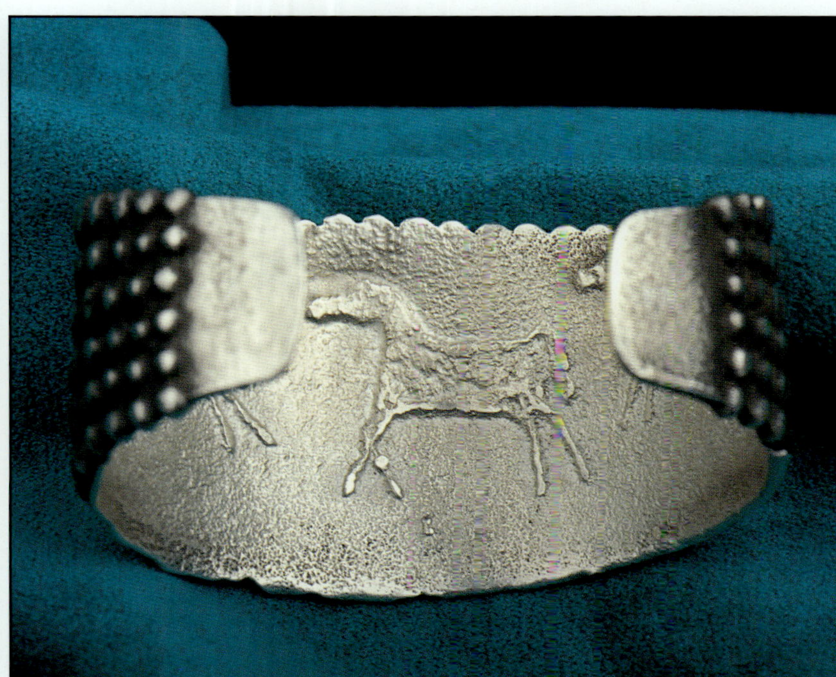

Sterling silver and Australian Boulder opal corn bracelet with inside horse design, by Anthony Lovato, Santo Domingo, 3-1/2" long x 1-1/4" wide, 2002. *Courtesy of Gerald Peters Gallery, Santa Fe, New Mexico*. (800)

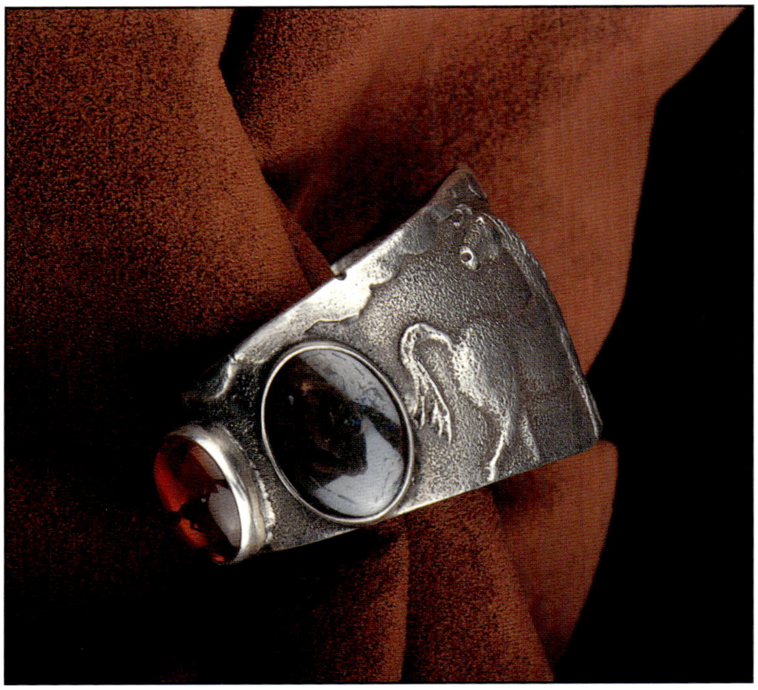

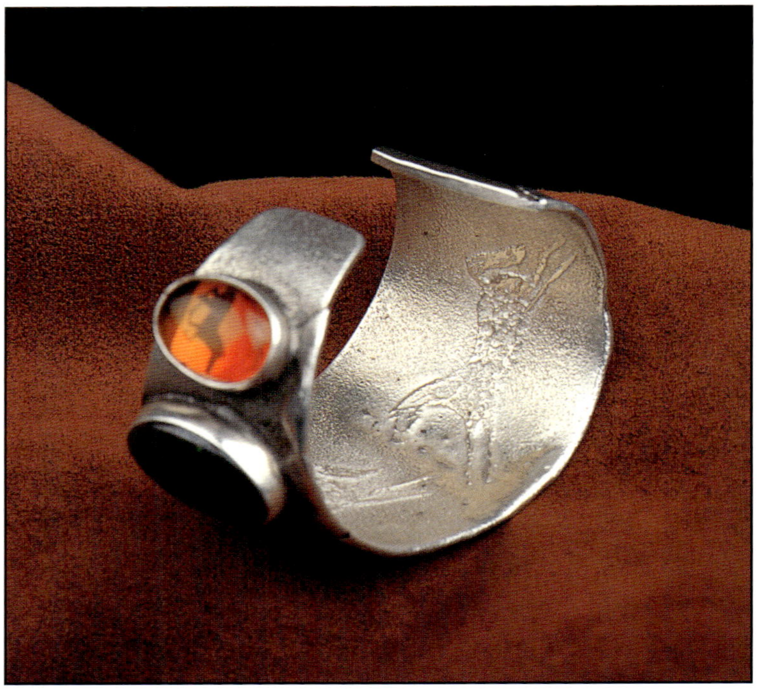

Sterling silver, Australian Boulder opal, and amber horse bracelet with inside three horse design, by Anthony Lovato, Santo Domingo, 3-1/2" long x 1-1/4" wide, 2002. *Courtesy of Gerald Peters Gallery, Santa Fe, New Mexico* (900)

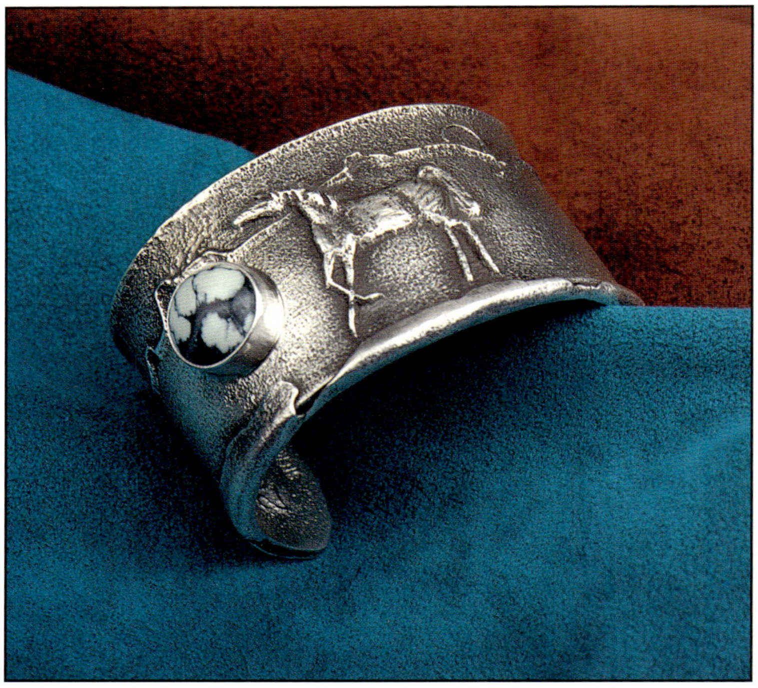

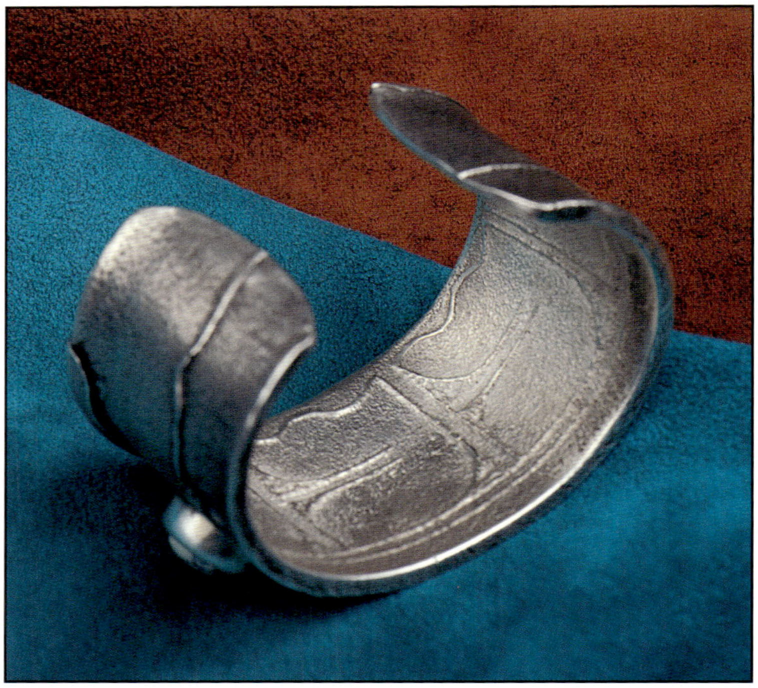

Sterling silver and variegated turquoise horse bracelet with inside pottery design, by Anthony Lovato, Santo Domingo, 3-1/2" long x 1-1/4" wide, 2002. *Courtesy of Gerald Peters Gallery, Santa Fe, New Mexico* (800)

The love for colorful displays led Southwest Indians to use materials from beyond their native area. Traders were able to get coral from Italy, which the Indians loved to combine with turquoise and shell. In the early days, large necklaces of coral beads were rare and valuable.

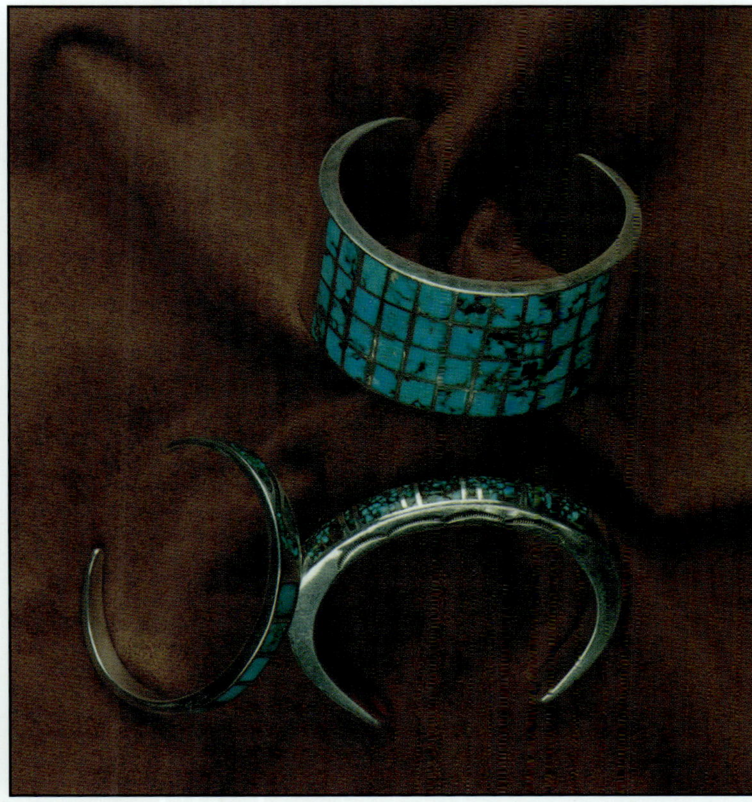

Wide cuff with four rows of channel inlay from the 1930s. / Narrow silver bracelet with curved and rectangular cut turquoise channel inlay. / Silver bracelet with stamped side decoration and #8 spiderweb turquoise channel inlay. *Turquoise Lady collection*

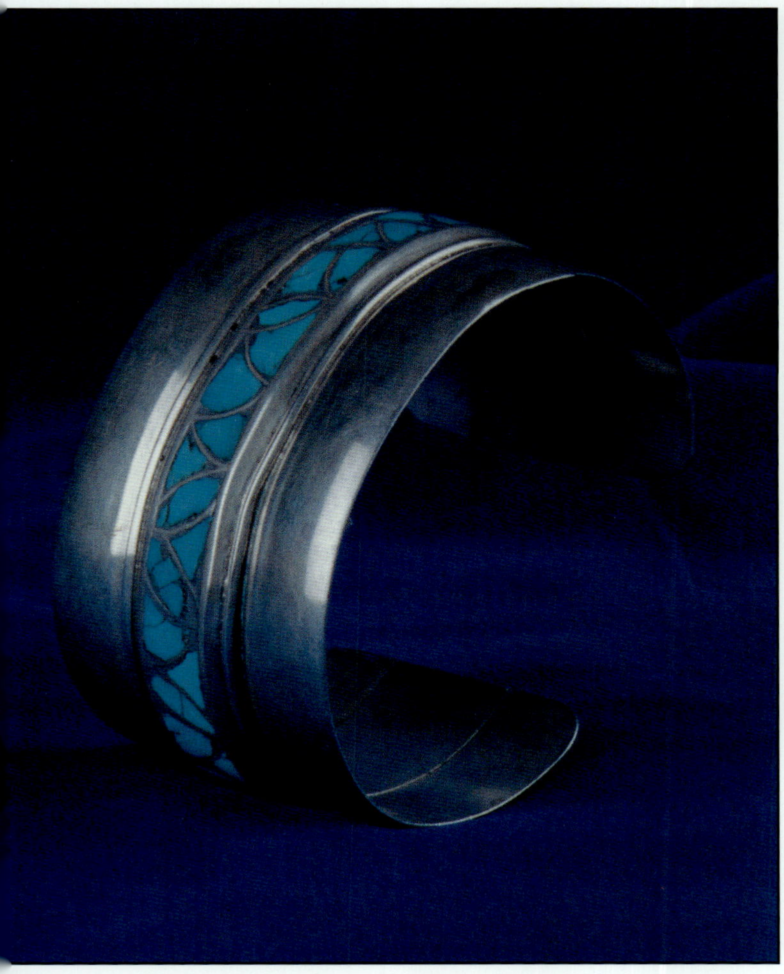

Sterling cuff with Morenci turquoise channel inlaid design by Rosita Wahlela, Zuni, circa 1971.

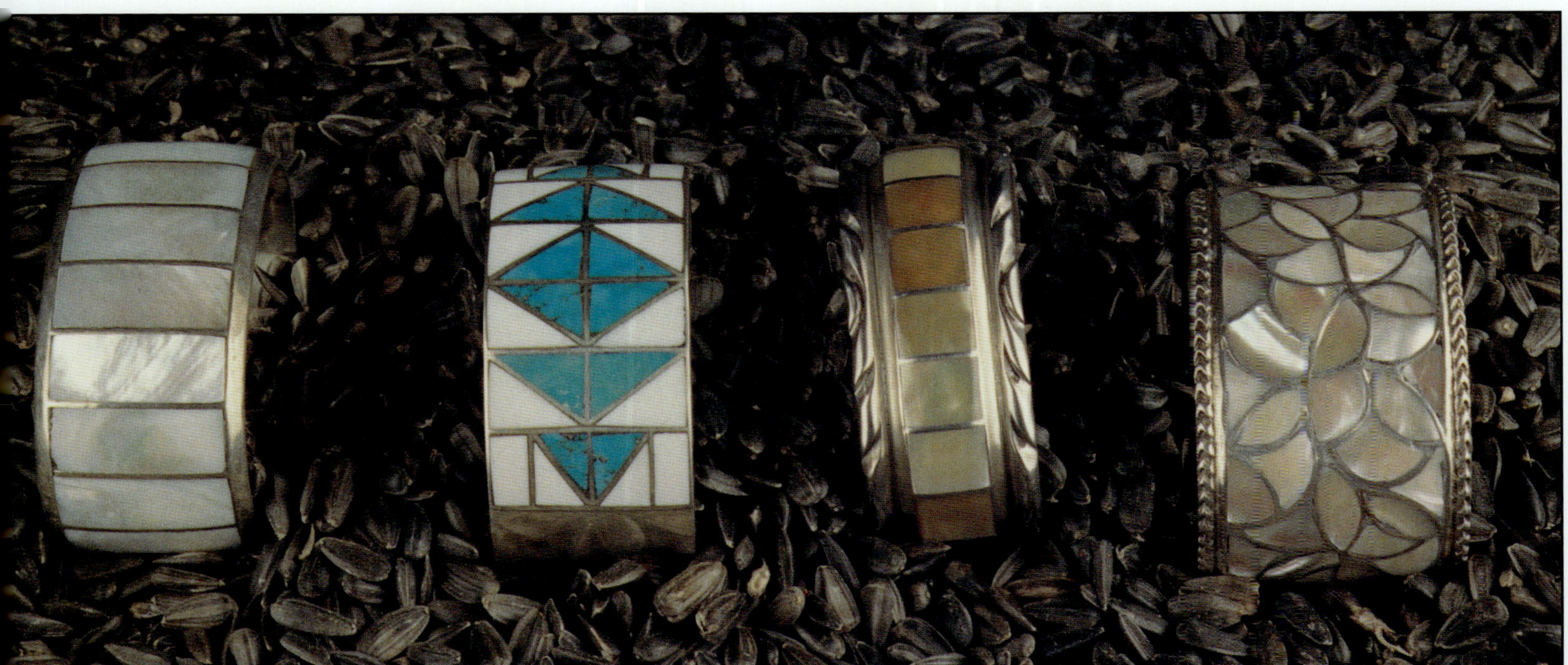

Four silver cuffs decorated with different shell and turquoise channel inlay by Zuni jewelers. *Enchanted Mesa collection*

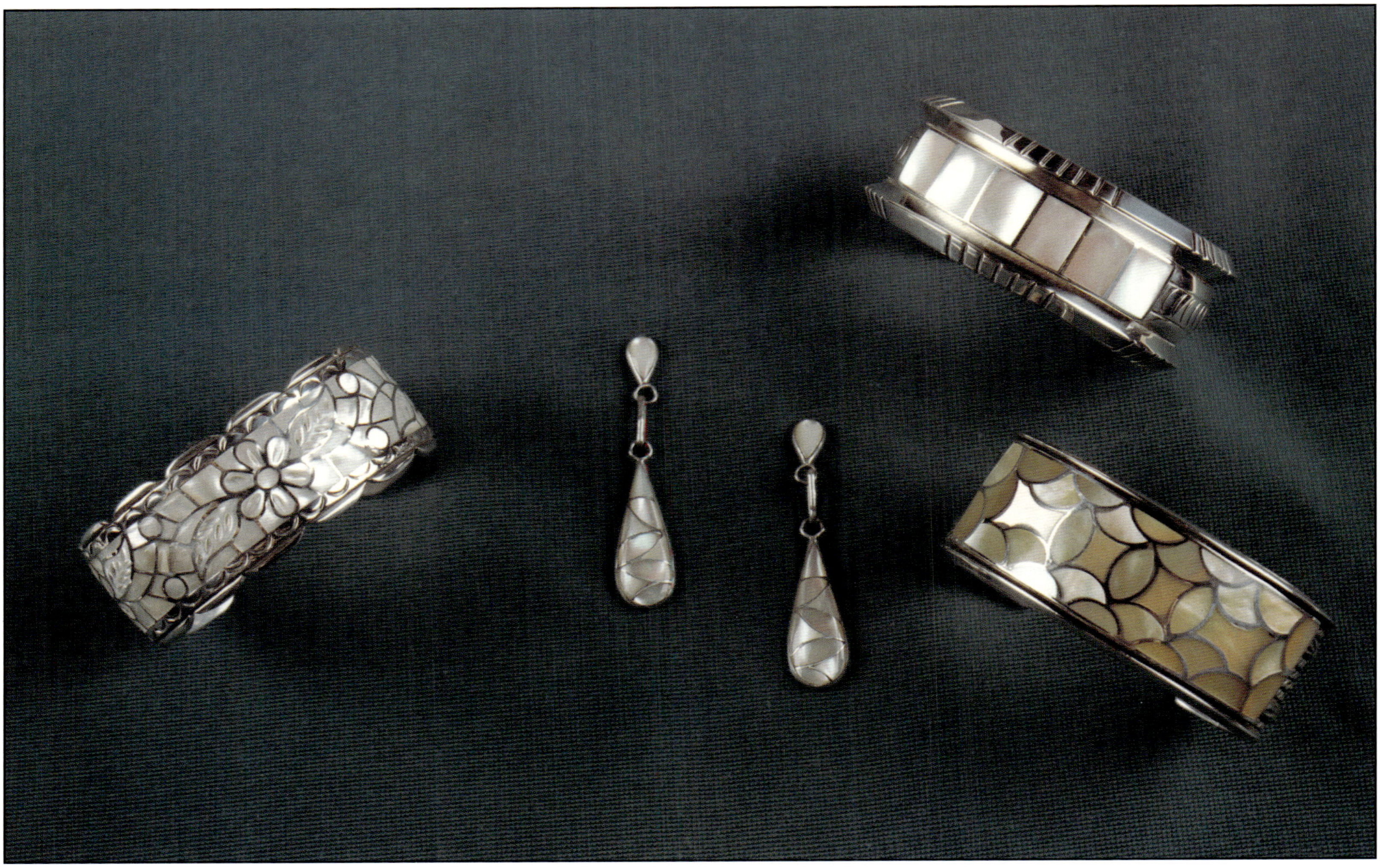

Zuni bracelets and earrings of silver with shell channel inlay decoration from the 1980s: Left, lacy green snail shell inlay by Rick Leekela. / Right, yellow clamshell channel inlay by Neil and Shirley Natewa. *Indian Post collection*

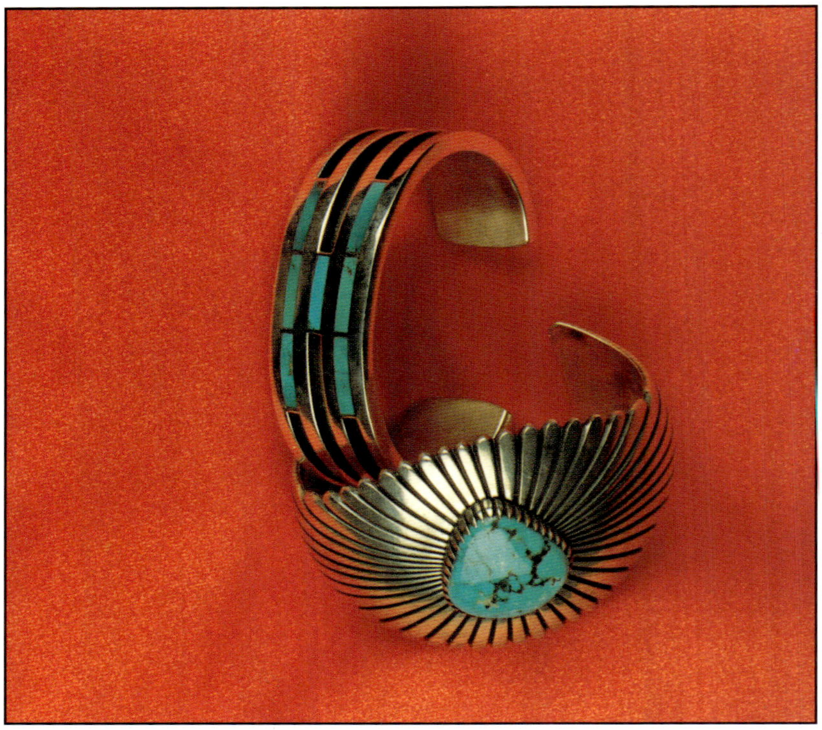

Two bracelets of heavy silver ornamented with turquoise set in channel inlay and in a serrated bezel, made by Navajo artist Kee Joe Benally, 1970s. *Private collection*

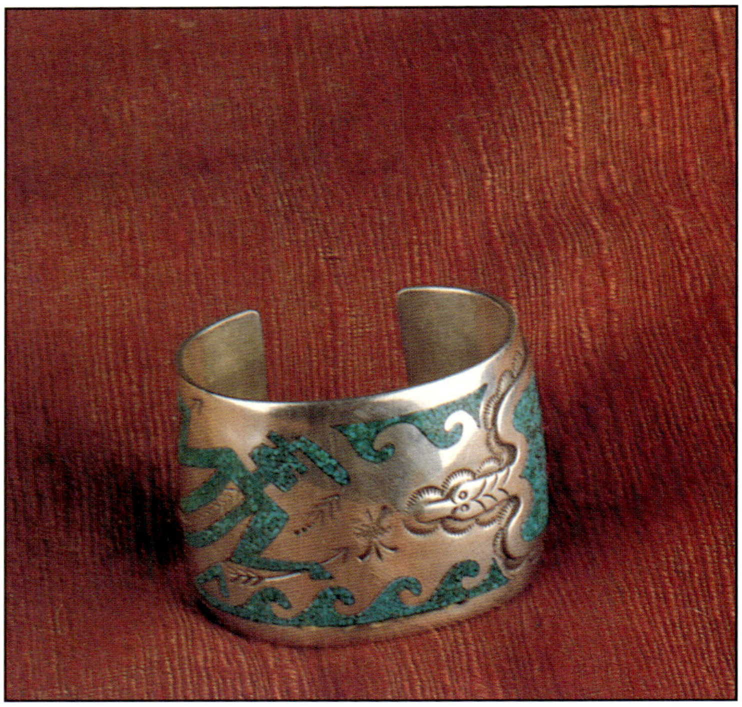

Silver cuff decorated with stamped work and turquoise chips mixed and inlaid with resin. The origin of this "chip inlay" technique is credited to Navajo jeweler Dean Kirk about 1961. Navajo artist Tommy Singer made this bracelet in the 1970s. *Enchanted Mesa collection*

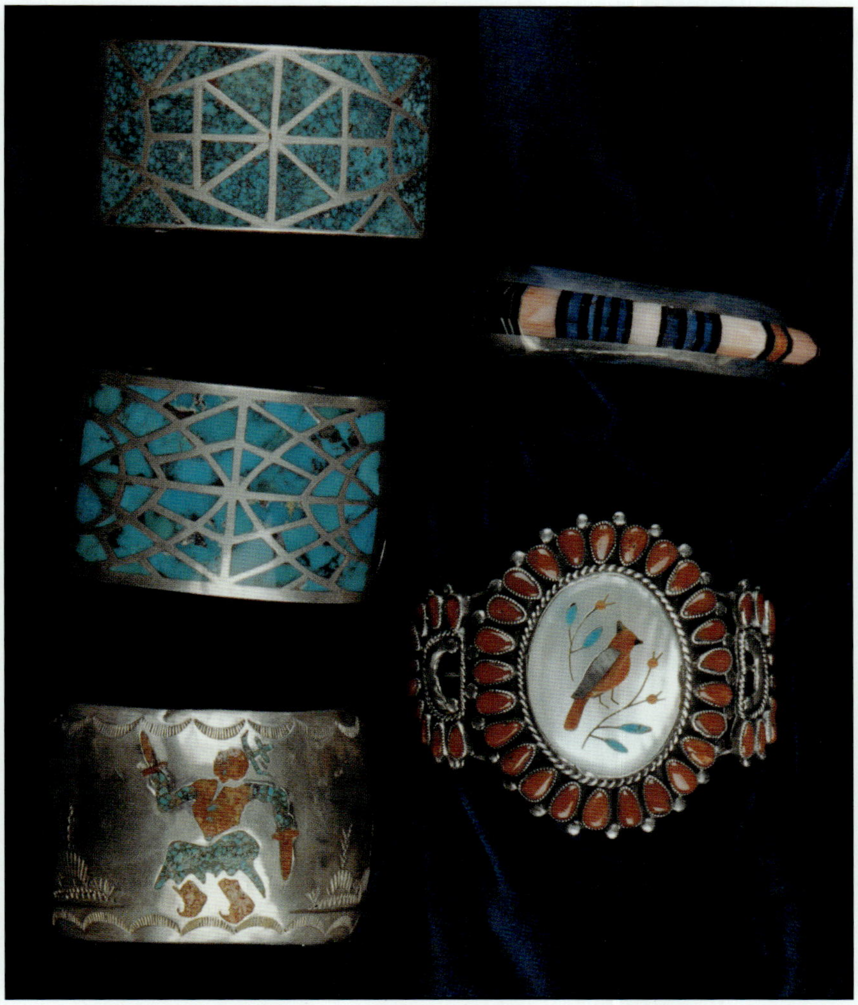

A wonderful assortment of bracelets displaying various forms of inlaid decoration including channel, stone to stone, and direct techniques of figural and geometric designs. *Private collection on permanent loan to Ohio University*

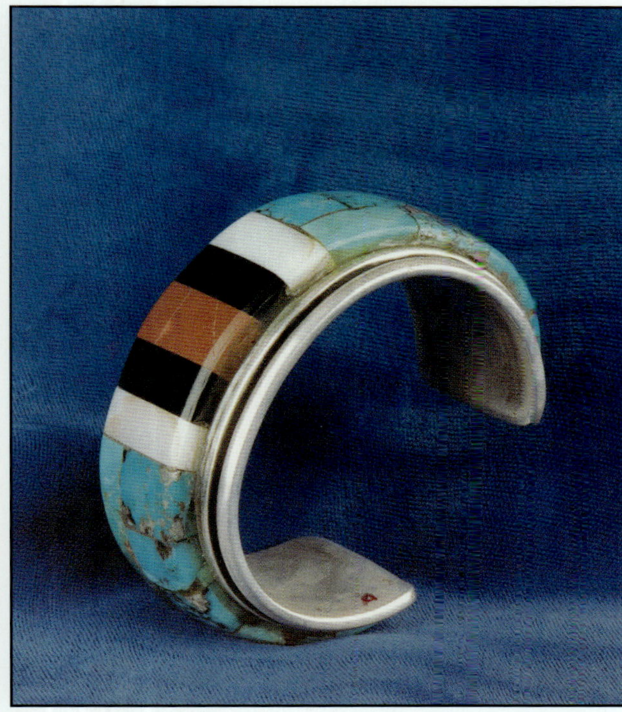

Cuff bracelet in silver with turquoise, shell, onyx and coral stone to stone inlay by P S (unlisted), circa 1980. *Maxwell Museum collection*

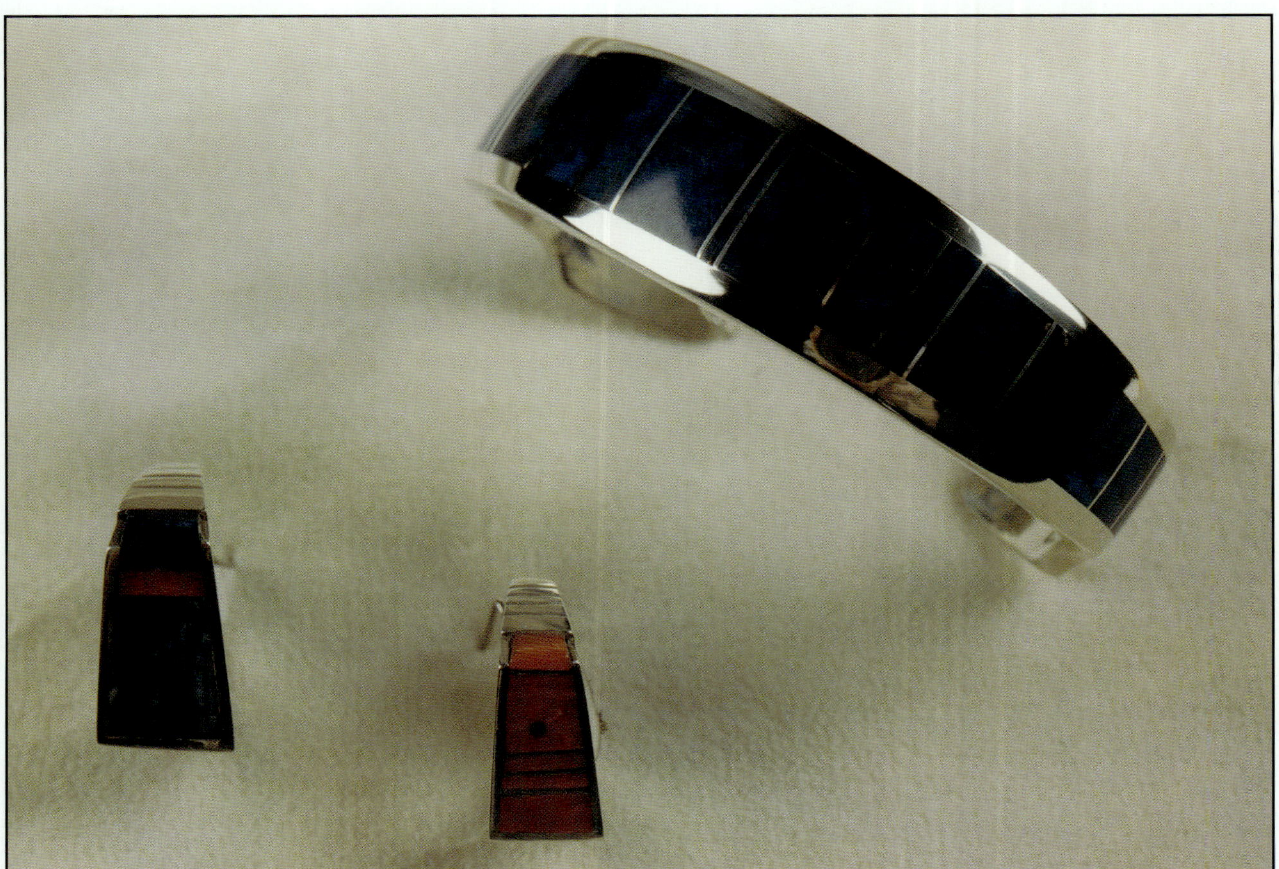

Two finger rings and a bracelet of silver set in channel inlay with lapis lazuli and coral, made by Navajo Ray Tracy's Knifewing workshop, late 1980s. *Indian Post collection*

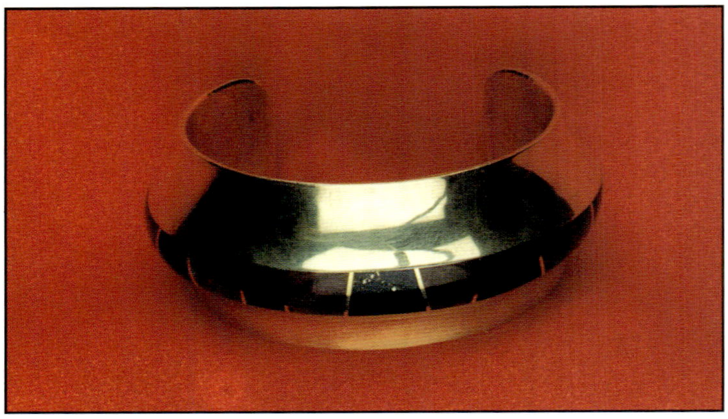

Cuff bracelet of sculpted silver with a lavulite and lapis lazuli channel-inlaid band, late 1980s. *Private collection*

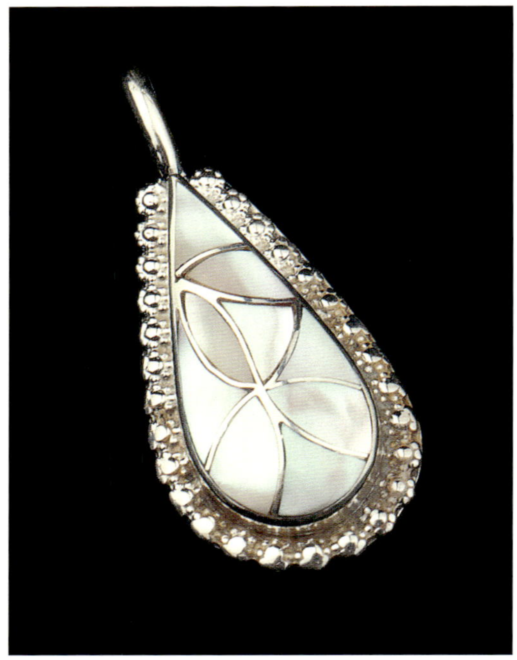

Sterling silver teardrop pendant with inlayed green snailshell by Orlinda Natewa, Navajo, 2002. *Courtesy of Palms Trading Company* ($54)

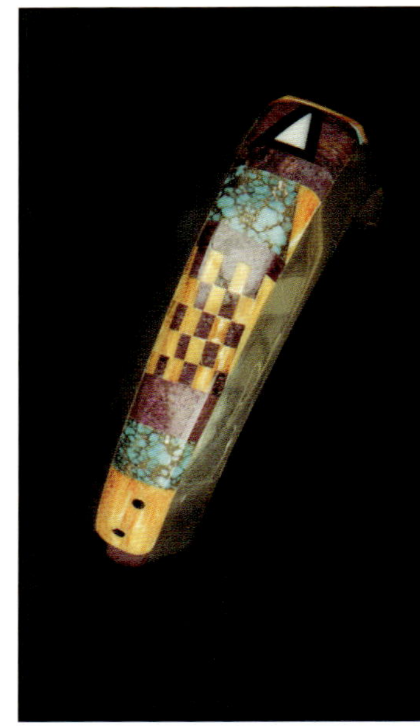

Silver bracelet with imaginative mosaic stone inlay design by Larry C., late 1980s. *Turquoise Lady collection*

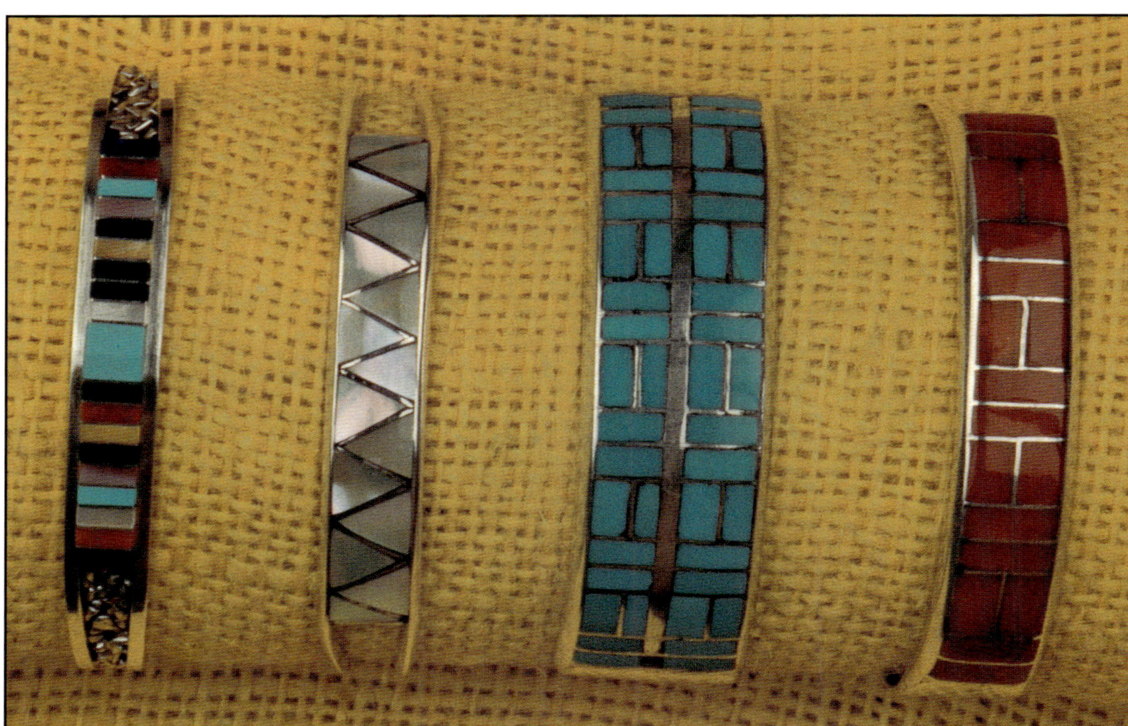

Four inlaid bracelets made in 1989: Stone to stone inlaid silver bracelet by S J T. / Yellow shell channel inlay in silver. / Turquoise channel inlay by Tsadiase, Zuni. / Coral channel inlay bracelet on silver. *Bing Crosby collection*

Channel inlay bracelets

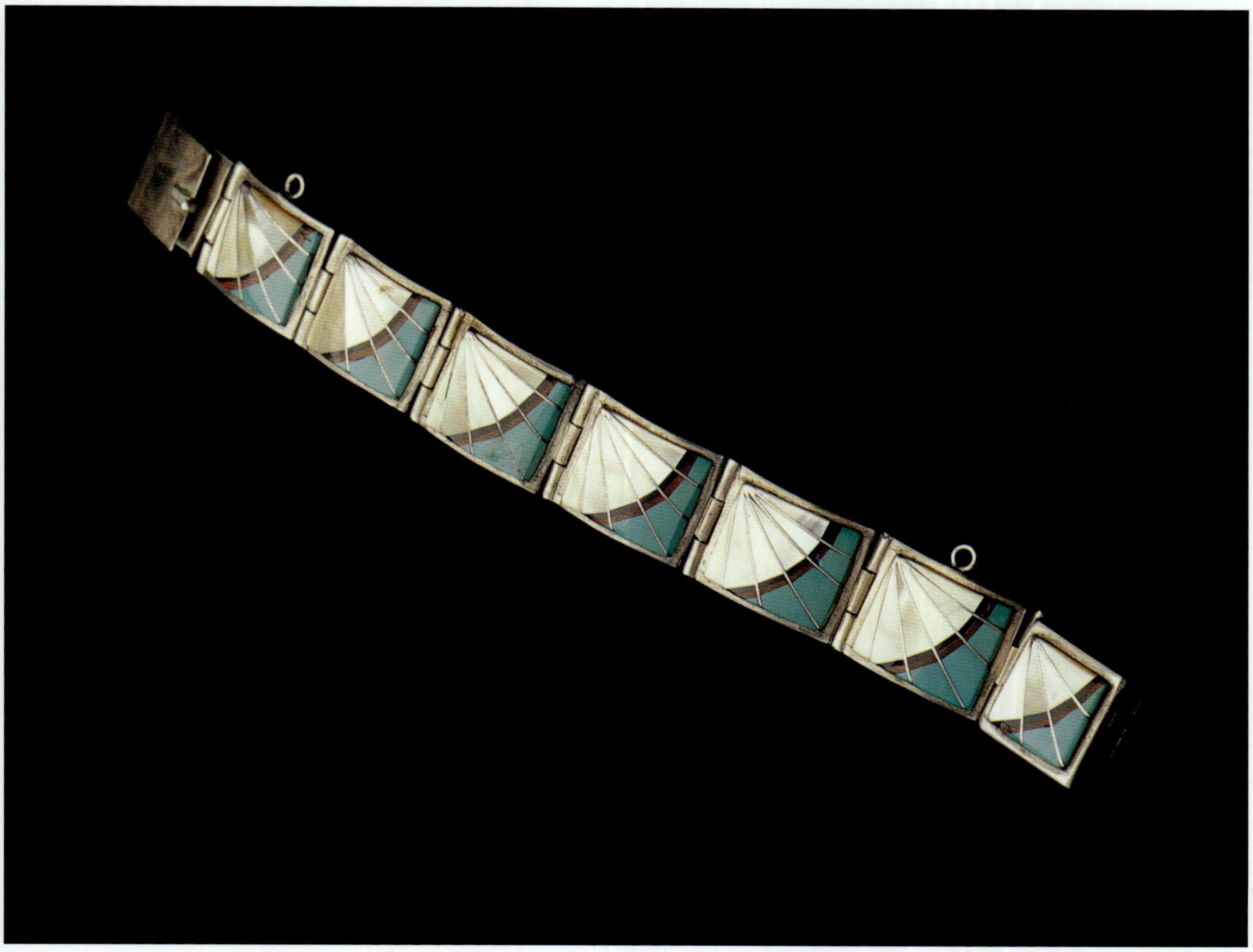

Zuni link bracelet with shell, turquoise, coral, and jet channel inlayed pattern, c. 1990.

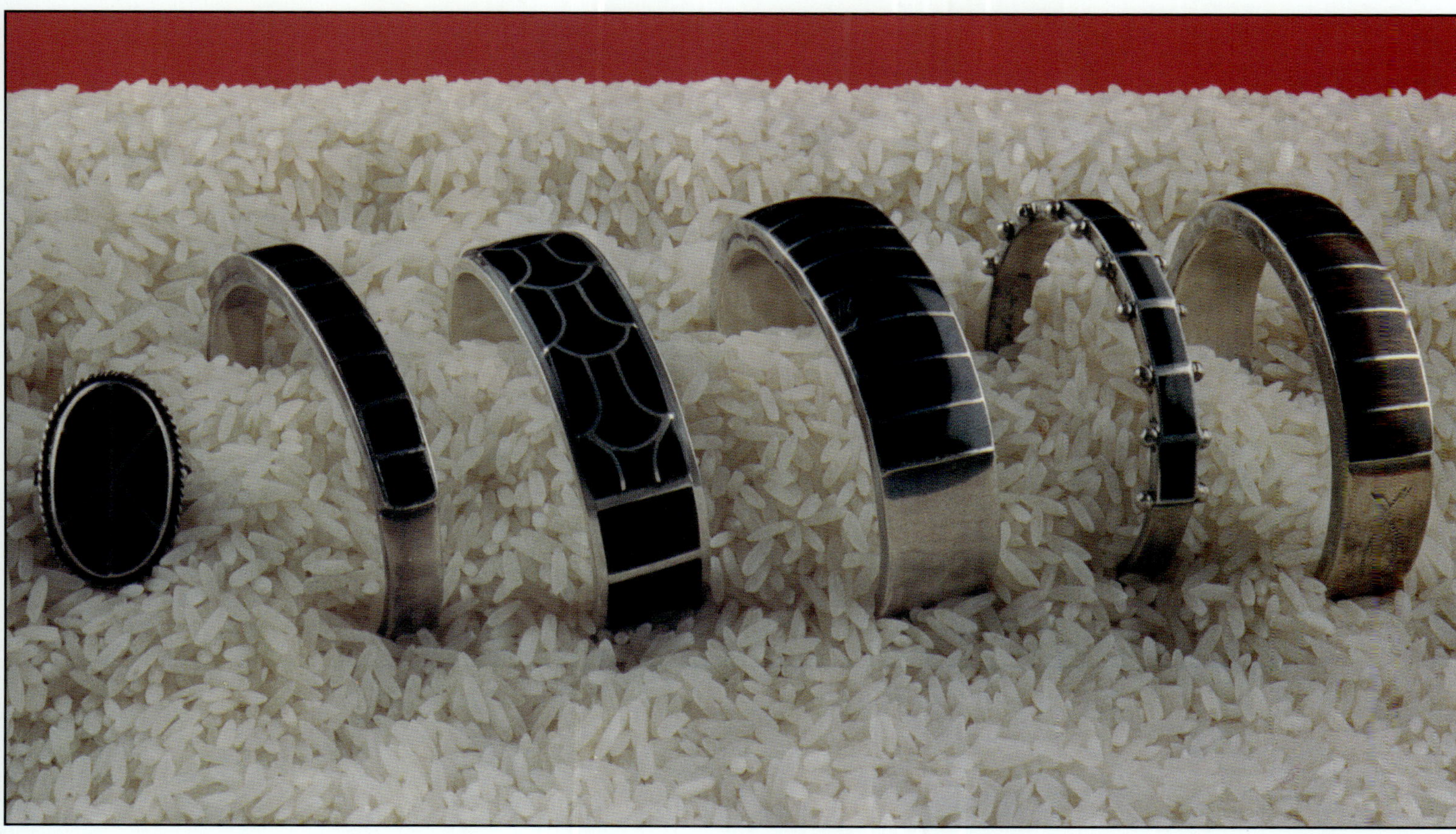

Zuni artists made this ring and group of five bracelets with channel-inlayed ironwood and jet in the 1980s. *Enchanted Mesa collection*

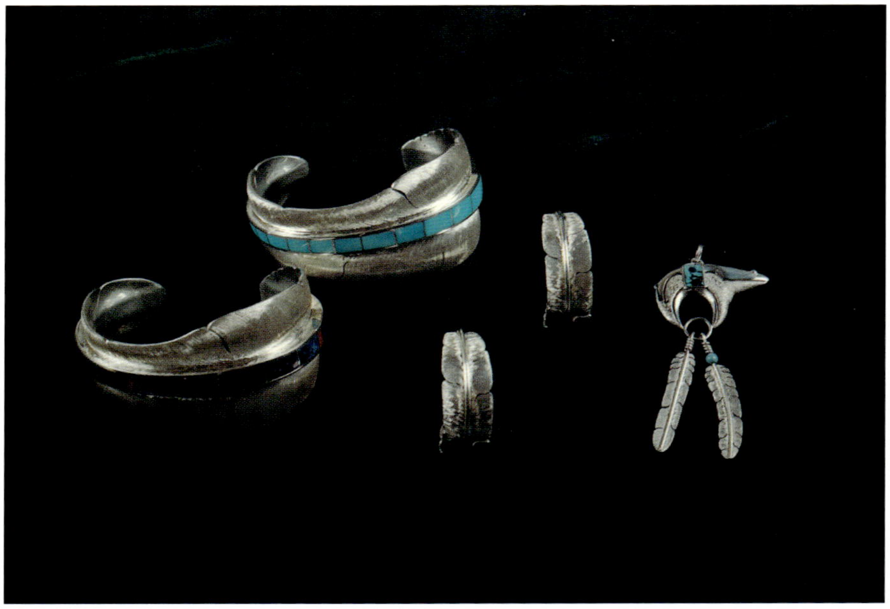

Modern bracelets

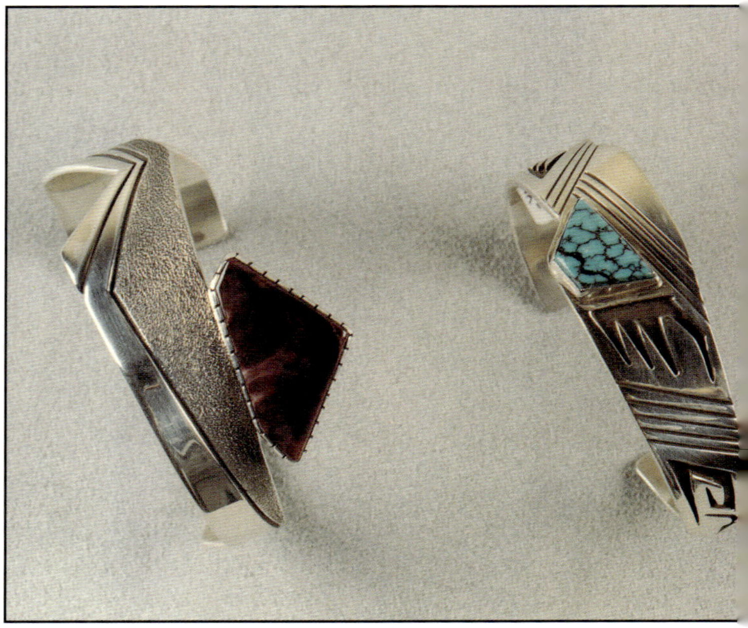

Silver bracelets of modern design from the late 1980s: angular design with attached purple spiny oyster shell by Mike Platero. / Overlay design with turquoise inlay by Aaron Tsadlena. *Indian Post collection*

Group of silver jewelry in feather design by Michael Kirk, Navajo, circa 1989, including bracelets inlaid either with turquoise or lapis lazuli band, earrings, and pendant with a bear figure. *Indian Post collection*

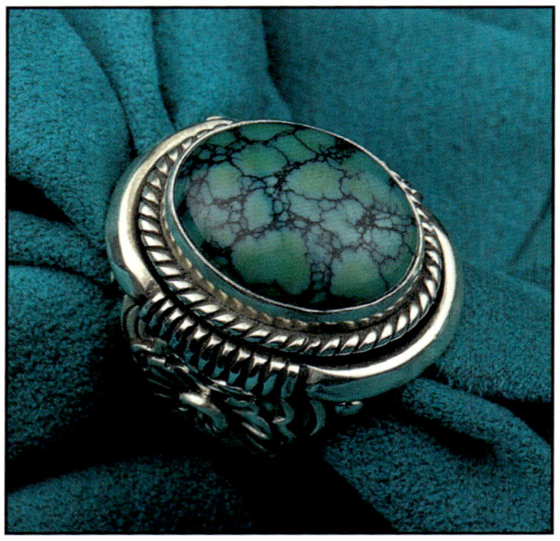

Ring with an oval, green stabilized turquoise by Ben Begay, Navajo, 2002. *Courtesy of Palms Trading Company* ($189)

Jet and silver are combined to form classic fashion designs from the 1980s: Left, bracelet by Zuni lapidarist and silversmith Clara Gasper. / Wire band bracelet with large jet stone by Joe Rosetta, Santo Domingo. / Cuff by Navajo silversmith D. A. Jackson. / Pair of earrings by David Yellowhorse, Navajo. *Indian Post collection*.

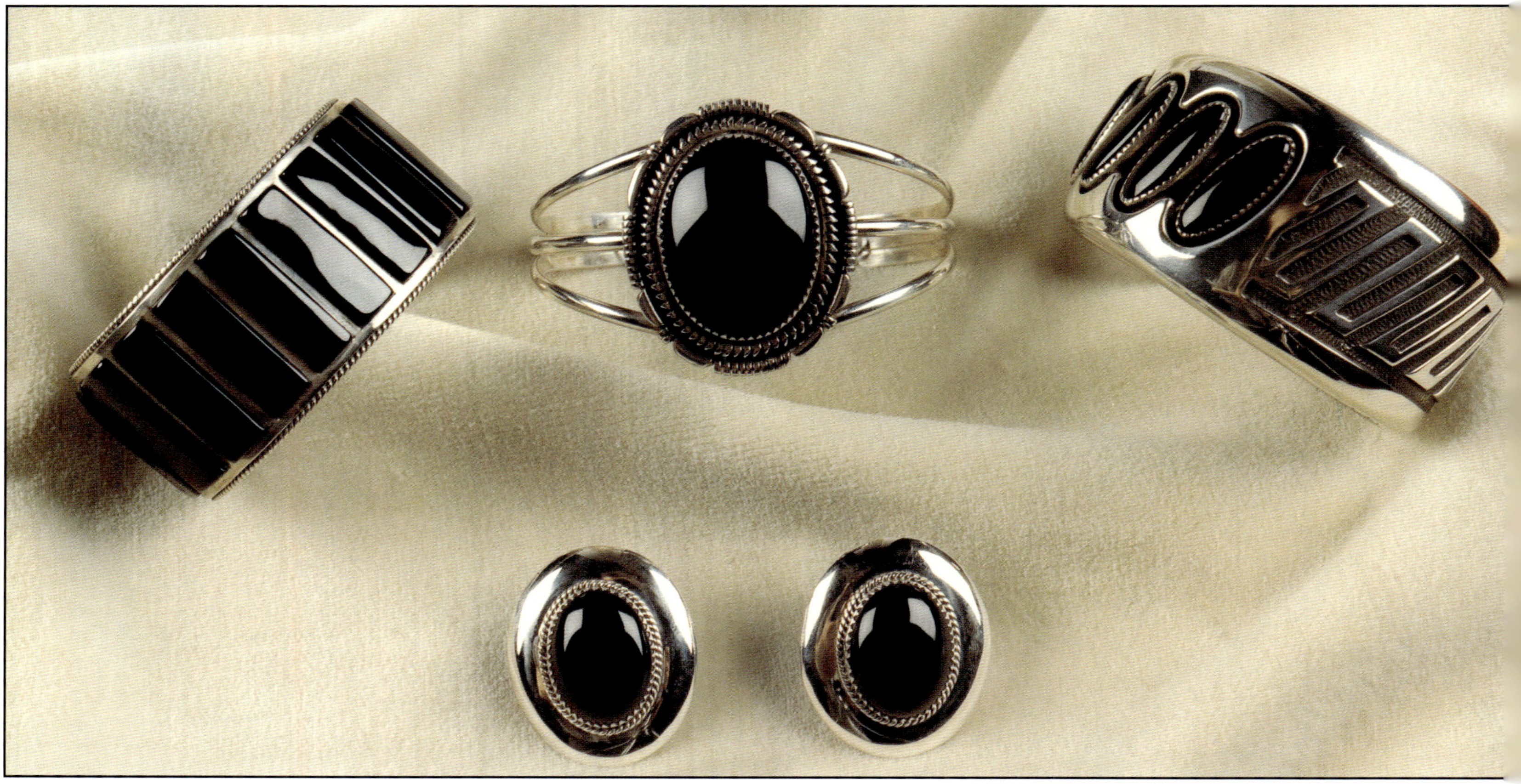

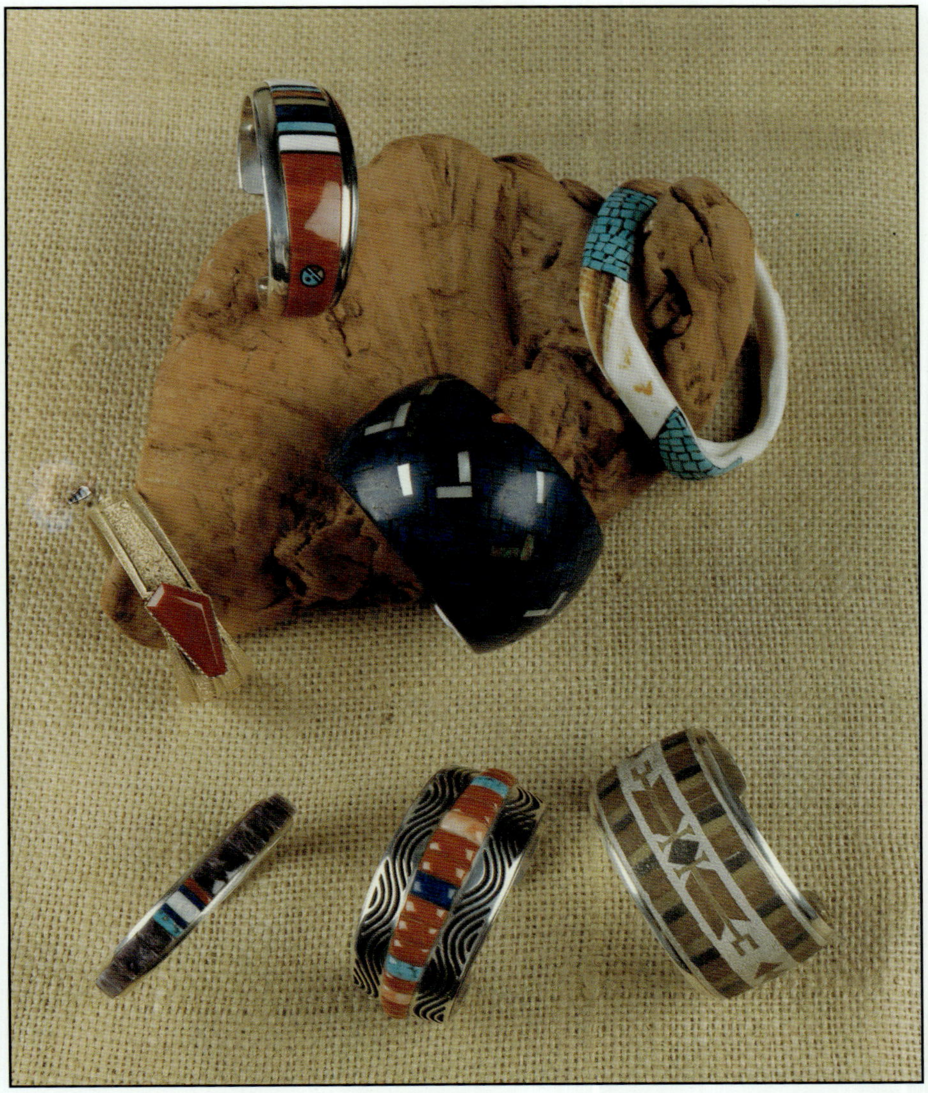

Seven bracelets from the 1980s representing a variety of modern decorative ideas. Clockwise on the wood: silver bracelet with a variety of colorful flat stone inlay by Jessie Monongye, Navajo. / Shell disc inlaid with turquoise by Angie Reano Owen, Santo Domingo. / Shell covered with stone and shell mosaic by Angie Reano Owen, Santo Domingo. / Gold bracelet with coral by Al Nez, Navajo. / Below left: Mosaic stone to stone inlay in a line design by Phil Russell. / Stamped silver bracelet with a line of coral and stone inlay by Lee Yazzi, Navajo. / Sterling and metal inlay bracelet decorated with old Cheyenne beadwork designs by Ben Nighthorse, Cheyenne, 1989. *Indian Post collection*

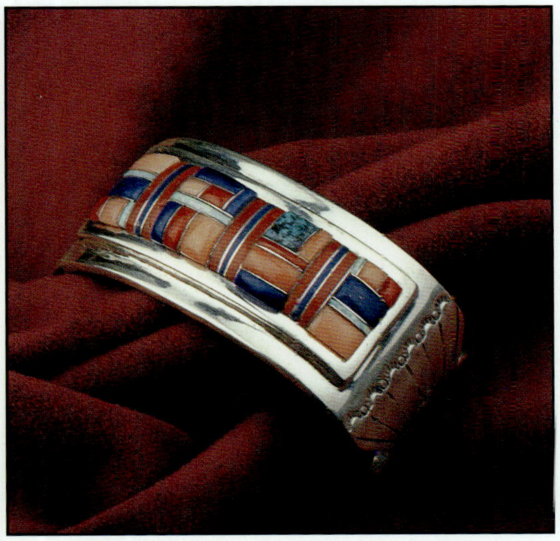

Silver cuff bracelet with assorted stone inlay by Cathy Sanchez, Navajo, 2002. *Courtesy of Palms Trading Company* ($750)

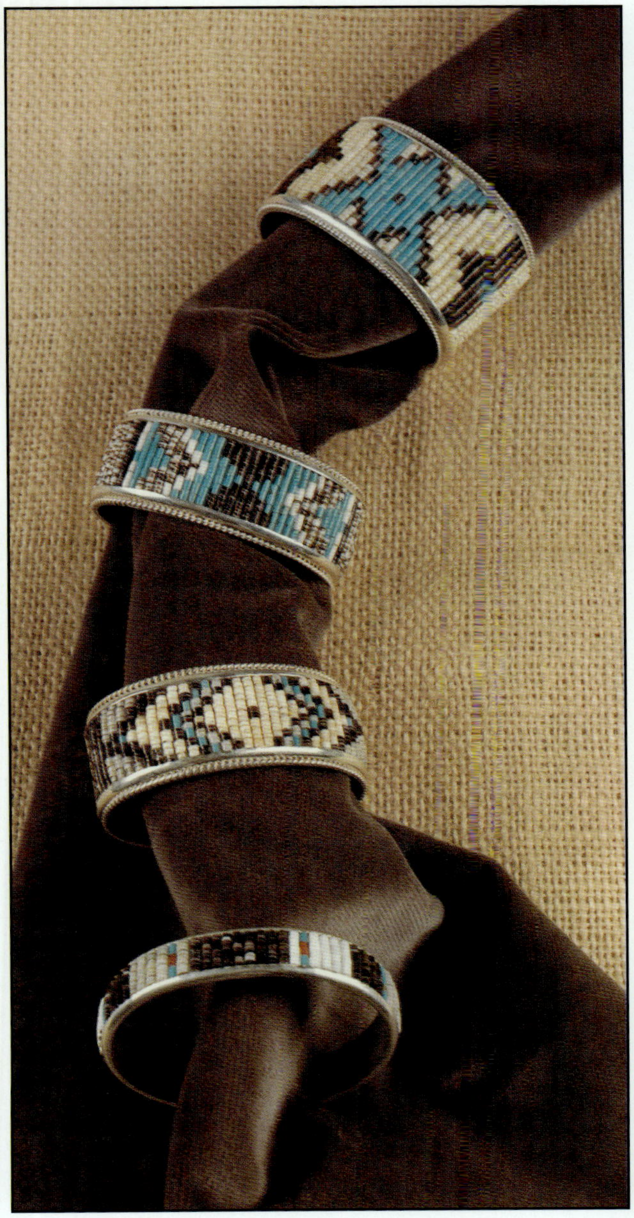

Colorful beadwork creates an innovative style on these silver bracelets by Navajo artist Louise Clark. *Indian Post collection*

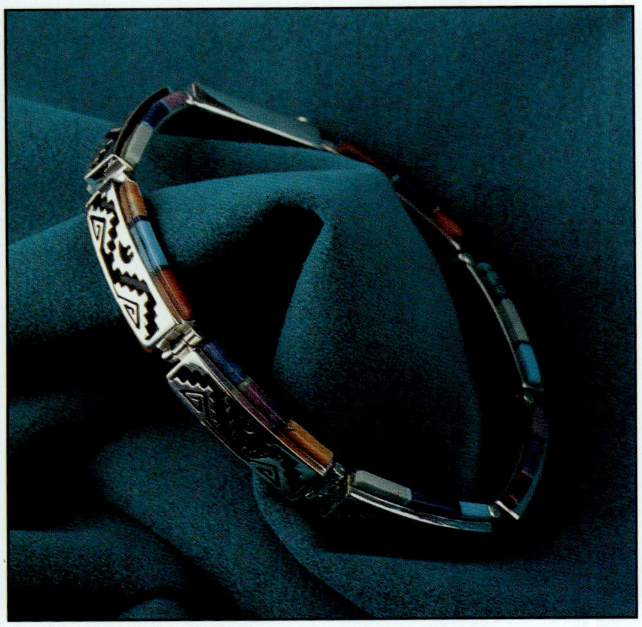

Bracelet by Earl Plummer, Navajo, 2002. *Courtesy McGee's, Holbrook*

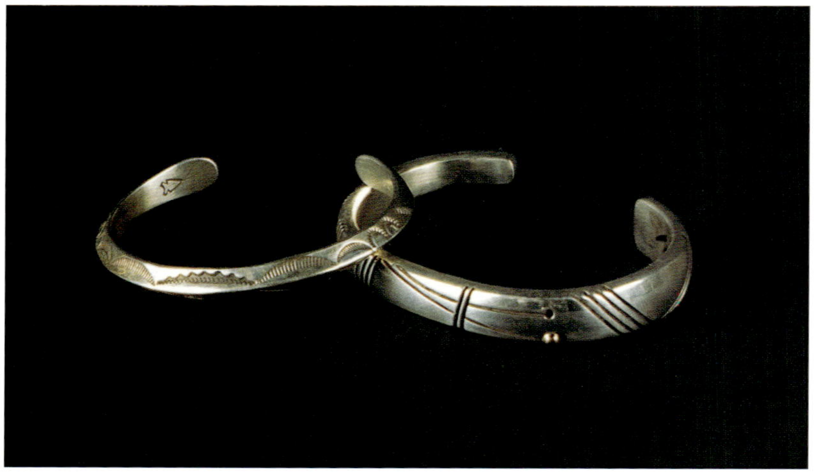

Two Navajo sterling bracelets from the 1980s: stamped triangular band by Charlie Singer. / Rectangular band with geometric stamping by Jimmy King, Jr. *Shiprock Trading Company collection*

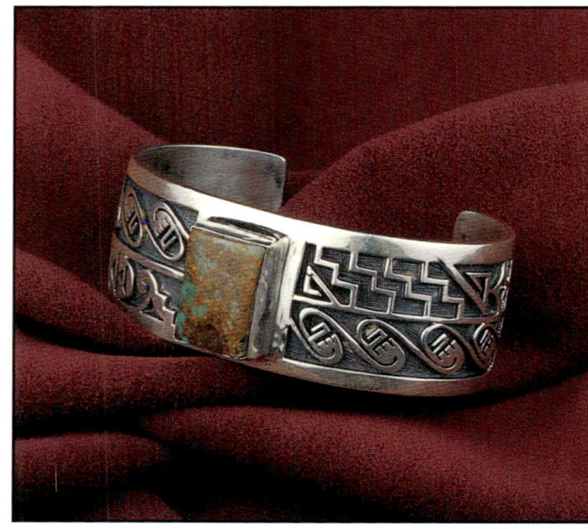

Silver cuff bracelet with rectangular green turquoise stone, by Tim Yazzie, Navajo-Hopi. *Courtesy of Palms Trading Company* ($450)

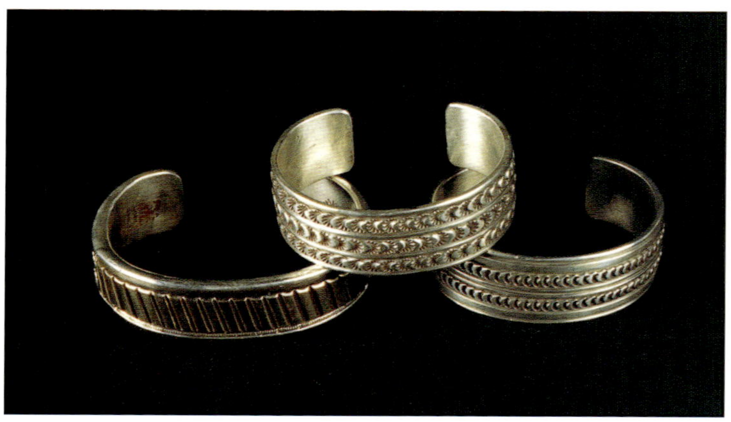

Three beautifully stamped sterling silver bracelets by Bruce Morgan, 1989. *Shiprock Trading Company collection*

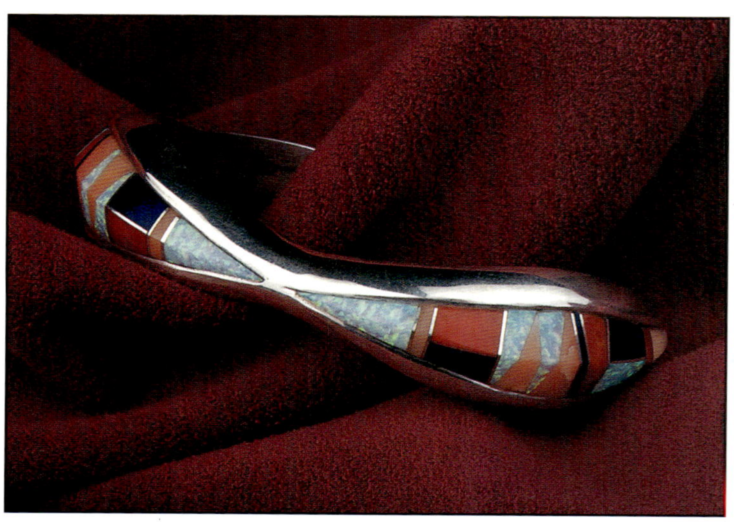

Silver cuff bracelet with various stone inlay by Juan Aguilar, Isleta. *Courtesy of Palms Trading Company* ($330)

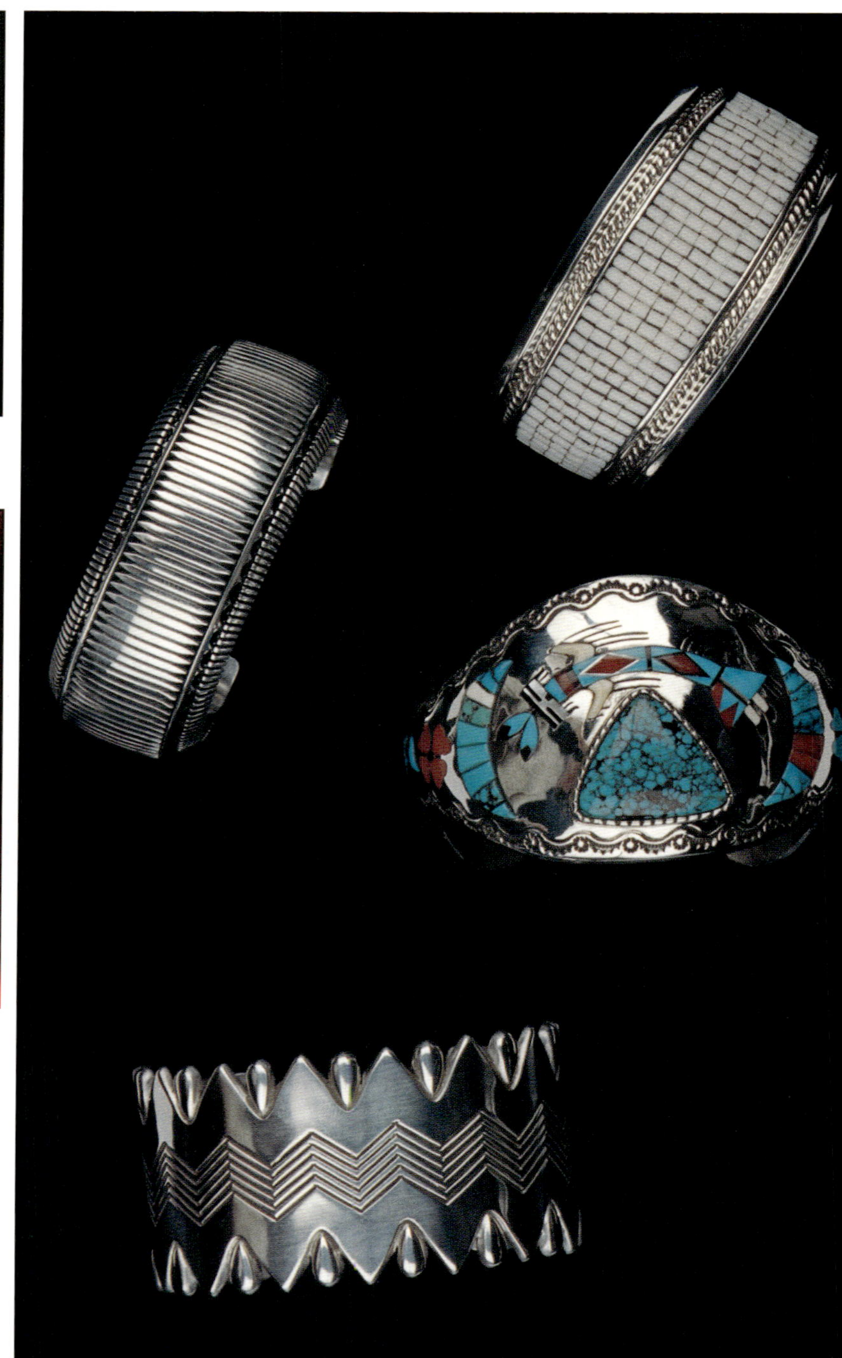

Four exceptional bracelets of contemporary designs in sterling silver by Navajo artists, 1989: From the top, with white beadwork mosaic decoration by D. A. Jackson. / Precision silverwork creates a mosaic effect, by Howard Nelson. / Colorful inlay of turquoise and coral including a Yei figure and triangular turquoise stone in shaped and stamped silver by Jacob I. (Jake) Livingston. / Zigzag lines both form and decorate this silver bracelet by Thomas Curtis. *Keams Canyon Arts & Crafts collection*

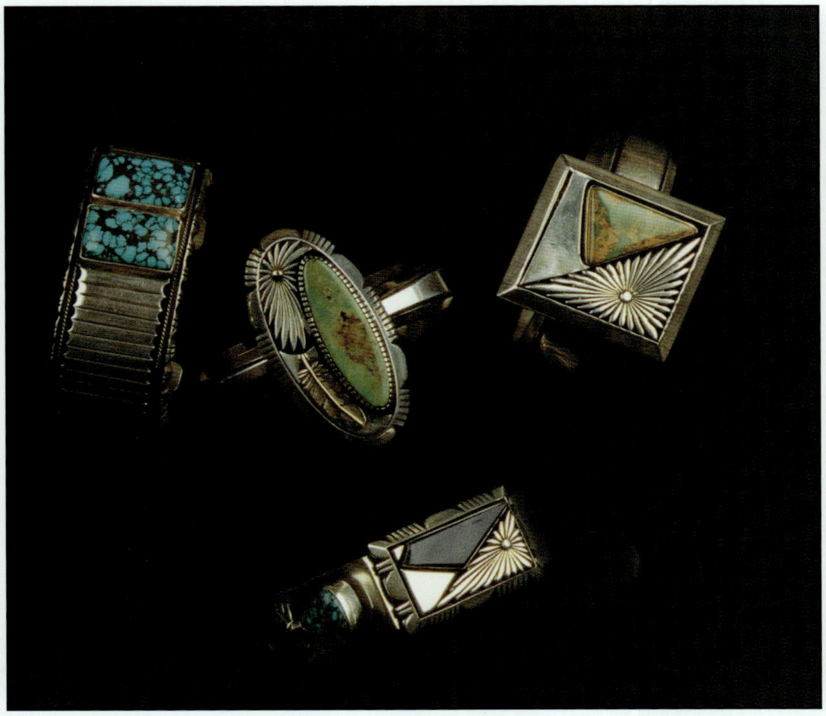

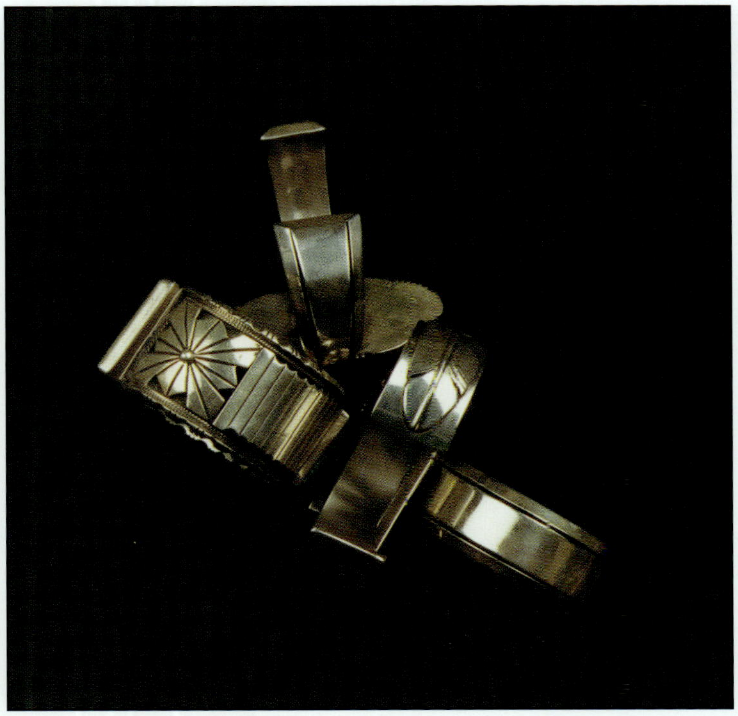

The fronts and backs of these bracelets are equally interesting as the designs are carried out in the round bands. At left: turquoise and heavy silver cuff bracelet by Calvin Martinez, late 1980s. / Three silver band bracelets with silver stamped plaques inlaid with various blue and green turquoise and jet by Navajo artist Delbert Vanderver, late 1980s. *Turquoise Lady collection*

Victor Beck combined coral and opal stone to stone inlay with gold to created this beautiful ring and bracelet set, 1980s, Navajo. *Artist's collection*

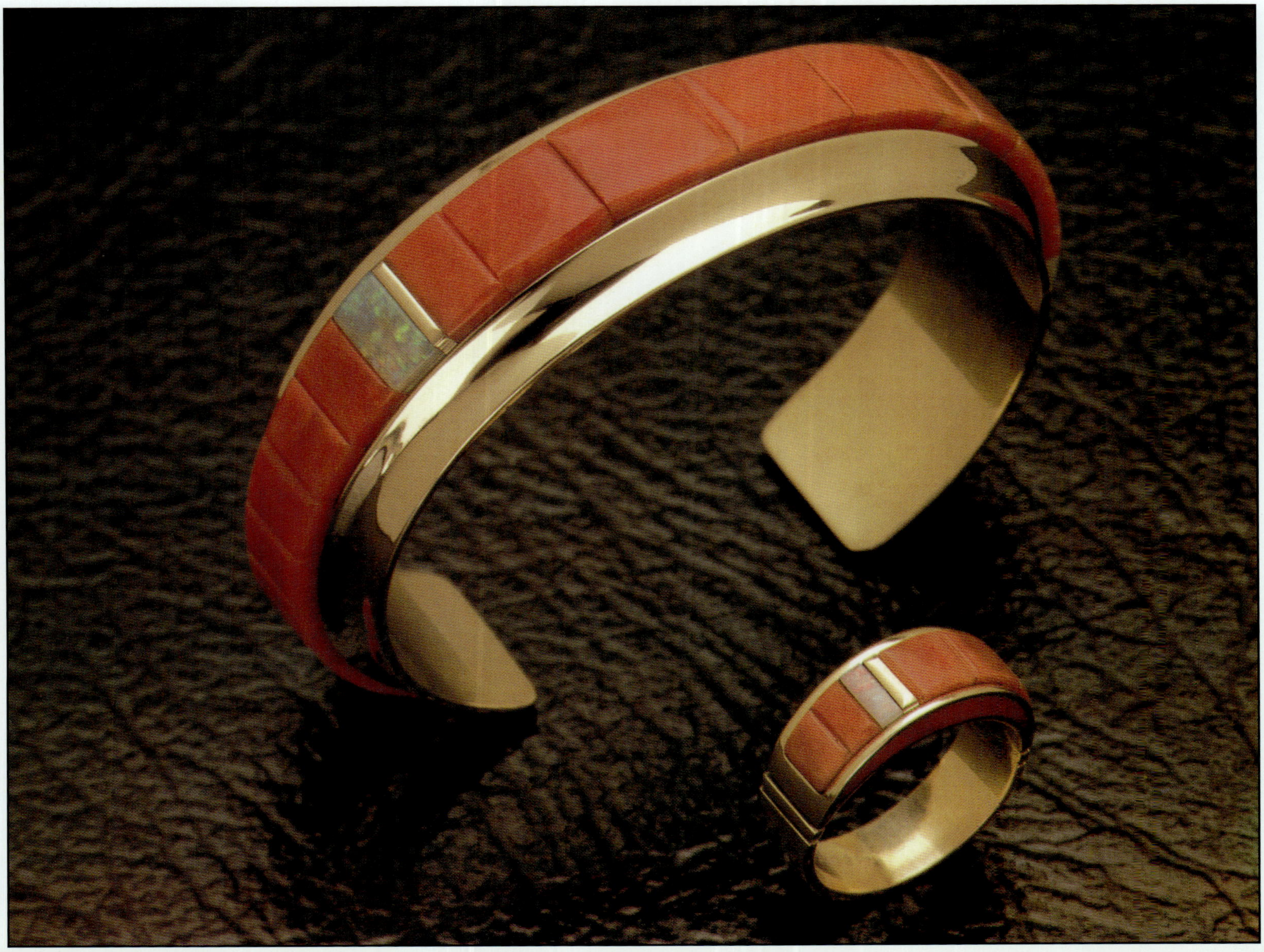

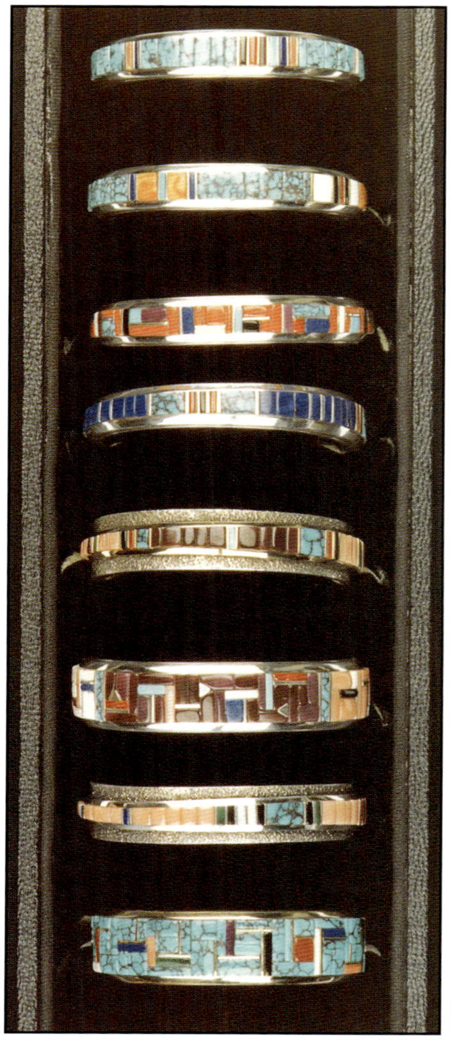

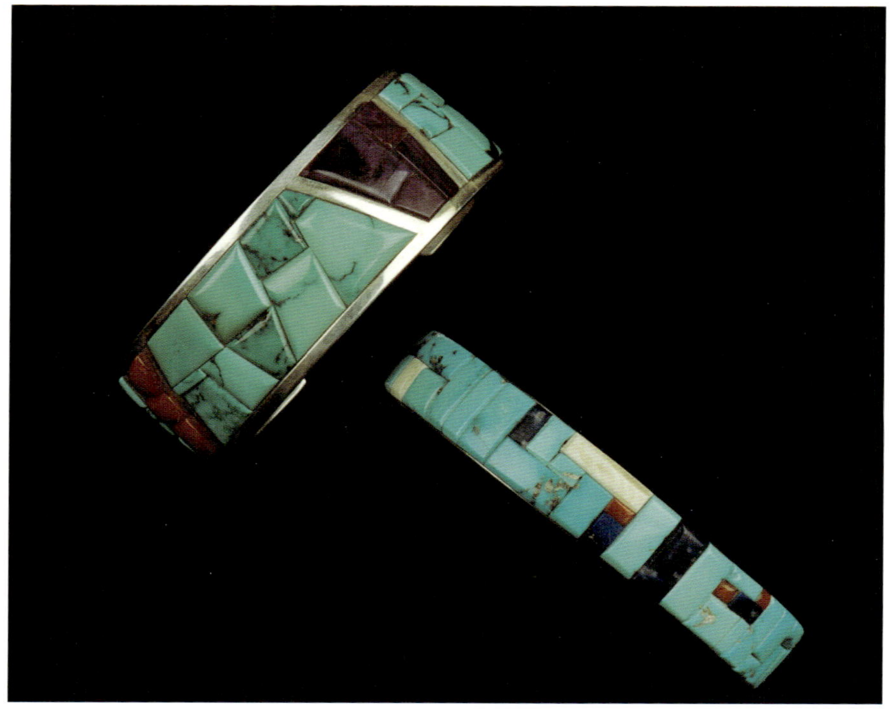

Stone to stone inlay completely defines the dynamic designs of these silver bracelets by Paul Arviso, 1980s. *Turquoise Lady collection*

Colorful stones have been combined in mosaic inlays to create diversity in these gold and silver bracelets by Phil and Fannie (Bitsui) Russell, Navajo. *Keams Canyon Arts & Crafts collection*

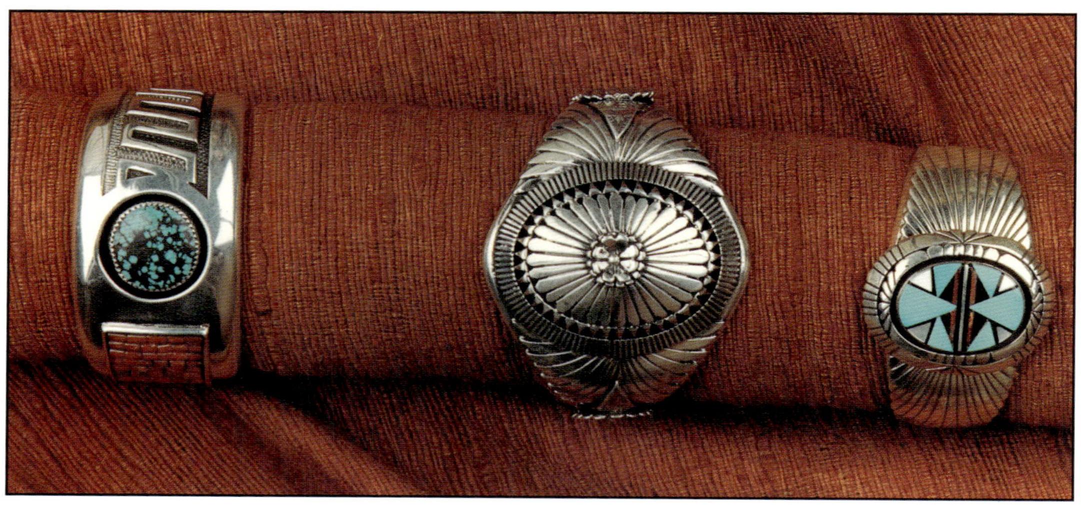

Contemporary Navajo silversmiths put extensive work into the ornament of these cuff bracelets, all late 1980s: Top, turquoise shadowbox and coral bead inlay give contrasting color and texture to the overlaid band, by D. A. Jackson. / Careful chisel work completes the symmetrical design on this all-silver bracelet by Eddy Chaco. / A bold mosaic stone plaque ornaments this chiseled band by Wilson Begay. *Bing Crosby collection*

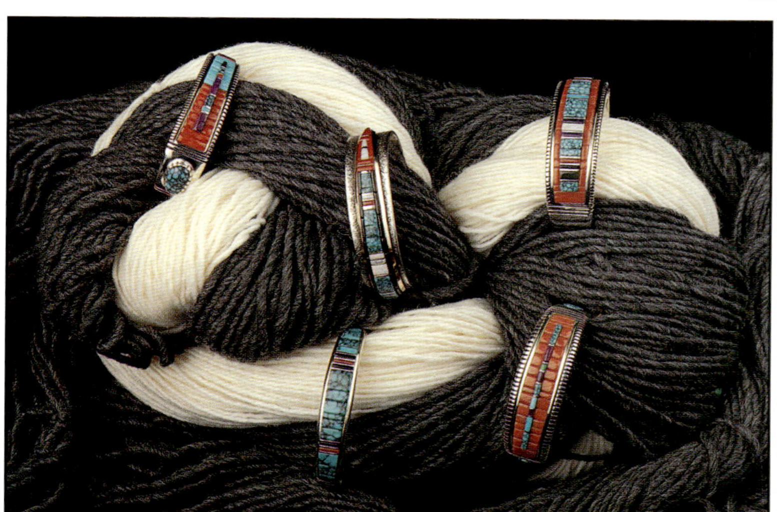

Five stone inlayed bracelets by Phillip Russell, 2002. *Courtesy McGee's, Keams Canyon*

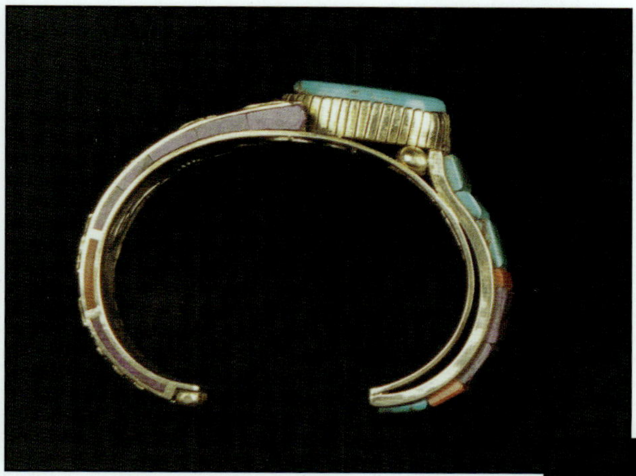

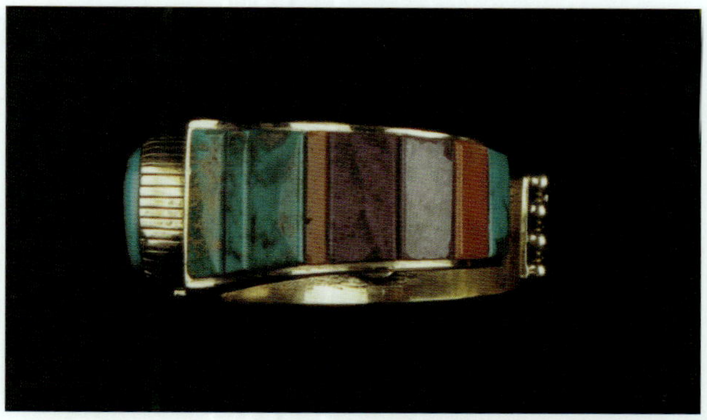

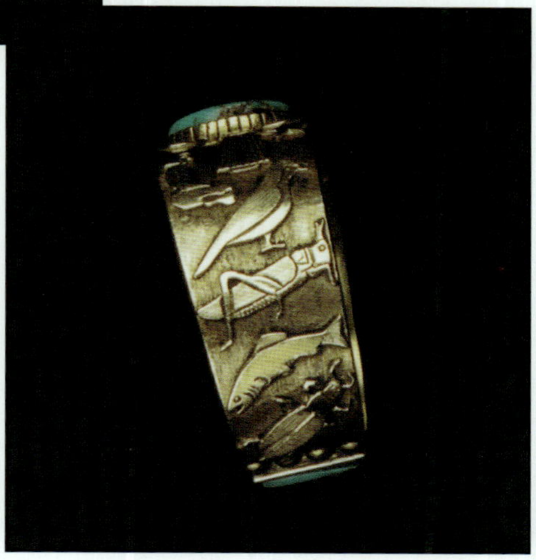

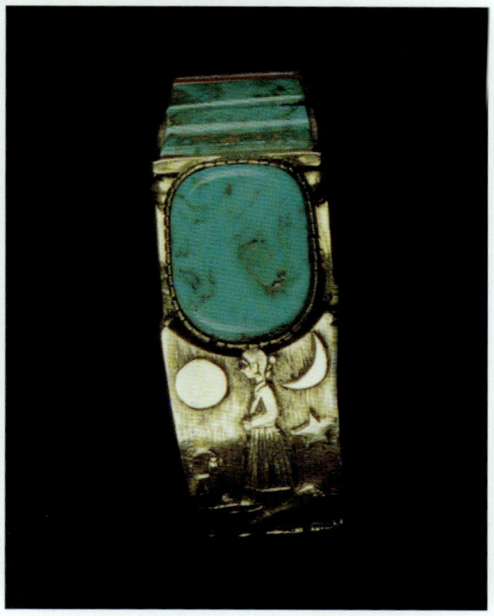

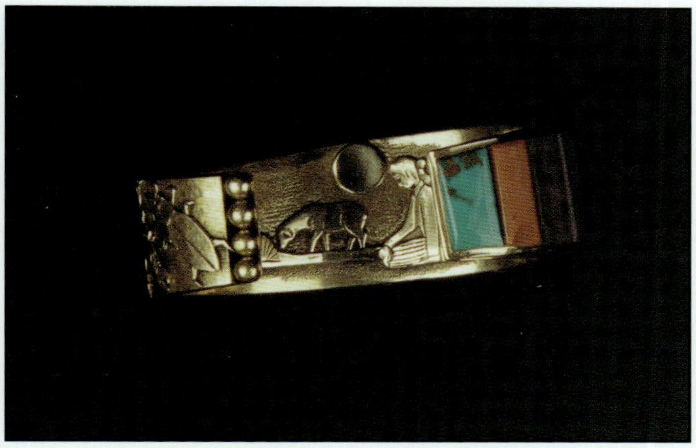

Storytelling jewelry is full of personal meaning to the maker for the wearer. This jewelry transcends design as ornament and becomes a means of communication. Few jewelers attempt to interpret the deep meanings of their cultural heritage in their work, and fewer meet the tremendous challenge with refined technical skill to succeed.

"The Emergence" bracelet depicts the Navajo creation story through different forms of its metamorphosis as interpreted by Paul Arviso in gold appliqué and stone inlay in many layers. The inside (bottom picture) shows their current place still emerging, late 1980s. *Turquoise Lady collection*

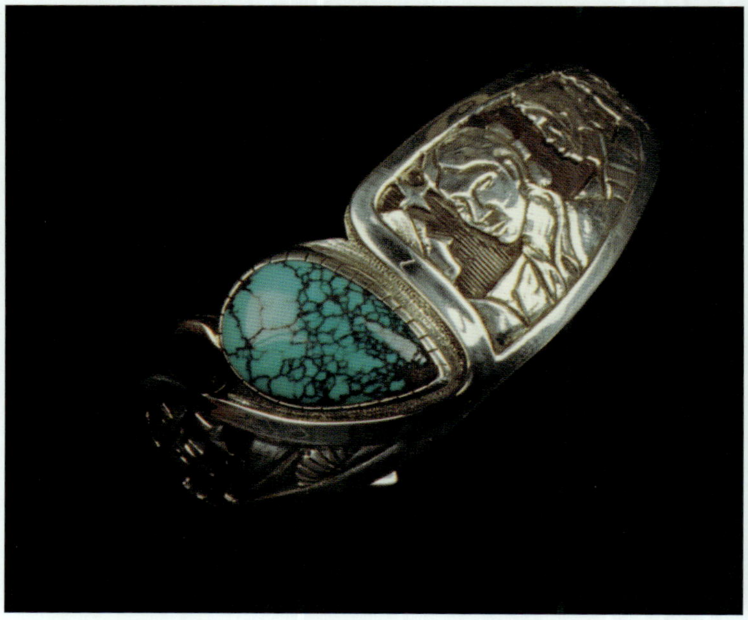

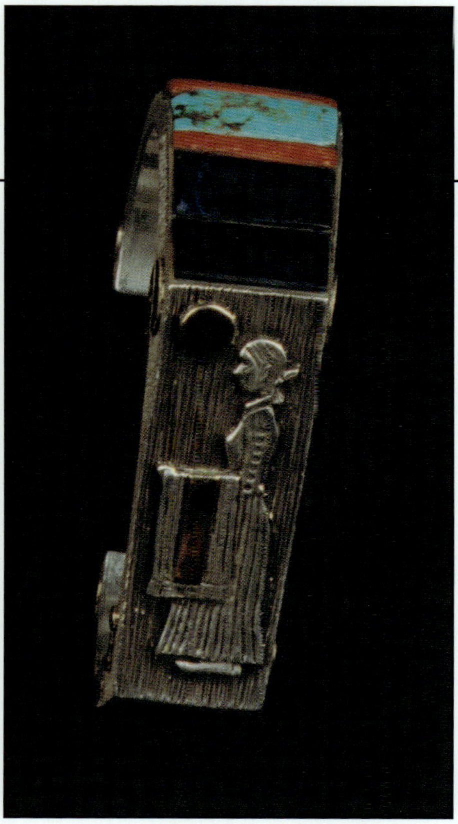

Two storytelling bracelets of silver and gold appliqué technique include stone inlay decoration and continued narrative design on the side and inside surfaces, by Paul Arviso, Navajo, late 1980s. *Turquoise Lady collection*

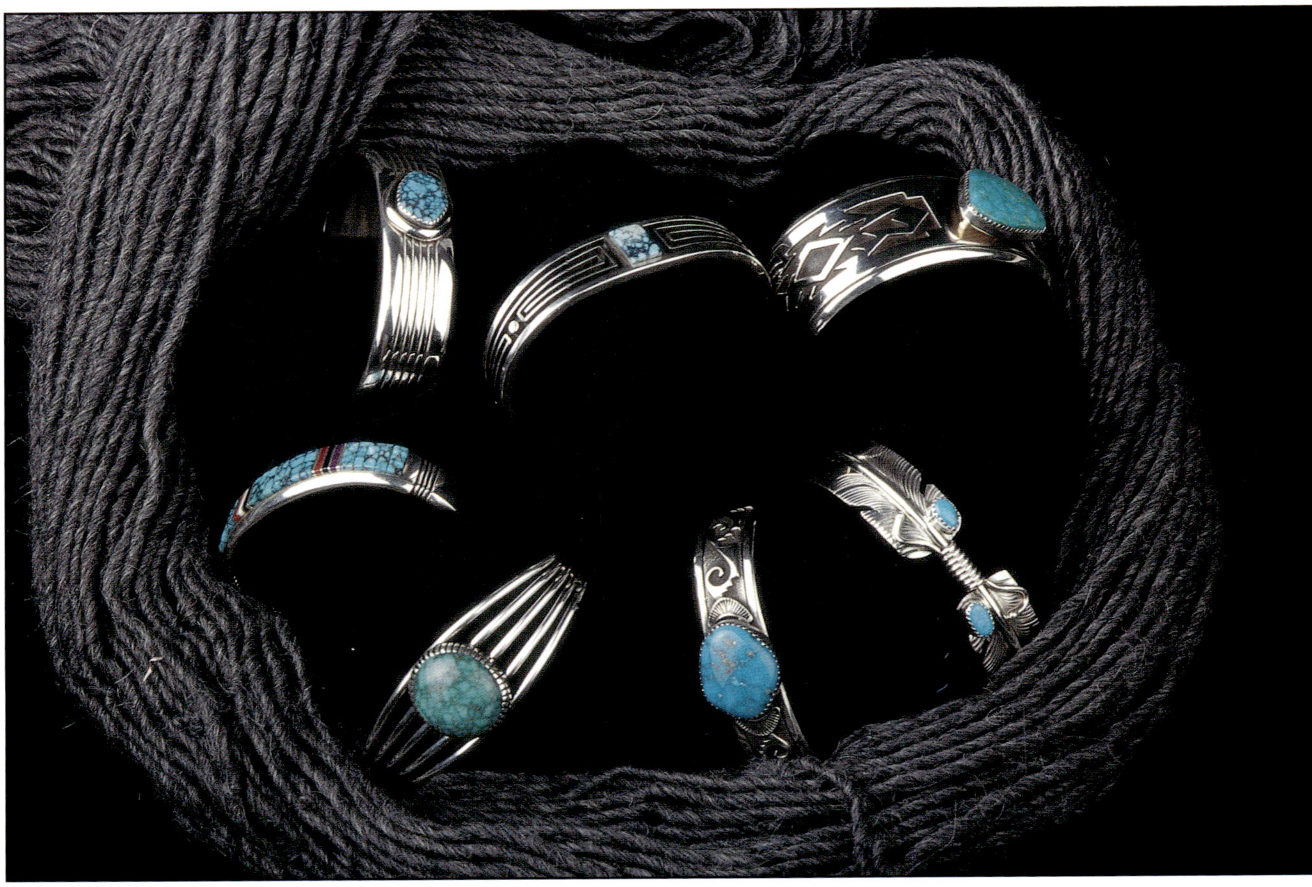

Group of seven Navajo silver bracelets, 2002. *Courtesy McGee's, Holbrook*

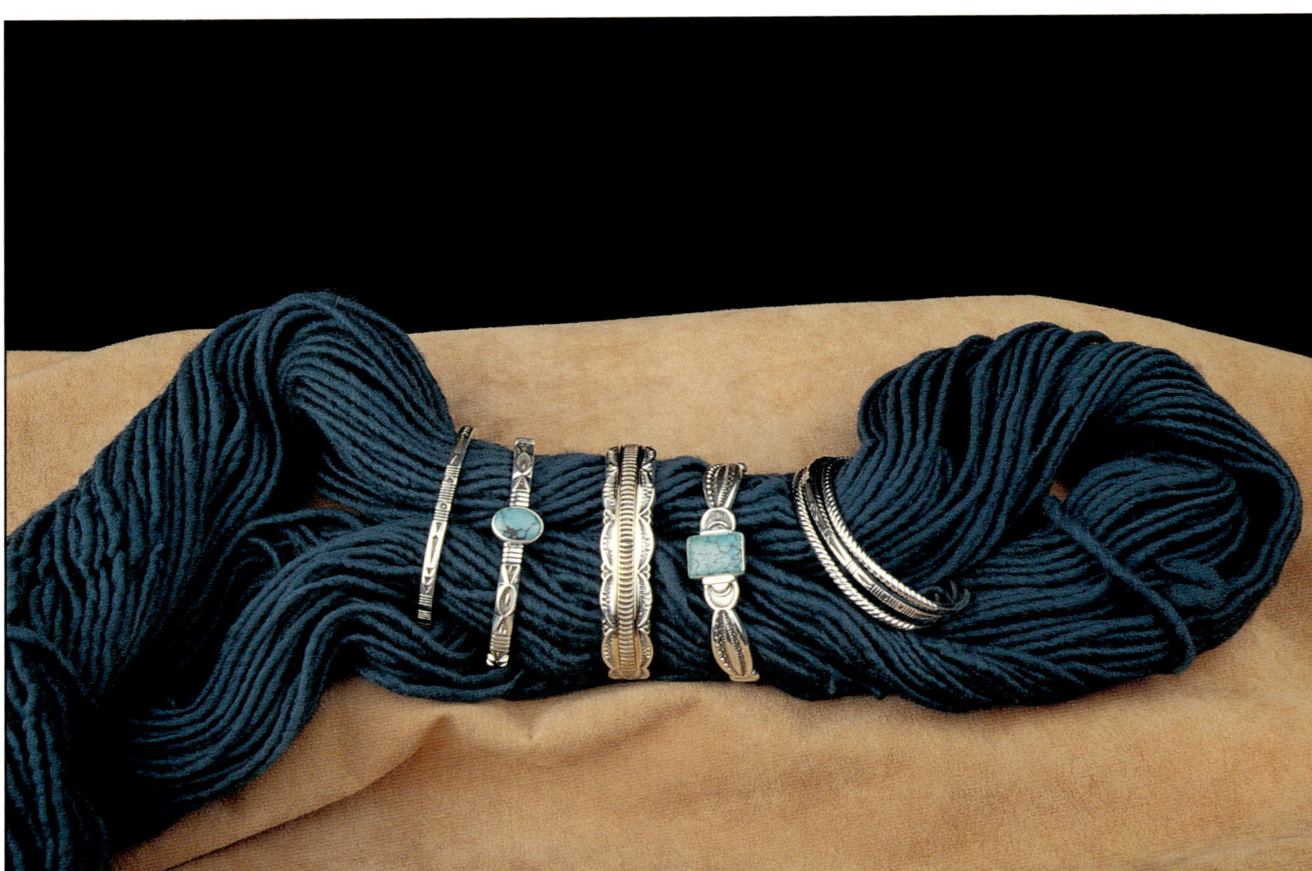

Five silver bracelets by Howard Nelson, Navajo, 2002. *Courtesy McGee's, Keams Canyon*

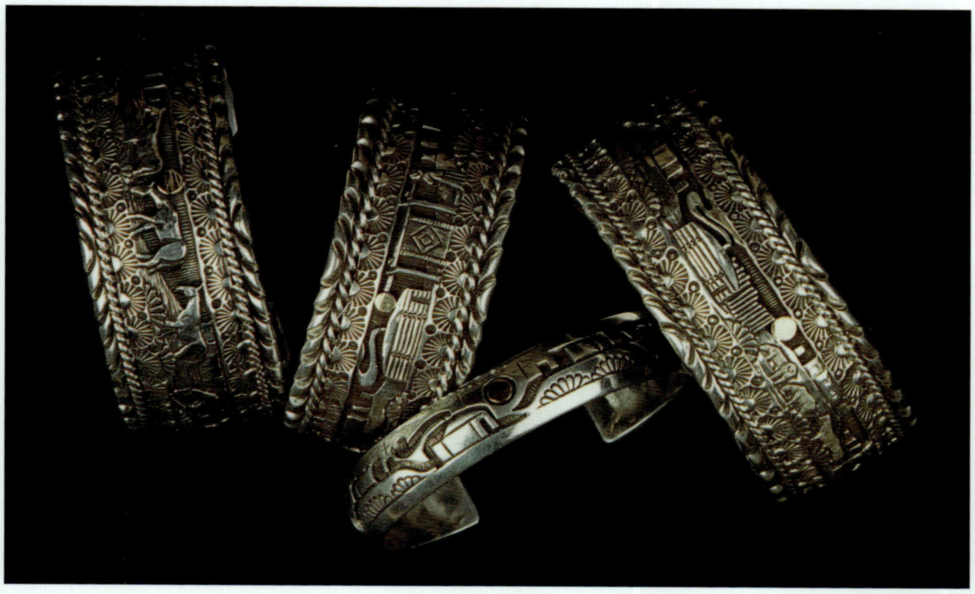

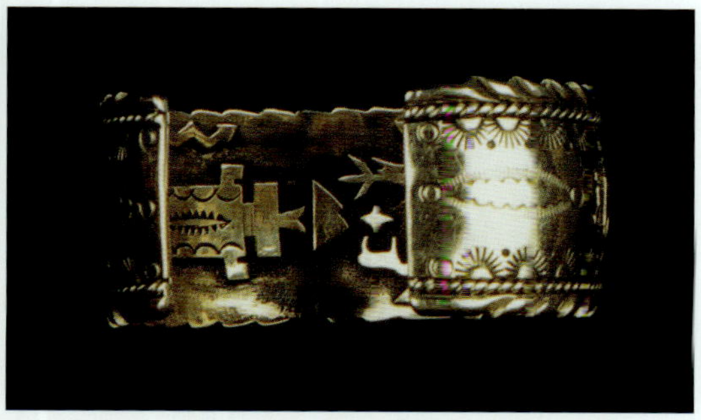

Group of four narrative bracelets in gold and silver appliqué with stamping, including an inside view of symbolic design, by Paul Arviso, Navajo. *Turquoise Lady collection*.

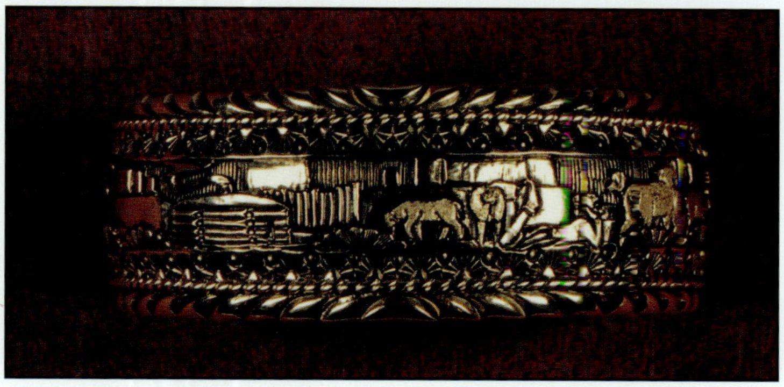

"New Design" narrative bracelet in gold overlay with stamping by Paul Arviso, Navajo, 1989. *Private collection*

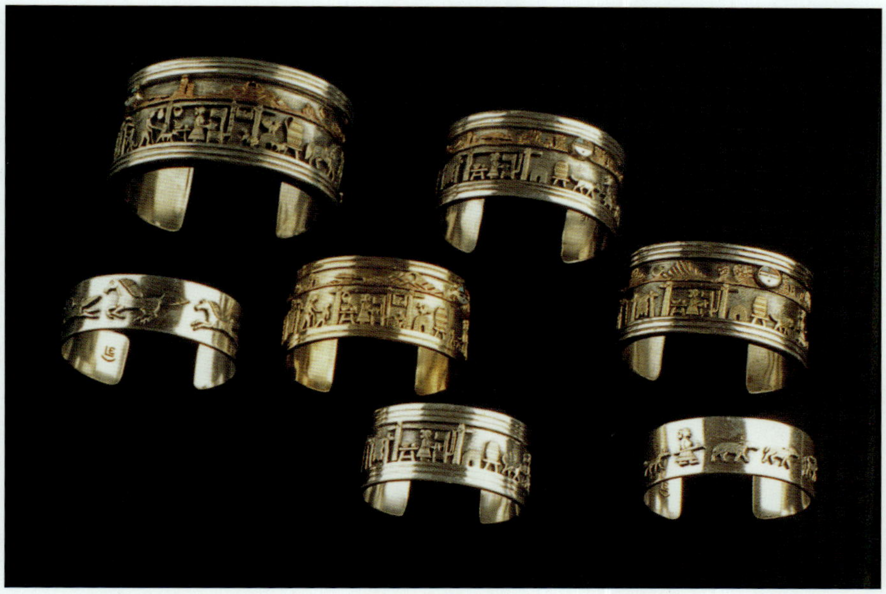

Seven storytelling bracelets in silver appliqué with copper and gold details by Clarence Lee, Navajo, 1989. *Clarence Lee collection*

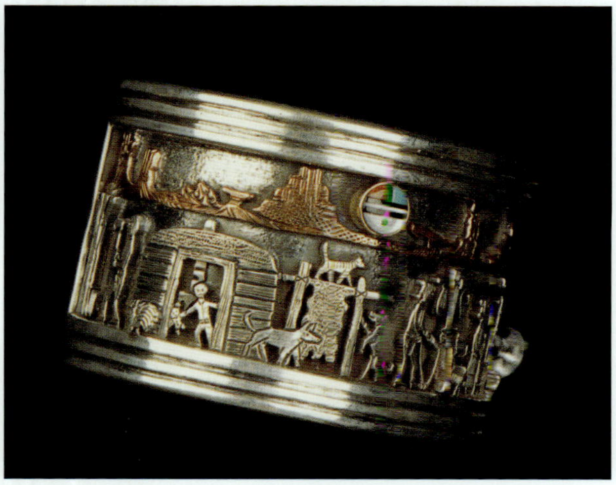

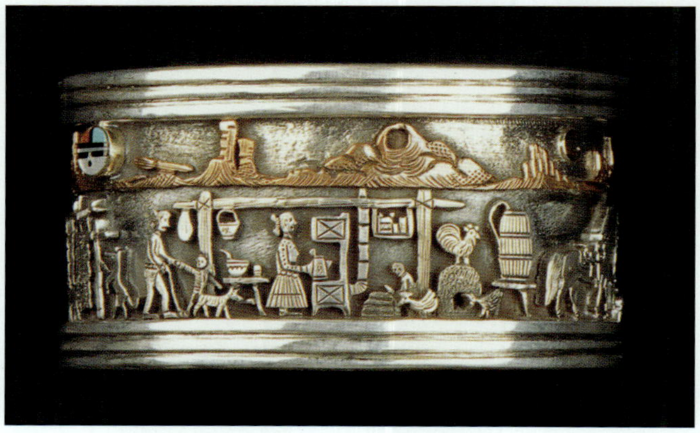

Details of the storytelling bracelets by Clarence Lee from the group above, showing traditional Navajo summer domestic scenes. *Clarence Lee collection*

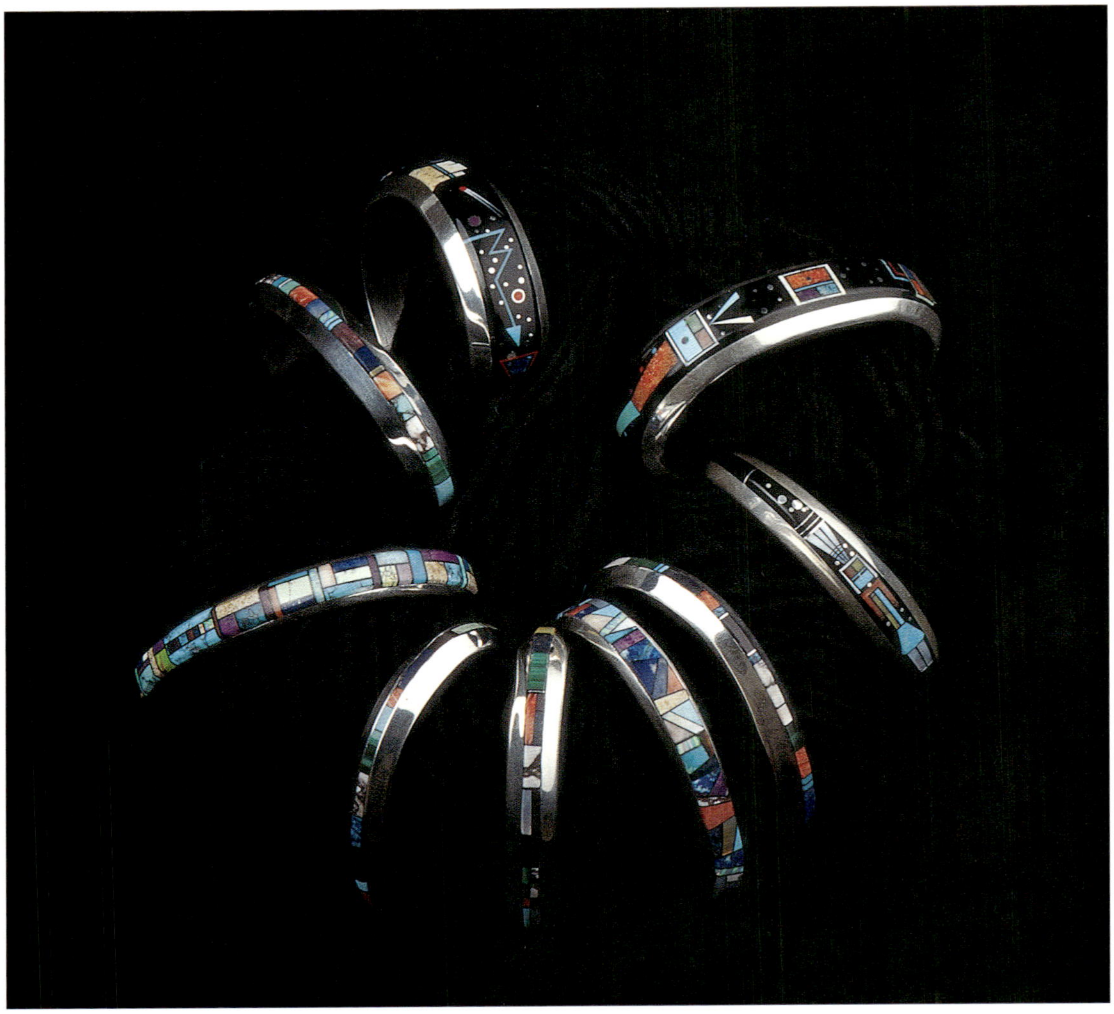

Nine bracelets with stone to stone inlay designs by Melvin Cleveland, Navajo, 2002. *Courtesy McGee's, Holbrook*

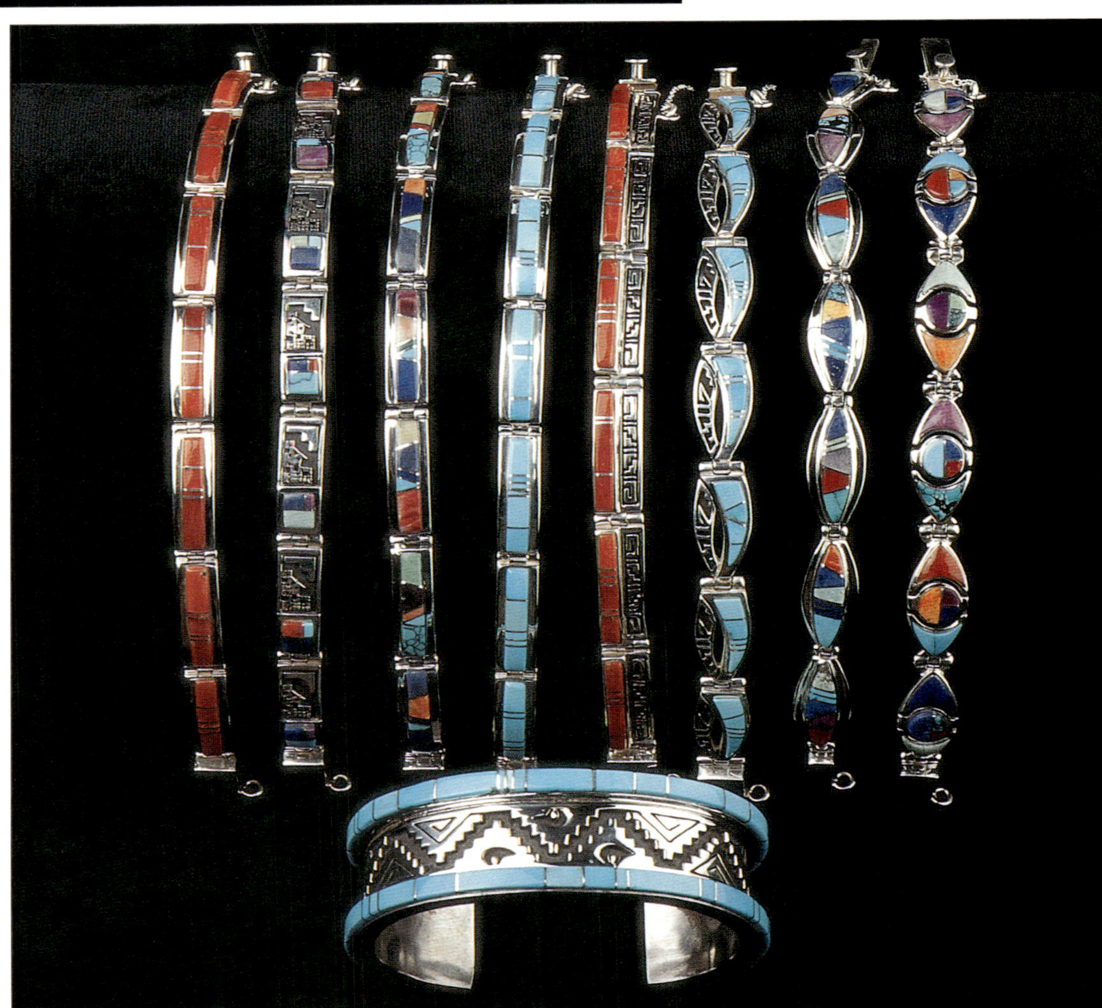

Group of silver and stone inlay bracelets by Earl Plummer, Navajo, 2002. *Courtesy McGee's, Holbrook*

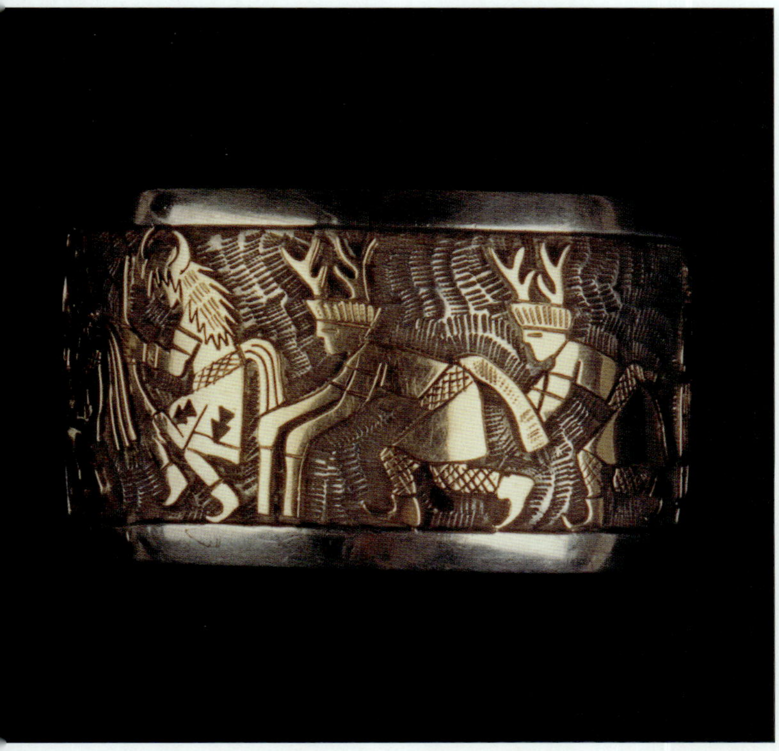

Storytelling bracelet showing Hopi mountain sheep dancers in gold and silver over/appliqué by Watson Honanie, Hopi, 1980s. *Bromberg collection*

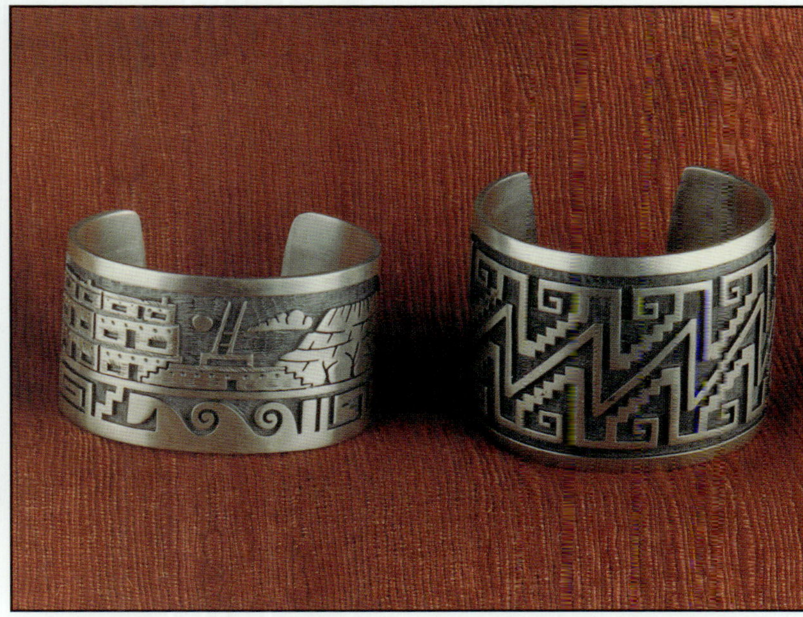

Large silver overlay bracelet with geometric decoration by Dan A. Jackson, Navajo, late 1980s. / Three small silver overlay bracelets, unmarked. *Enchanted Mesa collection*

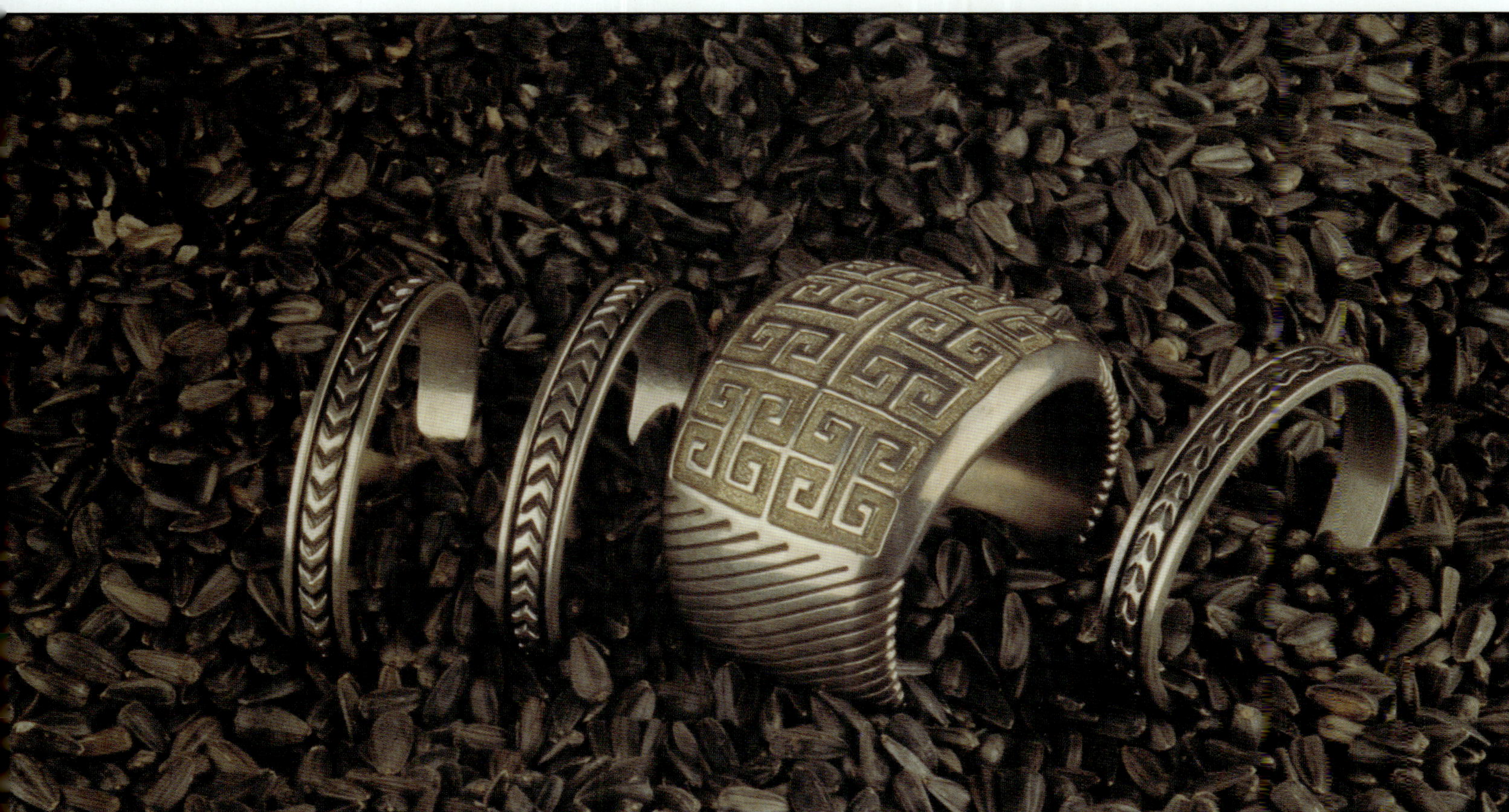

Two silver overlay cuffs with finely detailed ornamentation by Billy Sekakuku, Hopi, 1980s. *Enchanted Mesa collection*

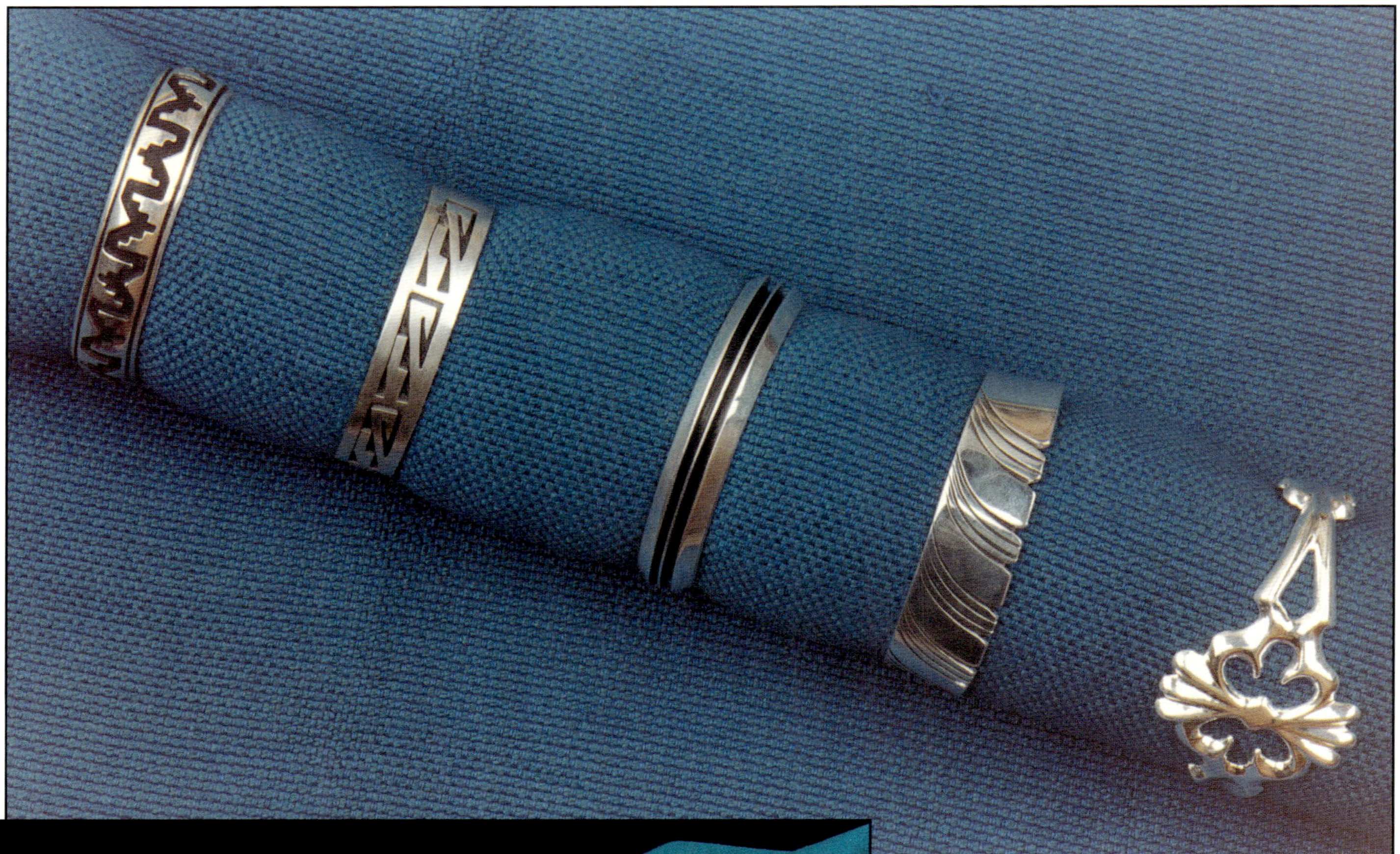

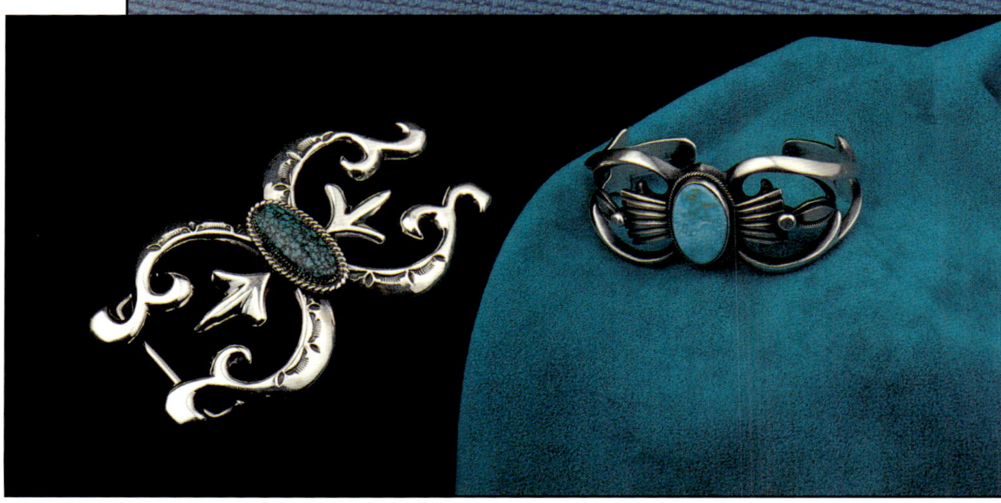

Silver sand-cast bracelet, unmarked. / Wrought silver bracelet with feather edge design by S Y. / Wrought silver bracelet with one "rail" of "railroad tracks" design by Navajo Yazzie Johnson, 1989. / Silver overlay bracelet with geometric design. / Meandering design in silver overlay on a bracelet by Thomas Curtis, Navajo. *Bing Crosby collection*

Sand-cast silver buckle with oval turquoise by WB ($150) and cuff bracelet with oval turquoise by Morgan, both Navajo. *Courtesy of Palms Trading Company*

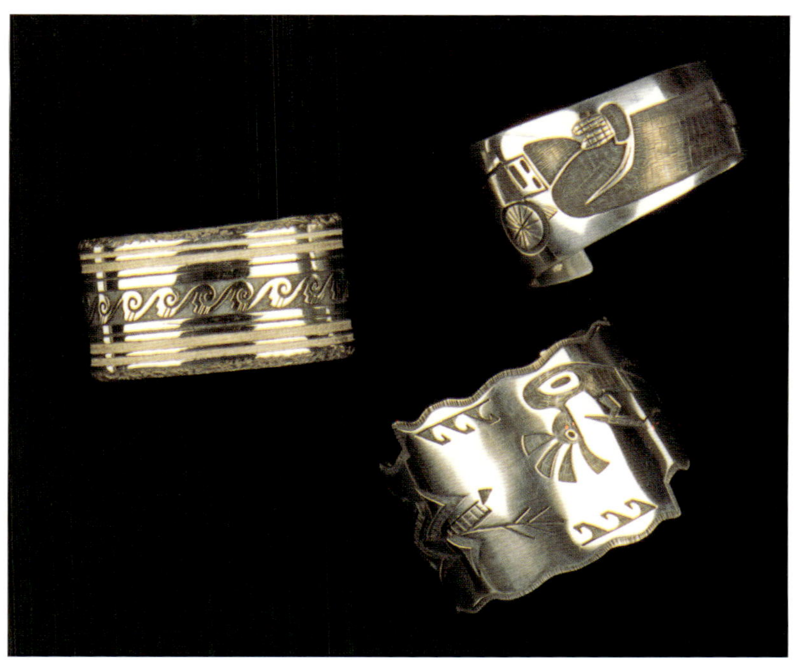

Hopi silversmiths continue to design in silver overlay technique to ever-higher standards as these bracelets from the late 1980s demonstrate. From the top, Roy Talaheftewa created contrasting textures in the design of this bracelet. / The irregular outline gives a more naturalistic character to this bracelet with corn stalk and flute player design by Richard Powiki. / The corn maiden fertility design dominates the bracelet which itself expands in width as it curves upward, made by Richard Powiki.

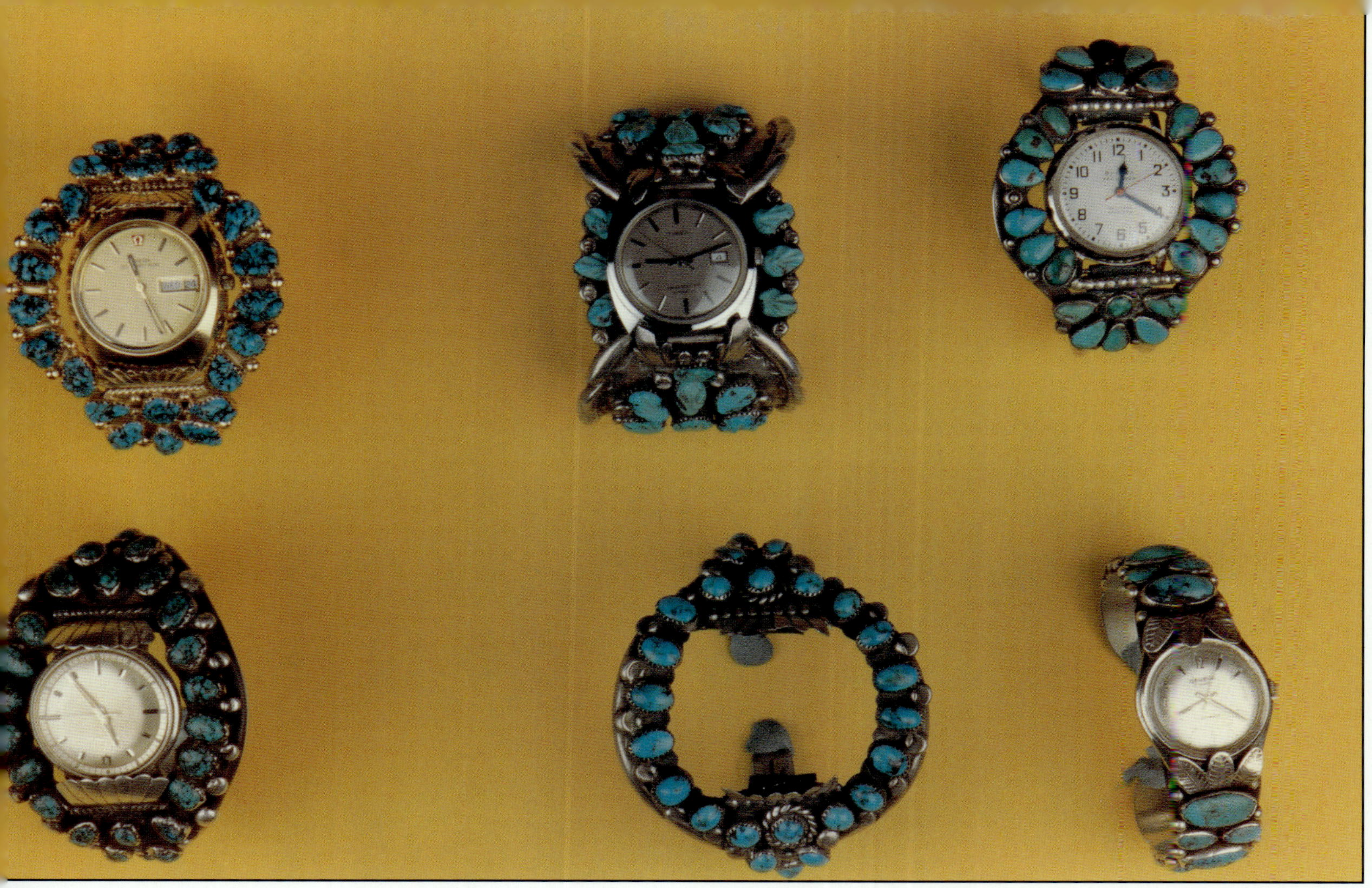

Watchbands

Above: Navajo silversmiths have created wristbands and elaborate frames for men's' wristwatches since the 1960s. This group of six includes turquoise ornamental stones. *Private collection*

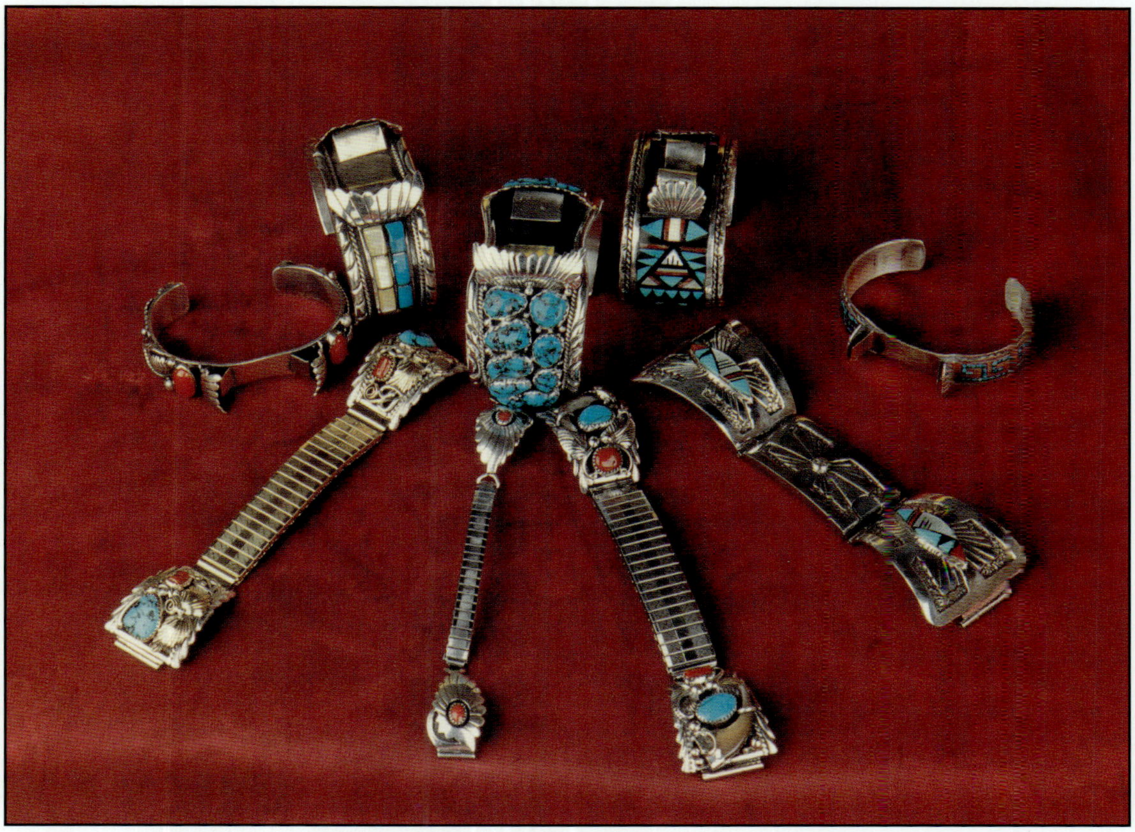

By the late 1980s, men's watchbands were also made as highly decorative as the most elaborate women's bracelets, far surpassing their usefulness to hold a watch. This group includes ornamental silverwork and much embellishment with inlay and colored stones. *Bing Crosby collection*

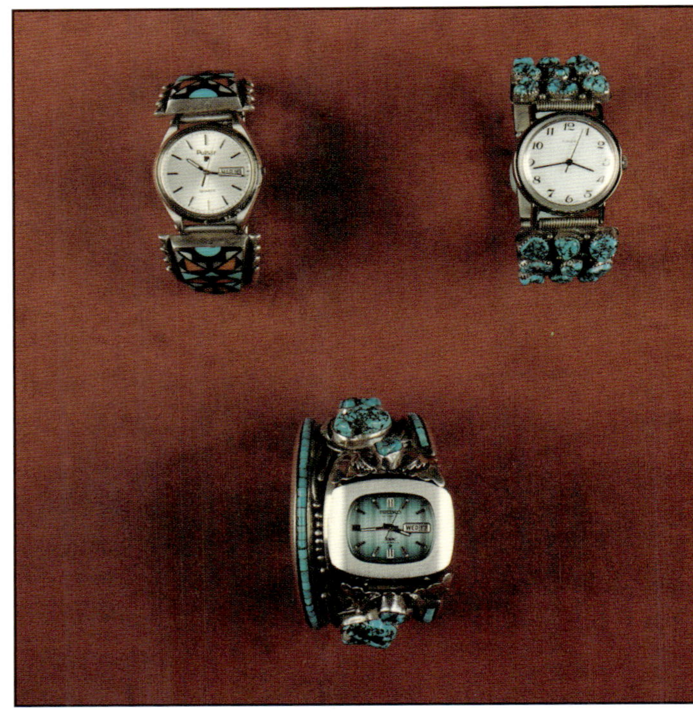

A Pulsar wristwatch is held in a band with colorful stone inlay made by Wayne and Virginia Quam, Zuni, in 1982. / The Timex wristwatch is supported by a silver band set with nuggets of Kingman turquoise by Raymond Bennett, Navajo, early 1980s. / The blue Seiko wristwatch harmonizes with an elaborate band inlaid and set with Kingman turquoise nuggets by Larry Begay, an Anglo silversmith. *Private collection on permanent loan to Ohio University*

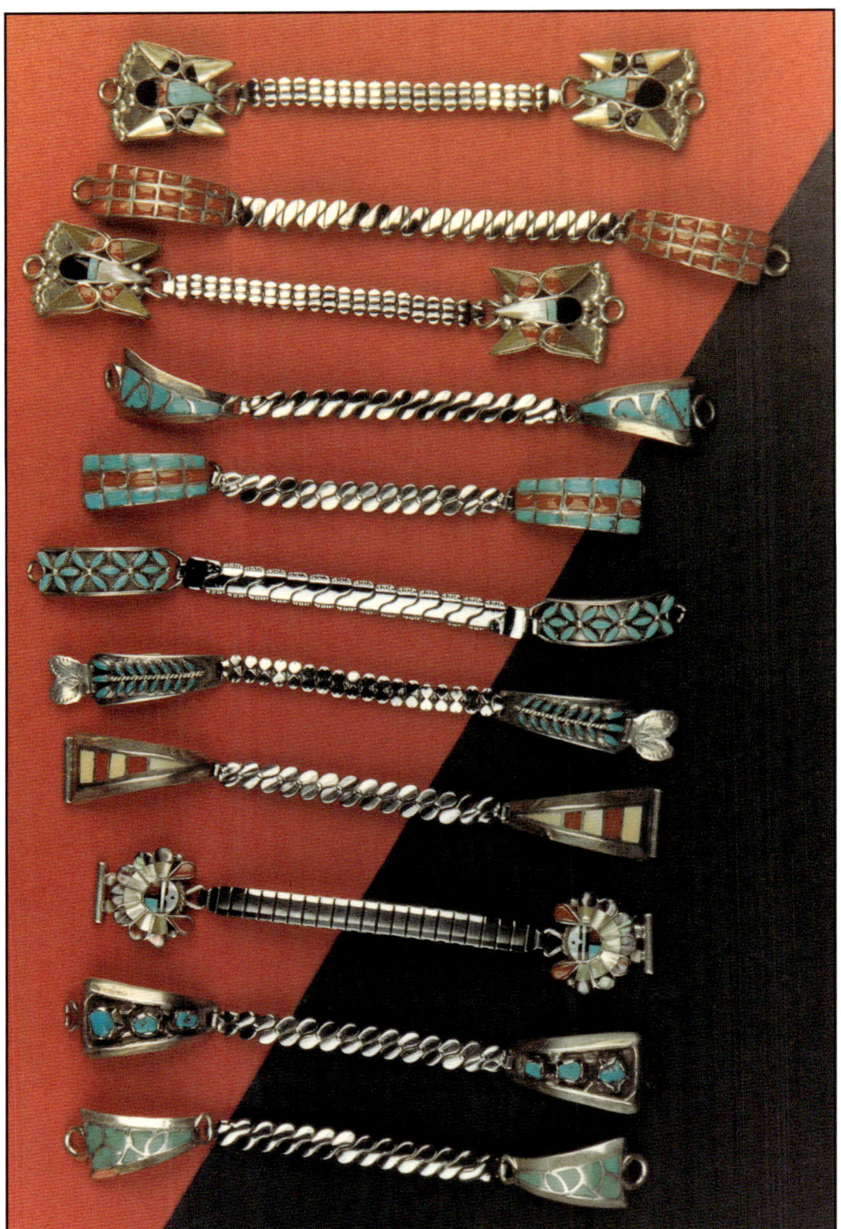

Zuni artists have applied their skill with stone inlay to decorate this group of watchbands from the late 1980s. *Enchanted Mesa collection*

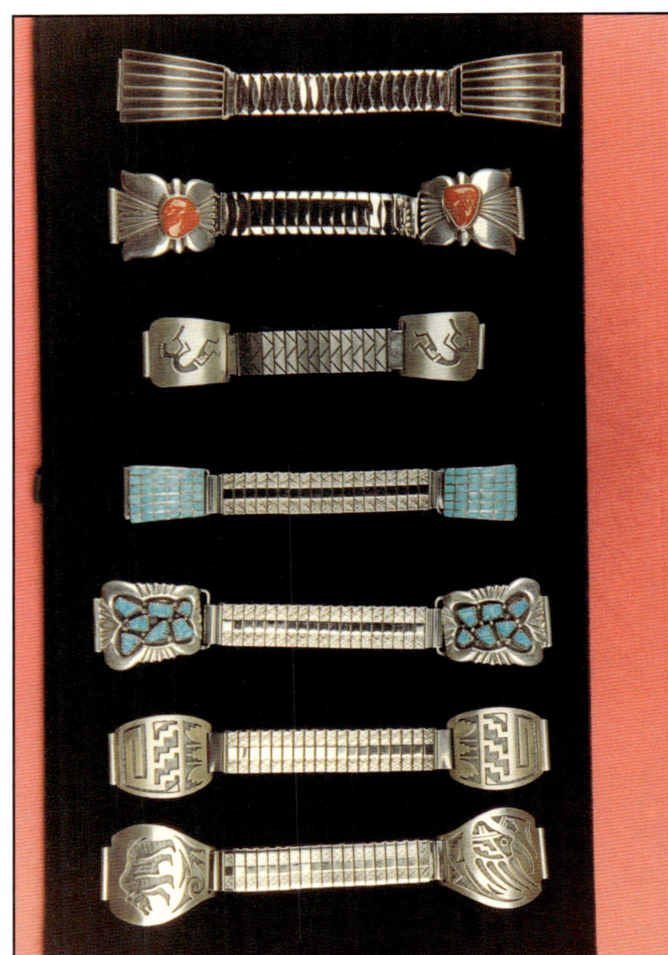

Comparisons in ornamental techniques can be made among these silver watchbands. From the left, two silver overlay designs by Bobby Sekakuku, Hopi. / G. & L. Leekity, Zuni, set turquoise chunks. / Turquoise was inlaid by L. Melani, Zuni. / Three Navajo-made watchbands have an overlay figure, coral stones, and "railroad tracks" ornamentation respectively. *Enchanted Mesa collection*

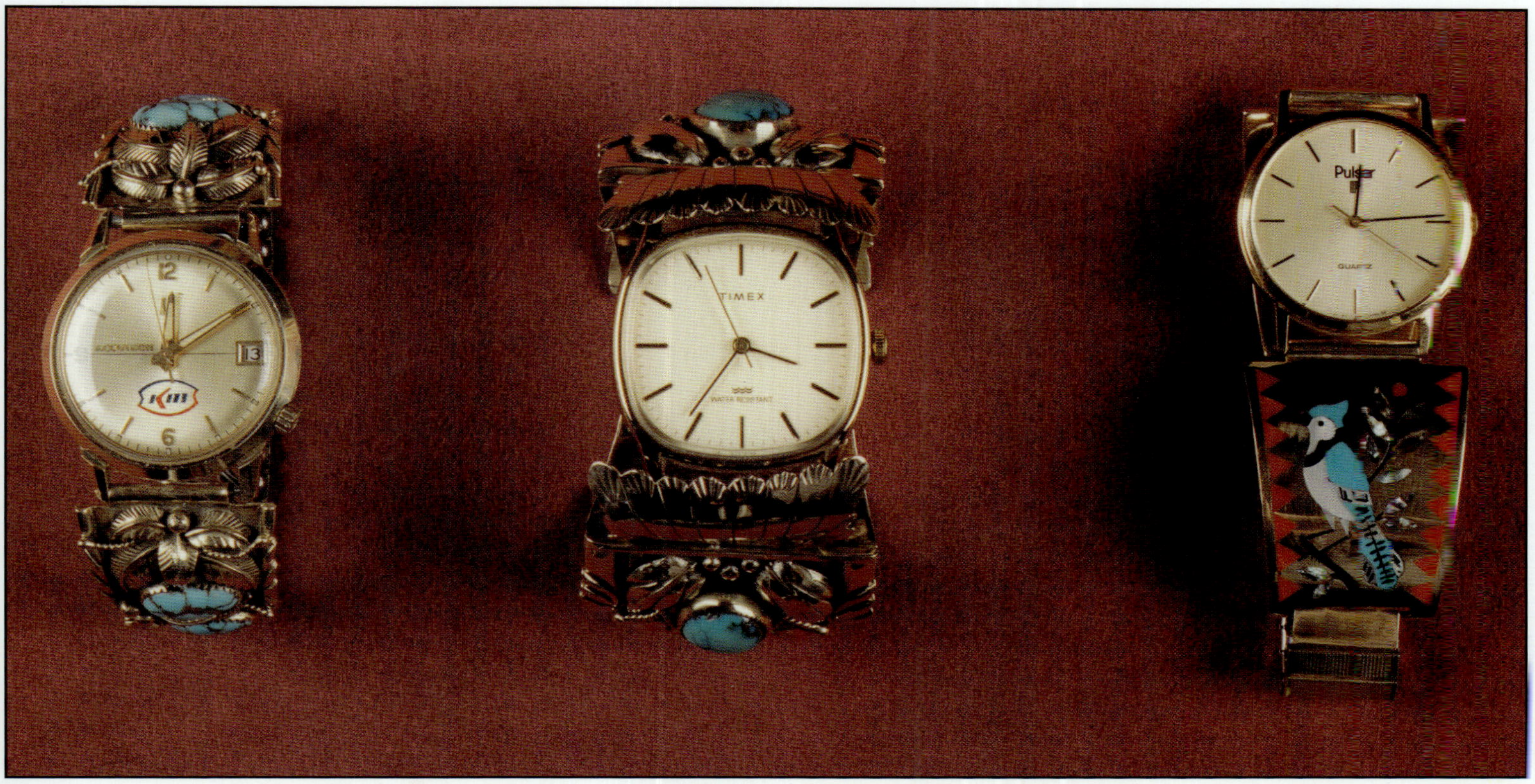

Accutron watch on a gold band with appliqué work and turquoise made by Ivan Valencia in 1976. / Timex watch on a wide gold band with appliqué and turquoise decoration by Larry Begay, an Anglo, in 1976. / Pulsar watch on a gold band with colorful blue jay design inlay by Dennis and Nancy Edaakie, Zuni, in 1984. *Private collection on permanent loan to Ohio University*

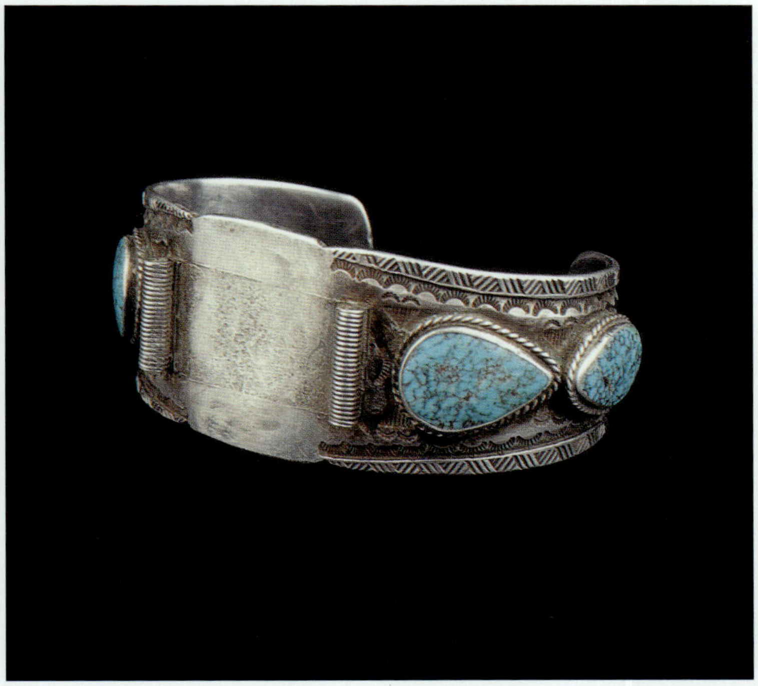

Navajo silver watch band decorated with four #8 Spiderweb turquoise stones, made for tourists, *Lynn D. Trusdell, Crown & Eagle Antiques*

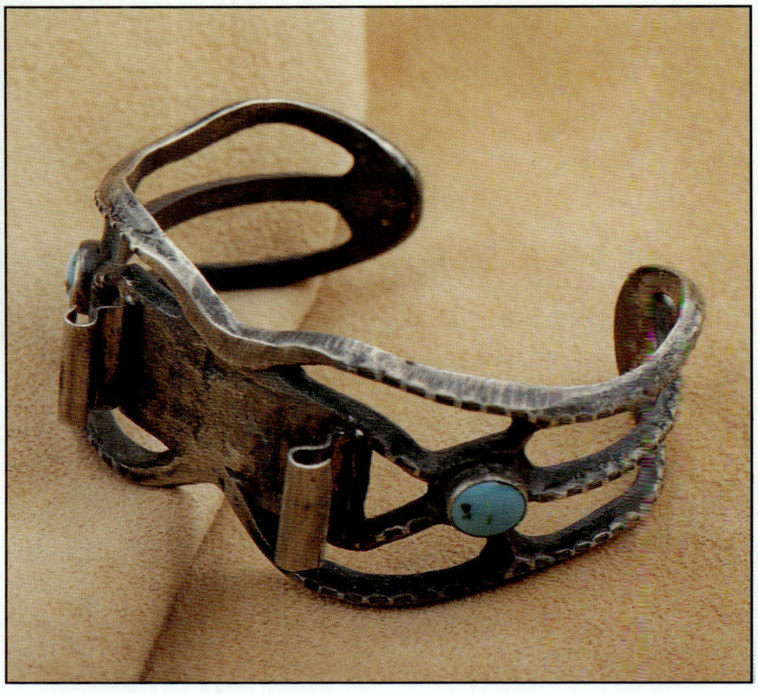

Sand cast silver watch band of unusual design with early style file work and two small turquoise accents, perhaps 1920s. *Lynn D. Trusdell, Crown & Eagle Antiques*

Bolo Ties

Bolo ties were made popular in the 1950s. Ed Houters, a former employee of the Hickok Leather Company of Rochester, New York, remembers the company originating the designs for bolo ties in the late 1940s or early 1950s. He recalls their being based upon South American gaucho's string ties with ornaments, and having been named for the bolo weapon they used. In early 1990 the Hickok company's successor, Tandy Brands Accessories Company of Fort Worth, Texas, reintroduced bolo ties to its product line. A 1976 article in *Turquoise Annual* credits Vic Cedarstaf of Wickenburg, Arizona, with the first bolo tie in 1949, and the possible first Indian-crafted tie slide in 1953. (King, *Indian Silverwork*, p. 61.)

Lynn Trusdell owns a silver and turquoise tie slide that appears to be of earlier origin, comparable to Navajo pins of the 1920s but with a simple hinged locking slide.

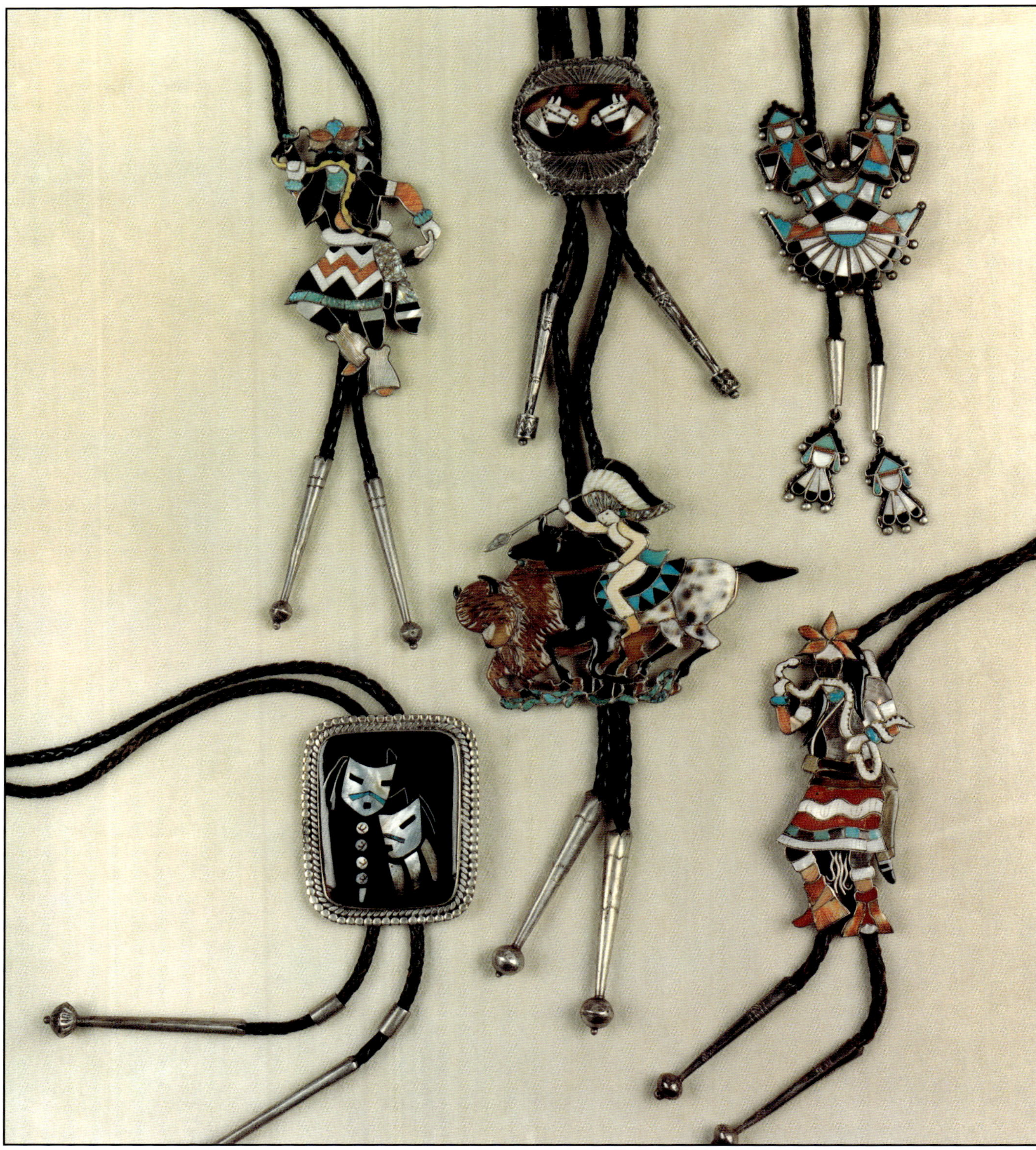

A selection of Zuni bolo ties, all set in silver and with silver tips. Top row, from left: Channel set snake dancer, 1940s. / Two horse heads in tortoise shell, 1940s. / Double kachina, 1950s. Bottom row, from left: Ghost masks of mother of pearl set in tortoise shell, 1970s./ Indian spearing a buffalo, 1950s. / Snake dancer, 1940s. *Lynn D. Trusdell collection*

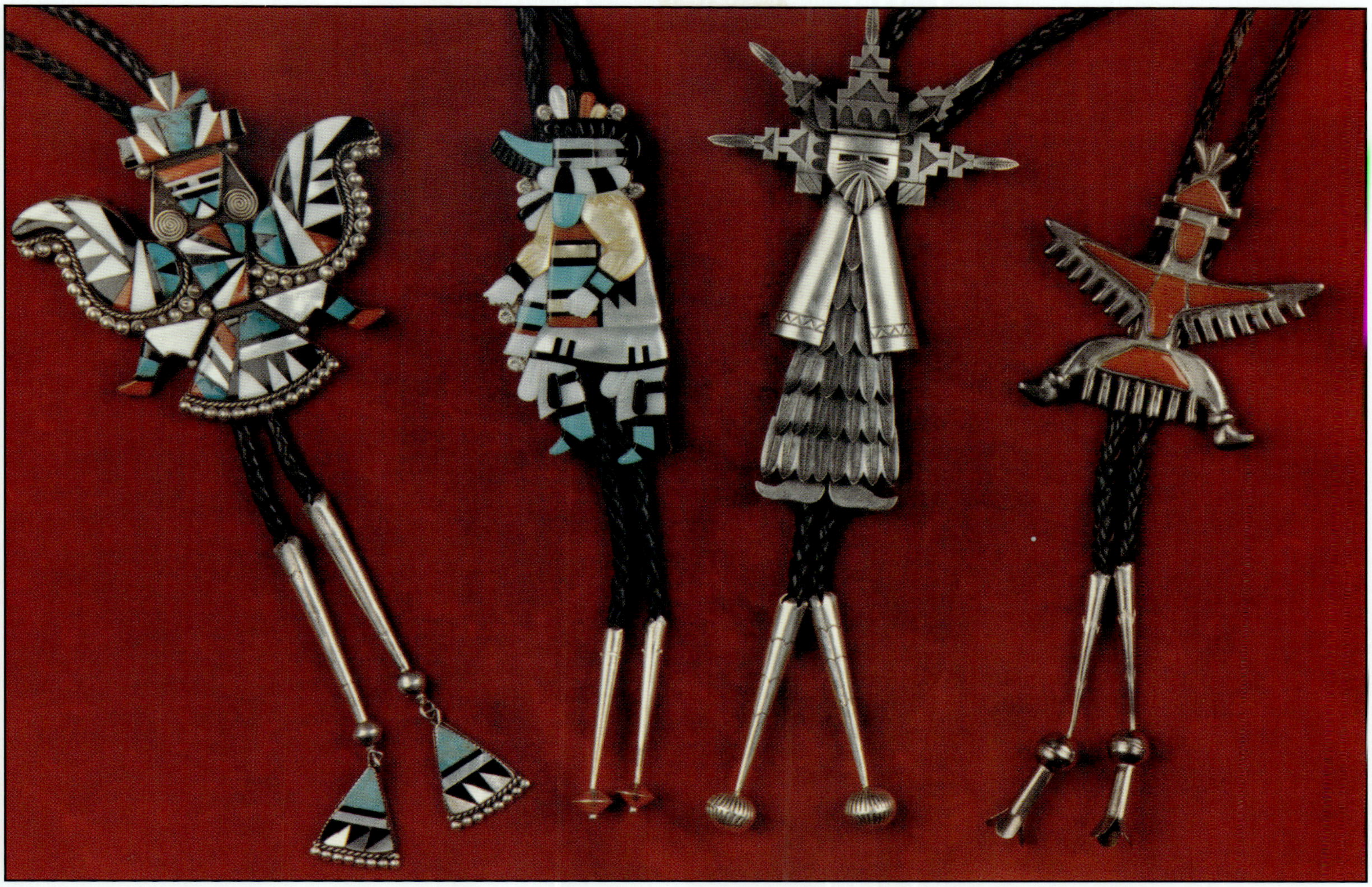

Six silver Zuni bolo ties set with turquoise, including a three-dimensional kachina. / Blue dancer with details of gold and gold tips with turquoise tips by Edward Beyuka. / A rainbow dancer with small rainbow dancers hanging from each tip made by A.O. / A small inlaid dancer made by V.I. *Private collection*

Four figural bolo ties: Knifewing with Blue Gem turquoise and pendants on the tips by Oliver Cellicion, Zuni, and Robert Napoleon. / Shalako with colorful inlay by A. Dewa, Zuni, 1978. / Silver Shalako by Mike Shirley, 1983. / Thunderbird design of silver and coral by Tobe Turpen (shop mark). *Private collection on permanent loan to Ohio University*

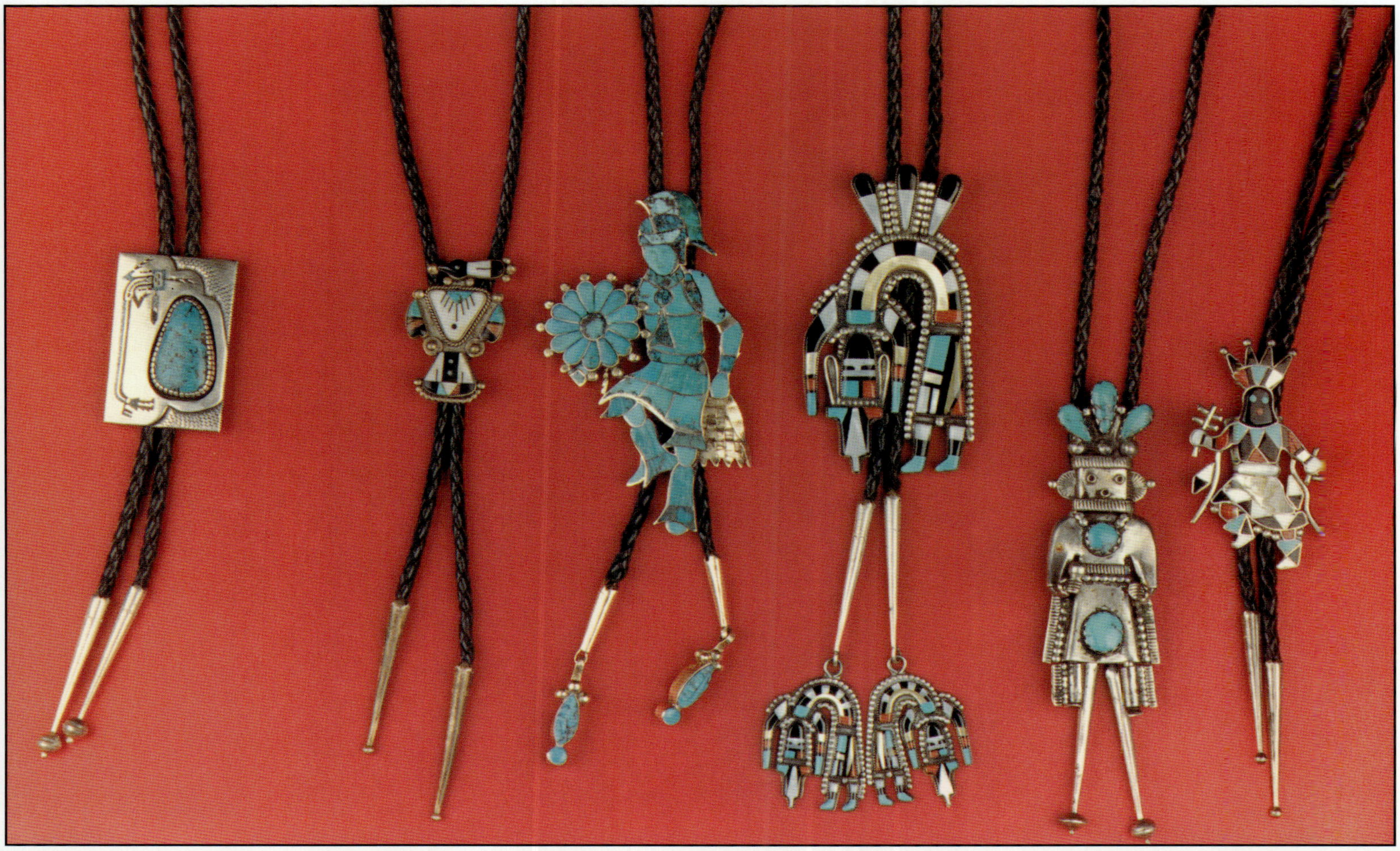

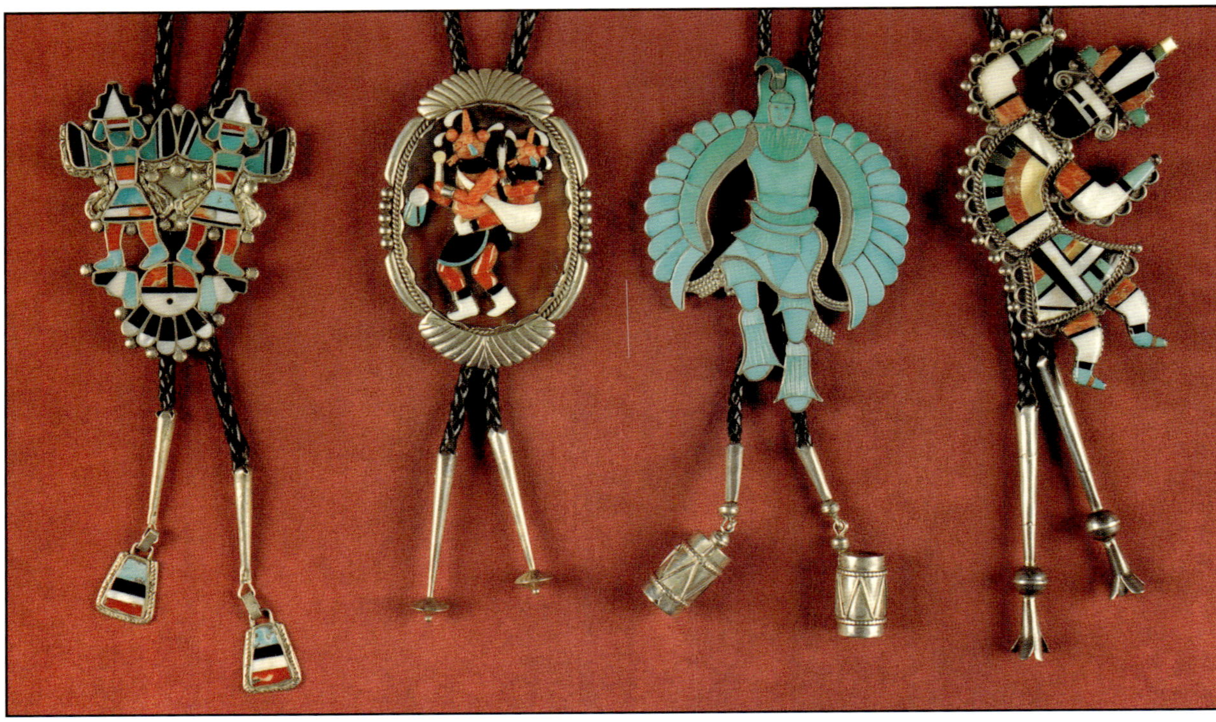

Four Zuni bolo ties: Twin Knifewing gods with pendant inlays on the tips by Lee Edaakie, 1977. / Mudhead with young mudhead by Rosalie Pinto, 1979. / Channel inlaid Eagle dancer with pendant drums by Edward Beyuka. / Rainbow god with squash blossom tips. *Private collection*

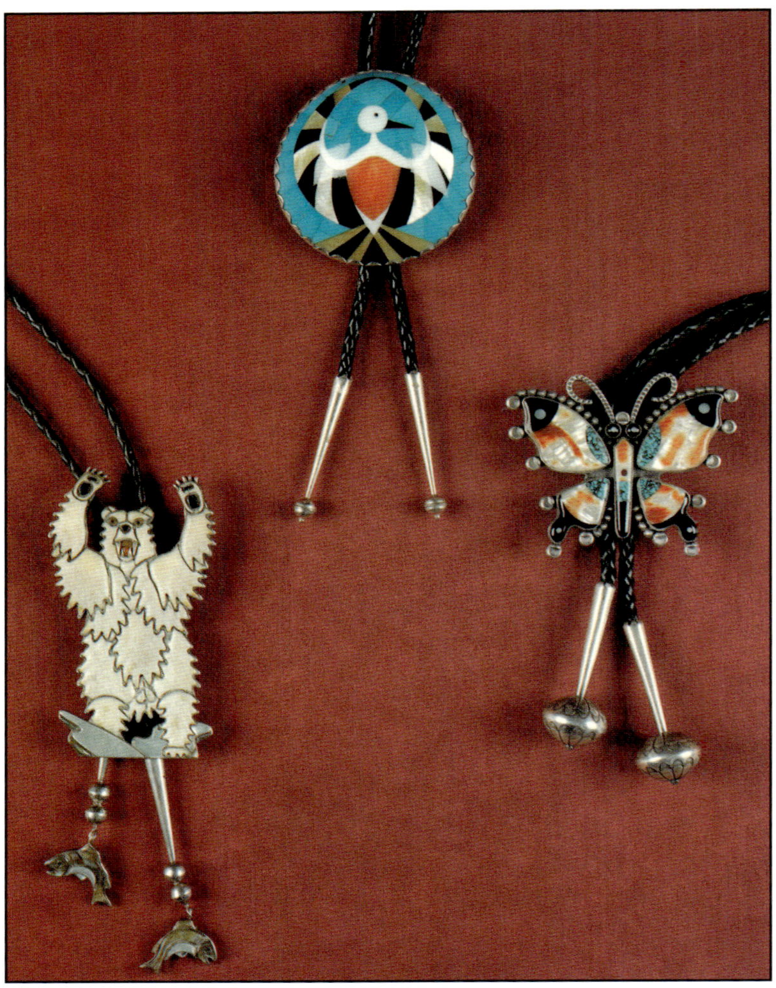

Representational bolo ties, including an ivory polar bear with pendant fish on the tips by Tom Z., 1985. / Shell with bird inlay by Ernest Medina, 1978, mounted as a bolo in 1982, silverwork by Mary Martin of Tobe Turpen's shop. / Butterfly by Michael, made in 1988. *Private collection*

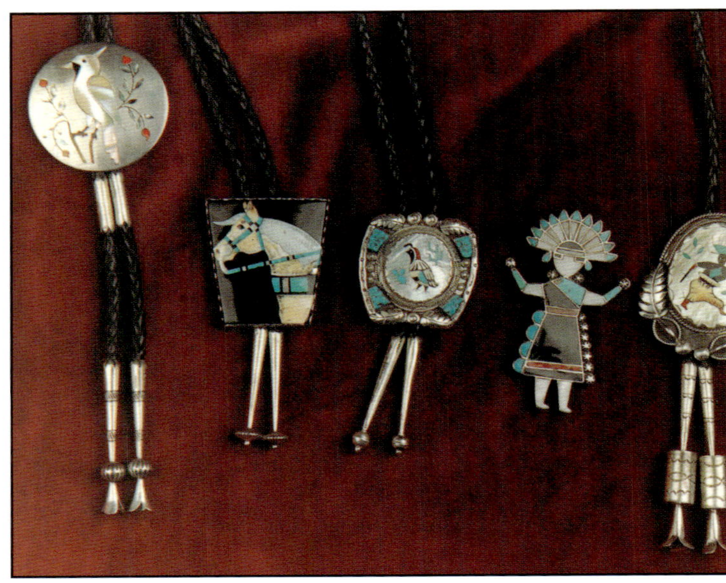

This distinctive Zuni jewelry includes a bolo tie medallion, featuring a white bird. / An inlaid horse's head, late 1950s. / A quail by Leonard Lonjose. / A pin of a female dancer. / A crown dancer by L.H. Lonjose. *Enchanted Mesa collection*

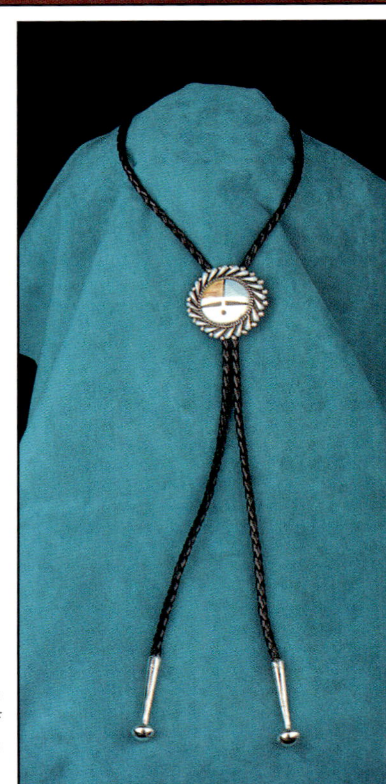

Bolo slide of sterling silver inlayed with a sunface design by C.Tsipa, Zuni. *Courtesy of Palms Trading Company* ($225)

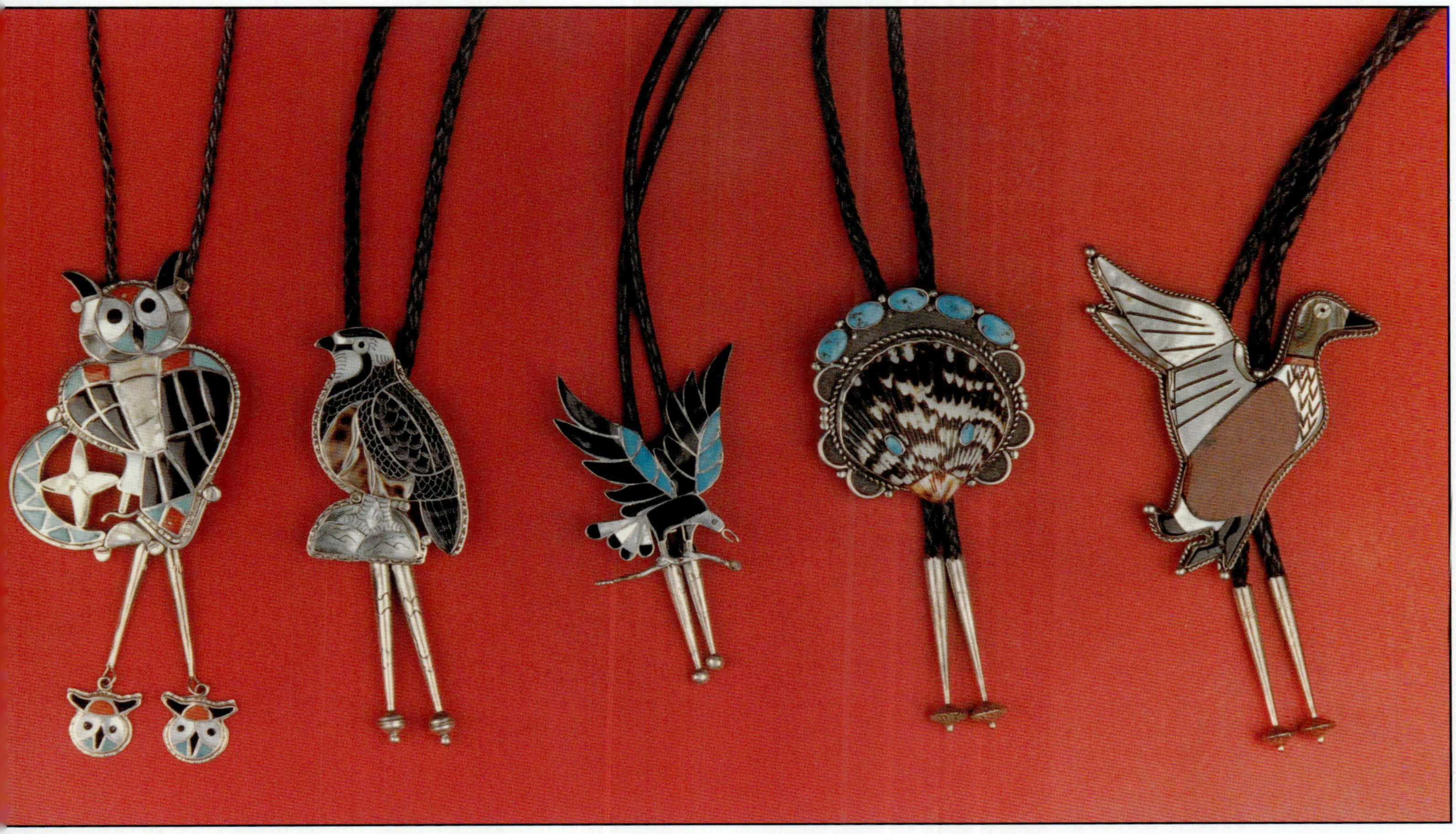

Birds are popular subjects for Zuni bolo ties. An inlaid owl with owl pendant heads by L.L.Y. / Grouse of intricate inlay by Porfilio Sheyka. / Eagle inlay marked Art. / Shell as an owl's head and with turquoise inlay by L.L.Y. / Flying duck, unmarked. *Private collection*

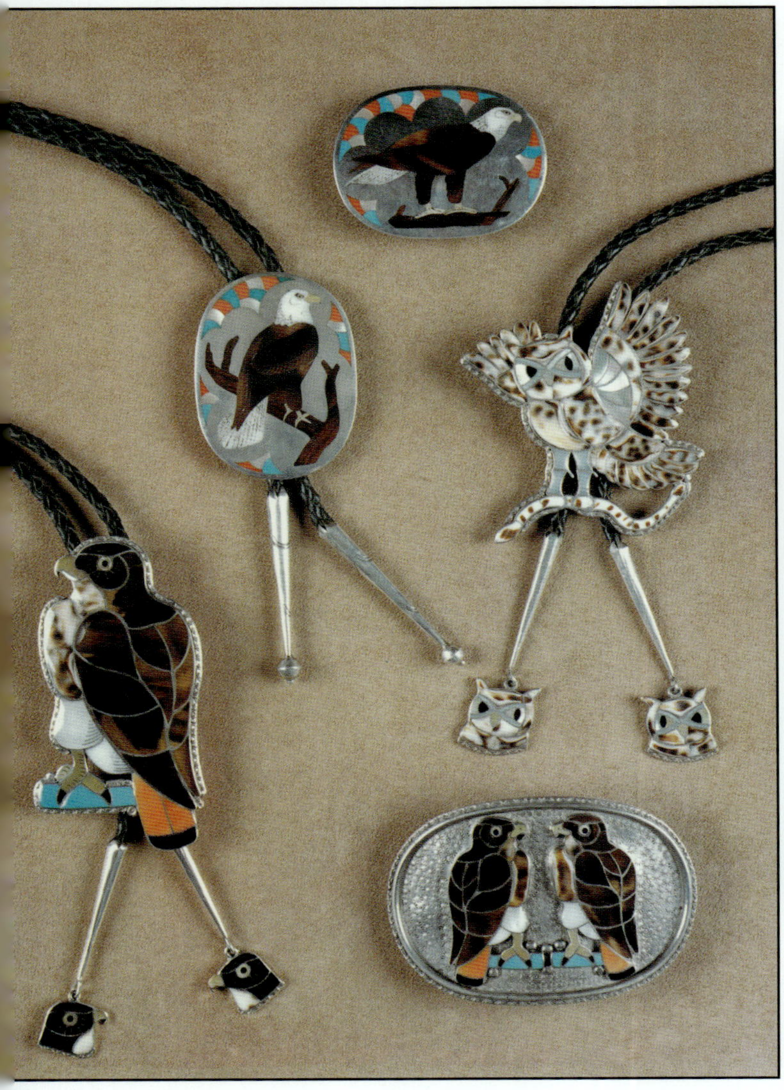

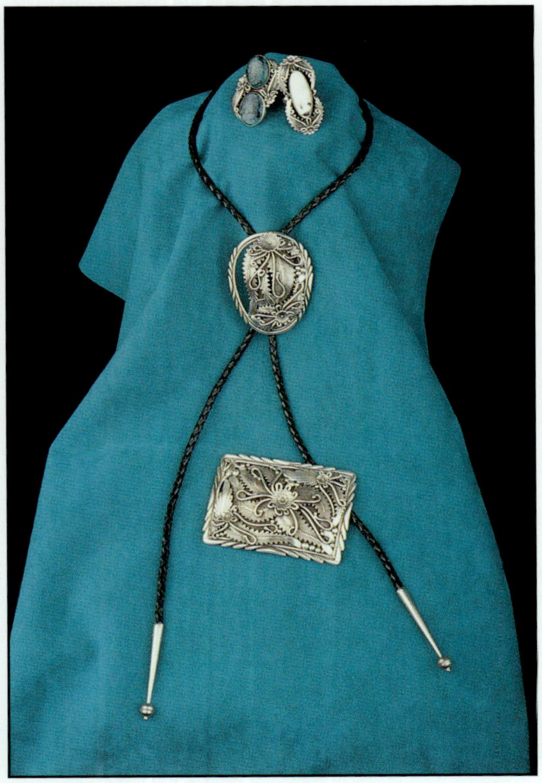

Bolo slide ($330), buckle ($435), and two rings ($120 and $87) by Peterson Johnson, Navajo, 2002. *Courtesy of Palms Trading Company*

In the 1970s matching buckles and bolo slides were made primarily for sale. Porfilio and Ann Sheyka made this strong hawk bolo with pendant heads and matching buckle in 1978. / A.D. Panteah made the eagle bolo slide and buckle in 1979. / Porfilio Shekya made the owl slide and pendants with tiger shell and mother of pearl in 1977. *Private collection*

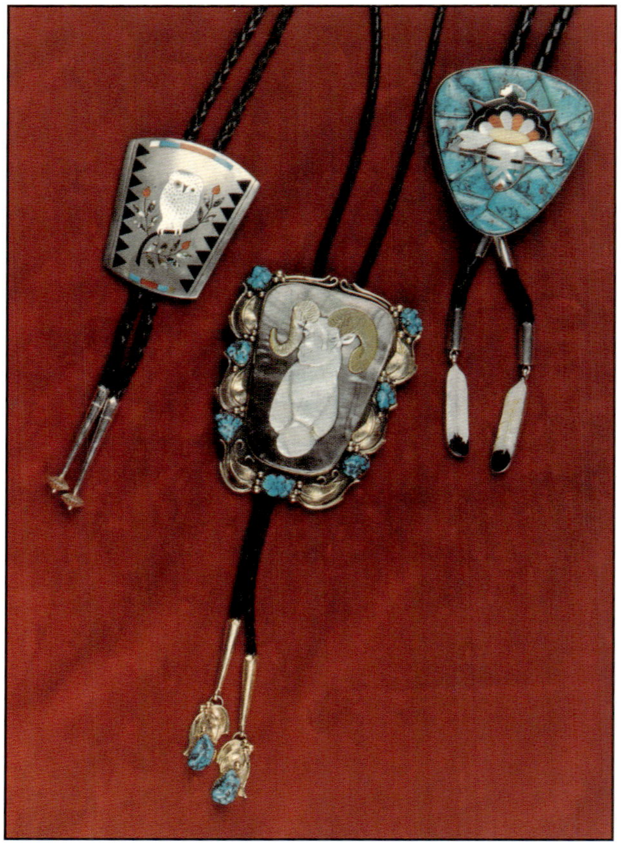

A trio of Zuni bolo ties: Dennis and Nancy Edaakie made the white owl inlay. / The gold work and ram's head inlaid bolo slide with nine turquoise nuggets is by Martin Muskett. / A mosaic kachina head bolo slide with carved feather tip ends was made by J. Frazee and William C.Shotts. *Private collection*

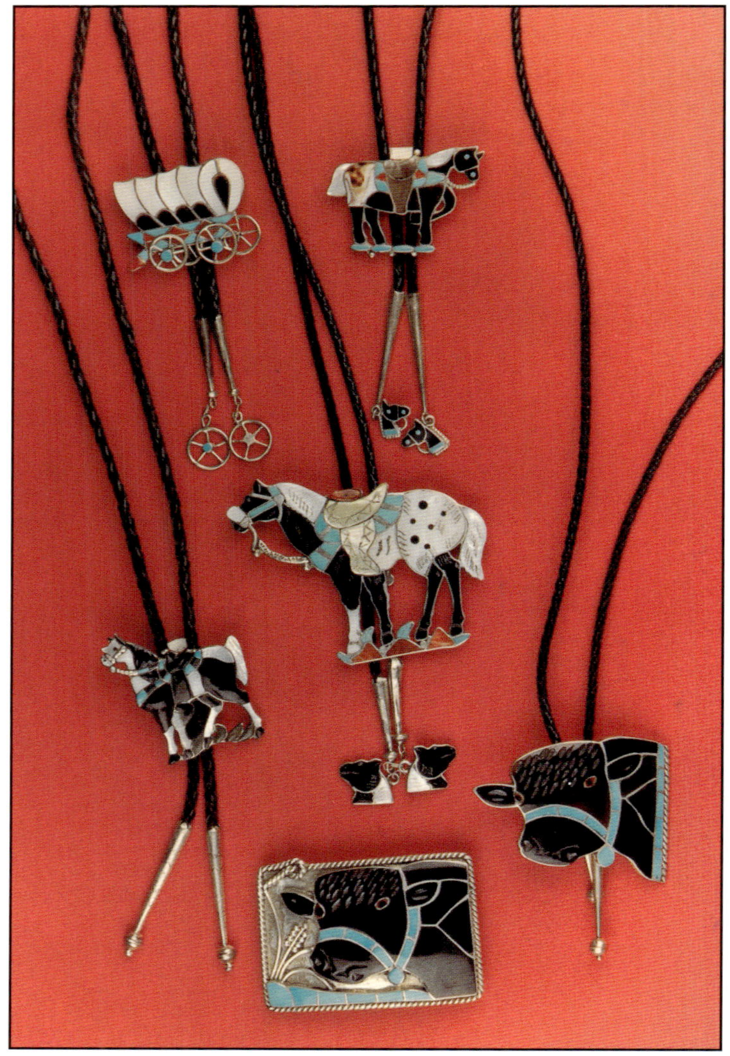

Animals are frequent subjects for Zuni bolo ties. Two small inlaid horses are unmarked. Joe Zuni made the big horse with small head pendants. / D.J. Lamy made a covered wagon with gold wheels and wheel pendants. / The cow's head bolo slide and buckle are amusing designs made by Helen and Lincoln Zunie. *Private collection*

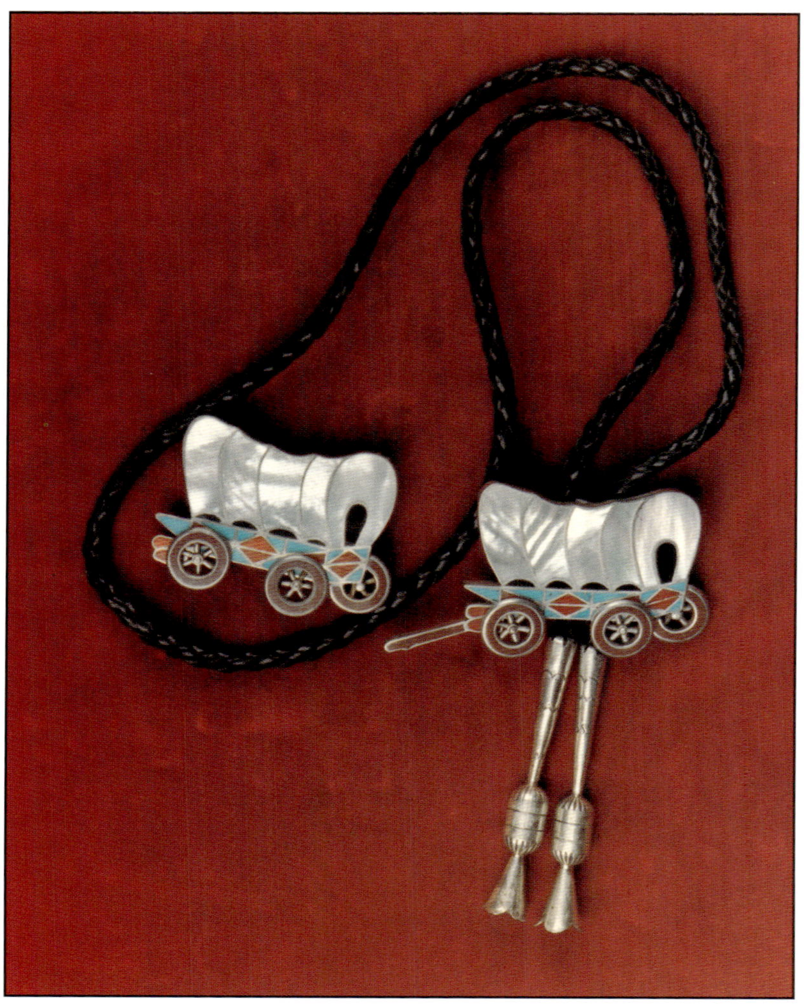

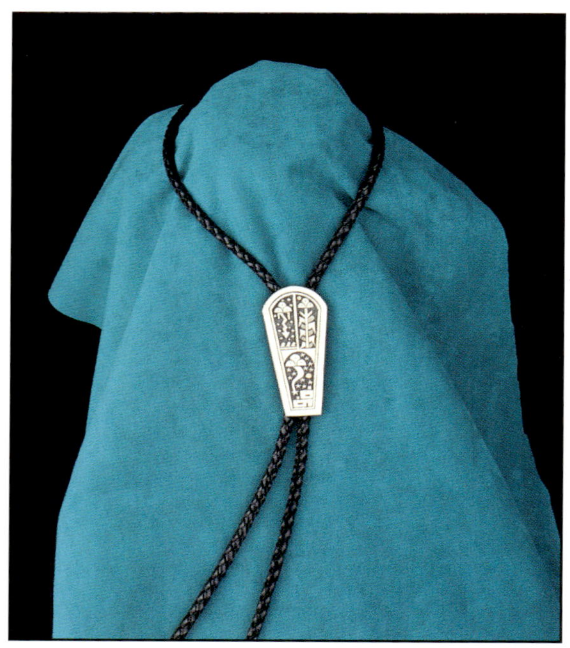

Bolo slide of sterling silver and 14k gold by Joseph Coriz, Santo Domingo ($390)

Mike Shirley made the covered wagon bolo and buckle set with mother of pearl inlay, circa 1978. *Private collection*

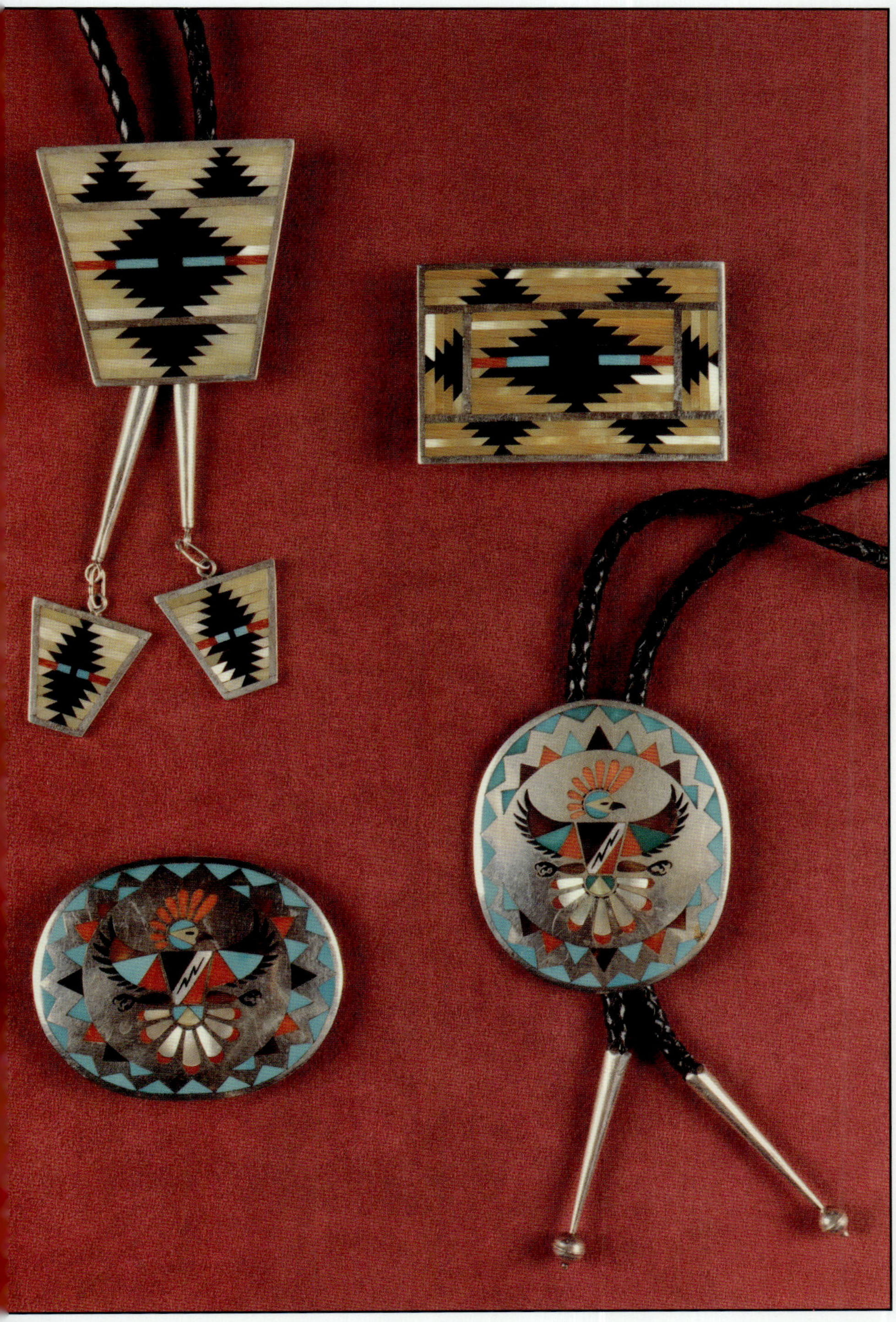

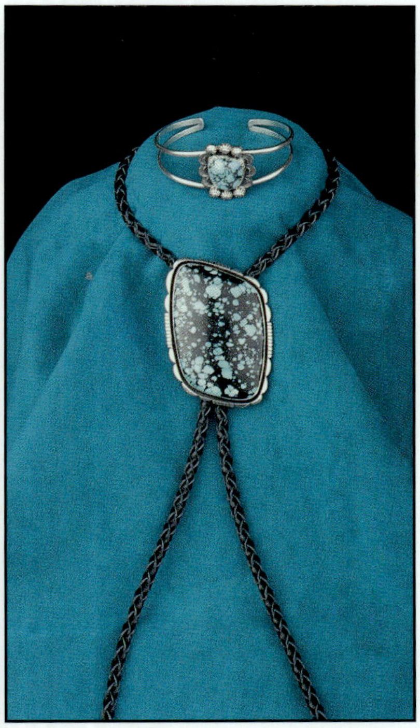

Bolo slide by Nat Skyhorse with black matrix turquoise ($210) and a two-wire silve bracelet with turquoise in a medallion by Lonnie Willie. *Courtesy of Palms Trading Company*

These Zuni bolo sets have different styles of inlay. The rug design of close stonework inlay is fashioned as a bolo slide with pendants and a buckle made by Charlene Dishta, 1988. / Ruddell and Nancy Laconsello made the eagle man buckle and bolo slide of inlay set in silver in 1982. *Private collection on permanent loan to Ohio University*

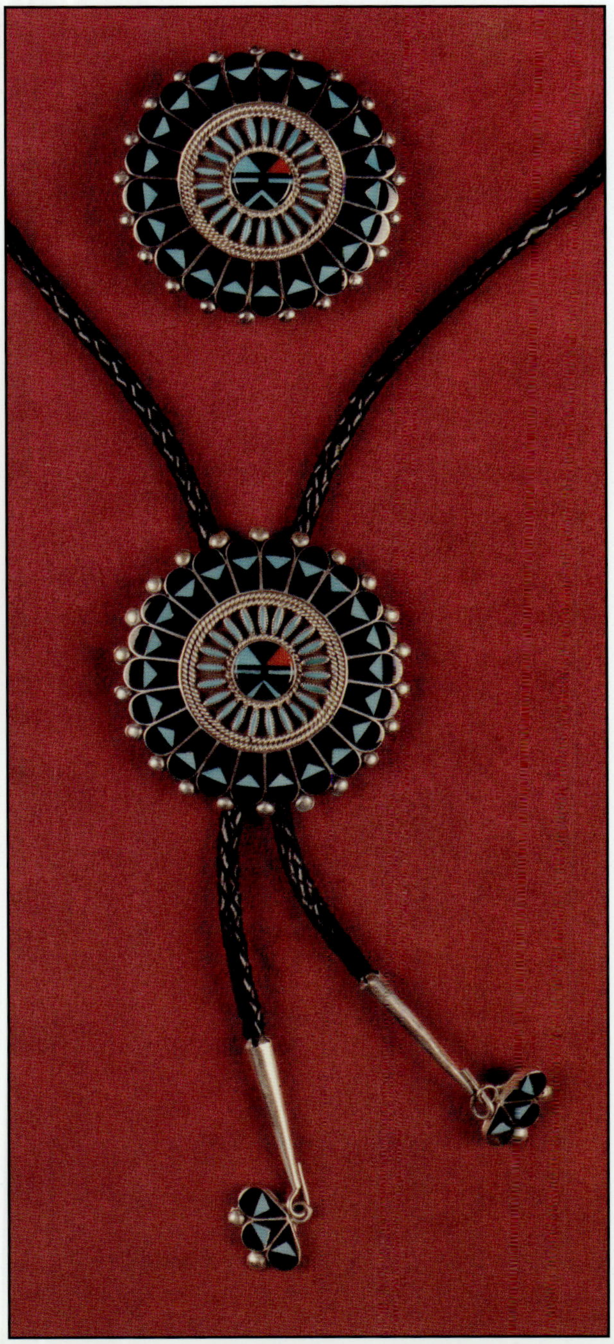

Very fine inlay work is exhibited by the black sunface bolo slide with pendants and buckle by Benjamin and Shirley Zuni of Zuni in 1982. *Private collection*

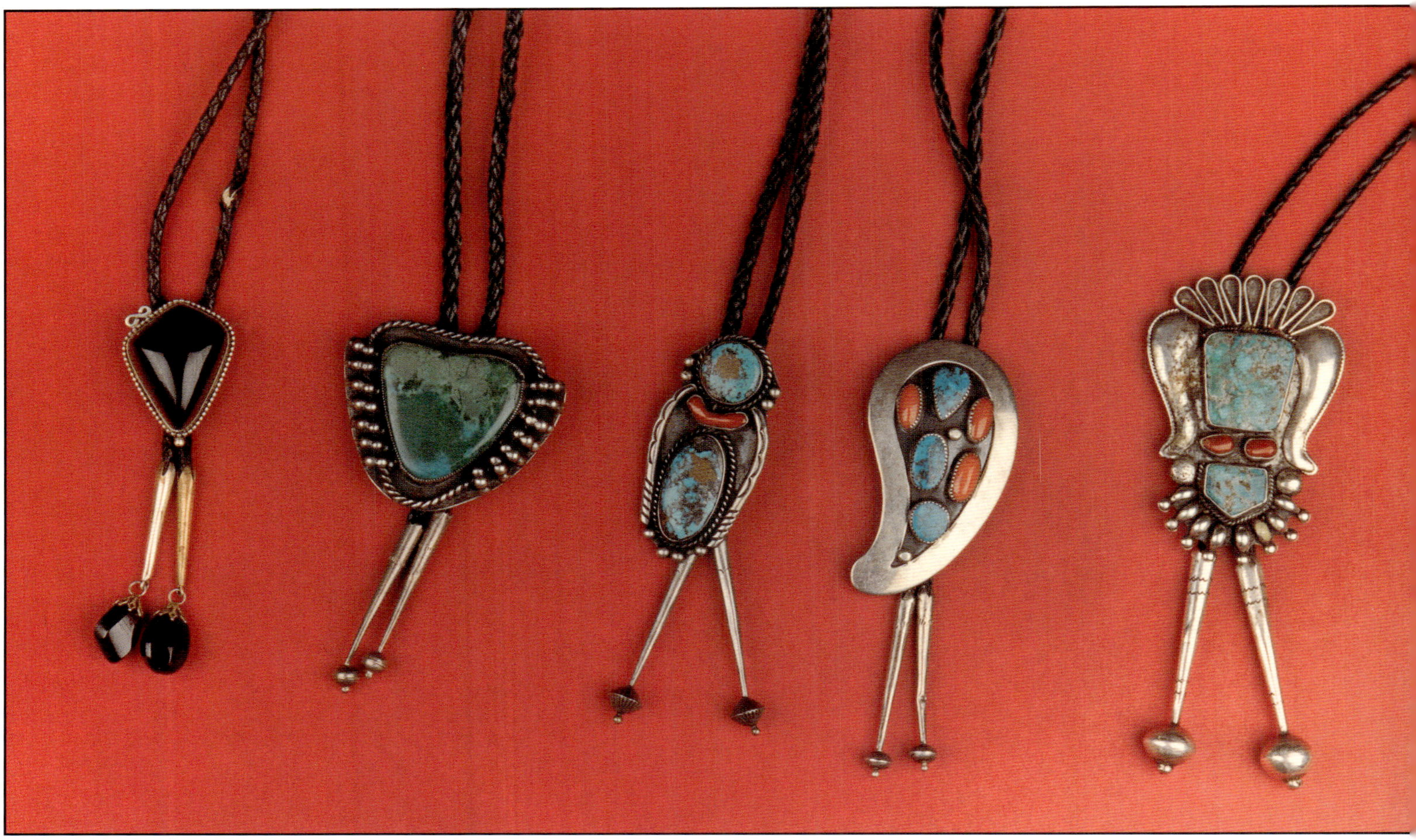

Bolo slides from the 1970s set with various types of turquoise and coral. *Private collections*

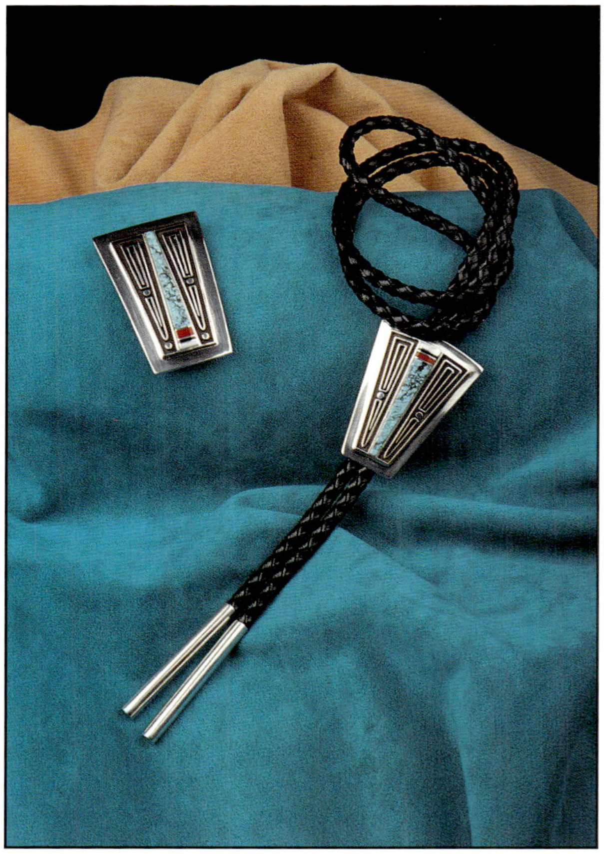

Buckle and bolo by Albert Nells, Navajo. *Courtesy McGee's, Keams Canyon*

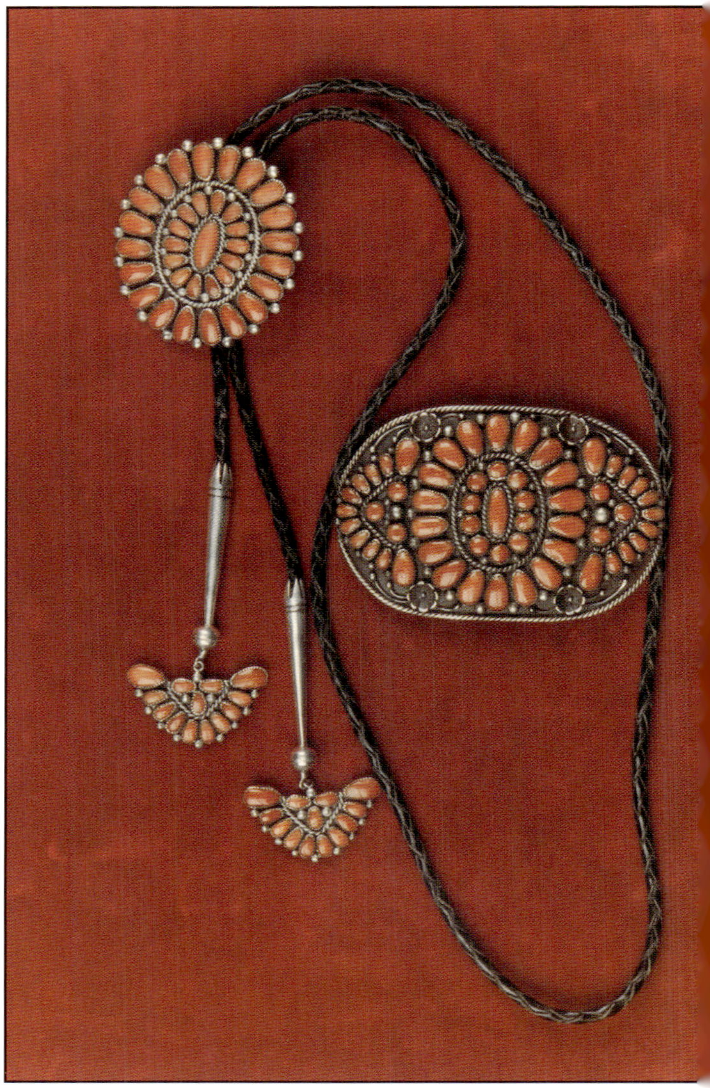

Silver bolo and matching buckle set with coral clusters, circa 1980. *Private collection*

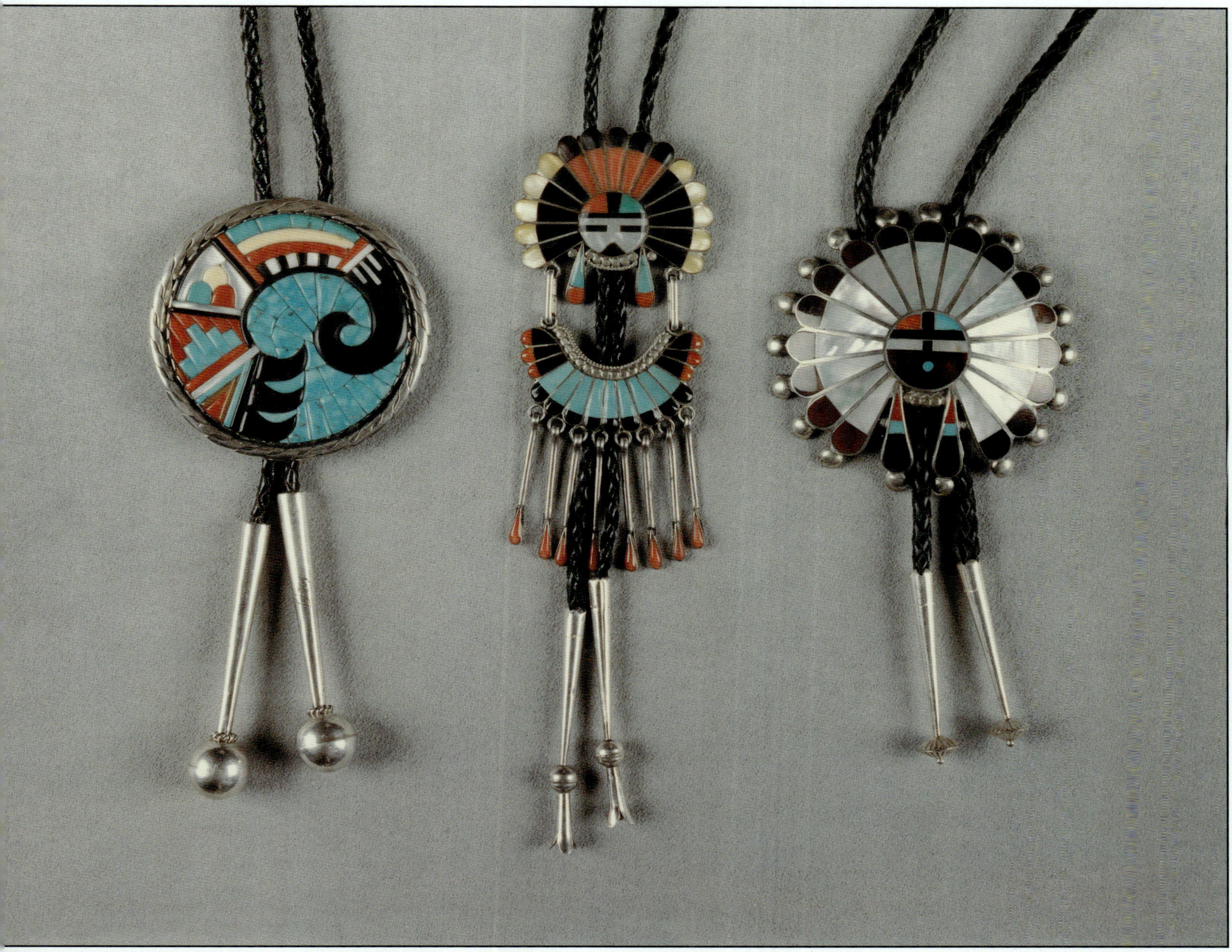

Three handsome bolo slides featuring contemporary designs: Disc with Morenci turquoise by Lee and Mary Weebothee, Zuni, 1979. / Sunface figure with fringed bib by Dexter and Eva Cellicion, Zuni, 1979. / A white sunface by T.P.B., Zuni. *Private collection on permanent loan to Ohio University*

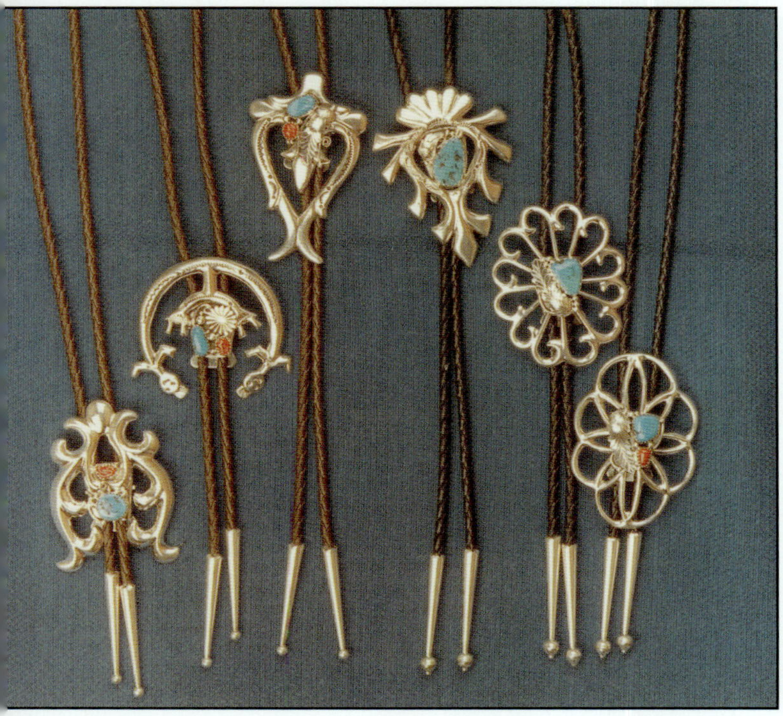

These finely detailed sand-cast silver and turquoise bolo slides show the design variations made in the 1980s. *Bing Crosby collection*

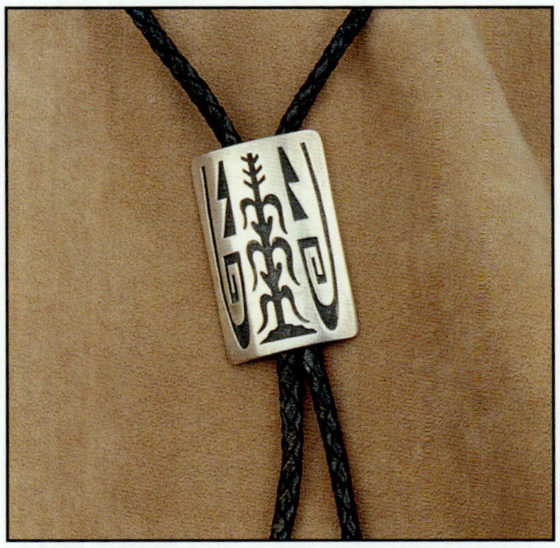

Hopi silver bolo slide with the fertility design of a corn stalk, late 20th century. *Lynn D. Trusdell, Crown & Eagle Antiques*

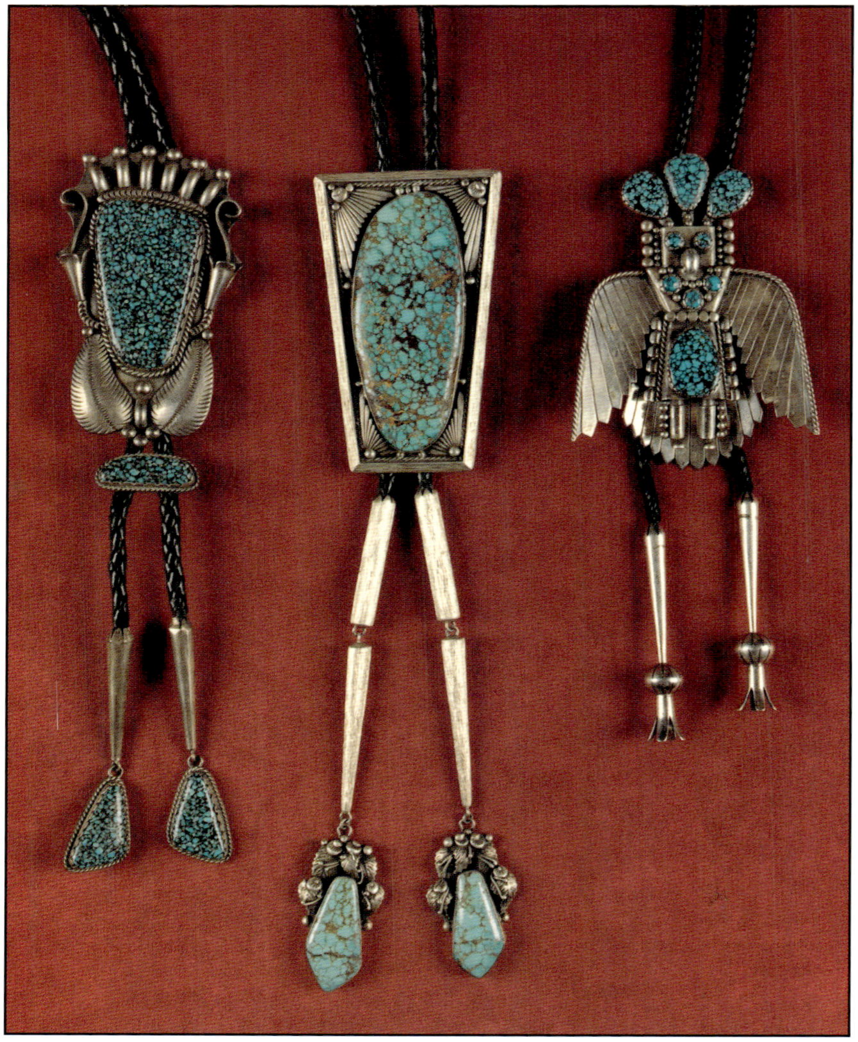

From left, silver bolo slide with applied leaf designs and turquoise chips in black matrix, 1975. / Spiderweb turquoise set in a silver slide, shell tubular tips and pendants set with Spiderweb turquoise made by Boyd Tsosie, Navajo, 1971. / Eagle kachina figure as a bolo slide set with turquoise and tips with squash blossoms, 1982. *Private collection on permanent loan to Ohio University*

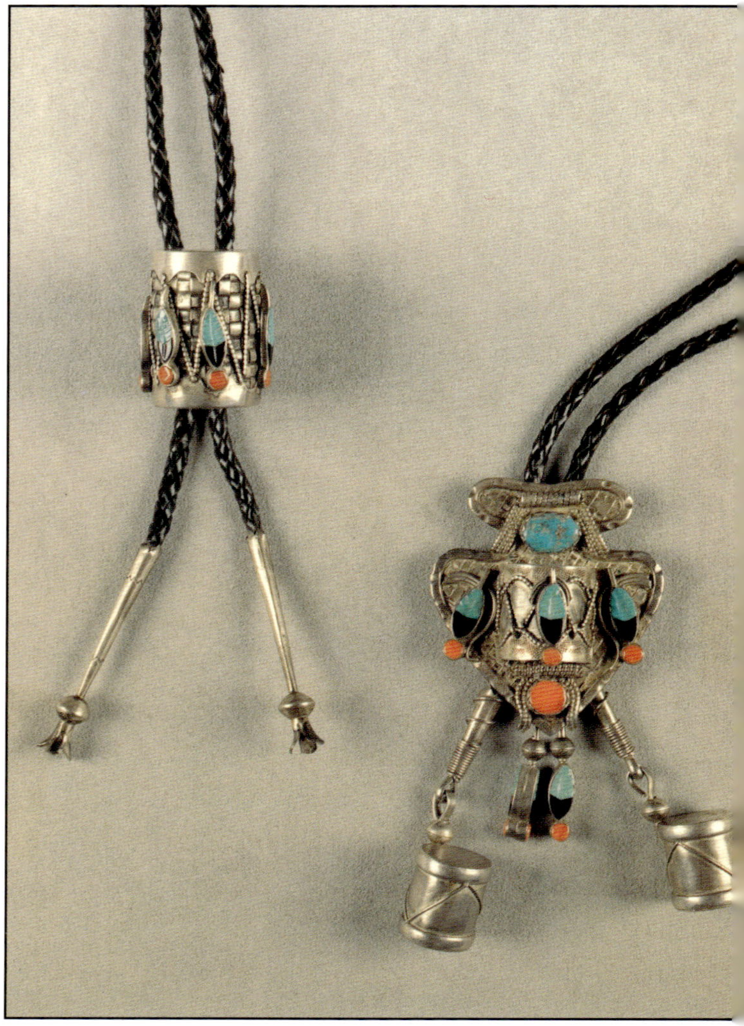

Two Zuni bolo ties, one in the shape of a drum and the other shaped as an arrowhead, with drum pendants, both made by E.A.E., 1976. *Private collection on permanent loan to Ohio University*

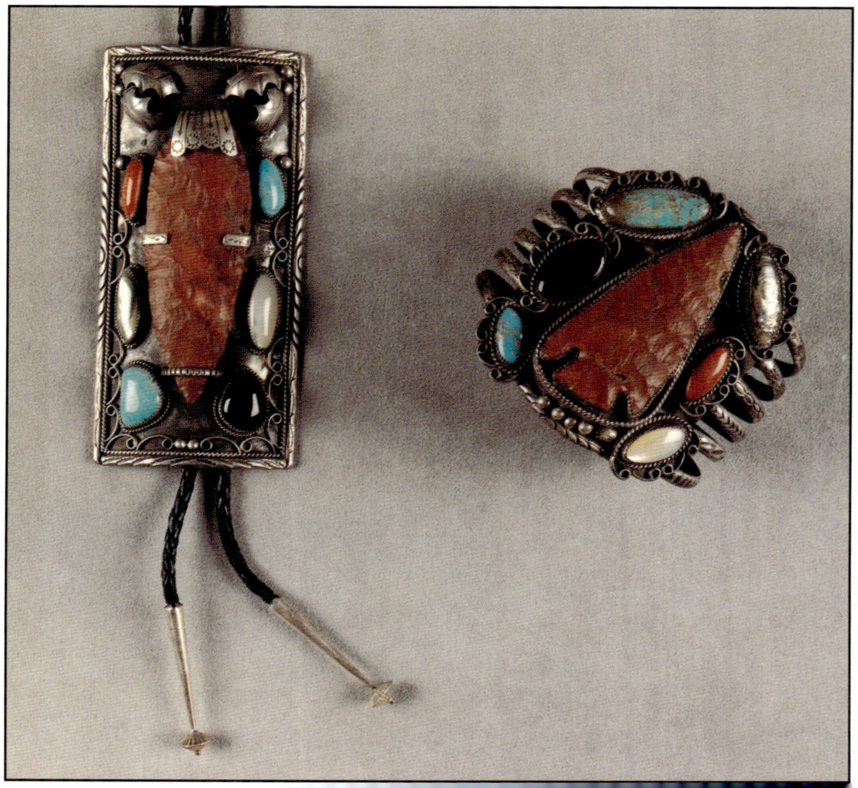

Bolo and matching man's bracelet set in silver with assorted colored stones and a flint spear point on the slide and a flint arrowhead on the bracelet, made by Paul Stover, Navajo, 1975. *Private collection on permanent loan to Ohio University*

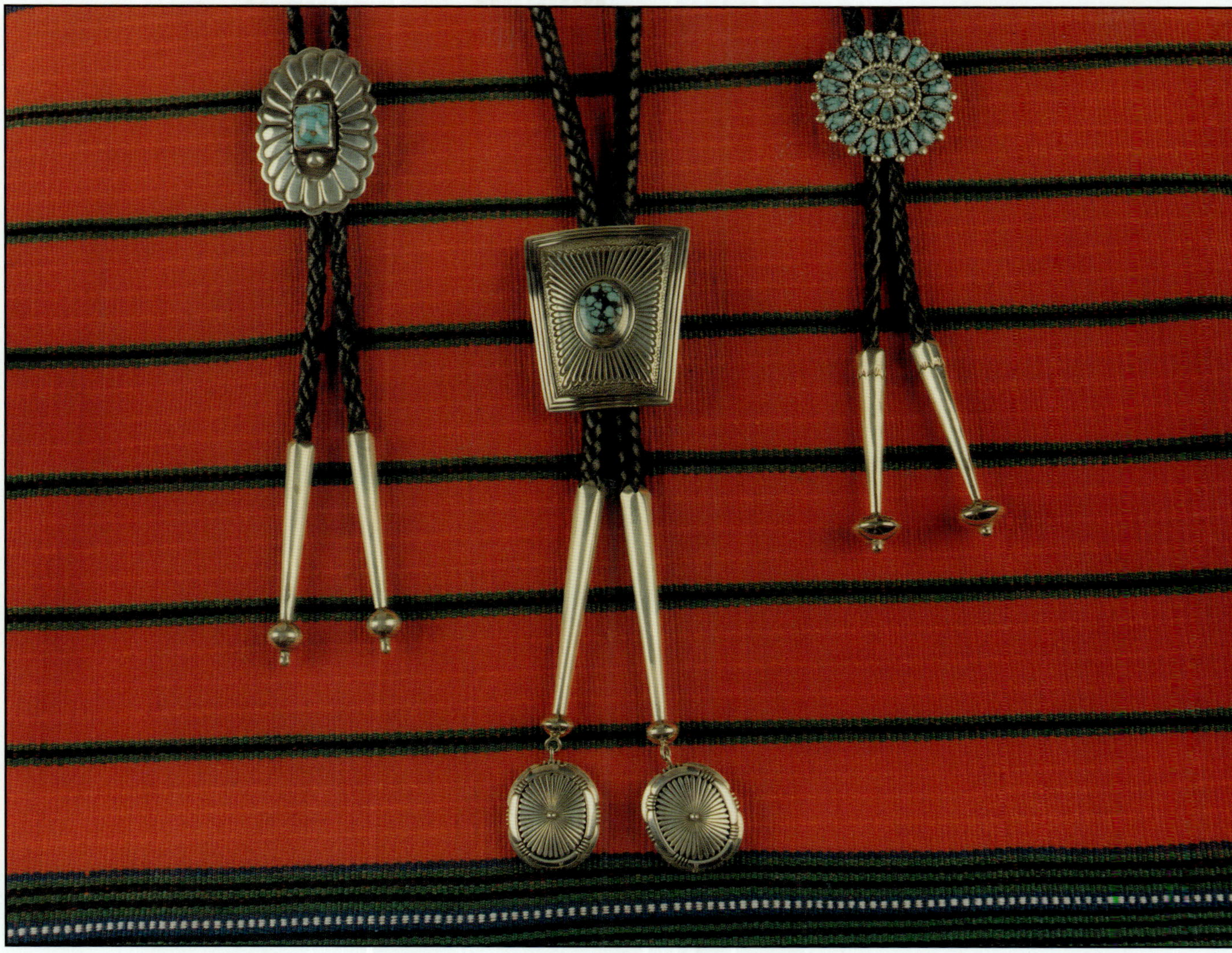

Distinctive bolo ties: From left, Oval wrought silver slide with turquoise stone by Joseph H. Quintana, Cochiti. / Sterling silver slide with wrought details and turquoise, and wrought oval pendants at the tips, made with stone by Howard Nelson, Navajo. / Chinese turquoise petite point clusters set in silver by Lorraine Waatsa, Zuni. *Indian Post collection*

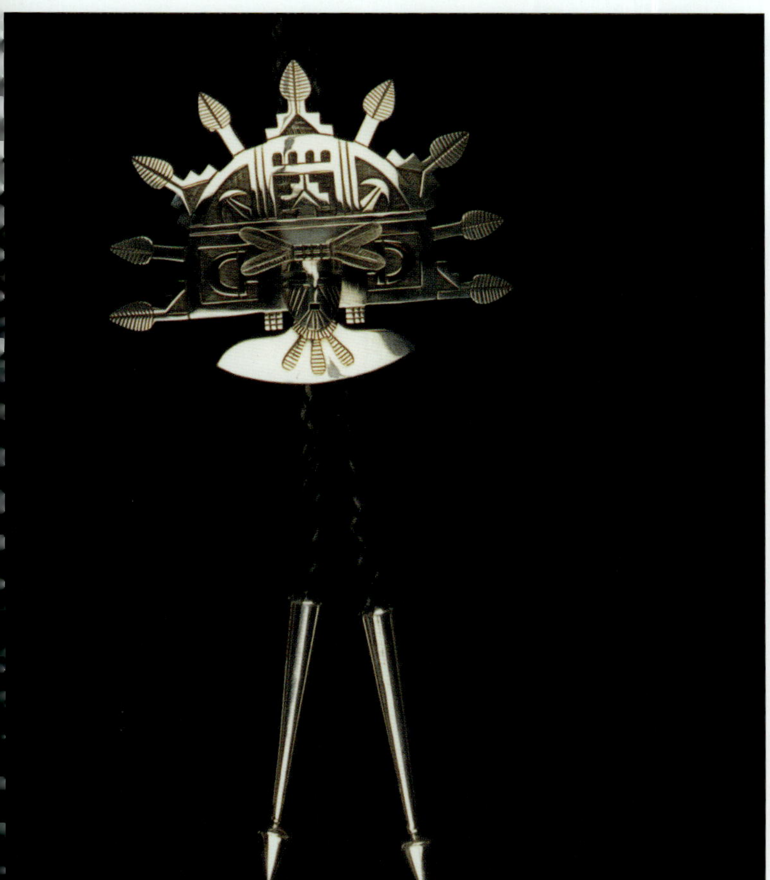

Bolo tie by Lawrence Saufkie, Hopi. *Keams Canyon Arts and Crafts collection*

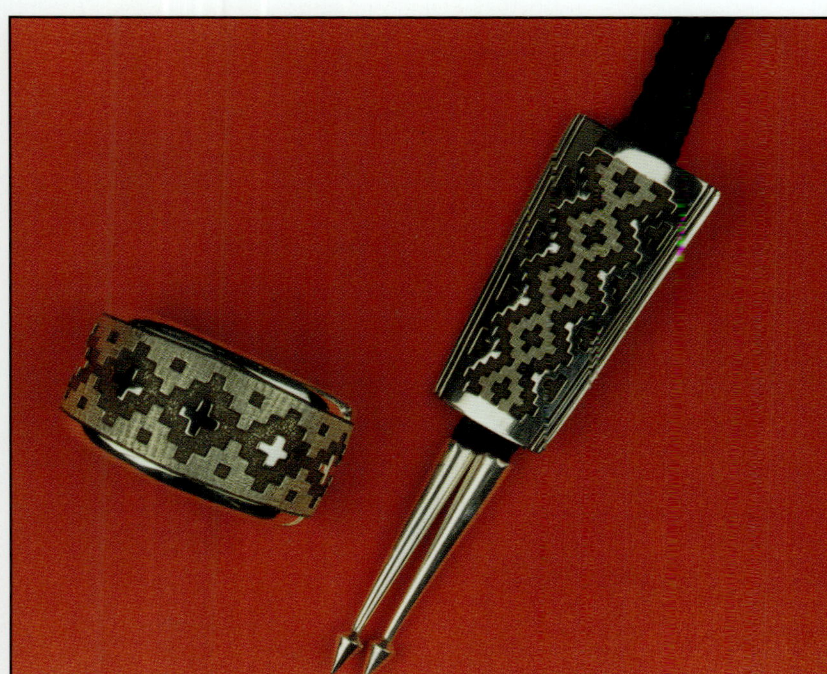

Unique bolo tie and bracelet by D.A. Jackson, Navajo. *Keams Canyon Arts and Crafts collection*

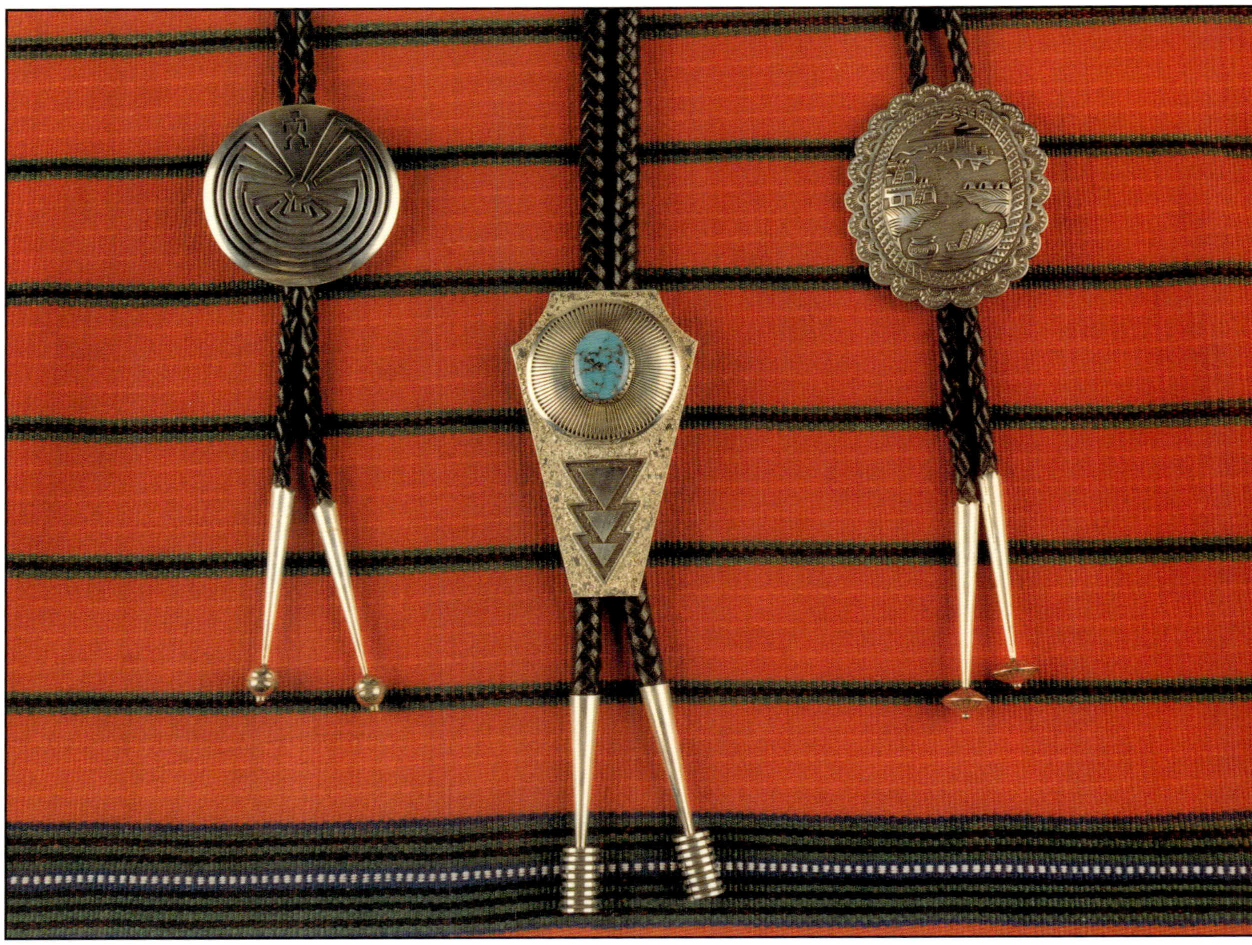

Three bolo ties: From left, sterling Man in the Maze by Riley Polequaptewa, Hopi. / Textured sterling design with turquoise made by Howard Nelson, "Kee Nez," Navajo. / Sterling oval with landscape of mesa, pueblos, beehive ovens, and bowl with corn in stamped and filed border made by D. Morgan. *Indian Post collection*

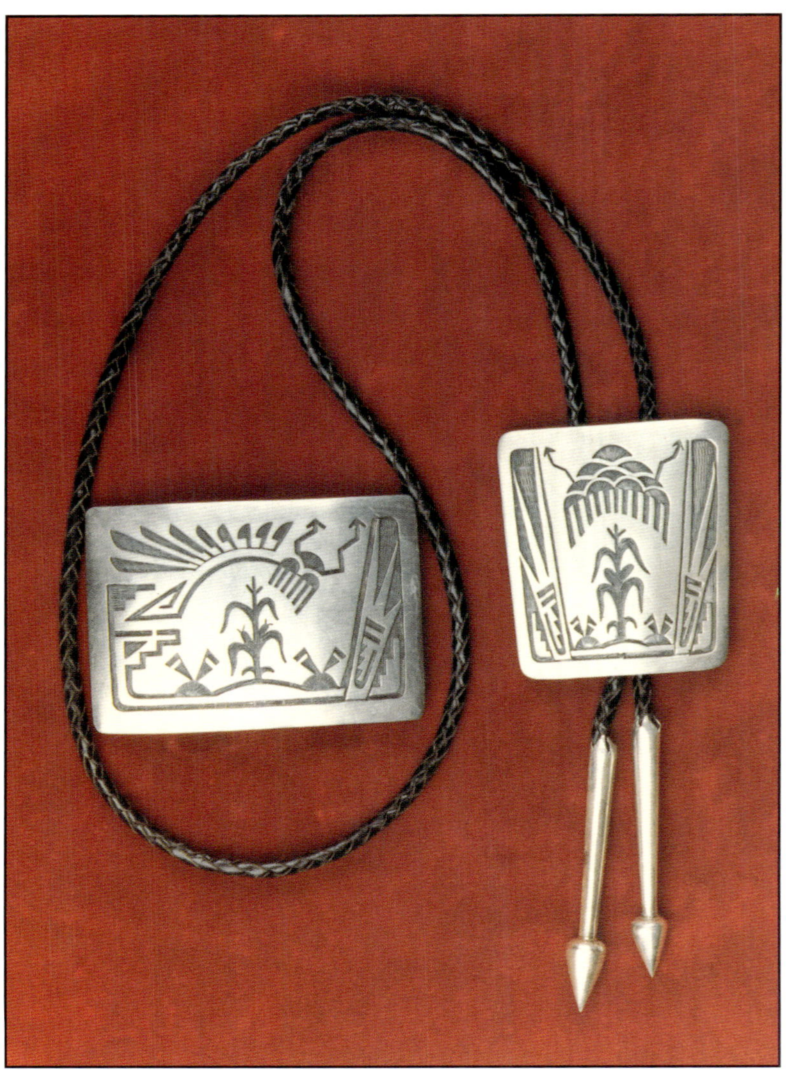

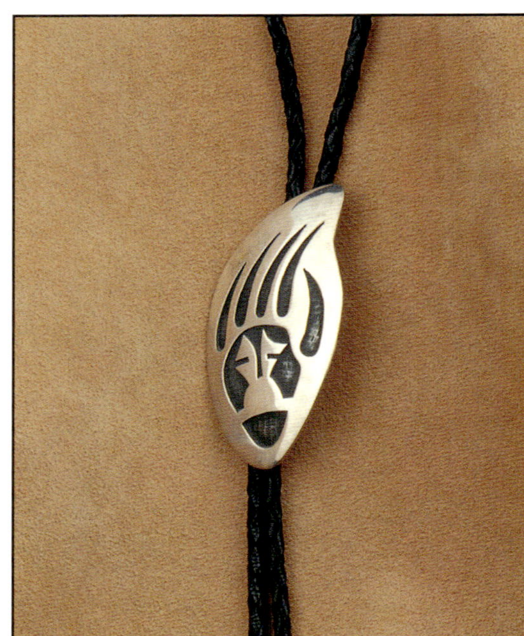

Hopi bolo slide with bearpaw design, late 29th century. *Lynn D. Trusdell, Crown & Eagle Antiques*

Bolo slide and belt buckle decorated in overlay design with corn plants, made by Watson Honanie, Hopi, circa 1978. *Private collection on permanent loan to Ohio University*

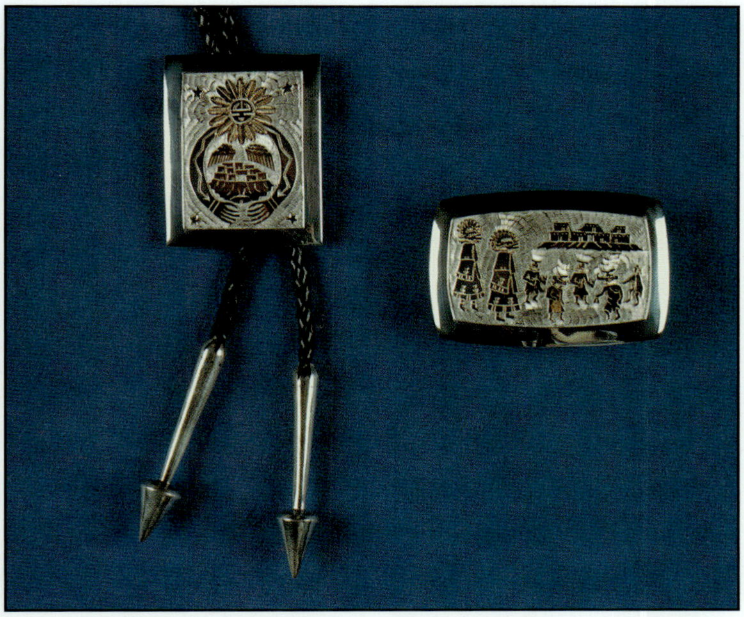

Five bolo slide and belt buckle with silver and 14-k gold overlay of delicate figurative design, made by Watson Honanie, Hopi, late 1980s. *Private collection*

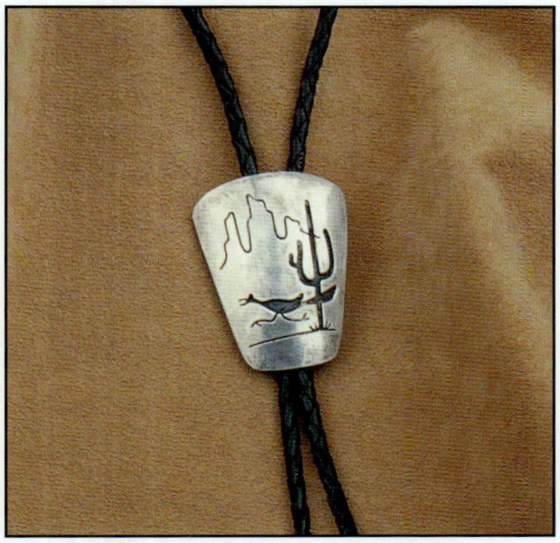

Hopi bolo slide with road-runners, cactus, and mountains design, late 20th century. *Lynn D. Trusdell, Crown & Eagle Antiques*

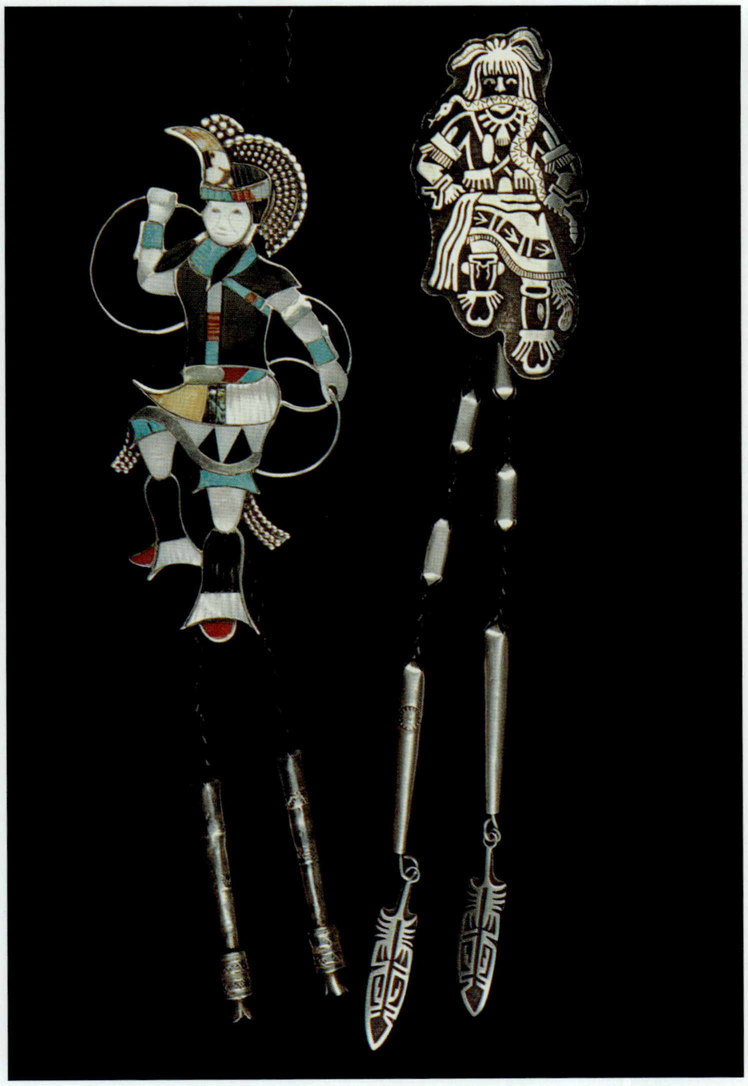

Bolo tie with extensive inlay by Eddie Beyuka, Zuni. / Silver bolo slide of silver overlay design by Bobby Secakuku, Hopi. *Turquoise Lady collection*

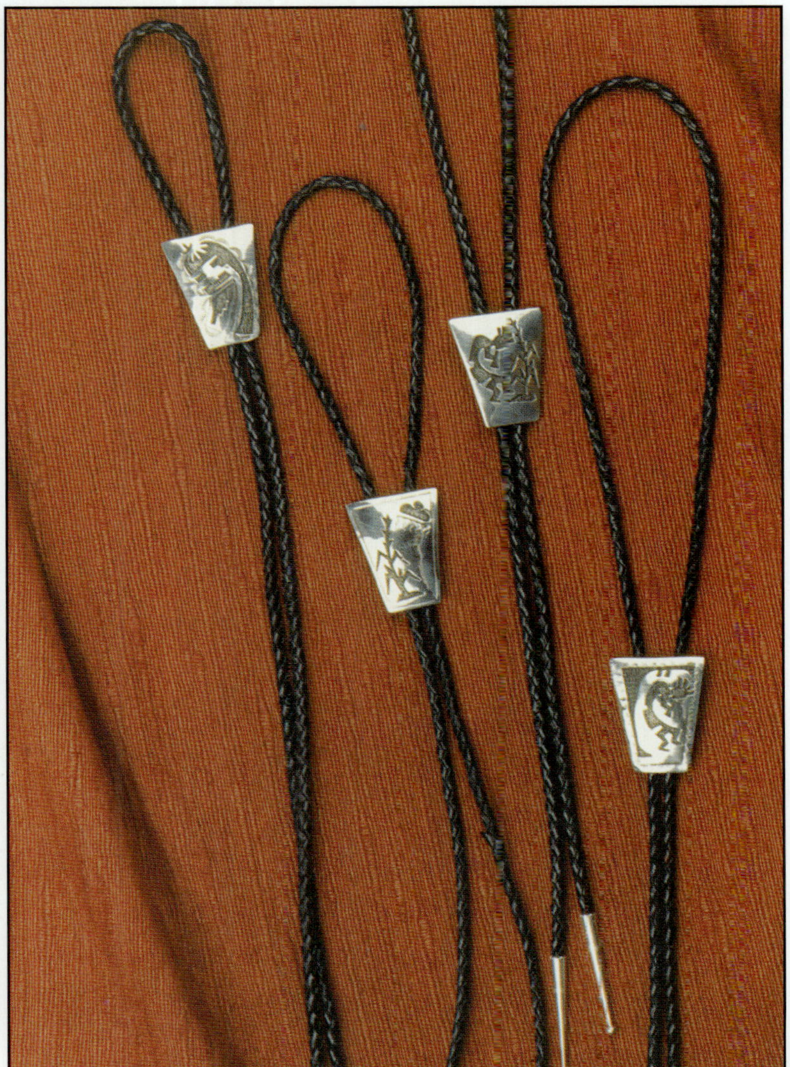

Four sterling silver Hopi overlay bolo slides from the late 1980s. *Bing Crosby collection*

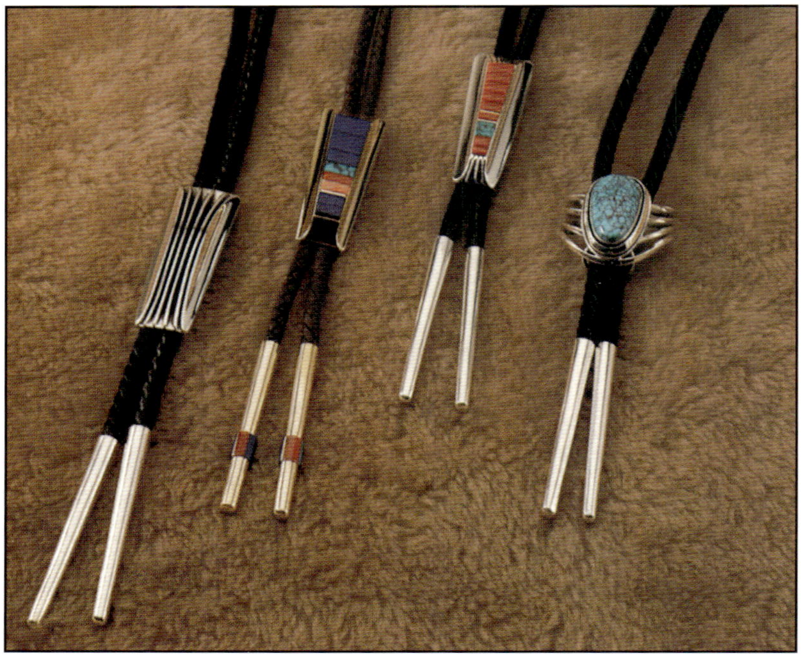

Four stone inlay bolo slides of streamlined designs by Victor Beck, Navajo.

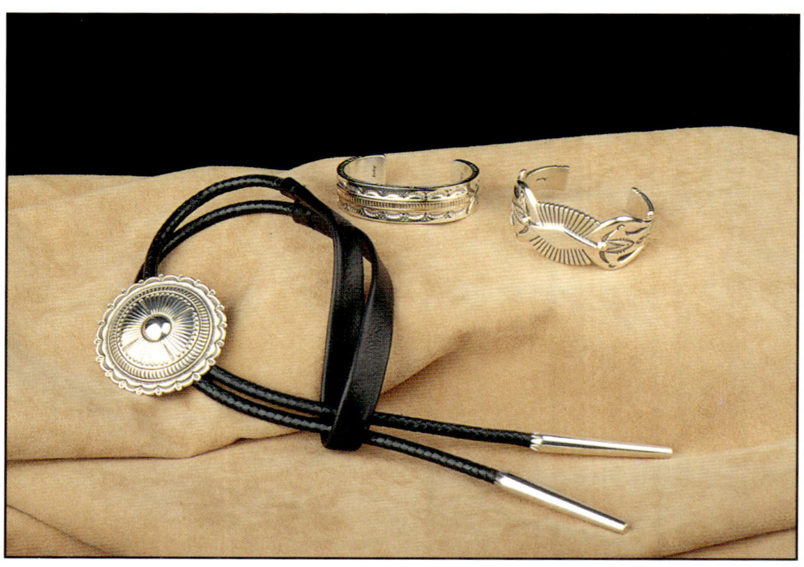

Bolo tie and two bracelets with gold by Thomas Curtis, Navajo. *Courtesy McGee's, Keams Canyon*

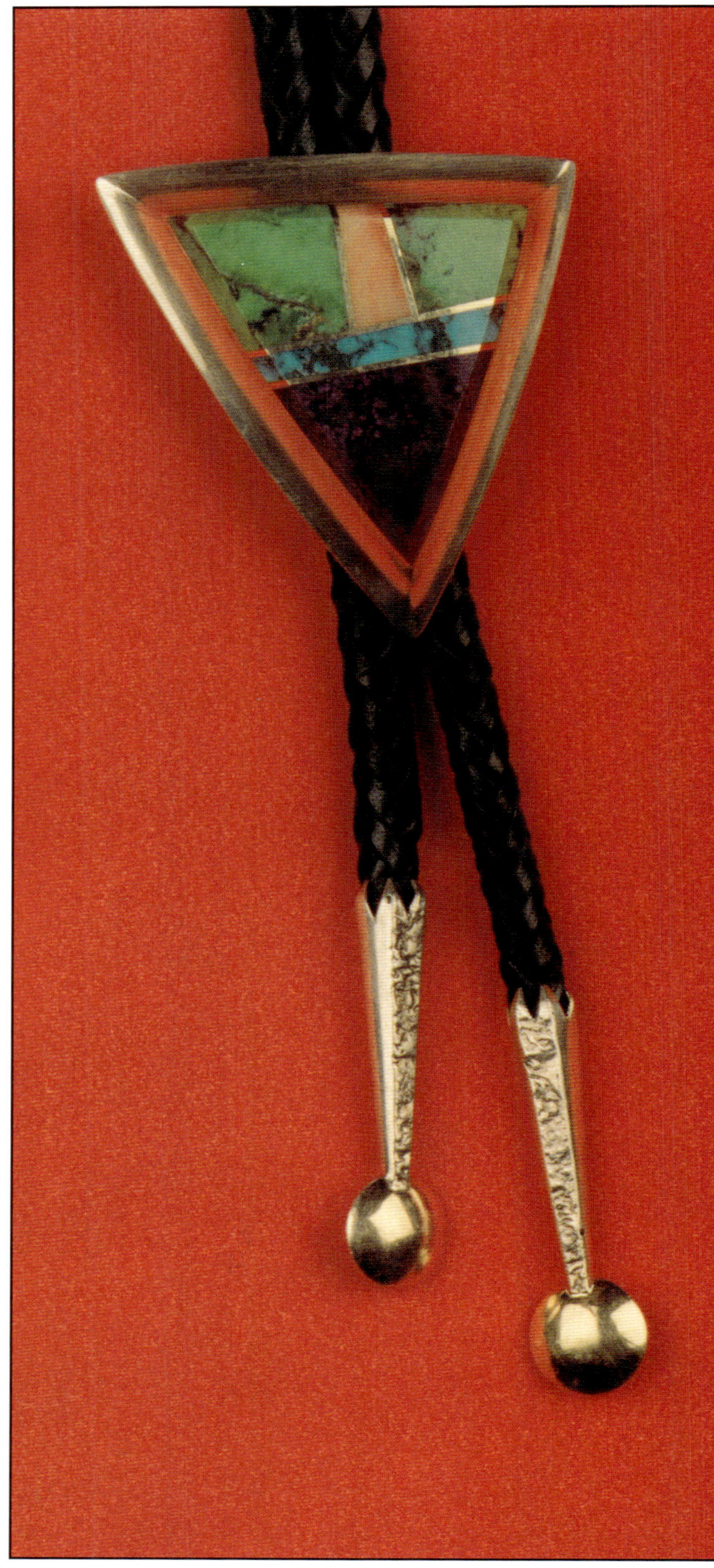

Lovely, colorful mosaic stone bolo slide made by Duane Maktima, Hopi, late 1980s. *Private collection*

Earrings

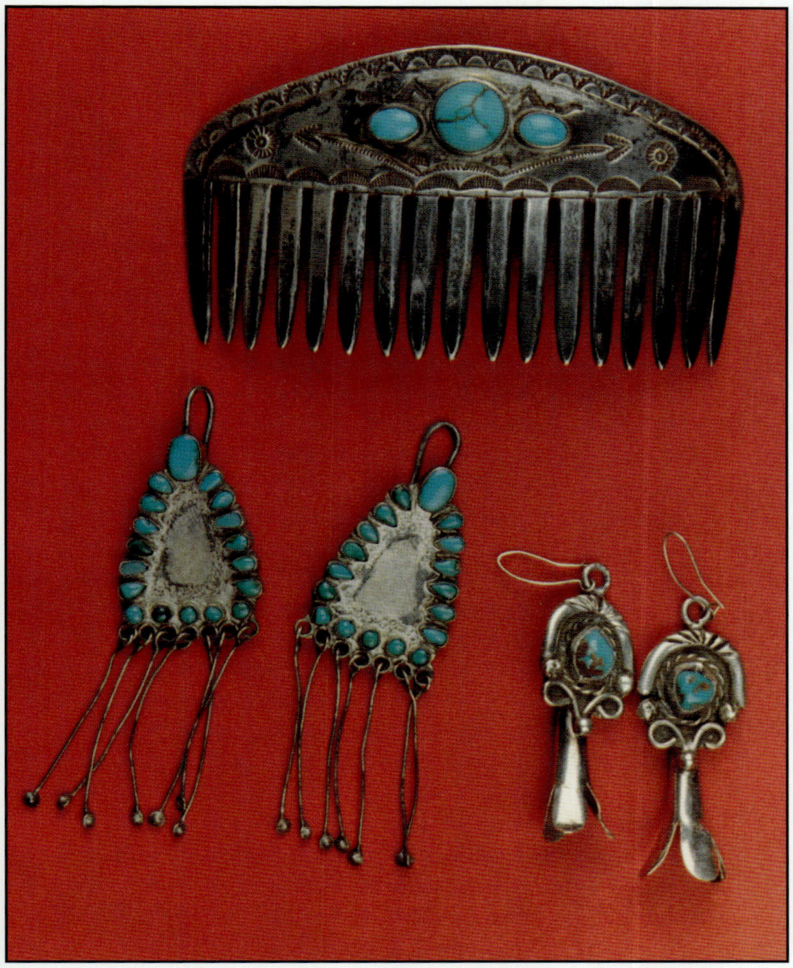

Old Navajo-made silver hair comb with stamped borders and three turquoise stones, designed in the colonial Spanish tradition. / One pair of silver Navajo earrings with small turquoise stones along the edges and six long fringed dangles. / Pair of silver earrings with wrought design and turquoise stones and squash blossom dangles. *Maxwell Museum collection*

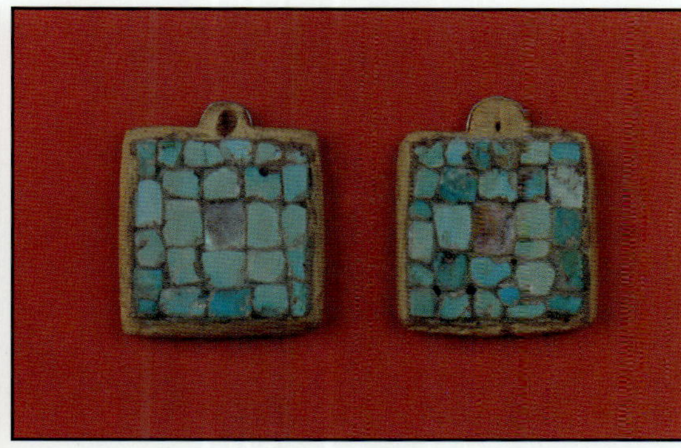

Pair of old-style Hopi earrings of square wood backing with turquoise mosaic inlay made by Washington Tahayuhptewa, Hopi. *Maxwell Museum collection*

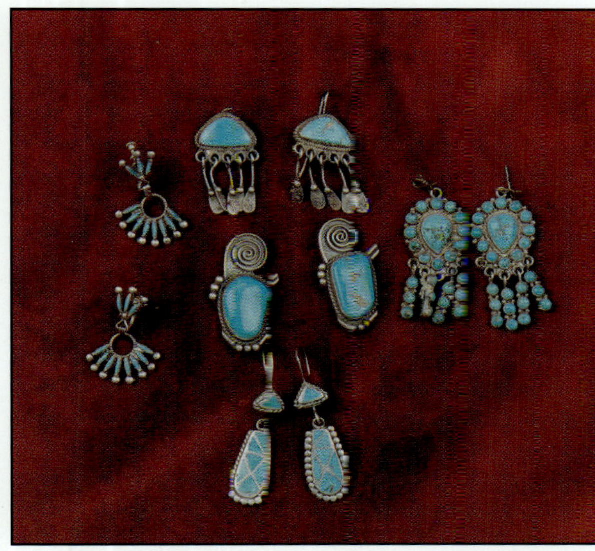

Five old-style pairs of earrings: From left, Zuni needle-point Morenci turquoise earrings, circa 1960. / Triangular turquoise-set earrings with silver drops. / Two Navajo pins set with turquoise. / Navajo dangle earrings set with Morenci turquoise, circa 1960. / Navajo cluster earrings set with Morenci and other turquoise stones, circa 1930. *Dennehotso collection*

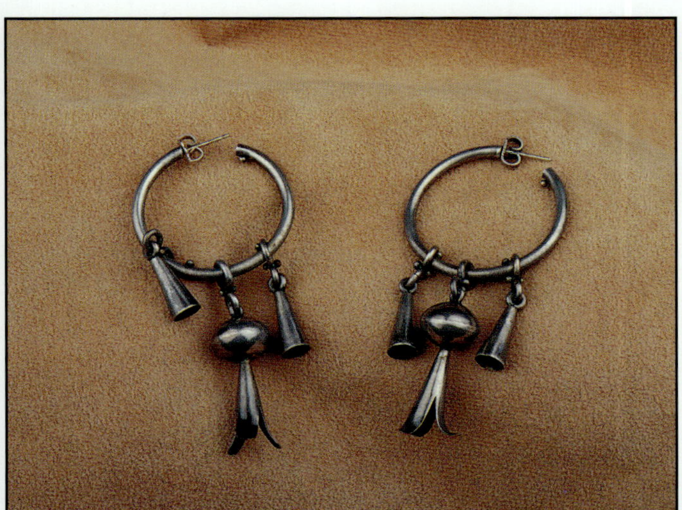

Pair of Navajo silver earrings of the earliest style of simple silver wire ring and a single squash blossom with a dangle on each side, late 19th century. *Lynn D. Trusdell, Crown & Eagle Antiques*

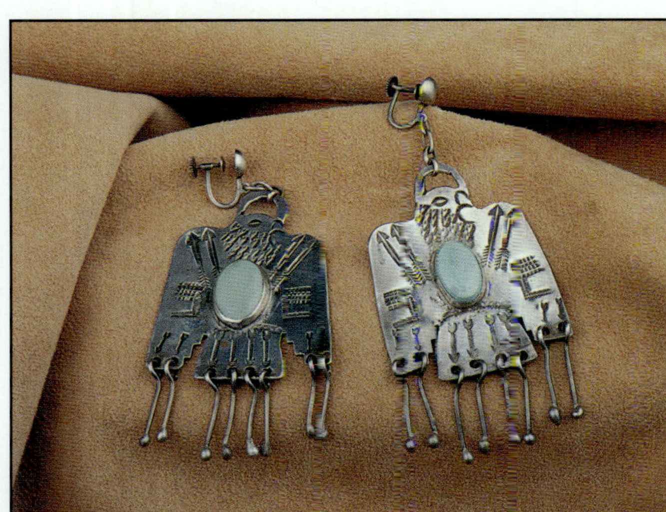

Large and unusual silver Navajo earrings of thunderbird design with attached dangling tail feathers, c. 1930. *Lynn D. Trusdell, Crown & Eagle Antiques*

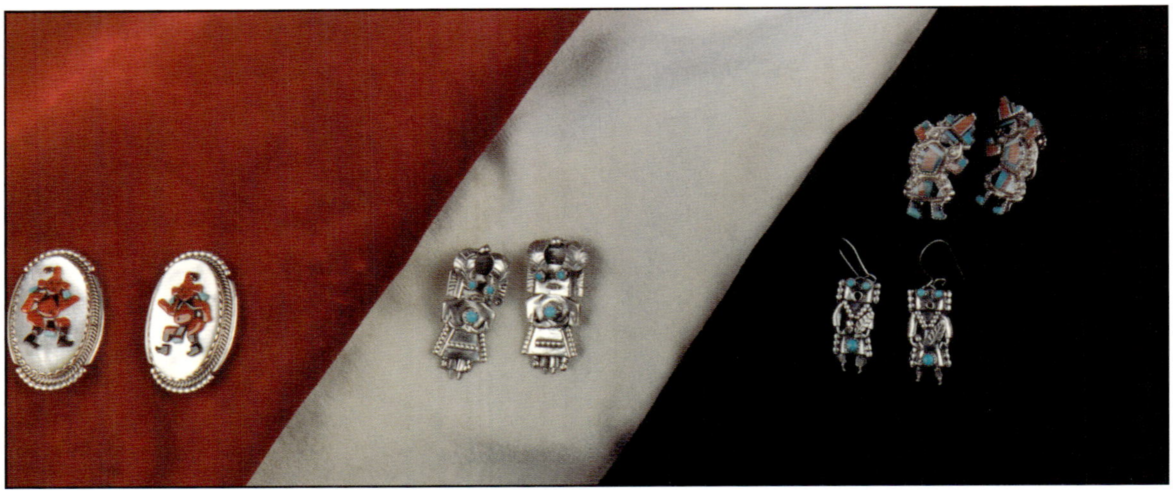

Four pairs of earrings featuring human figures: From left, Zuni oval earrings of mother of pearl decorated with coral kachina inlay. / Kachina figures set with turquoise. / Kachina figures set with coral and turquoise inlay, Zuni. / Small silver kachina figures with turquoise details. *Private collection on permanent loan to Ohio University*

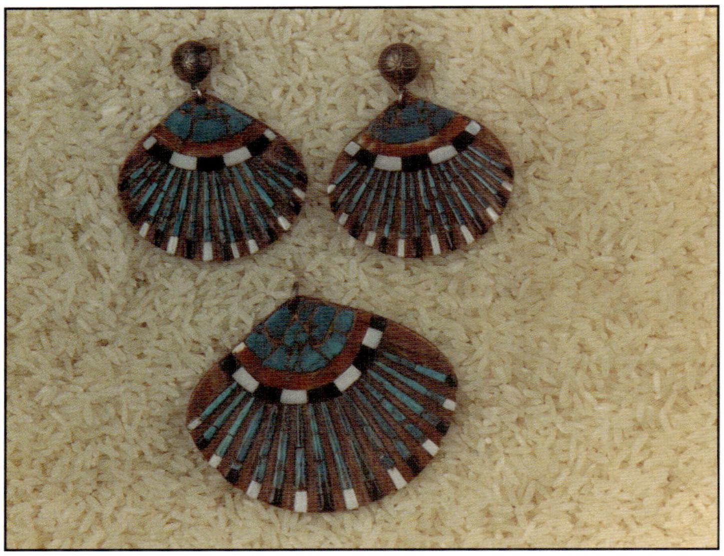

Matching pair of earrings of shell shape and pendant and decorated with extensive stone inlay, Zuni, circa 1950. *Enchanted Mesa collection* .

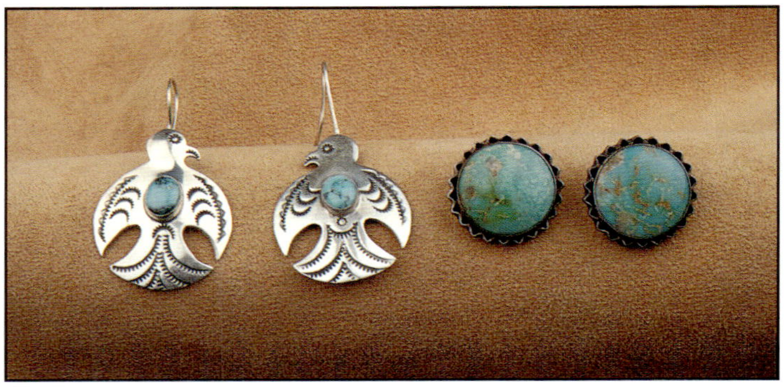

Two pair of Navajo tourist style earrings from the 1930s-'40s. *Lynn D. Trusdell, Crown & Eagle Antiques*

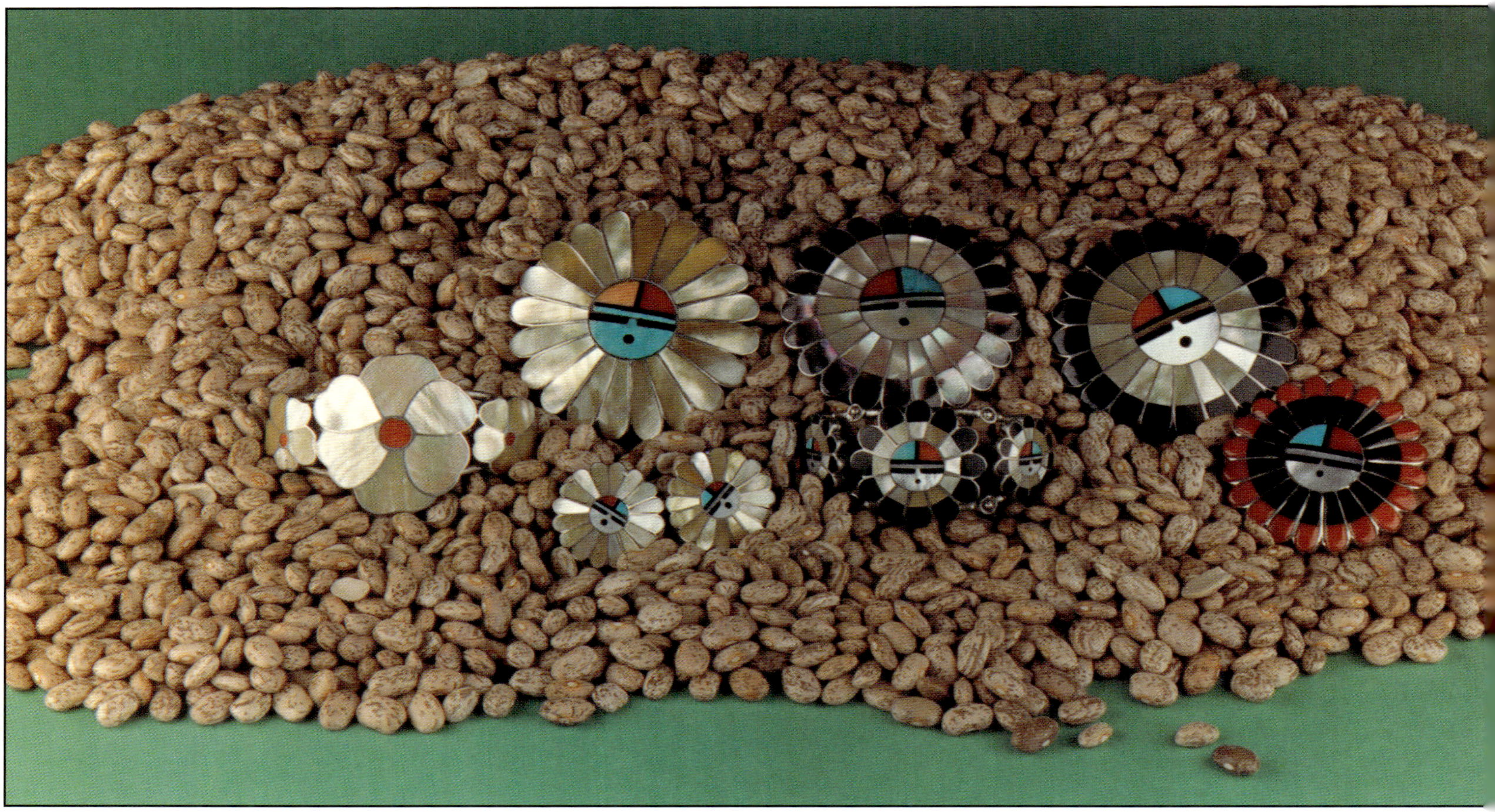

Zuni pins, earrings, and bracelets with gold shell inlay, featuring the sunface design in a variety of color combinations, and a floral inlay bracelet. Circa 1950s. *Enchanted Mesa collection* .

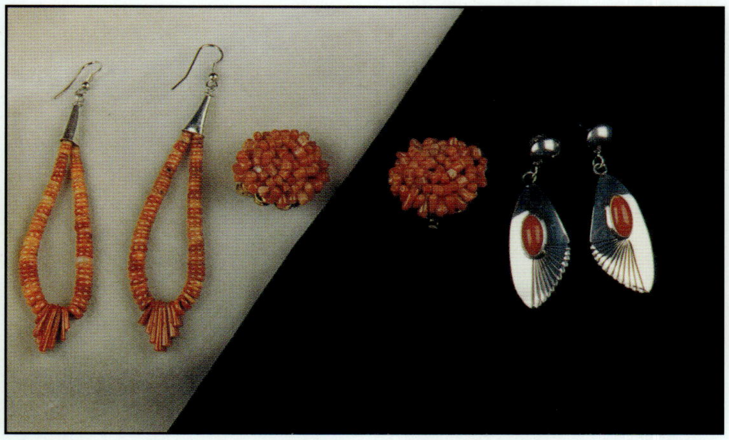

Beads have been used in different methods to create these three pairs of earrings: From left, Bead joclas of spiny oyster form miniature necklace forms. / Shell beads are grouped in clusters. / Silver dangle earrings are accented with single coral stones. *Private collection on permanent loan to Ohio University*

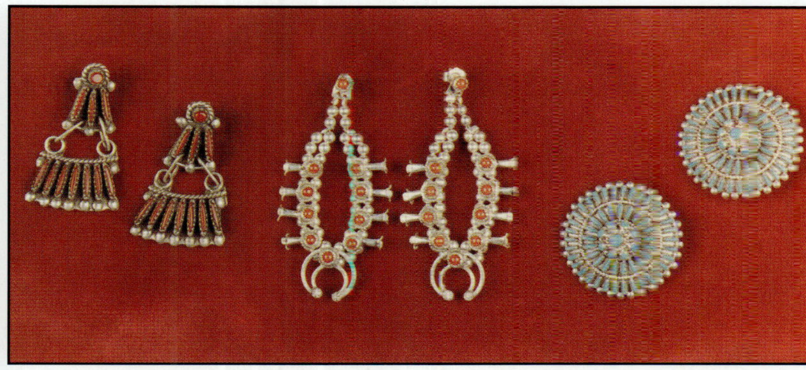

Three pairs of Zuni silver earrings: From left, a pair with dangling coral inlay. / Small version of a coral-set squash blossom necklace. / Fine quality round turquoise needlepoint pair by Rosemary Q. Panteah, Zuni *Private collection on permanent loan to Ohio University*

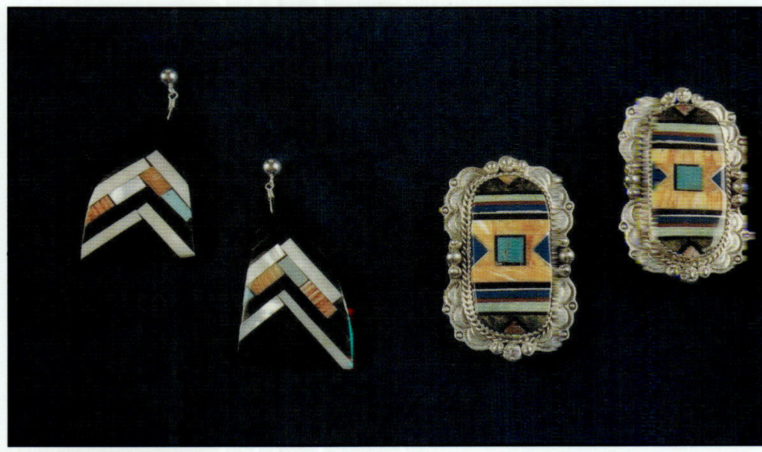

The experimentation of new decorative designs in the 1980s produced these forms: From left, Triangular earrings on shell with shell and stone inlay by Sanchez. / Large silver stamped rectangles with geometric inlay by Albert Platero, Navajo. *Indian Post collection*.

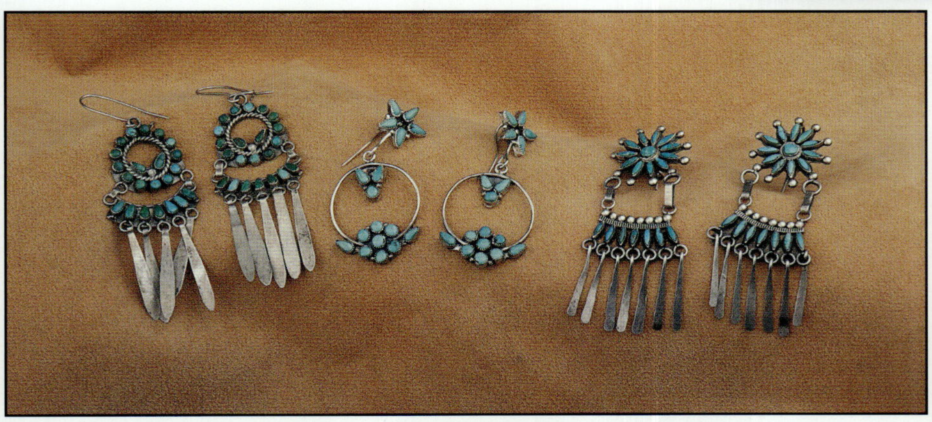

Zuni silver dangling earrings set with turquoise. Left: early 20th century. Center: mid-20th century. Right: early 20th century. *Lynn D. Trusdell, Crown & Eagle Antiques*

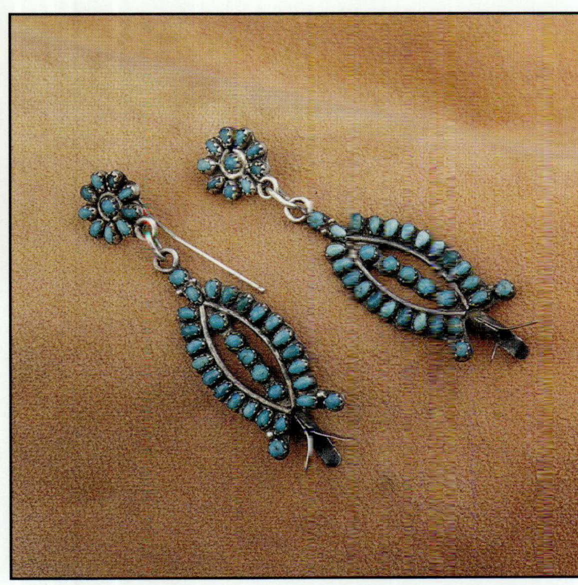

Pair of Zuni silver earrings set with turquoise in a design derived from earlier squash-blossom tradition, c. 1950. *Lynn D. Trusdell, Crown & Eagle Antiques*

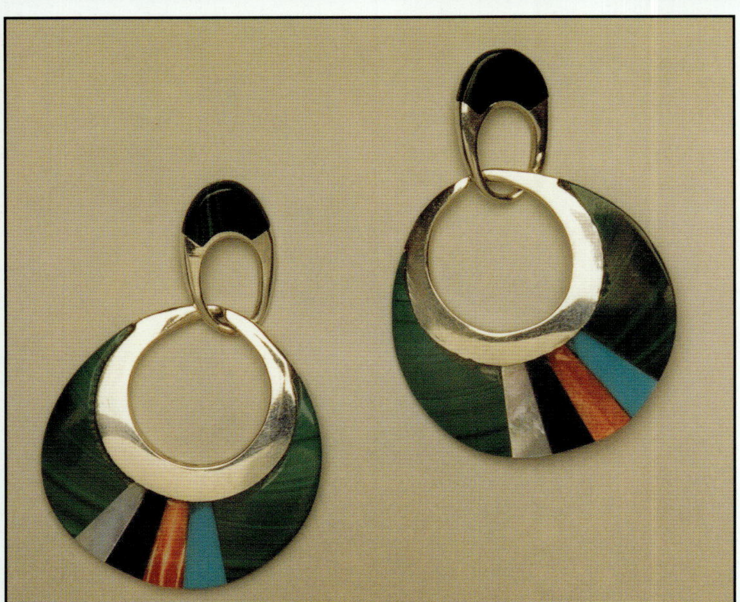

Zuni stone mosaic earrings which combine malachite, mother of pearl, jet, shell and turquoise in a dangling hoop design, made by T.C.A., late 1980s.

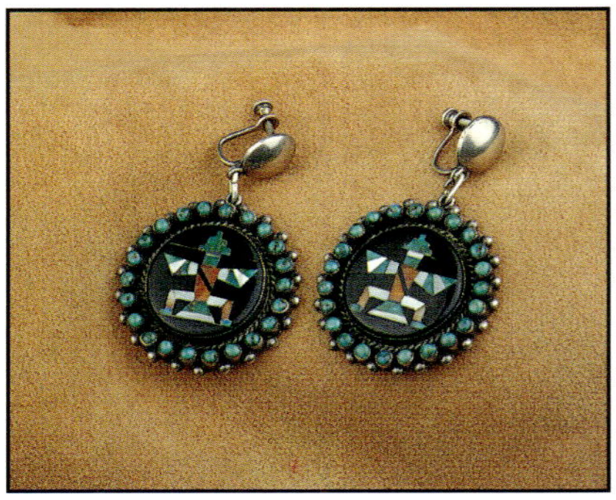

Zuni earrings probably by Dan Simplicio demonstrating the finest quality inlay work in a Knifewing Dancer design set in jet. Formerly in the collection of Carl Druckman. *Lynn D. Trusdell, Crown & Eagle Antiques*

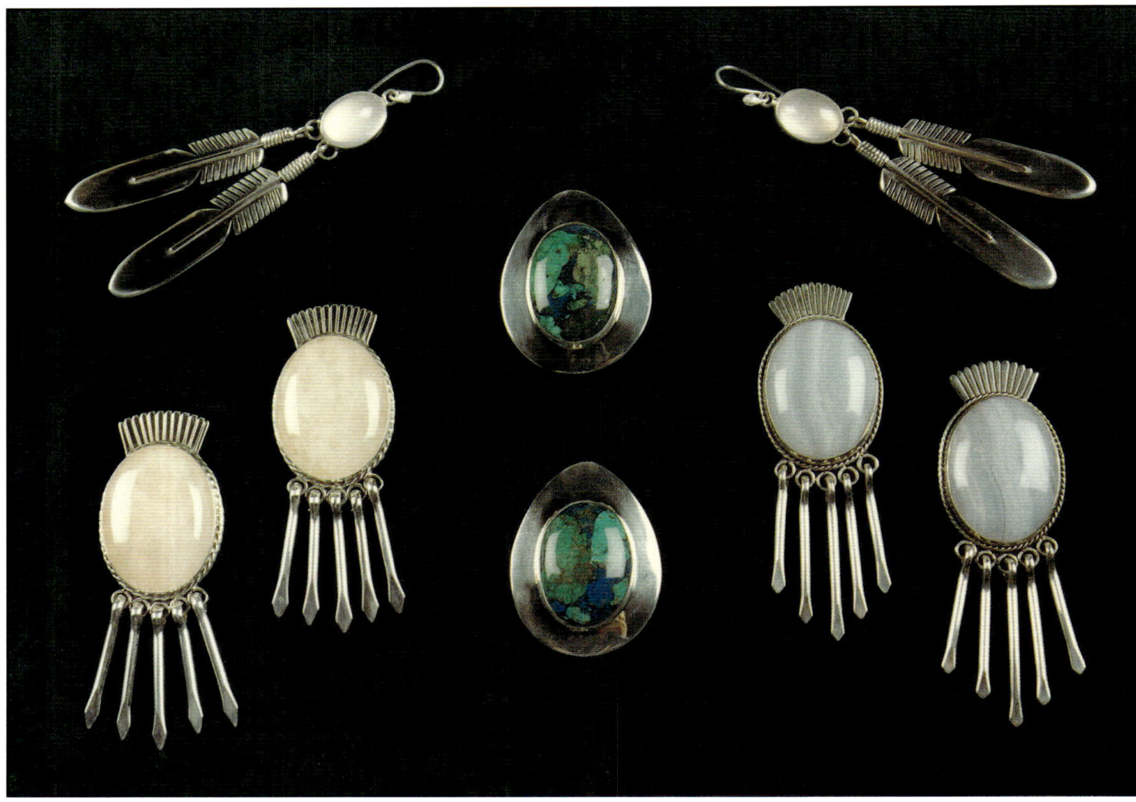

Larger, bolder designs with new varieties of stone accents were made in the 1980s: From left, Rose quartz earrings with silver feather dangles by Mike Nez, Navajo. / Rose quartz ovals set in silver with dangles. / Variegated turquoise stones in silver frames. / Oval Azurite stones set in silver with fine dangles made by M. Lee. *Indian Post collection*.

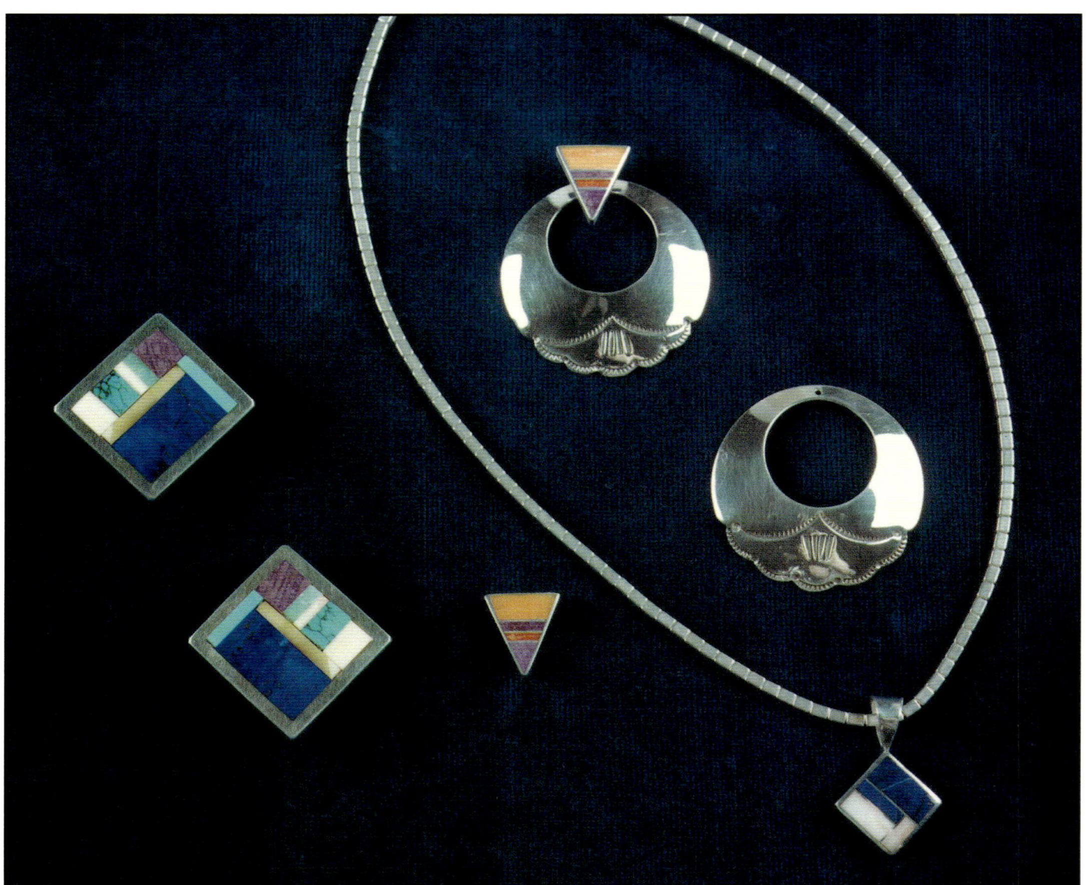

Colorful mosaic stone inlays were beautifully crafted in the late 1980s. Large square earrings set in silver by Coriz. / Square pendant and small triangular earrings with silver hoop jackets by Knifewing. / Square silver bead chain by Joe Herreras-Suina. *Indian Post collection*.

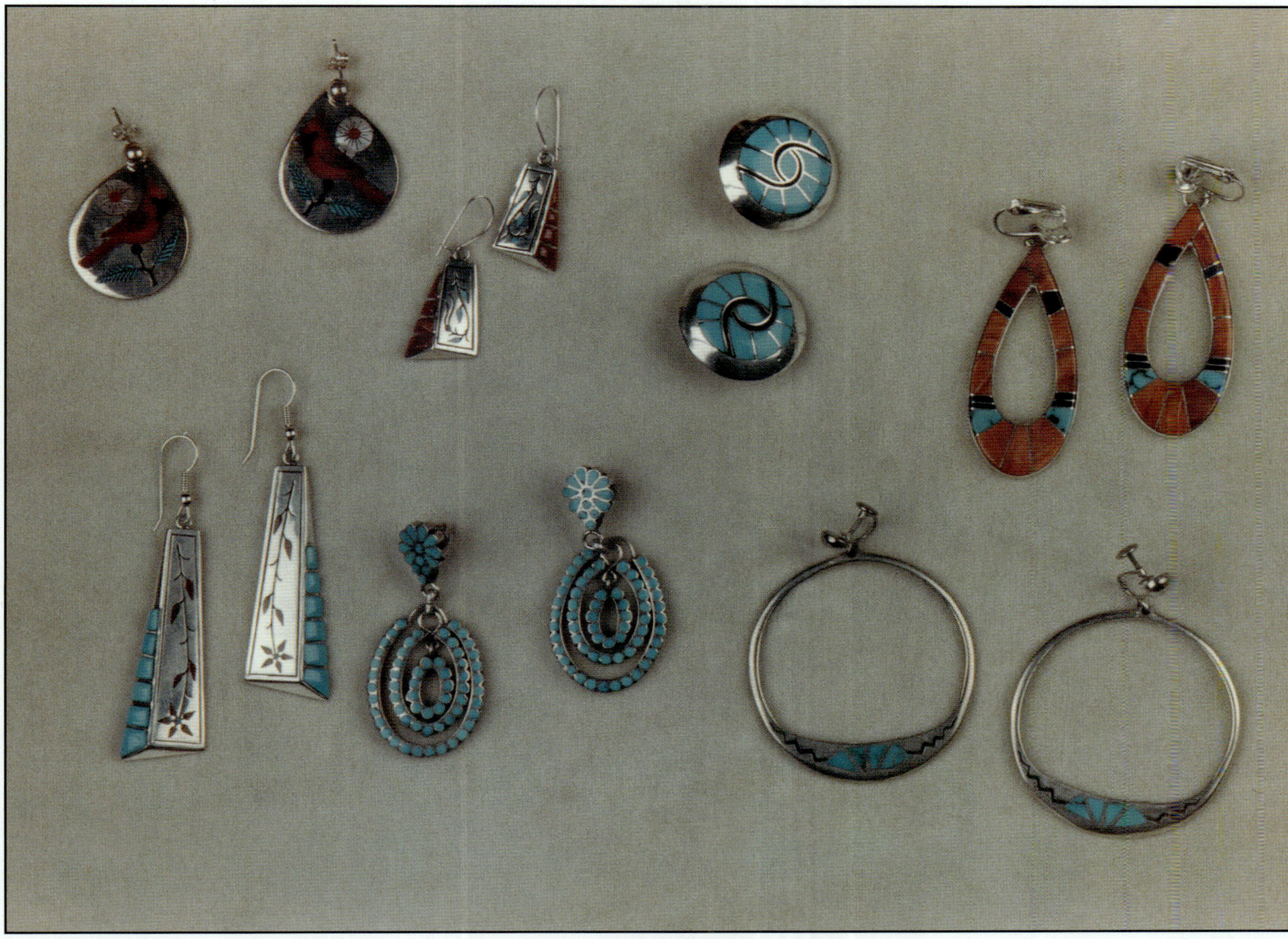

Zuni earrings of great diversity were made in the late 1980s: From left, Coral cardinals inlaid in silver. / Silver earrings with coral edging. / Circular earrings with spiral turquoise inlay. / Silver oval loops with coral and stone inlay. / Silver with turquoise edging. / Multiple turquoise-set loops / Silver hoops with turquoise. *Private collection on permanent loan to Ohio University*

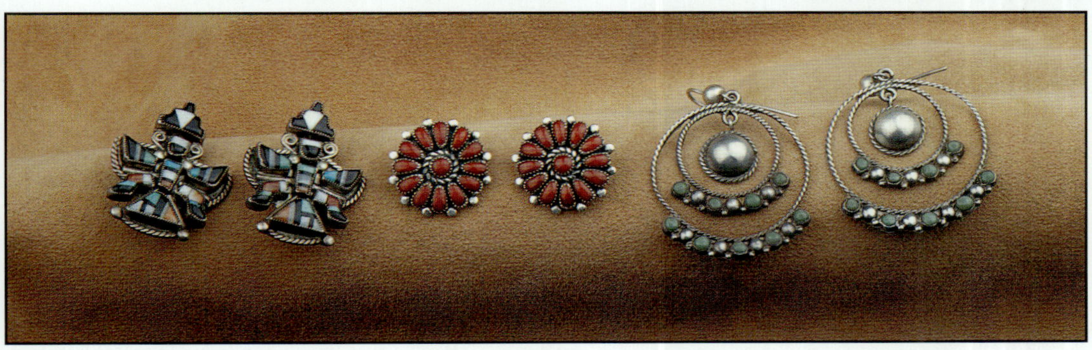

Left: Fine quality Zuni inlay earrings of silver with a Knifewing Dancer design, 1930s.
Center: Zuni cluster earrings of silver and coral, 1950s.
Right: Zuni silver double hoop earrings with turquoise, 1930s. *Lynn D. Trusdell, Crown & Eagle Antiques*

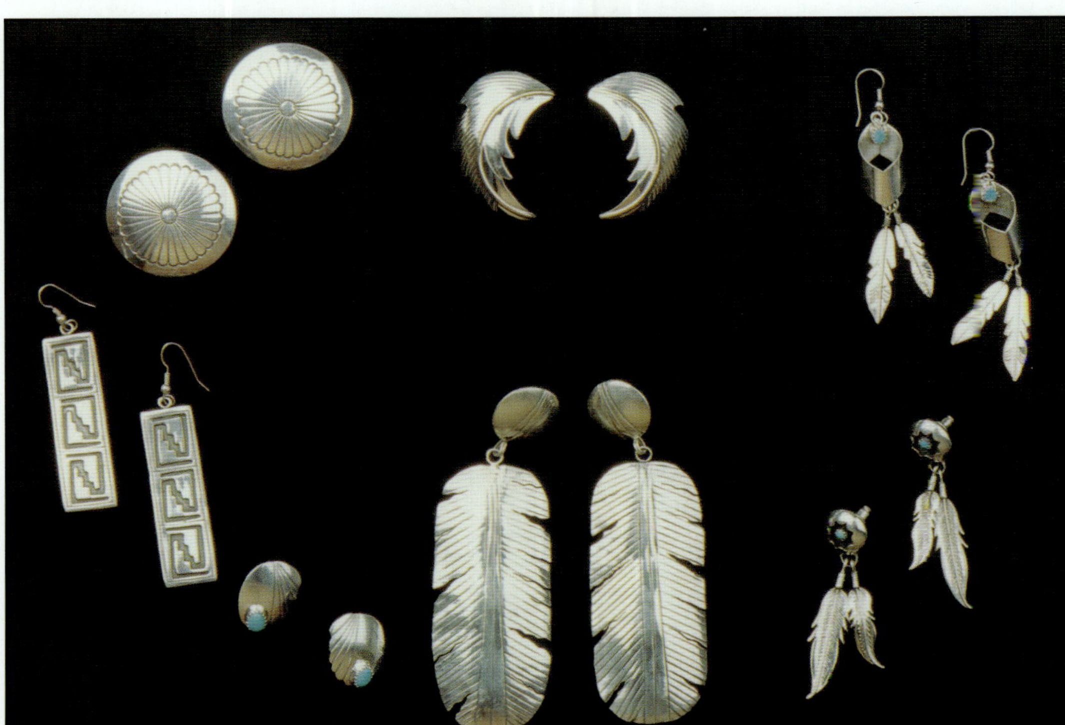

Seven pairs of sterling silver earrings (clockwise from top): Short feathers / Ovals with turquoise stones and feather dangles / Round with turquoise stones and feather dangles / Large feather dangles / Oval with turquoise stones / Rectangular / Circular with blossom patterns. *Bing Crosby collection*

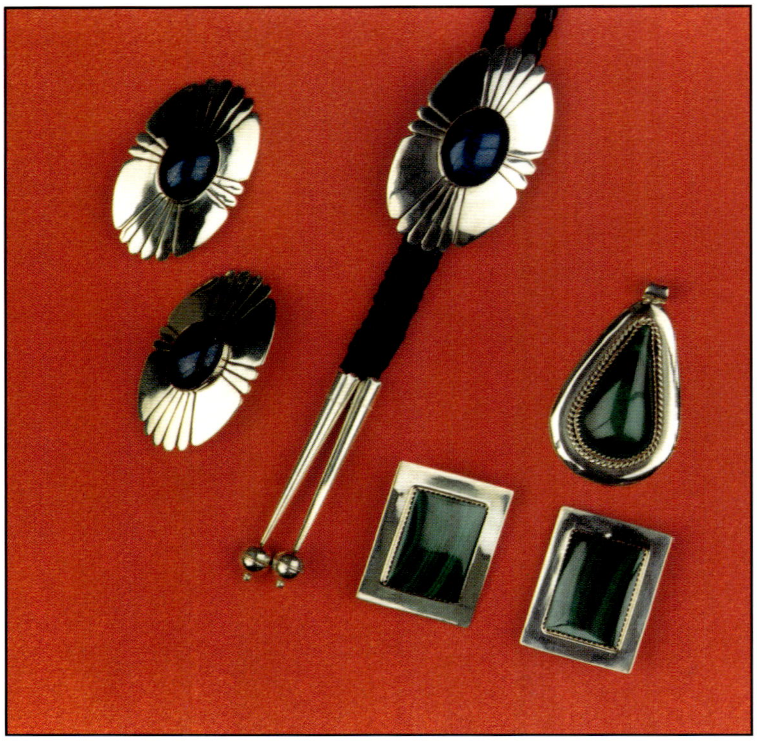

Matching bolo tie slide and earrings with blue stones set in wrought silver by M. Jackson, Navajo. / Matching green malachite pendant and earrings set in silver, unmarked, both late 1980s. *Keams Canyon Arts and Crafts collection.*

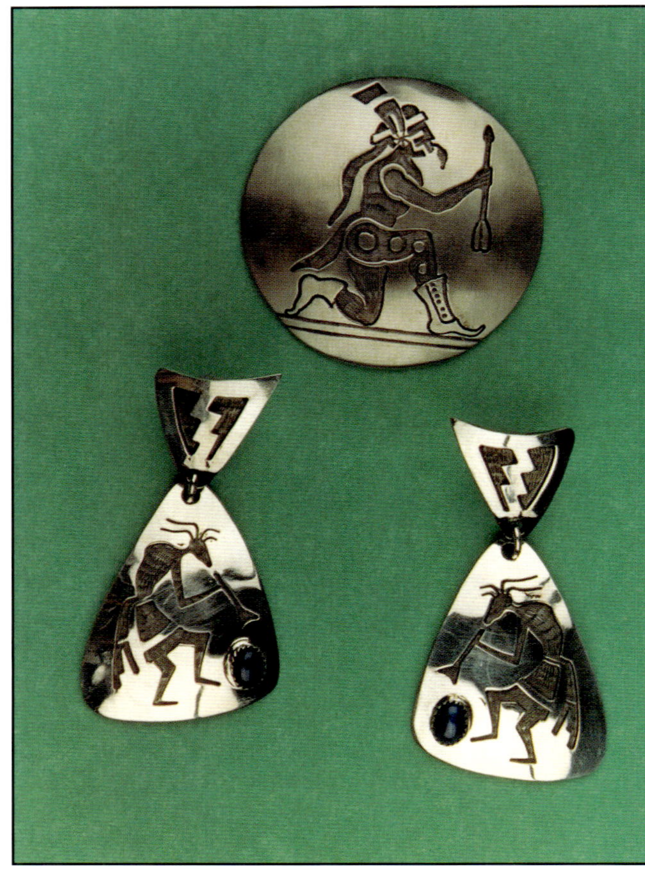

Wonderfully designed Hopi overlay silver pendant and earrings with representative figural decorations of a kneeling man (above) and the famous flute player (below). Earrings also set with small blue stones. Unmarked. *Enchanted Mesa collection*.

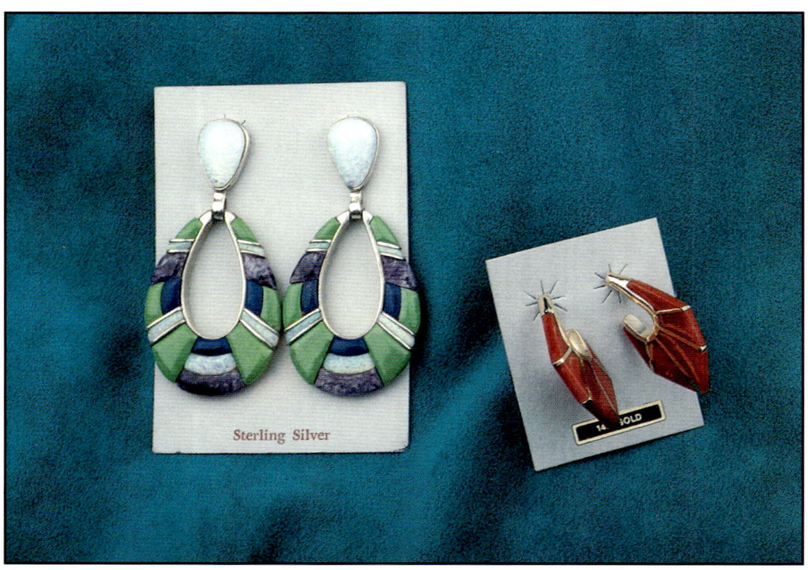

Pair of Navajo drop earrings with assorted stone inlay in silver. ($600) Pair of Navajo earrings with red stone inlay in gold, Navajo. ($3,000) *Courtesy of Palms Trading Company*

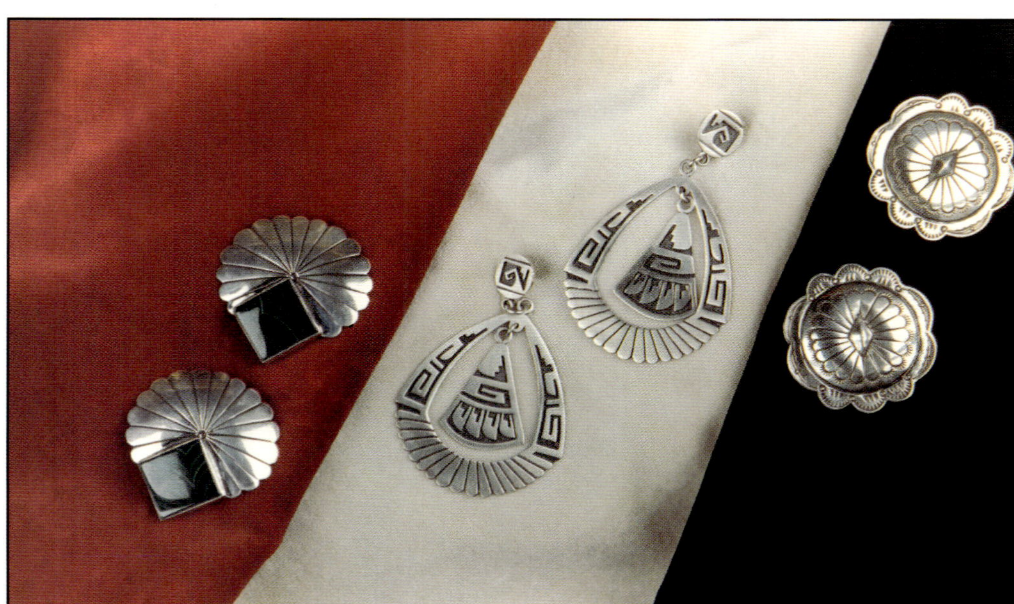

Three pairs of earrings: Shell pattern silver wrought earrings set with malachite. / Hopi silver overlay designed earrings made with inside dangle. / Circular button-type wrought earrings, Navajo. *Private collection on permanent loan to Ohio University*

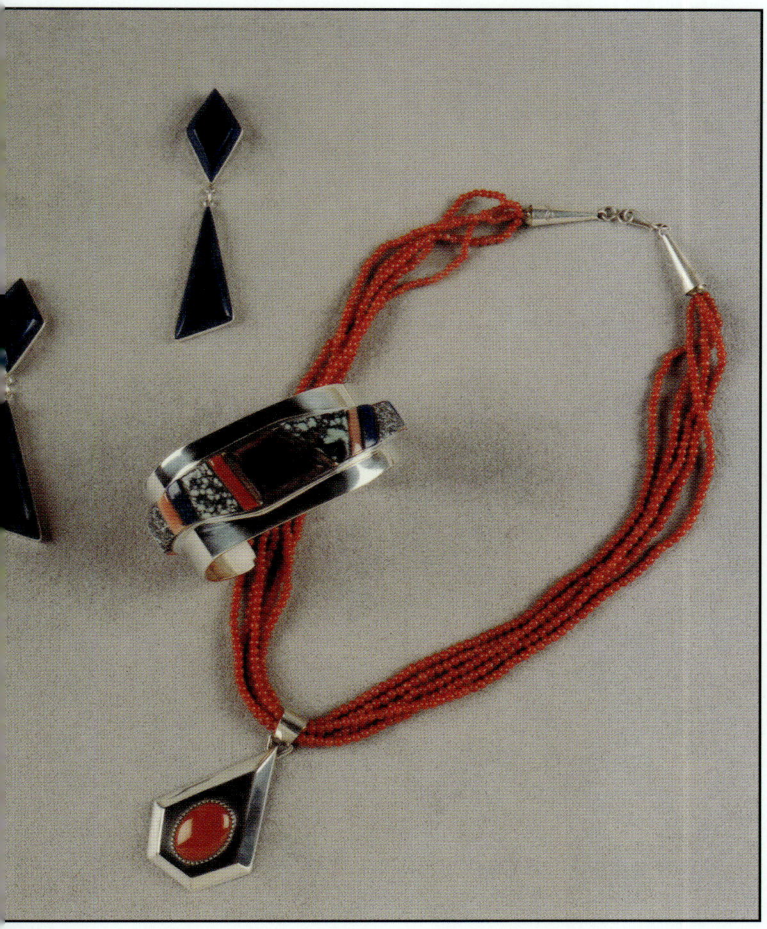

Lapis lazuli dangle earrings by Sam Lovato, Navajo, late 1980s. / Coral, lapis lazuli, and turquoise inlaid silver bracelet. / Five-strand coral bead necklace with a silver shadowbox pendant framing a coral stone. *Indian Post collection*.

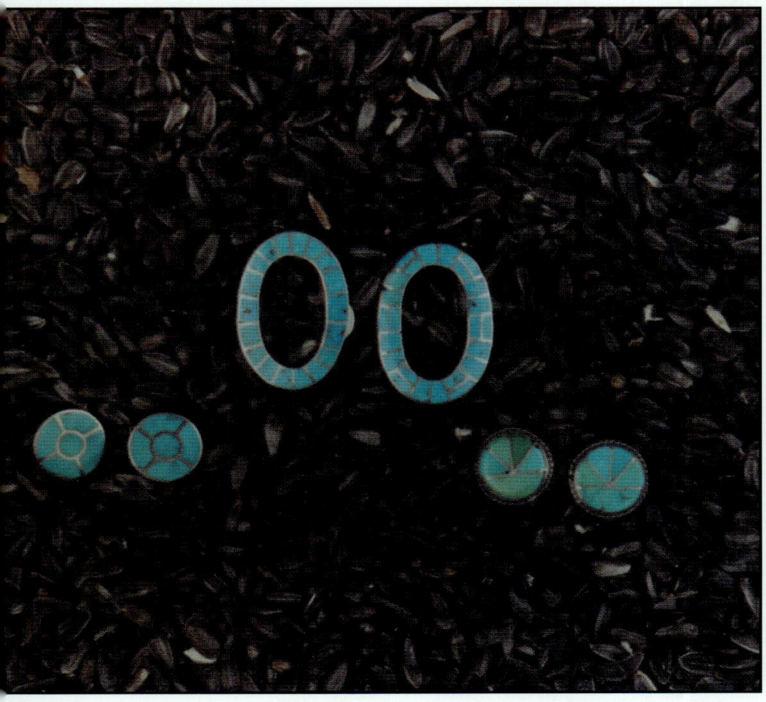

Three pairs of Zuni earrings with channel inlay turquoise and silver, circa 1970s. *Enchanted Mesa collection* .

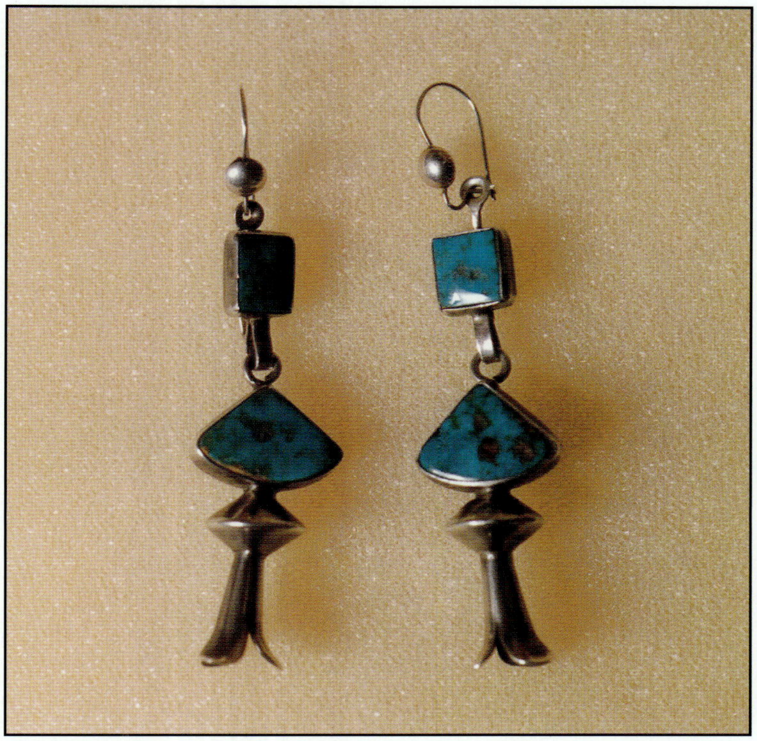

Pair of earrings with squash blossom dangles made by Nettie Wilson, circa 1940s. *Adobe Gallery collection*

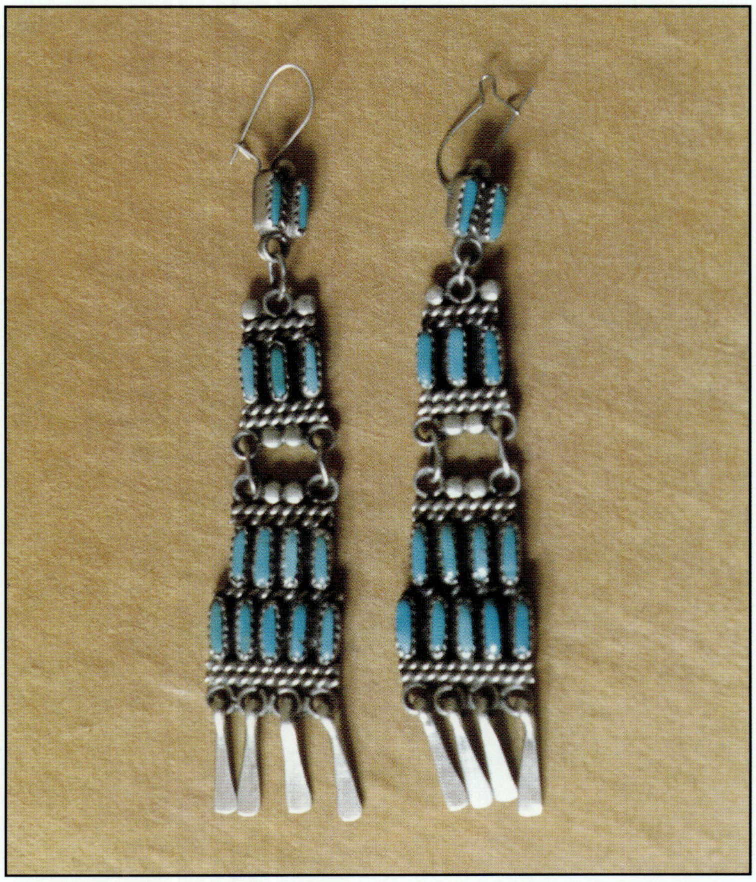

Zuni dangle earrings with needlepoint turquoise, 1940s. *Adobe Gallery collection*

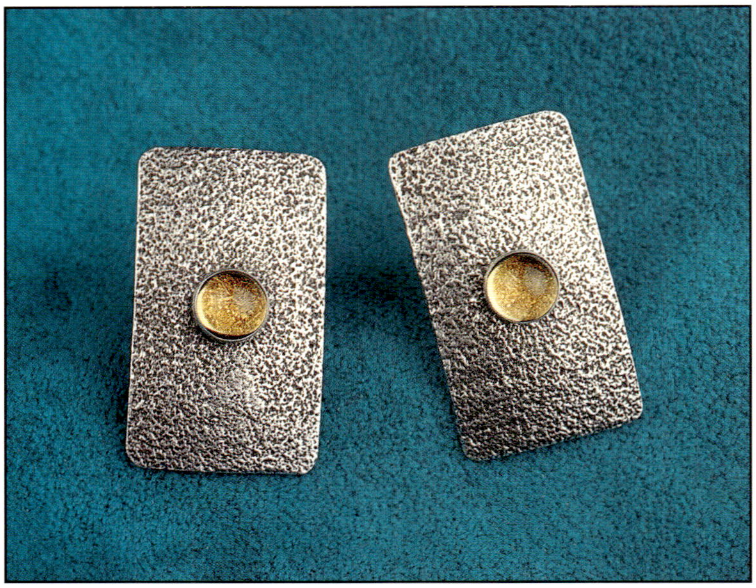

Textured silver and citrine "rain drop" earrings by Anthony Lovato, Santo Domingo, 2002. *Courtesy of Gerald Peters Gallery, Santa Fe, New Mexico* ($160)

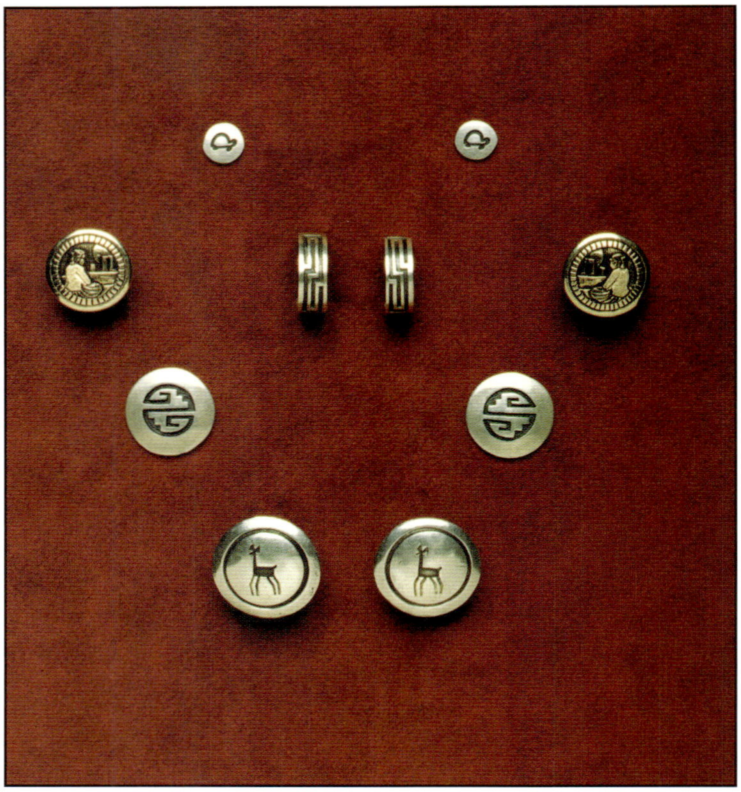

Four pair of Hopi silver overlay earrings with figural and geometric designs, 1980s. / Pair of large round button shape by Manuel Hoyungua. / Pair of gold button earrings with appliqué design of woman and landscape by Paul Arviso, Navajo, late 1980s.

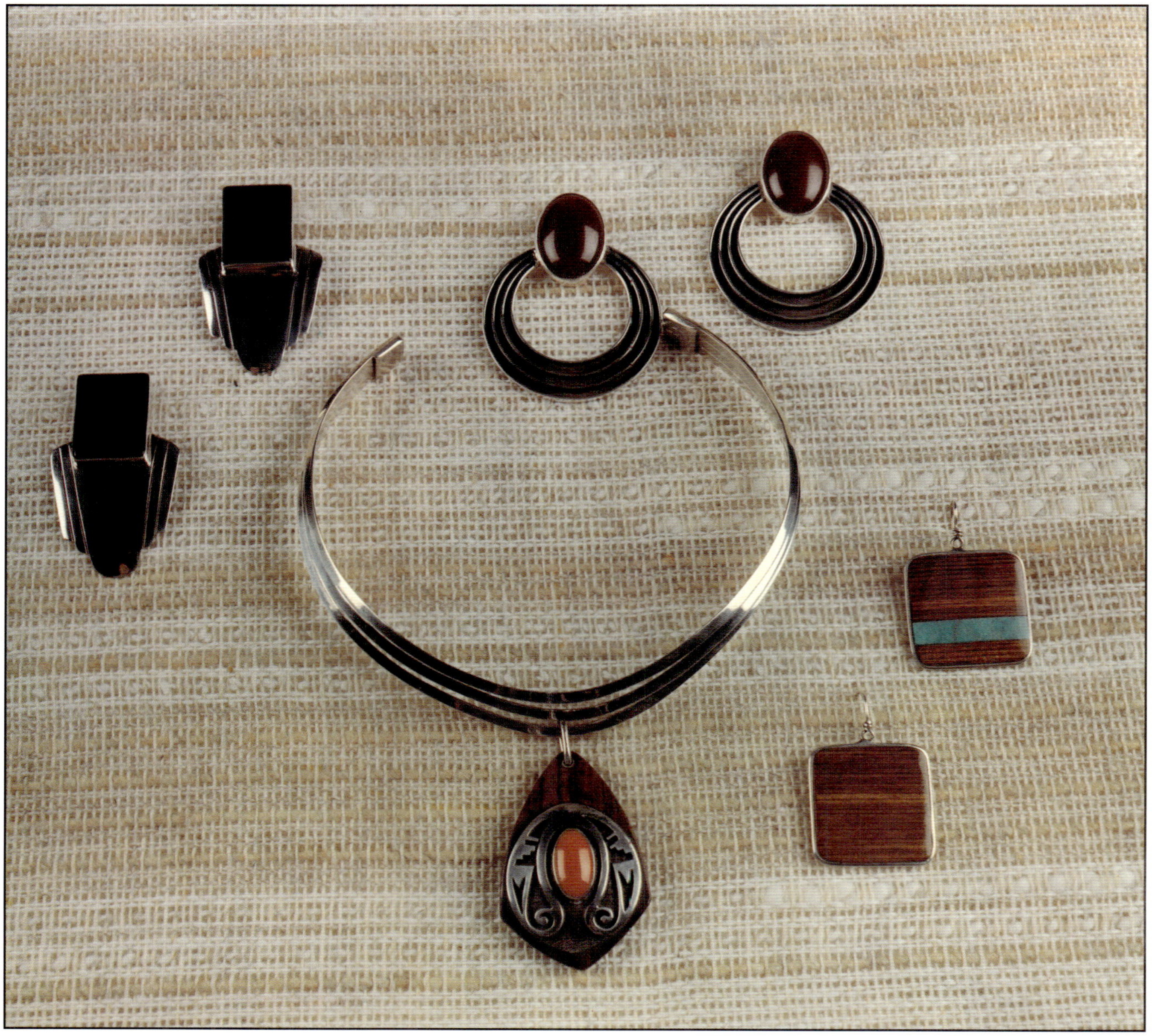

Modern designs blend excellent craftsmanship with a new combination of materials: From left, Silver and onyx earrings by Mike Nez, Santo Domingo. / Silver and carnelian hoop earrings by Frances Jones, Santo Domingo. / Coco bola wood square earrings with turquoise, and a silver necklace with wood, silver, and coral pendant by Phillip Sekaquaptewa, Hopi, all late 1980s. *Indian Post collection*.

Necklaces

Among the earliest forms of jewelry were trade beads formed of materials from local and distant origins that had some accepted value in the community. Continuing to this day, beads have been popular ornaments to all peoples through the generations.

Indians of the Rio Grande pueblos in particular have become particularly skilled in making stone beads, which they have traded with their Navajo neighbors for centuries. Santo Domingo, for example, has a reputation as the origin for some of the finest beads of uniform shapes and small size, very hard to make.

Stone Bead Necklaces

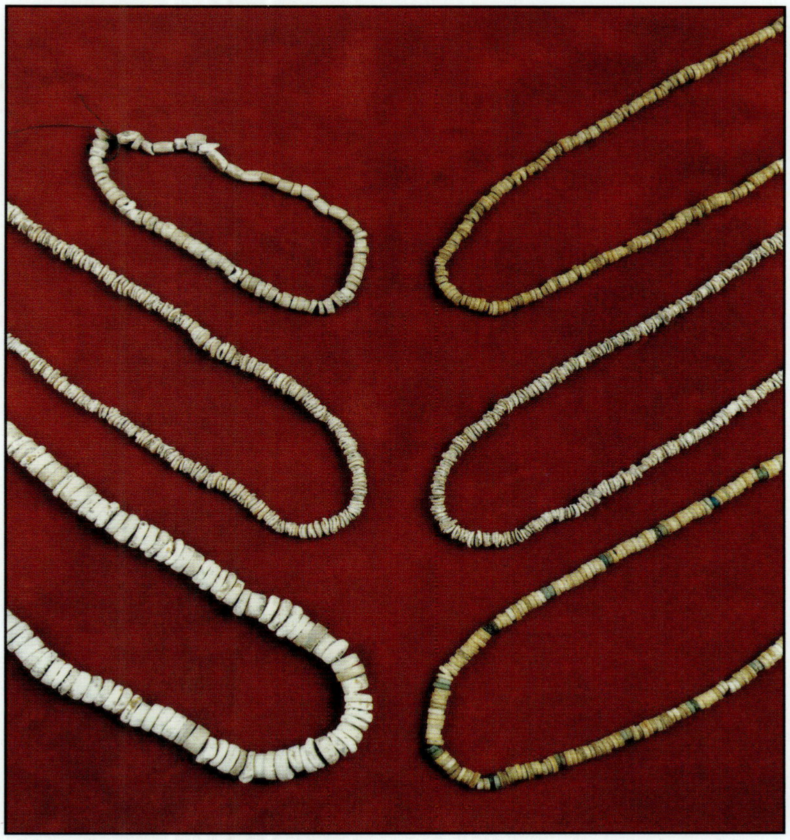

These six strings of wampum trade beads are made of shell from the eastern woodlands, which were exchanged with fur-trading Indians who in turn traded with the Southwest Indians. These date from the Hohokam (pre-historic) period. *Lynn D. Trusdell collection*

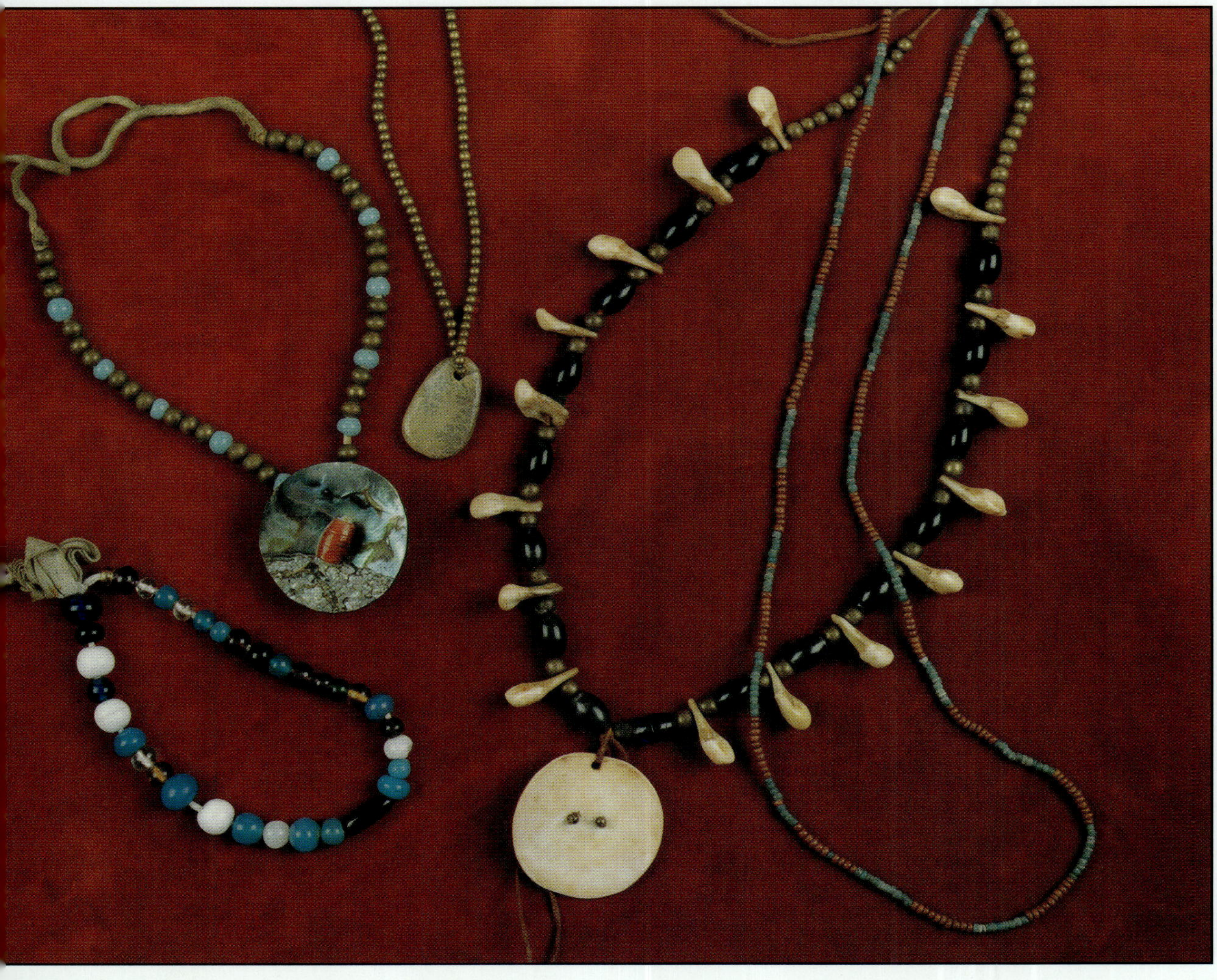

The early trade beads in this group include shell, blue glass, teeth, and brass beads, some strung on hide. *Lynn D. Trusdell collection*

Many bead necklaces were made with matching beaded ear decorations know as "jocla" which, when not worn in the ears, were looped over the necklace and carried as a pendant group. Many old necklaces can be found with jocla this way.

Small and uniform strings of rolled beads are known as "heishi" and they can be found in many materials including turquoise, coral and shell.

Old, large Blue Gem turquoise beads were strung in recent times by James Pete, Navajo, and are shown with two old jocla (beaded ear decorations) and four strands of jocla restrung as a choker necklace. *Indian Post collection*.

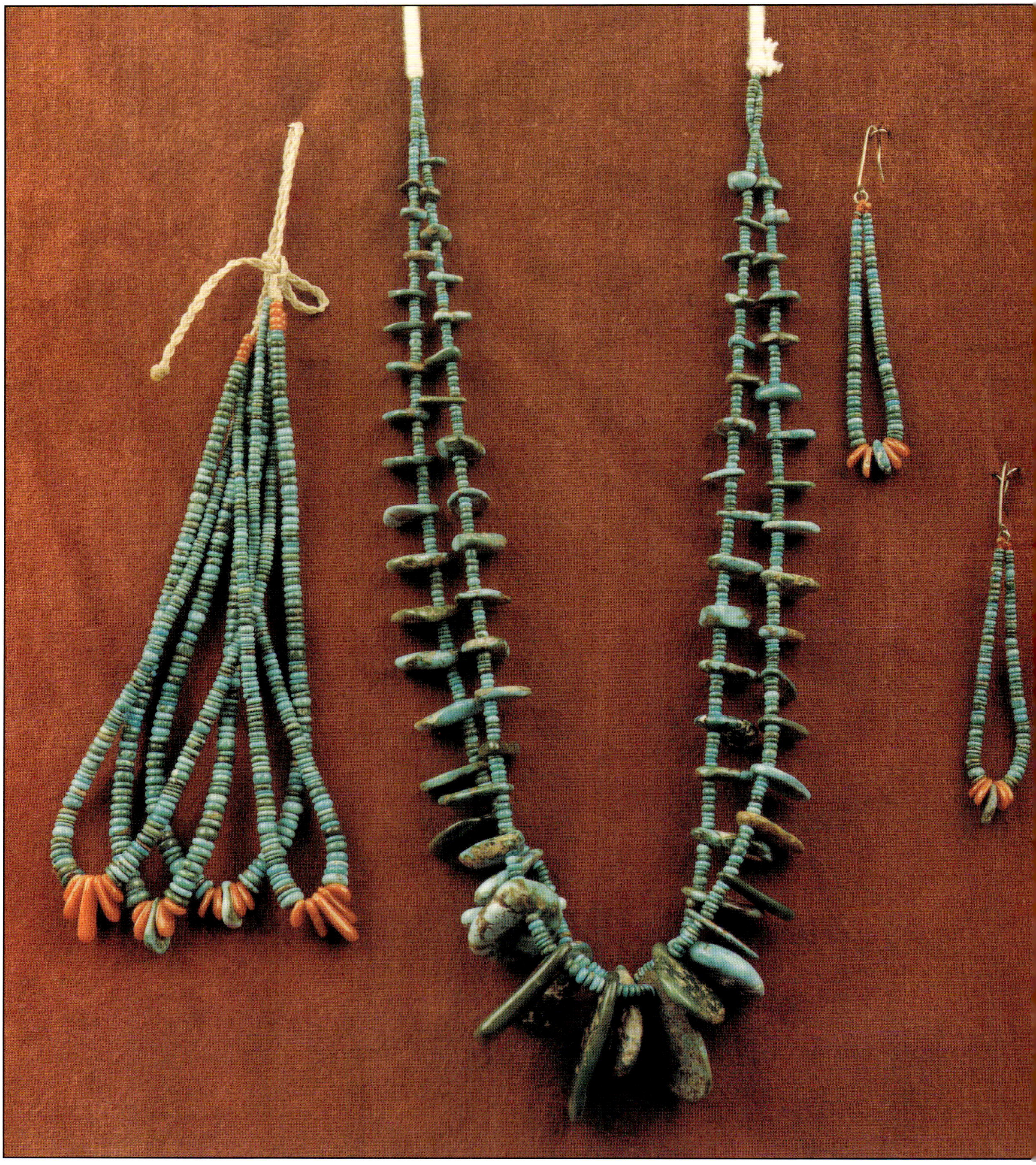

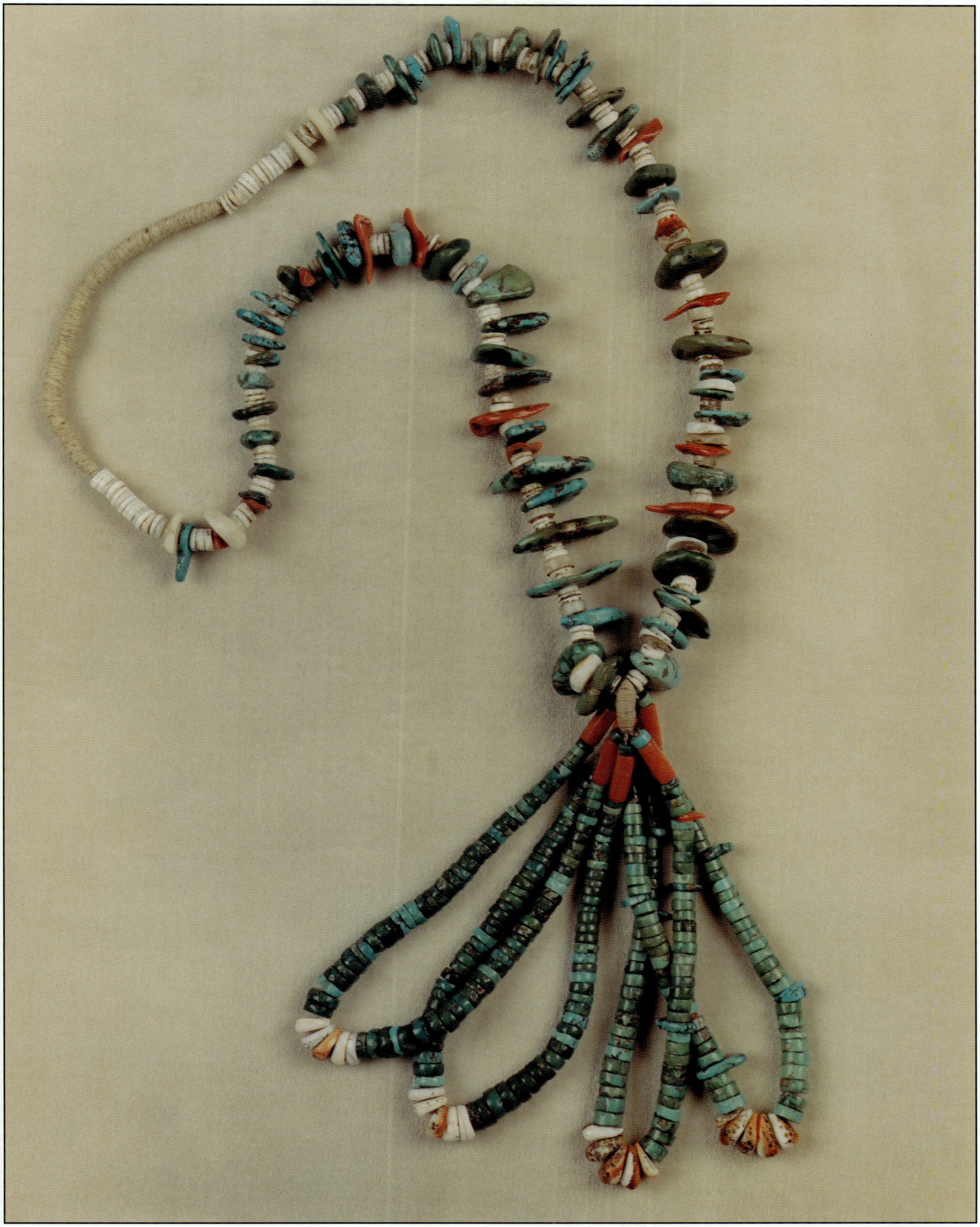

Necklace and double jocla of pump-drilled beads, including coral, Blue Gem turquoise and shell, dating from the 1920s. *Lynn D. Trusdell collection*

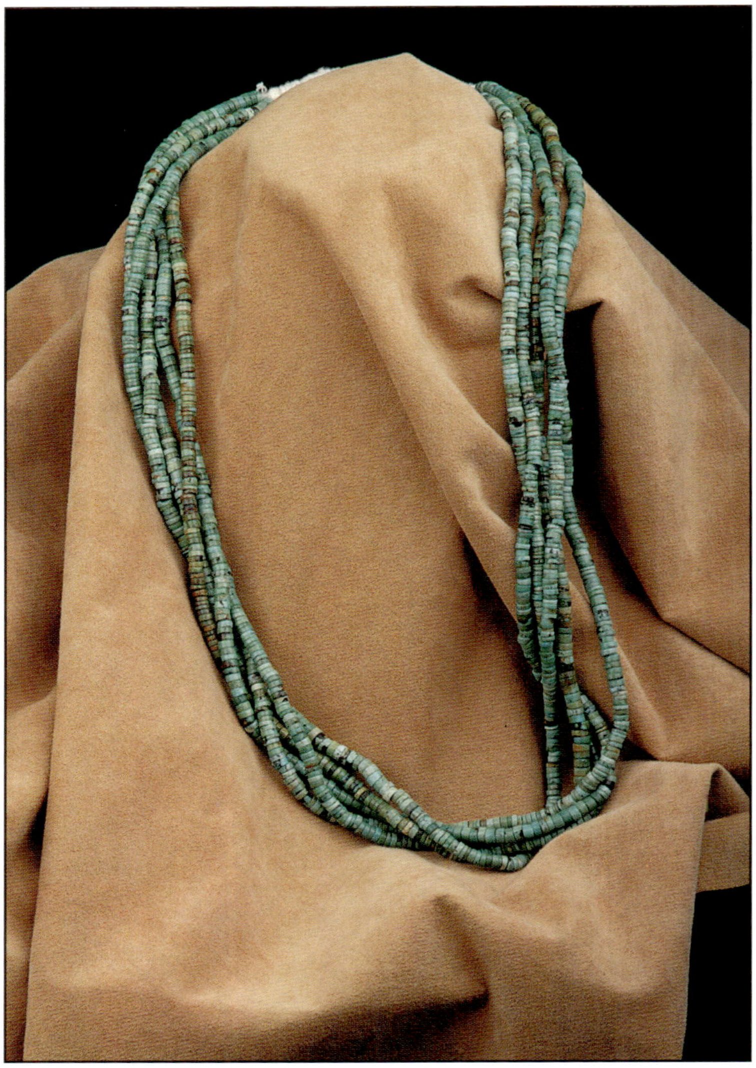

Santo Domingo turquoise 8-strand heishi necklace of pump-drilled stones, c. 1930s. *Lynn D. Trusdell, Crown & Eagle Antiques*

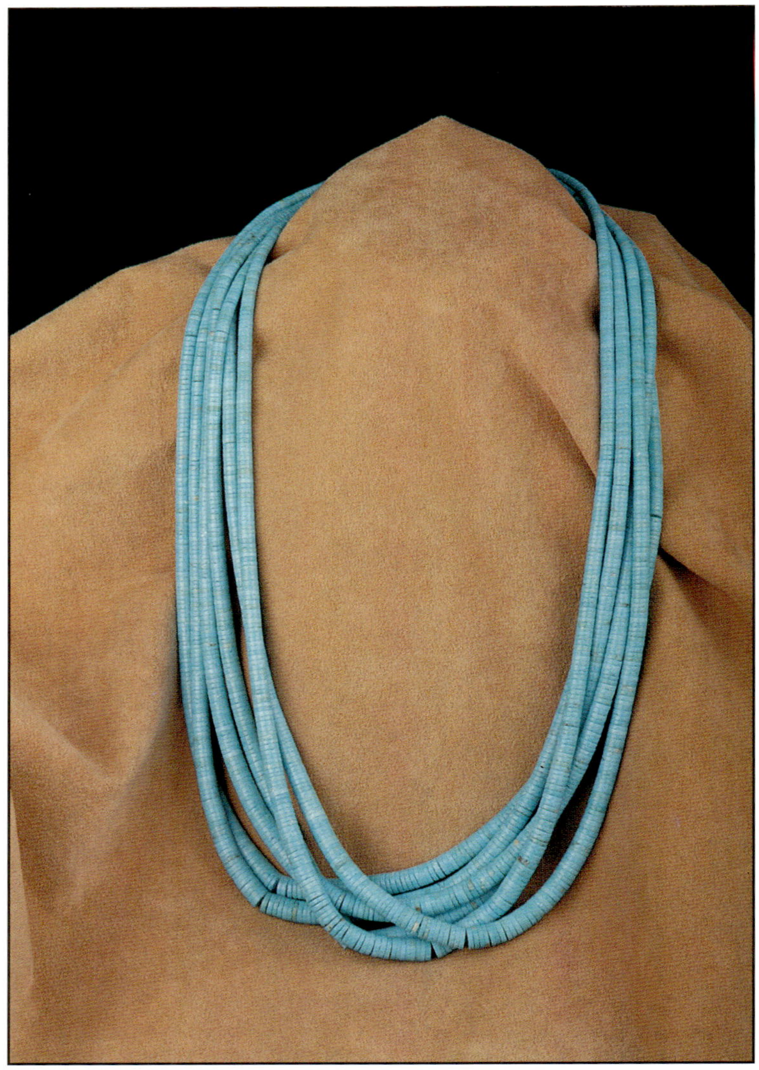

Santo Domingo heishi necklace of six-strands of graduated Sleeping Beauty turquoise beads by Joe Cate. *Courtesy of Palms Trading Company*

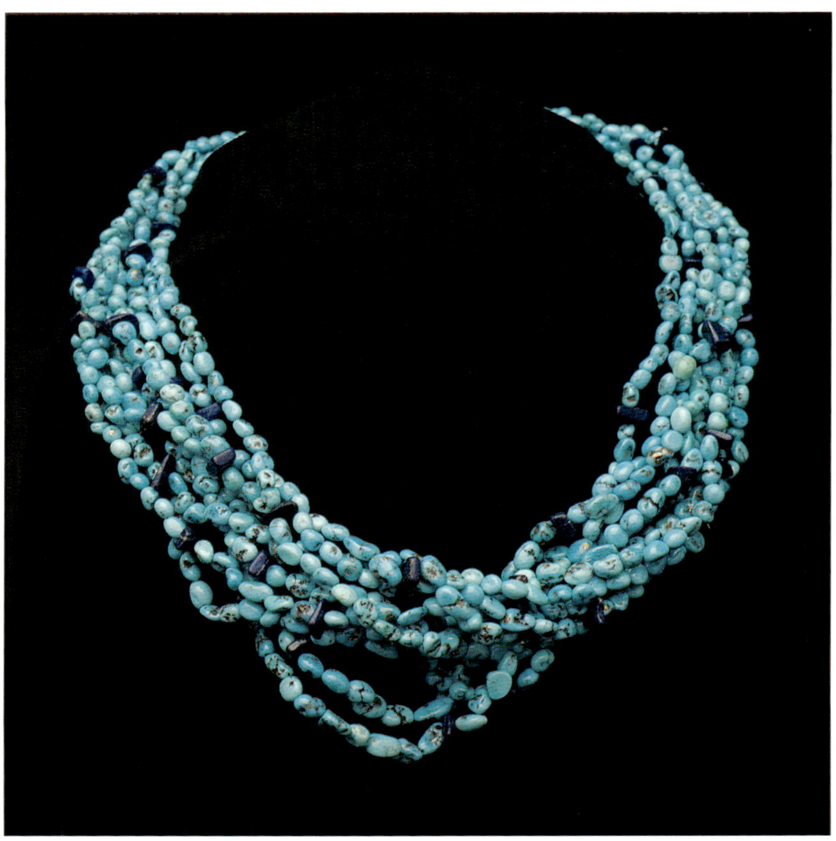

Santo Domingo turquoise and lapis lazuli bead necklace, 2001.

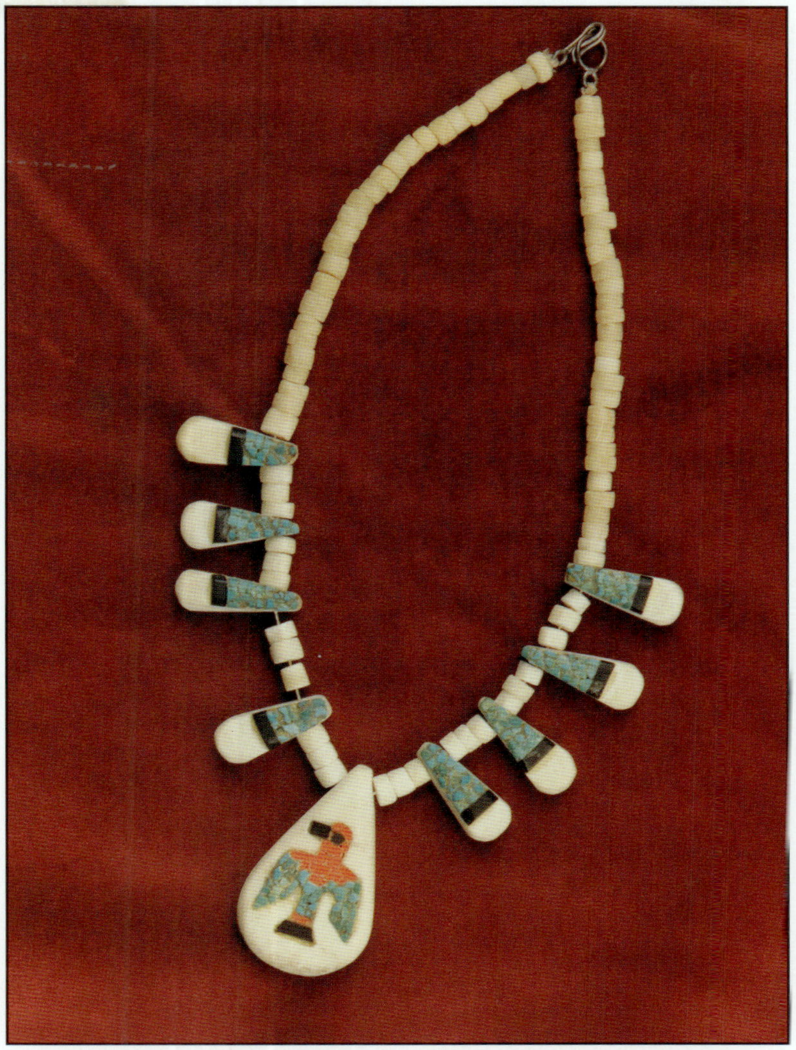

This necklace was made at the Santo Domingo pueblo in the 1930s with assorted materials, which gave colorful contrasts: turquoise chips (blue), gypsum (white), broken phonograph record (black), and pieces of a plastic comb (red). *Enchanted Mesa collection*

Small 6-strand necklace of coral and silver beads with squaw-wrap closure. / Large 6-strand light coral and turquoise necklace made by Pueblo Indians around 1900. / Four-strand coral necklace with 23 silver crosses and miscellaneous beads from the Lukachukai Mountains area of the Navajo reservation, circa 1930. *Private collection on permanent loan to Ohio University*

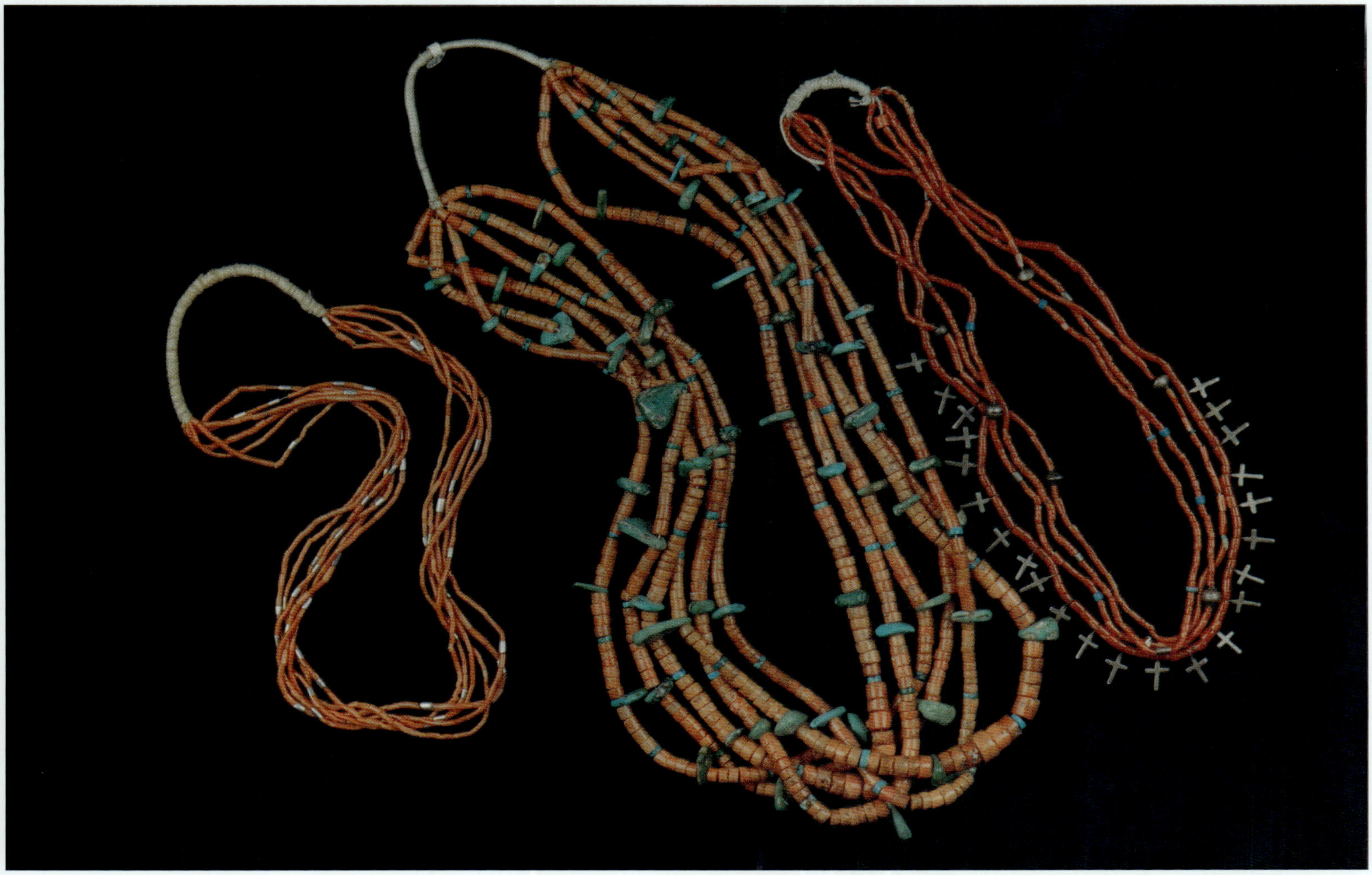

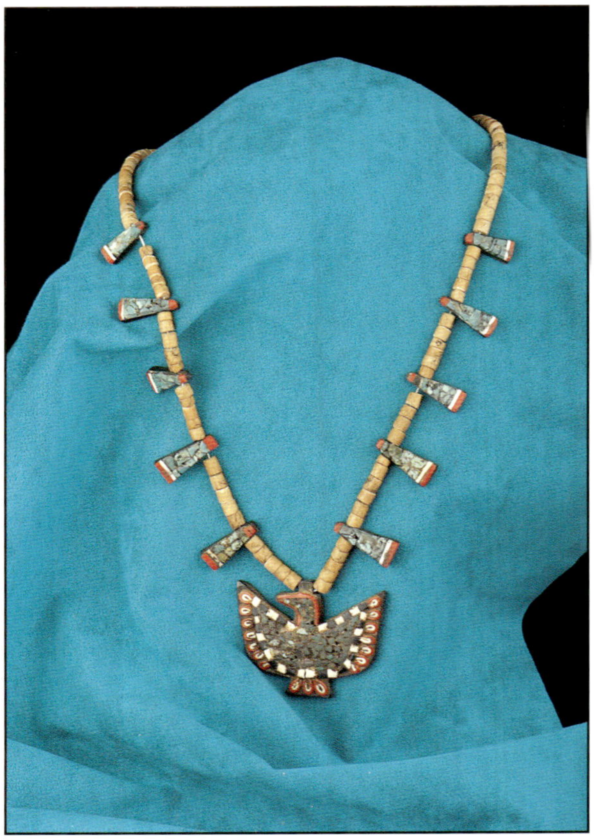

Santo Domingo heishi necklace with a single strand of beads made from assorted materials, including bone, rubber, plastics, and turquoise chips with eagle pendant, c.1930s. *Courtesy of Palms Trading Company*

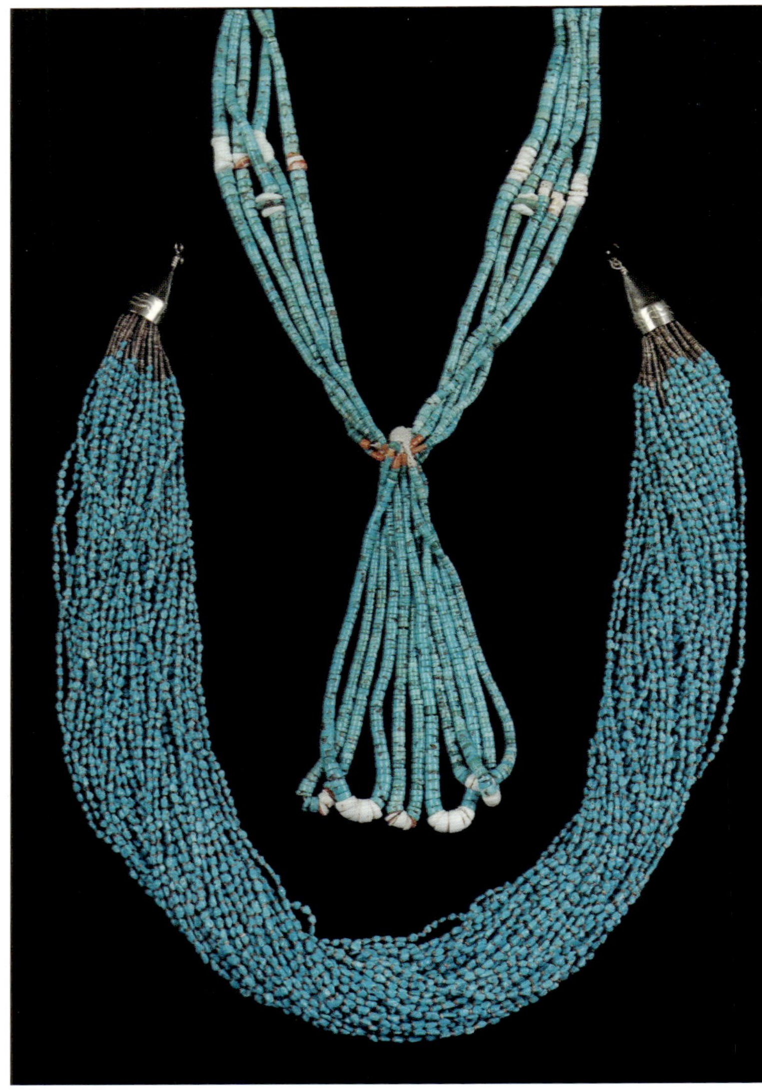

Old five-strand necklace of Lone Mountain turquoise, coral, and shell beads with six joclas. / 46-strand turquoise and brown shell heishi necklace with gold clasps made in the 1970s. *Private collection on permanent loan to Ohio University*

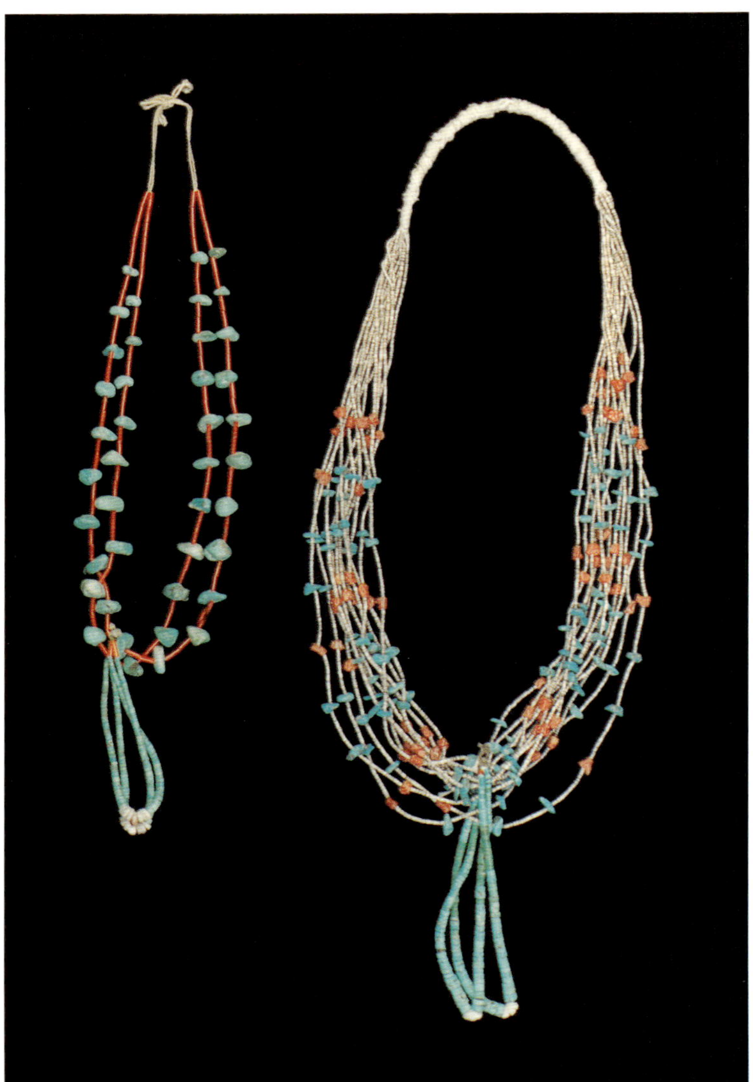

Look-alike materials must be watched for on the market and identified for what they are, attractive ornaments. The two-strand necklace at the left has red glass beads and treated turquoise beads with two jocla, made in the 1940s. / On the right is a fine 12-strand necklace of genuine coral, treated Kingman turquoise and Olivella shell heishi with two jocla and a squaw wrapped closure, circa 1960. *Dennehotso collection*.

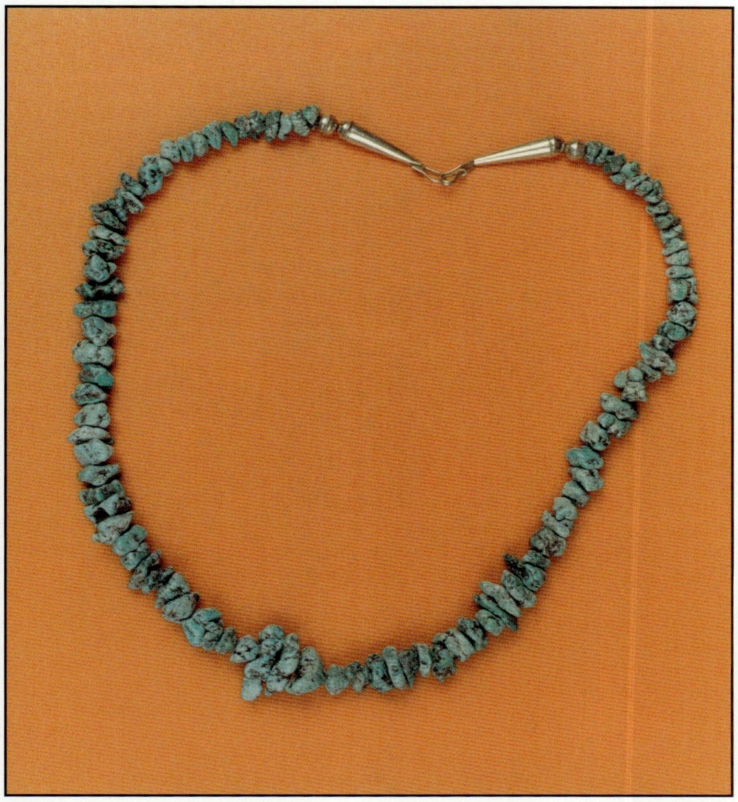

Bead necklace of Fox turquoise chunks from the 1950s. *Maxwell Museum collection*

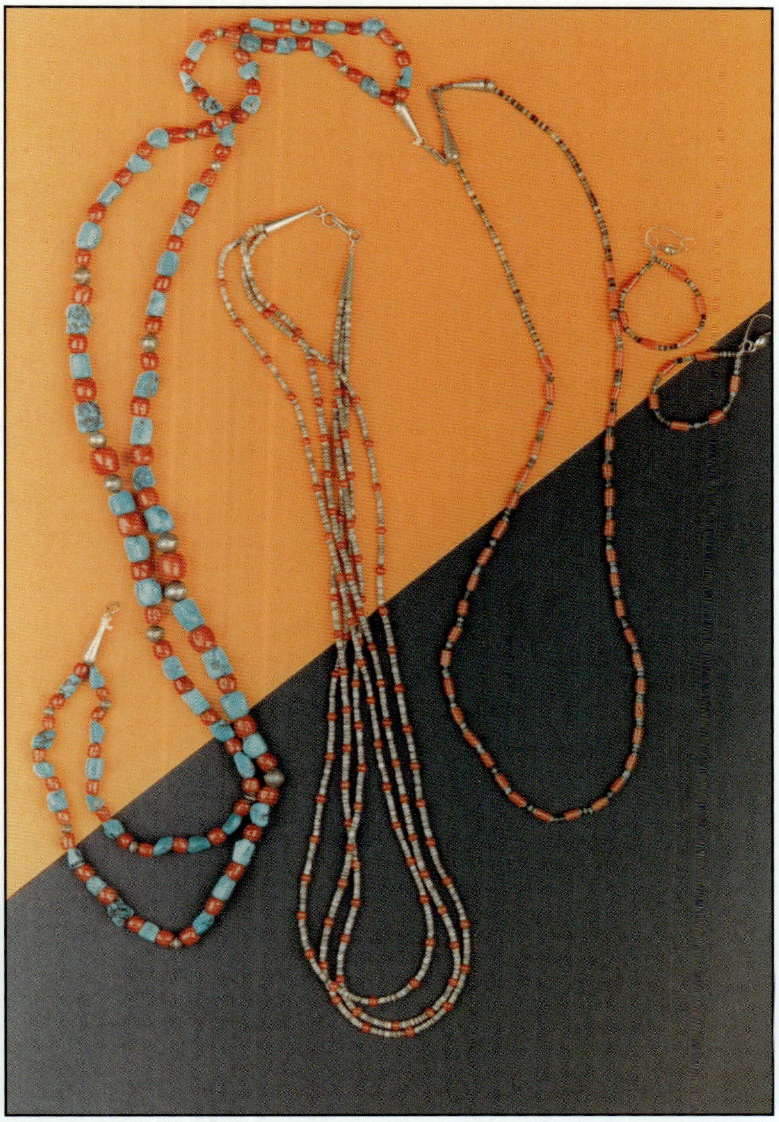

Turquoise, silver and coral beads are combined in this two-strand necklace. / A fine coral and silver heishi necklace of three strands. / A single strand of coral and silver beads with matching earrings. *Private collection*

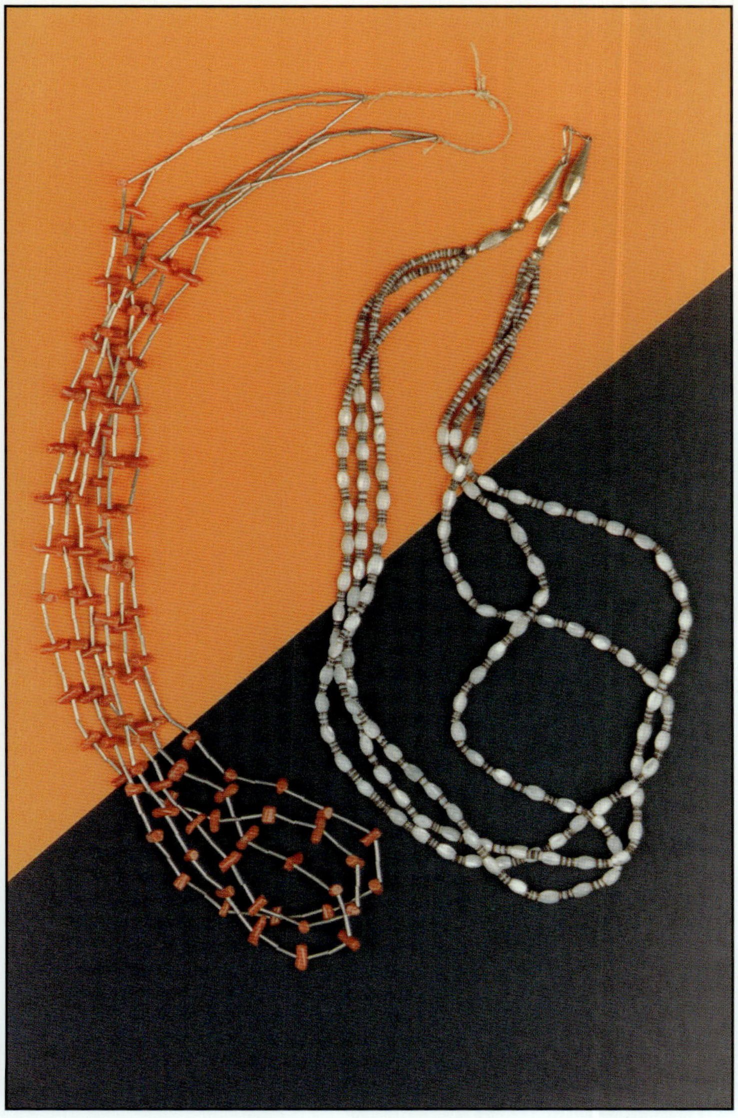

Three strands of coral beads and very fine shell heishi make a delicate necklace. / Brown and white shell beads and heishi are combined in this three-strand necklace. *Private collection*

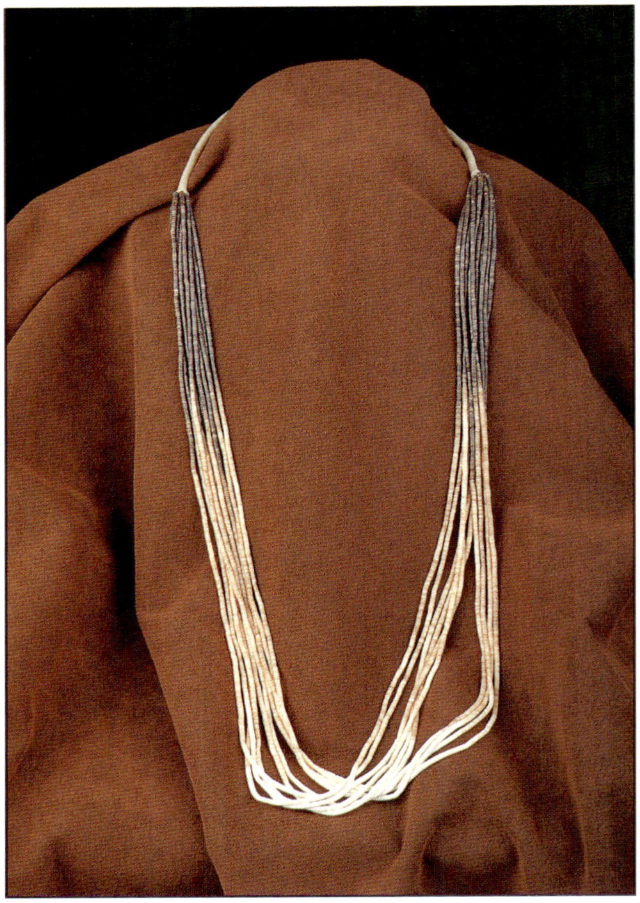

Santo Domingo heishi necklace of ten strands of white and shaded brown beads with a squaw wrap closure. ($300) *Courtesy of Palms Trading Company*

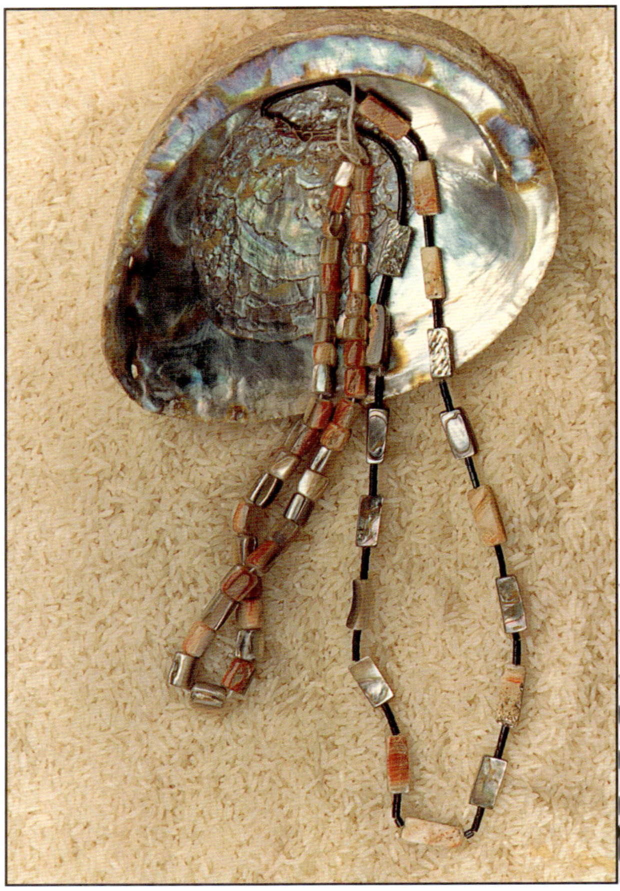

These two single-strand necklaces of abalone shell beads were made at the Santa Domingo pueblo in the 1980s. The use of diverse materials creates such interesting variety of this traditional form of ornament. *Enchanted Mesa collection*

Coral varies in color from light pink to very dark red and black, making for interesting tonal differences among jewelry pieces. Here a light colored coral heishi necklace of four strands with a squaw wrap is shown with a single strand dark coral choker. *Enchanted Mesa collection* .

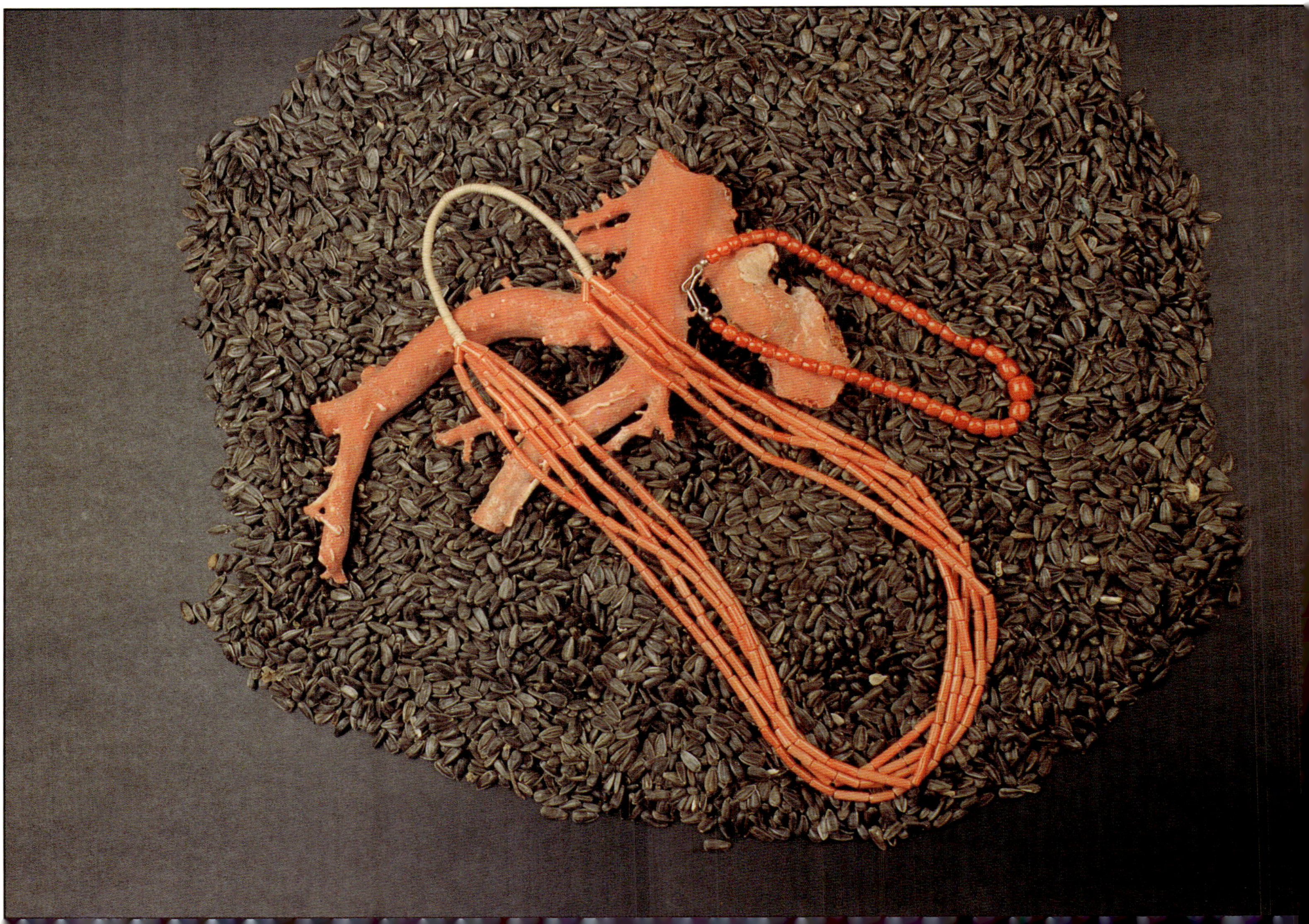

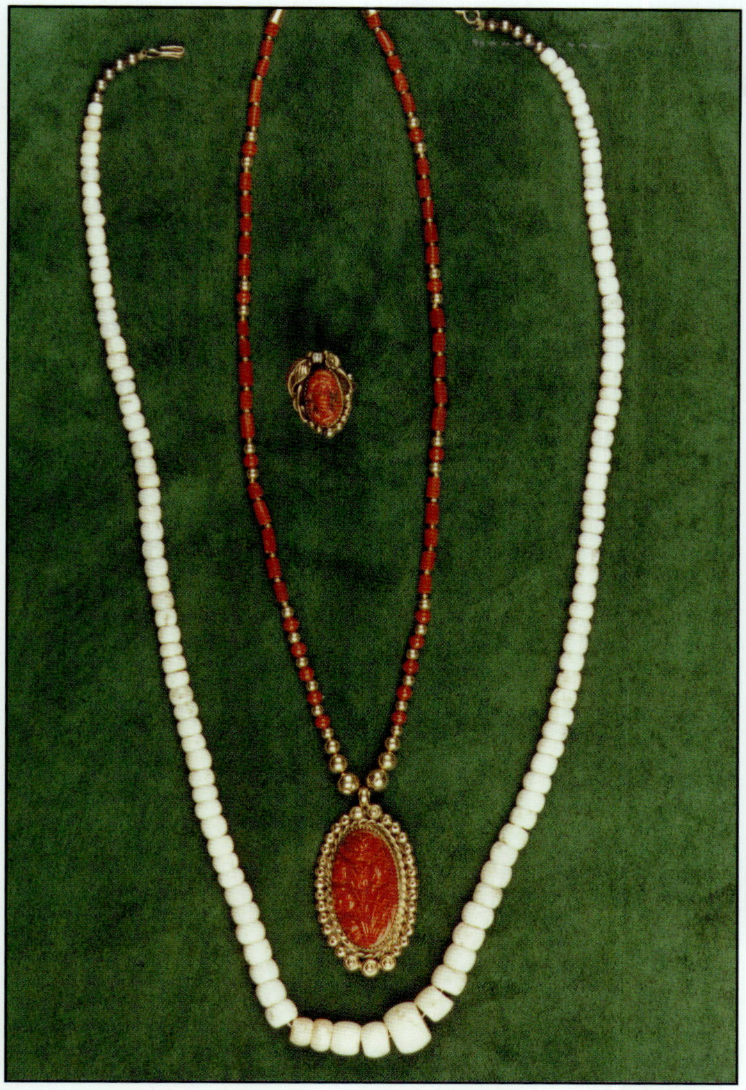

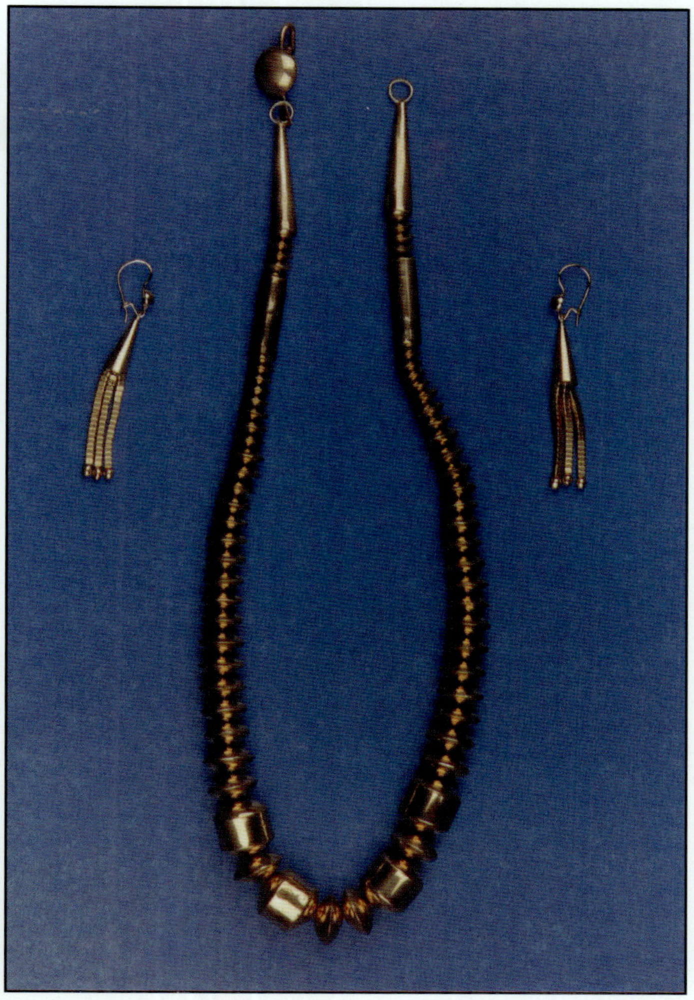

Brass beads of graduated size and diverse shapes were combined to create this necklace and pair of earrings, circa 1970s. *Enchanted Mesa collection*

A white coral and silver bead single-strand necklace is an unusual piece. / The red coral and gold bead necklace with carved coral pendant is marked JC 1970 HK. / The finger ring of carved red coral, gold and small diamond is marked BM. *Turquoise Lady collection*.

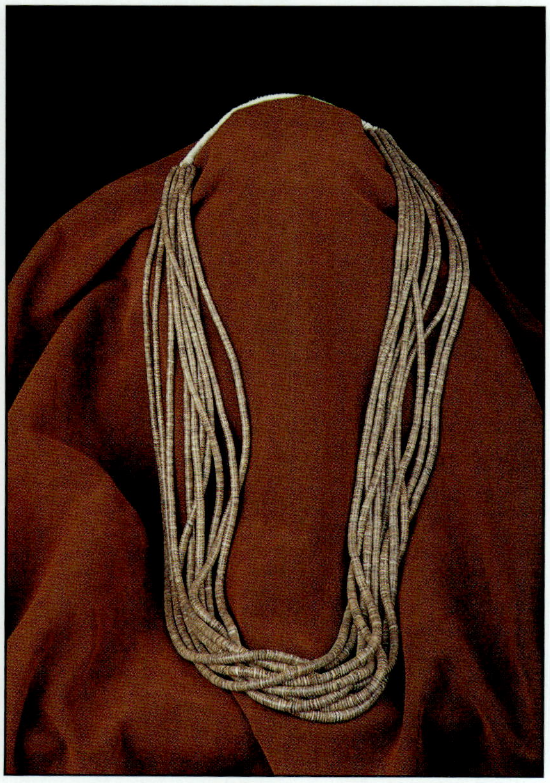

Santo Domingo long 10-strand heishi necklace of finely matched dark baby olive shell beads with a squaw wrap closure, by Joe Cate. ($2400) *Courtesy of Palms Trading Company*

Center: Jet and silver 5-strand choker by Ed Aguilar, Santo Domingo. / Four-strand shell heishi necklace. / Brass hand-drawn heishi necklace of many strands made at Santo Domingo pueblo, circa 1960. *Private collection on permanent loan to Ohio University*

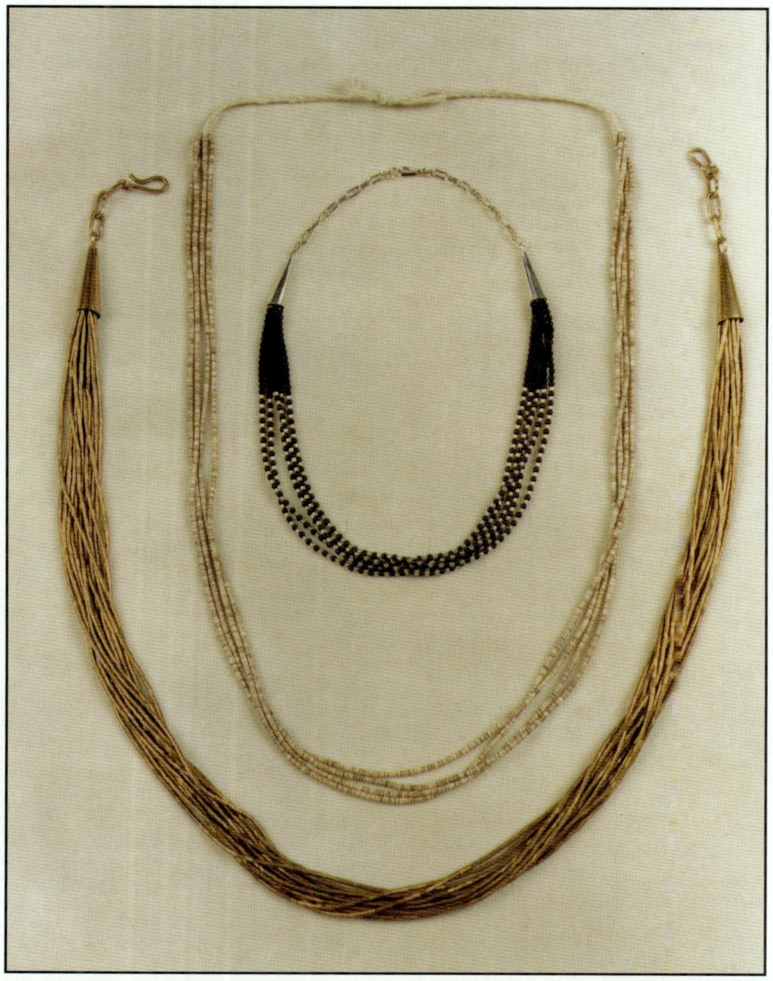

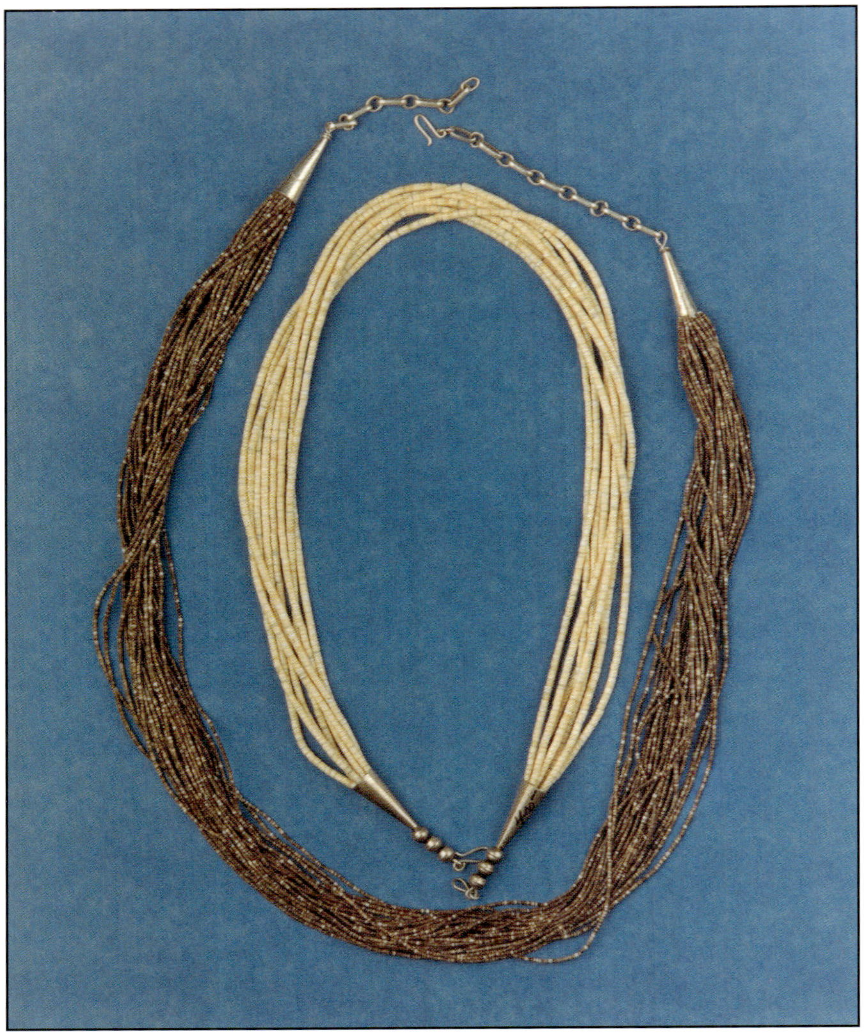

Two multi-strand shell heishi necklaces, one of white shell and one of dark brown shell, made in the 1970s. *Private collection*

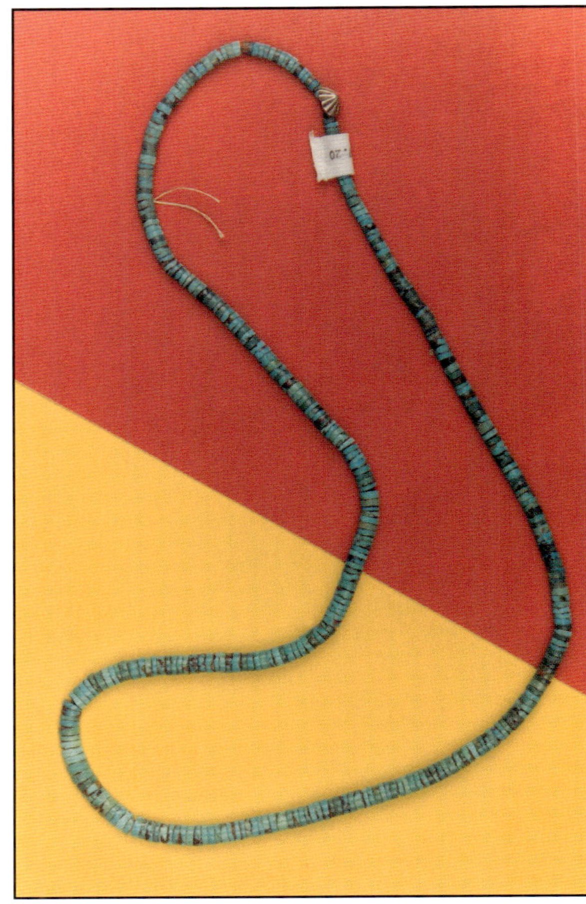

Turquoise heishi necklace from Santo Domingo in the 1950s. *Maxwell Museum collection*

Old 15-strand coral necklace with three pair of turquoise and shell jocla. / Coral and turquoise necklace of 13 matched strands made in the 1970s with a squaw wrap closure. *Private collection on permanent loan to Ohio University*

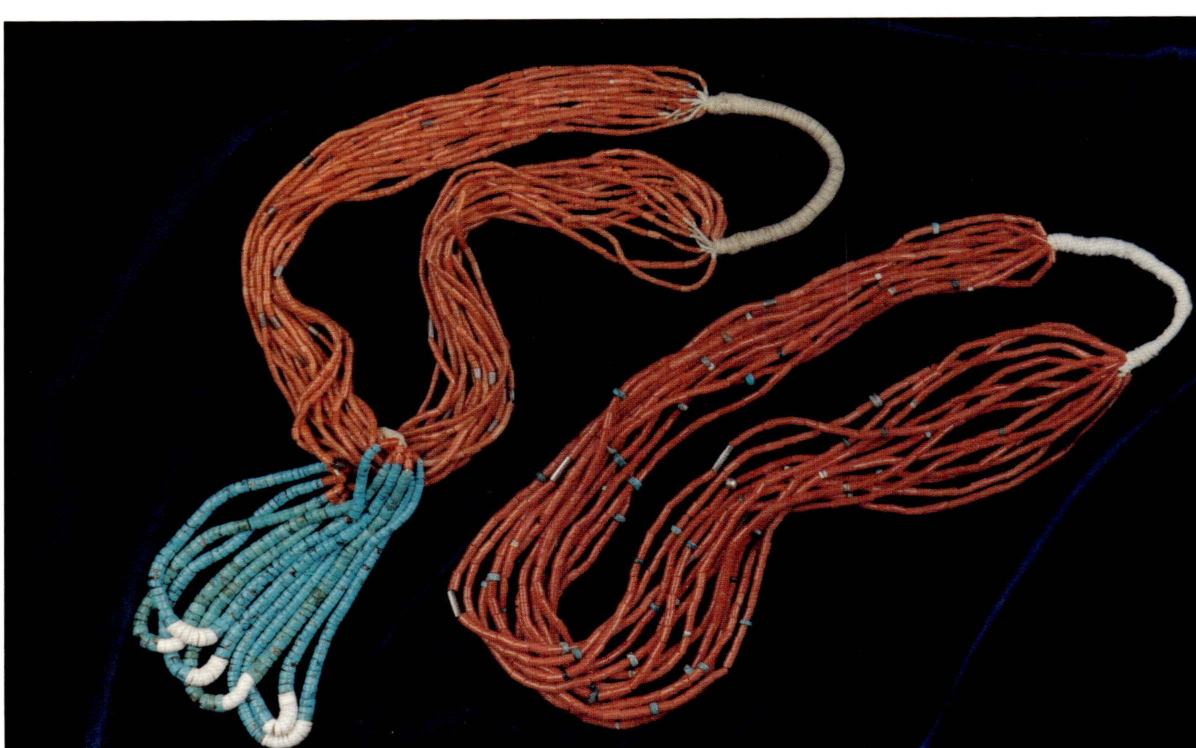

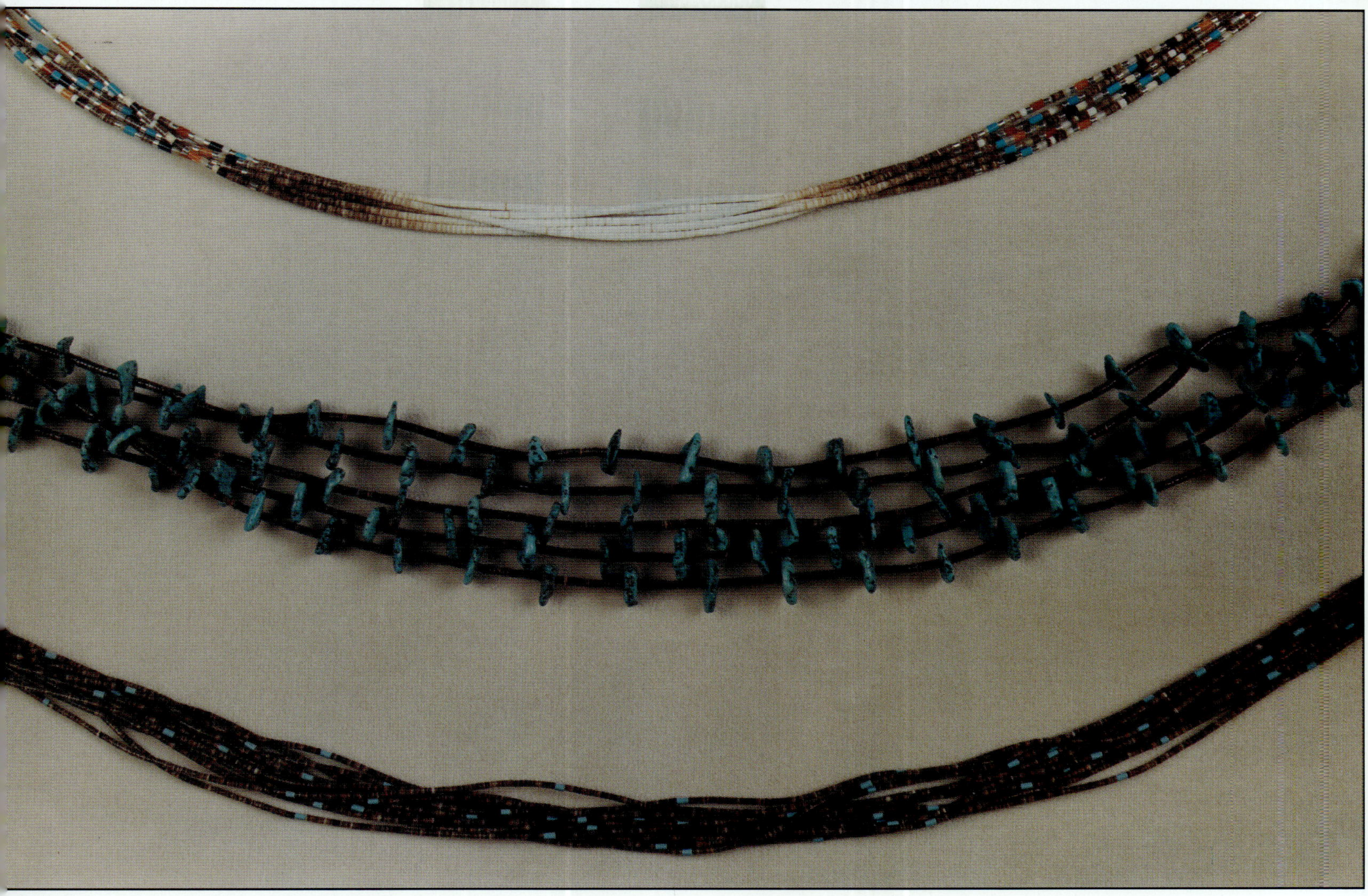

Three heishi necklaces of shell, turquoise, and assorted stone beads, the center one with larger Fox turquoise beads, all made in the 1980s. *Private collection on permanent loan to Ohio University*

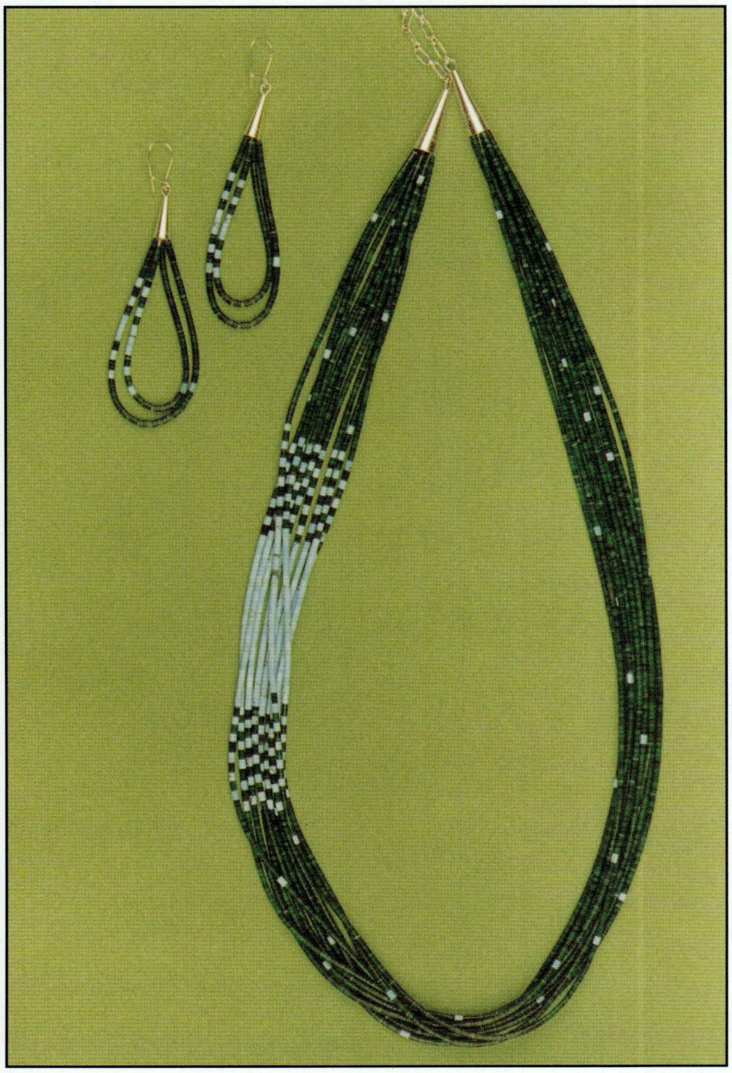

The use of African malachite with turquoise heishi indicates the growing use of new materials in all areas of contemporary jewelry design. This attractive necklace and earring set was made by Frank Ortiz of San Felipe pueblo in the late 1980s. *Turquoise Lady collection*.

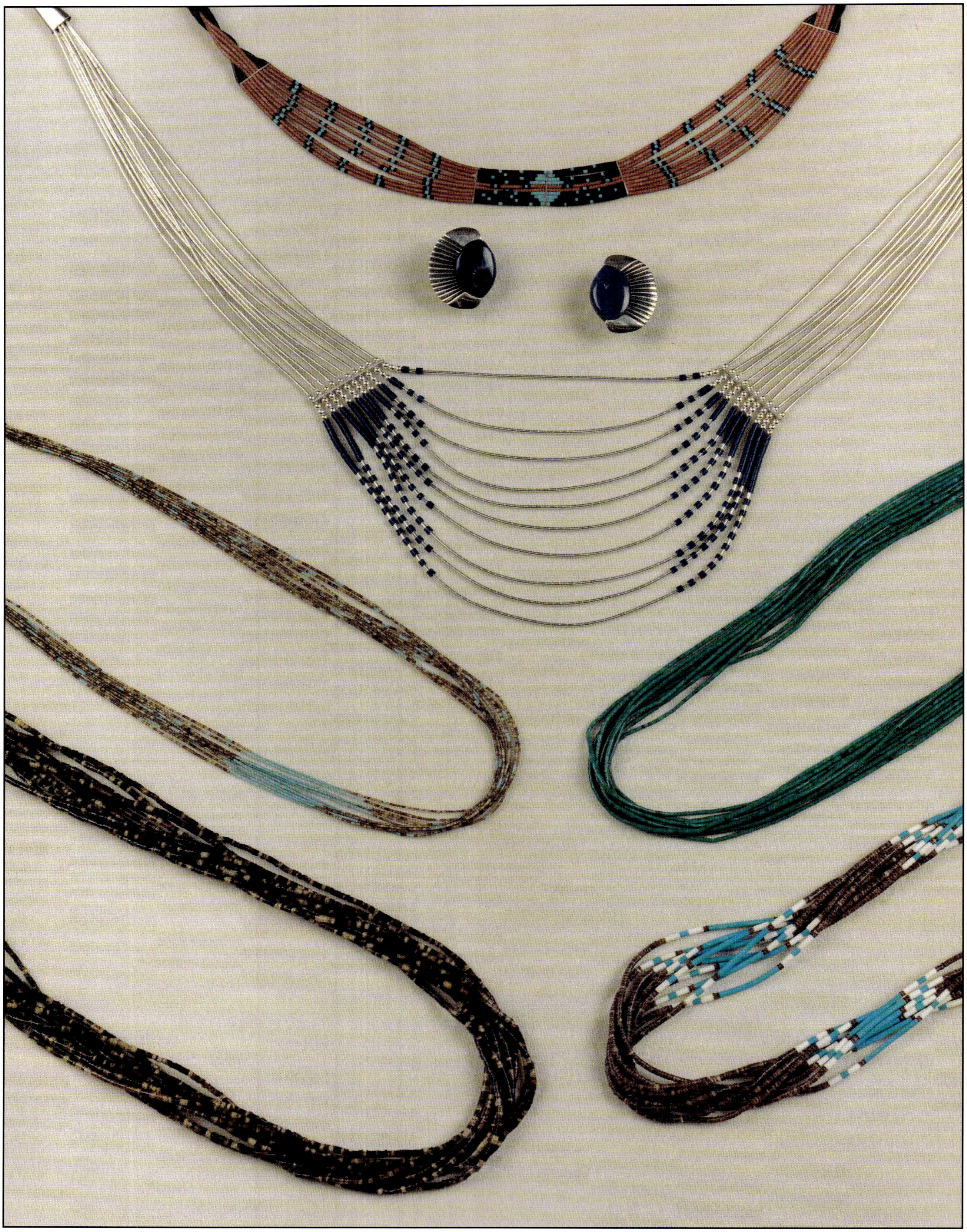

Assorted heishi necklaces from the 1980s show the variety of designs and materials, which were used to create the new styles. From the top: a ten-strand woven choker is made with pipestone, jet and turquoise beads. / Silver and lapis lazuli are combined in this pair of earrings and woven choker. / Ten tiny strands of tortoise shell, turquoise and silver beads form this short necklace. / Dark brown tortoise shell heishi in ten strands comprise a long necklace. / Ten strands of deep green malachite heishi make a long necklace. / An interesting striped design was achieved by combining brown and white shell with turquoise heishi in this necklace by the Tenorio family of Santo Domingo pueblo. *Private collection on permanent loan to Ohio University*

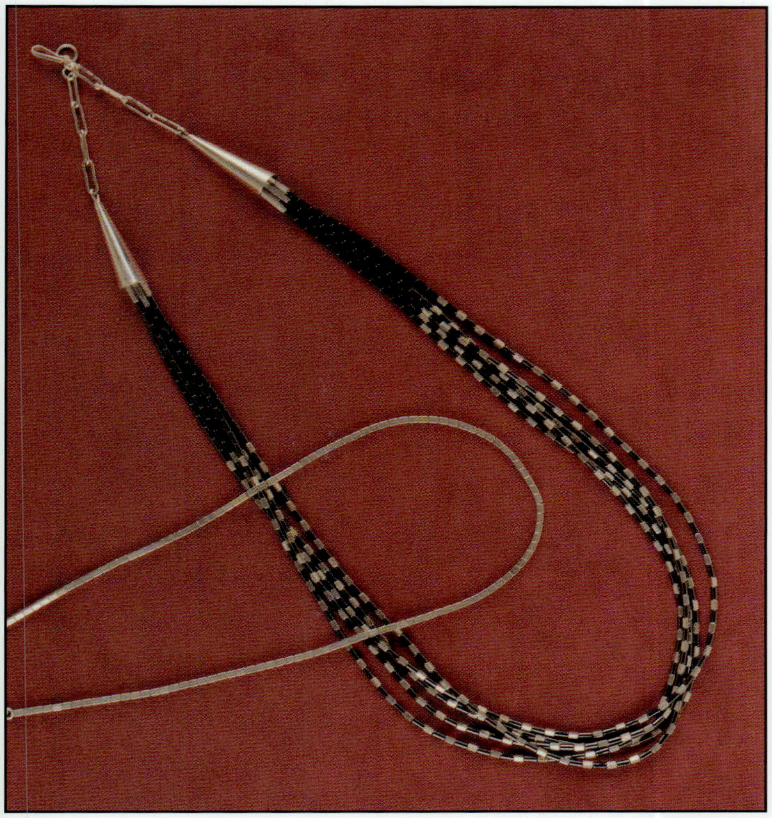

Single strand necklace of hand-drawn silver beads by Joseph Herrera Suina. / Five-strand silver and hematite bead necklace by Ed Aguilar, Santo Domingo. *Indian Post collection*.

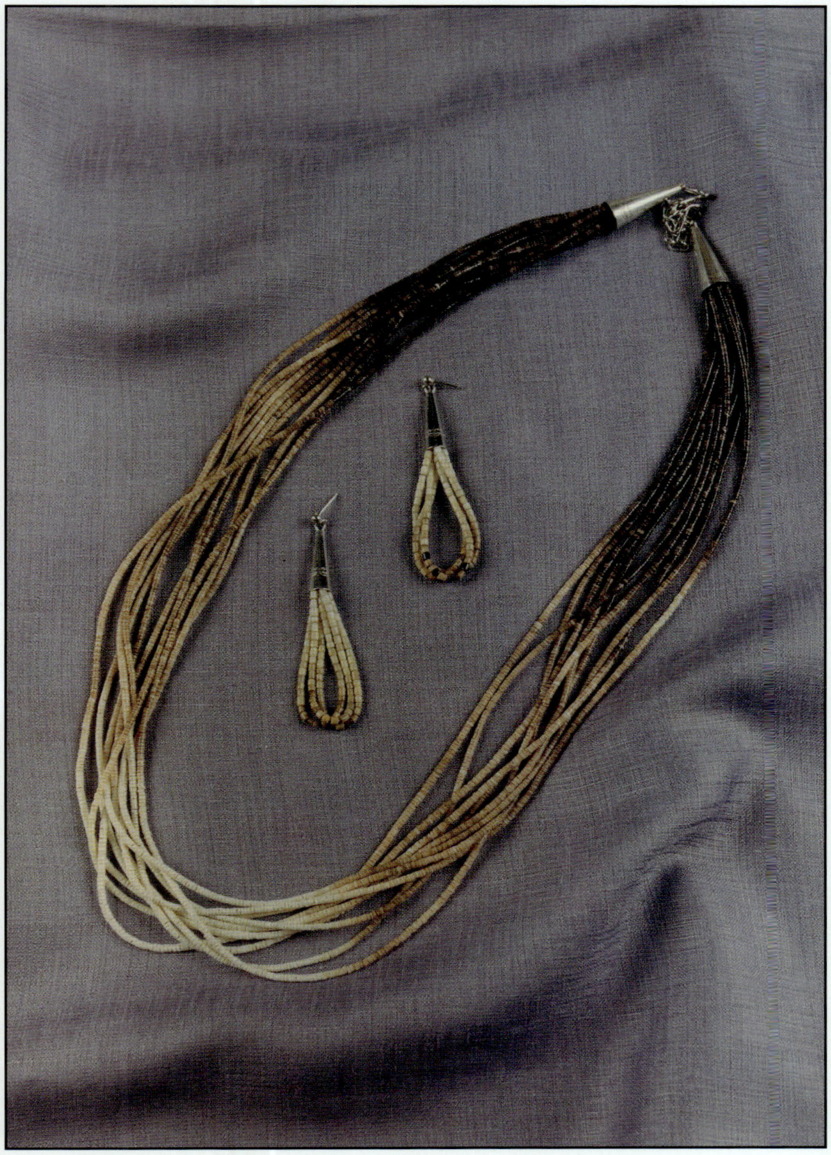

Shell heishi necklace by Mary Coriz, Santo Domingo. / Pair of shell heishi earrings by Louise Padille, San Felipe pueblo, both made in the late 1980s. *Indian Post collection*.

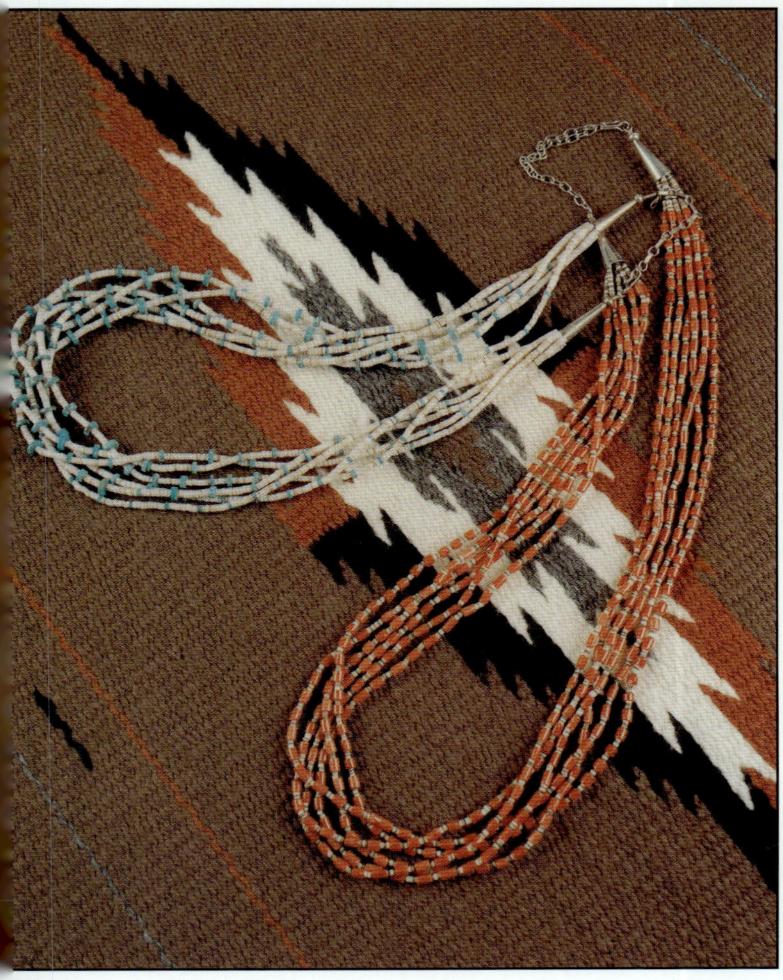

Two lovely six-strand heishi necklaces from the 1980s: left with shell and turquoise beads, right with coral and silver beads. / Right of. *Indian Post collection*.

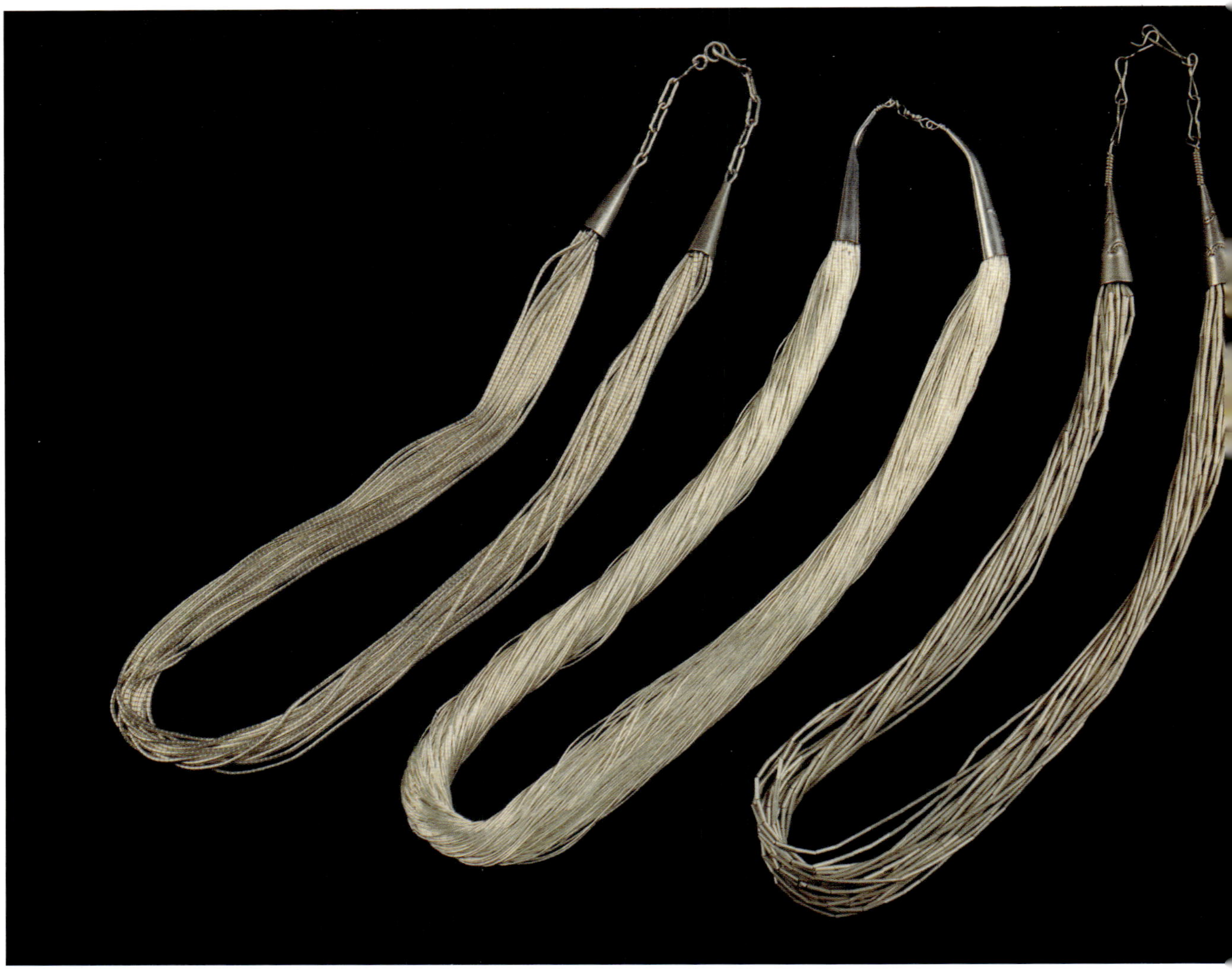

Three heishi necklaces of hand drawn silver beads: 15 strands, 27" long, by Ed Aguilar, Santo Domingo. / 100 strands of very fine silver, 25 1/2" long. / 20 strands made in 1967. *Private collection*

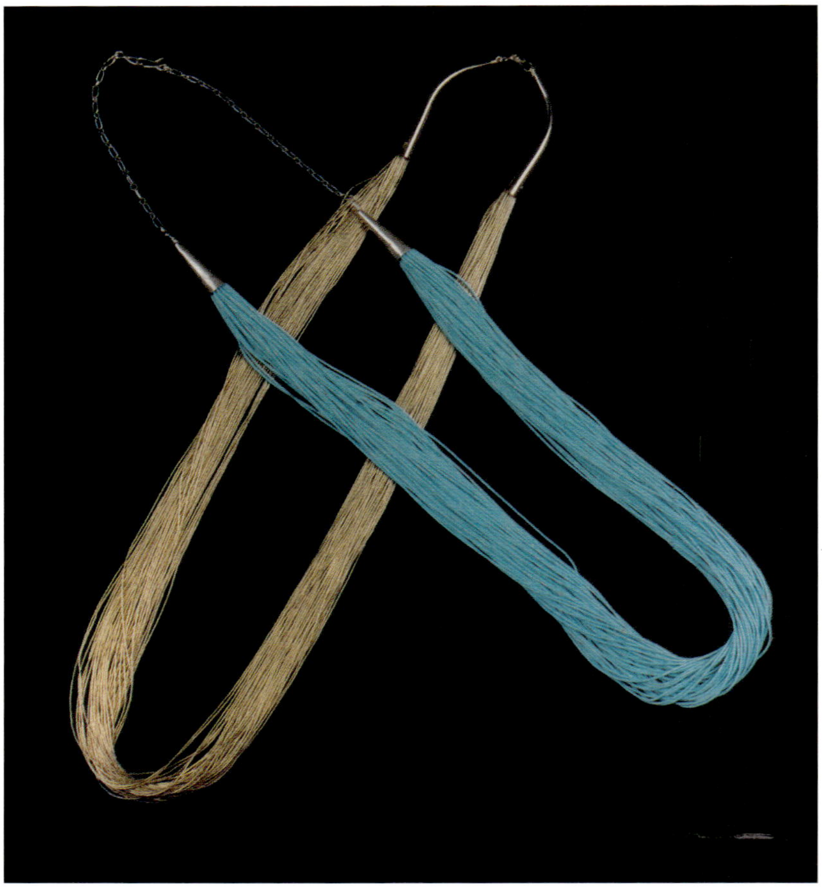

Very fine beads of 14 K gold on 40 strands comprise the elegant necklace on the left. / 50 strands of minute turquoise beads of uniform color and size make the right necklace, both from the 1980s. *Private collection on permanent loan to Ohio University*

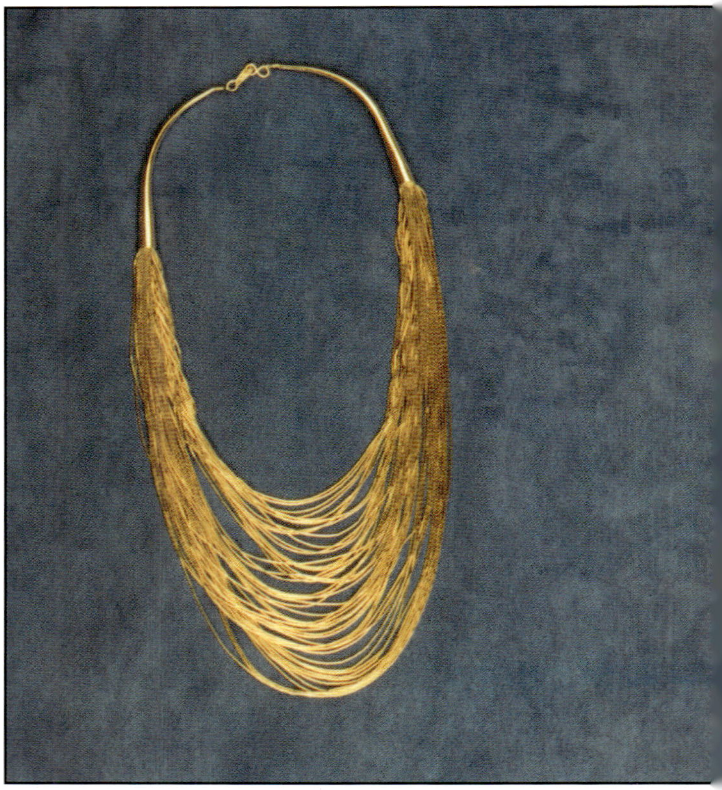

Tiny 14 K gold heishi in 50 graduated strands made by Johnnie (Juan) and Marlene Rosetta, Santo Domingo. *Keams Canyon Arts & Crafts collection*

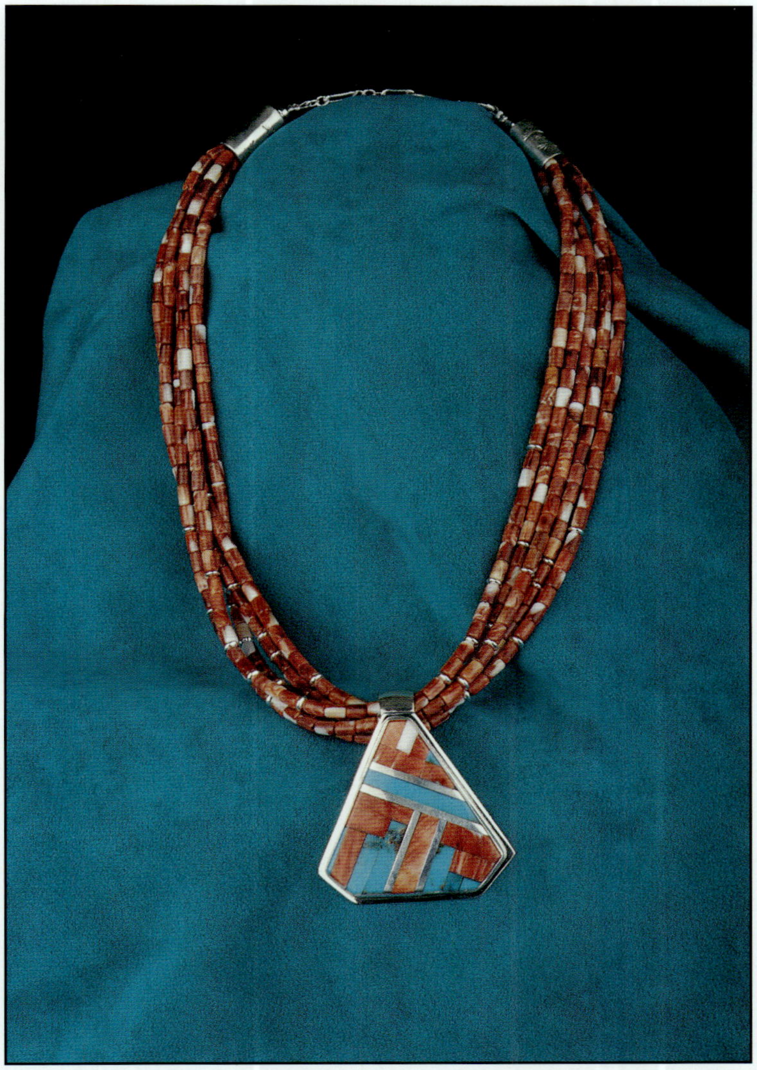

Heishi necklace of 5-strands of coral and silver beads and a pendant with turquoise and coral inlay, by Daniel Coriz. Santo Domingo. *Courtesy of Palms Trading Company* ($705)

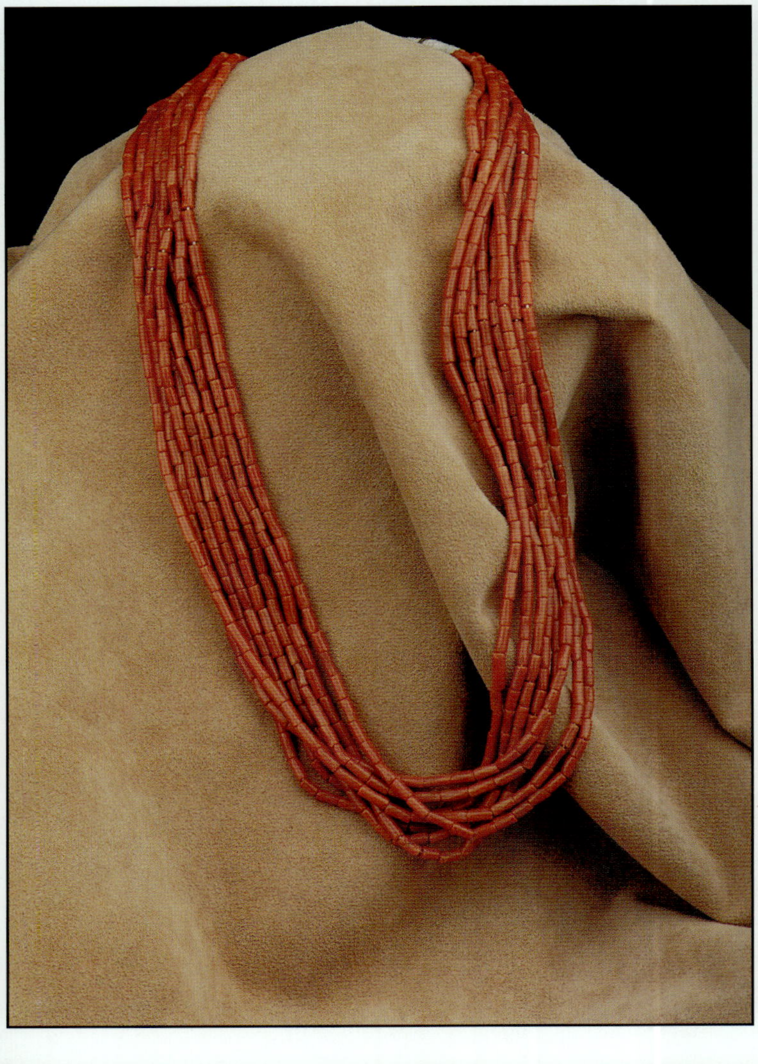

Light coral bead necklace of 10 strands, Santo Domingo, c.1940s-'50s. ($1500) *Lynn D. Trusdell, Crown & Eagle Antiques*

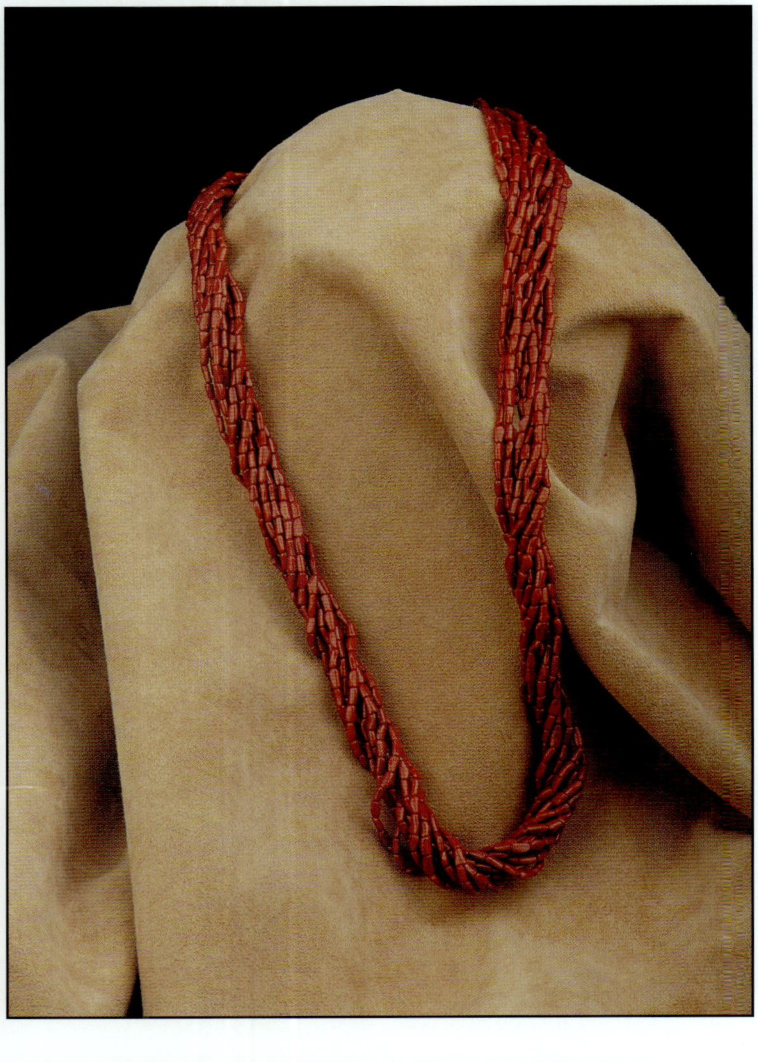

Dark coral heishi necklace of 8 strands, c. 1930s. ($1200) *Lynn D. Trusdell, Crown & Eagle Antiques*

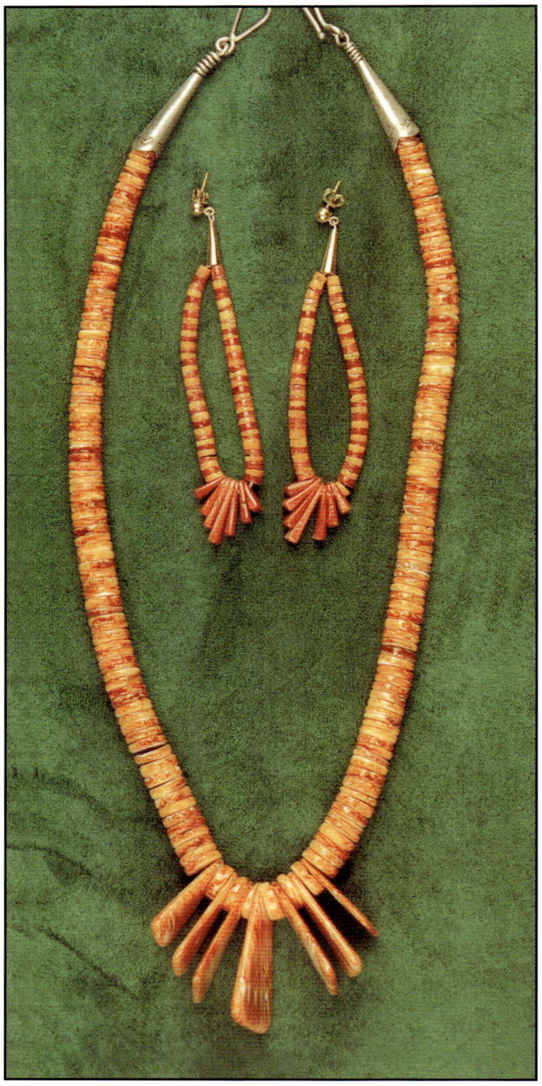

Necklace and matching earrings of graduated shell heishi with flat shell beads made in the 1980s. *Turquoise Lady collection*.

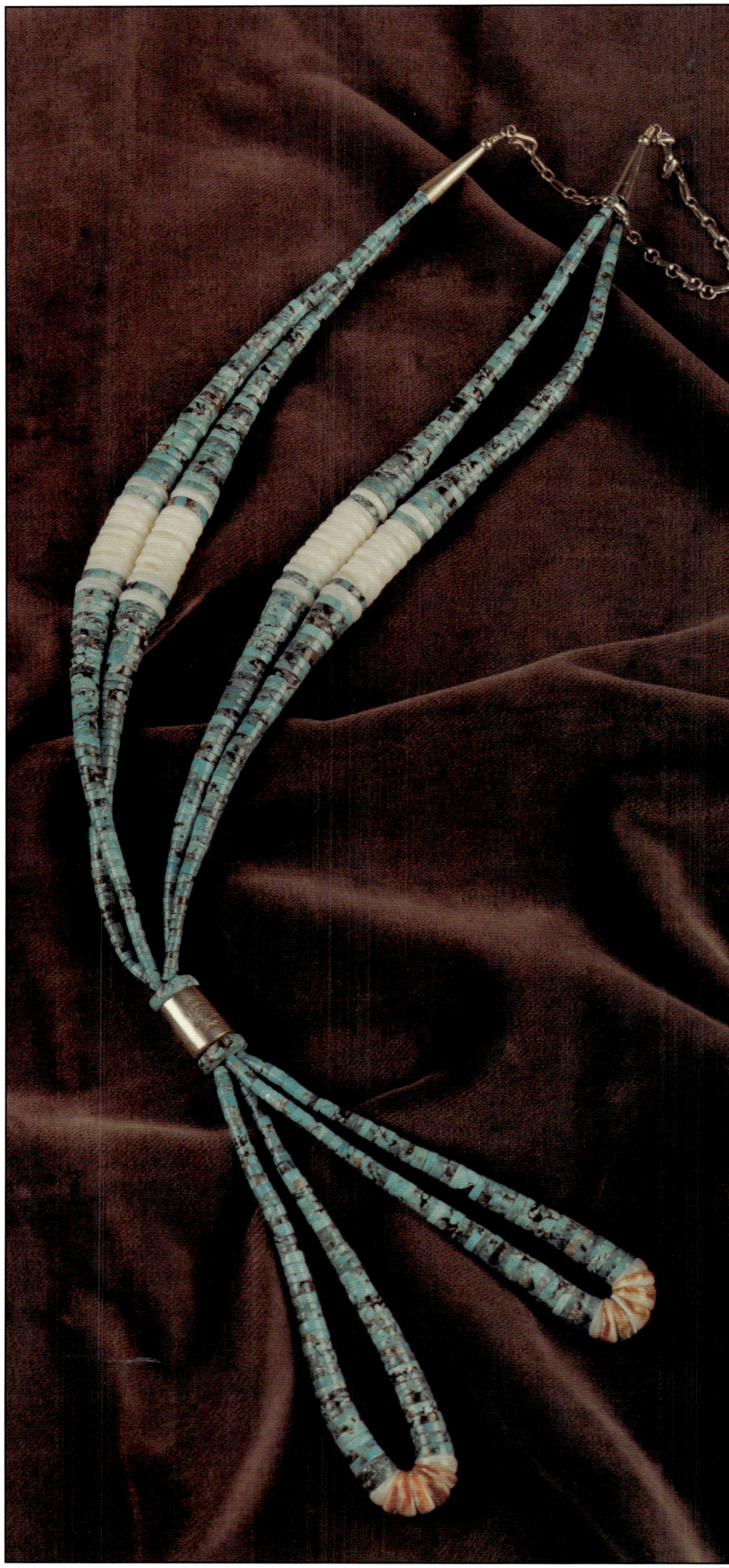

Double strands of graduated turquoise and quartz beads bound with a silver tube and two graduated turquoise and shell jocla-style pendants from the late 1980s. *Indian Post collection*.

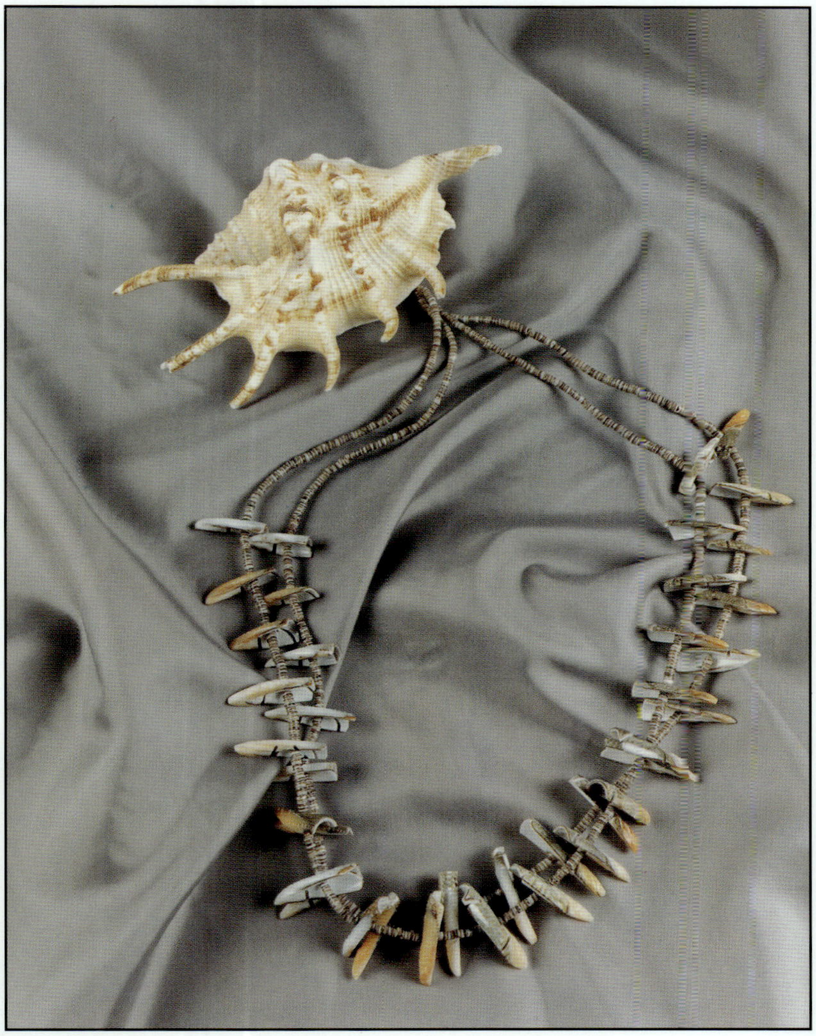

Shell heishi and spiny shell beads are combined in this attractive two-strand necklace from the 1980s. *Indian Post collection*.

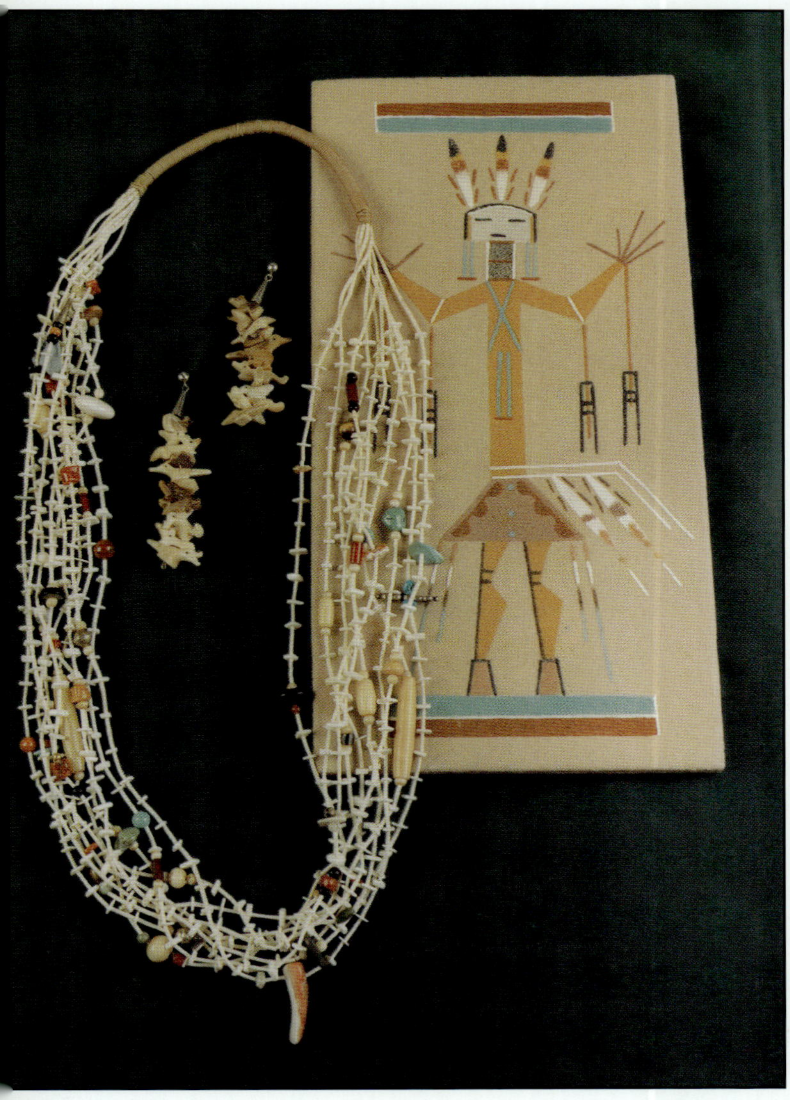

Ivory heishi and colored stone 10-strand necklace, sometimes called a "treasure necklace," made by Mary Coriz, Santo Domingo, late 1980s. / Pair of stone fetish earrings. *Indian Post collection*.

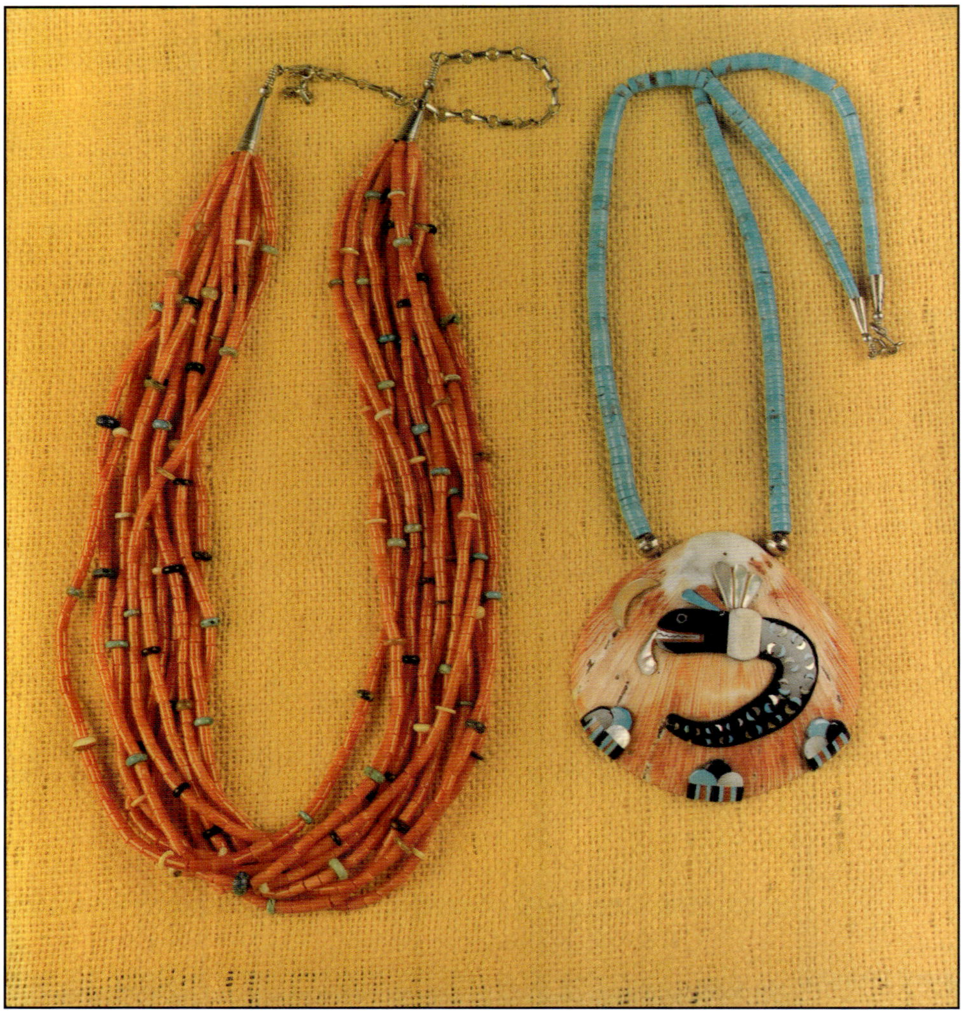

Ten-strand coral bead necklace with turquoise and colored shell bead accents made in the 1980s by Charles Lovato, Santo Domingo. / Pendant necklace with colored stone mosaic designs on a spiny oyster shell suspended from a strand of graduated turquoise heishi from the late 1980s. *Indian Post collection*.

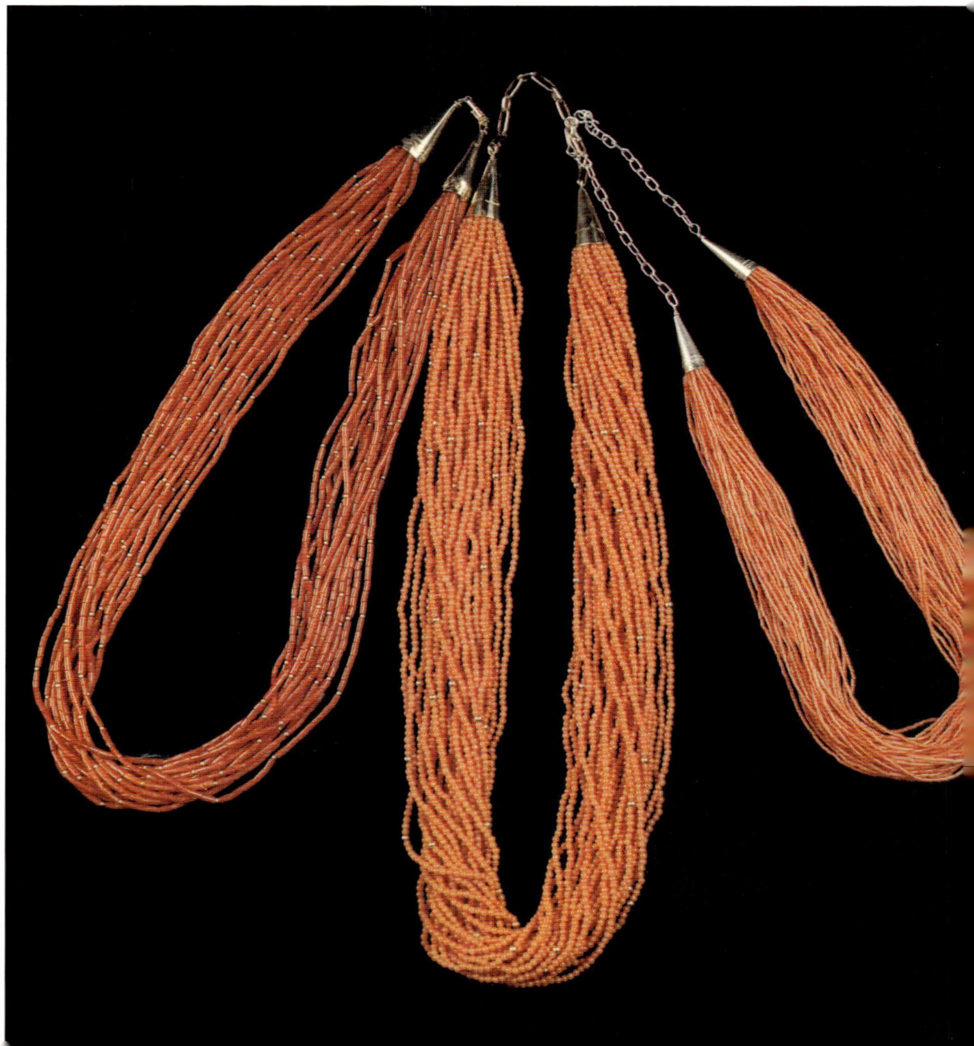

Coral heishi and gold bead 15-strand necklace. / Coral and gold 2mm beads form a 24 1/2 "-long, 26- strand necklace. / Tiny coral heishi are gathered into a 32-strand choker from the 1980s. *Private collection on permanent loan to Ohio University*

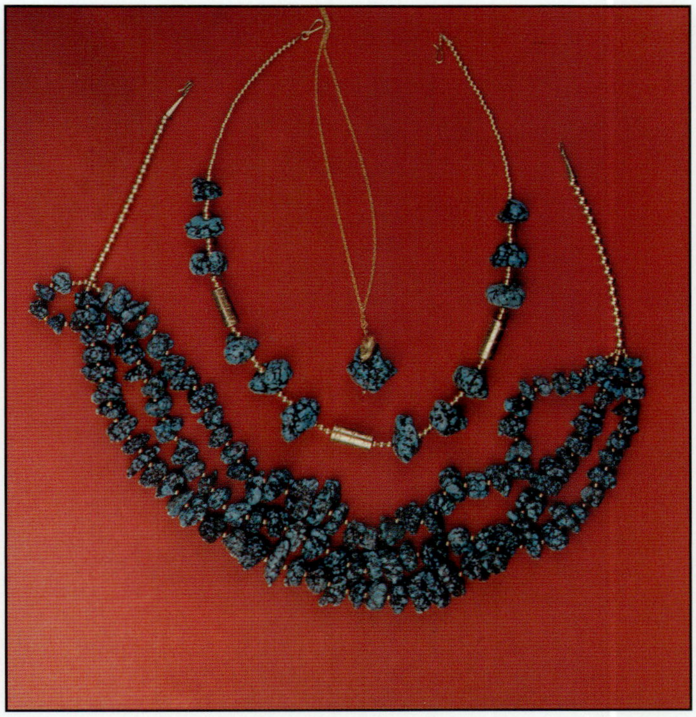

Turquoise chunks have been drilled and strung with gold chains to create a pendant, a choker, and a three-strand necklace all from the 1980s. *Private collection*

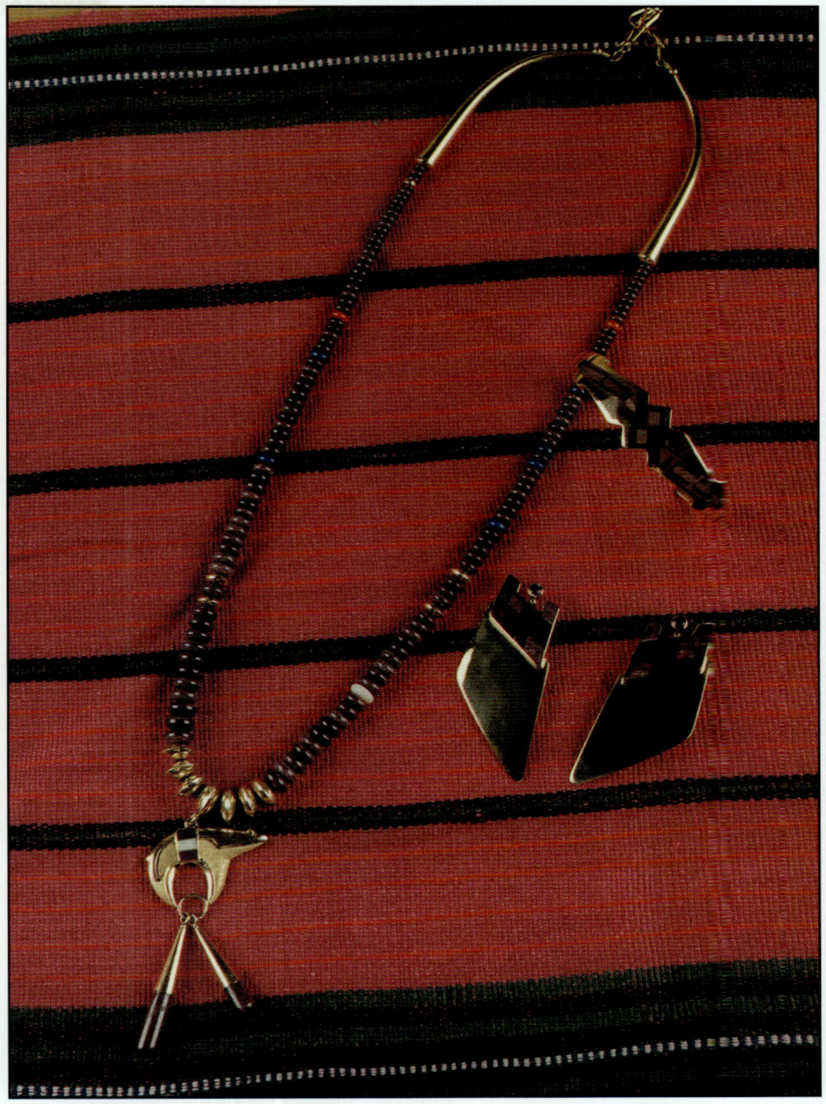

Purple sugalite, colored stone, and gold graduated beads form a necklace with bear and drop pendant by Andy Kirk, Navajo, late 1980s. / Shown in harmony with the necklace are a bracelet and earrings with sugalite mosaic designs by Ray Tracy, Navajo. *Indian Post collection*.

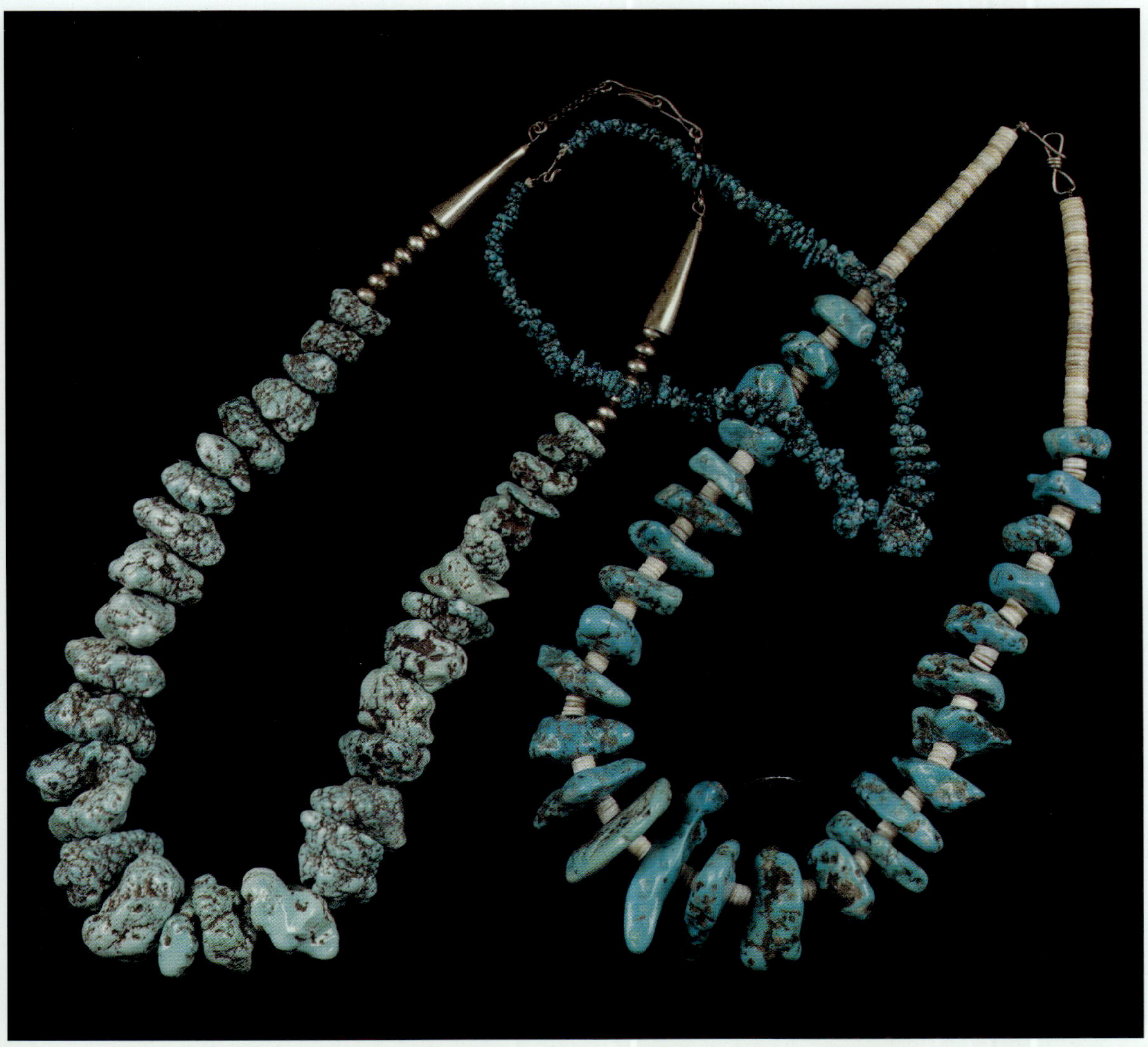

Necklace of 32 enormous graduated nuggets of Lone Mountain turquoise totaling 4,600 k fastened with silver beads and terminals. / 27 irregular and large Morenci turquoise stones of 3,630 k and white shell heishi strung together as a necklace 32" long. / To dramatize the scale of these necklaces, a normal size choker of Lone Mountain turquoise, 22 1/2" long, is included. *Private collection on permanent loan to Ohio University*

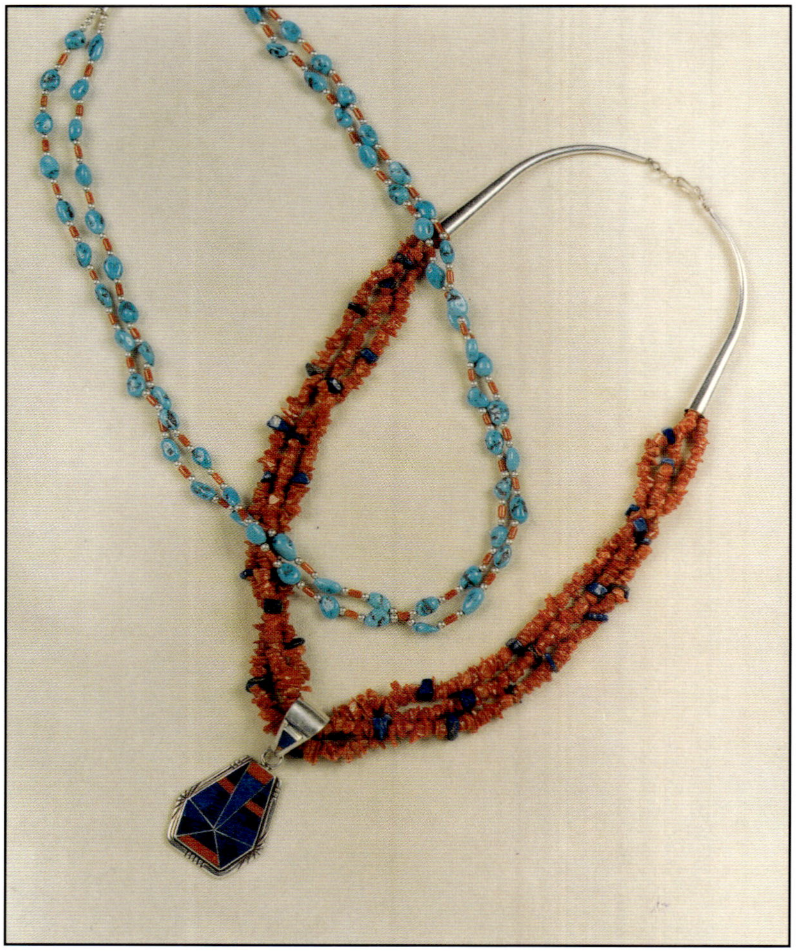

Two strands of turquoise, coral and silver beads, 26" long, made in 1988 by members of the Tenorio family of Santo Domingo pueblo. / Three strands of coral and lapis lazuli beads, 22 1/2" long, with a pendant of silver with coral and lapis lazuli inlay, 1988. *Private collection on permanent loan to Ohio University*

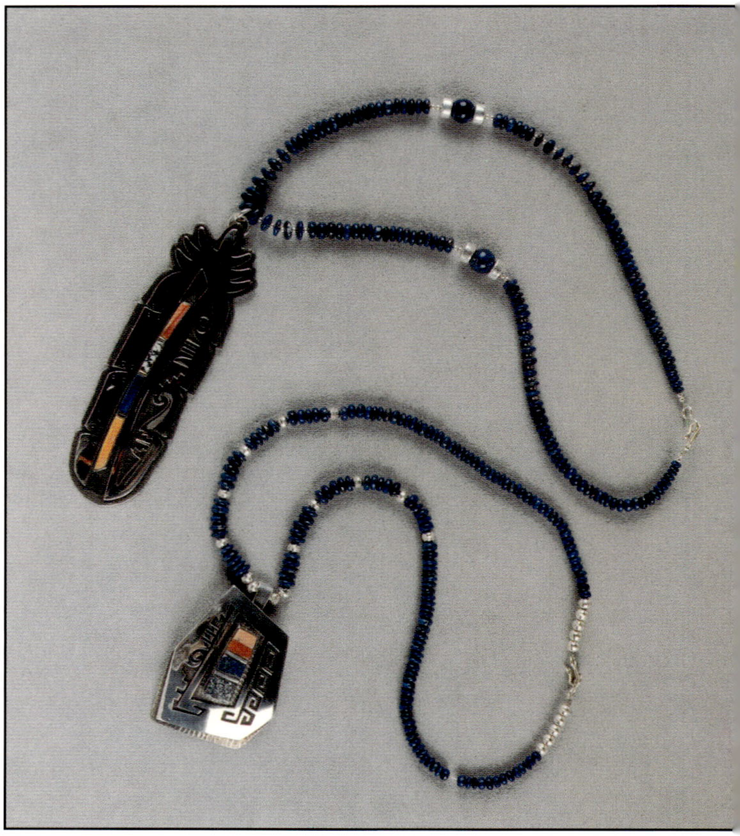

Two Hopi necklaces of lapis lazuli and silver beads with silver pendants inlaid with lapis lazuli, turquoise, coral and shell, 1980s. *Indian Post collection*.

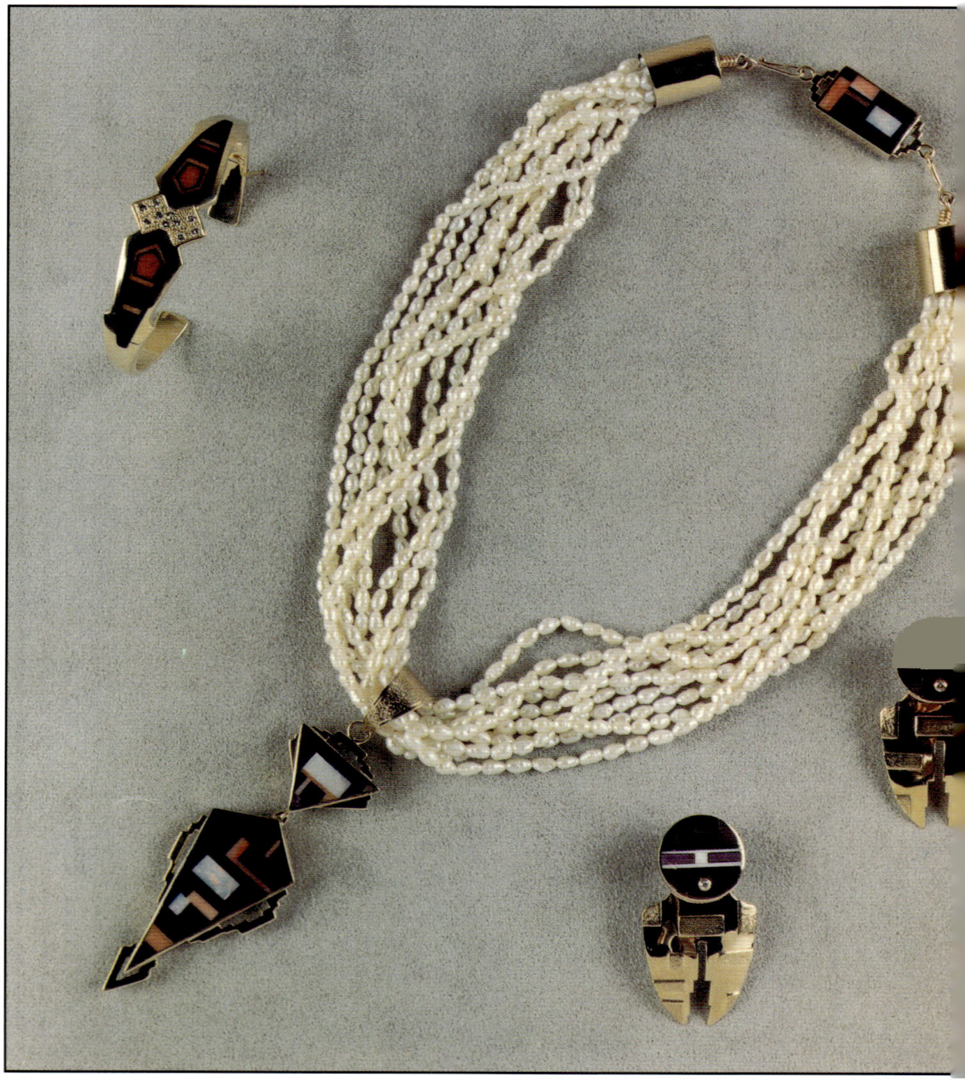

Necklace of eight strands of white beads fastened with gold ends and a clasp matching the stone mosaic inlaid pendant. / Earrings and bracelet of stone mosaic inlaid in gold. All by Ray Tracy, Navajo. *Indian Post collection*.

Fetish Necklaces

Zuni fetishes have been carved from stone for centuries. In the 1930s Zuni makers began to make very small stone figures to add to bead necklaces, and eventually to completely make up necklaces with no other forms. Their popularity soared in the 1970s and this type of necklace is still made today.

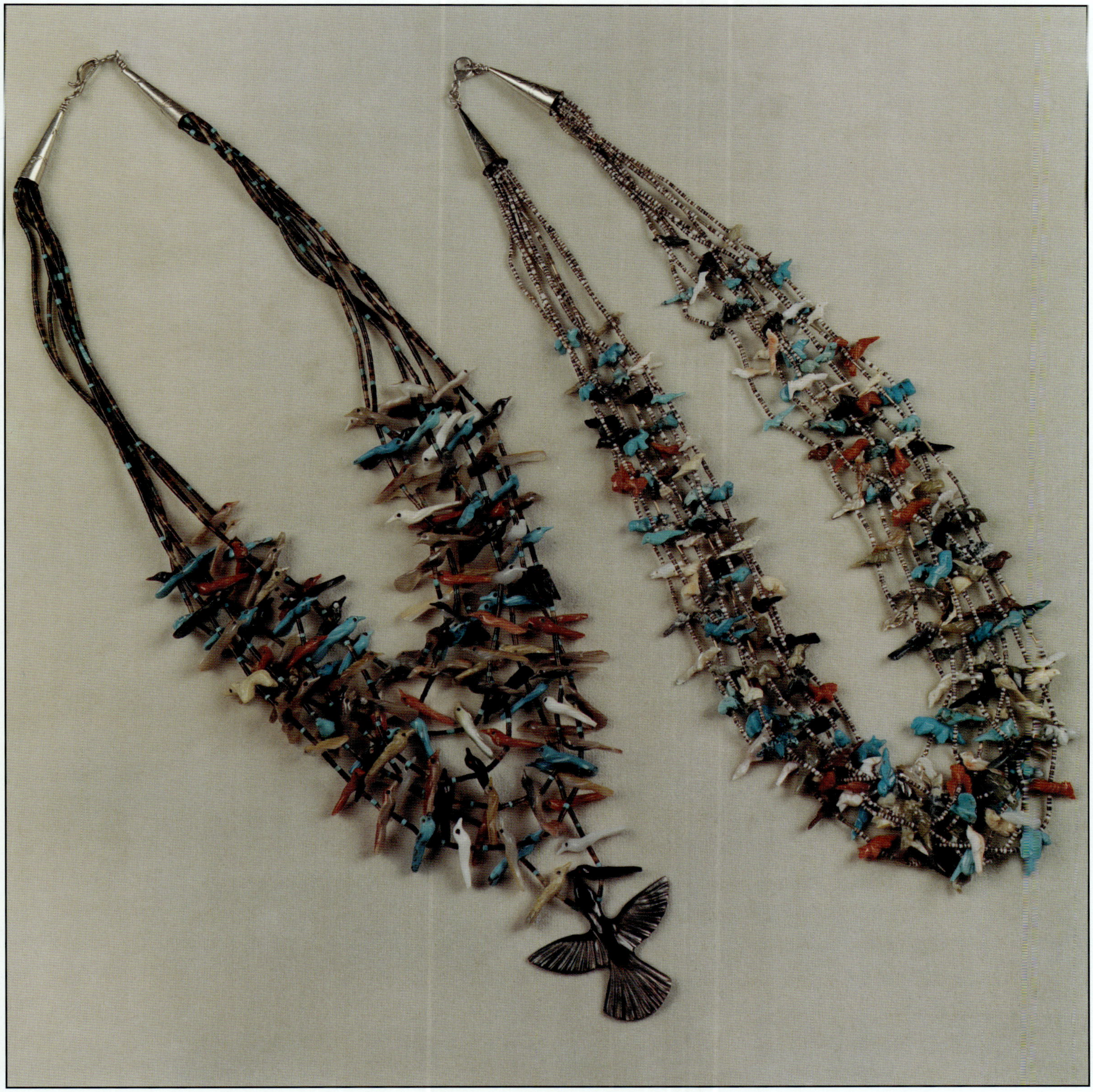

Seven-strand fetish necklace of carved stone animal- and bird-shaped beads with a large black stone pendant eagle figure marked G. H. C., circa 1978, probably Zuni. / Eight-strand fetish necklace made from a five-strand necklace with 23 birds on each strand and a three-strand necklace with 25 birds on each strand, joined by the owner, all made in the 1970s by James Feischter. *Private collection*

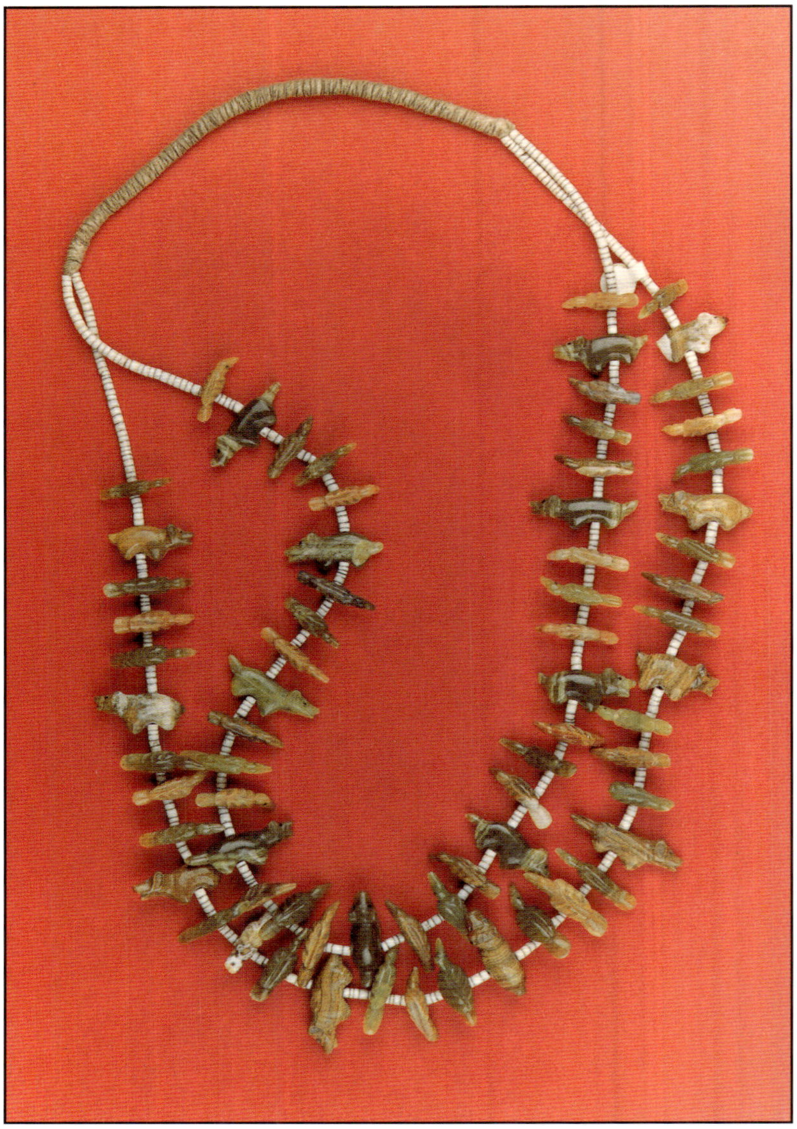

Two-strand Zuni fetish necklace of carved stone animal figures and shell heishi with a squaw-wrapped closure, 1970s. *Private collection*

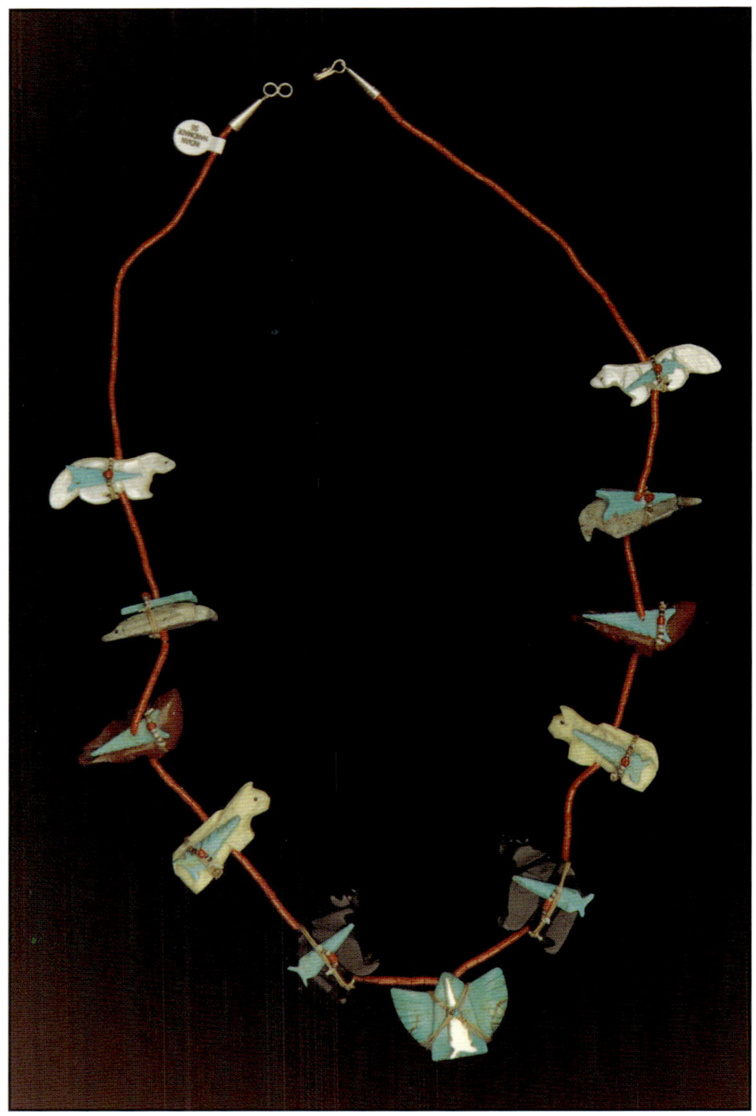

Single-strand necklace depicting the six Zuni prey gods in stone carvings with coral heishi beads. Arranged in pairs to the center, the fetishes represent six directions by their animal representations: South, badger / Below, mole / East, wolf / North, mountain lion / West, bear / and at the center, Above, eagle. *Bing Crosby collection*

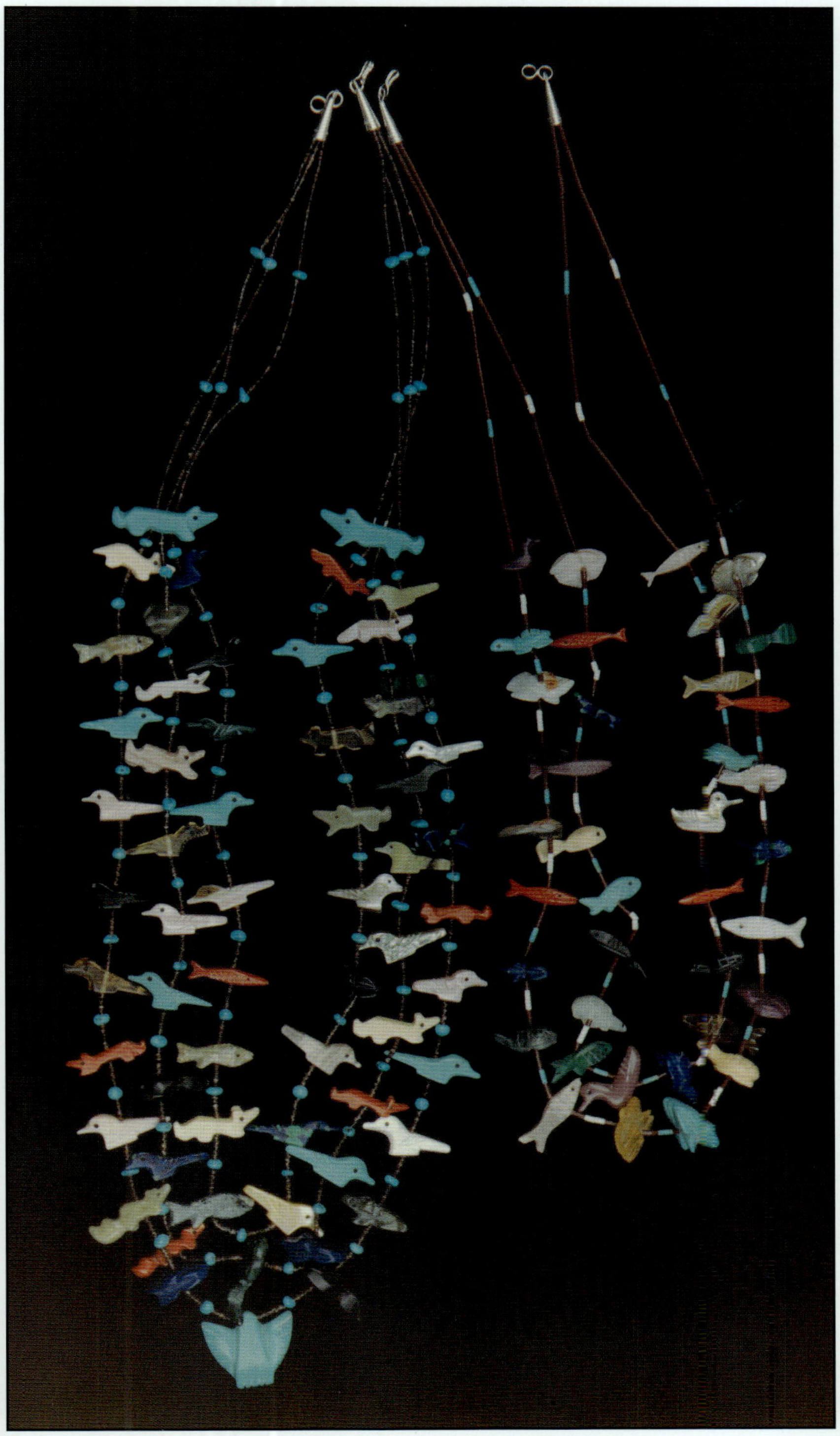

Three-strand fetish necklace with extra fancy carved stone bird and animal figures. / Two-strand fetish necklace with stone carved waterfowl figures, both necklaces by Anthony Upshaw, Navajo, late 1980s. *Bing Crosby collection*

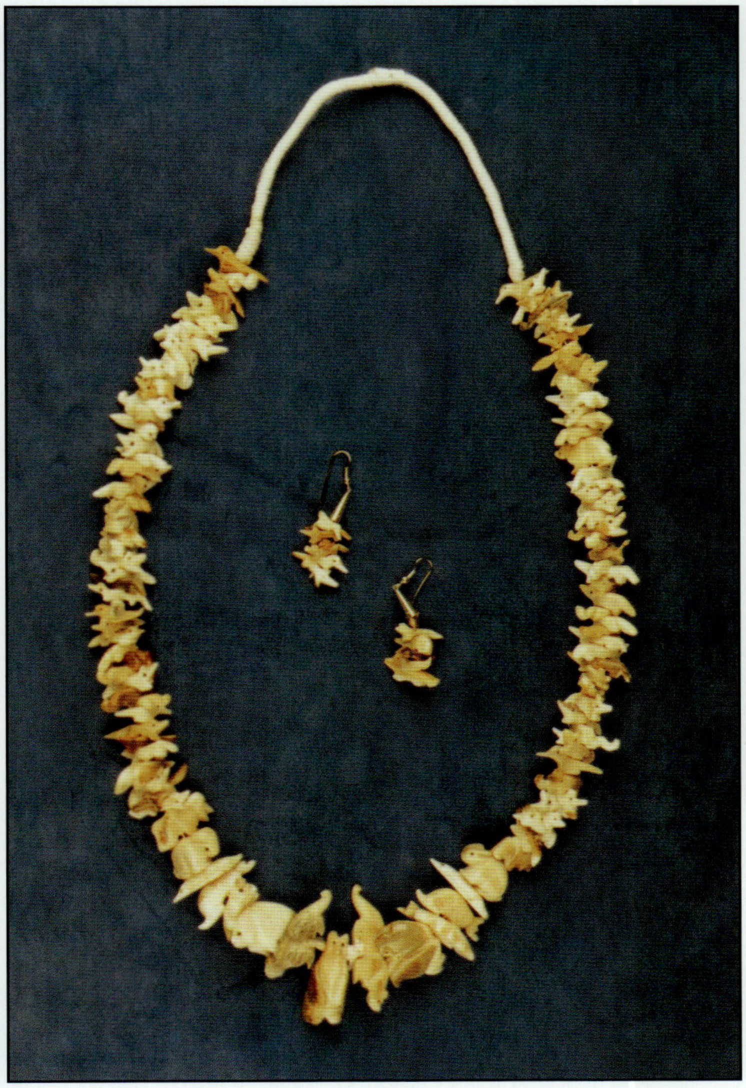

Stone animal fetish necklace and earrings by the Upshaw brothers, Navajo, late 1980s. *Keams Canyon Arts & Crafts collection*

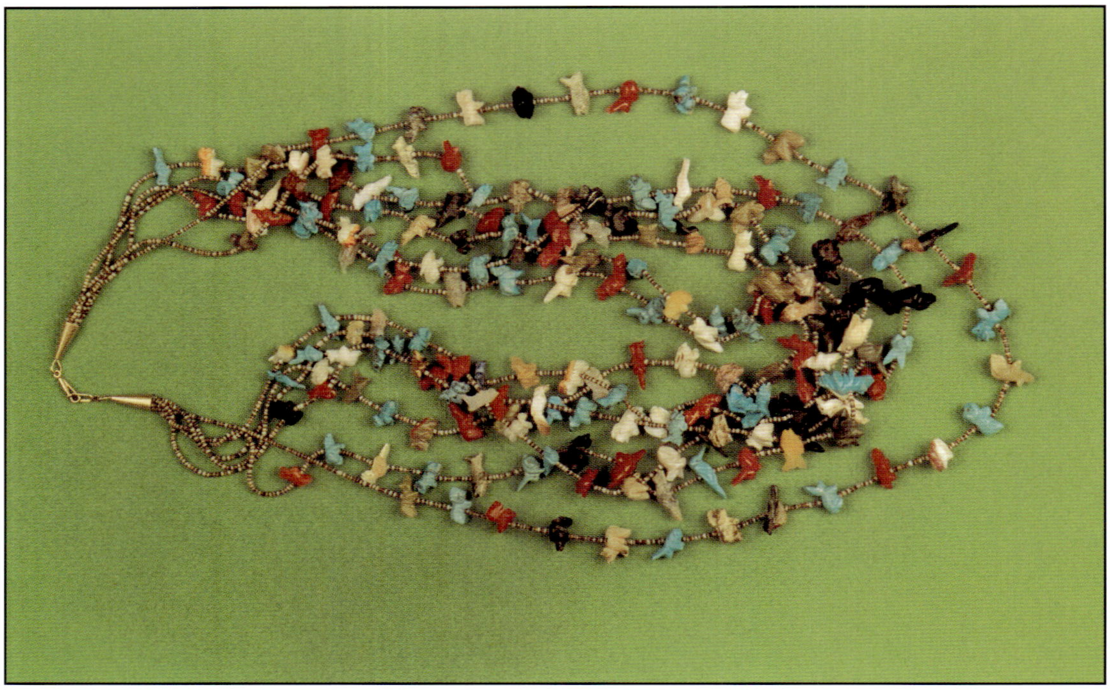

Six-strand fetish necklace of carved stone beads with shell heishi made in the 1980s by James Feischter. *Turquoise Lady collection*.

Three-strand fetish necklace of carved turquoise. / Three-strand carved shell fetish necklace. / Seven-strand fetish necklace of carved stone, all from the 1970s, Zuni. *Private collection*

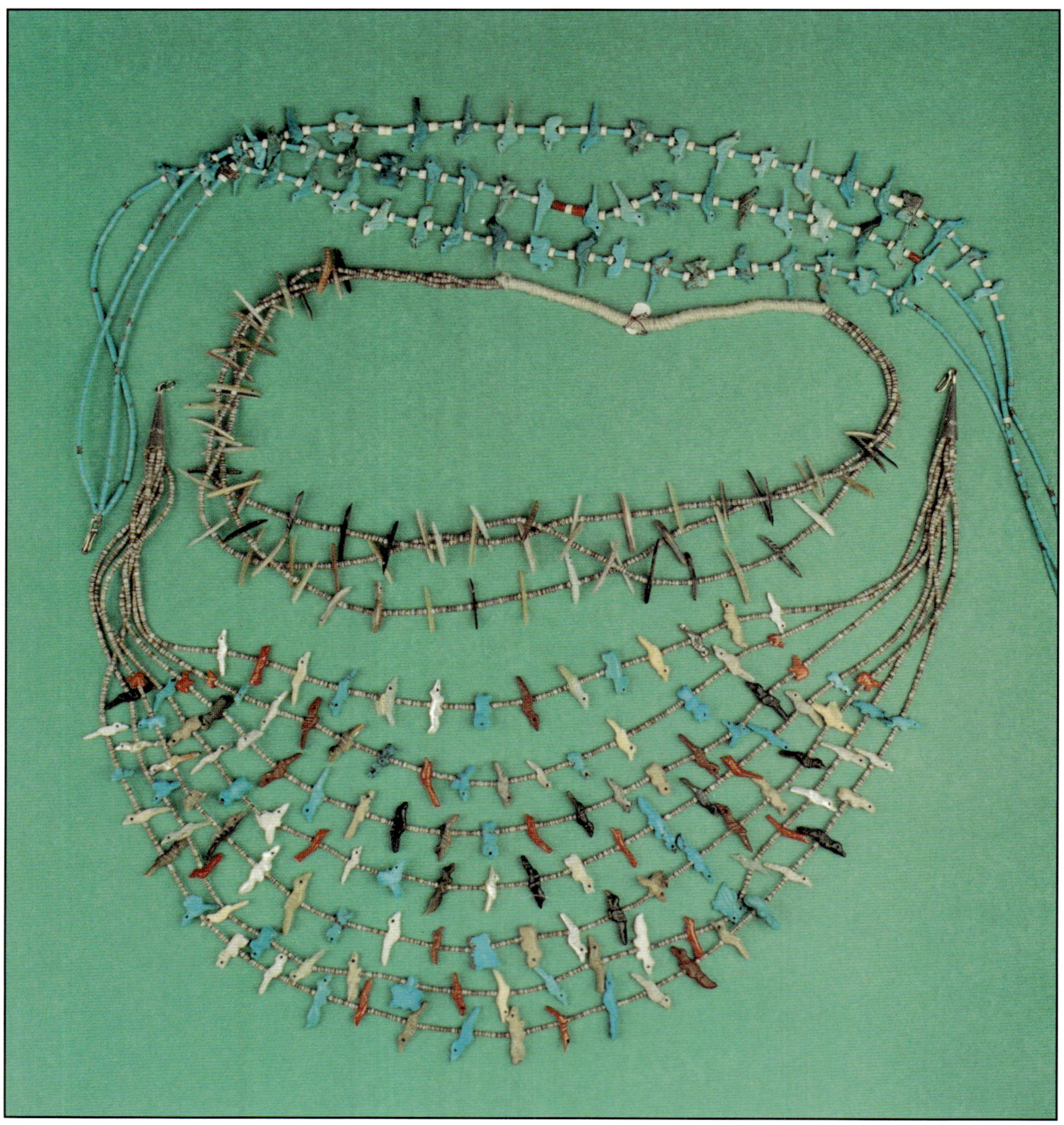

Eight-strand fetish necklace with carved stone figures, coral heishi, and silver beads at the closure, by Leekya Deysee, Zuni. *Private collection on permanent loan to Ohio University*

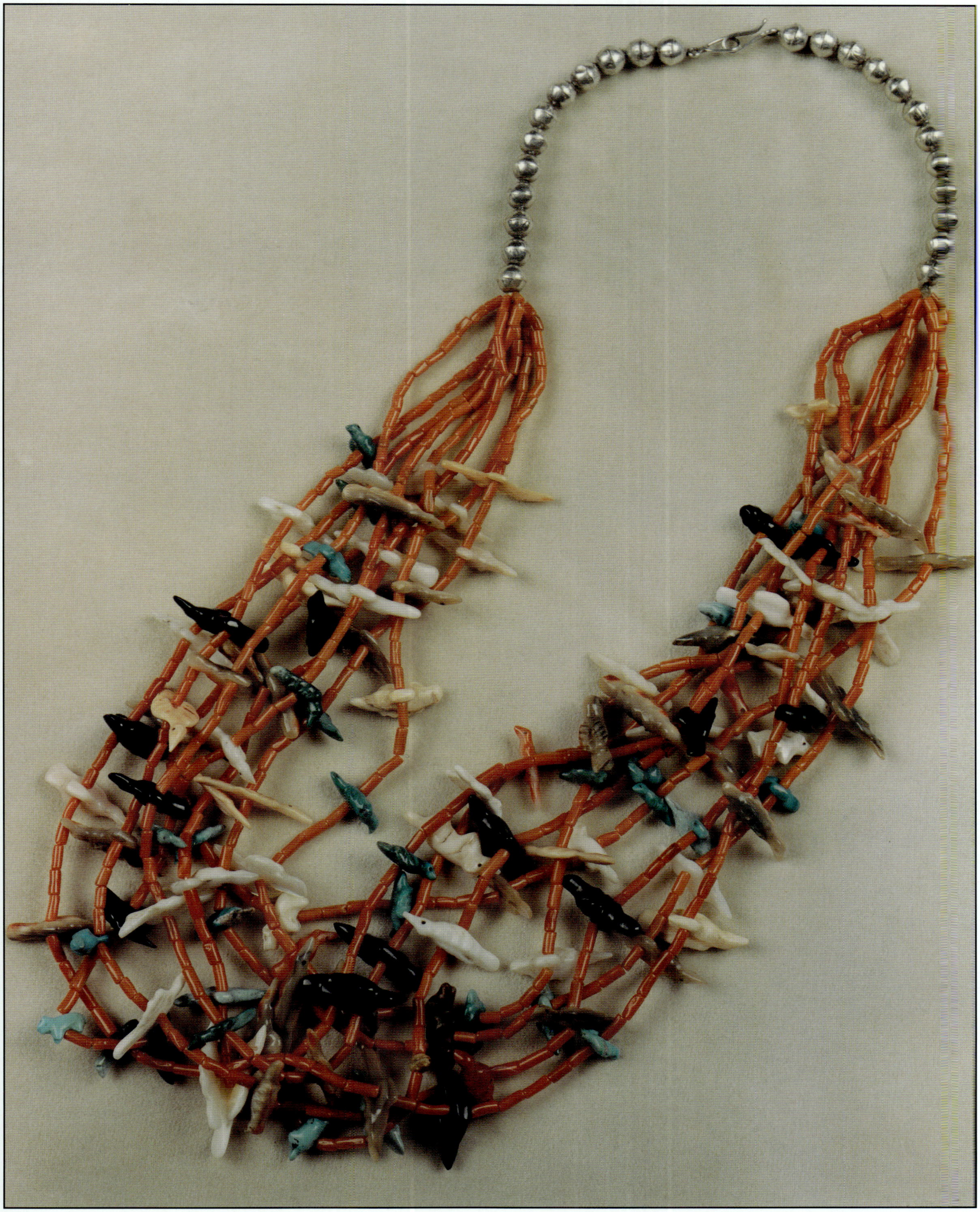

Silver Bead Necklaces

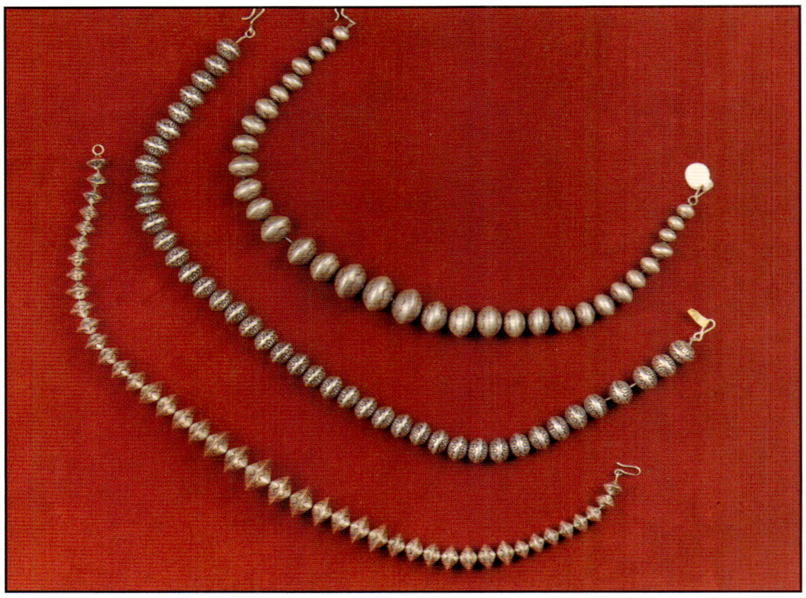

Single strand of 33 old, graduated, hand-made silver beads, Navajo, 16" long. / 41 old, hand-made, Navajo, round silver beads strung together. / Strand of triangular, hand-made, silver beads, 17 3/4" long, by Felix Coan, Navajo. *Private collection on permanent loan to Ohio University*

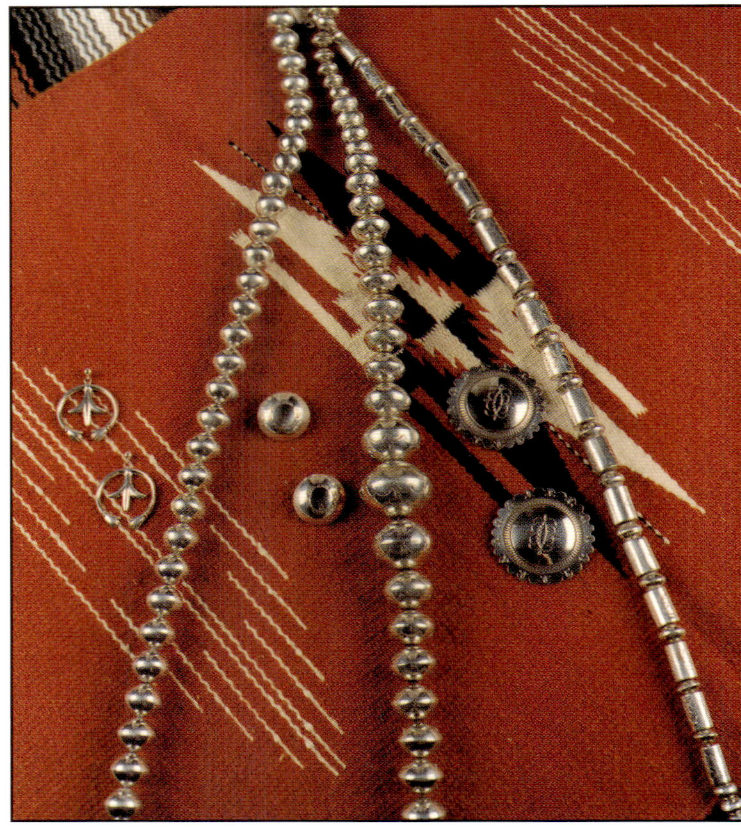

Classic silver jewelry made in the 1980s: Earrings replicating a naja design with two hands as terminals and a pendant squash blossom. / Necklace of plain uniform beads by Cipi Crazyhorse, Cochiti. / Round button style earrings. / Graduated Navajo beads in a single strand necklace. / Concho-style earrings with stamped and filed edges. / Tubular beads of graduated sizes create a single strand necklace, Navajo. *Indian Post collection*.

A necklace of buttons originally strung onto a hand-made chain, Navajo, 1920s-'30s, and sold in gift shops. *Lynn D. Trusdell, Crown & Eagle Antiques*

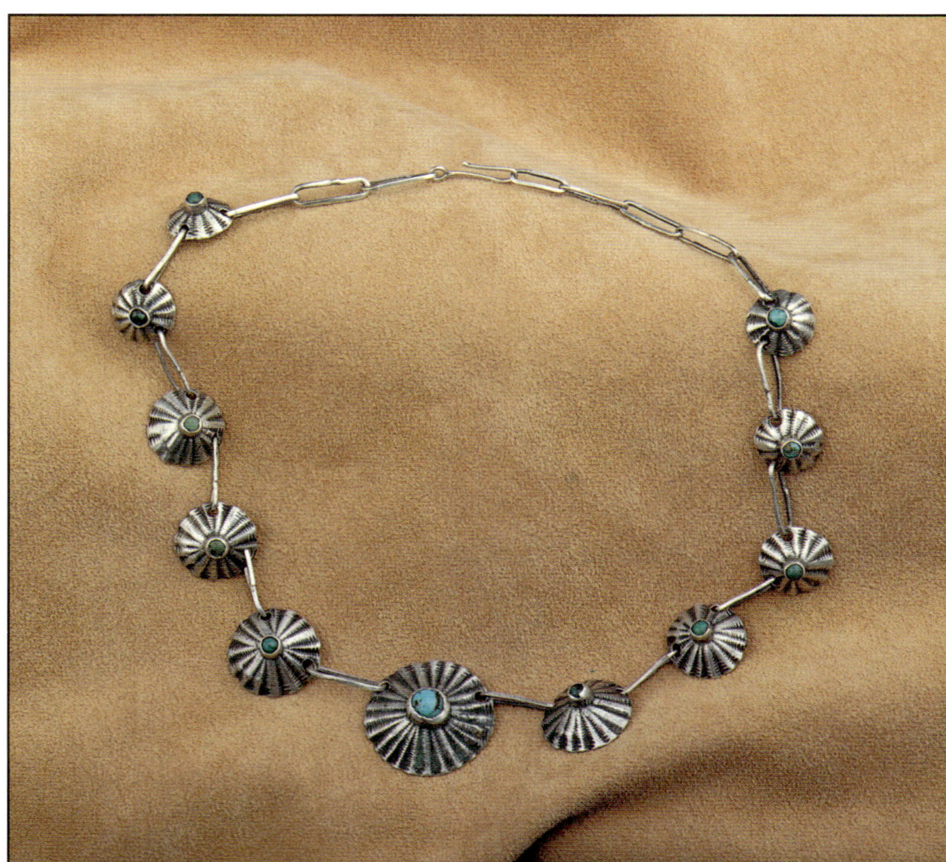

Long strand of coin silver beads with stamped decorations, 1930s. *Lynn D. Trusdell, Crown & Eagle Antiques*

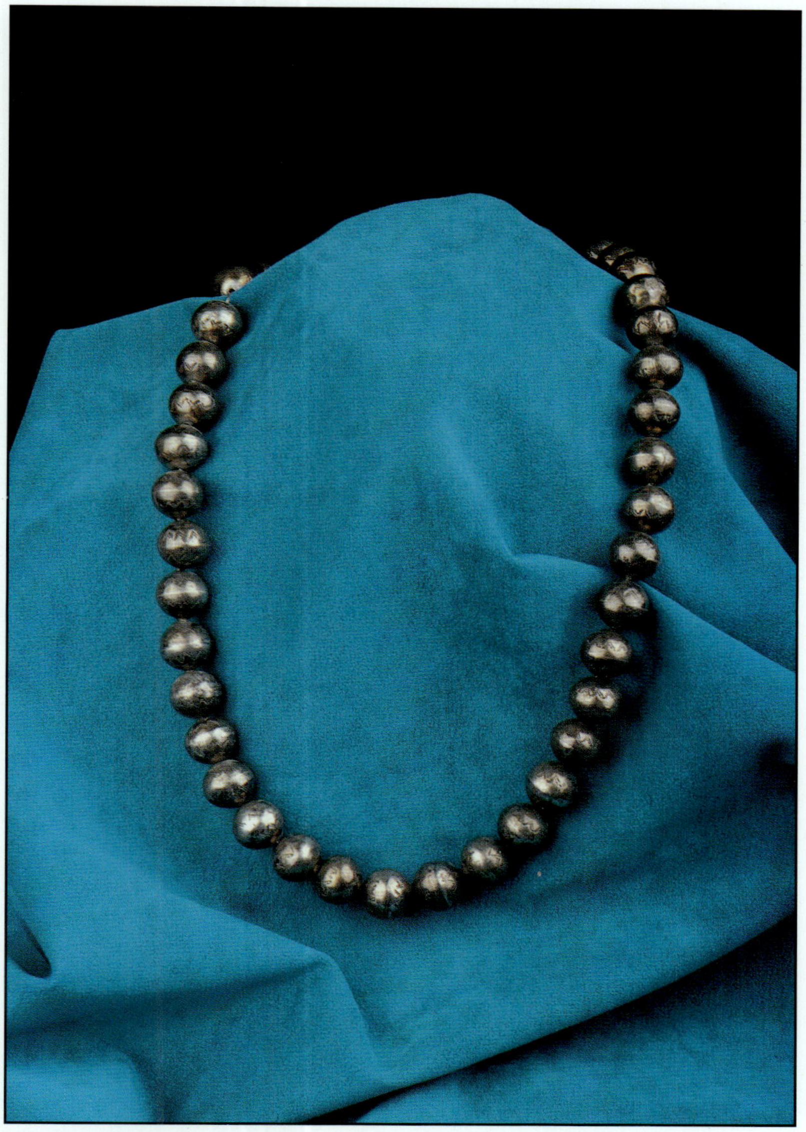

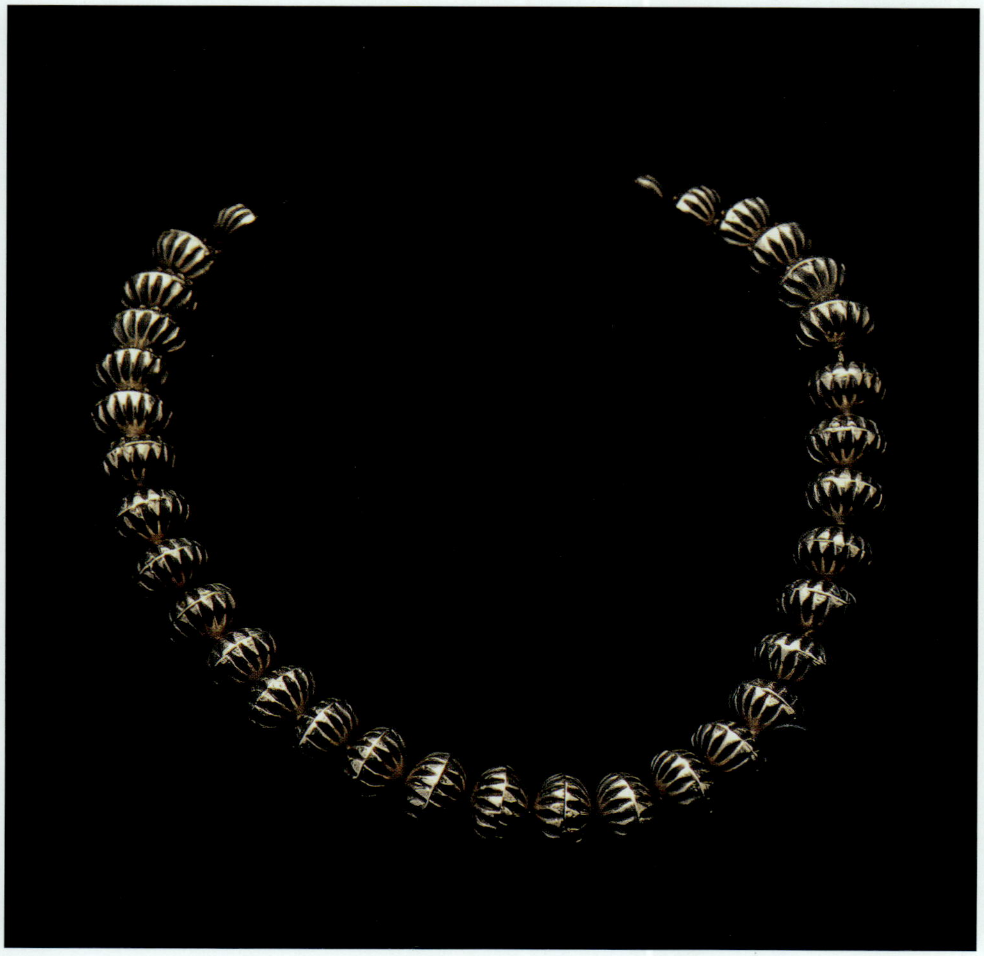

Coin silver beads with ribbed decoration strung as a choker necklace, 1930s.

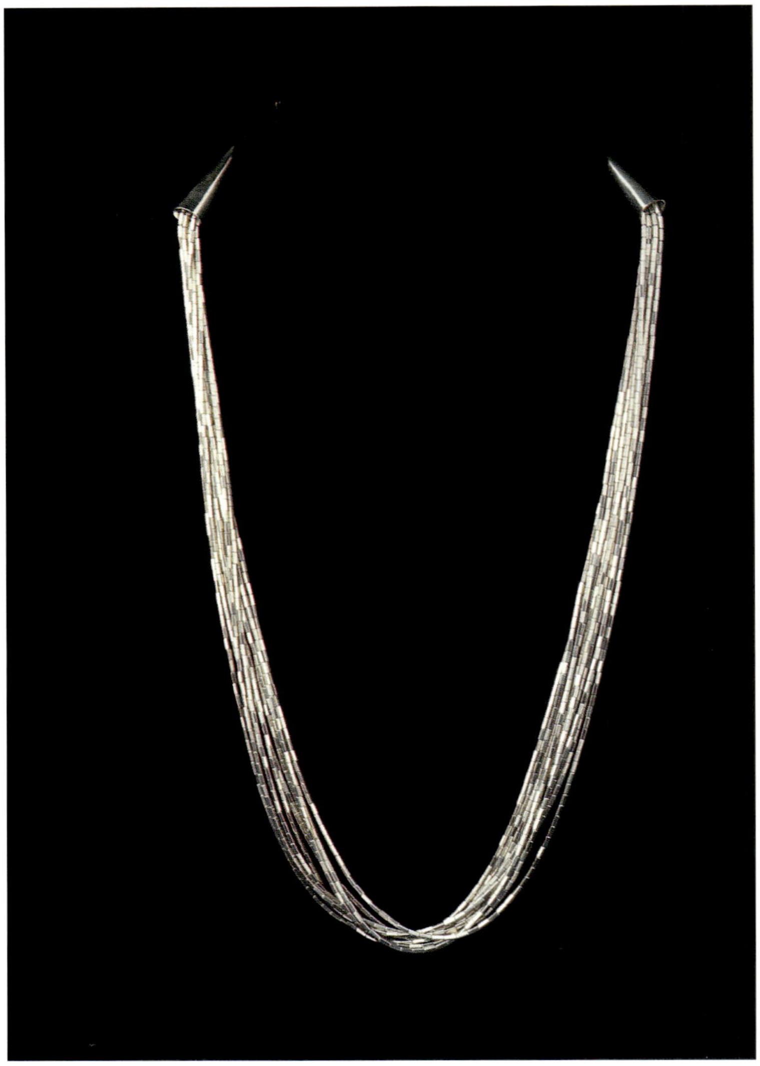

Navajo silver bead 10-strand necklace, called "liquid silver," made by Ed Aguilar. *Courtesy McGee's, Holbrook* ($385)

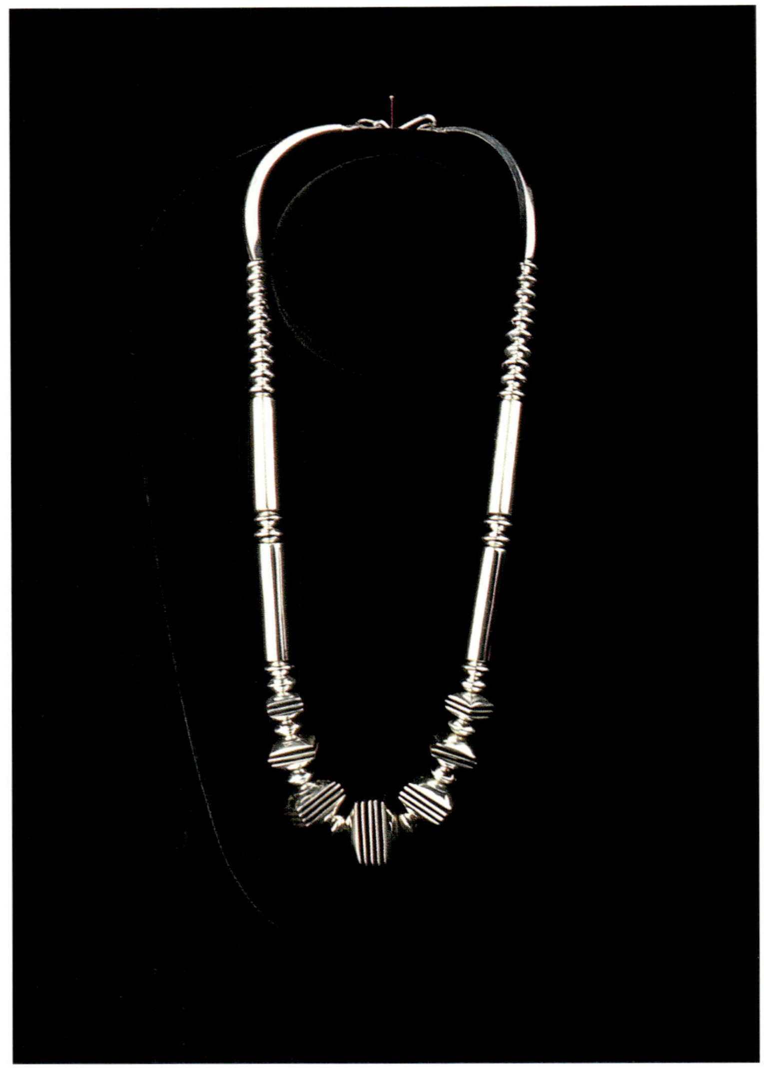

Necklace of silver beads of original shaped styles by Jack Tom, Navajo, 2002. *Courtesy McGee's, Keams Canyon*

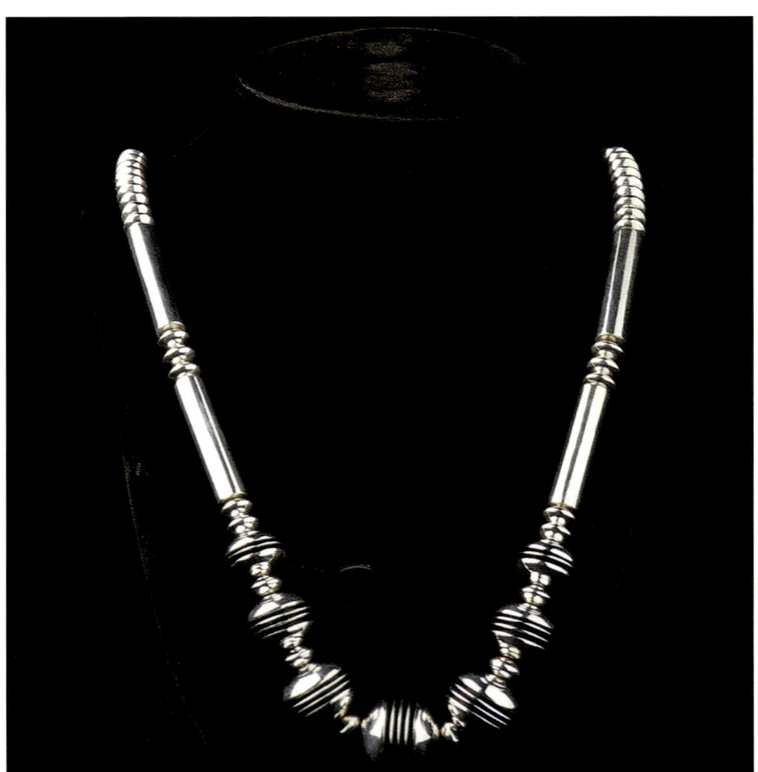

Silver bead necklace by Jack Tom, Navajo, 2002. *Courtesy McGee's, Holbrook*

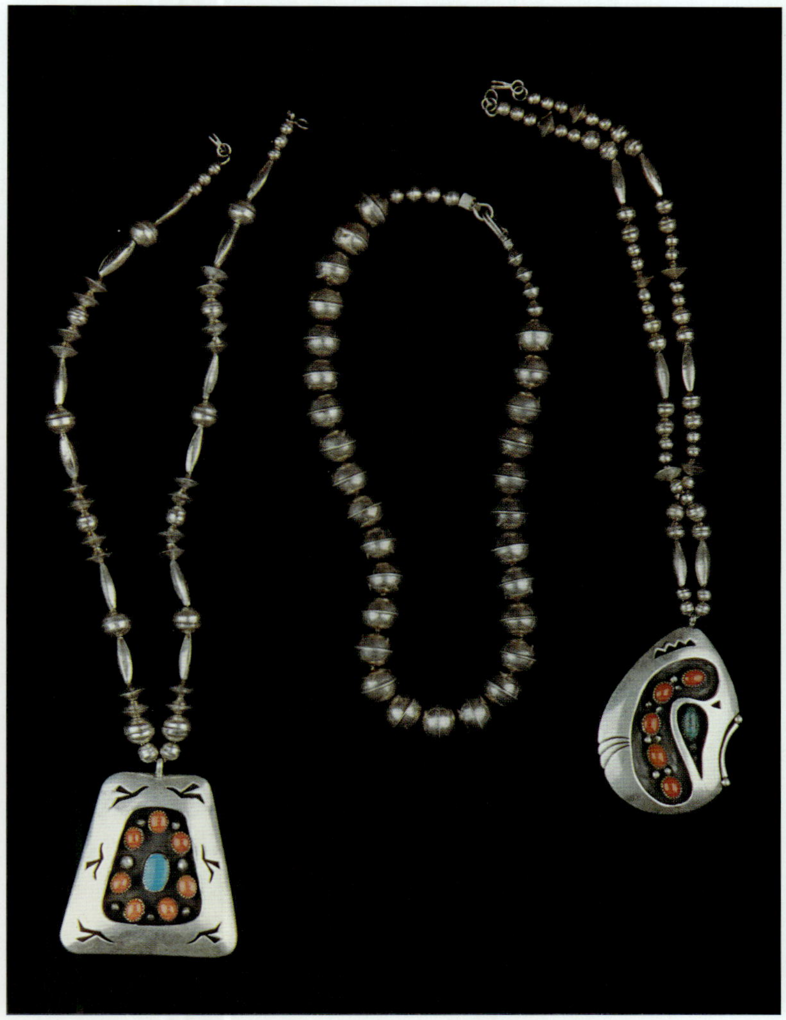

Three Navajo bead necklaces with differently designed beads and two with shadow-box pendants with coral and turquoise stones, 1970s. *Private collection*

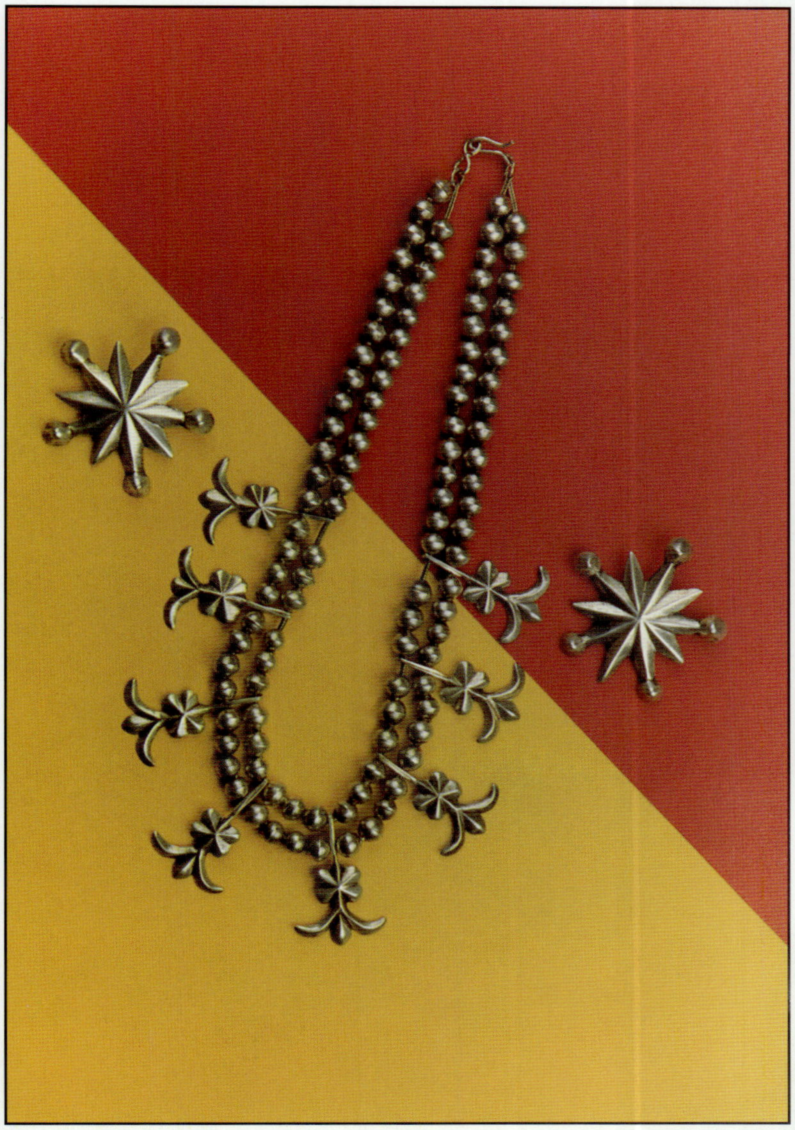

Double strand of silver beads joined by eight bars with cast squash-blossom pendants, shown with two cast snowflake design pins, all from the 1950s, Navajo. *Enchanted Mesa collection* .

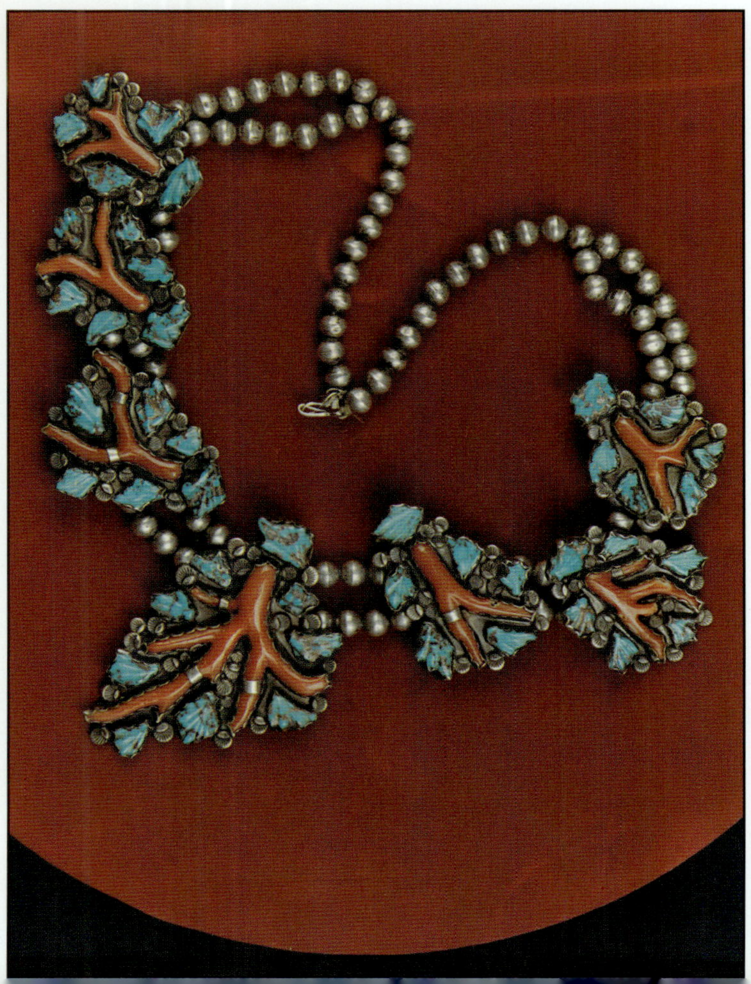

Dan Simplicio, Zuni, made this important necklace with silver beads and plaques of Villa Grove turquoise and branch coral in 1933. *Private collection on permanent loan to Ohio University*

Squash Blossom Necklaces

The design sources of squash blossom necklaces are intertwined with the history of Southwest jewelry. From the Spanish influence through Mexico came the crescent-shaped naja design which itself derives from a Medieval European shape devised to ward off the "evil eye" from those who wore it. The Spanish used this crescent shape as the central pendant on the headstall of their horse bridles, to protect their horses, and from there the Southwest Indians of the nineteenth century adopted it in their squash blossom necklace designs.

The design of the flaring blossoms themselves derive from a European pomegranate blossom through Spanish and Mexican silver clothing decorations and finally to Navajo silversmiths who, or whose white traders, called it "squash blossom", for they were familiar with the blossoms of the squash plants in their gardens.

Silver beads, as described in the first section of this book, were made from metal coins of European origin which were traded by white men to the Eastern woodland, then Plains, then Southwest native peoples from the sixteenth century onwards. By the time silversmithing skills reached the Southwest in the late nineteenth century, beads were prized possessions of tribal leaders.

When Navajo silversmiths combined the silver beads, squash blossoms, and naja in a necklace form around 1885, a tradition was born which remains strong to this day in both its classical and interpreted forms.

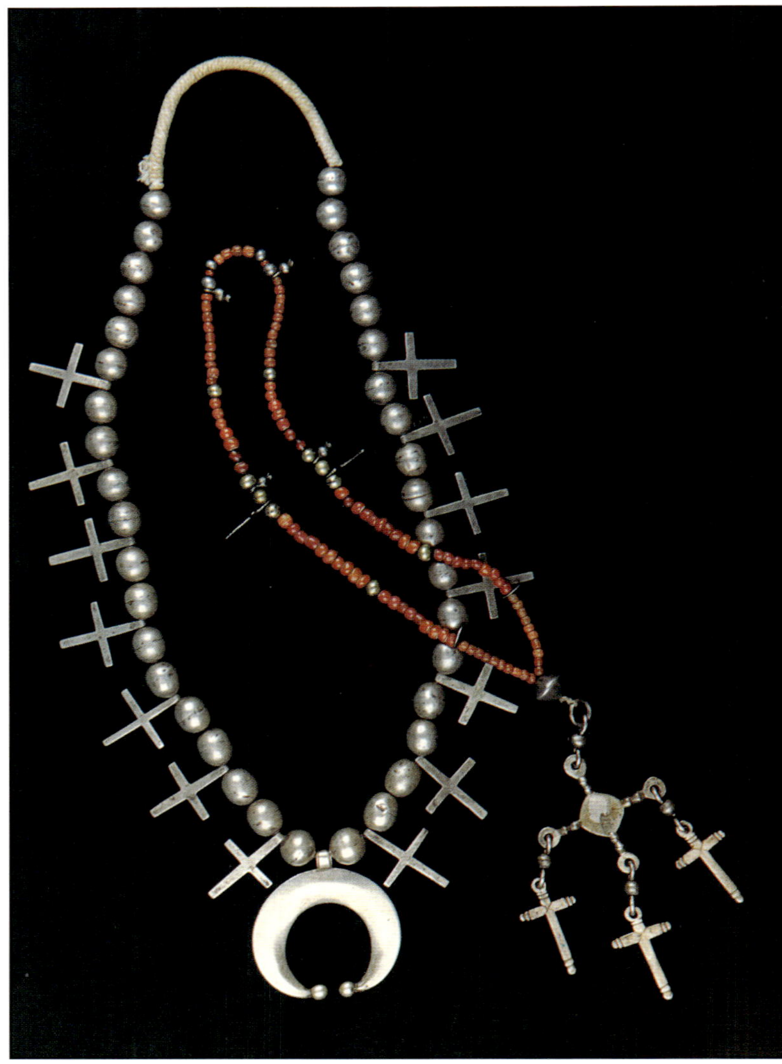

Two Navajo silver necklaces which preceded the "squash blossom" form: On the right, a truly early single strand of red glass trade beads 21 3/4" long with four silver, ten gold and four wax letter seals and two Mexican silver one-cent coins dated 1807 and 1810, with a pendant of three silver crosses (similar to pendants found in Mexico in the 19th century). / On the left, a silver necklace of 38 beads, 33" long, 14 flat crosses, a crescent naja and squaw-wrapped closure dating circa 1875. *Private collection*

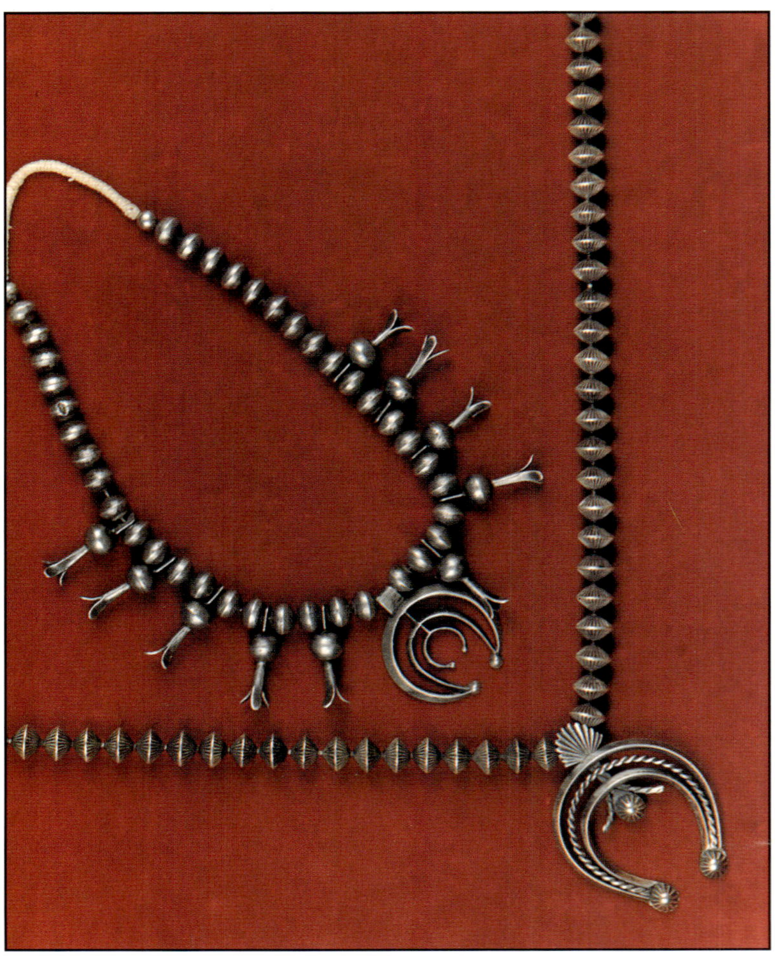

A very early Navajo squash blossom necklace of coin silver, 23 1/4" long, with three petals on the blossoms and a cast naja, circa 1885. / Below is a contrasting necklace of fifty fluted silver beads with a triple naja that was made circa 1949. *Private collection on permanent loan to Ohio University*

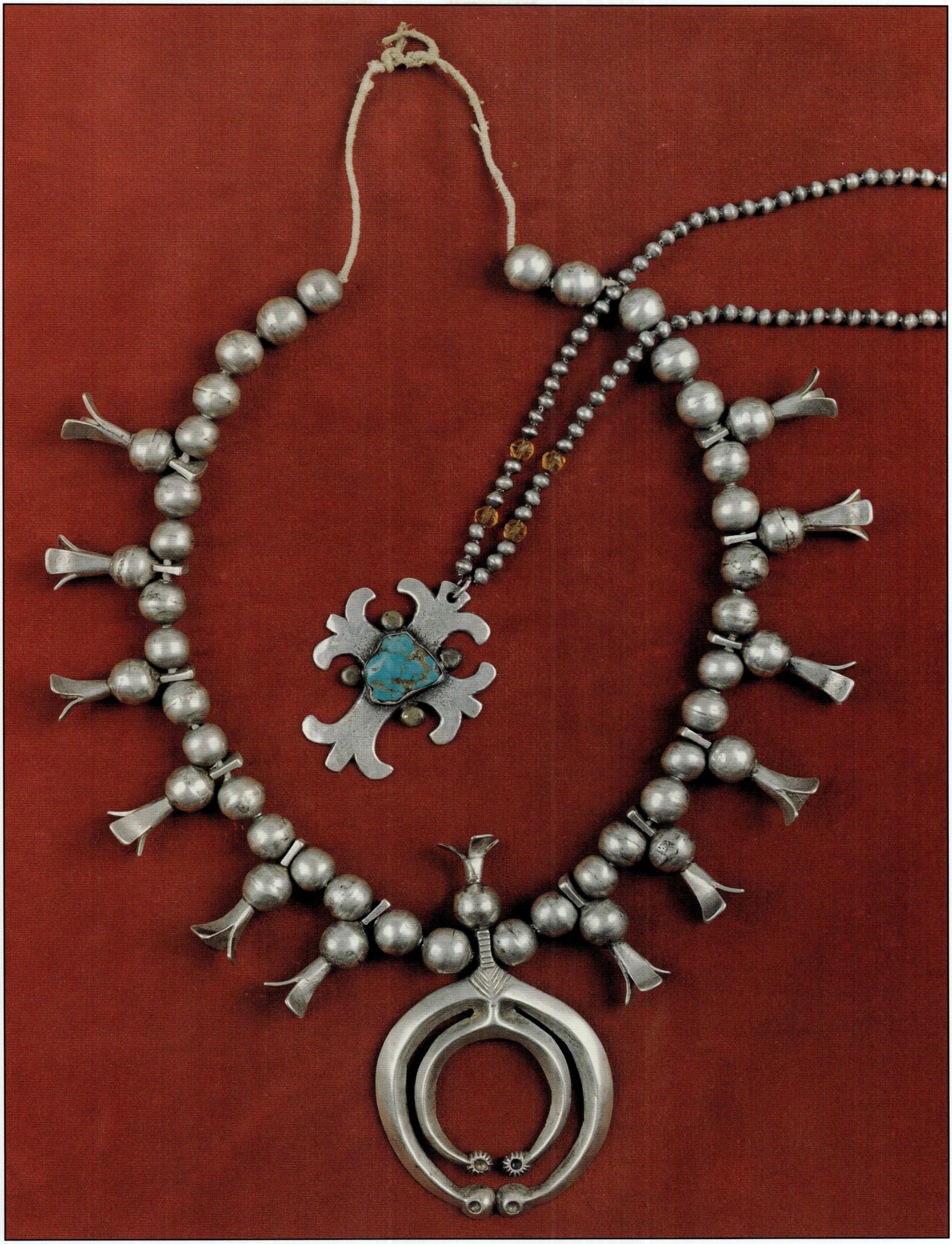

Navajo squash blossom necklace of silver with three petals on the blossoms , a cast double naja, and an up-turned blossom on the crown of the naja, circa 1885. / Silver bead necklace with four copper beads and a sand cast pendant cross with turquoise dating from the 1920s. *Lynn D. Trusdell collection*

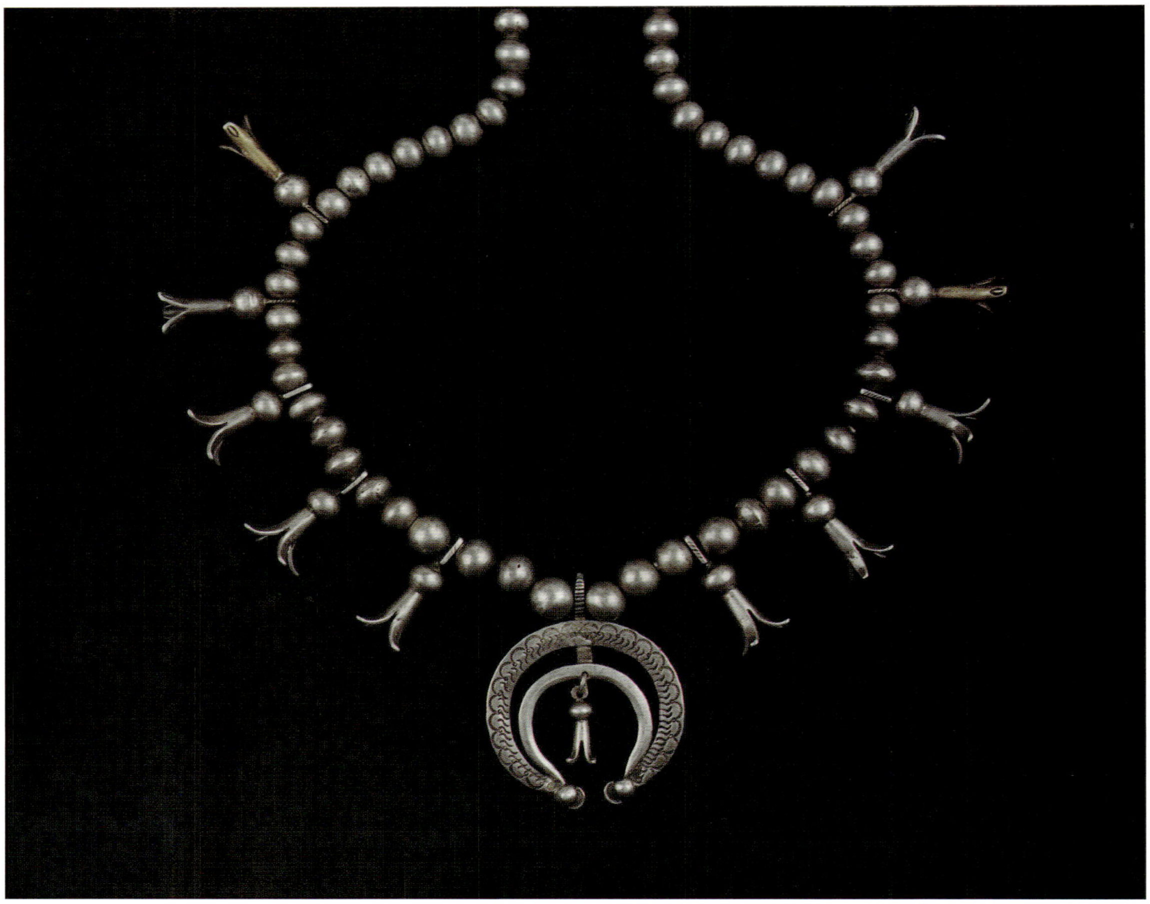

Refined Navajo squash blossom necklace made of coin silver, circa 1890, with three-petal blossoms bearing stamped designs, uniform round beads and a double naja, the outer crescent stamped and filed and with a pendant blossom. *Lynn D. Trusdell collection*

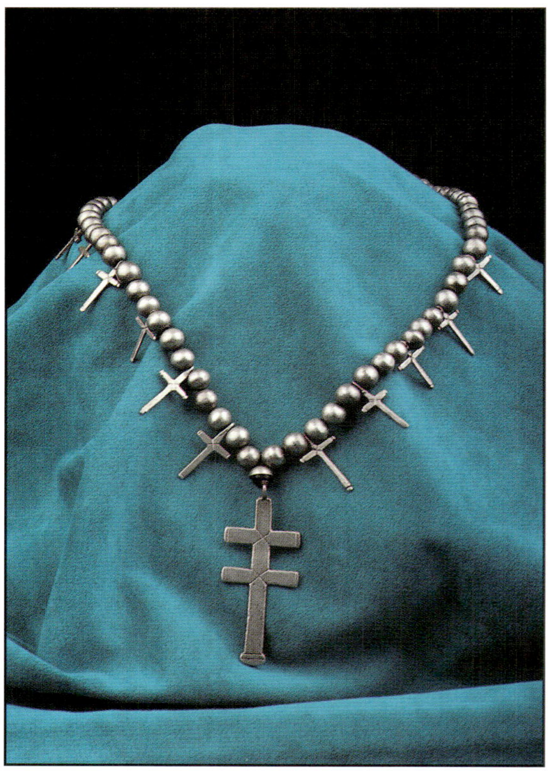

Early silver cross necklace with uniform beads, c.1890s. *Lynn D. Trusdell, Crown & Eagle Antiques*

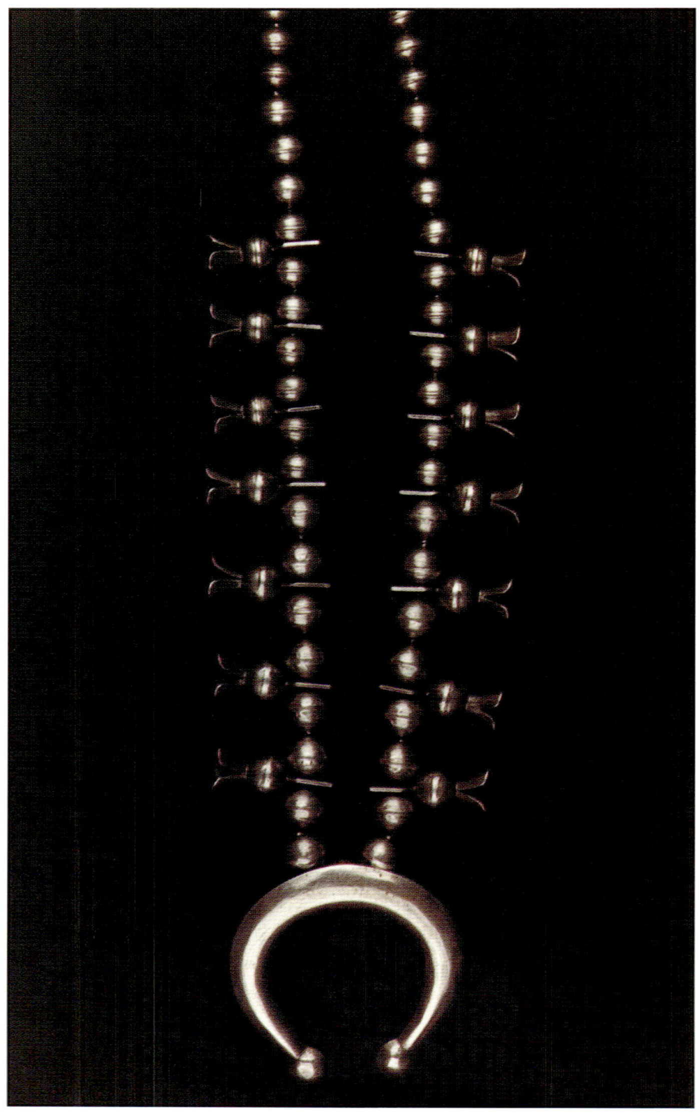

Classic Navajo coin silver squash blossom necklace of uniform beads, three-petal blossoms, and a plain naja, circa 1900. *Turquoise Lady collection*

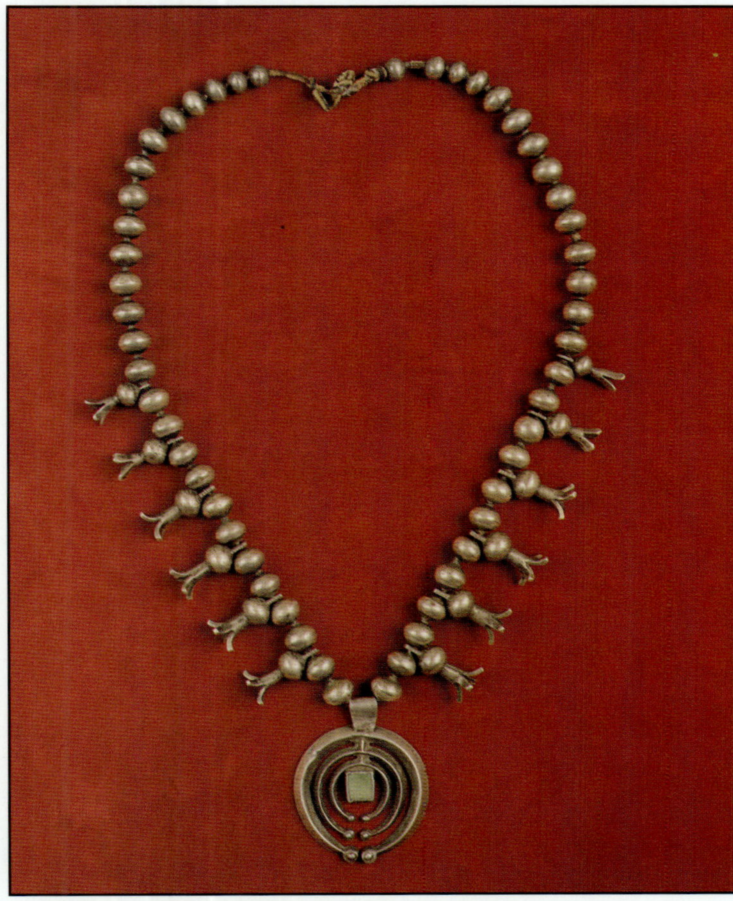

Early silver Navajo squash blossom necklace of silver beads with triple petal blossoms and a triple cast naja with square Cerillos turquoise stone, circa 1885. *Lynn D. Trusdell collection*

Unique necklace with small Pueblo pump-drilled Cerillos turquoise heishi with flat silver crosses, silver beads, and a single crescent naja with closed terminals and a single pendant turquoise, pre-1915. / Large Pueblo silver bead necklace with wrought silver crosses and cast naja with triangular drilled pendant Cerillos turquoise set in silver, circa 1917, formerly from the Fred Harvey collection. *Lynn D. Trusdell collection*

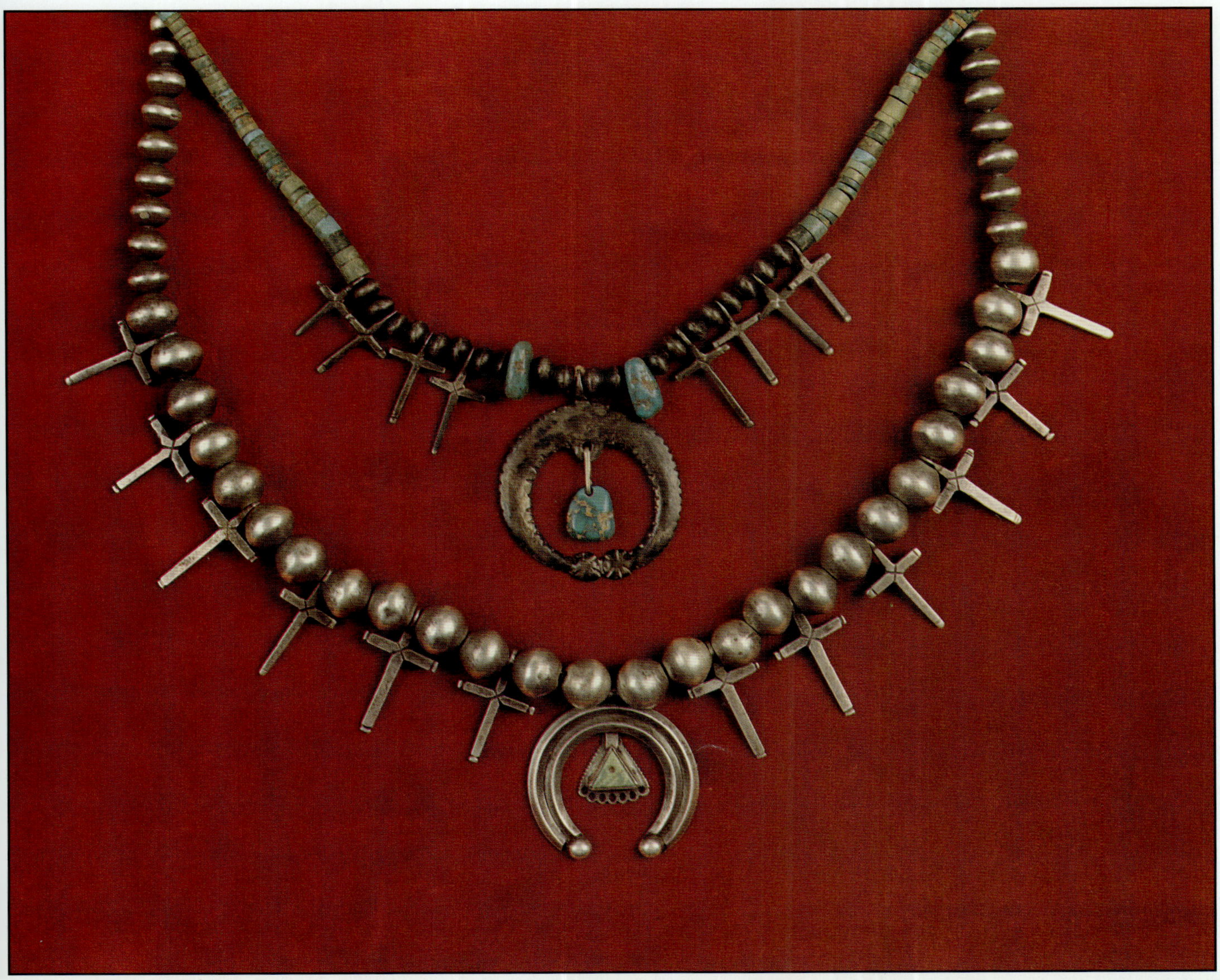

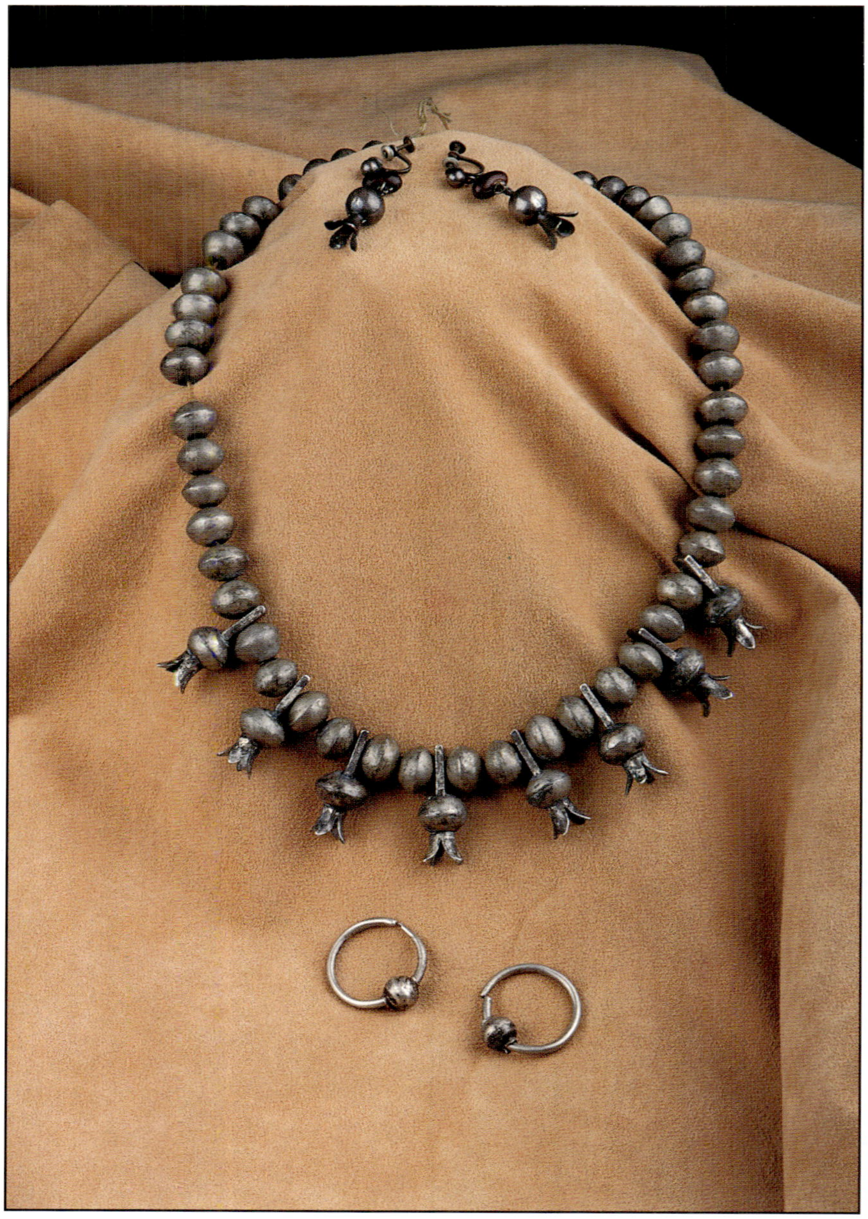

Heavy coin silver bead necklace with the earliest pomegranate squash blossoms, Navajo, c.1880s. / Below: Pair of silver rings with a single silver bead is the earliest Navajo silver earring style. / Above: Later squash blossom earrings with screw-on backs date from the 1940s. *Lynn D. Trusdell collection*

Coin silver Navajo squash blossom necklace of fluted beads and blossoms grouped near the naja with three turquoise stones, circa 1930s. *Private collection on permanent loan to Ohio University*

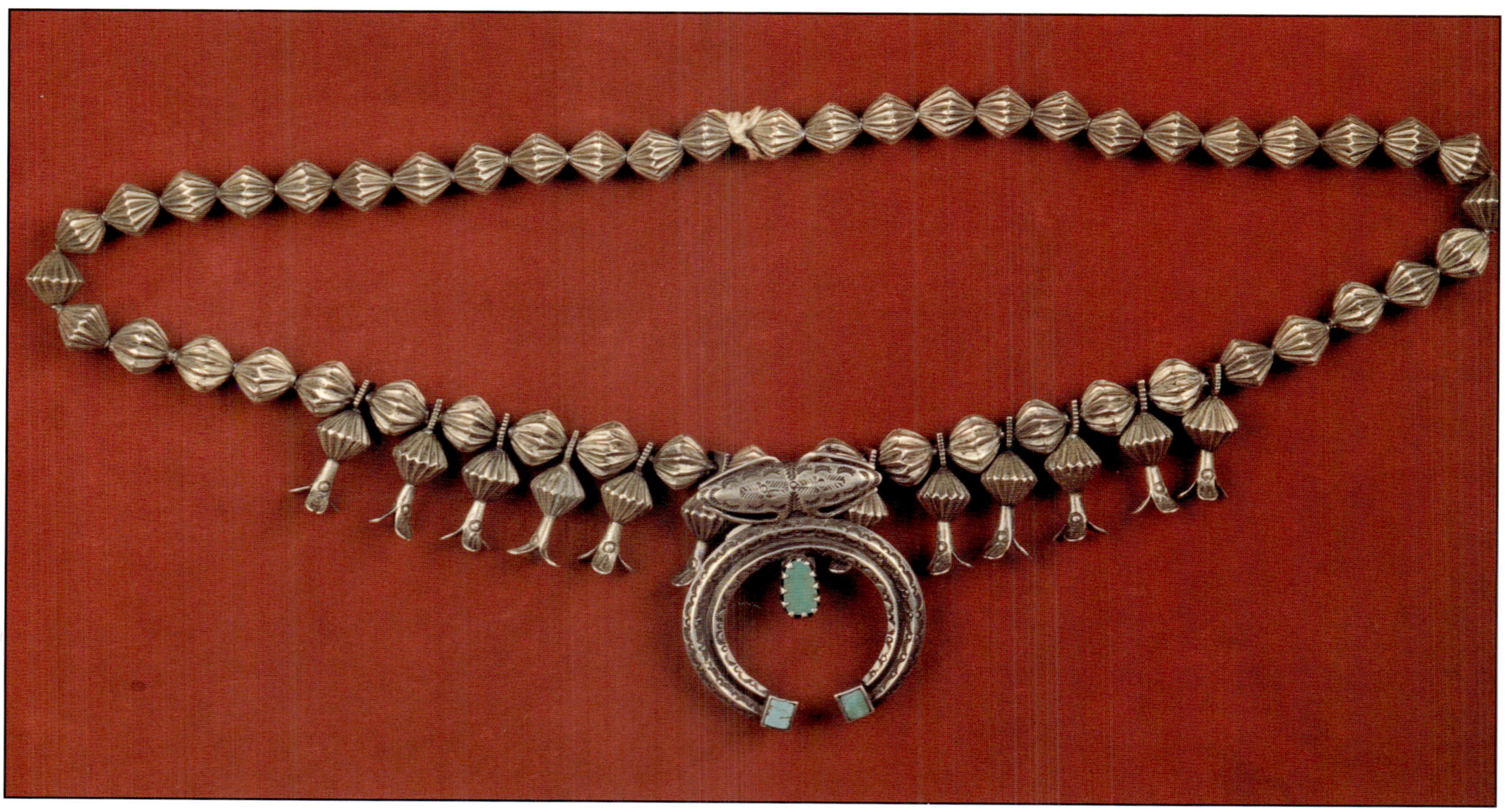

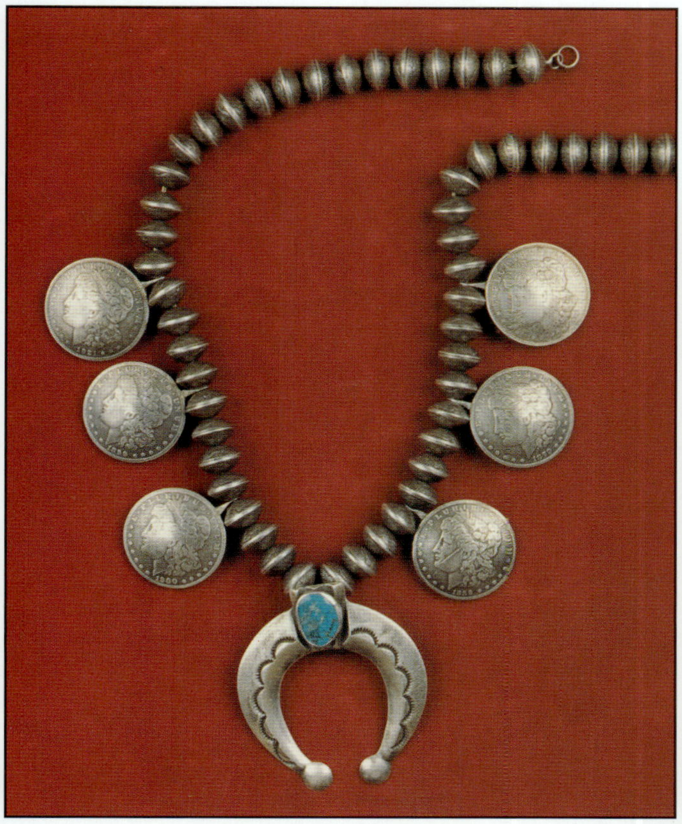

Navajo silver bead necklace made from 58 U.S. dimes as the small beads and pendant U.S. silver dollars dated 1879, 1889, 1899, 1900, and two 1921. The naja has stamped decoration and a turquoise stone, 25" long, circa 1922. *Private collection on permanent loan to Ohio University*

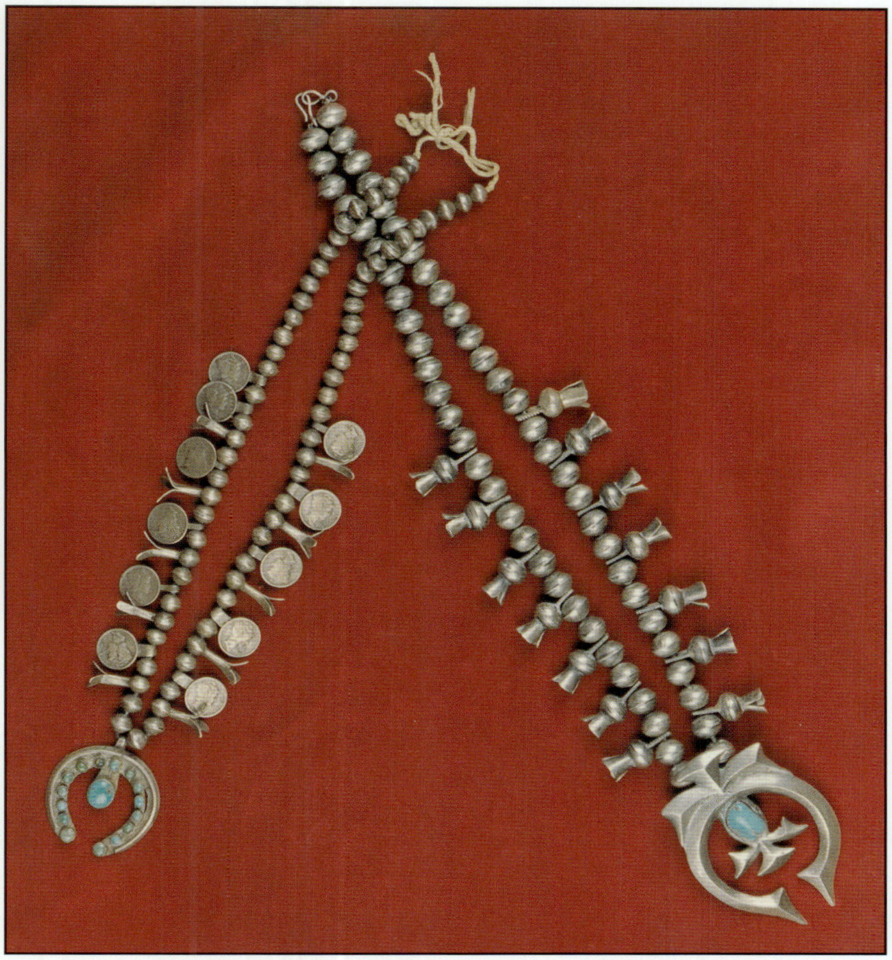

A Navajo necklace of squash blossom design with the added embellishment of U.S. dimes dating from 1924 to 1939, 26" long, circa 1940. / Old coin silver Navajo squash blossom necklace with a particularly dynamic sand-cast naja with unusual flaring terminals, crown and mounting for the pendant turquoise stone. *Private collection on permanent loan to Ohio University*

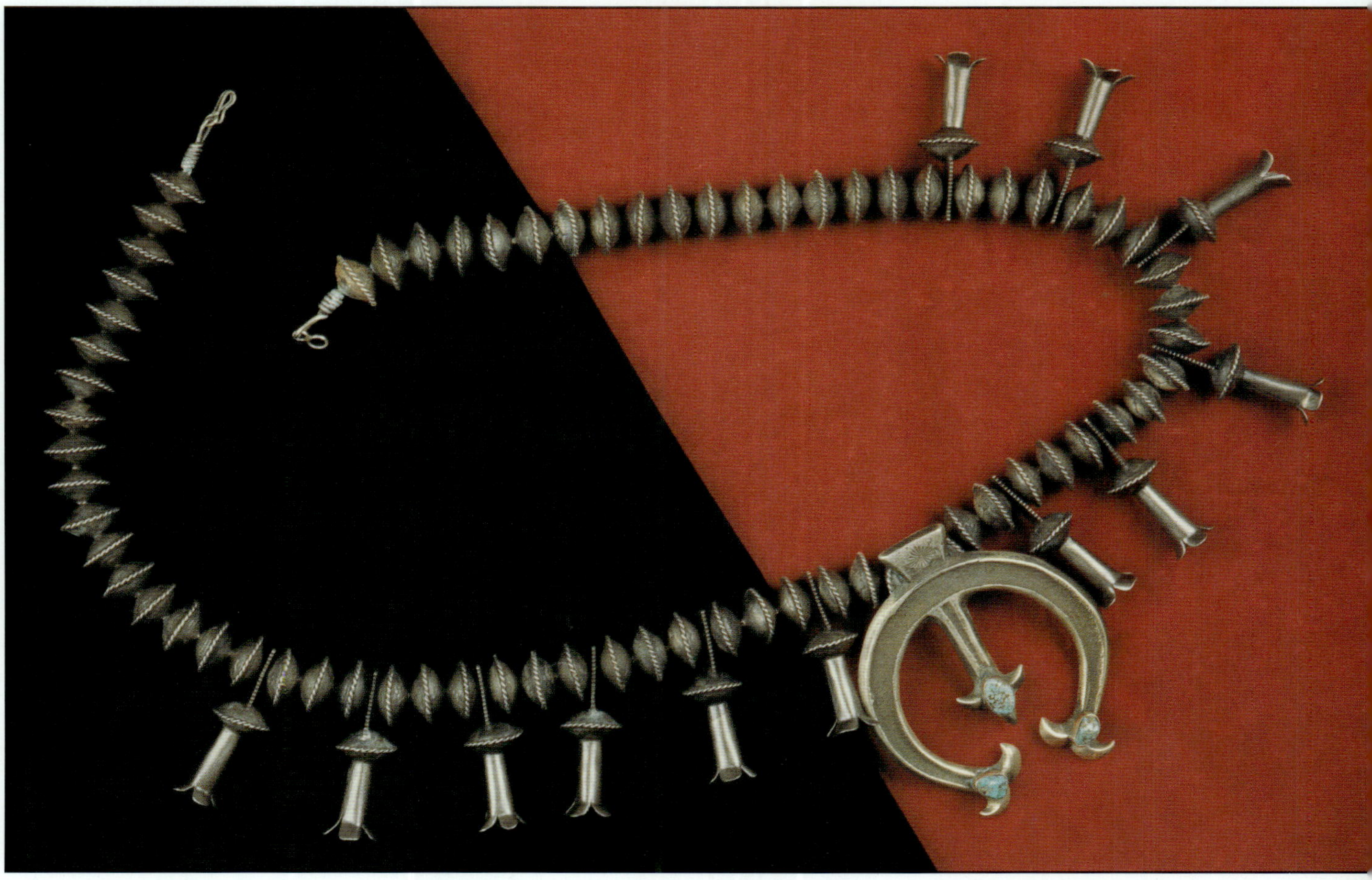

Squash blossom necklace made with 70 oval beads constructed from U.S. Liberty dimes, 34 1/2" long, squash blossom beads and a cast naja with three turquoise stones. *Private collection on permanent loan to Ohio University*

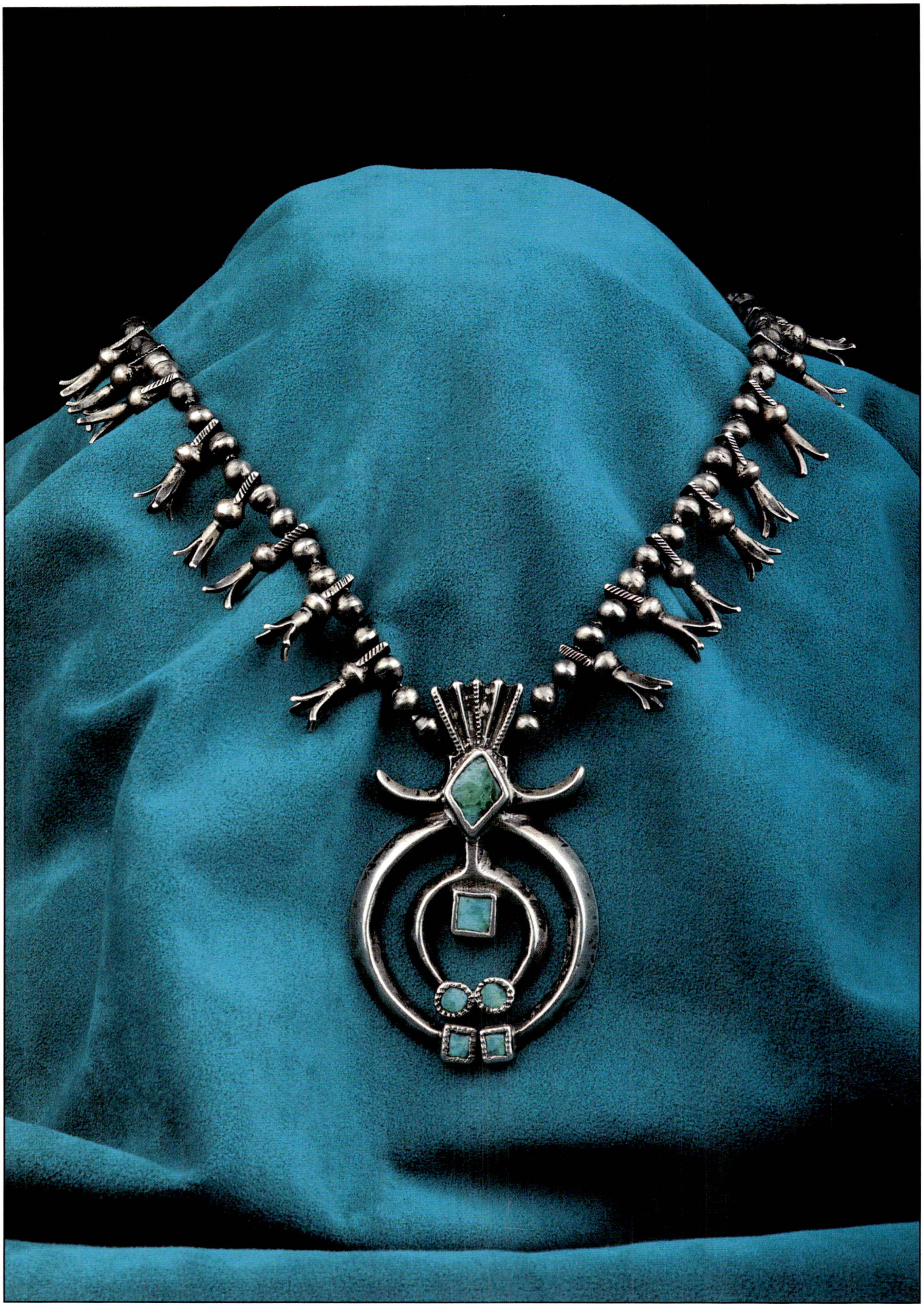

Heavy-weight silver beads and squash blossoms strung on rawhide. The unusual double naja has a large crescent with diamond-shaped turquoise stone at the top and two small square turquoise stones at the terminals. Enveloped within the larger naja is a smaller crescent with a square turquoise drop at the top and two round turquoise stones set in serrated bezels at the terminals, c.1915. *Lynn D. Trusdell, Crown & Eagle Antiques*

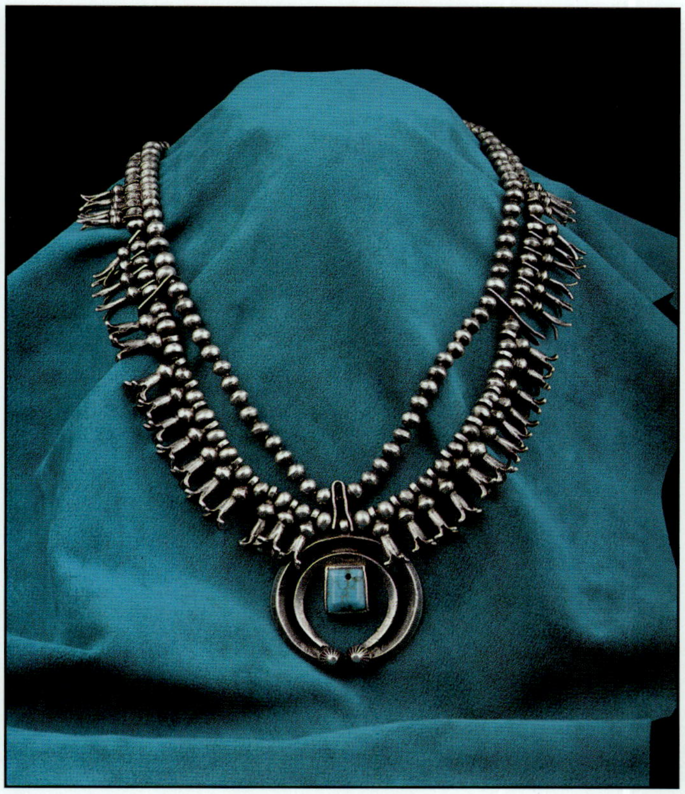

Beautiful and intricate silverwork is displayed here. Many squash blossoms and a double strand of beads support a refined double naja with a drilled square Spiderweb turquoise stone, c.1880. *Lynn D. Trusdell, Crown & Eagle Antiques*

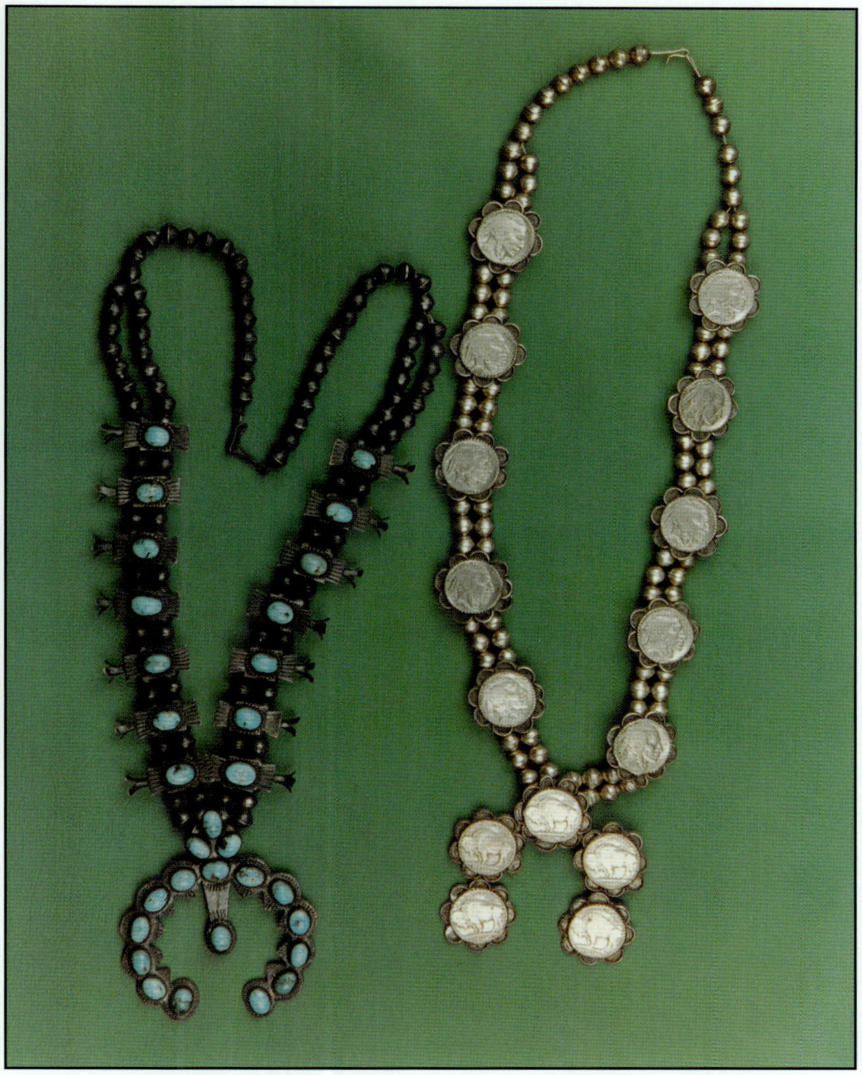

Oxidized silver Navajo squash blossom necklace with Persian turquoise and "bow box" beads made circa 1940. / Silver necklace of two strands of beads and 15 U.S. Buffalo nickels dating from the 1920s and 1930s, probably made circa 1950, and signed Keith Morton. *Dennehotso collection*.

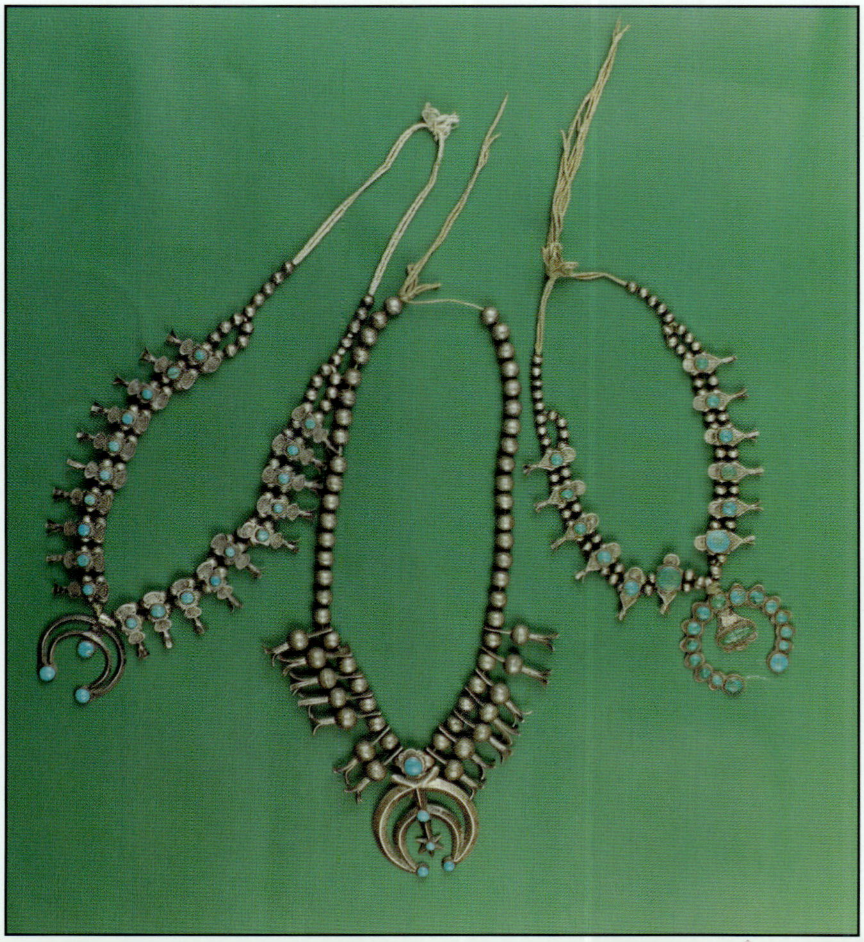

The evolution of styles in Navajo coin silver squash blossom necklaces can be seen in the contrasting examples shown here. In the center, a traditional form circa 1910. / To the left and right are two necklaces made circa 1930, with Morenci turquoise on "bow box" squash blossom beads. Still, the ridges of the silver coins used to make the naja can be seen on the necklace to the right. *Dennehotso collection*.

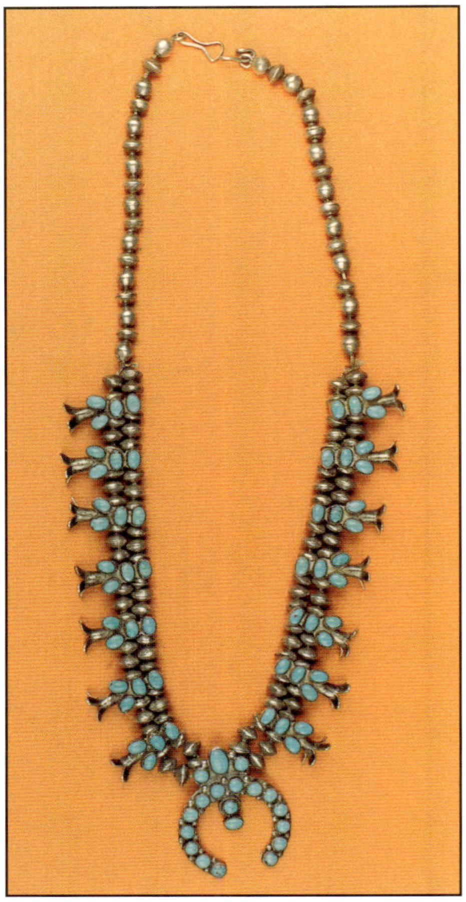

Light colored turquoise enhances this squash blossom necklace made in 1942 by Josephine Buqua. *Maxwell Museum collection*

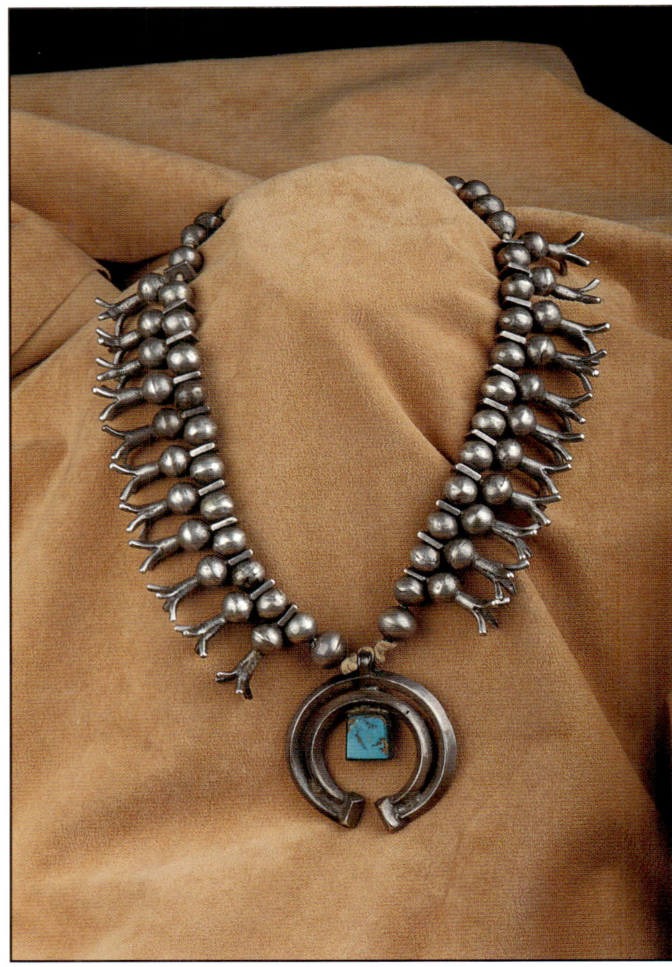

Sophisticated 1920s squash blossom necklace strung on its original store string and with a single Blue Gem turquoise stone in the naja. *Lynn D. Trusdell, Crown & Eagle Antiques*

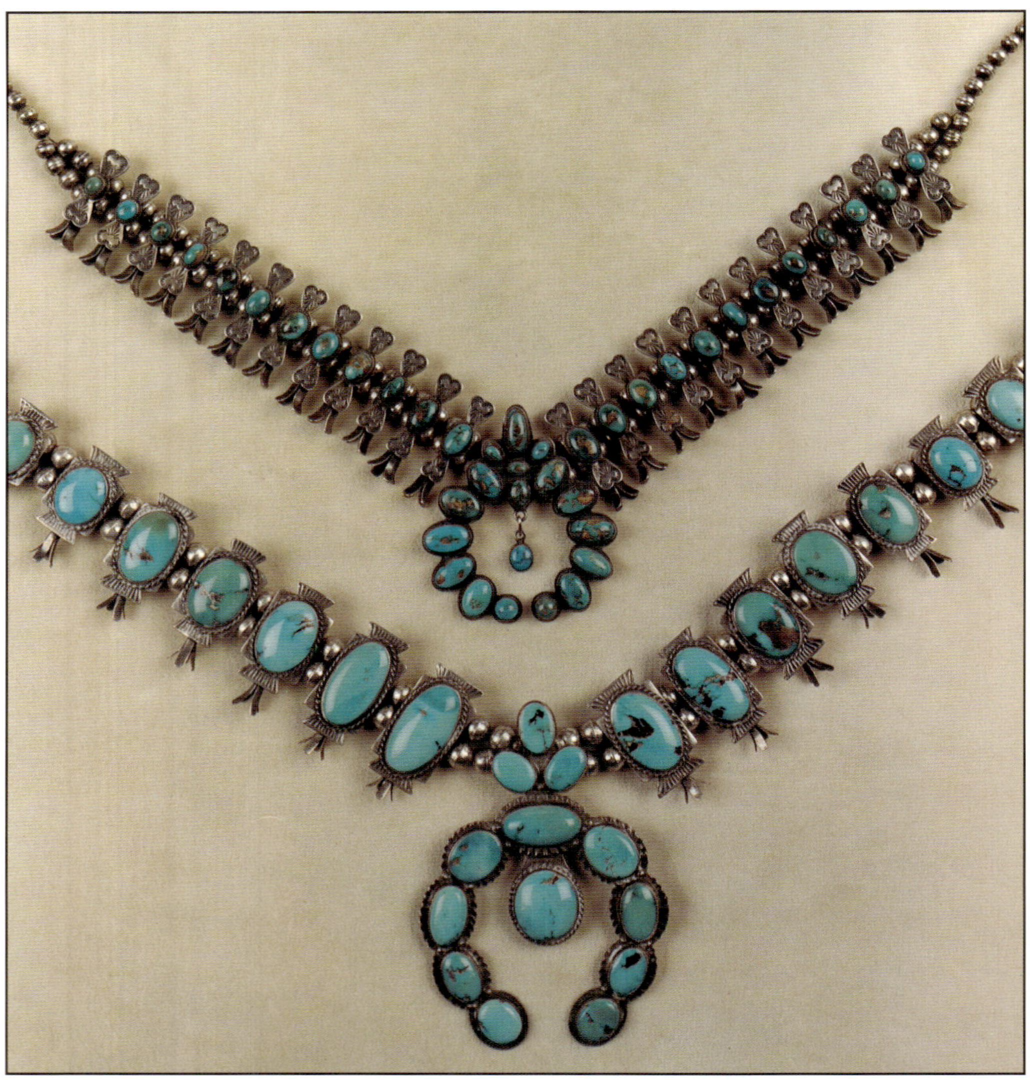

These two necklaces from the 1940s demonstrate the evolving "bow box" use in squash blossom necklaces. The smaller one at the top features Blue Gem turquoise. / Below, Fox turquoise stones of large size are mounted on the squash blossoms and the naja. *Lynn D. Trusdell collection*.

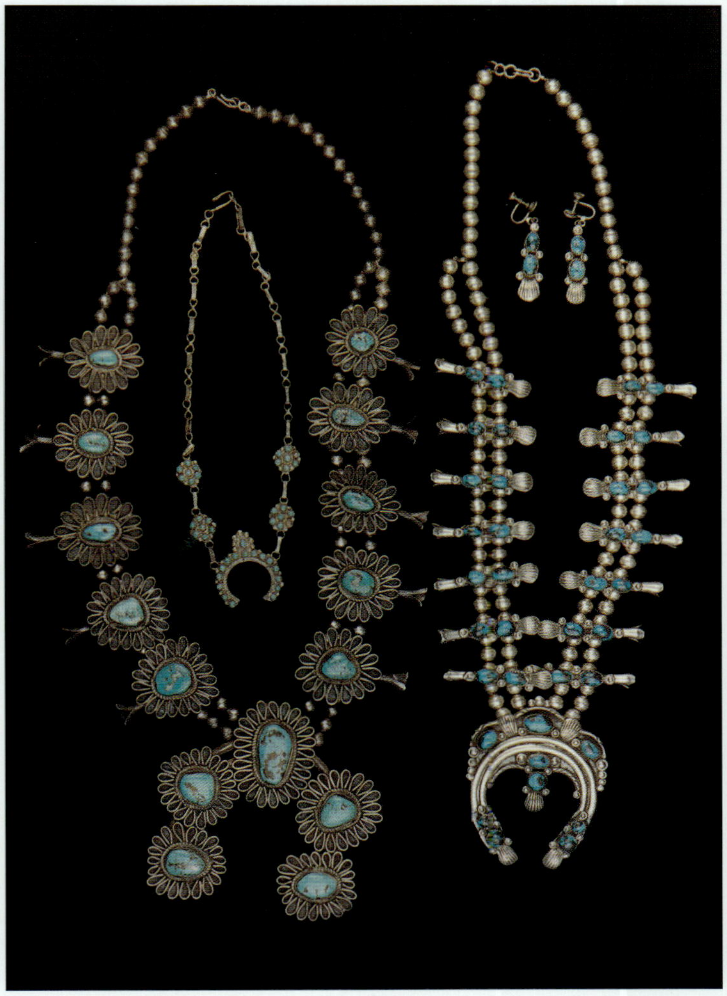

Large dark silver squash blossom necklace with turquoise made during the "boom period" in the 1970s without great skill or care. / In contrast, is a tiny child's necklace of Zuni origin set with Kingman turquoise from the 1930s when skills for making jewelry were a source of pride. / On the right, a Navajo necklace and earrings set with Persian turquoise from the 1960s. *Dennehotso collection*.

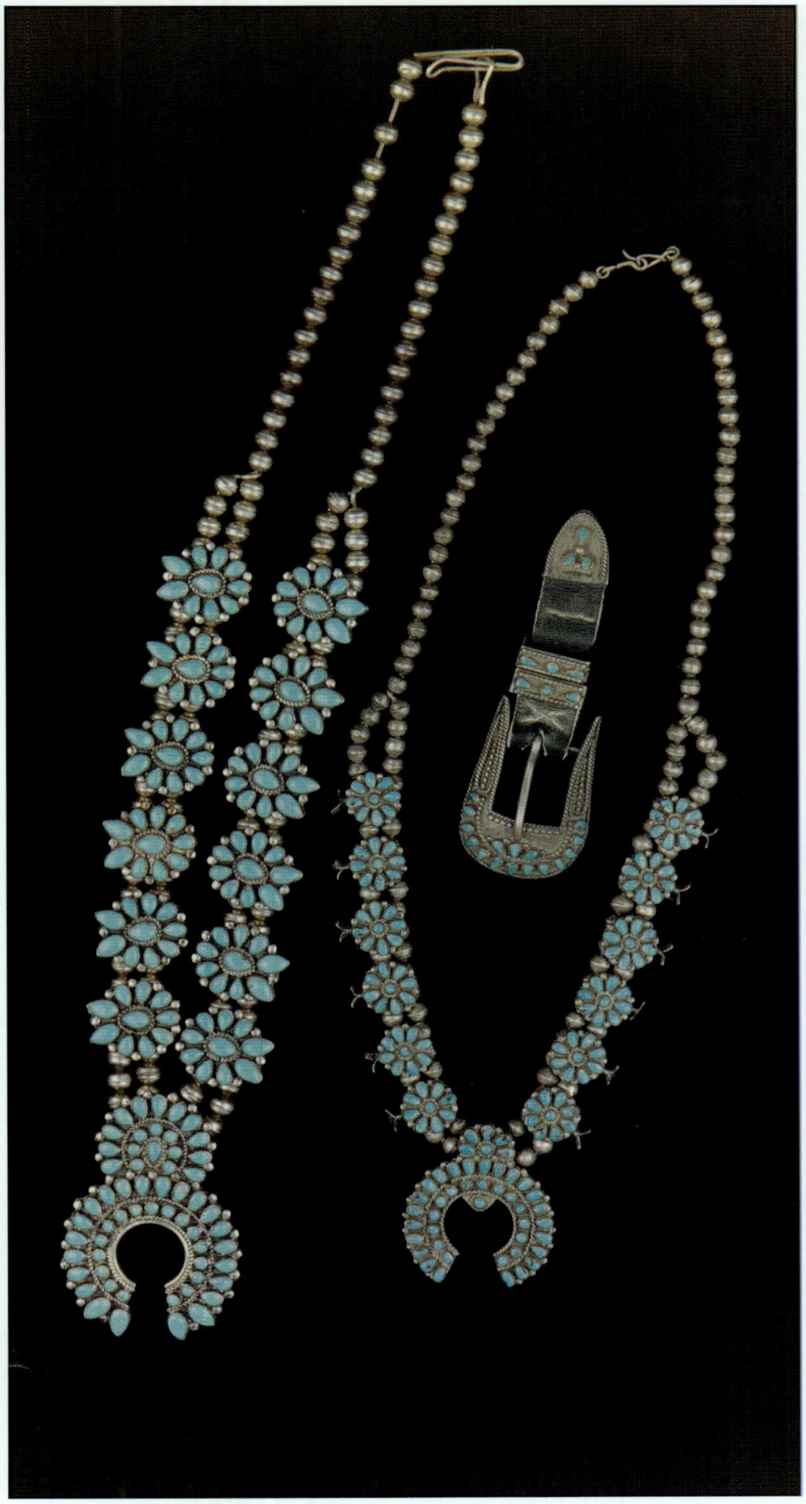

Zuni silversmiths interpreted the Navajo squash blossom style of necklace with the addition of their skill setting turquoise into these examples. The necklace on the left has turquoise floral clusters replacing the squash blossoms and a two-tier naja set with small turquoise stones, marked A B. / The smaller necklace on the right is set with Lone Mountain turquoise, circa 1940s. / Ranger buckle set with four Morenci turquoise stones, circa 1930. *Dennehotso collection*.

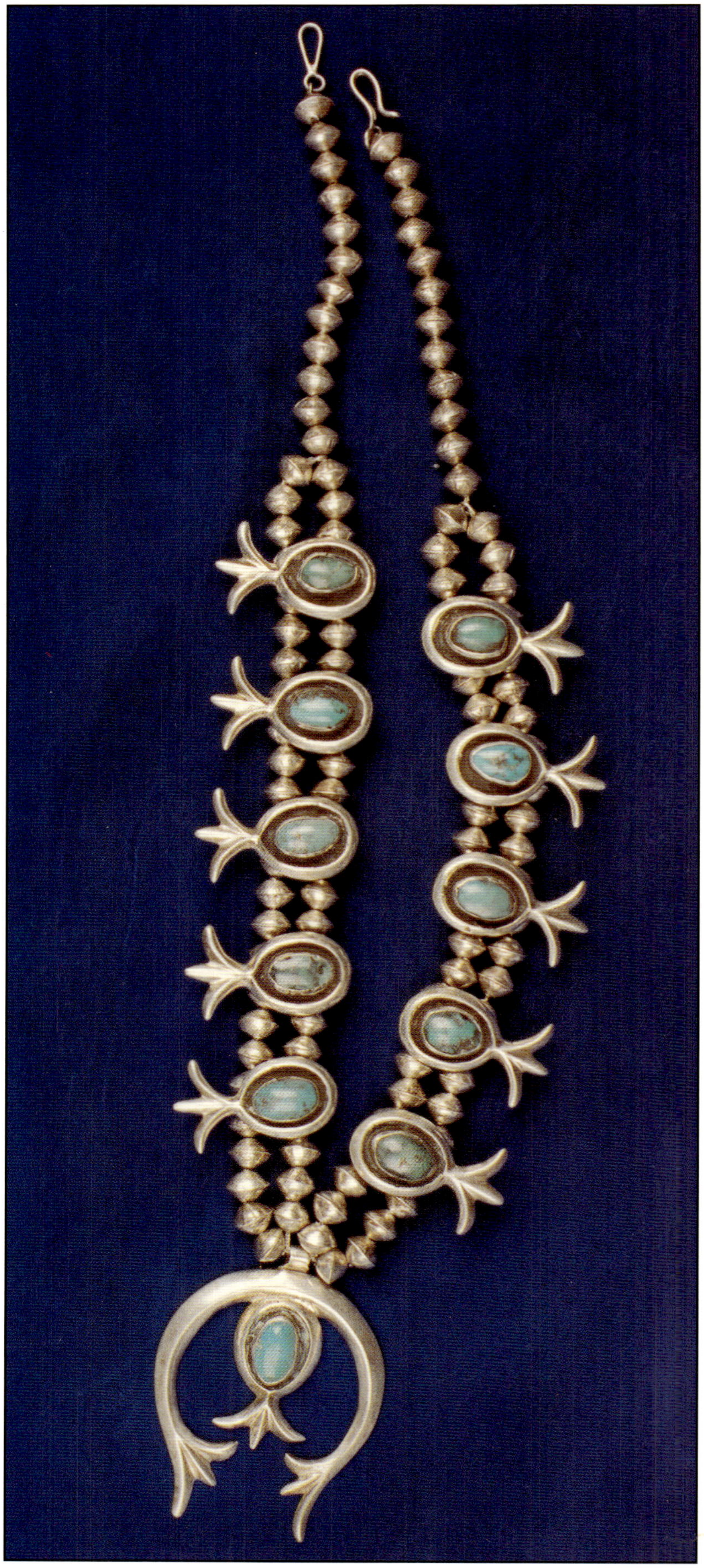

Stylized squash blossom necklace with cast silver blossoms and naja set with Smoky Mountain turquoise, circa 1965, Navajo. *Maxwell Museum collection*

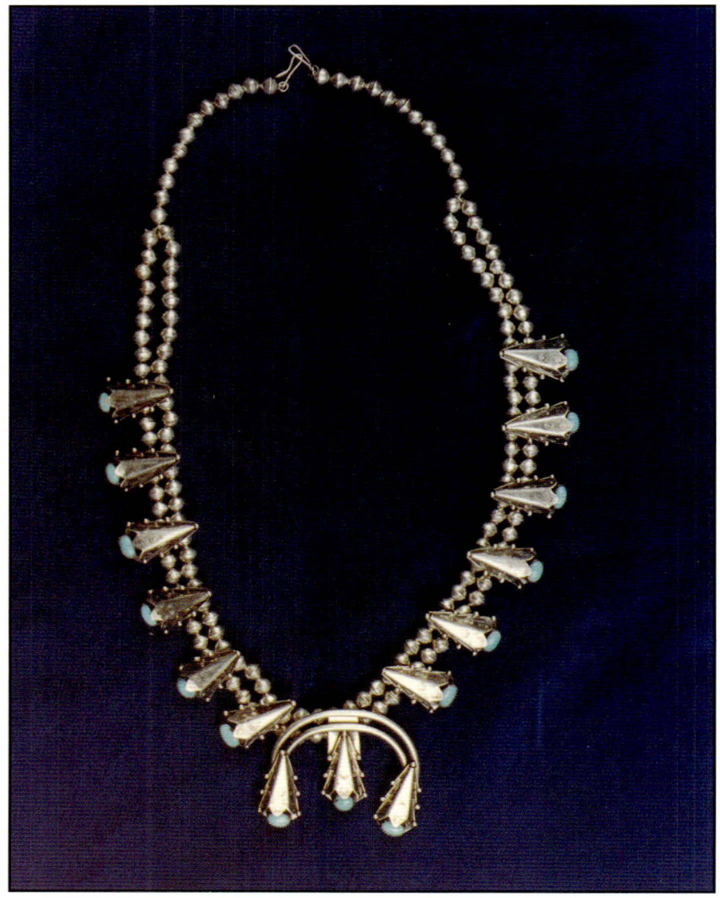

Navajo silver squash blossom style necklace with turquoise settings in place of the blossoms, made in the 1970s by Lucille Joe. *Maxwell Museum collection*

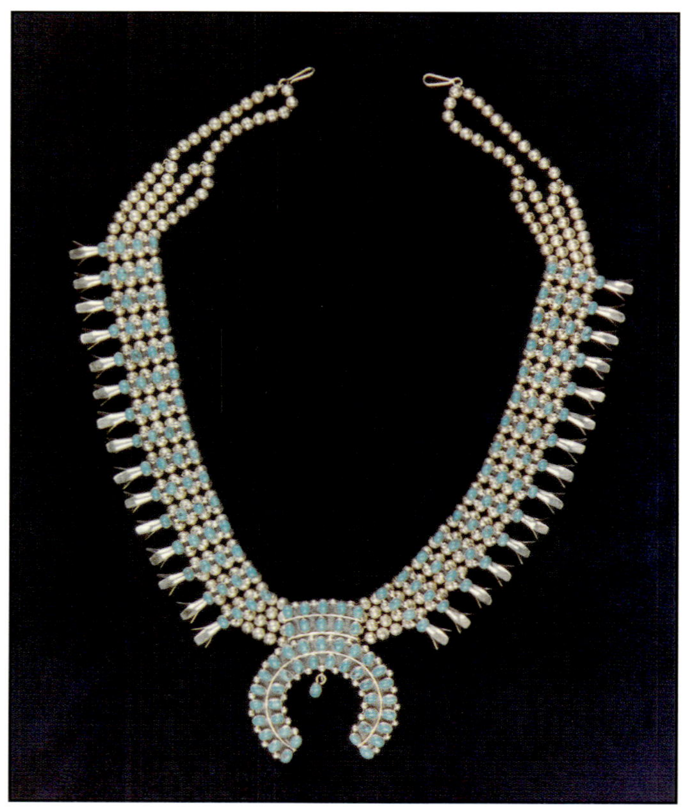

Large and original interpretation of a squash blossom necklace by Navajo silversmith Marie Silver, 1976, 31" long. *Private collection on permanent loan to Ohio University*

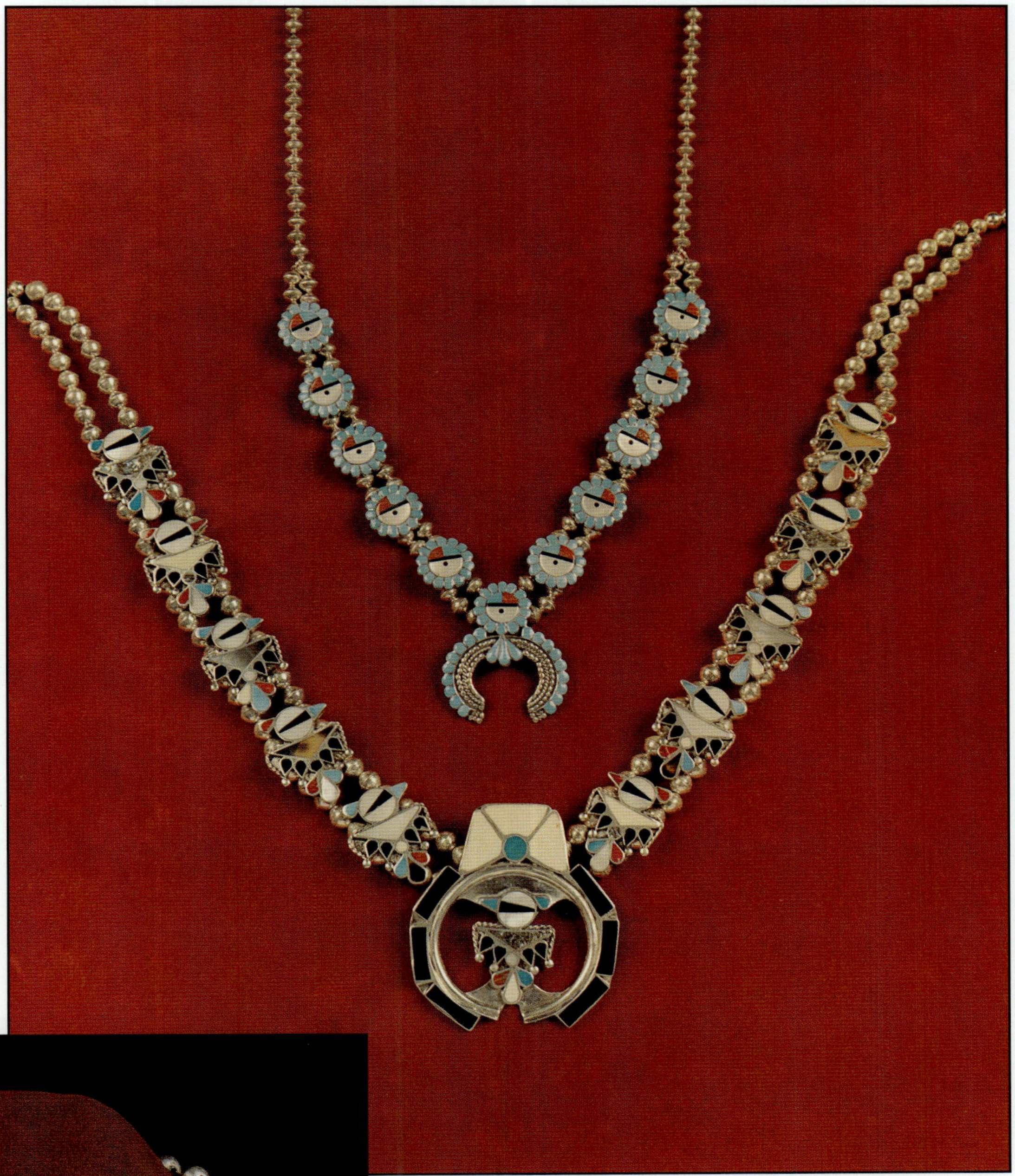

Two Zuni necklaces from the 1970s, which are interpretations of the squash, blossom style, both incorporating multiple stone inlaid medallions in place of the blossoms. The smaller necklace has sunface medallions and a turquoise-set naja, 23 1/2" long. / The larger necklace has thunderbird-designed medallions and a larger thunderbird in the naja. *Private collection on permanent loan to Ohio University*

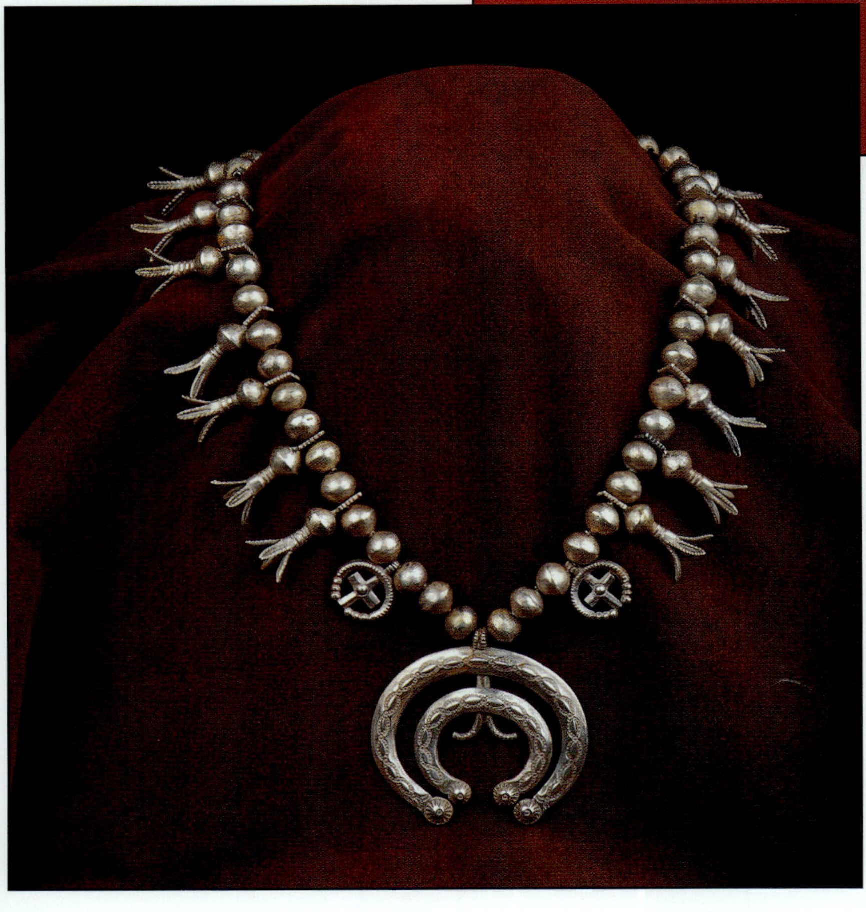

Navajo squash blossom ingot silver necklace with two small medallions containing a Christian cross in each flanking a double naja with elaborate stamping, c.1920s. *Lynn D. Trusdell, Crown & Eagle Antiques*

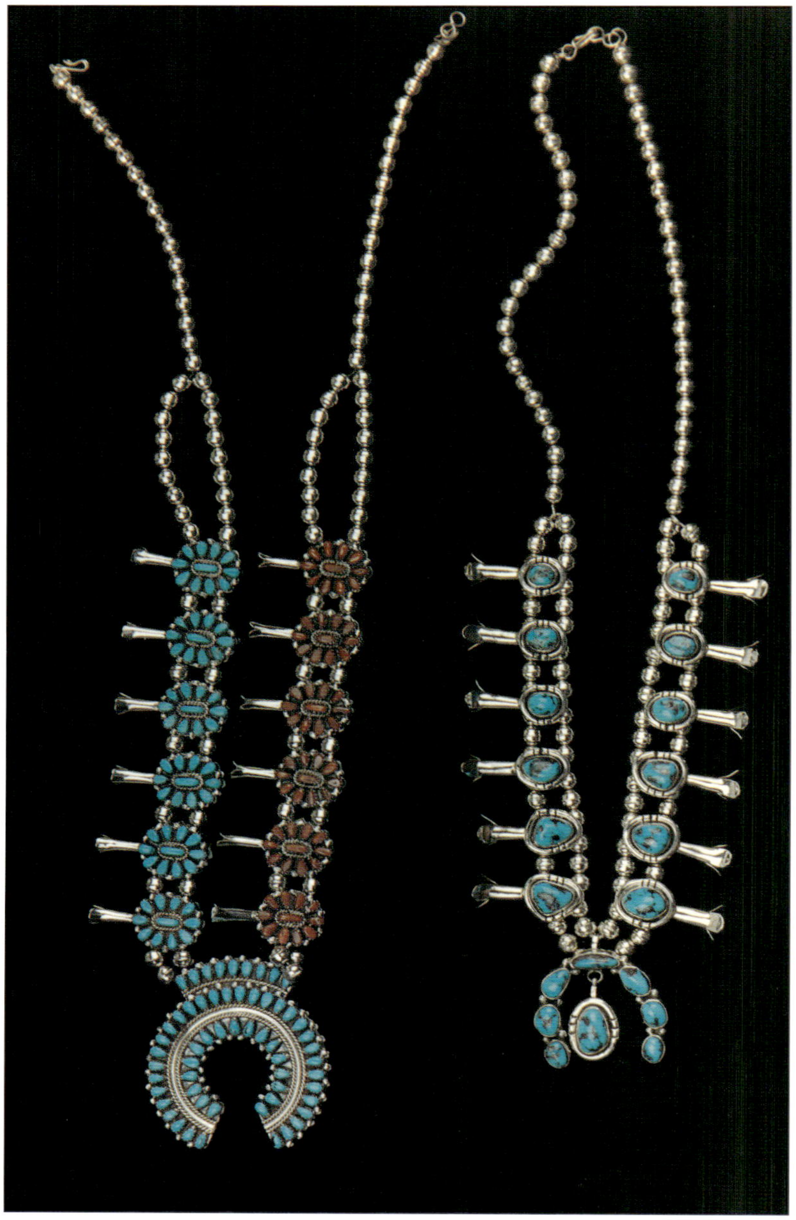

Reversible necklace of squash blossom style set with turquoise on one side and coral on the reverse, a truly novel design made by a Zuni craftsman in the 1980s. / Will Vandervér created the turquoise-laden squash blossom necklace of important size and bold design in the 1980s. *Bing Crosby collection*

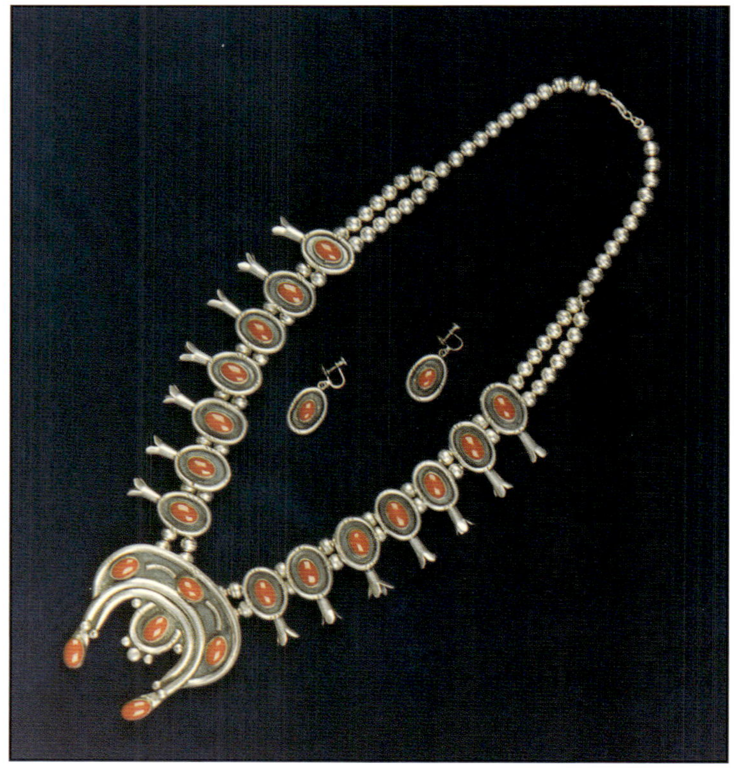

The naja has been designed in an original fashion and set with six coral stones on this large squash blossom necklace, 26 7/8" long. The coral blossom ornaments are repeated in the matching pair of earrings. *Private collection on permanent loan to Ohio University*

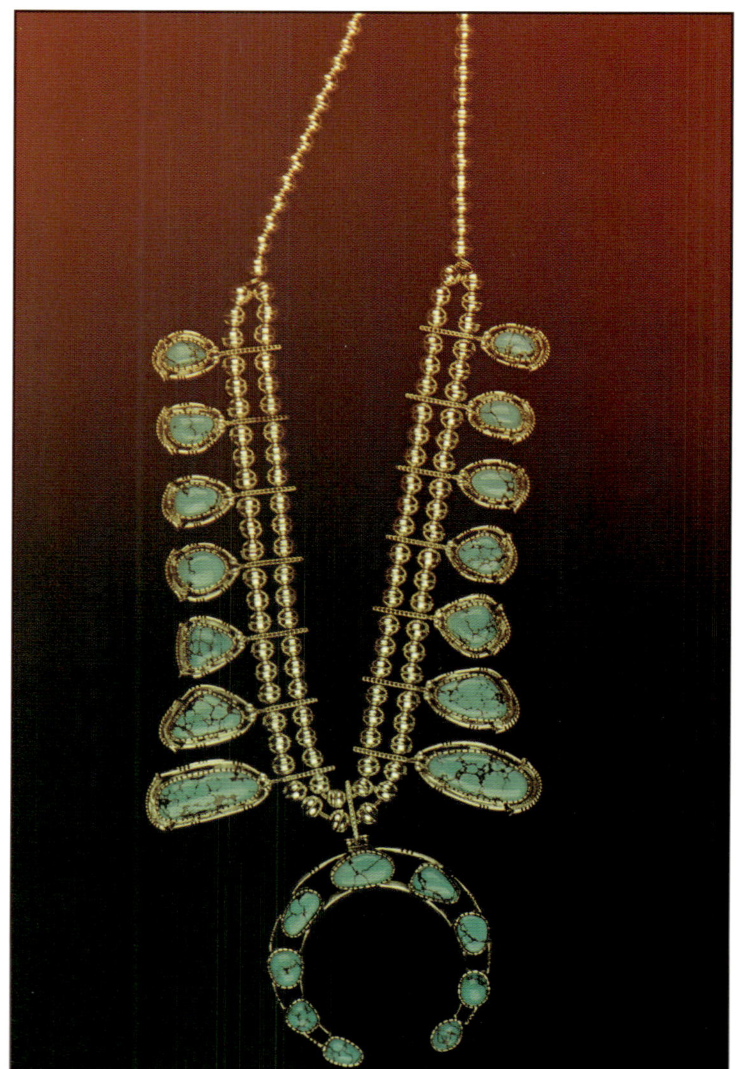

From the late 1980s, this variation of a squash blossom necklace has turquoise ornamenting the silver form. *Turquoise Lady collection*.

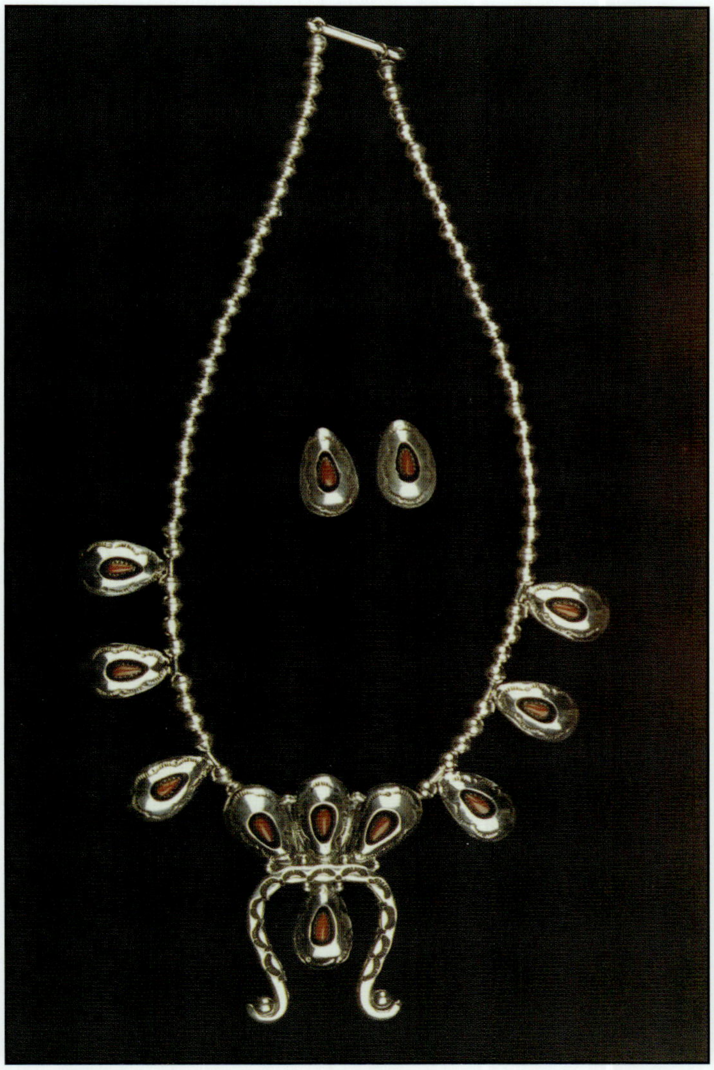

This "shadow box" variation of the squash blossom style necklace has been beautifully set with coral and made with a matching pair of earrings in the late 1980s. *Turquoise Lady collection*.

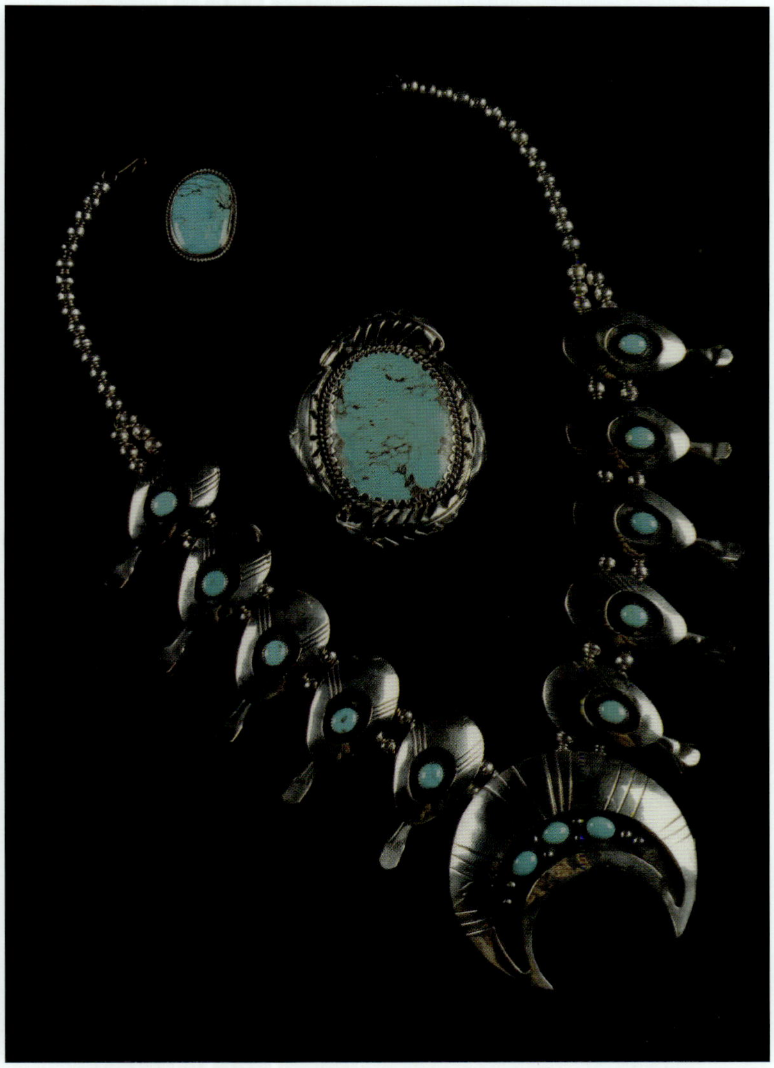

Another variation of the squash blossom design made in the 1980s is this large Navajo-made necklace with "shadow box" ornamentation set with turquoise. / Complementing the necklace are a dynamic and large bracelet set with a large turquoise stone and embellished with appliqué leaf designs, / A finger ring with turquoise set in a figured bezel. *Leonard D. Prins collection*

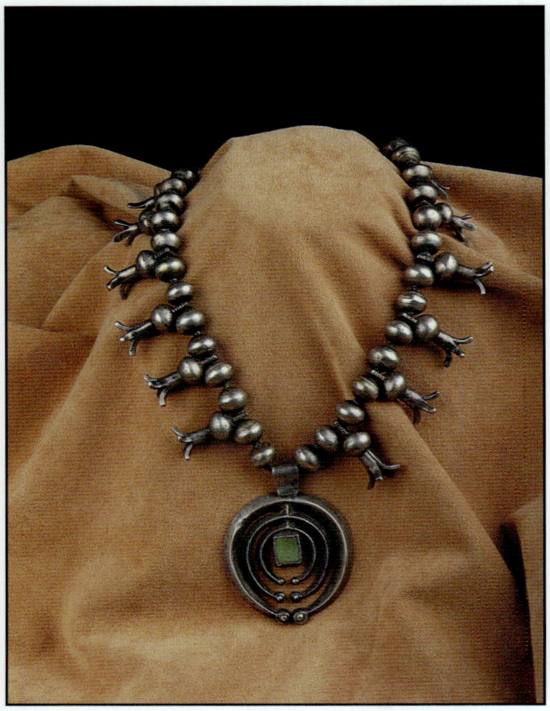

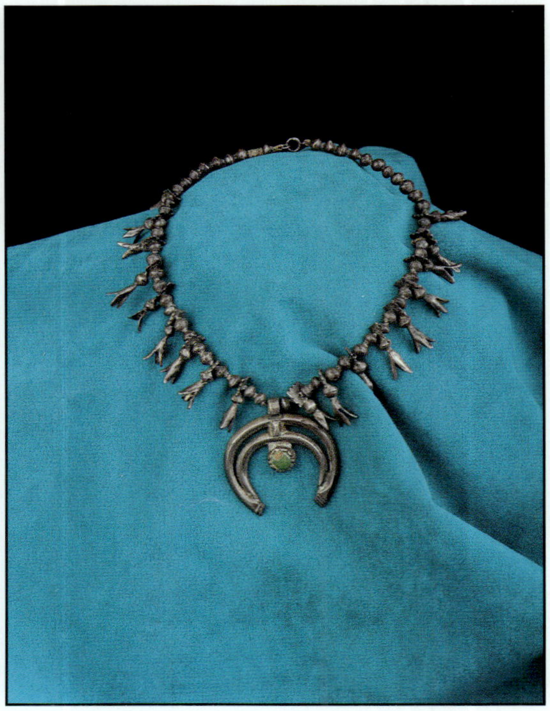

Left: Beautiful Navajo quash blossom necklace with a triple triangular bar crescent naja surrounding a square turquoise stone. The fine quality of this necklace suggests the work of the early silversmith known as Slender Maker of Silver, c.1880-1890. *Lynn D. Trusdell, Crown & Eagle Antiques*

Right: Small and early child's silver squash blossom necklace with a couble crescent naja holding a single Cerillos turquoise stone in a serrated bezel, c.1890. *Lynn D. Trusdell, Crown & Eagle Antiques*

Pendant Necklaces

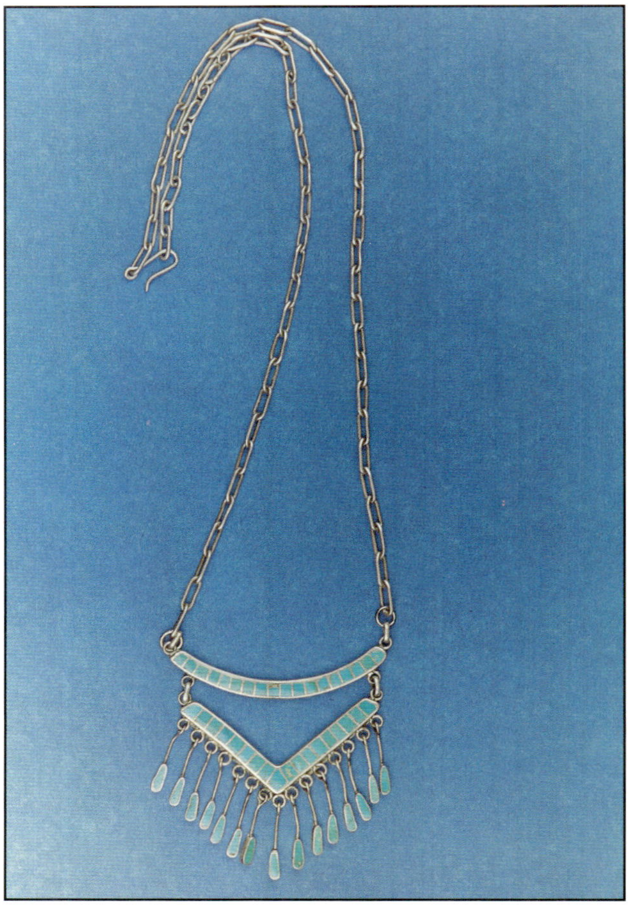

Necklace of fringe design with Zuni channel turquoise inlay and a silver link chain, 1960s. *Enchanted Mesa collection* .

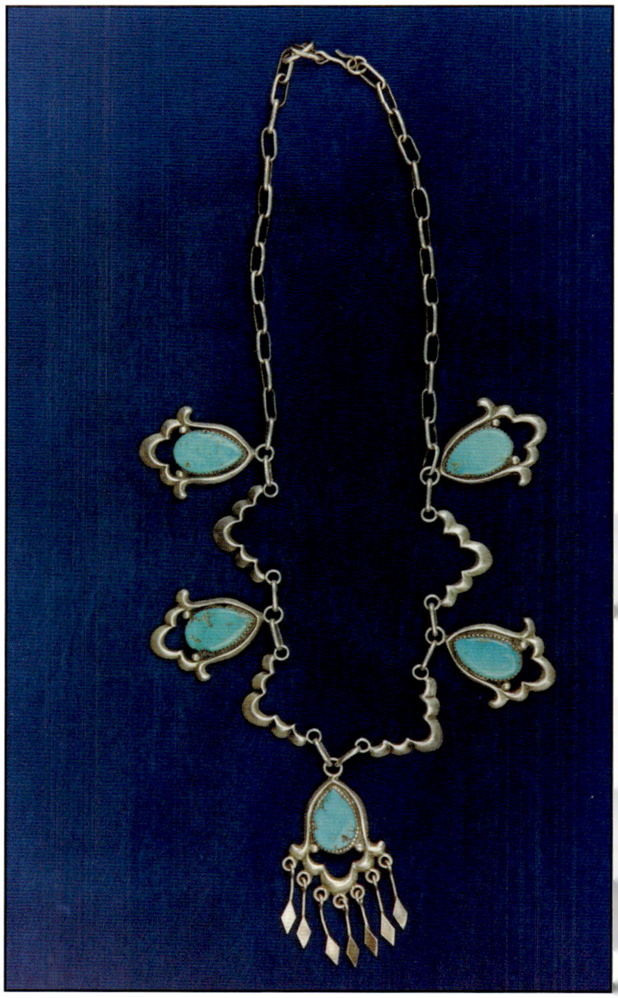

Necklace of original design made with five silver and turquoise pendants, one with fringe accents, made in 1965 by Elizabeth Kushi, Zuni, as a retirement gift for teacher Clara Gonzalez, from her friends. *Maxwell Museum collection.*

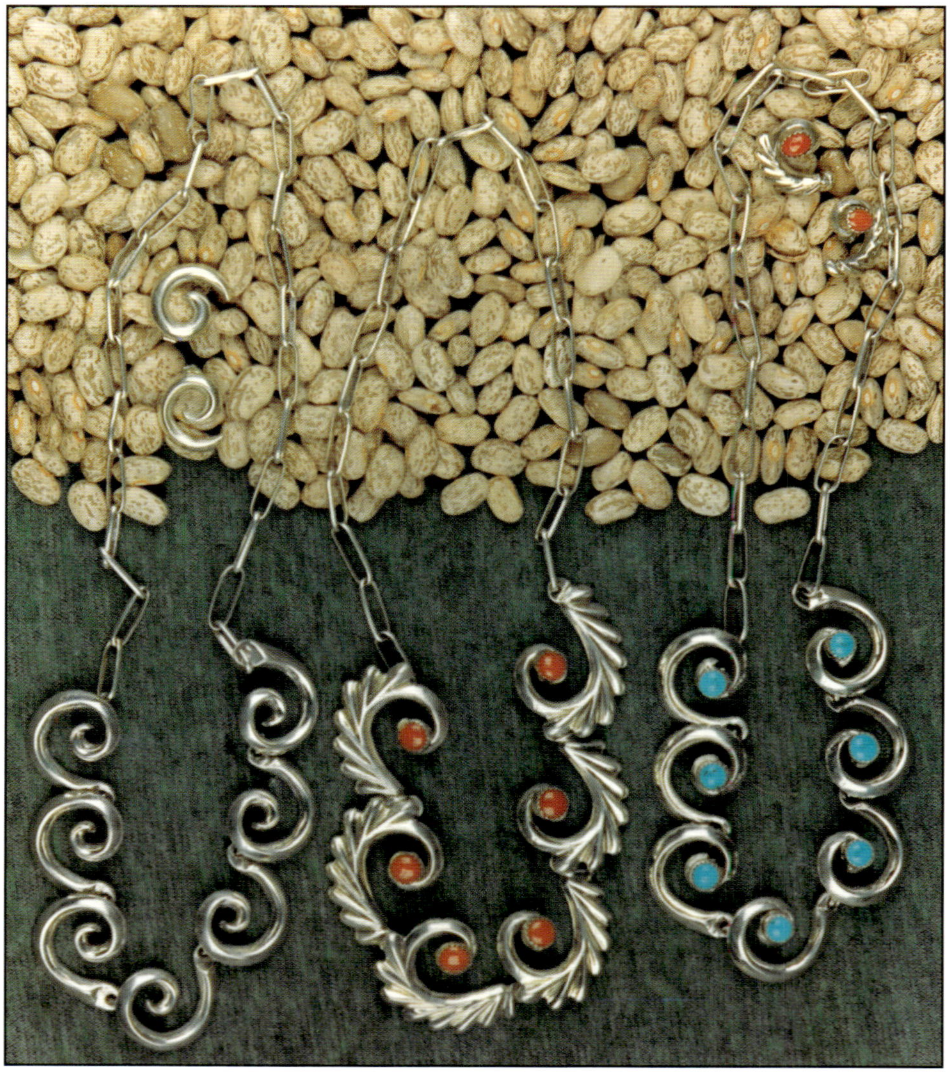

Three silver link necklaces and two pair of matching earrings, one set of silver only, one set with coral accents, and one necklace with turquoise stones, Navajo, late 1980s. *Enchanted Mesa collection* .

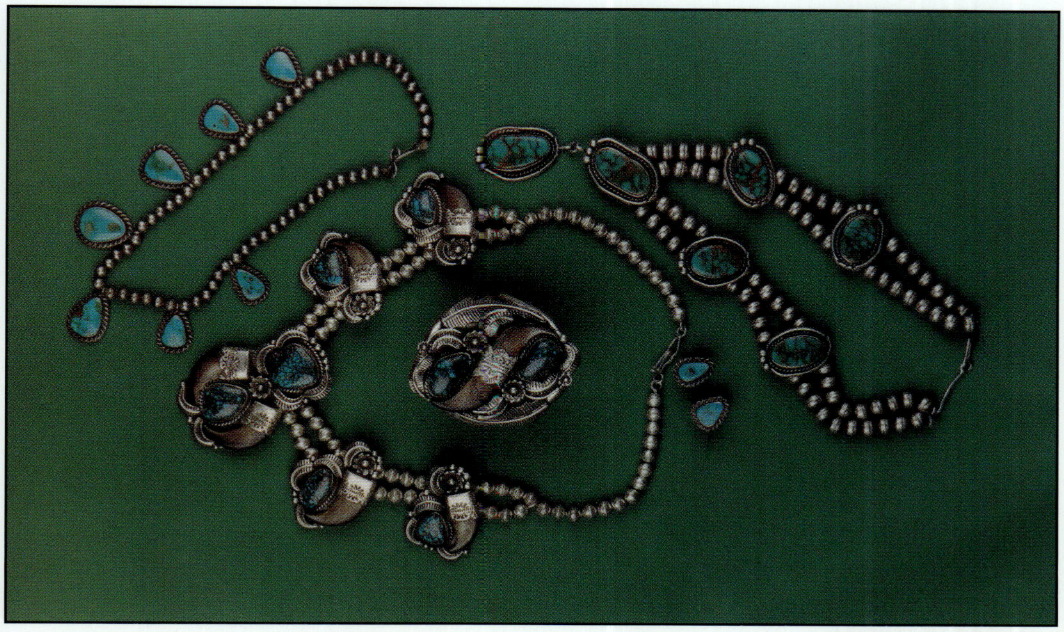

From the left: Silver bead necklace and seven pendants each set with Villa Grove turquoise. / Necklace and matching bracelet of silver with wrought and appliqué plaques set with Lander's Blue turquoise. / Necklace of silver beads and plaques set with Royston turquoise, and a matching pair of earrings. *Private collection*

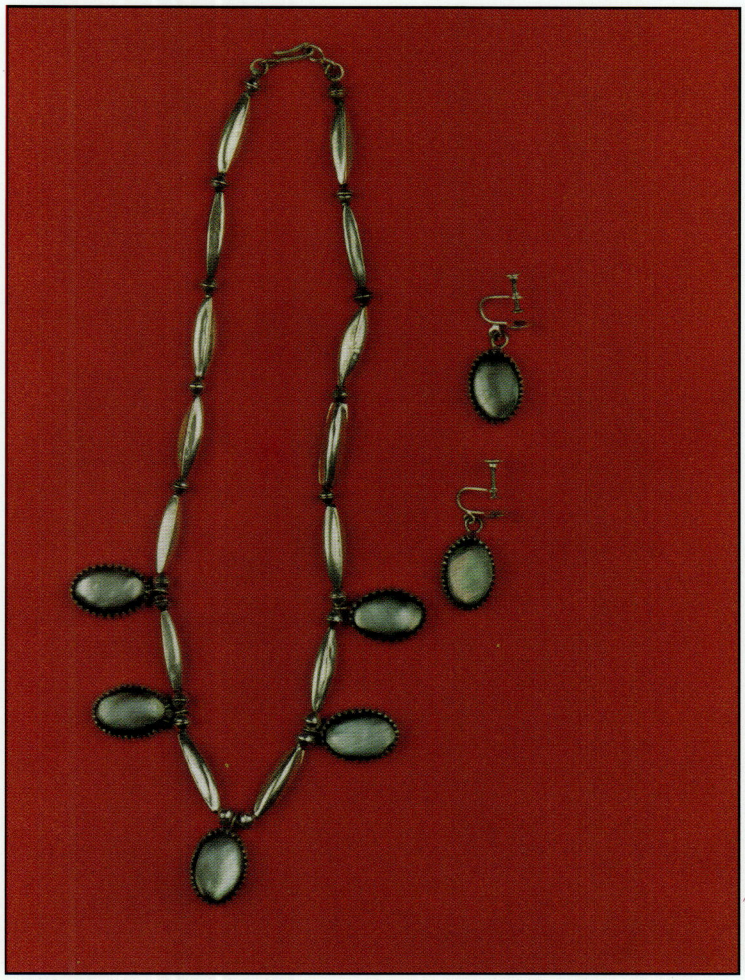

Silver bead necklace with oval pendants set with mother of pearl, and matching earrings, made by Betty Benally, Navajo. *Private collection*

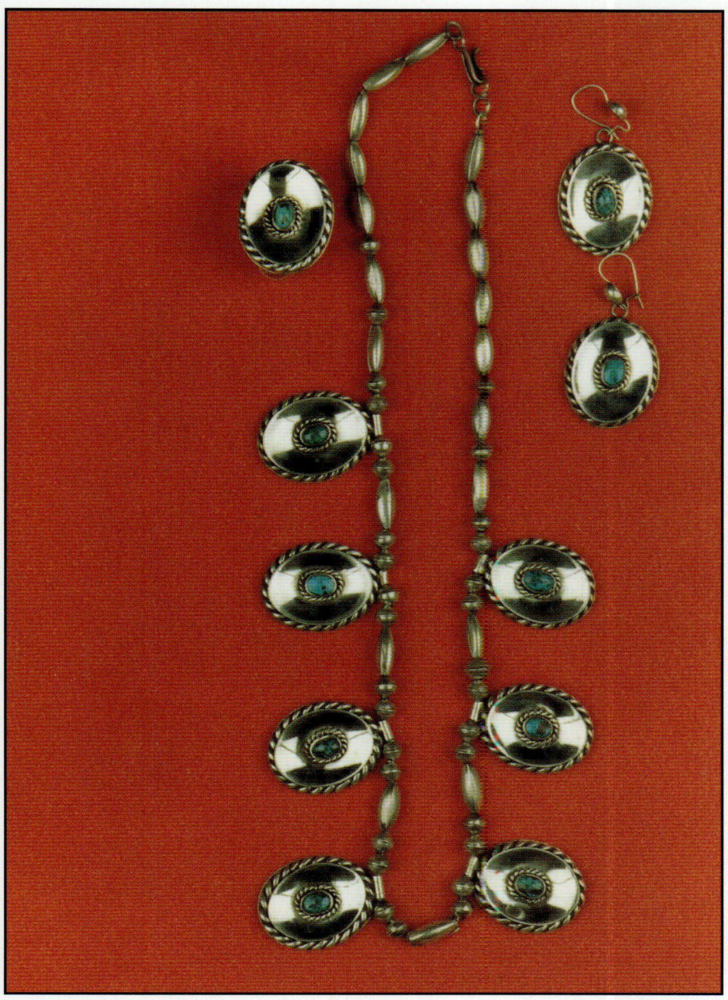

Navajo silver bead necklace with pendants set with turquoise, and matching earrings and ring. *Private collection*

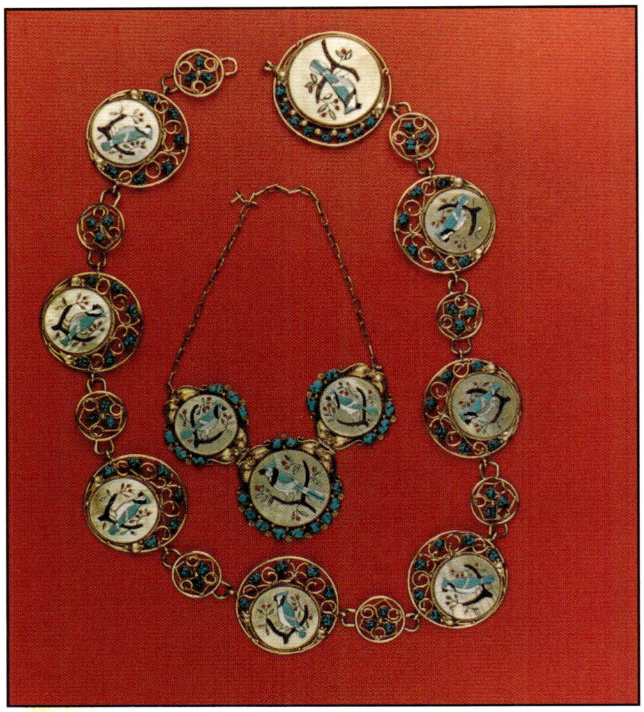

14 k gold and stone and shell inlay were used in these two pieces in an unusual combination in the 1980s. The necklace has three inlaid medallions by Bessie Manning with gold work by Tim Bedah. The link belt combines eight inlaid medallions by Sarah McCray with gold work by Martin Muskett. *Private collection*

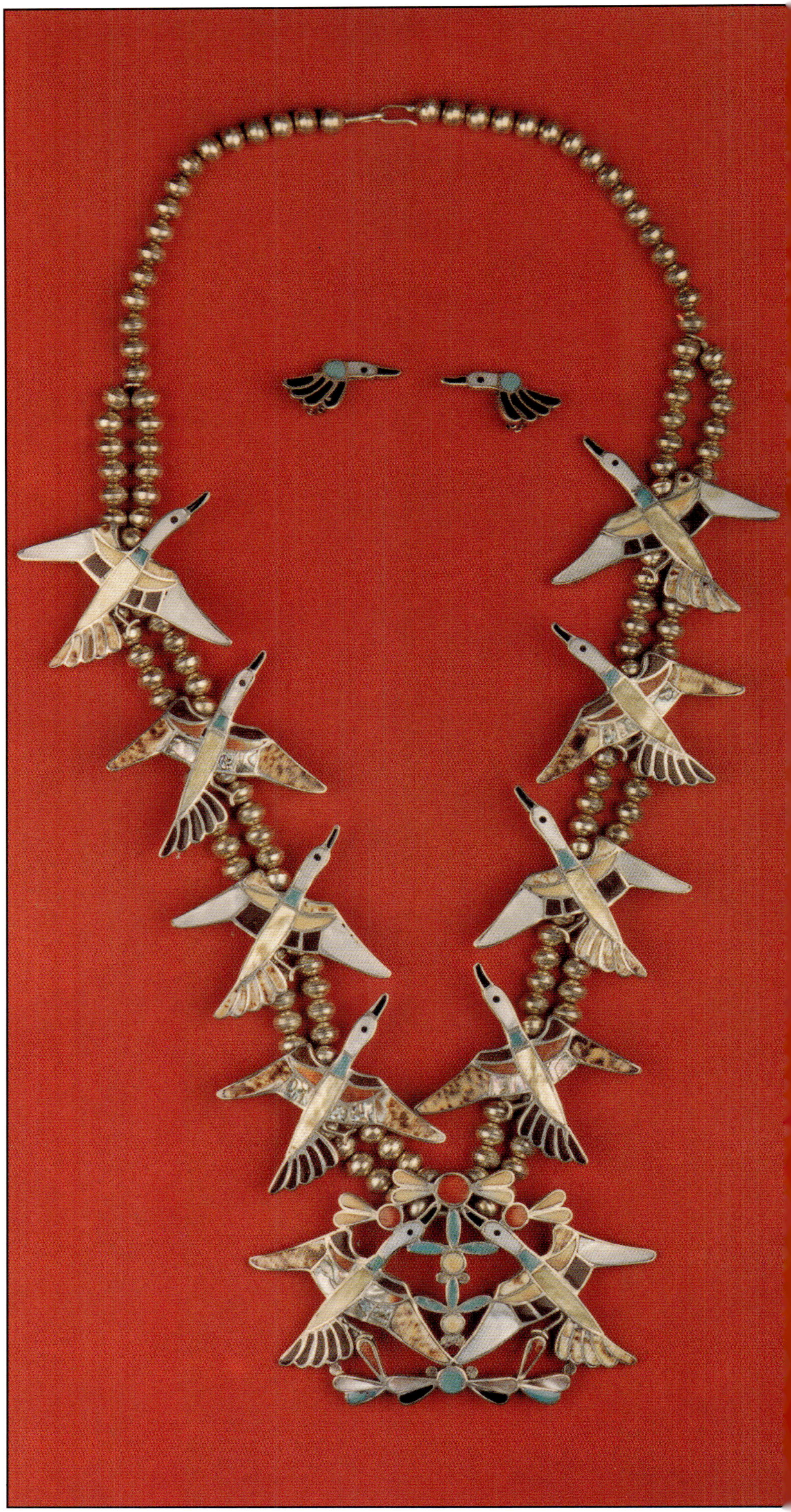

Shell and inlaid stone geese flock around a double strand of beads to create an unusual necklace, which is marked with a raised S. The pair of bird design inlaid earrings is unmarked. *Private collection*

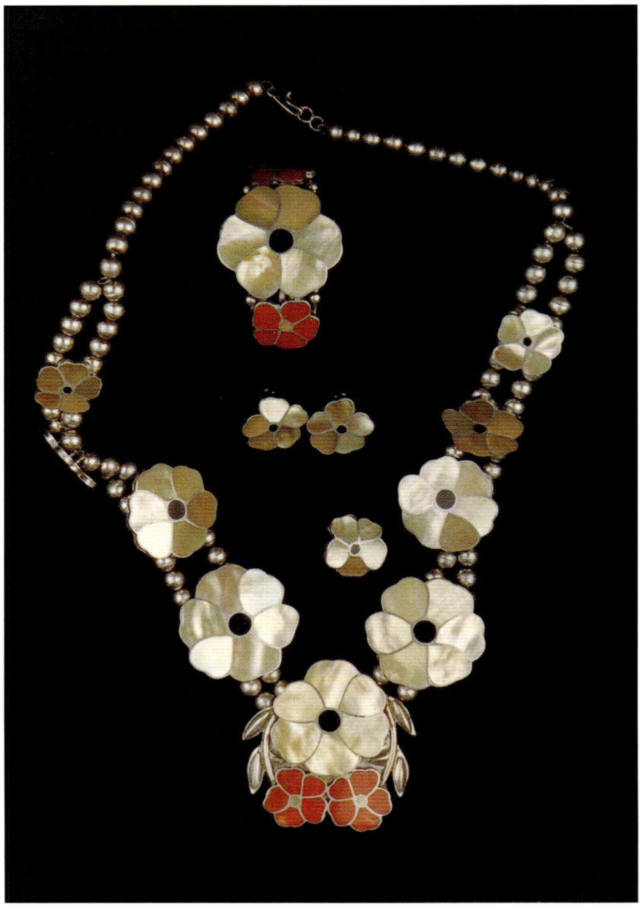

Shell, coral and jet inlay has been combined here in a floral design to create a necklace and matching bracelet, earrings and ring, Zuni. *Private collection*

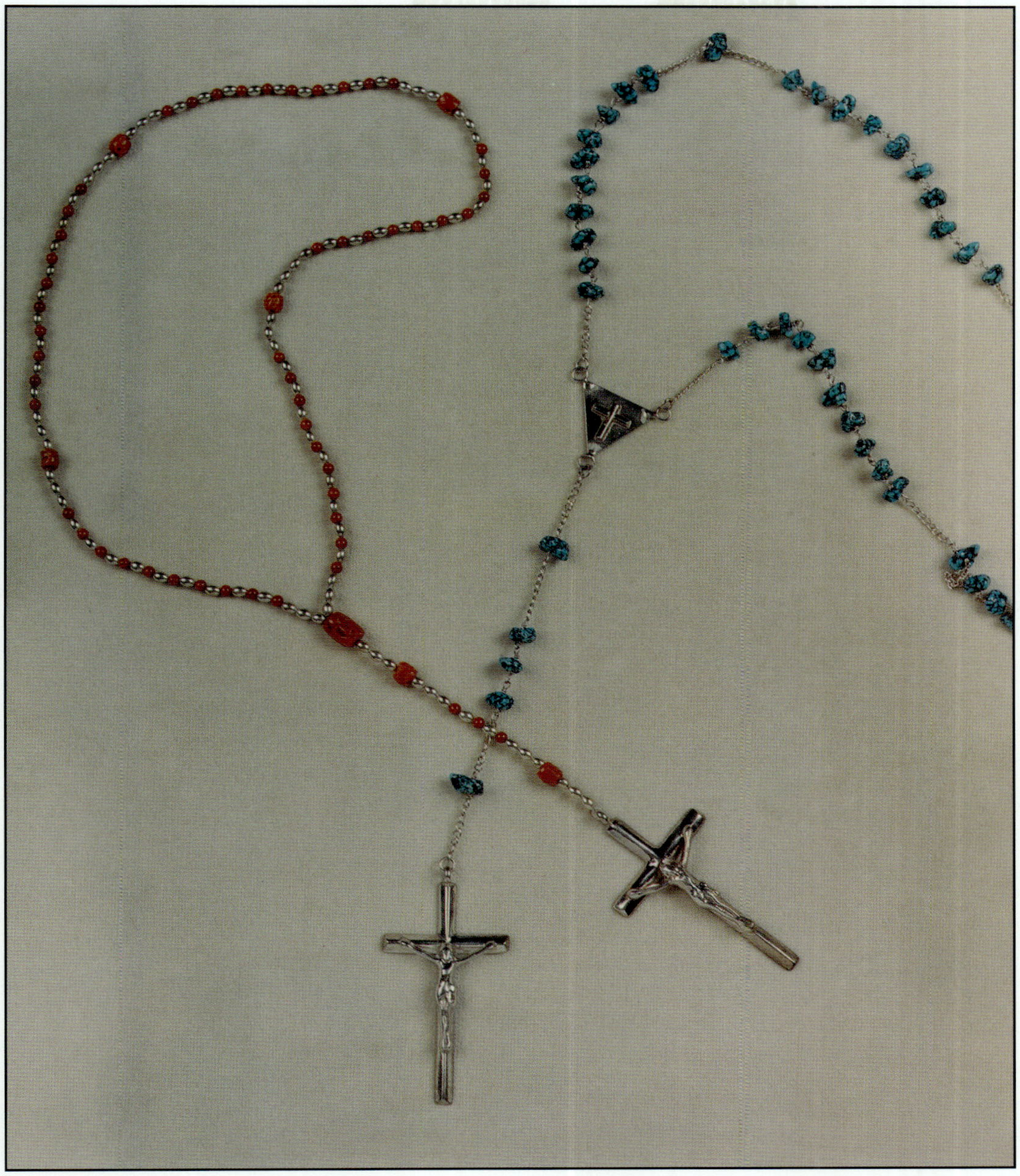

Two rosaries, with coral and turquoise beads respectively, each supporting a silver representation of the Crucifixion, 17" long, made in 1985. *Private collection*

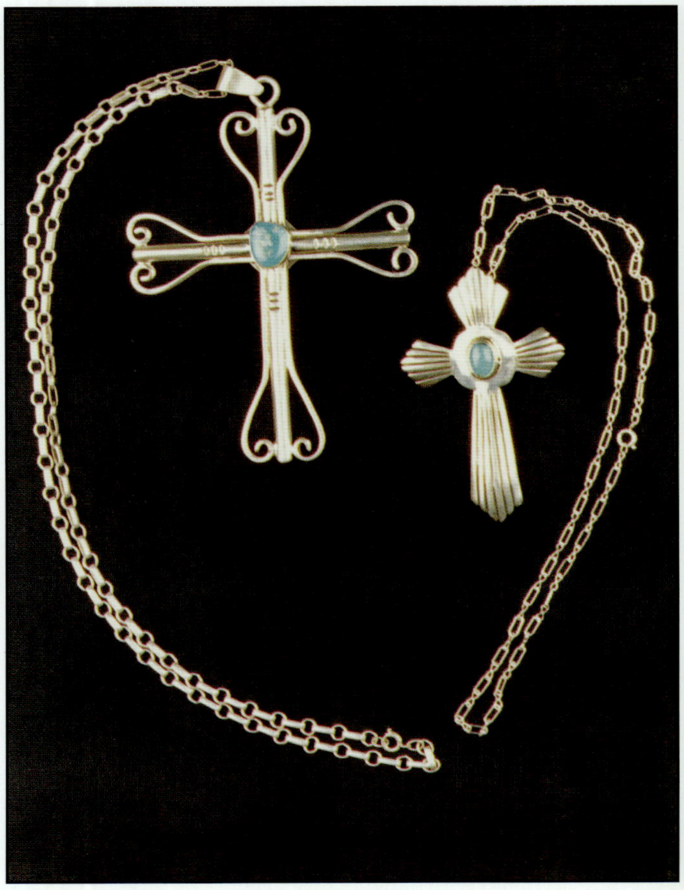

Large silver openwork pendant cross set with turquoise and link chain by Kee Joe Benally, Navajo. / Small solid silver cross set with turquoise and link chain by Benson Sam, Navajo, late 1970s. *Private collection*

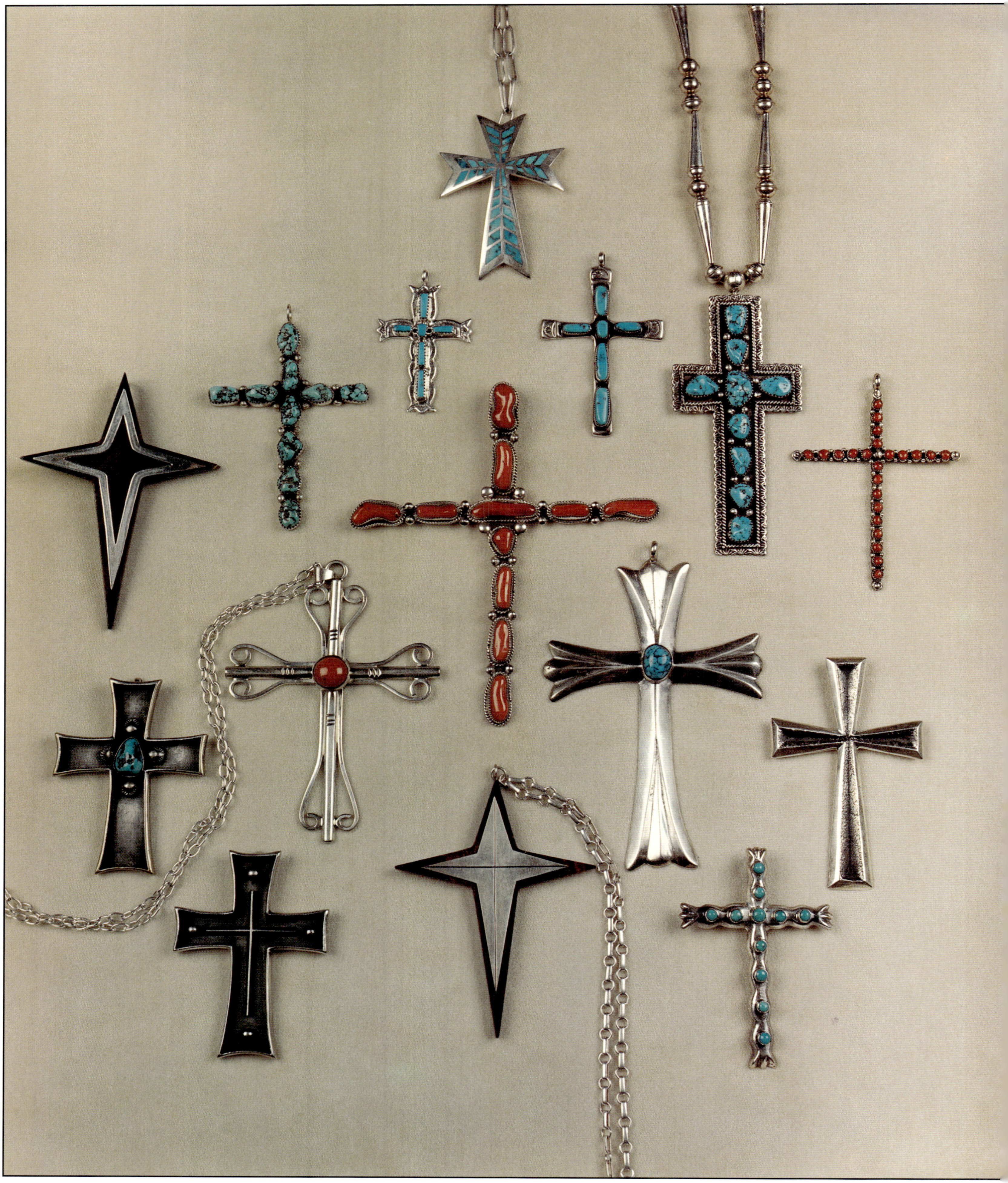

Group of pendant crosses from the 1970s and 1980s made by Navajo and Zuni jewelers for local use as well as for sale. *Private collection on permanent loan to Ohio University*

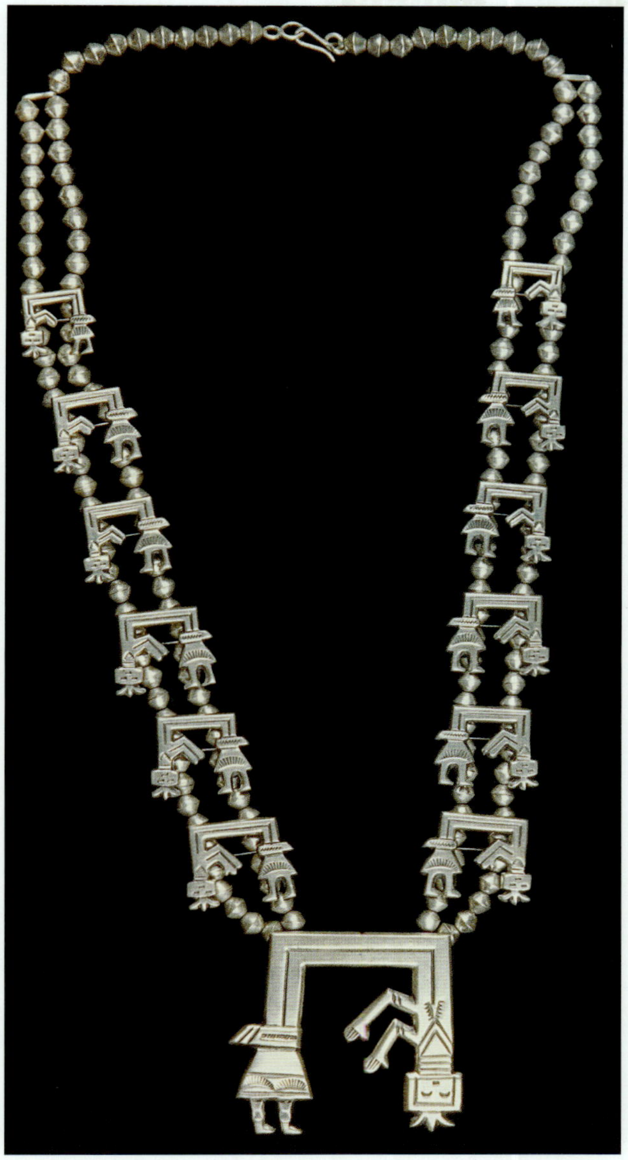

Double strand of silver beads supporting twelve cast silver rainbow god figures and a larger naja, made in 1978, Navajo. *Private collection on permanent loan to Ohio University*

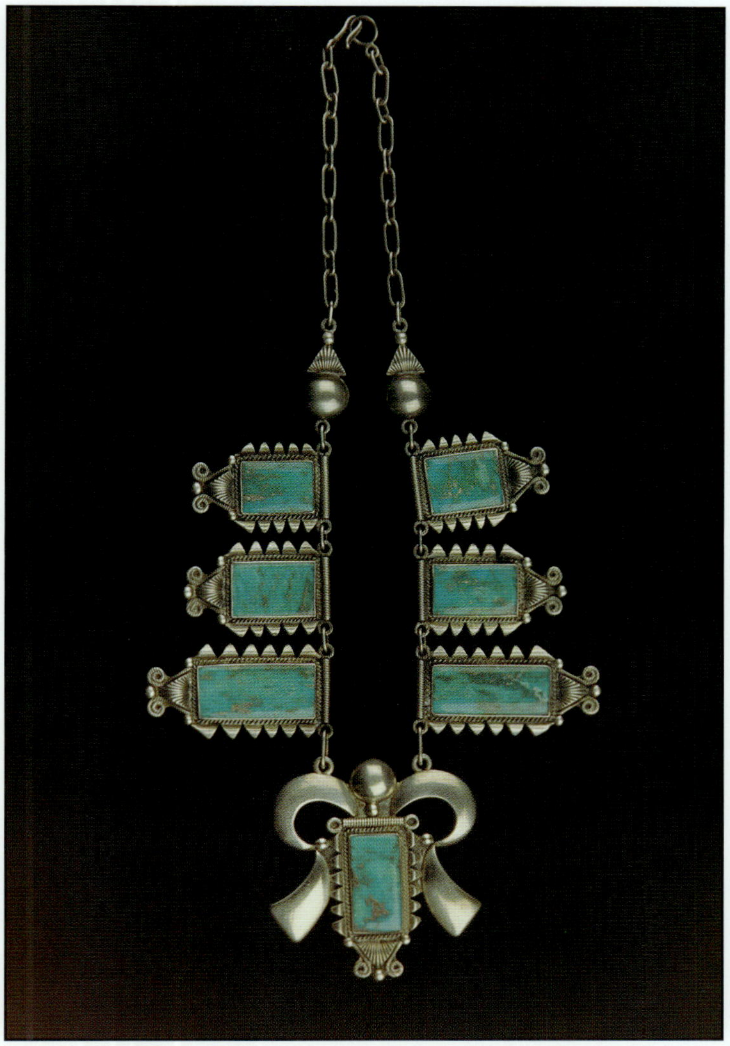

Stunning necklace of interesting symmetrical design with seven turquoise plates set in silver by Luke B. Yazzie, Navajo, 1970s. *Enchanted Mesa collection* .

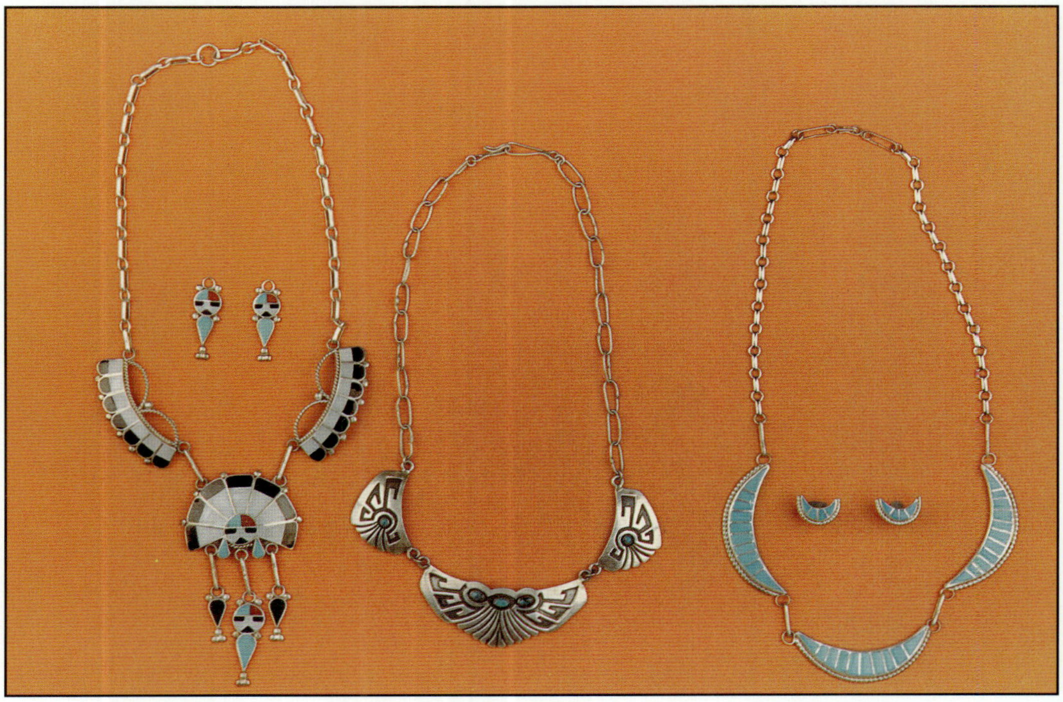

Link necklace of silver with inlaid plaques of black and white coral and turquoise, and matching earrings, by R. Lateyie, Zuni. / Silver overlay link necklace, Navajo. / Turquoise channel inlay necklace and matching earrings by Rose Bobelu, Zuni, 1977. *Private collection*

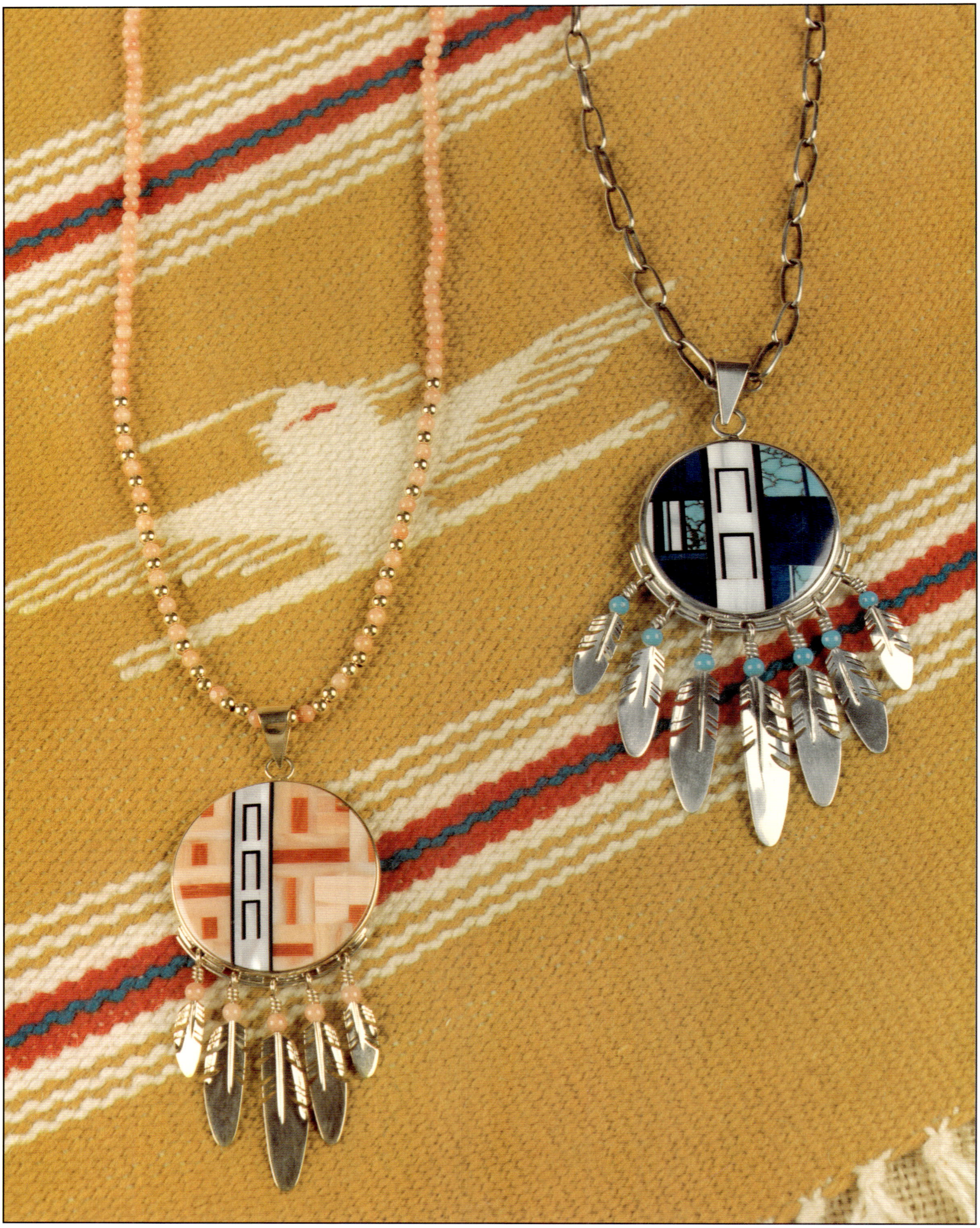

Two necklaces made by Ray Tracy, Navajo, in the late 1980s of pendant designs. On the left, coral and gold beads support the inlaid medallion with gold feather drops. / On the right, a silver link chain supports a medallion set with lapis lazuli, turquoise, jet and shell with silver feather and turquoise bead drops. *Indian Post collection*

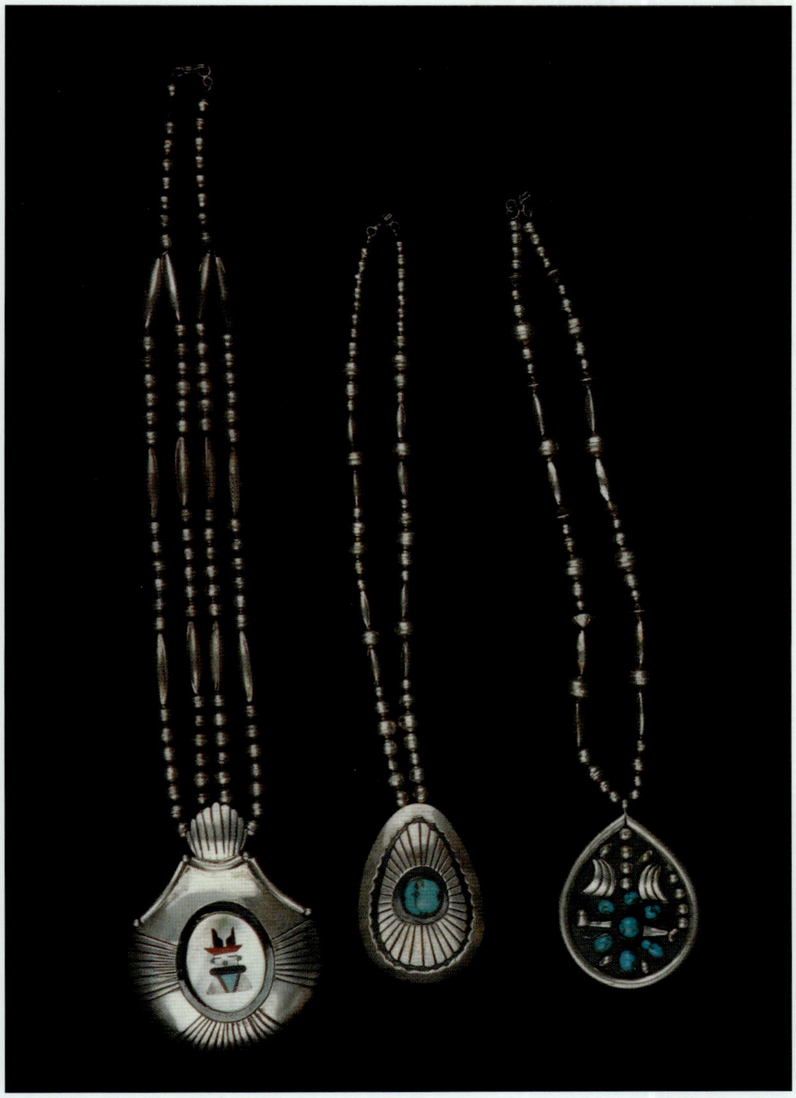

Double strand of silver round and melon beads and a silver pendant decorated with an inlay of green snail shell, mother of pearl, coral, turquoise and jet as a face design, circa 1970, Zuni. / Single strand of silver round and melon beads and a pendant of silver overlay with Persian turquoise, circa 1970. / Silver round and melon beads supporting a silver pendant set with Persian turquoise, made by Hardy T. in the 1960s. *Dennehotso collection*.

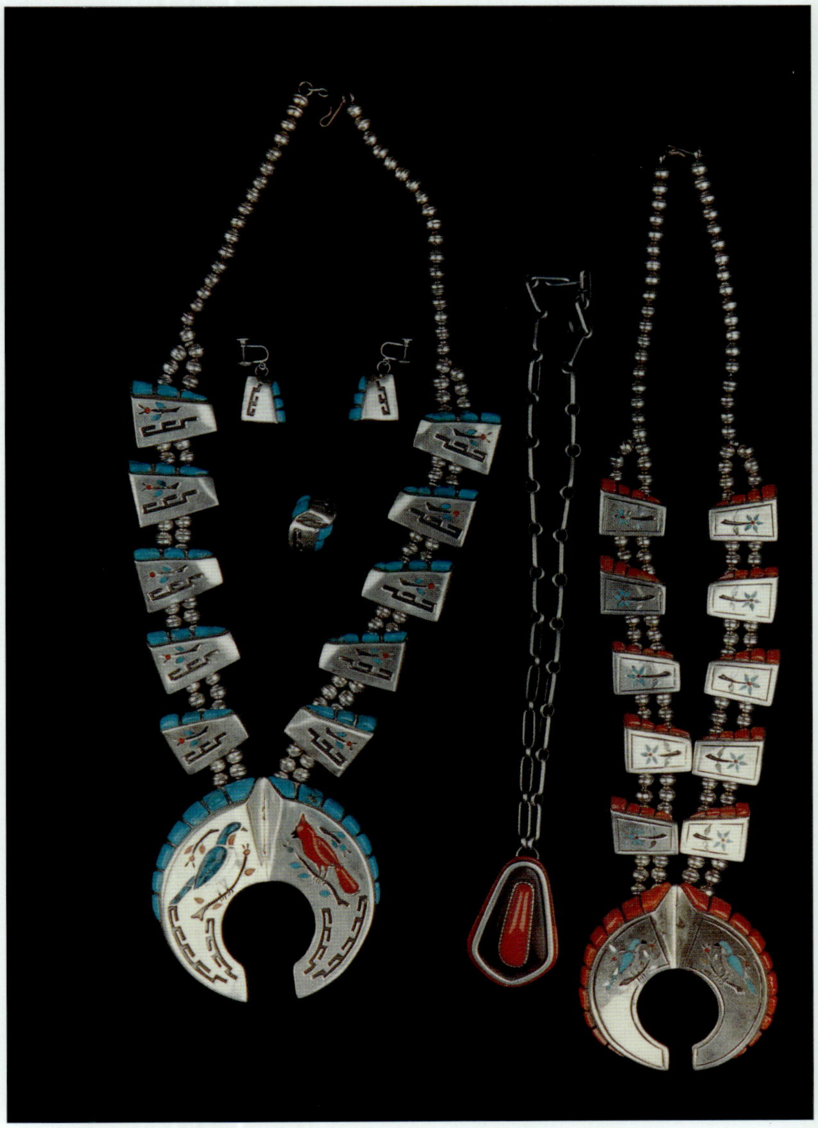

Zuni silver necklace with matching earrings and ring decorated with elaborate turquoise and coral inlay. / Pendant necklace of silver links with a coral set medallion. / Zuni necklace nearly matching the first in this group but smaller and with cZuni Zoral inlay predominating. *Private collection*

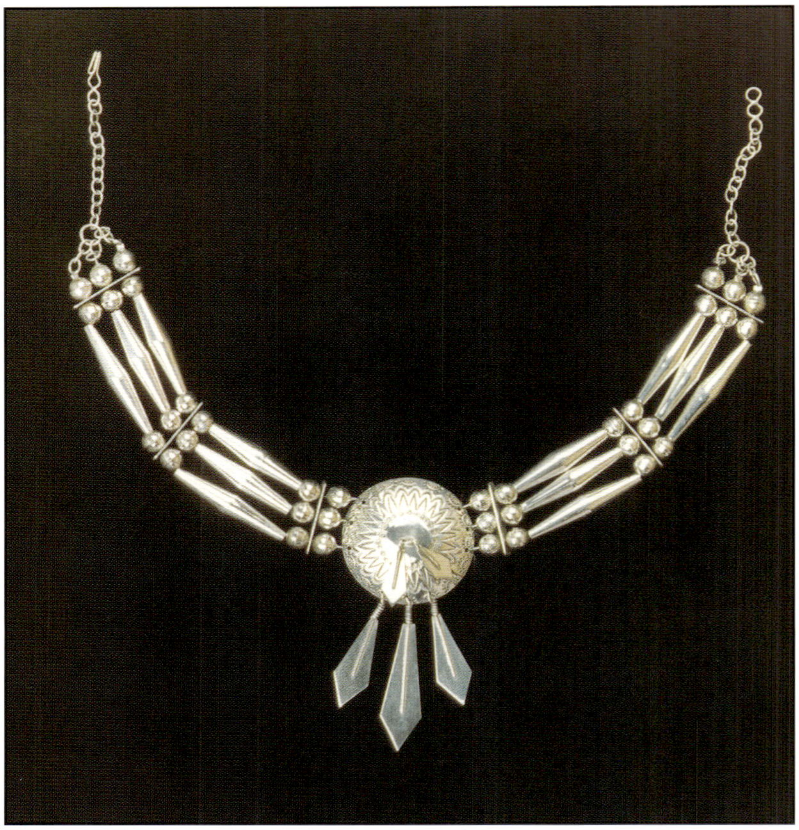

Navajo silver triple strand bead necklace with a central medallion and three drops, late 1980s. *Bing Crosby collection*

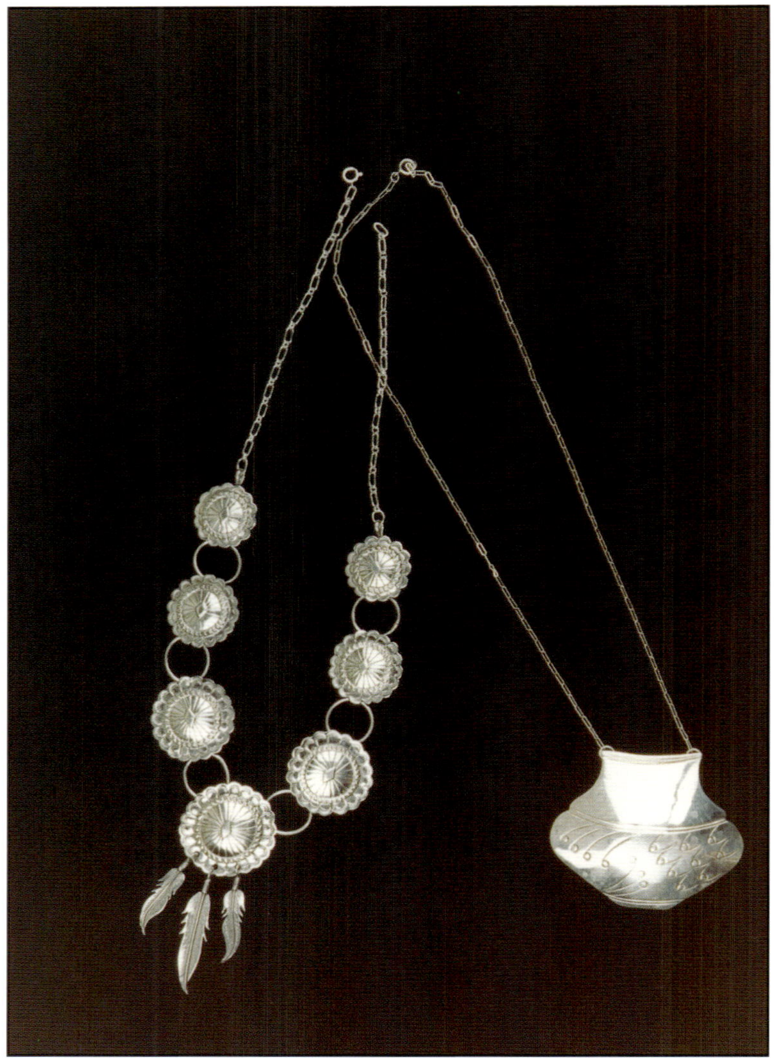

Silver link necklace of concho-style medallions and three feather designed drops made by A. Payton, 1980s. / Pendant necklace of silver with a pot-shaped medallion on a linked chain made by F. Ramone, 1980s. *Bing Crosby collection*

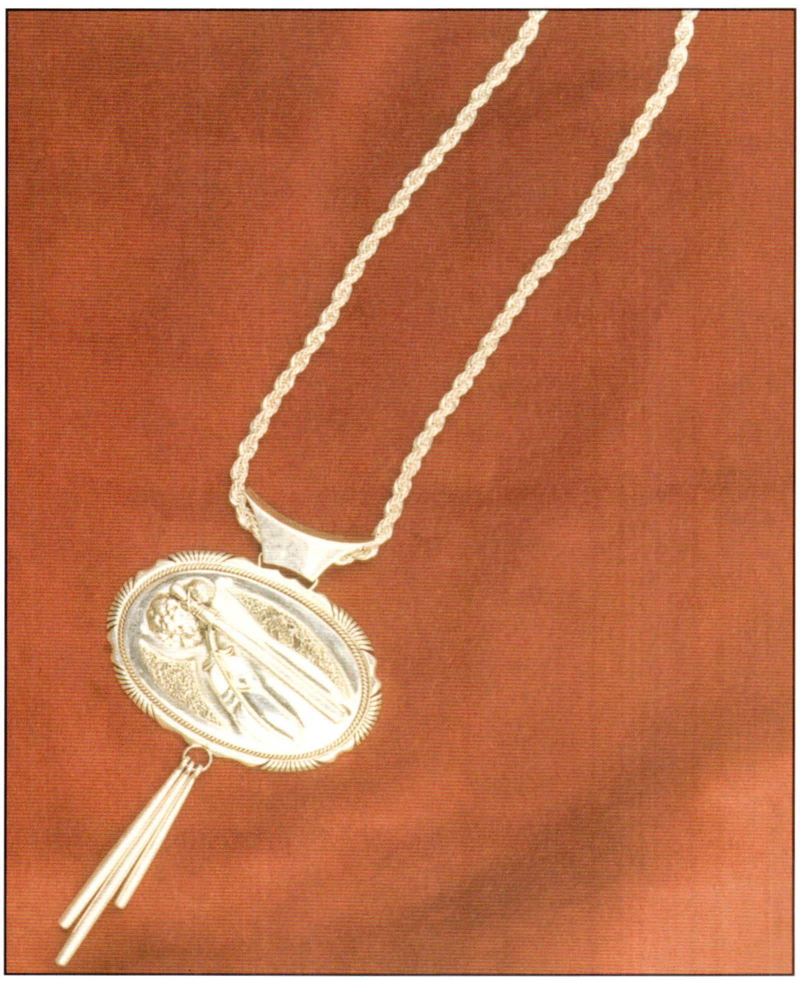

Oval silver pendant on a linked chain, decorated with a feather design and three rod-shaped drops, marked W C V, circa 1989. *Bing Crosby collection*

Silver necklace and earrings of feather design with pendants, made by Ben Begay, Navajo, 1980s. *Private collection on permanent loan to Ohio University*

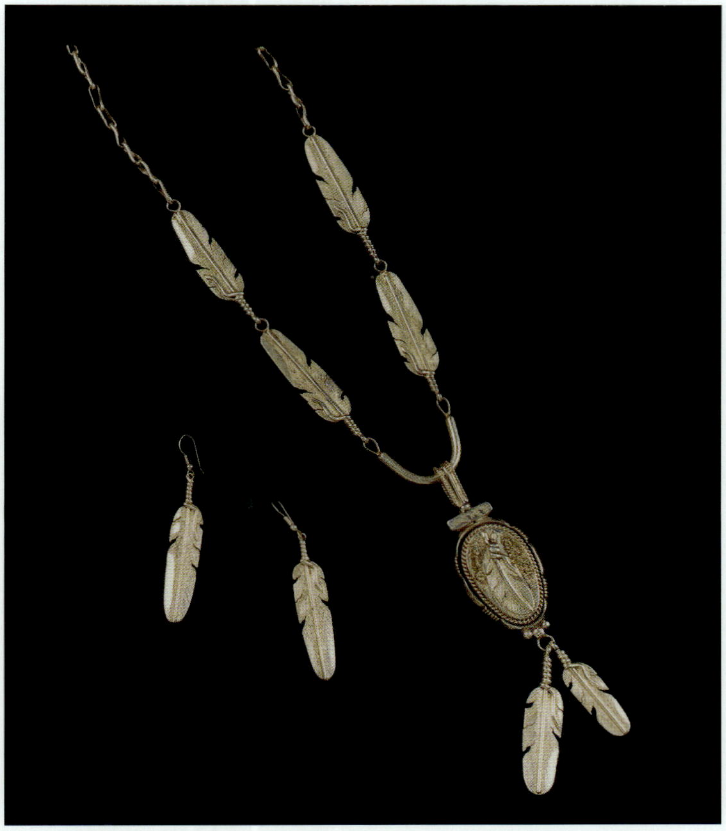

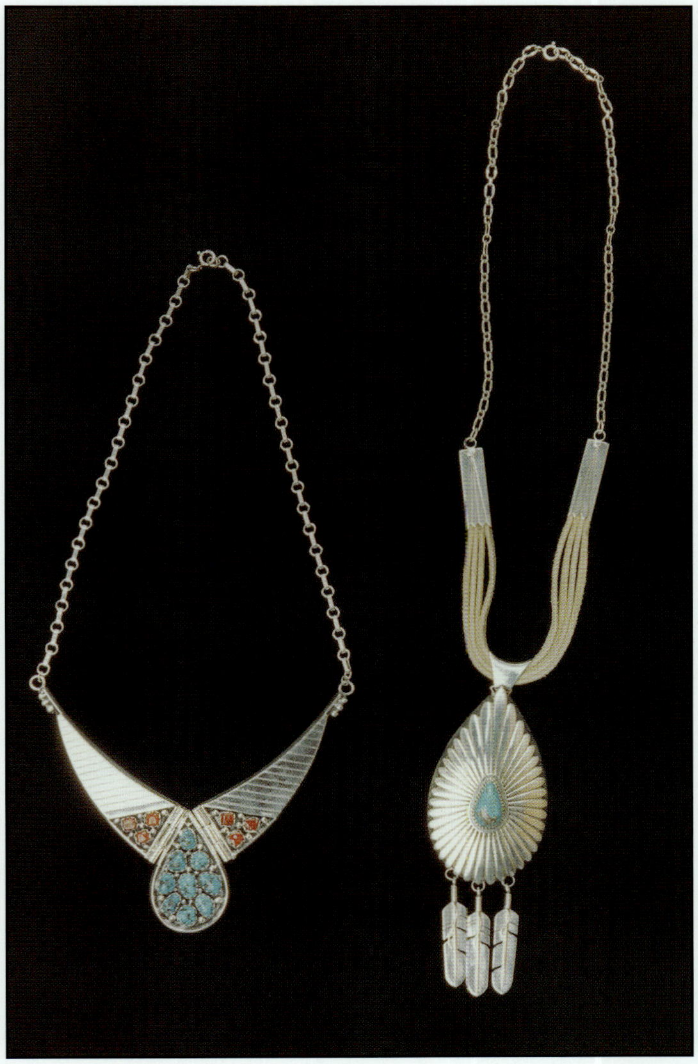

Necklace of silver with coral and Bisbee turquoise mounted on hinged plates, marked R. / Necklace of unusual design with four strips of rawhide joined to the silver chain and supporting a silver medallion set with turquoise and with three feather-shaped drops, marked W C V, late 1980s. *Bing Crosby collection*

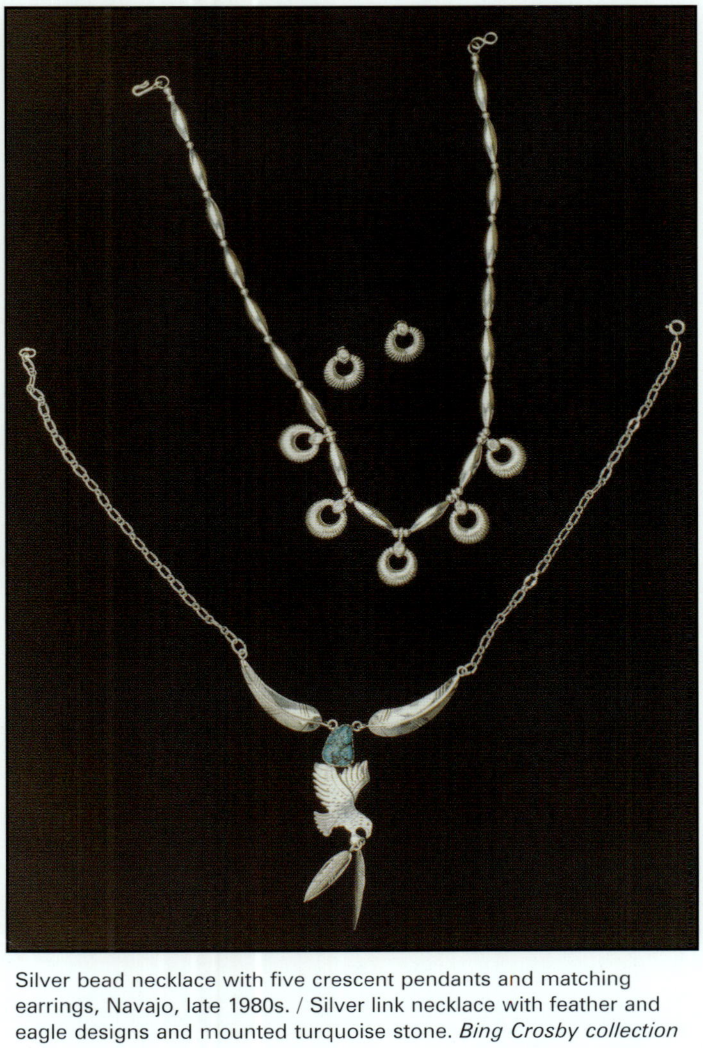

Silver bead necklace with five crescent pendants and matching earrings, Navajo, late 1980s. / Silver link necklace with feather and eagle designs and mounted turquoise stone. *Bing Crosby collection*

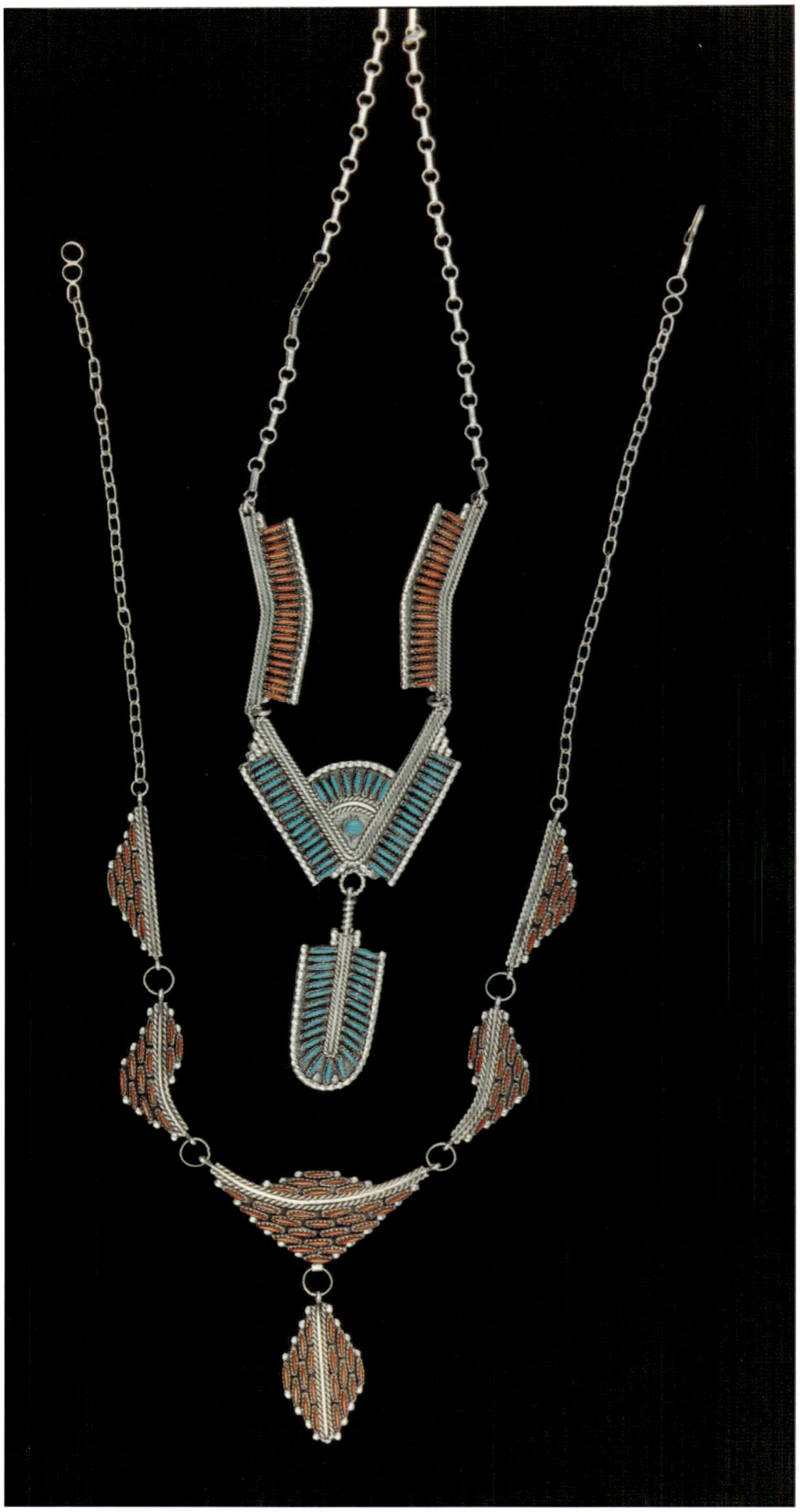

Two Navajo-made link necklaces in the Zuni style with needlepoint inlays, the top necklace in fact reversible with turquoise stones on one side and coral on the reverse. / The lower necklace is set with coral, late 1980s. *Bing Crosby collection*

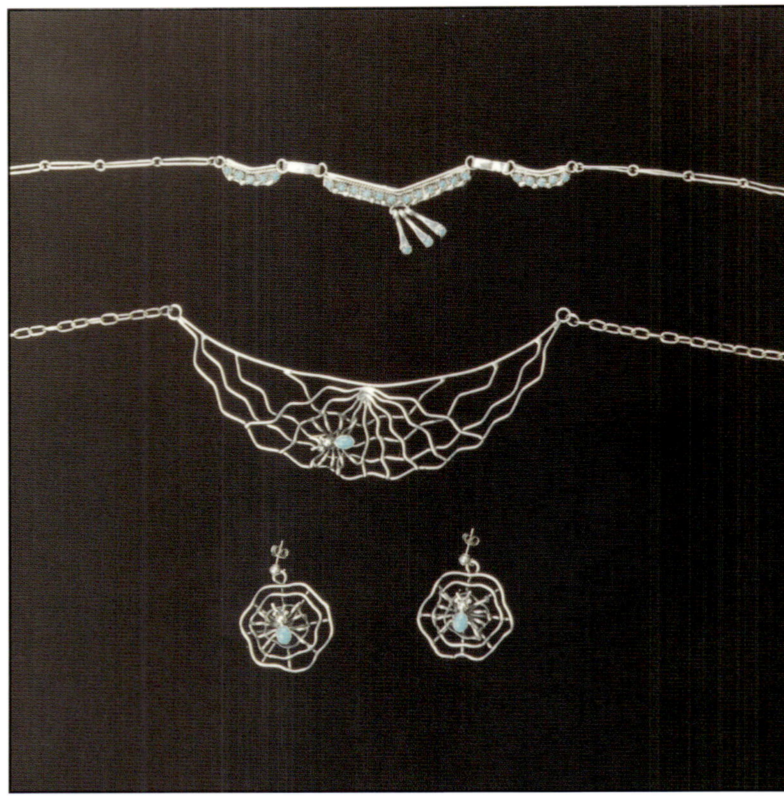

Navajo link necklace set with turquoise. / Unusual silver wire openwork necklace and earrings in a spiderweb design with turquoise set as the body of the spider, 1980s. *Bing Crosby collection*

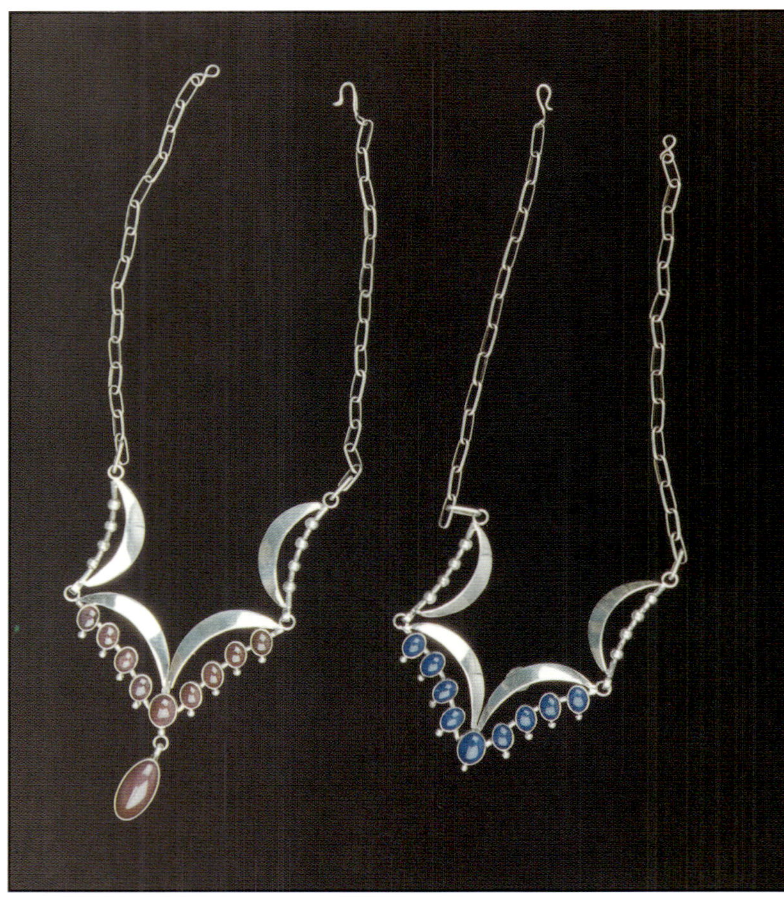

Two similar Navajo link necklaces of silver. On the left, the necklace and a pendant are set with red stones. / On the right, blue stones ornament the design. *Bing Crosby collection*

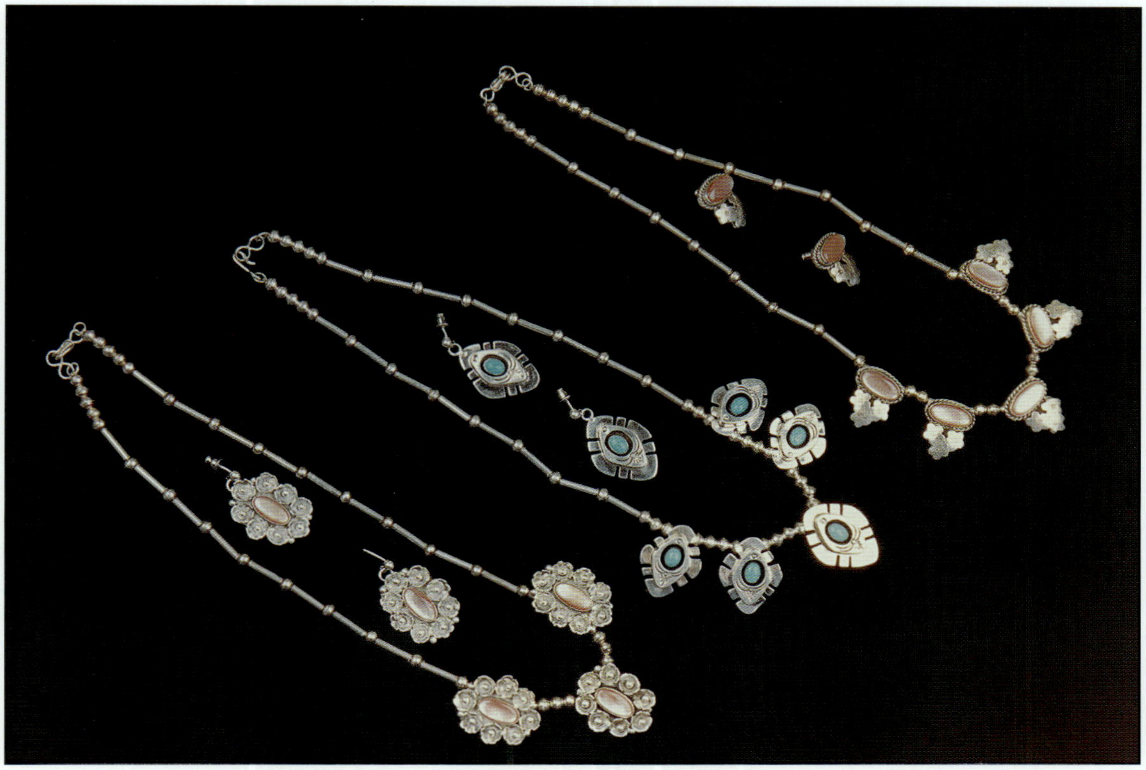

Three similar silver bead necklaces with matching earrings made by members of the Platero family, Navajo, in the late 1980s and set with pink shell or turquoise. *Bing Crosby collection*

Three sets of matching link necklaces and earrings bearing stone inlaid decorations by Adeline Bowannie, Zuni, late 1980s. *Bing Crosby collection*

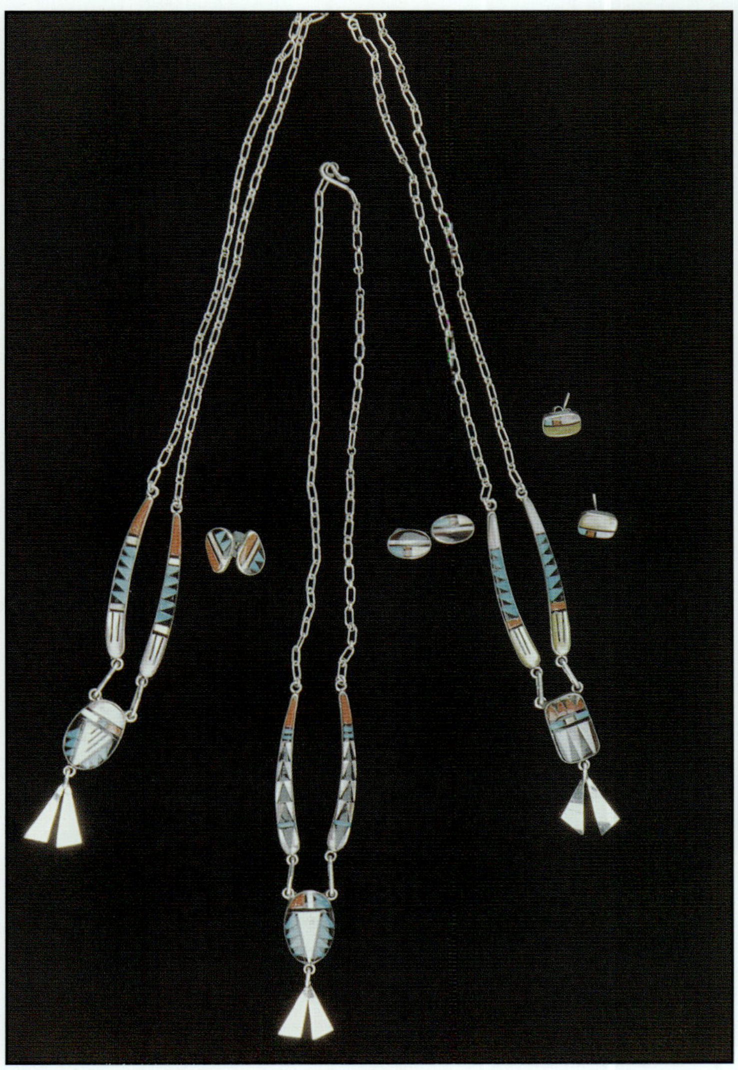

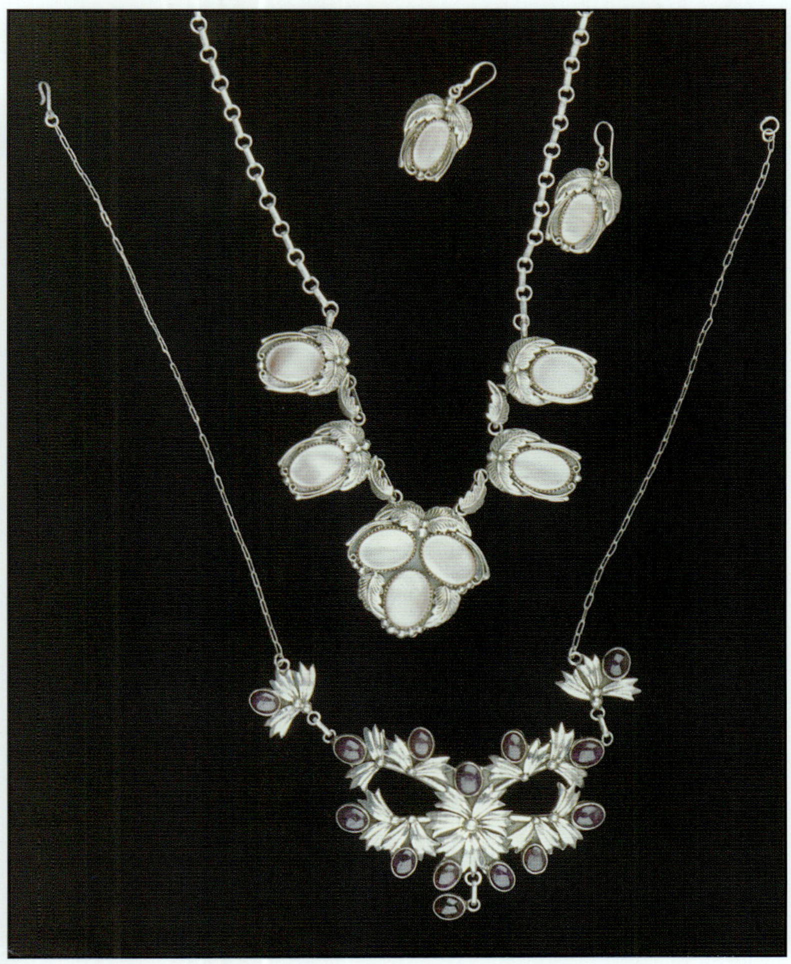

Silver link necklace and earrings of appliqué leaf design and pink shell, Navajo. / Link necklace of cast silver set with purple stones and marked B J P, a member of the Platero family, Navajo, late 1980s. *Bing Crosby collection*

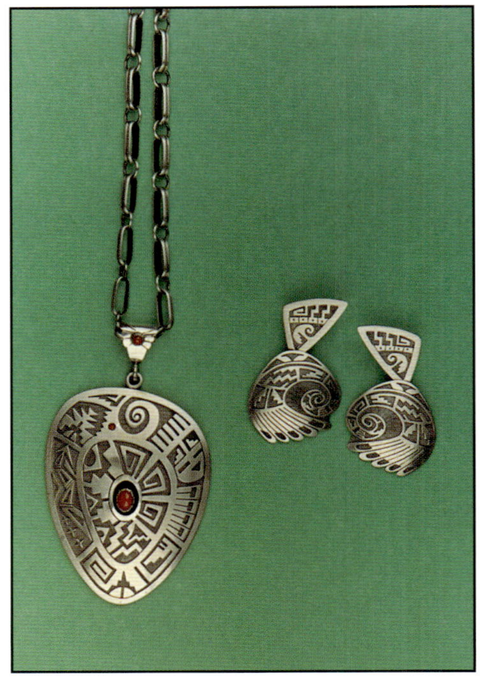

Hopi silver overlay pendant set with coral. / A pair of silver overlay earrings, late 1980s. *Enchanted Mesa collection* .

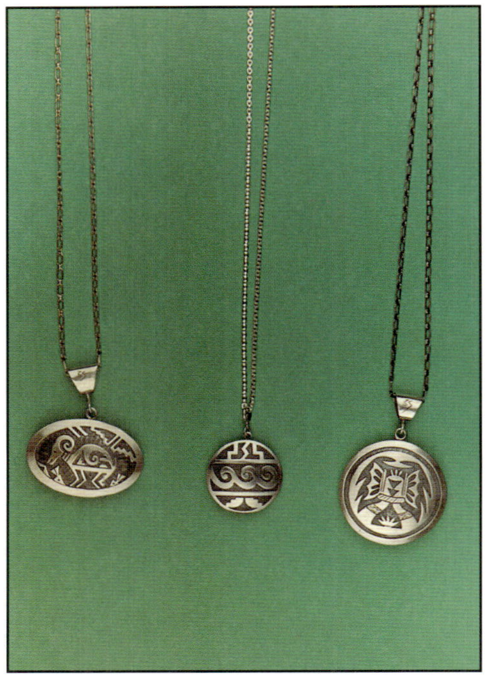

Three Hopi silver overlay pendants, which are decorated on both the front and back sides, late 1980s. *Enchanted Mesa collection*.

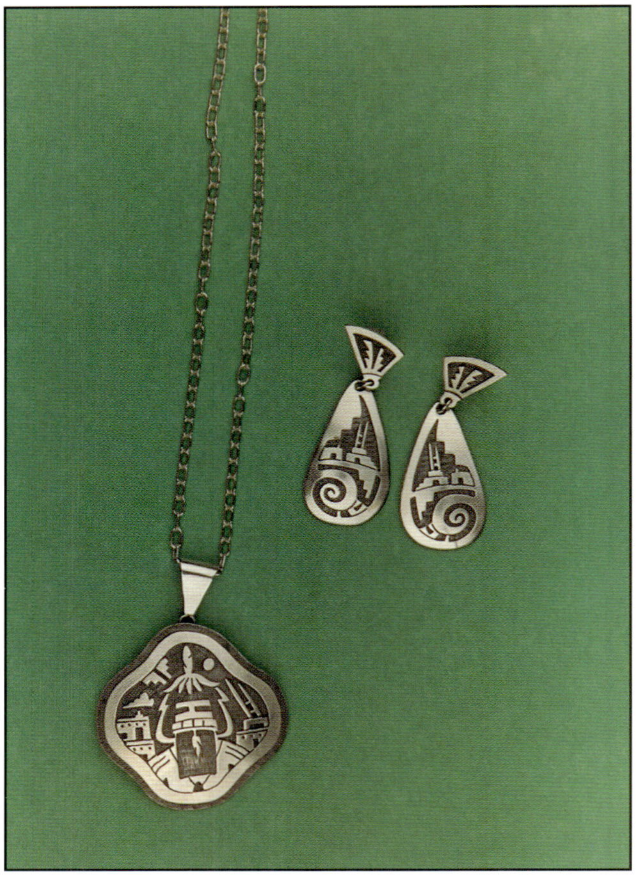

Hopi silver overlay pendant necklace and earrings, late 1980s. *Enchanted Mesa collection* .

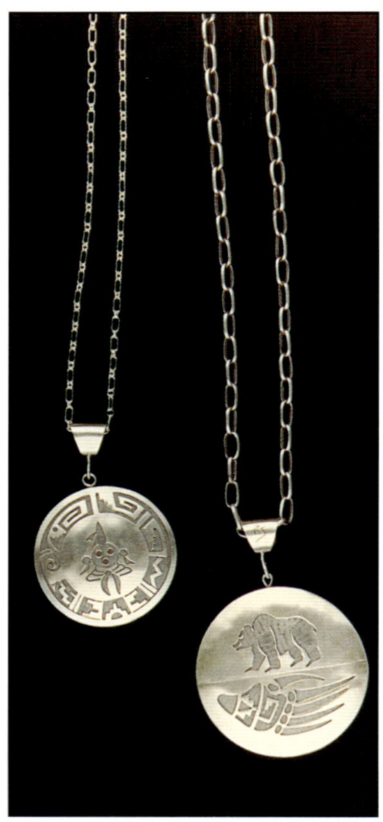

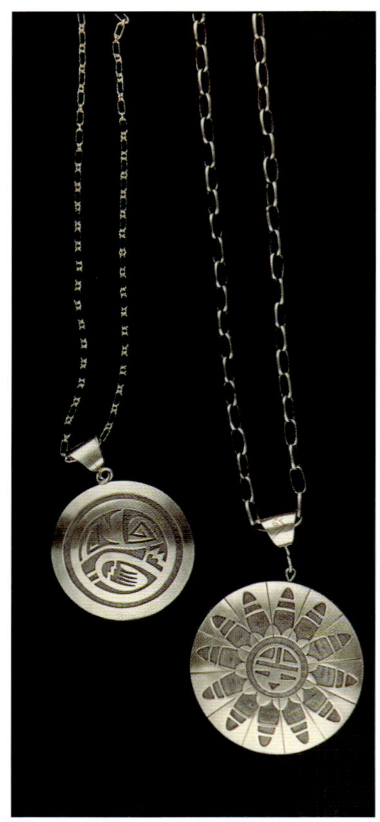

Two round pendants with overlay silver designs on the front and back sides, made by Hopi silversmith Bobby Sekakuku, late 1980s. *Enchanted Mesa collection* .

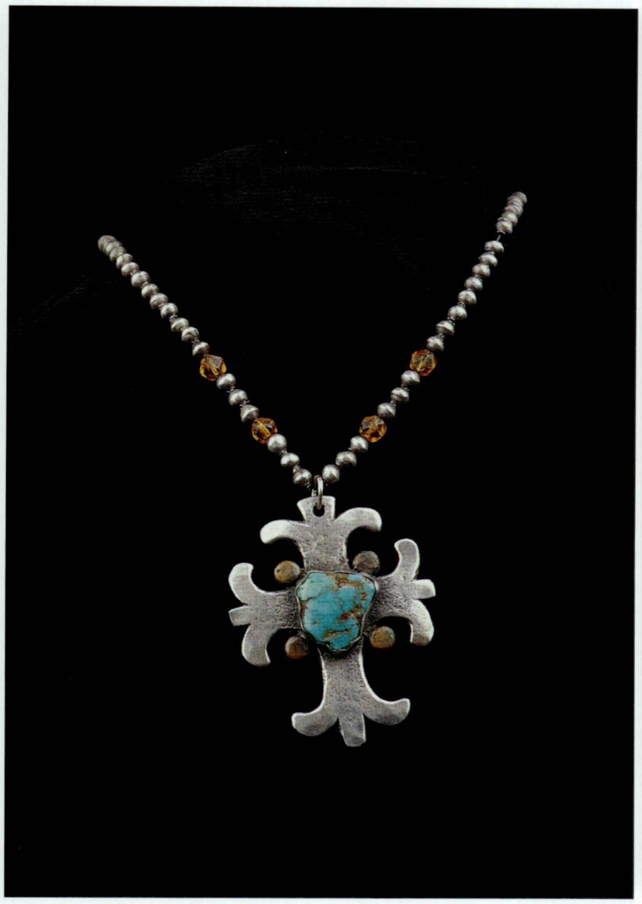

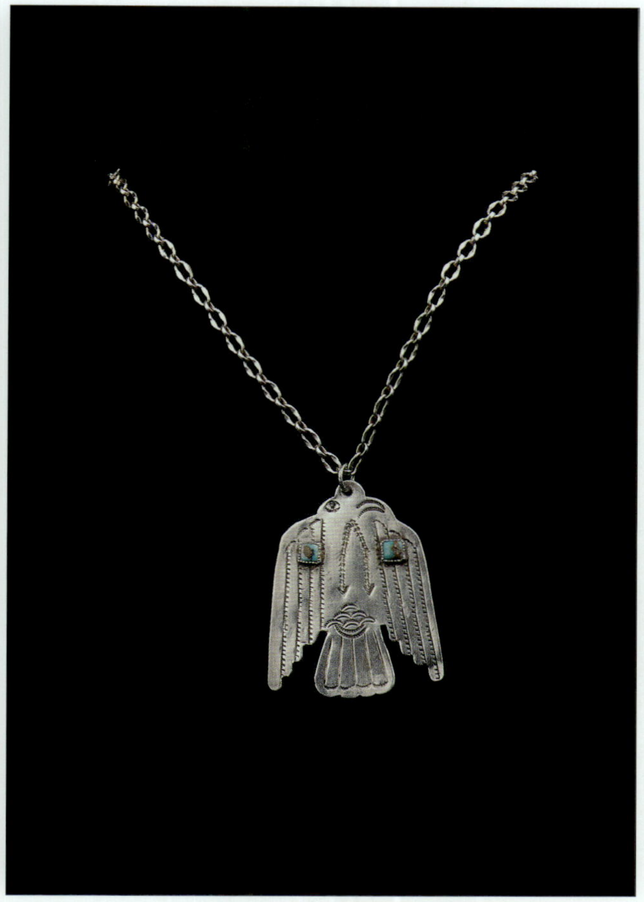

Left: Navajo necklace of small silver and citrine beads supporting a Christian cross pendant with squash blossom ends and a central turquoise nugget, c. 1920s. *Lynn D. Trusdell, Crown & Eagle Antiques*

Right: Navajo silver necklace with a link chain supporting a bird-shaped pendant and two small square turquoise stones, 1930s-'40s. *Lynn D. Trusdell, Crown & Eagle Antiques*

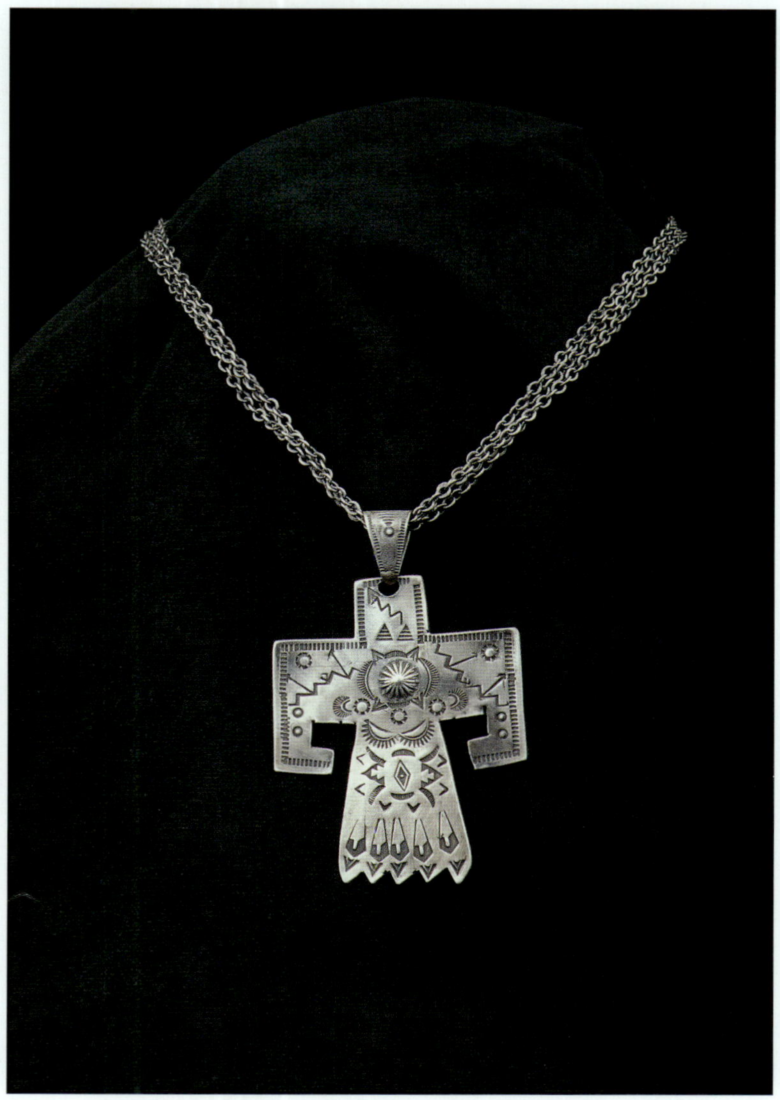

Navajo silver necklace with a double chain of links supporting a pendant of cross/man/thunderbird shape that is well stamped. *Lynn D. Trusdell, Crown & Eagle Antiques*

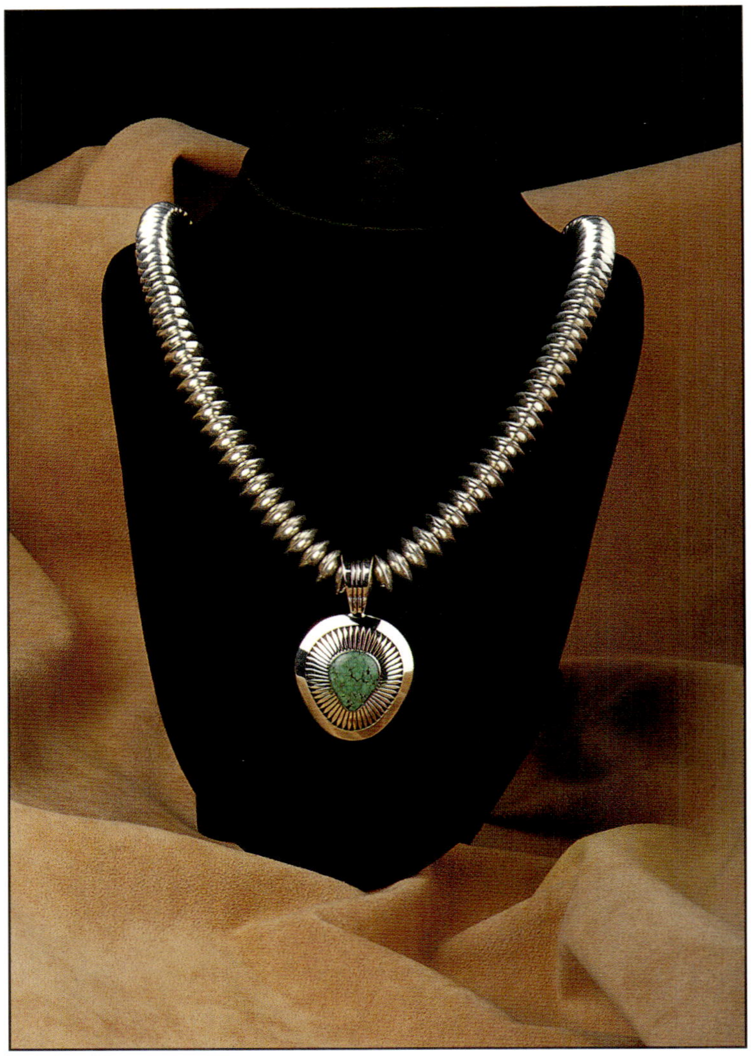

Silver bead necklace and pendant by Millie and Howard Nelson, 2002. *Courtesy McGee's, Holbrook* ($325)

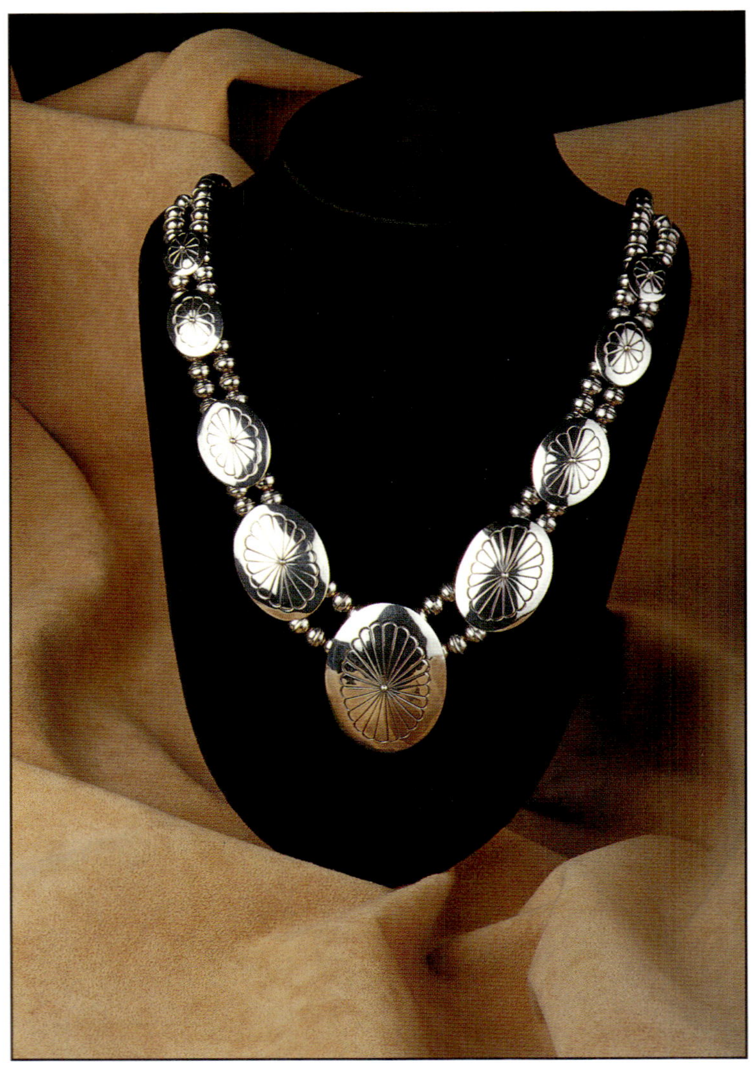

Silver necklace with round beads and oval conchas, 2002. *Courtesy McGee's, Holbrook* ($350)

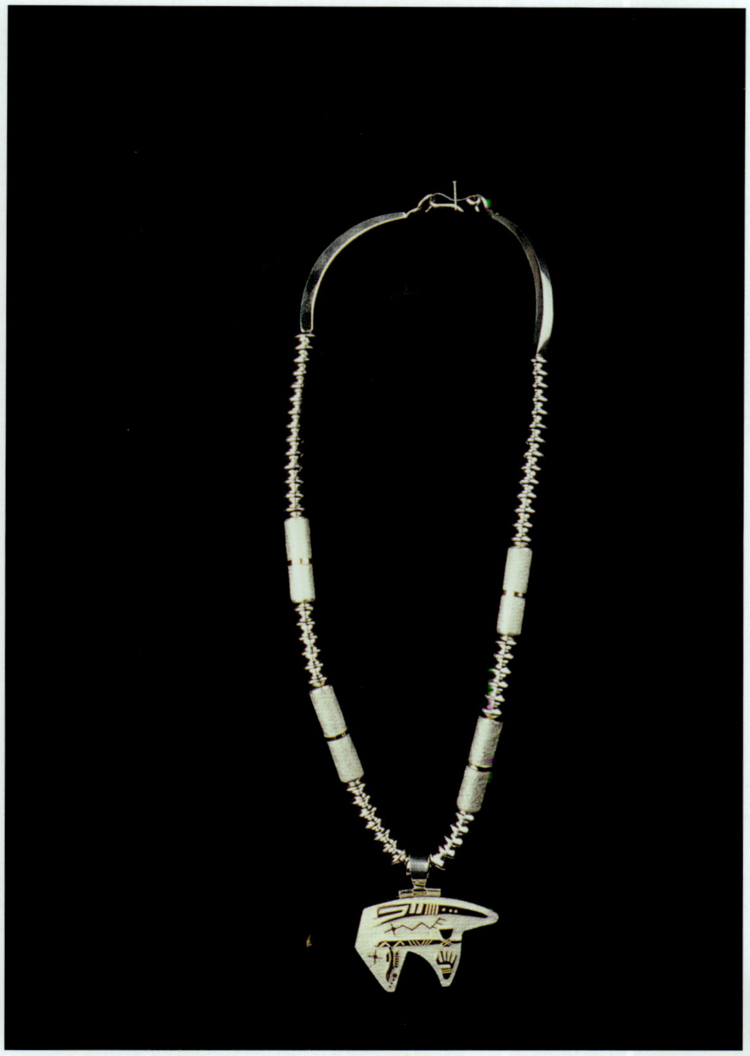

Necklace of silver beads with a pendant of Zuni fetish bear shape, by Jack Tom. *Courtesy McGee's, Keams Canyon*

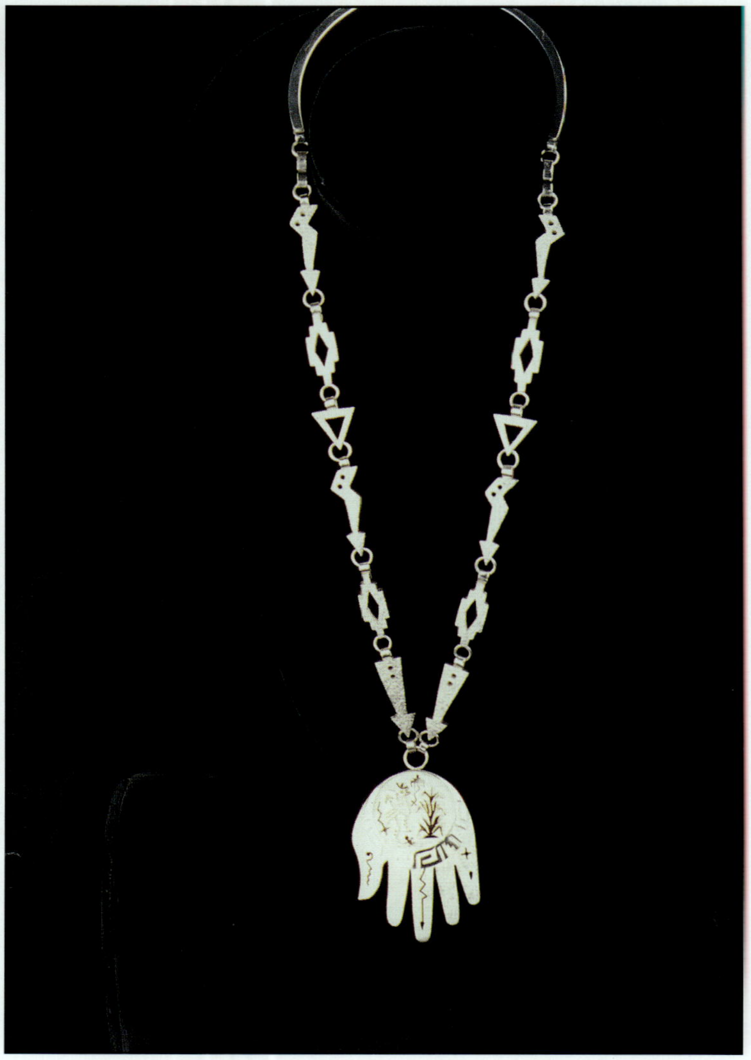

Necklace of silver links with a pendant of hand shape, by Jack Tom. *Courtesy McGee's, Keams Canyon*

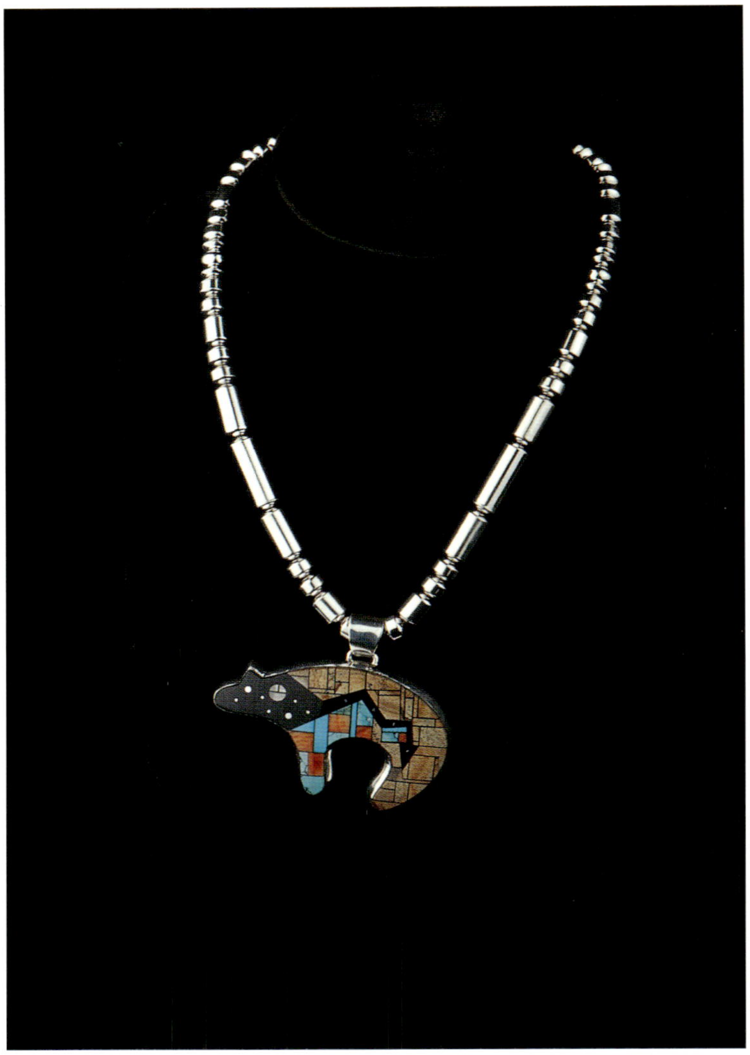

Necklace of tubular silver beads by Margaret Lee, Navajo ($150), and an inlaid bear pendant by Alvin Yellowhorse, Zuni. ($495)

Necklace of silver beads with five pendants of hand shape, and matching earrings, by Jack Tom. *Courtesy McGee's, Keams Canyon*

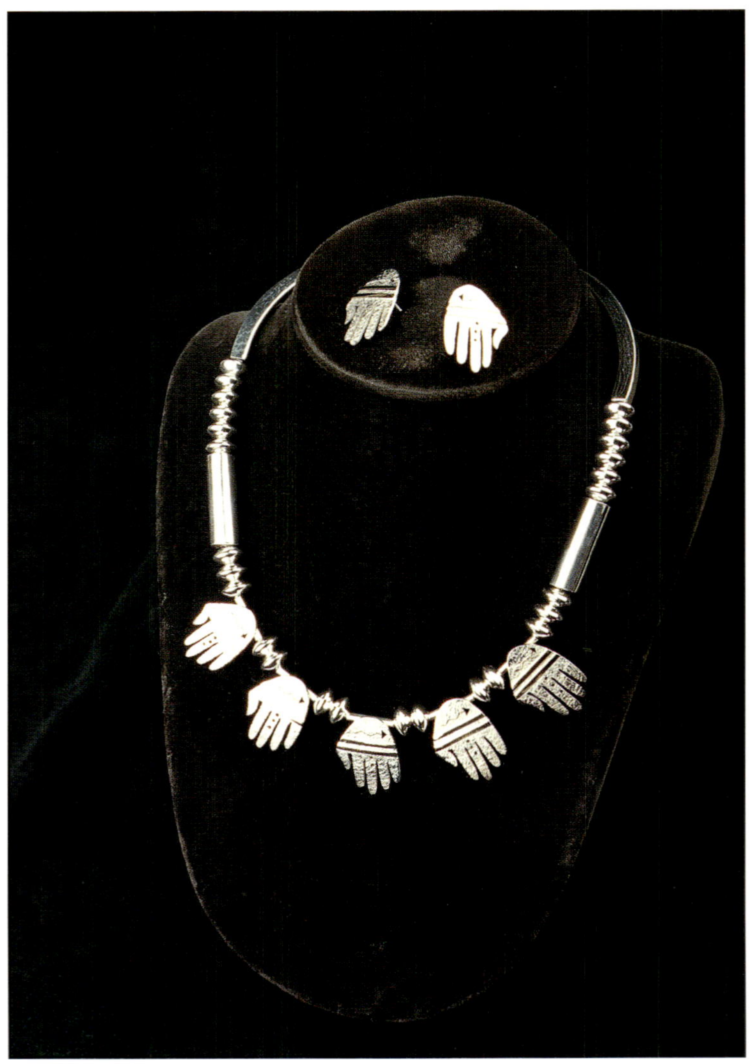

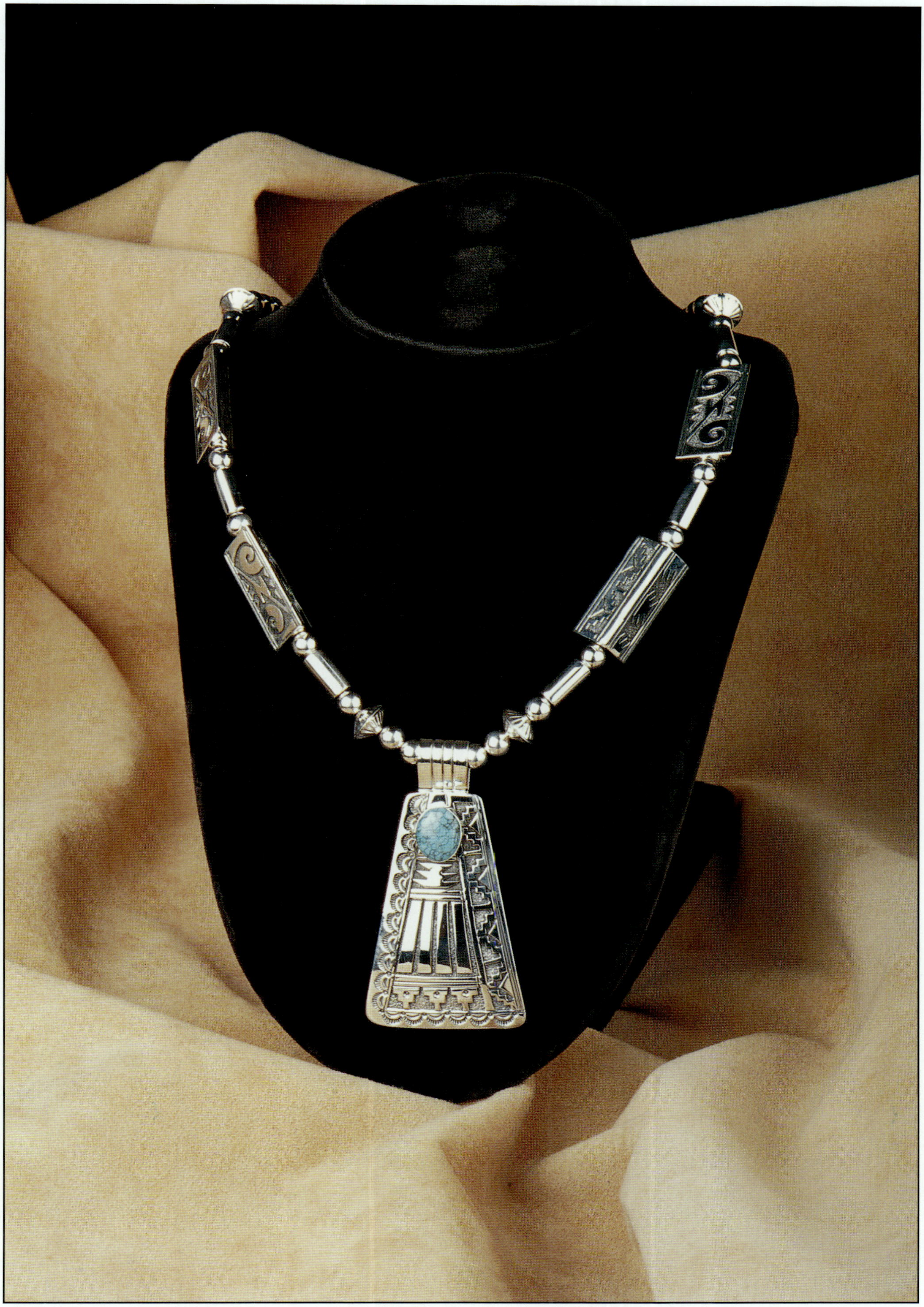

Navajo silver bead necklace with four triangular decorated beads and turquoise in the large pendant, marked Rew Dineh. *Courtesy McGee's, Holbrook*

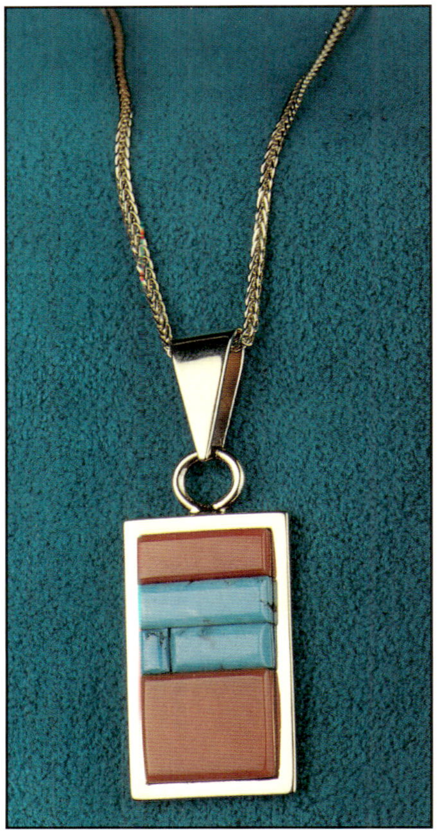

Gold rectangular pendant with coral and turquoise inlayed, suspended on an unusual chain, by Craig Agoody, Navajo. *Courtesy McGee's, Keams Canyon*

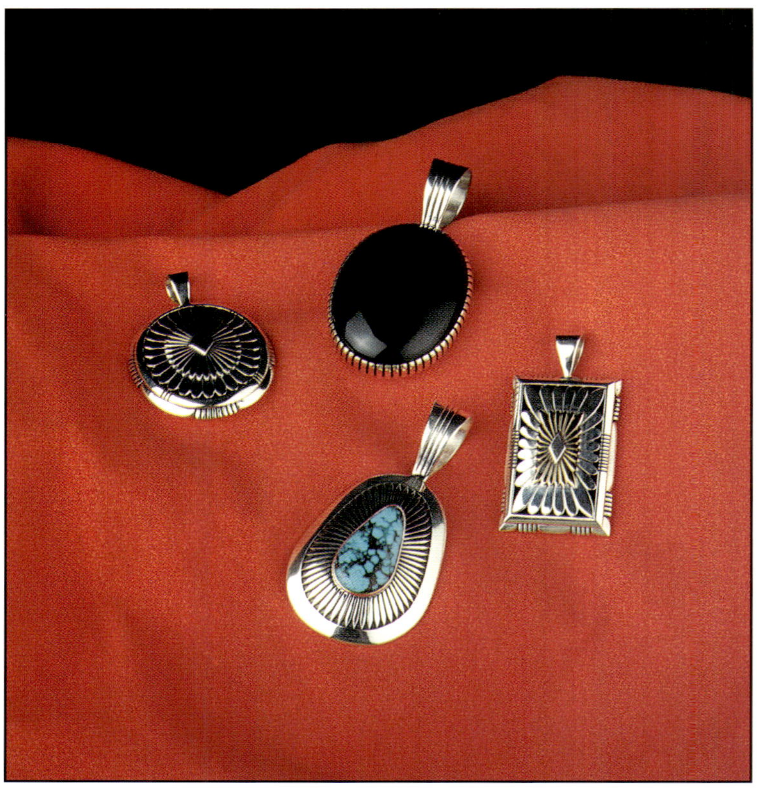

Four silver and gold pendants with fine detail and stone, by Howard Nelson, Navajo, marked Howard. *Courtesy McGee's, Holbrook*

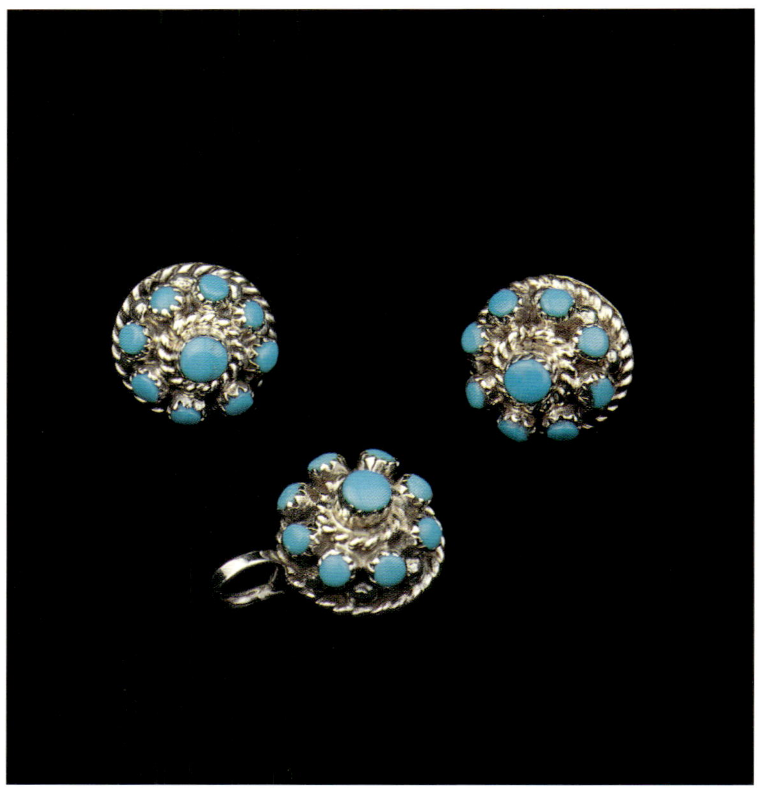

Matching Zuni silver pendant and pair of earrings set with small turquoise stones. *Courtesy of Palms Trading Company* ($27 and $49.50)

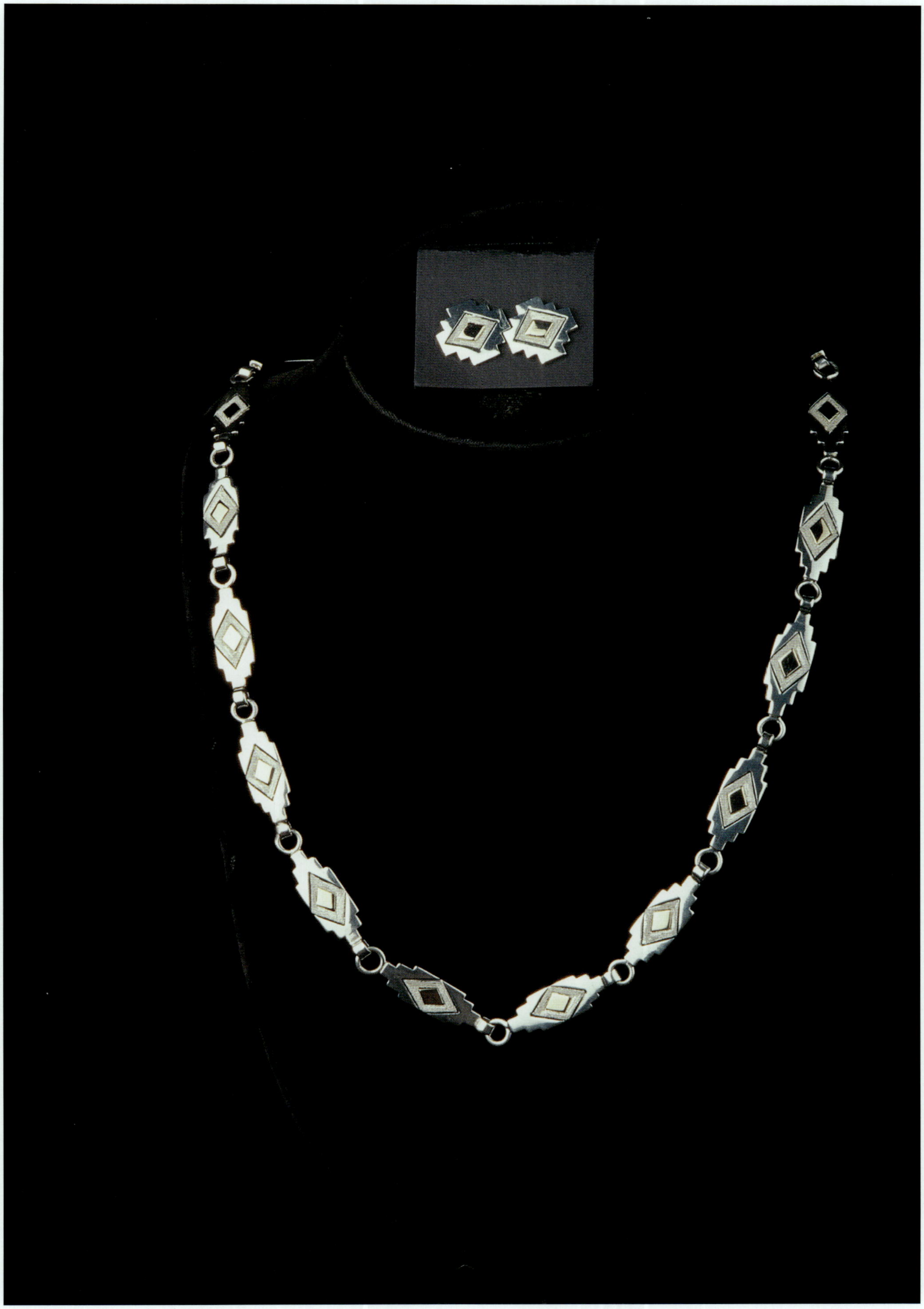

Silver link necklace and matching earrings with a gold diamond in the link centers, by Jack Tom. *Courtesy McGee's, Holbrook*

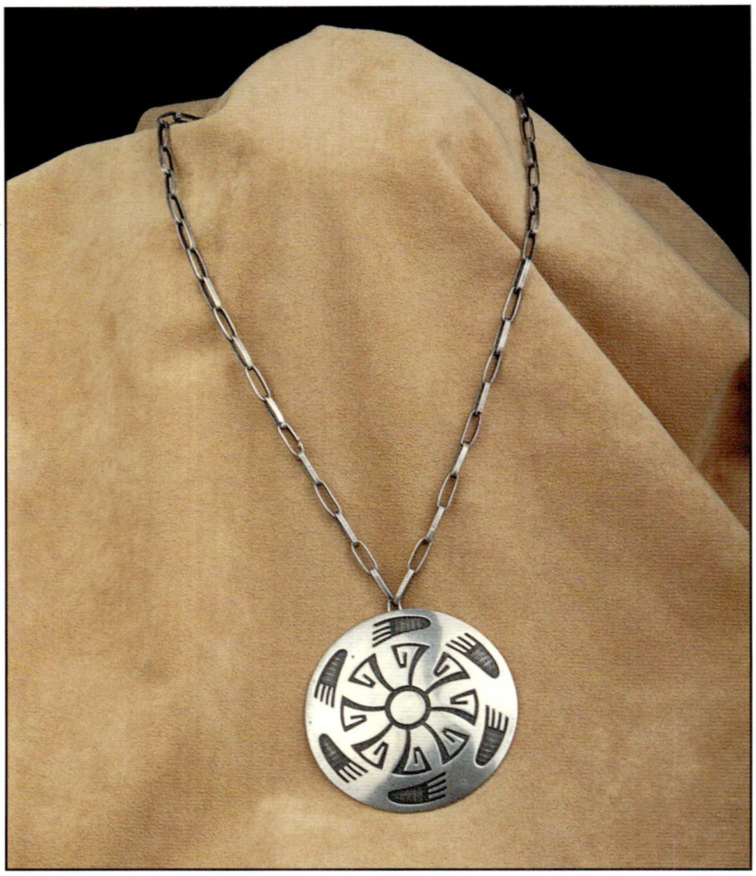

Hopi silver pendant with bear tracks completing a circle, 2002. *Lynn D. Trusdell, Crown & Eagle Antiques*

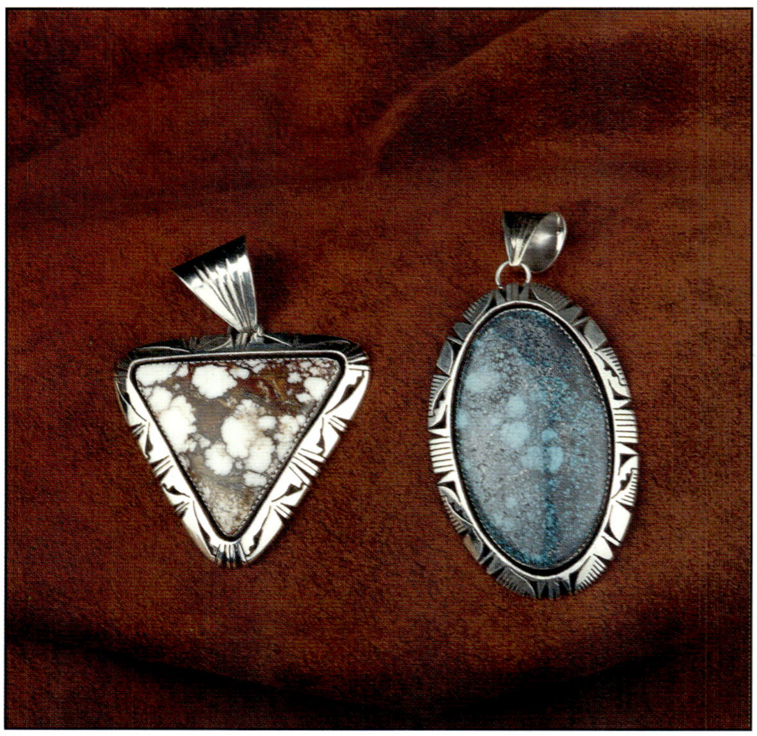

Triangular silver pendant with brown stone ($165) and oval silver pendant with Skyhorse turquoise ($330) by Bruce Wood, Navajo, 2002. *Courtesy of Palms Trading Company*

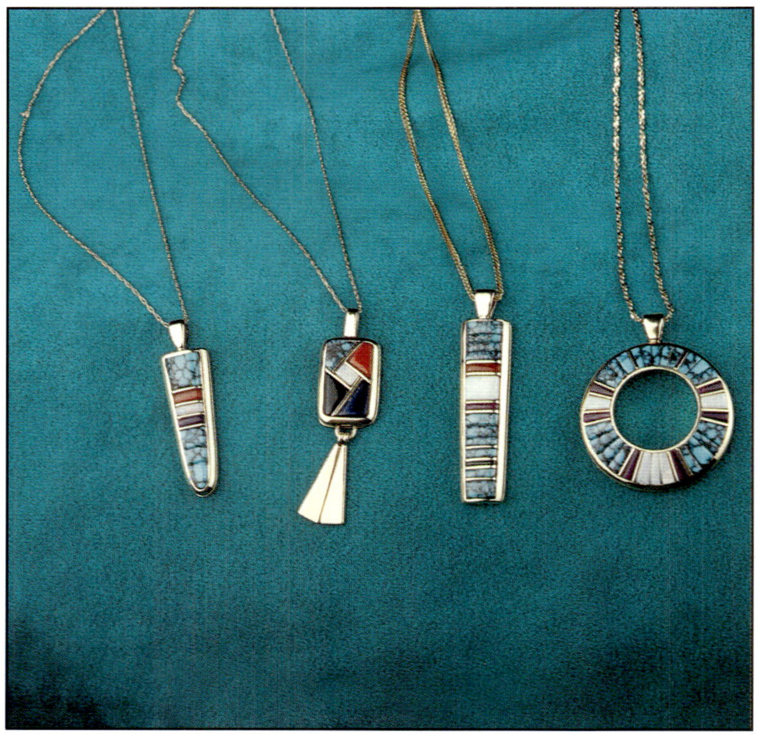

Four silver pendants with fine inlay of various stones by Fannie Bitsui, Navajo, 2001. *Courtesy McGee's, Keams Canyon*

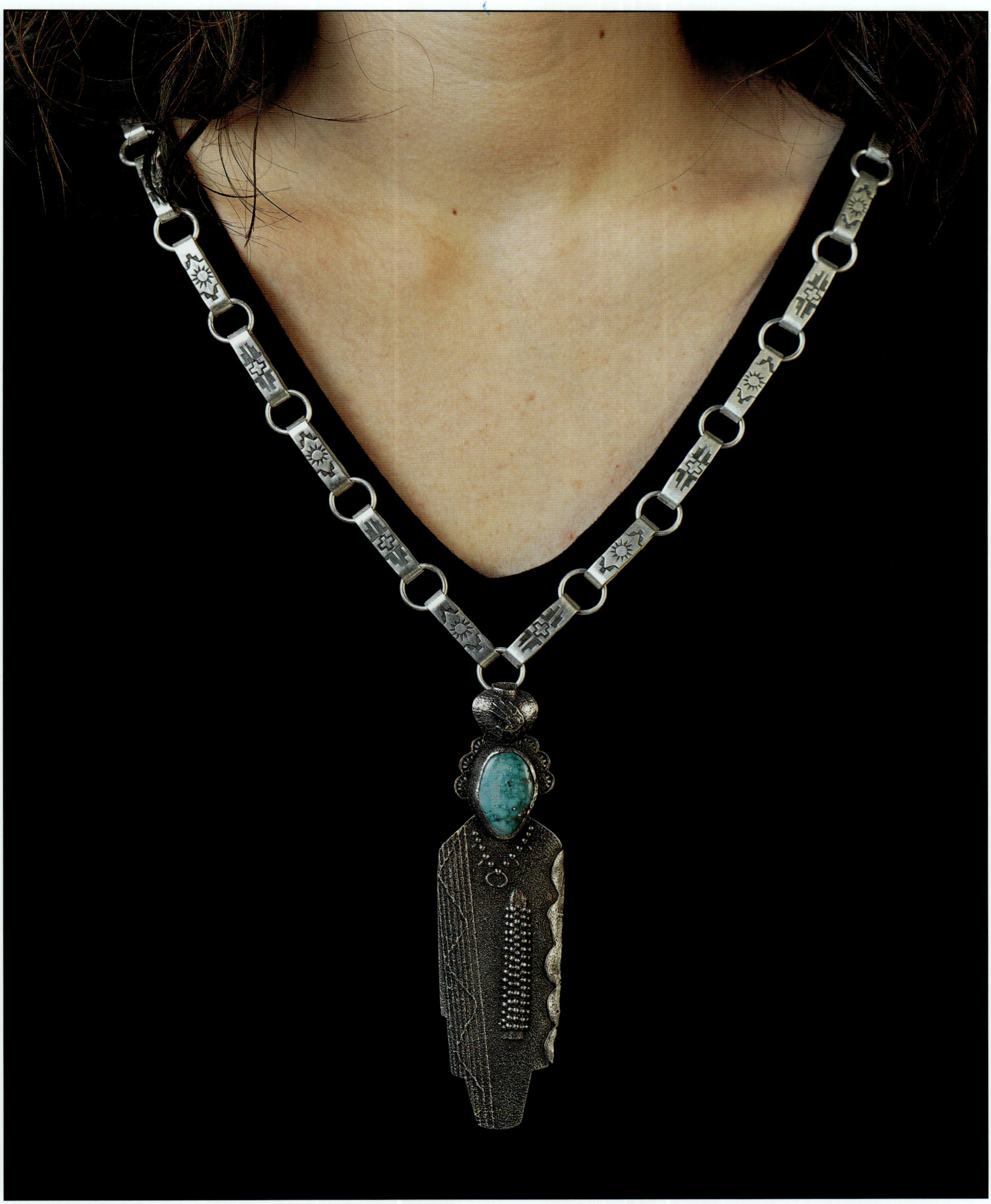

Sterling silver and Carico Lake turquoise spirit pin/pendant with decoration of the corn spirit and rain spirit designs suspended on a hand-stamped chain, by Anthony Lovato, Santo Domingo, 5" long, 2002. *Courtesy of Gerald Peters Gallery, Santa Fe, New Mexico* ($500 and $260)

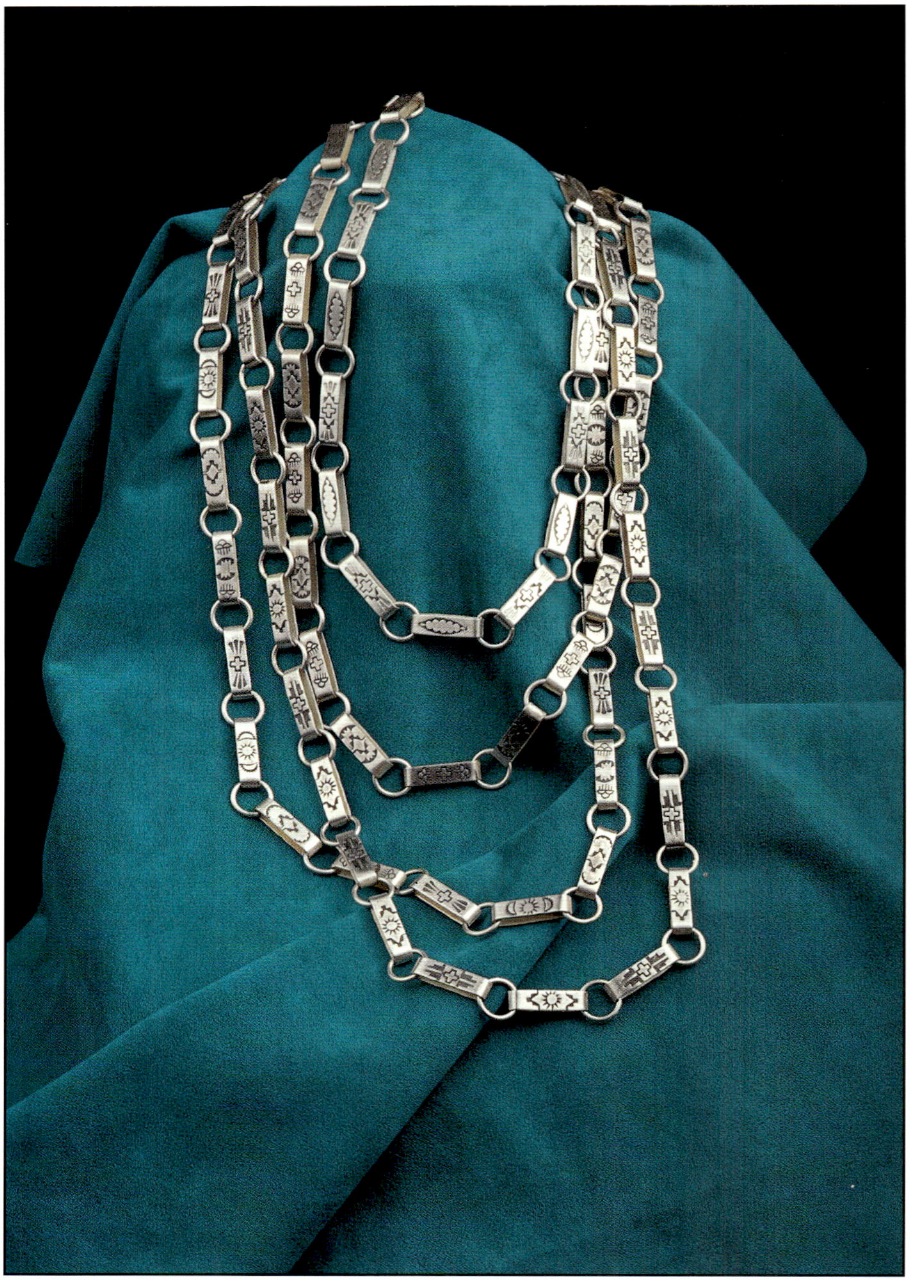

Lengths of hand-stamped, sterling silver chain by Anthony Lovato, Santo Domingo, 26" to 45" long, 2002. *Courtesy of Gerald Peters Gallery, Santa Fe, New Mexico* ($260 to $300)

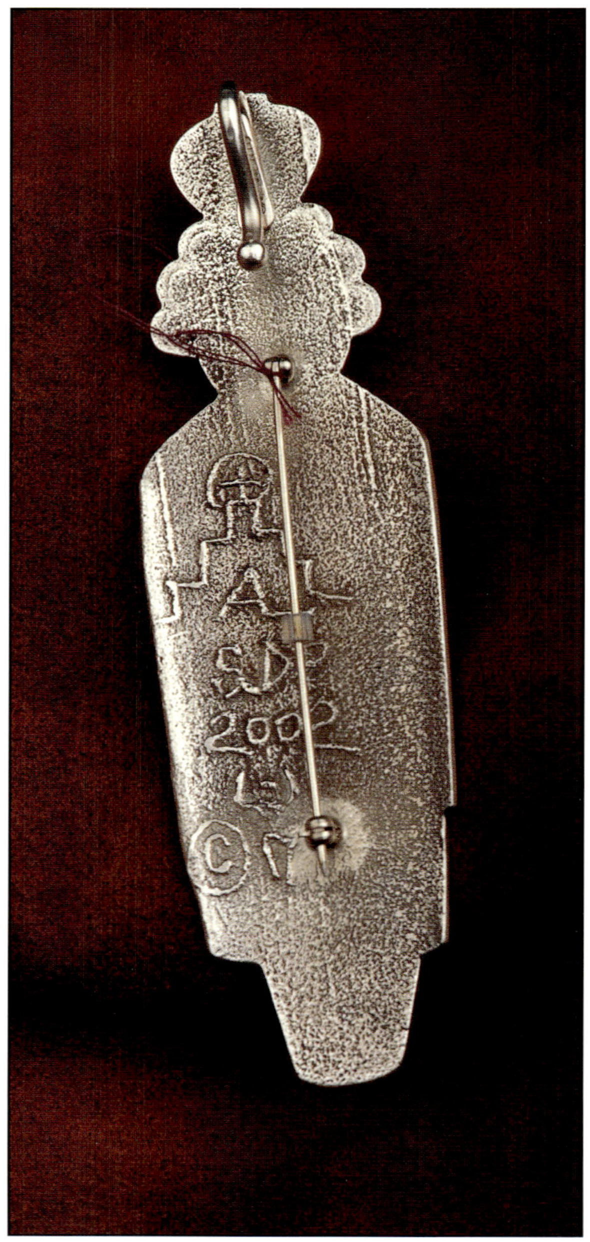

The back of the spirit pin/pendant by Anthony Lovato, Santo Domingo. *Courtesy of Gerald Peters Gallery, Santa Fe, New Mexico*

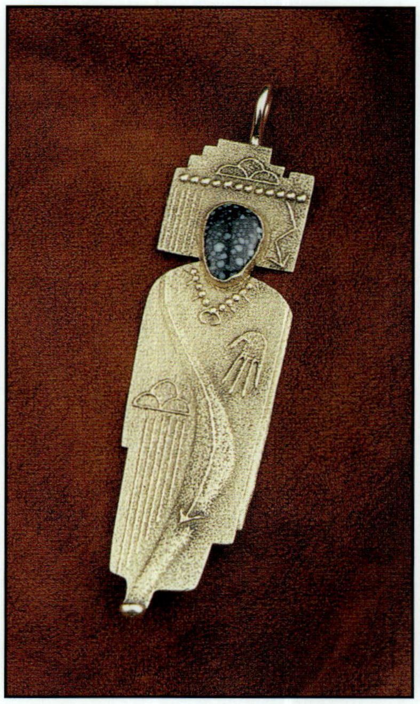

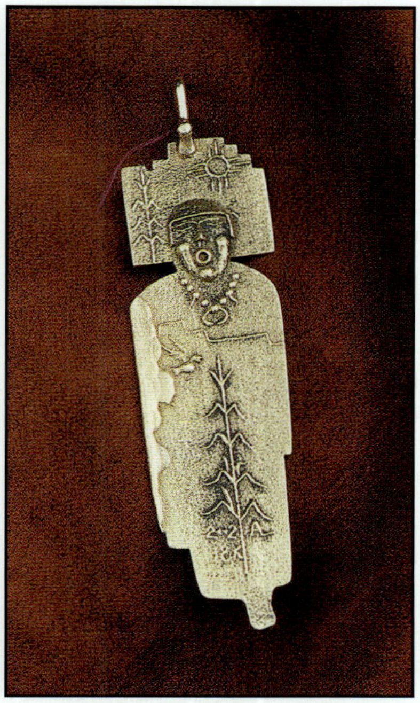

Reversible pendant of 18k gold and Tucker Mountain turquoise in a rain/corn spirit design by Anthony Lovato, Santo Domingo, 5-3/8" long, 2002. *Courtesy of Gerald Peters Gallery, Santa Fe, New Mexico* ($3000)

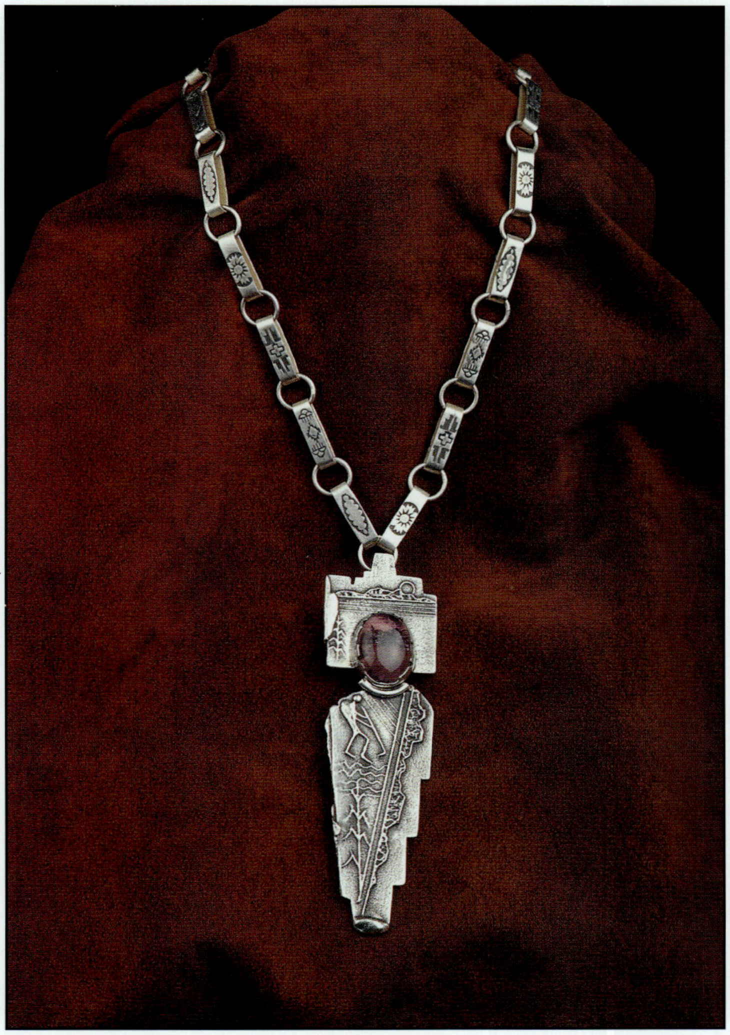

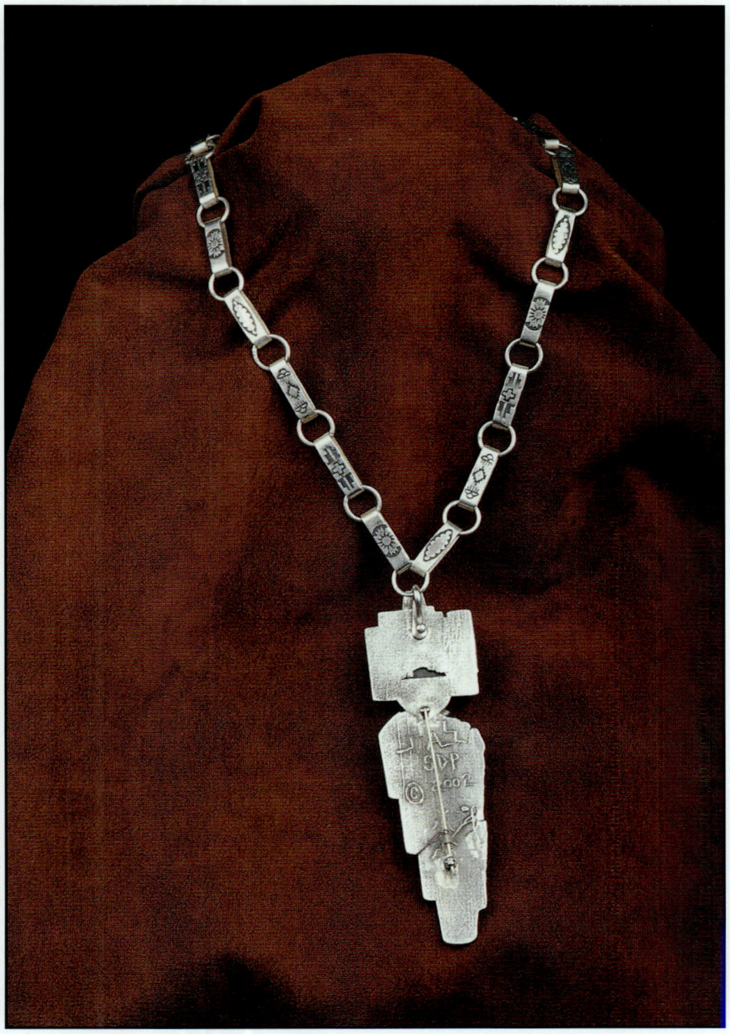

Sterling silver and pink tourmaline spirit pendant in "Sunset at the Corn Field" design by Anthony Lovato, Santo Domingo, 5-1/2" long, 2002. *Courtesy of Gerald Peters Gallery, Santa Fe, New Mexico* ($750)

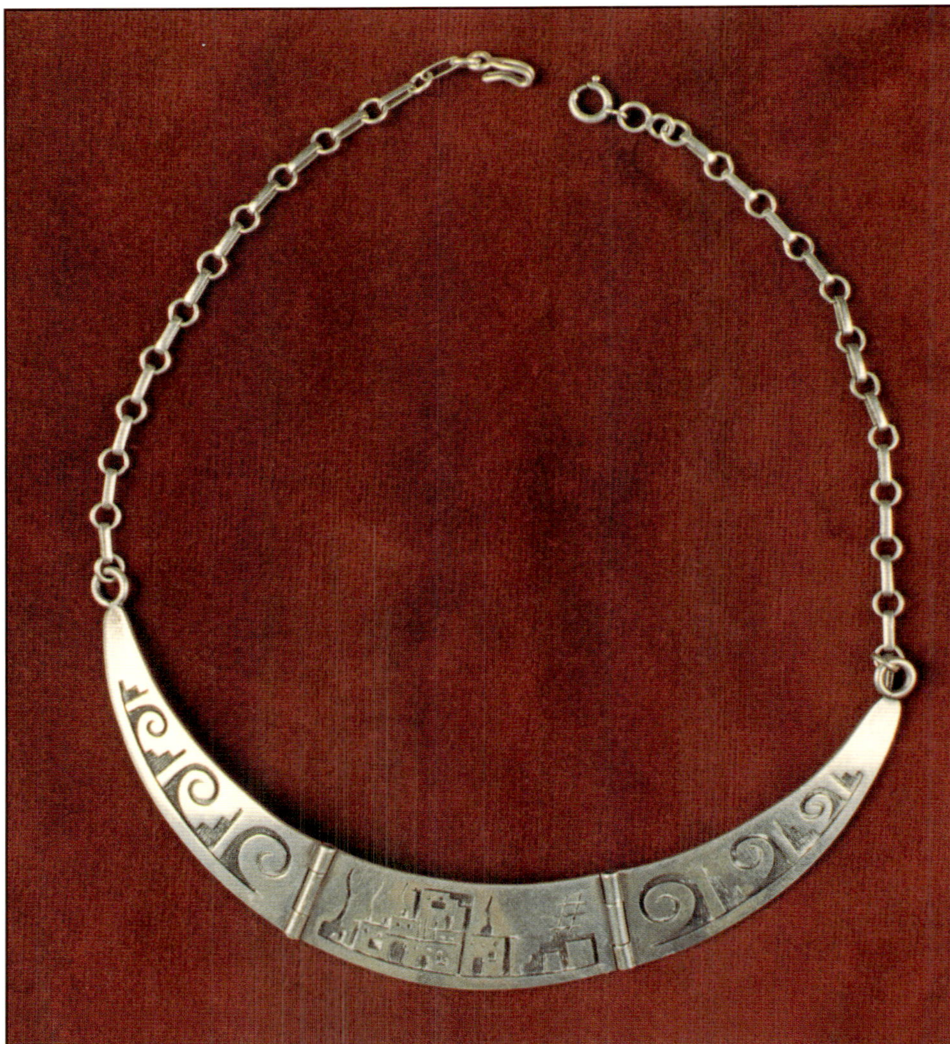

Modern Necklaces

Hopi silver overlay necklace of three hinged plates made by Myron Sekakuku in the 1980s. *Bromberg collection*

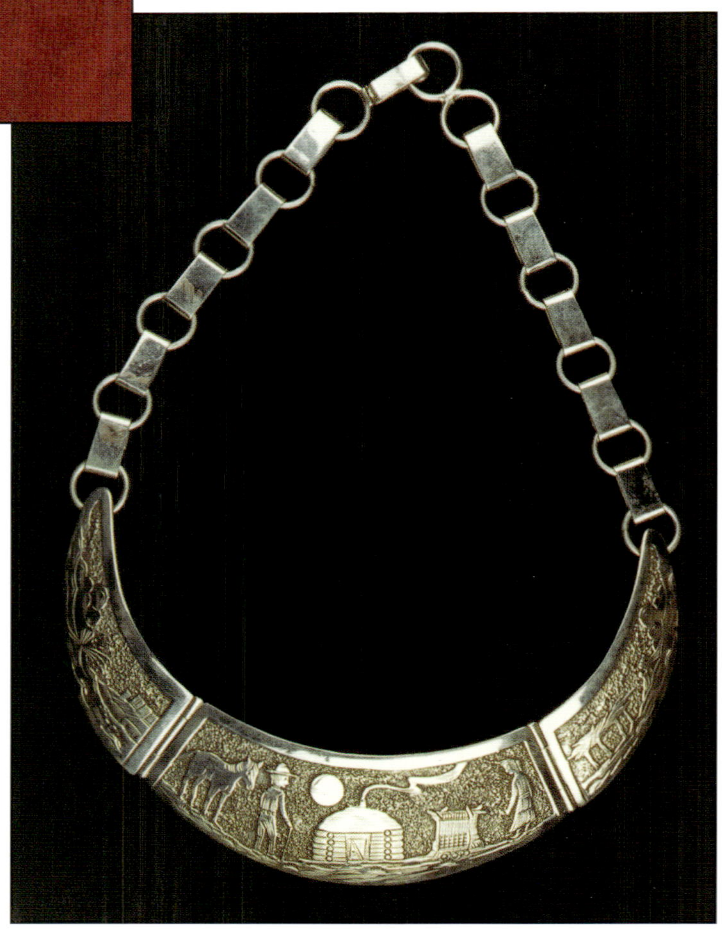

Navajo silver link necklace with three hinged plates decorated with an overlay narrative scene of family life from the 1980s. *Turquoise Lady collection*

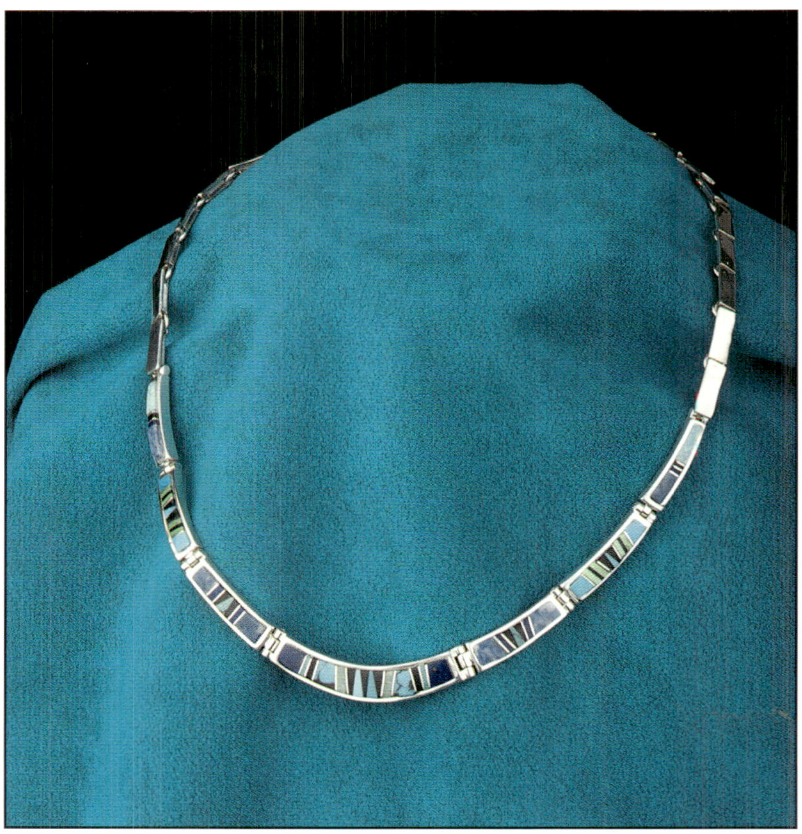

Silver link necklace with inlayed lapis lazuli and turquoise stone, signed by Calvin, Navajo. *Courtesy of Palms Trading Company* ($375)

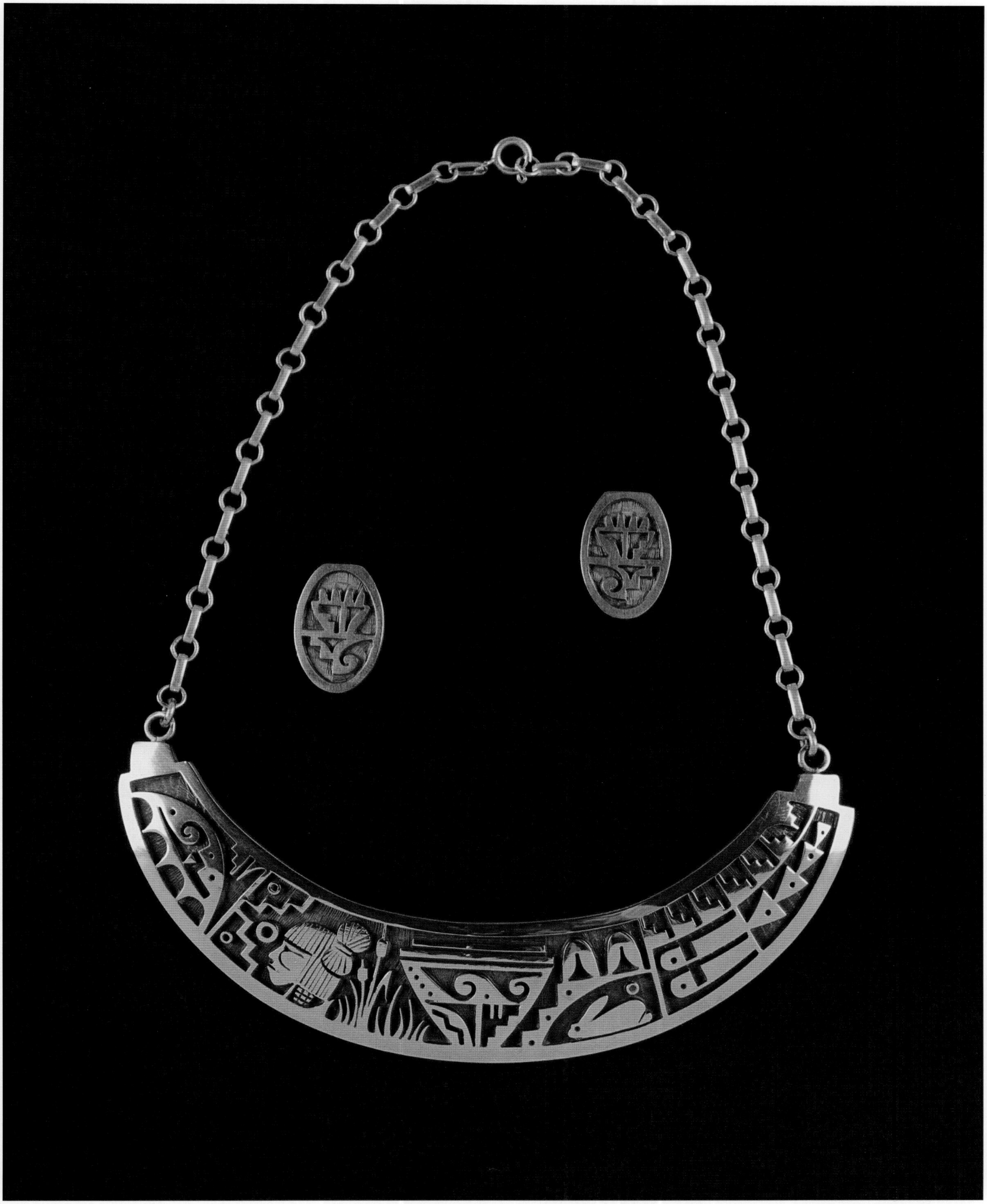

Hopi silver overlay link necklace and matching earrings, made by Chalmers Day, Hopi, 1989. *Indian Post collection*

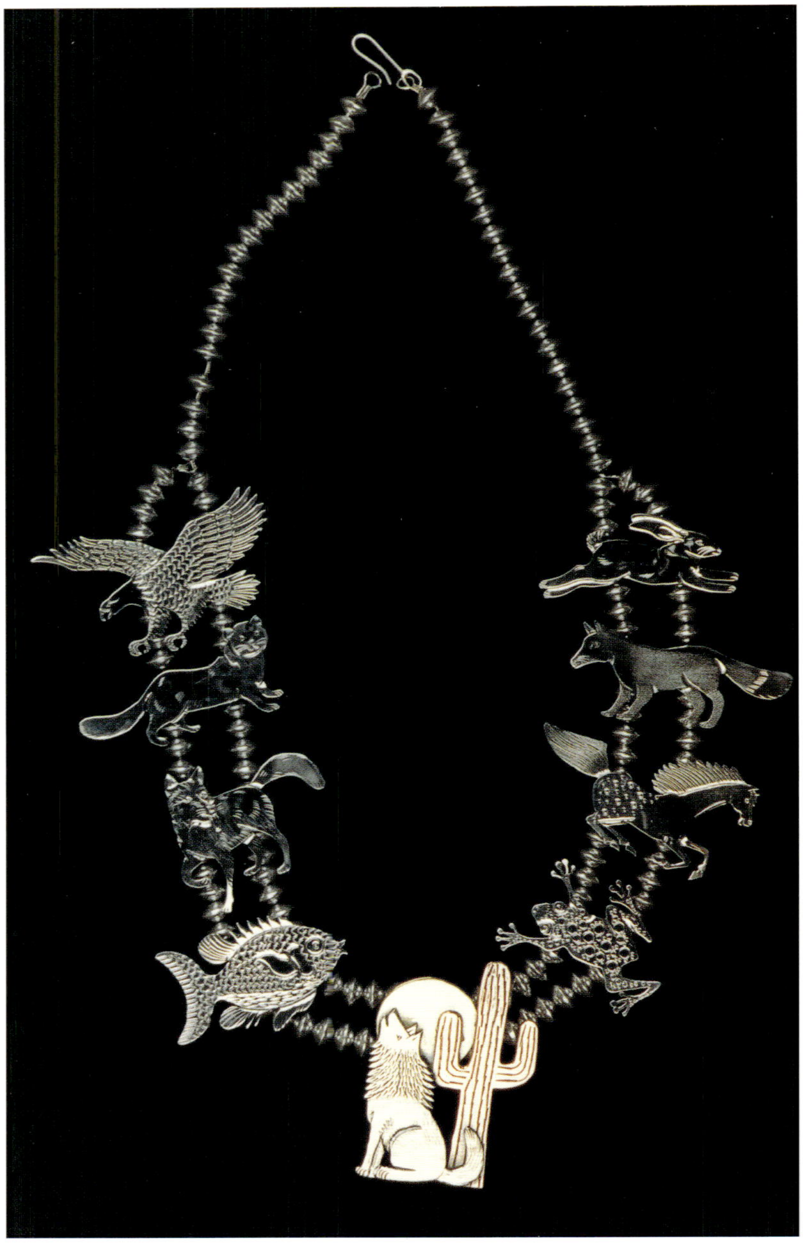

Silver bead necklace ornamented with silver animal plates, made in the late 1980s by Clarence Lee, Navajo. *Clarence Lee collection*

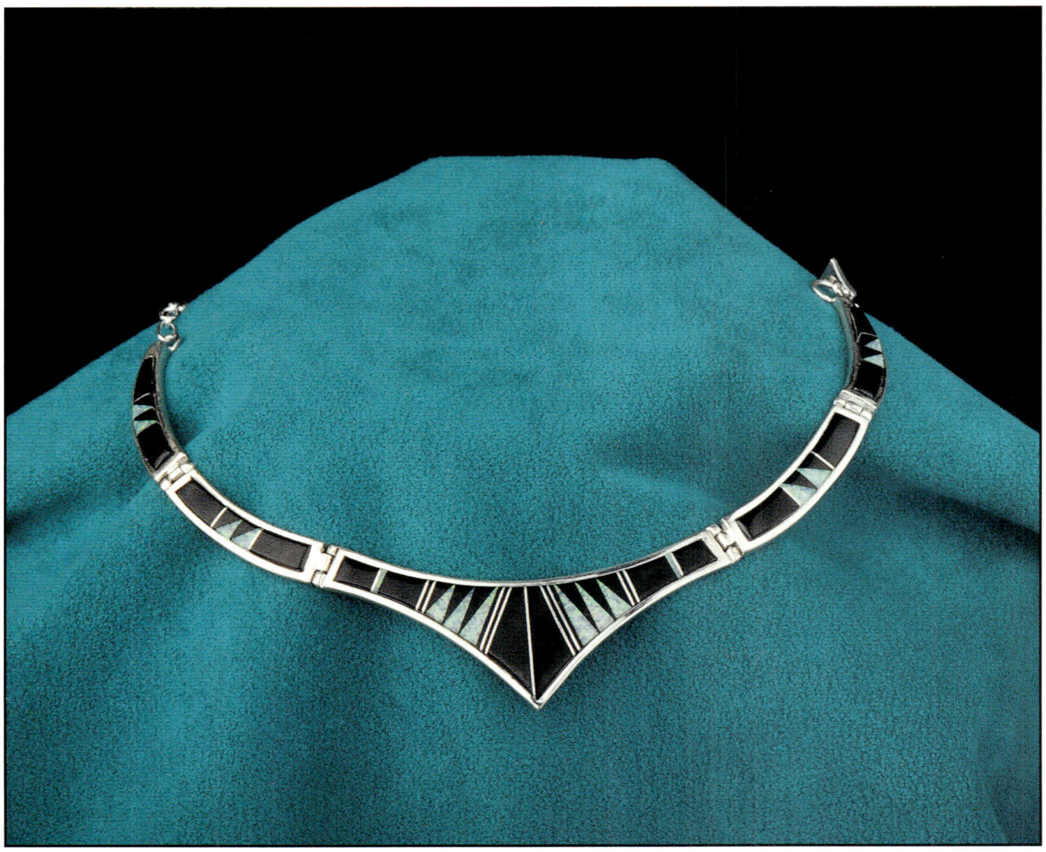

Link necklace and earrings set of cast silver and black and simulated opal inlay, by CB, Navajo. *Courtesy of Palms Trading Company* ($495)

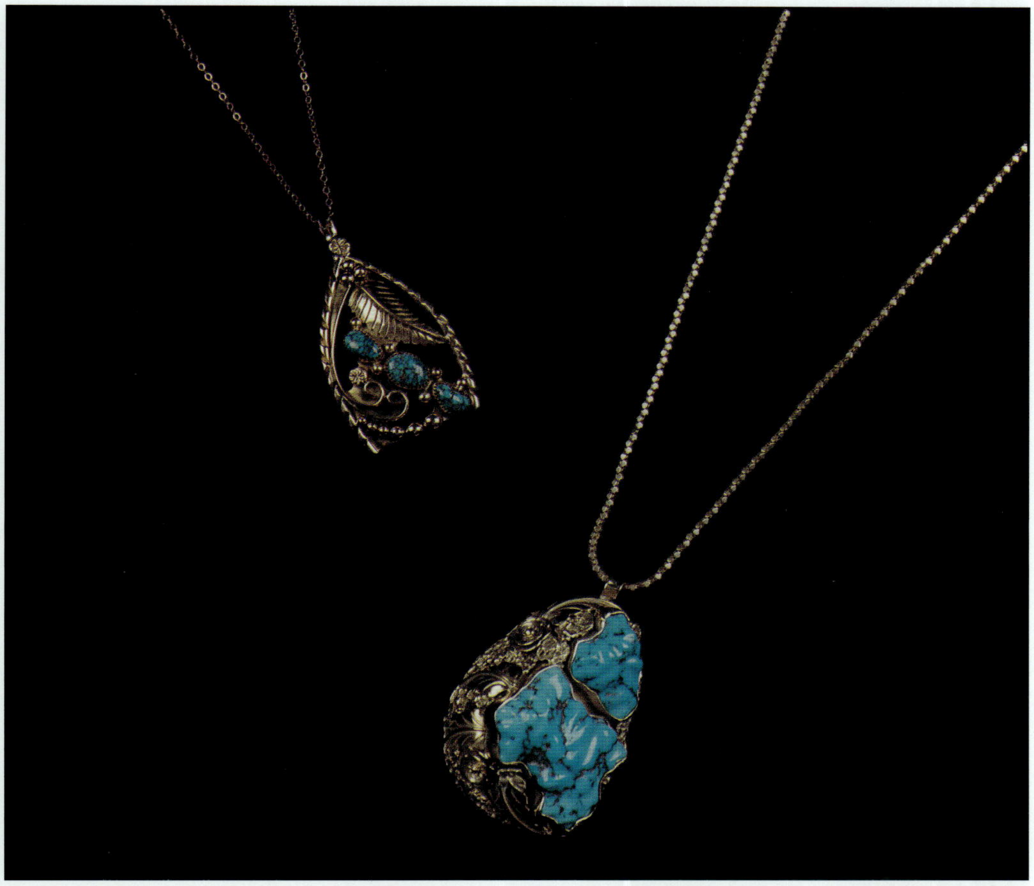

Two pendant and chain necklaces of gold and turquoise by Navajo goldsmith Leroy Benally, 1980s. *Private collection on permanent loan to Ohio University*

Gold necklace and earrings with an interesting change of textures in the design and oval turquoise stones set in serrated bezels, made by George and Nusie Henry, Navajo, 1989. *Indian Post collection*

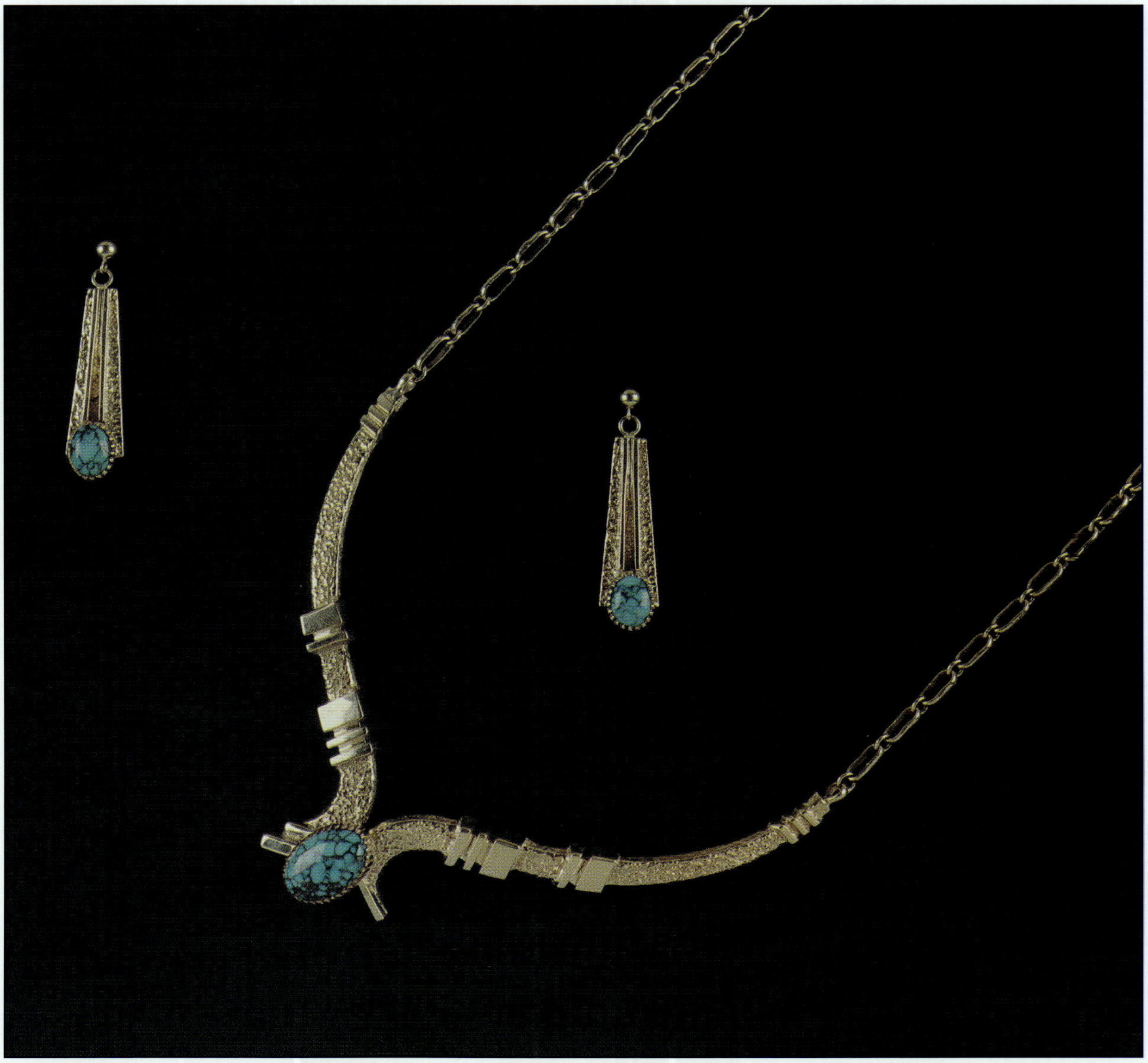

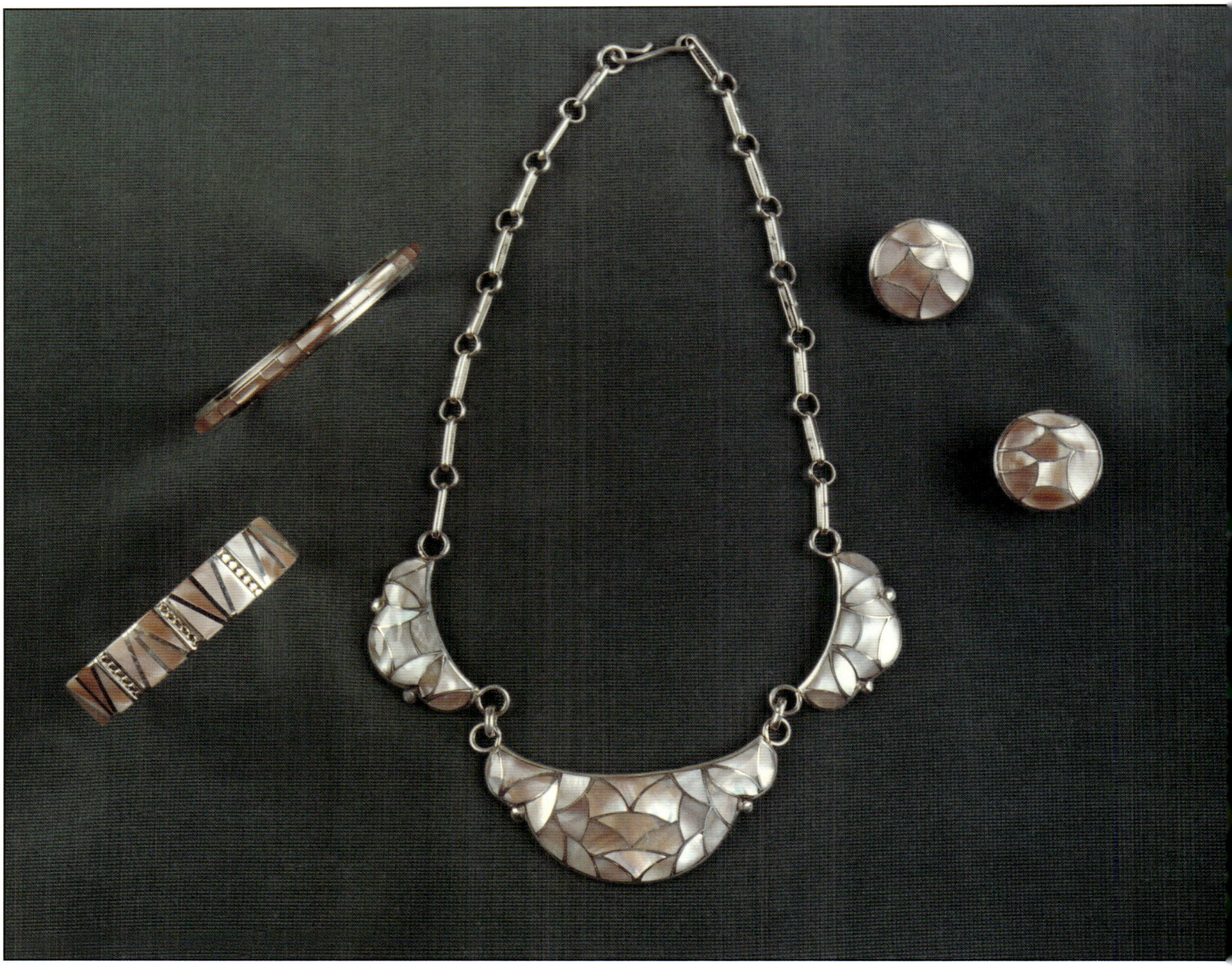

Zuni pink shell channel inlaid jewelry from the 1980s. The necklace was made by Orlinda Natewa and the thin bracelet by Velma E. Dewa. *Indian Post collection*

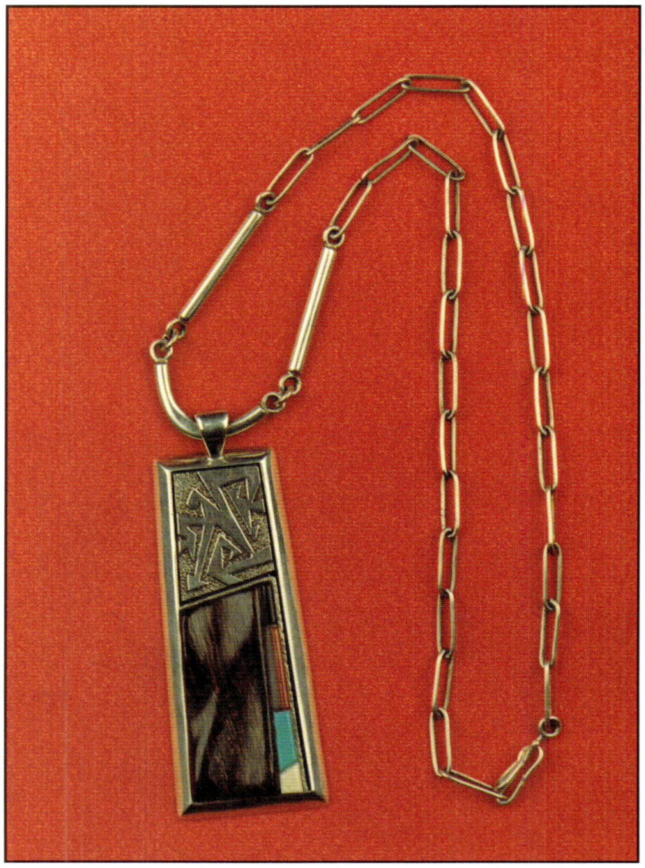

Pendant and customized chain of silver, the pendant with wood, jet, coral, turquoise and shell inlay in an original design made by Richard Tsosie, Navajo. *Private collection*

Pins

Women's pins

While pins have been a traditional ornament, especially for women in the Indian communities for a century, many have been made for sale to tourists who always liked a small and inexpensive souvenir of their trip to the Indian country. Quality, therefore, varies among pins probably more than any other form. In the Indian cultures, nickel silver and treated turquoise made a type of jewelry used for burial purposes, the family keeping the good old pieces.

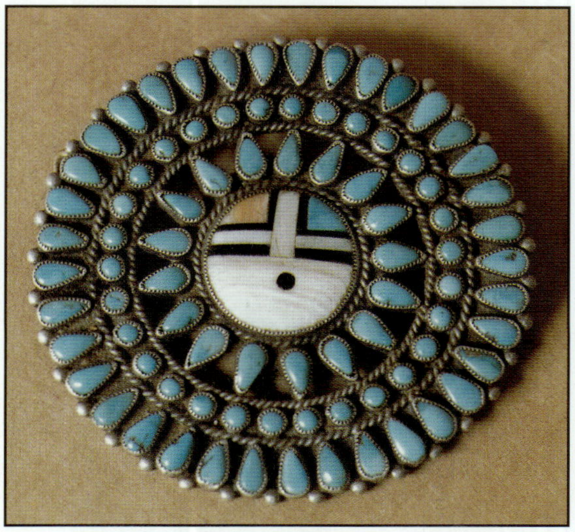

Zuni turquoise-set round cluster pin with sun face, circa 1985. *Adobe Gallery collection*

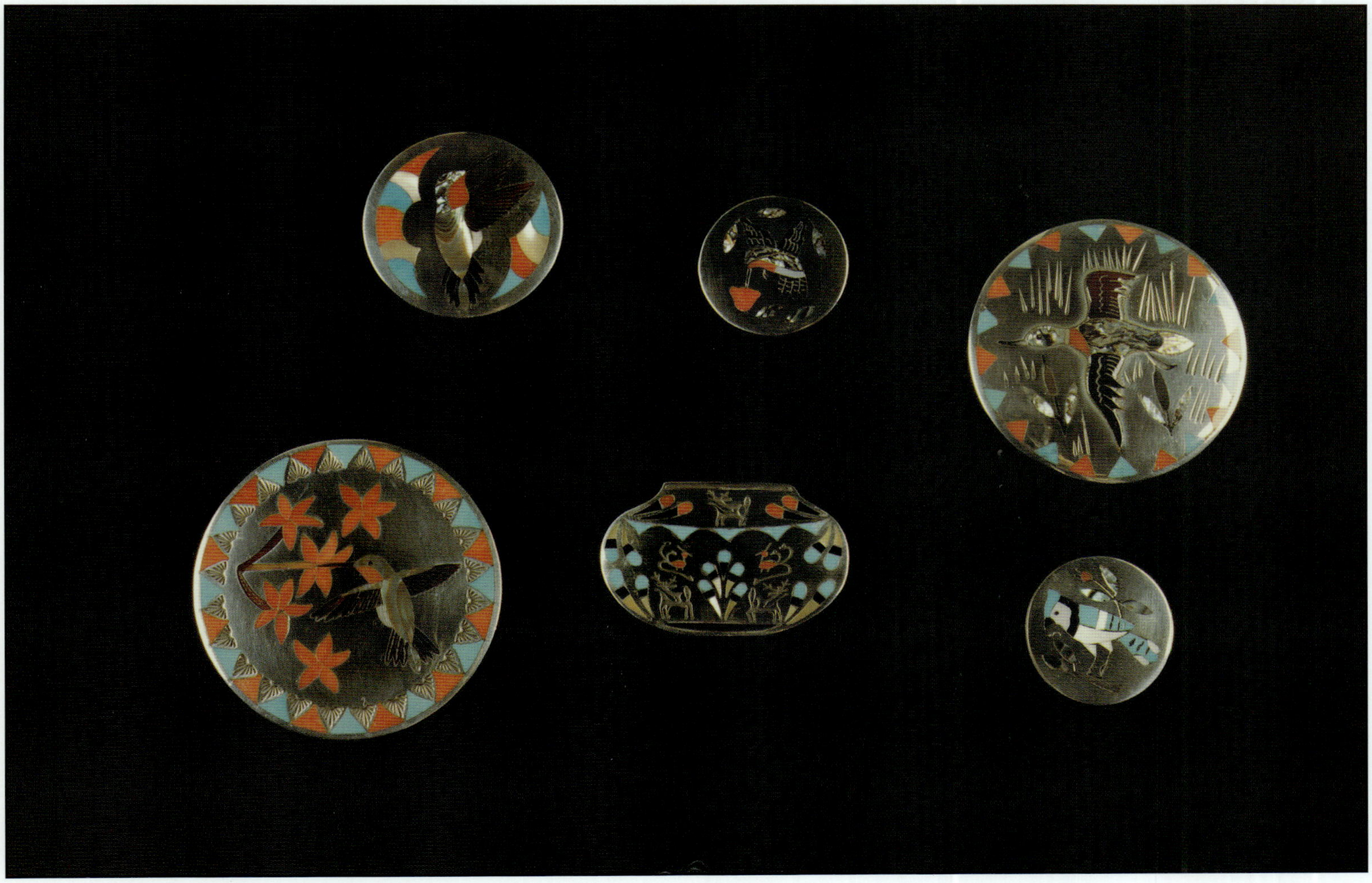

Six silver Zuni inlaid pins, circa 1980s. Top row from left: Small hummingbird pin by A.D. Banteah. / Small circular pin by S.C.Edaakie. / Large round pin with duck design by Jake L. / Below: Large round pin with hummingbird and floral inlay. / Bowl-shaped pin with floral inlay design by Q.P. / Blue jay on small round pin by S.C.Edaakie. *Indian Post collection*.

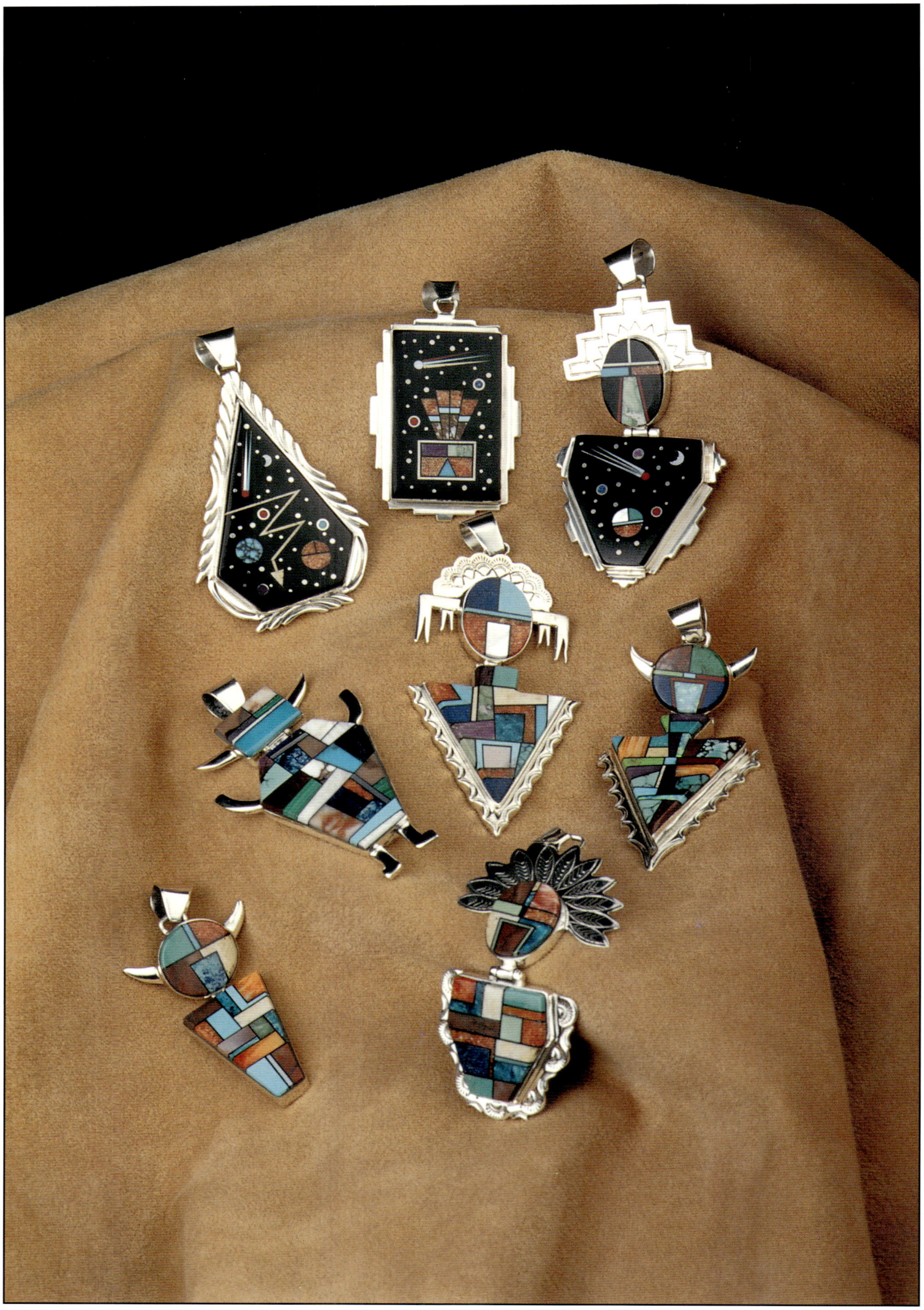

Group of eight pins and pendants with imaginative designs and fine quality stone inlay by Earl Plummer, Navajo, 2002. *Courtesy McGee's, Holbrook*

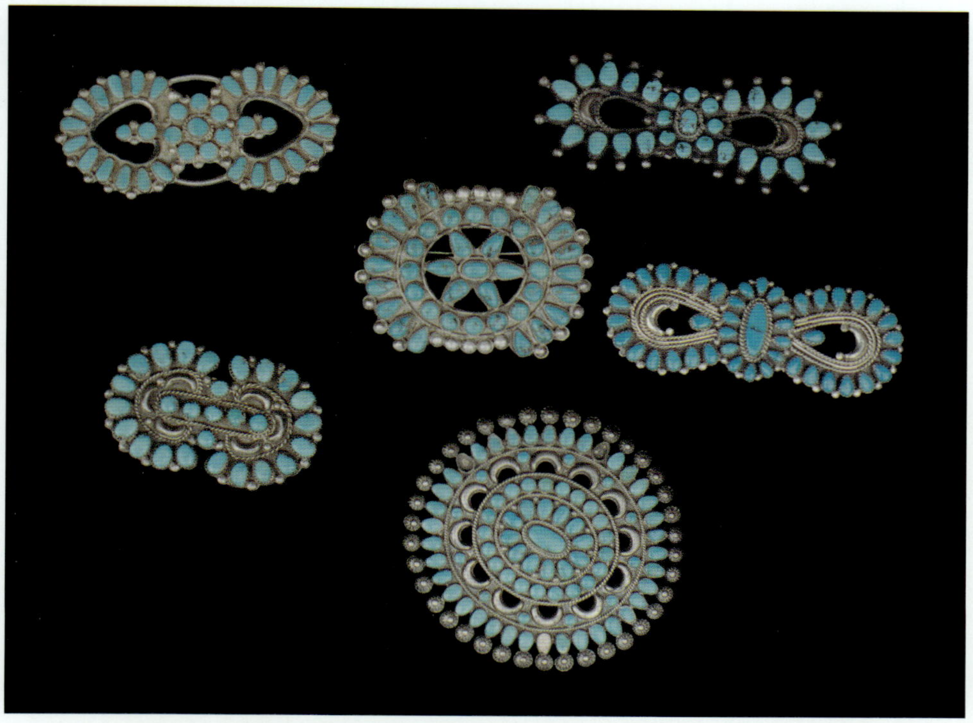

Old traditional-style Zuni pins of sterling silver set with small pieces of Kingman, Morenci, and Smokey Valley turquoise stones. One piece in this group is nickel silver with treated turquoise, probably made for burial purposes to replicate an old family piece. Circa 1940s. *Dennehotso collection*

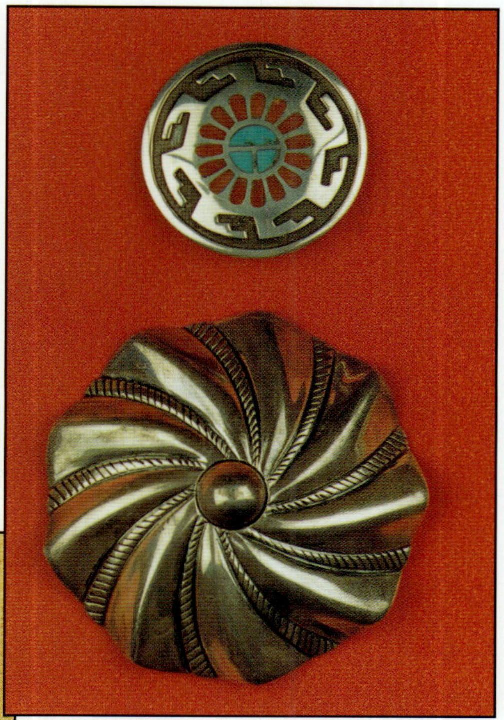

Two Navajo round silver pins of overlay (top) and stamped wrought decoration. *Private collection*

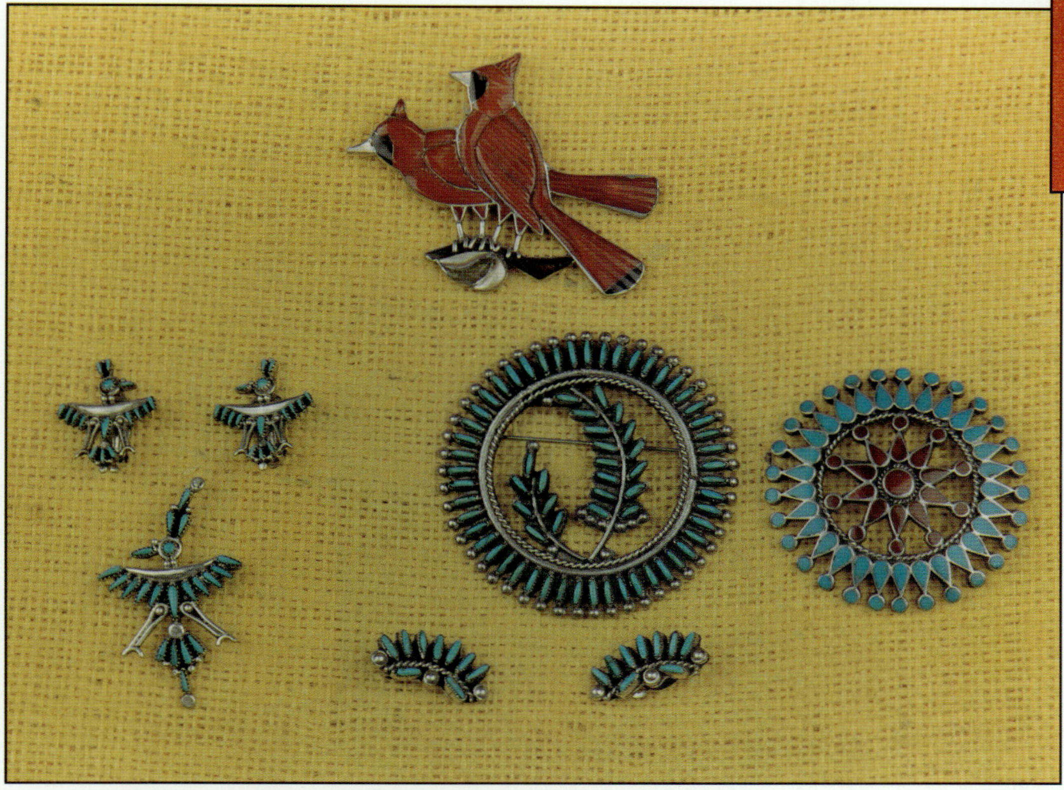

Zuni inlaid pins (coral-set cardinals) and earrings from the 1970s. The tiny turquoise needlepoint stones display fine quality stone-carving skills. *Private collection*

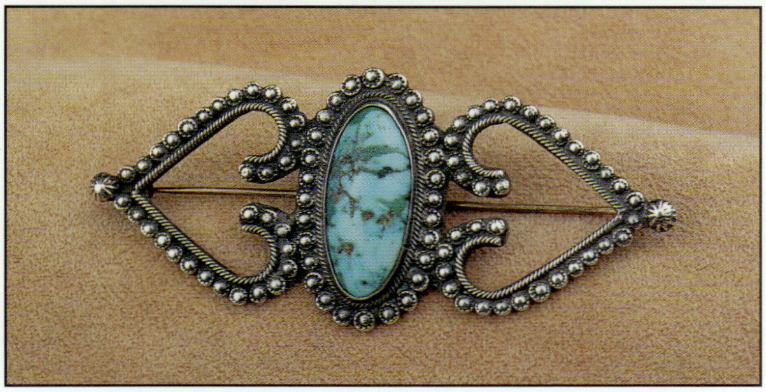

Navajo silver pin with turquoise and featuring a heart design that was such a favorite in the 1920s when it was made. *Lynn D. Trusdell, Crown & Eagle Antiques*

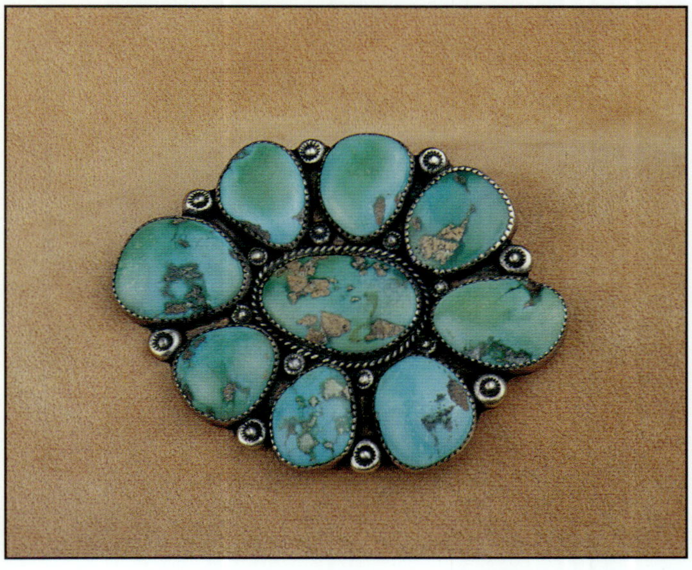

Large and beautiful Navajo cluster pin with turquoise stones, c.1930s-'40s. *Lynn D. Trusdell, Crown & Eagle Antiques*

Seven Zuni unmarked pins of bird and geometric inlay design, all made in the 1980s, surround an unusual Zuni-made sweater guard with chain by Shirley and Virgil Benn. *Indian Post collection*.

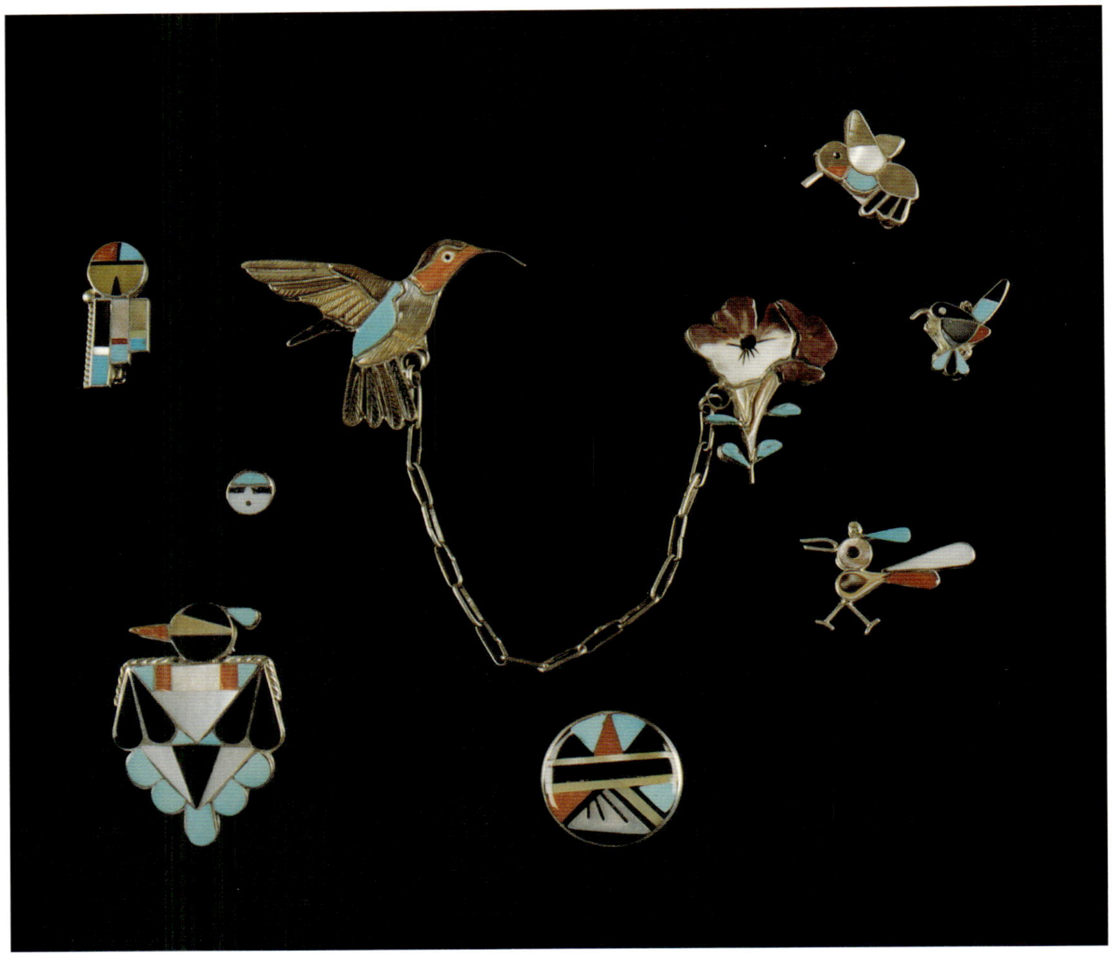

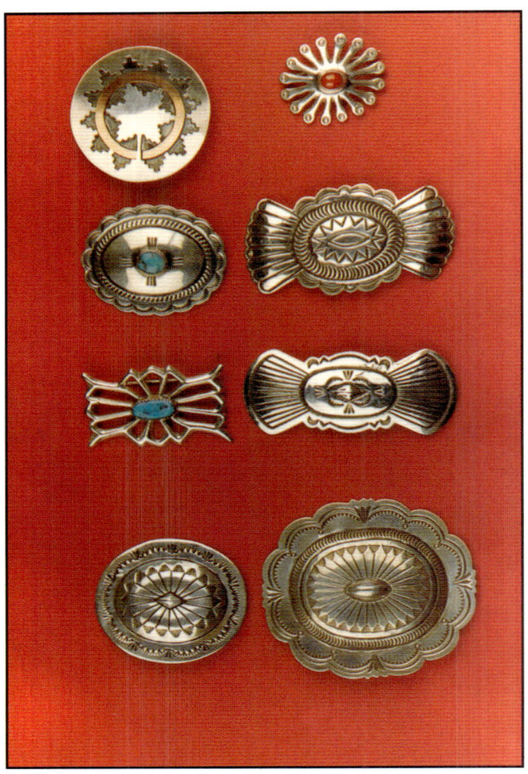

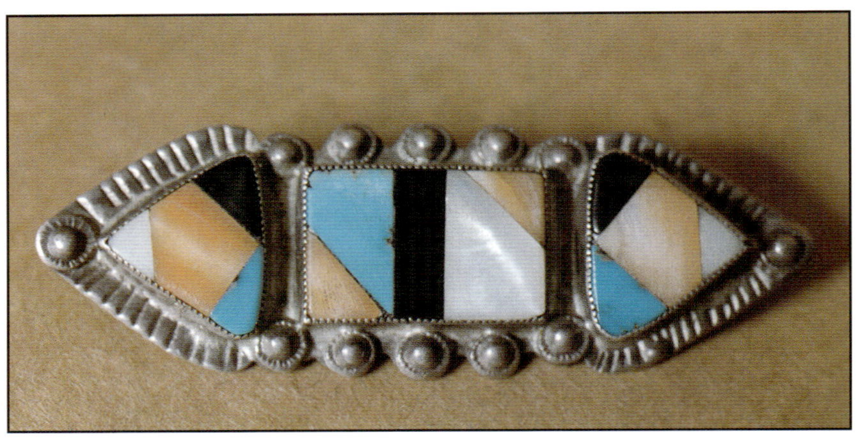

Bar pin with stone and shell inlay, 1985. *Adobe Gallery collection*

An assortment of Navajo-made pins of wrought and sand-cast silver from the 1980s include a round pin with copper Navajo wedding basket design. *Enchanted Mesa collection* .

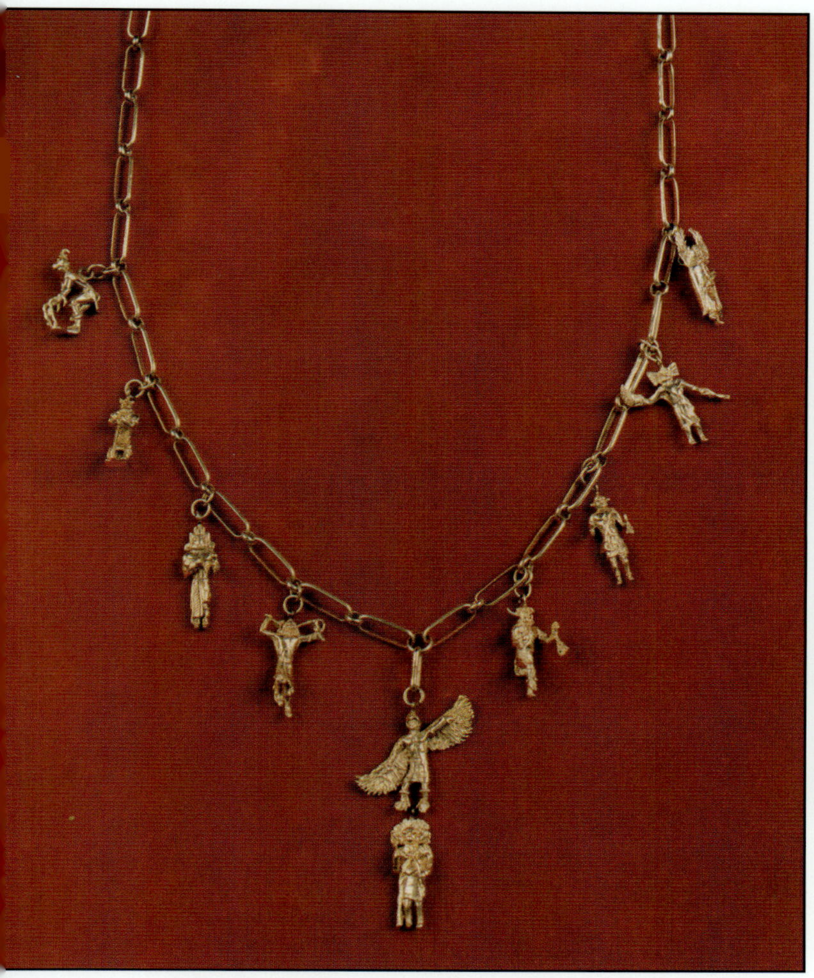

Cast and wrought figural gold charms mounted to a handmade gold chain. *Private collection on permanent loan to Ohio University*

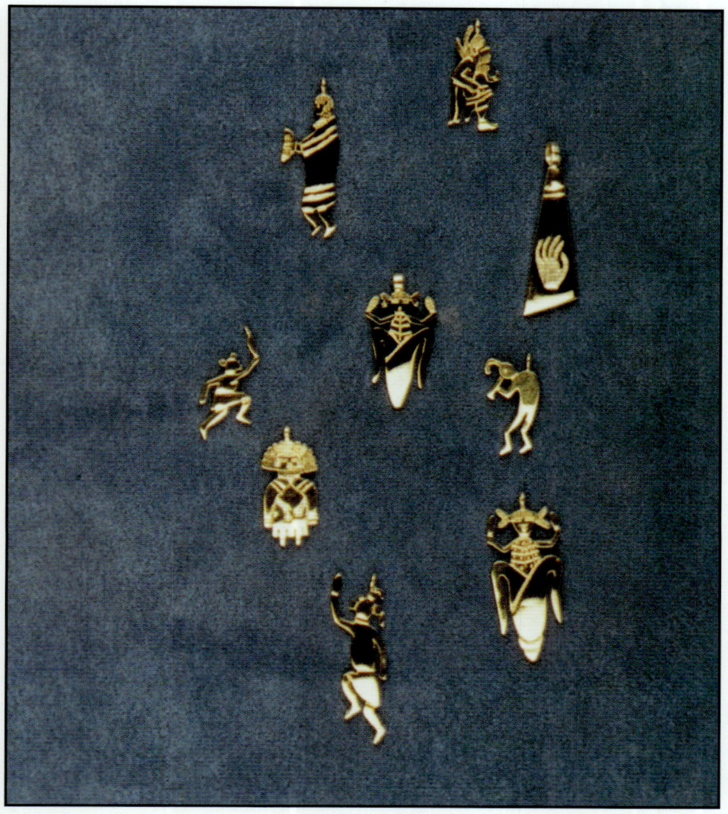

Nine figural gold-washed silver charms by Watson Honanie, Hopi, late 1980s. *Keams Canyon Arts and Crafts collection.*

Sterling silver overlay pins of assorted designs: From top left, Round Navajo pin with a stylized rabbit design. / Navajo round pin with a wading bird. / Hopi pin with a Man in the Maze design. / Triangular pendant of Hopi origin. All 1980s. *Enchanted Mesa collection*

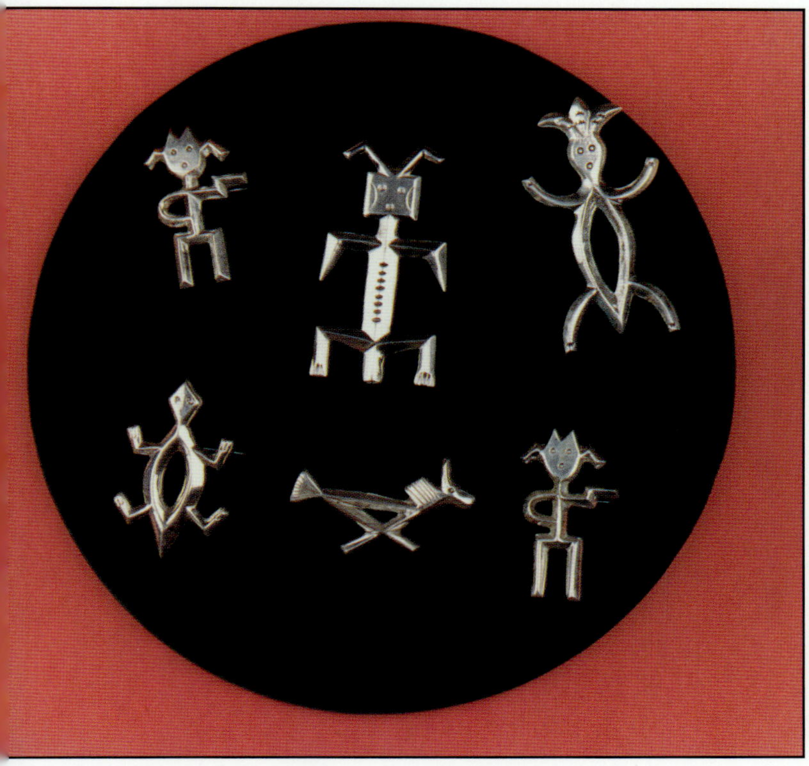

Six sand-cast Navajo pins from the 1980s. *Enchanted Mesa collection*

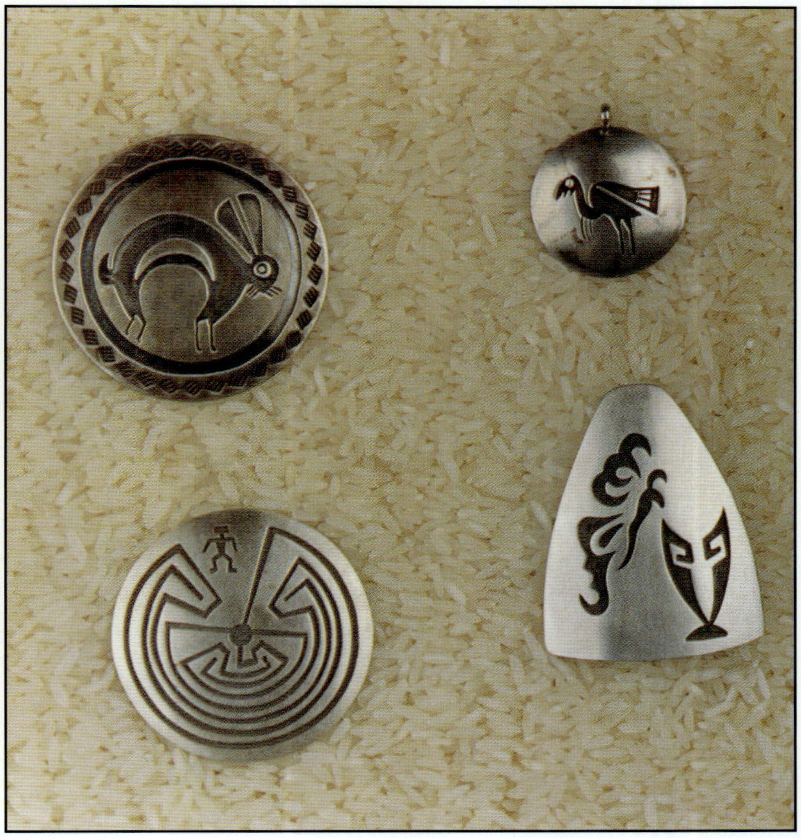

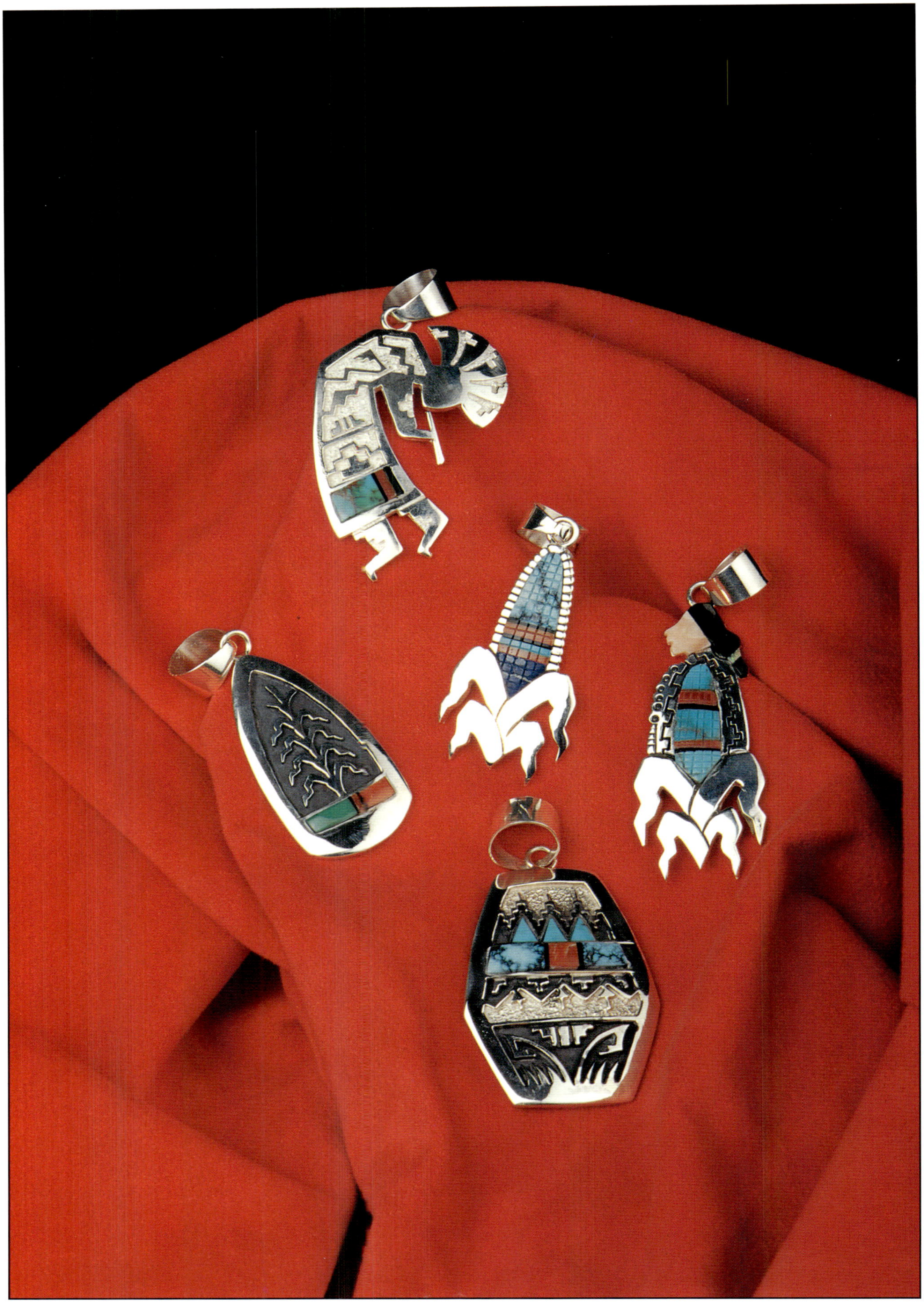

Group of five figurative pins and pendants with imaginative designs and fine quality stone inlay by Earl Plummer, Navajo, 2002. *Courtesy McGee's, Holbrook*

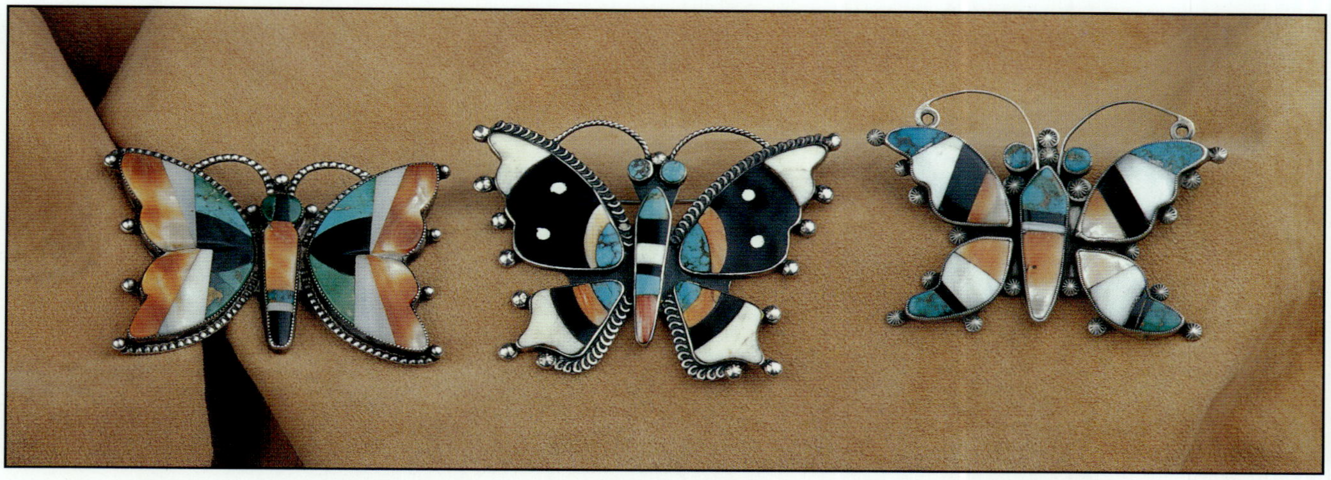

Three Zuni stone inlayed butterfly pins, 1930s. *Lynn D. Trusdell, Crown & Eagle Antiques*

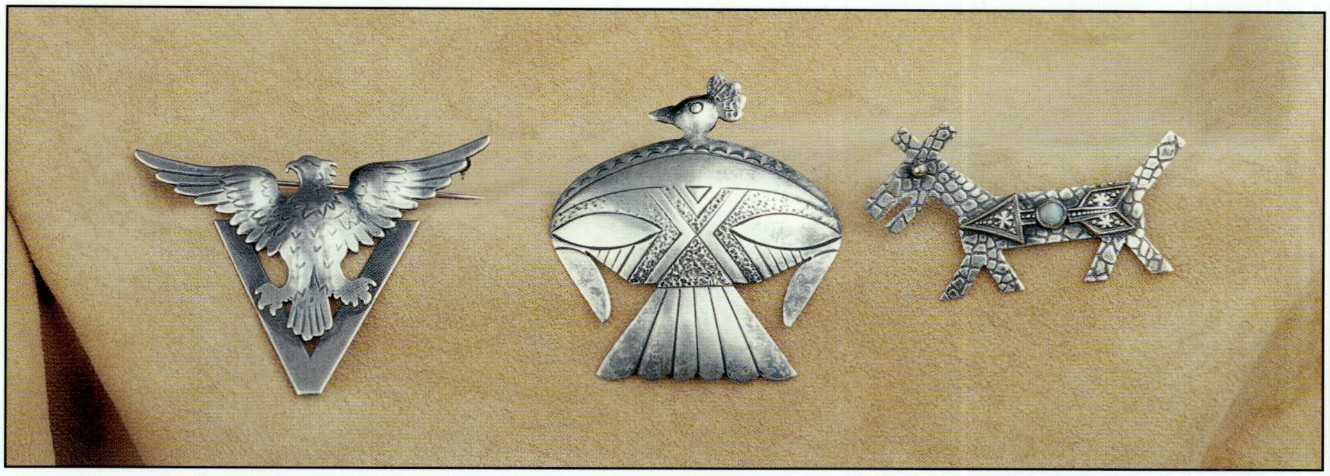

Three Navajo silver tourist-trade pins, including, on the left, an American eagle Victory design from the early 1940s. *Lynn D. Trusdell, Crown & Eagle Antiques*

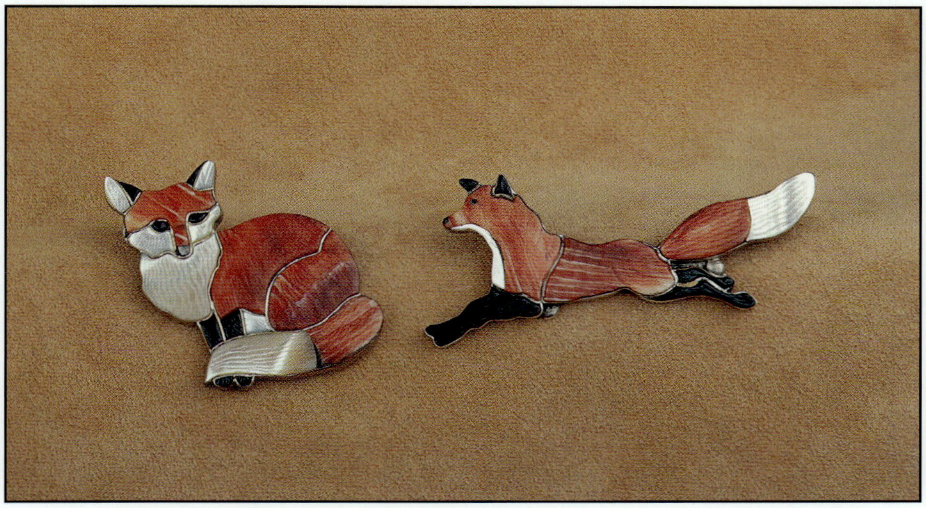

Two Zuni stone inlayed fox pins by Virgil and Shirley Benn, 1980s. *Lynn D. Trusdell, Crown & Eagle Antiques*

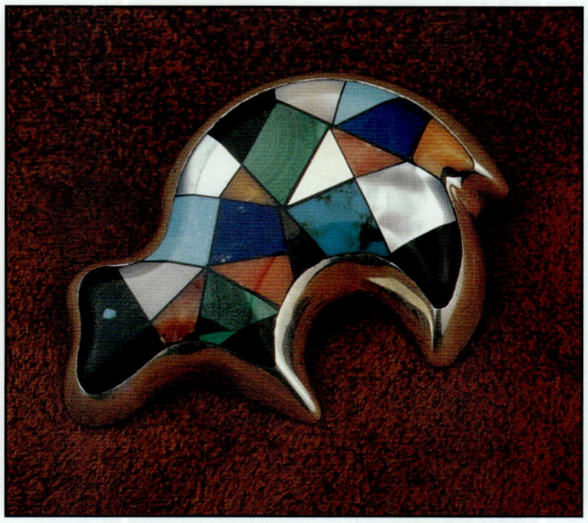

Pin/pendant in the shape of a bear and inlayed with various stones by Larry Bennett, Navajo, 2002. ($165) *Courtesy of Palms Trading Company*

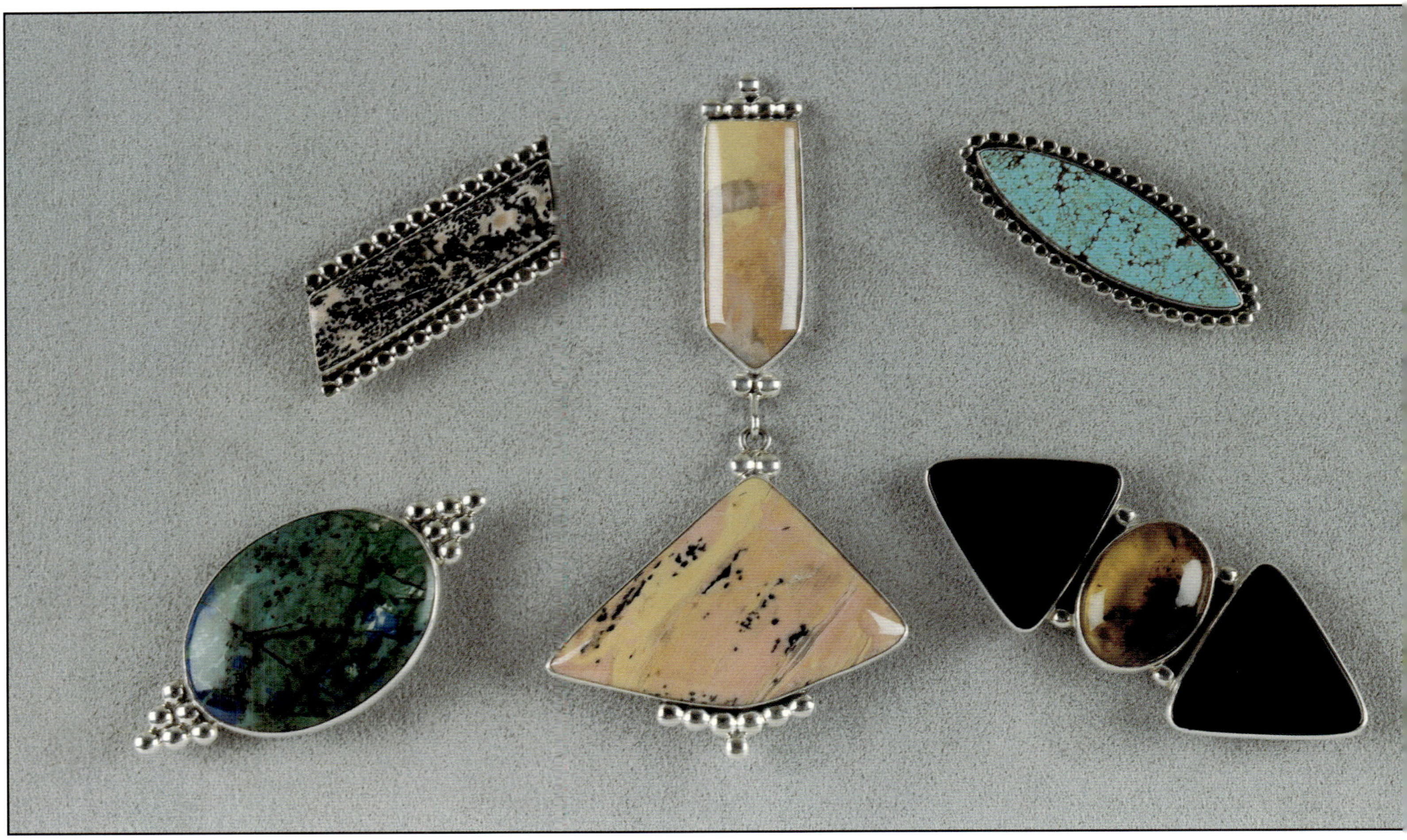

Six pins of contemporary design with a new selection of colored stones that include onyx, amber, pink rodelite, and turquoise, all made by Sam Lovato, 1989. *Indian Post collection*

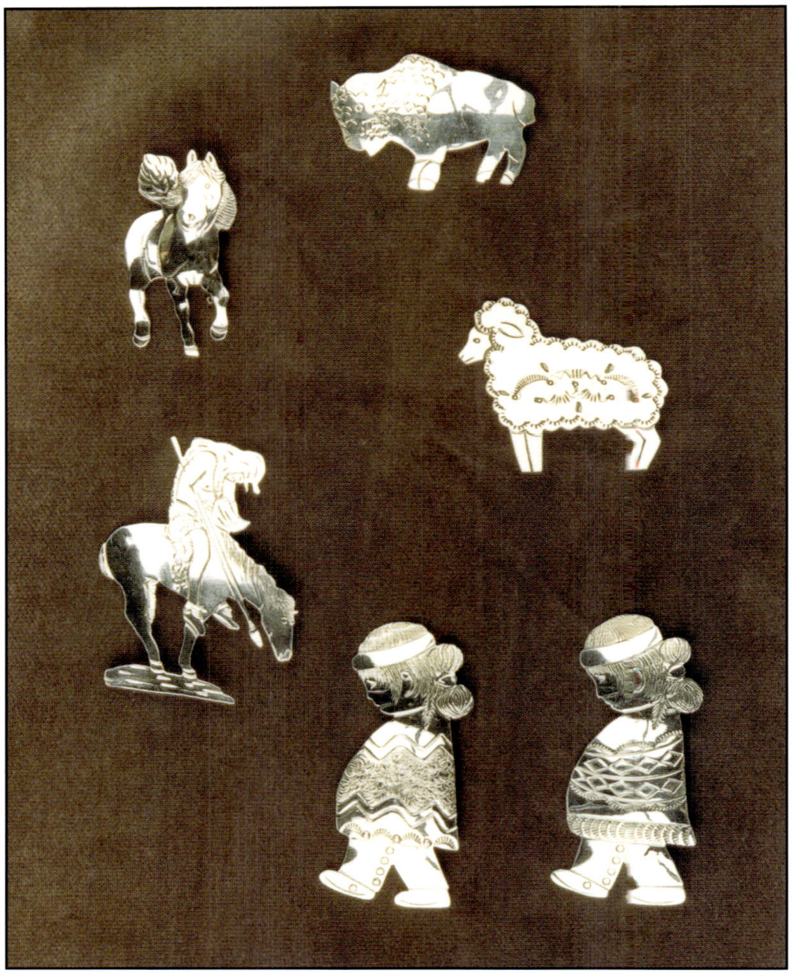

Filed and stamped silver pins of figural designs including animals and children. The horse and rider depict a design that has come to be known as "End of the Trail." *Bing Crosby collection*

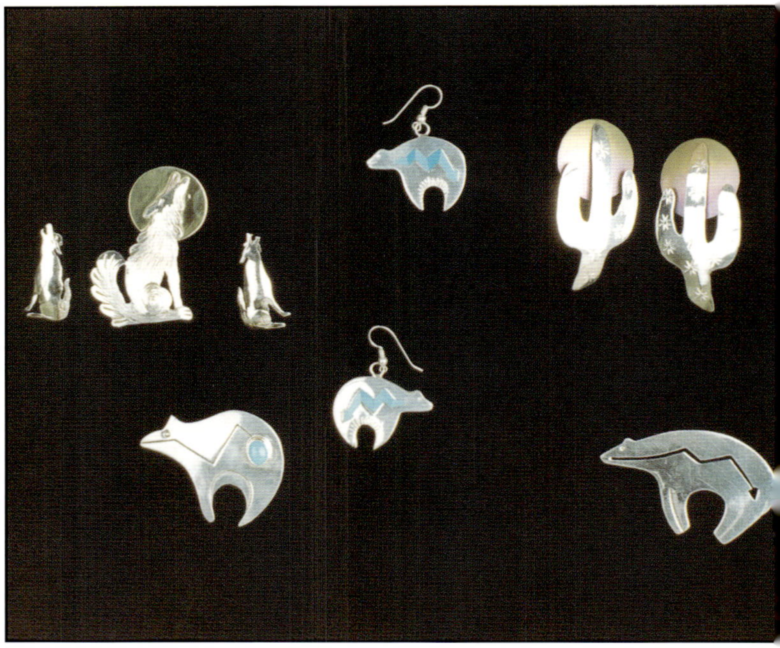

Pins and matching earrings made of silver in 1989. The coyote became a popular design much copied in lightweight silver. The Zuni bear fetish prompted this bear design, sometimes with turquoise inlay. *Bing Crosby collection*

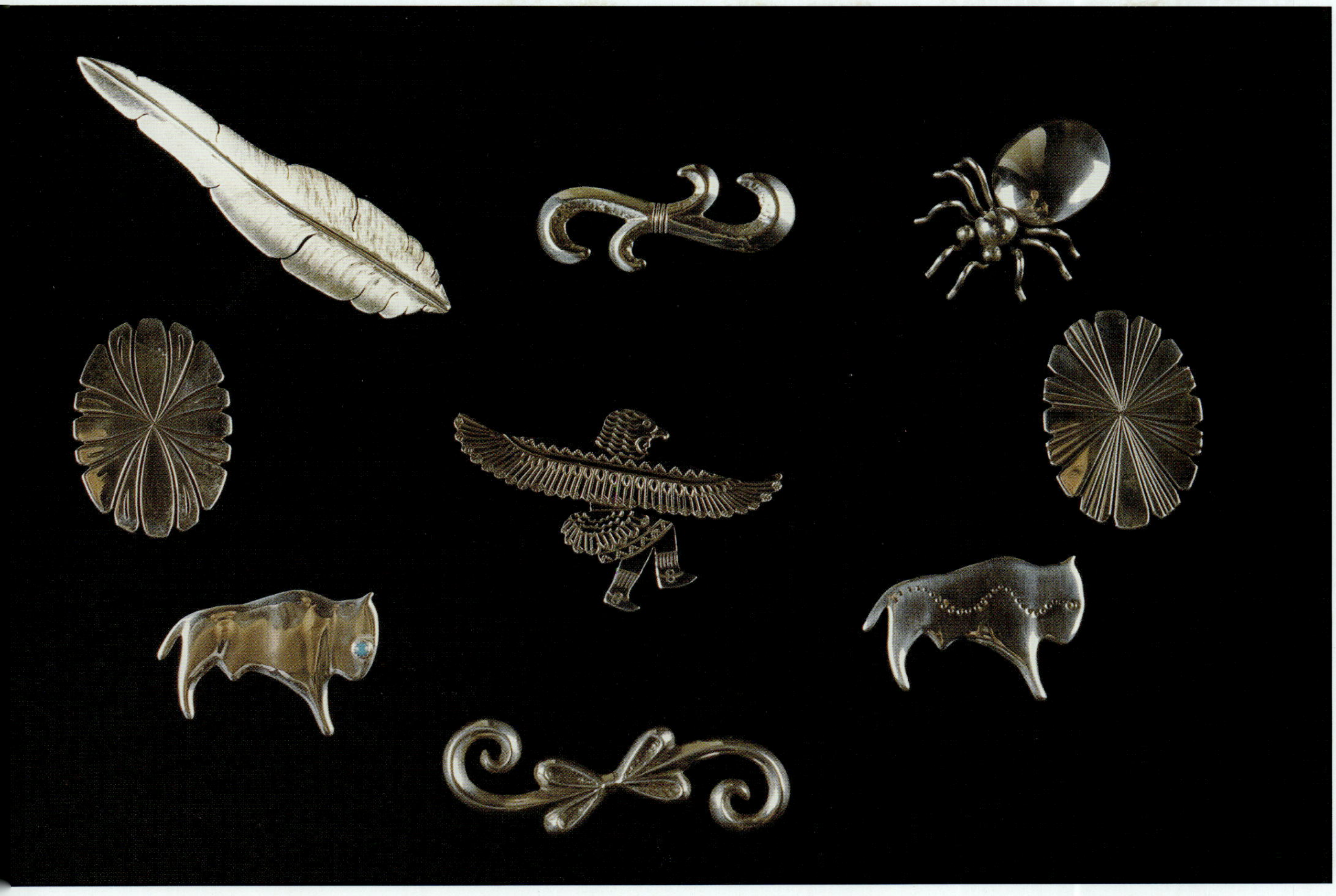

Nine sterling silver pins of assorted designs by Indian silversmiths, 1980s. *Indian Post collection*.

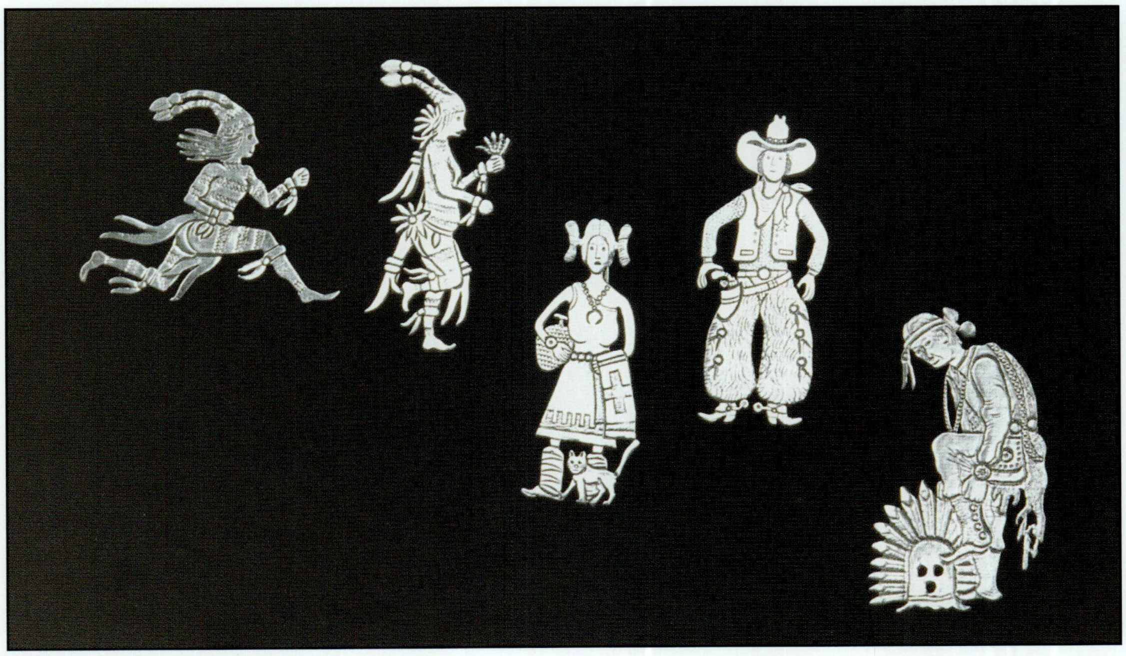

Five silver figural pins by Clarence Lee, from the 1980s: Running clown kachina. / Dancing yei dancer. / Lady and cat. / Cowboy. / Yei dancer dressing. *Clarence Lee collection*

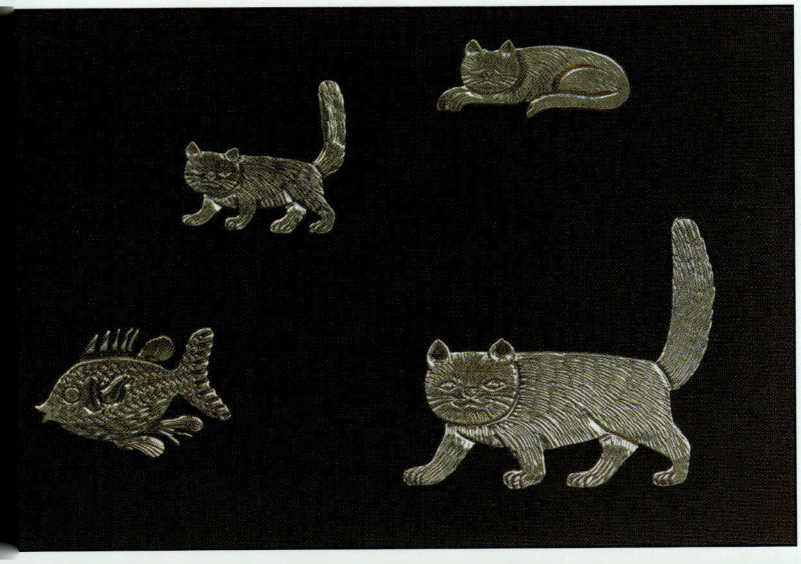

Four silver pins by Clarence Lee, 1980s: Three cats and a fish. *Clarence Lee collection*

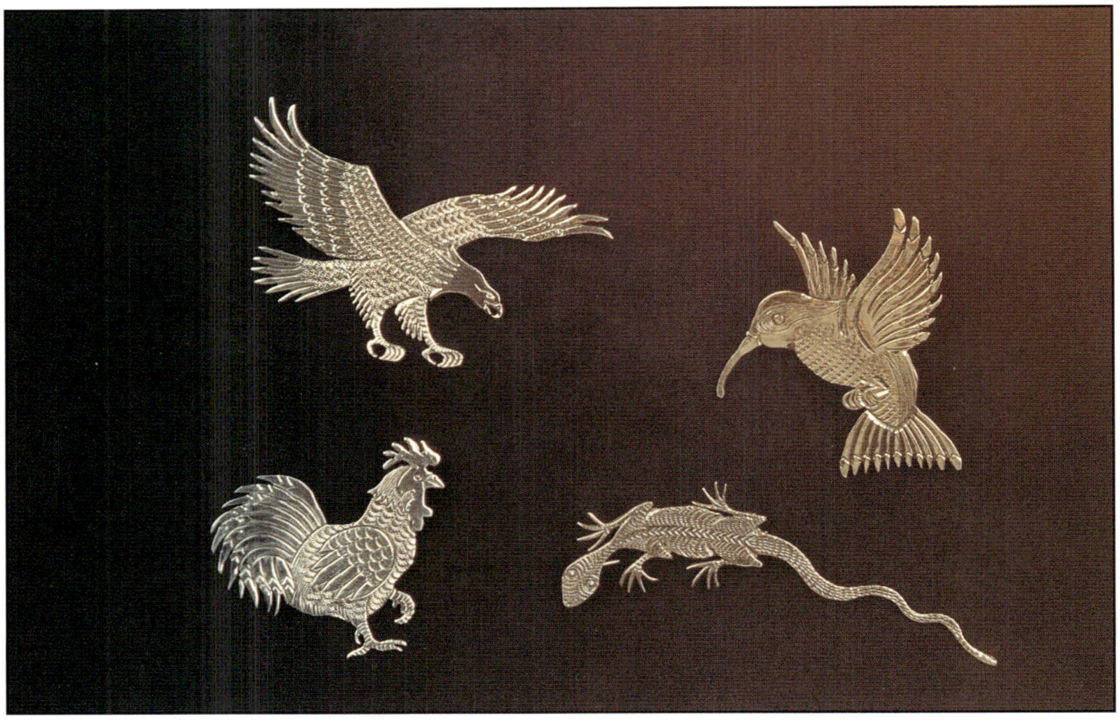

Four silver pins by Clarence Lee, made in the 1980s: Flying eagle, / Hummingbird, / Chicken, / Salamander. *Clarence Lee collection*

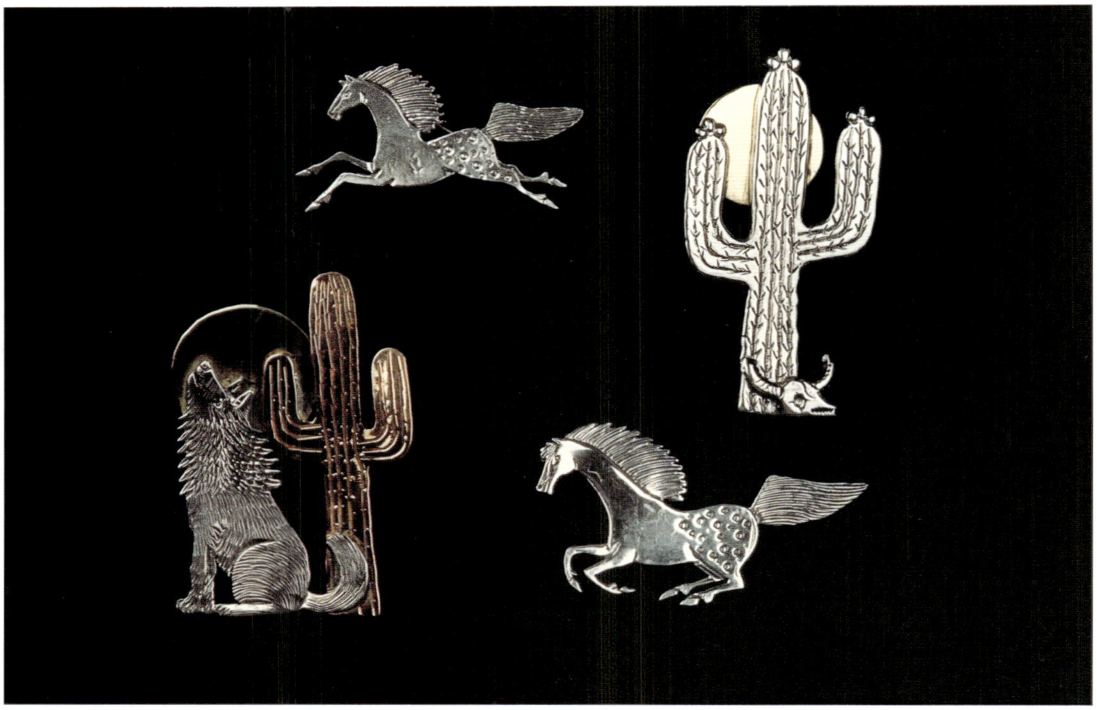

Four sterling silver pins by Clarence Lee from the 1980s: Small running horse. / Cactus and sun. / Cactus and howling wolf. / Large running horse. *Clarence Lee collection*

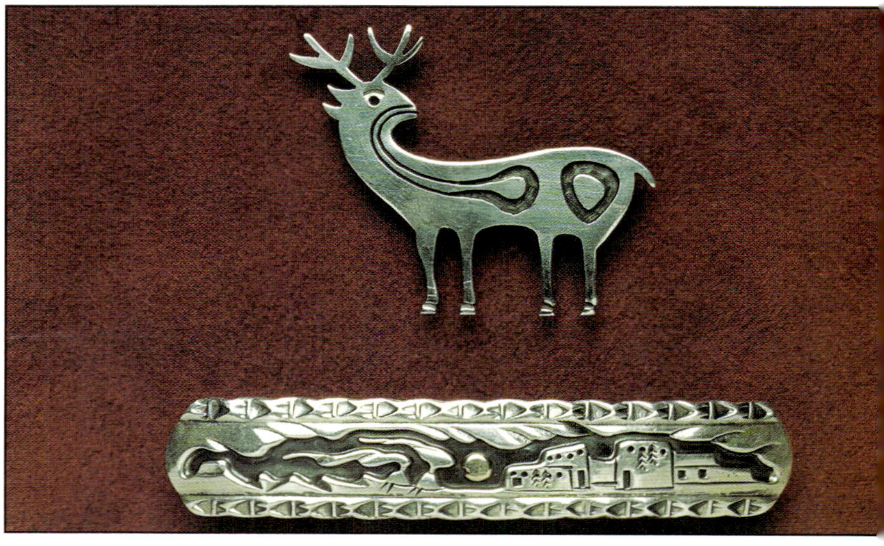

Silver pin of a Zuni-style deer made in Hopi overlay for Enchanted Mesa Indian Arts. / Hair-fastener (barrette) of silver overlay in landscape design with gold moon, Navajo, late 1980s.

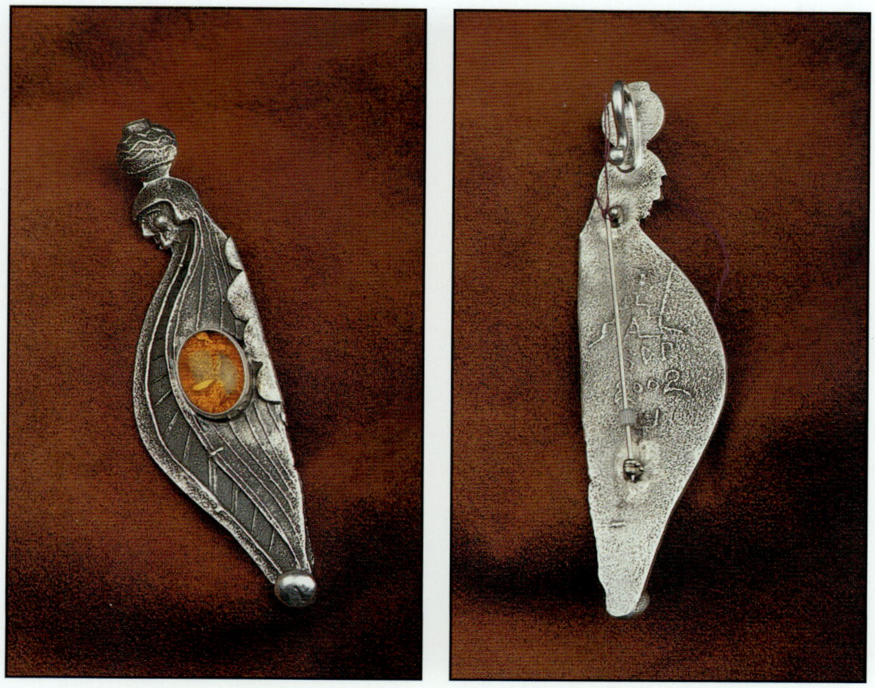

Sterling silver and amber spirit pin/pendant of "Baby in the Oven" design, by Anthony Lovato, Santo Domingo, 4-1/2" long, 2002. *Courtesy of Gerald Peters Gallery, Santa Fe, New Mexico* ($500)

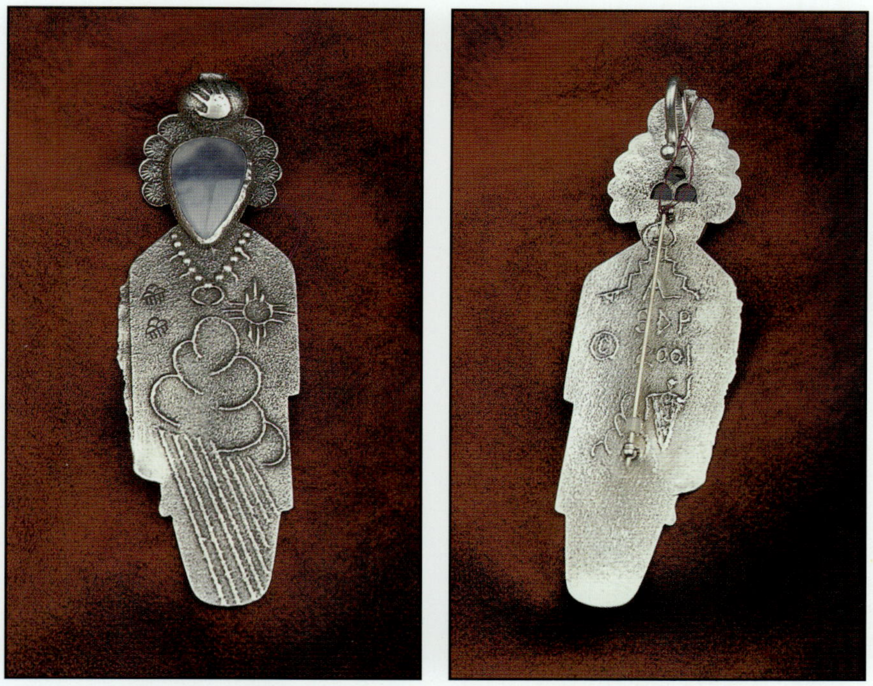

Sterling silver and blue chalcedony spirit pin/pendant of "Cloud Spirit" design, by Anthony Lovato, Santo Domingo, 5" long, 2002. *Courtesy of Gerald Peters Gallery, Santa Fe, New Mexico* ($620)

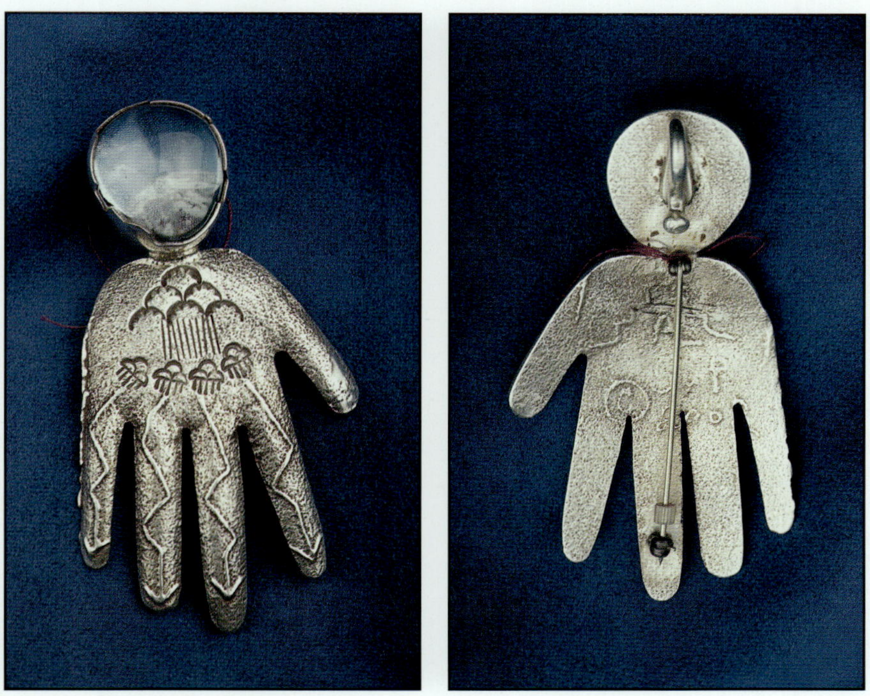

Sterling silver and Lander, Nevada blue topaz hand pendant of "Prayer for Rain" design, by Anthony Lovato, Santo Domingo, 3-1/2" long x 2" wide, 2002. *Courtesy of Gerald Peters Gallery, Santa Fe, New Mexico* ($420)

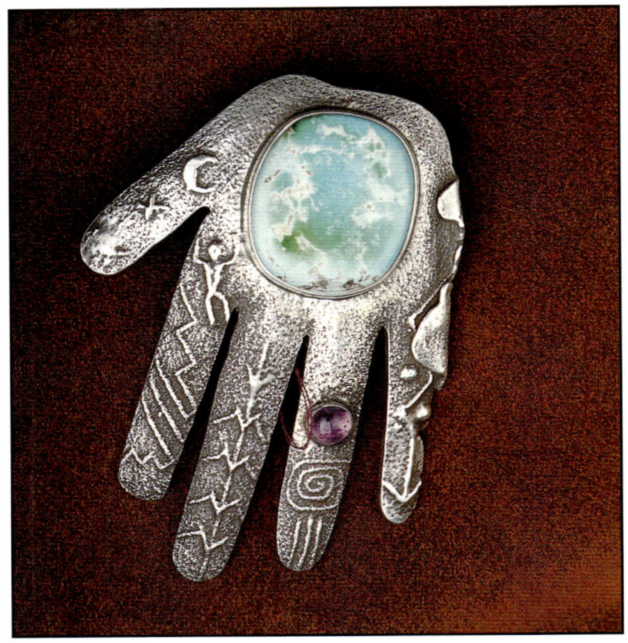

Sterling silver, Pilot Mountain turquoise, and amethyst hand pendant in "Prayer for Corn" design by Anthony Lovato, Santo Domingo, 2-1/4" long x 3" wide, 2002. *Courtesy of Gerald Peters Gallery, Santa Fe, New Mexico* ($450)

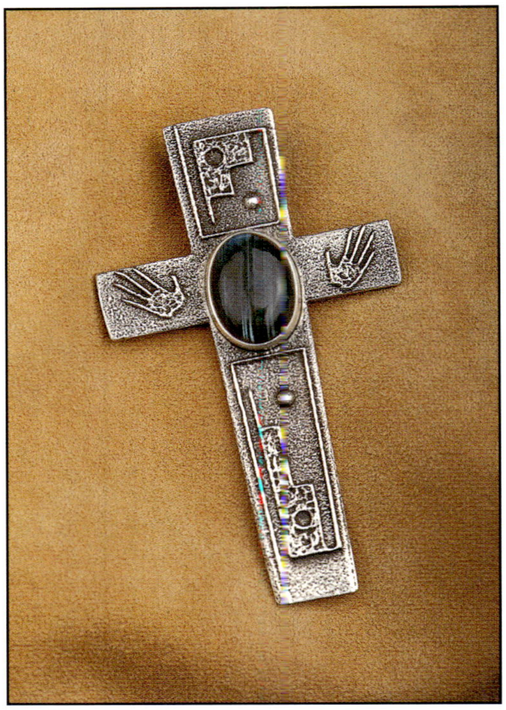

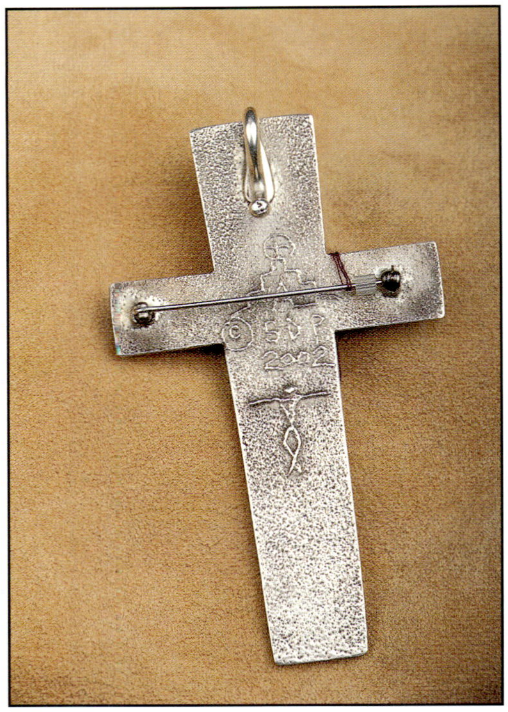

Sterling silver and Pietersite cross pin/pendant with hand and kiva designs by Anthony Lovato, Santo Domingo, 4" long x 2-1/4" wide, 2002. *Courtesy of Gerald Peters Gallery, Santa Fe, New Mexico* ($550)

Left: Sterling silver and Carico Lake turquoise double cross pin/pendant with landscape design by Anthony Lovato, Santo Domingo, 4" long x 1-4/4" wide, 2002. *Courtesy of Gerald Peters Gallery, Santa Fe, New Mexico* ($520)

Right: Sterling silver and Carico Lake turquoise double cross pin/pendant of bubble design, by Anthony Lovato, Santo Domingo, 3-1/2" long x 2-1/4" wide, 2002. *Courtesy of Gerald Peters Gallery, Santa Fe, New Mexico* ($520)

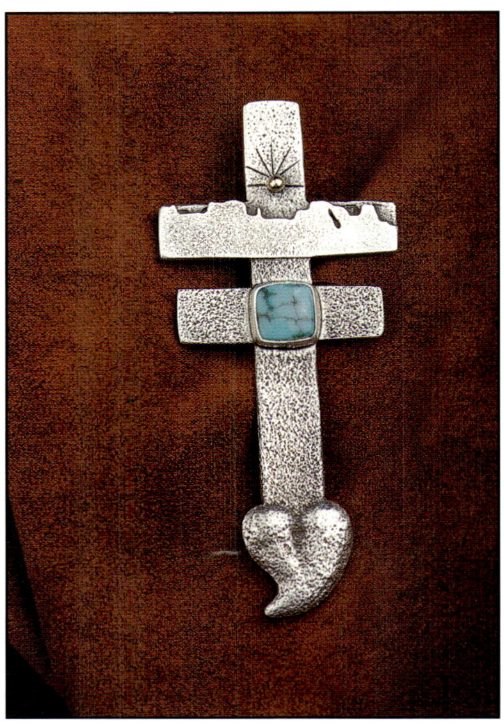

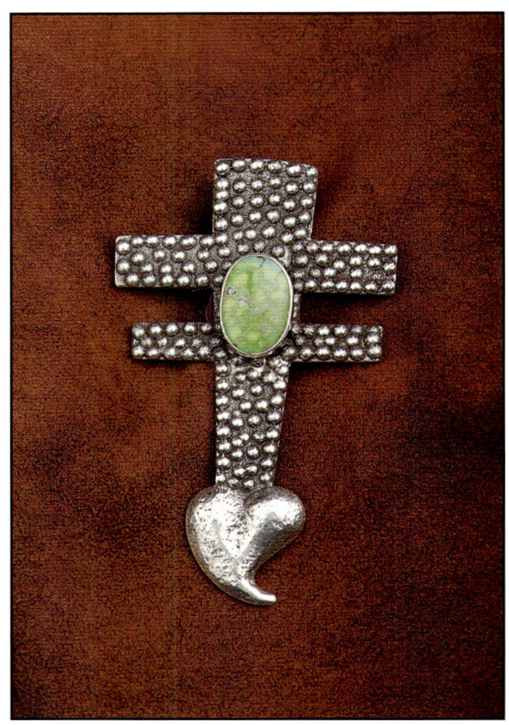

Hair Fasteners

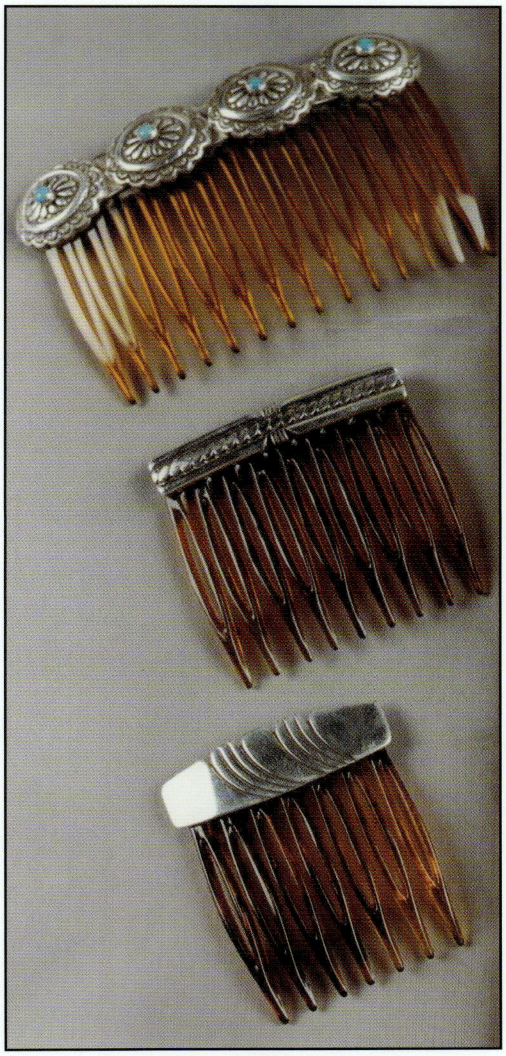

Silver Navajo hair jewelry from the 1980s: Large comb set with four turquoise stones in wrought silver. / Medium comb with stamped silver rim. / Small comb with wrought silver rim. *Indian Post collection*

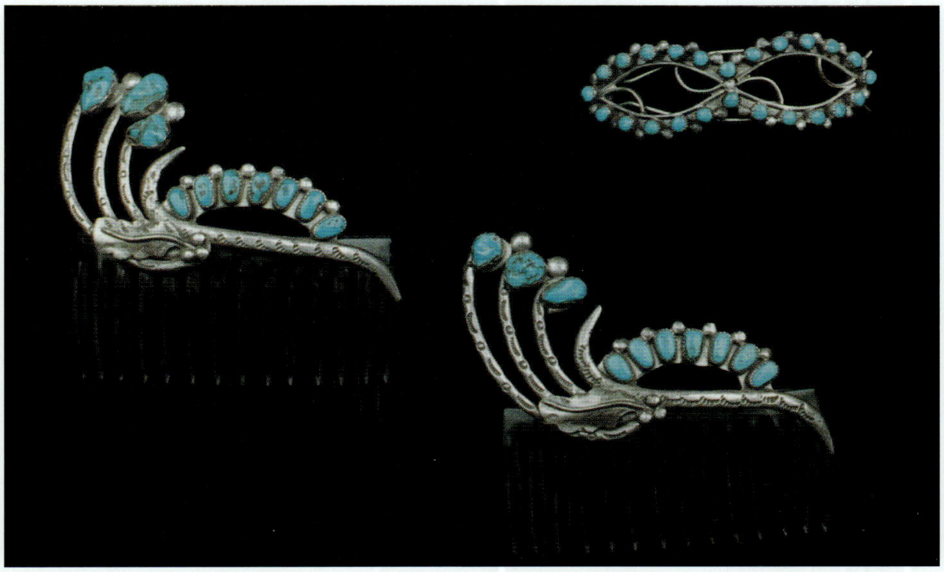

Sterling silver Navajo hair jewelry: Pair of silver hair combs set with Kingman turquoise, circa 1950s / Barrette with treated Kingman turquoise from Zuni, circa 1960s. *Dennehotso collection*.

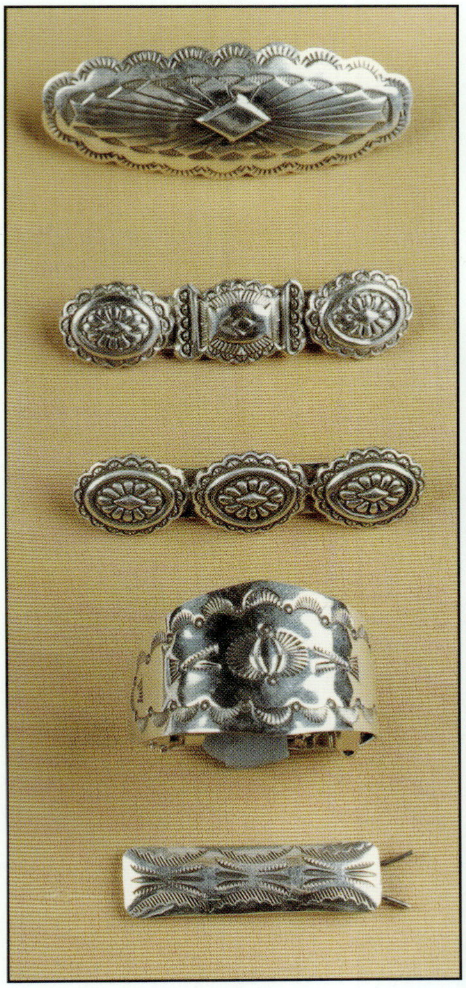

Large barrette of wrought and stamped design. / Two medium barrettes with wrought and stamped medallions. / Ponytail holder with stamped designs. / Small flat barrette with stamped designs. *Indian Post collection*

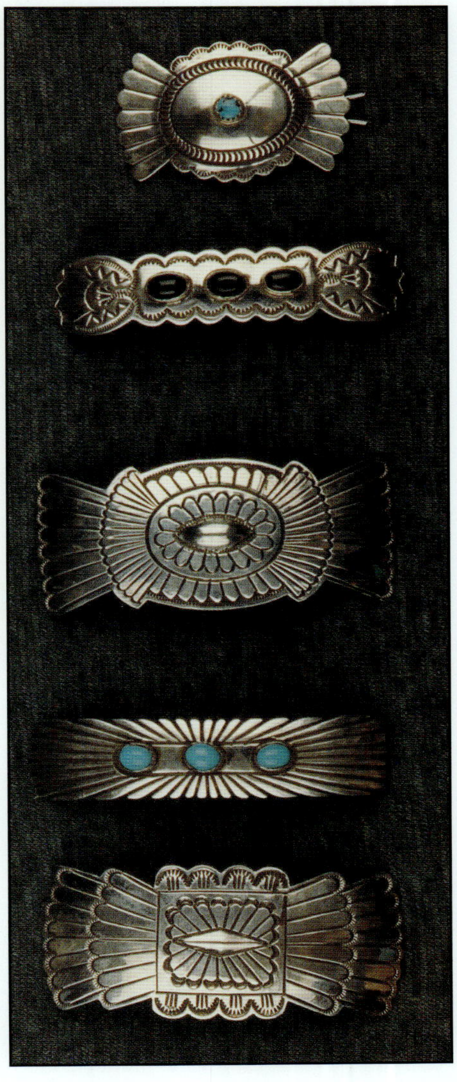

Five silver Navajo barrettes from the 1980s: Two set with turquoise, one set with jet, and two of wrought silver bow design. *Enchanted Mesa collection*

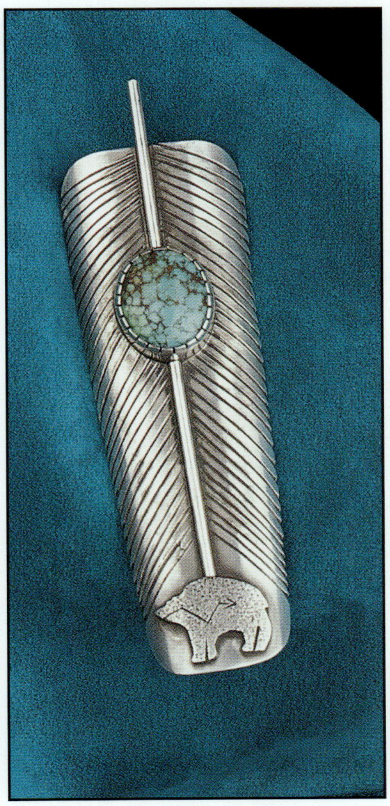

Feather-shaped hair tie of silver with Carico Lake turquoise and bear design by Anthony Lovato, Santo Domingo, 5-1/2" long x 1-3/4" wide, 2002. *Courtesy of Gerald Peters Gallery, Santa Fe, New Mexico* ($250)

Men's pins

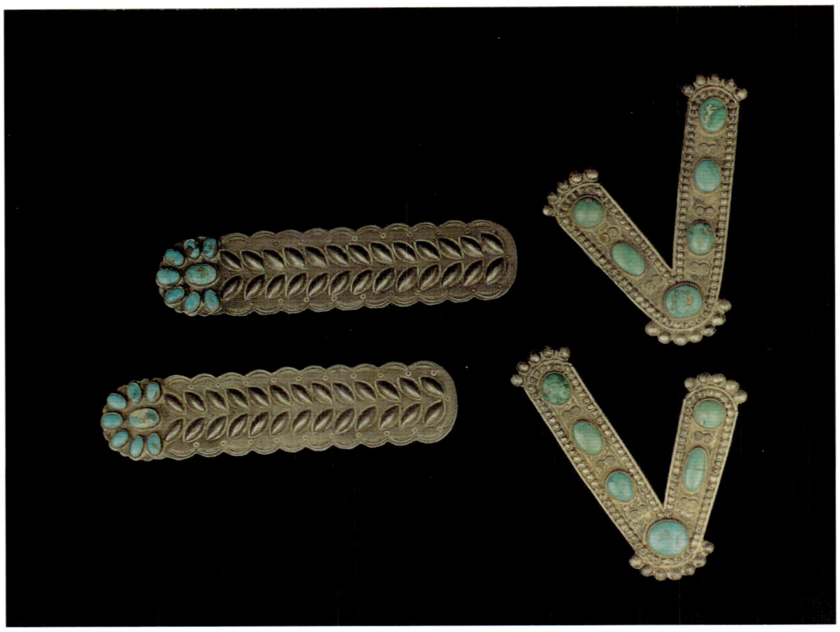

Two pair of Navajo shirt collar decorations, both made with Morenci turquoise and sterling silver, circa 1920s. *Dennehotso collection*

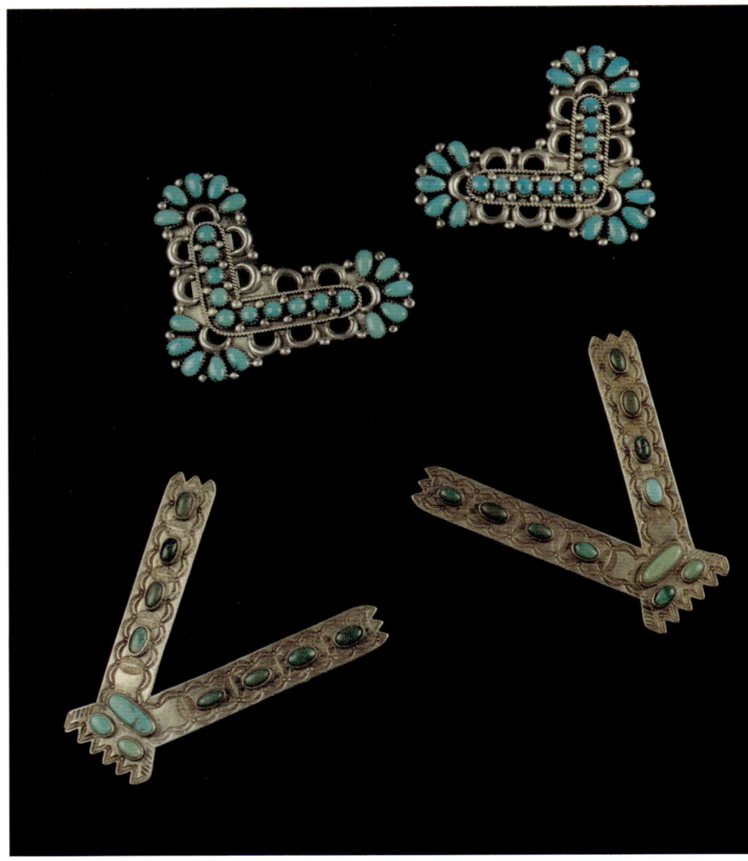

Showing the old and new designs are two pair of Zuni men's silver shirt collar points: Pair of modern openwork design set with turquoise, circa 1970s. / Old pair of stamped coin silver collar points with green turquoise, circa 1910-1915. *Private collection*

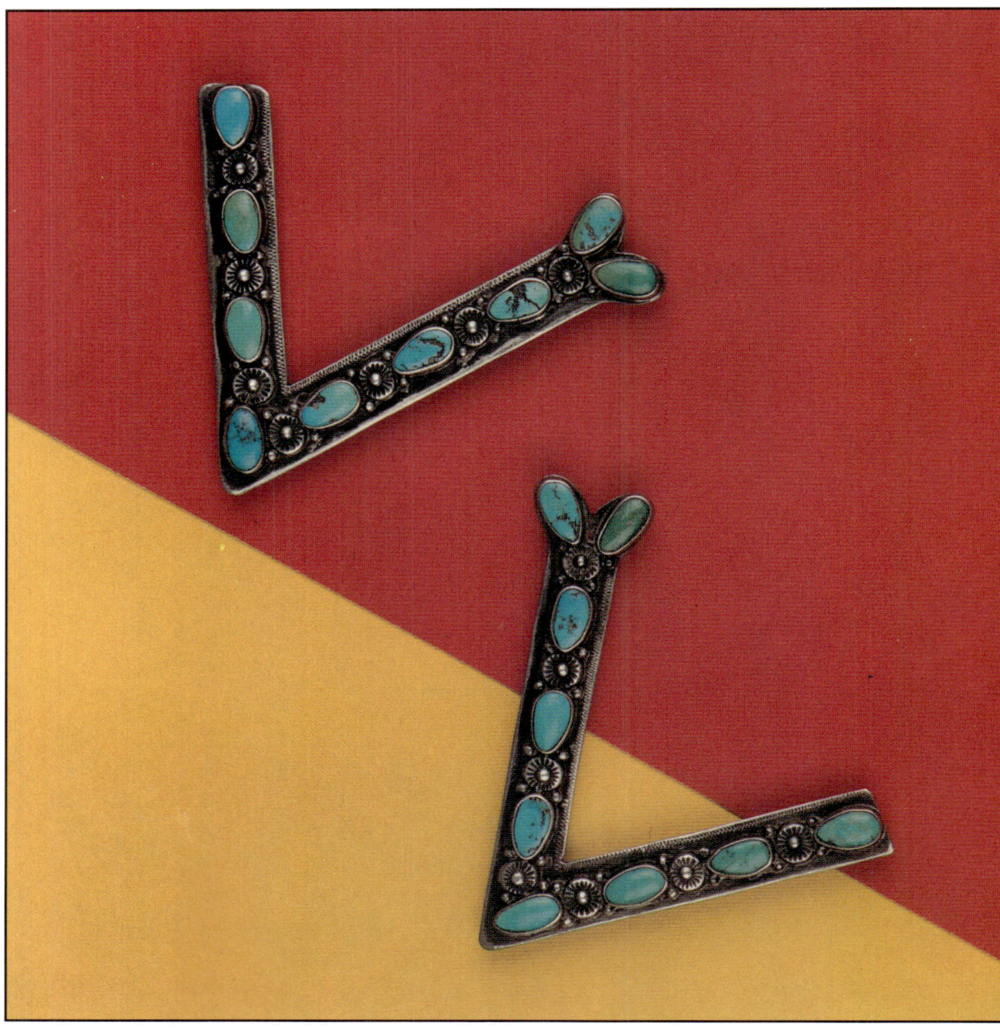

A pair of Navajo coin silver collar points set with turquoise from the 1930s. *Maxwell Museum collection*

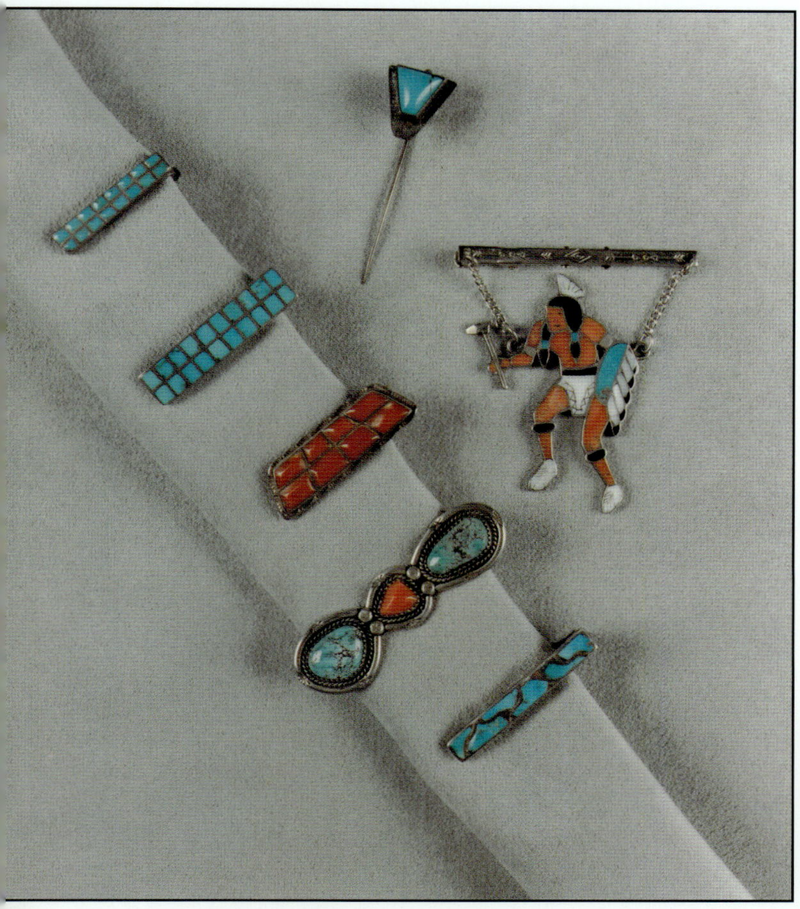

Necktie jewelry: From left, a necktie bar of silver set with sixteen turquoise stones in two lines. / Tie bar with twenty turquoise stones in two lines. / Navajo-made stickpin set with turquoise. / Tie bar of silver with dangling dancing male figure of inlaid stone, Zuni, circa 1940s. / Tie bar of eight coral stones in silver. / Two turquoise stones and one piece of coral on a Navajo tie bar. / Zuni tie bar with flat-set, irregularly shaped turquoise stones. *Private collection on permanent loan to Ohio University*

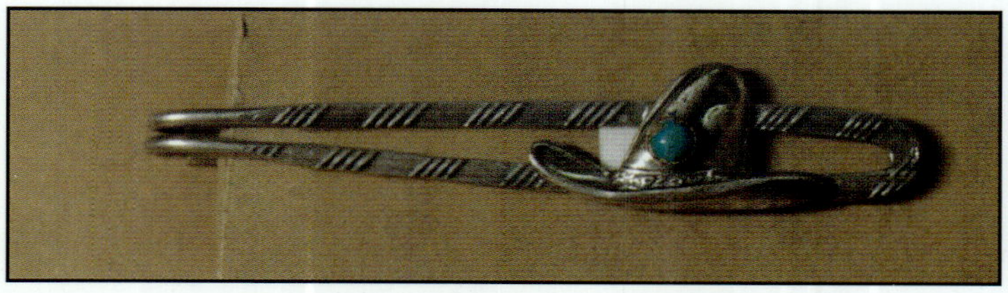

Old Navajo silver tie bar with cowboy hat decoration accented by a turquoise stone. *Adobe Gallery collection*

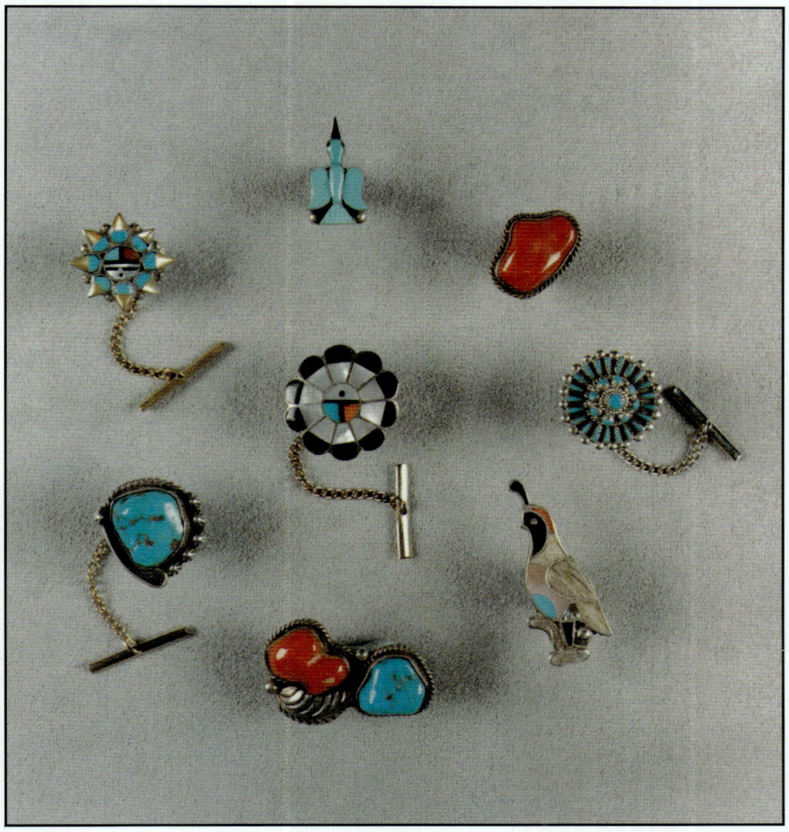

A group of silver tie tacks, clockwise from top: Turquoise and jet bird design. / Coral chunk with silver rope border. / Zuni needlepoint turquoise cluster. / Zuni quail of shell and stone inlay. / Coral and turquoise chunks set with silver leaf. / Turquoise chunk with silver dots. / Zuni star sunface of stone and shell inlay by A.L. / in center, round inlay with ten petals. *Private collection on permanent loan to Ohio University*

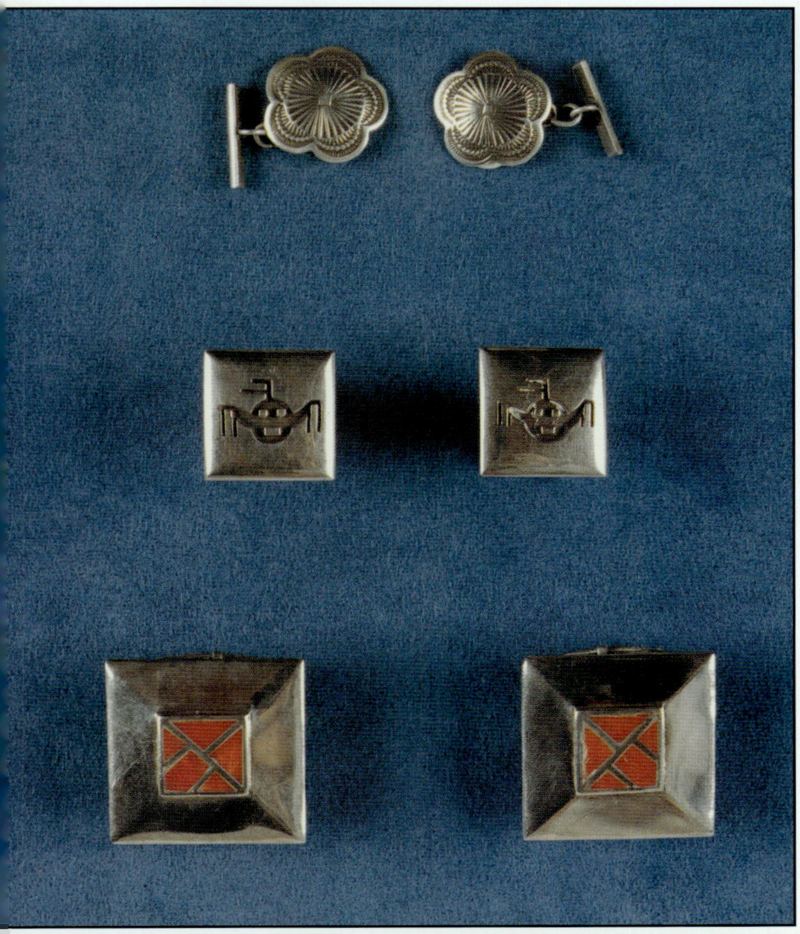

Old-style silver button cufflinks, circa 1980. / Square Hopi overlay cufflinks with mudhead face design. / Square cufflinks with coral channel inlay. *Private collection on permanent loan to Ohio University*

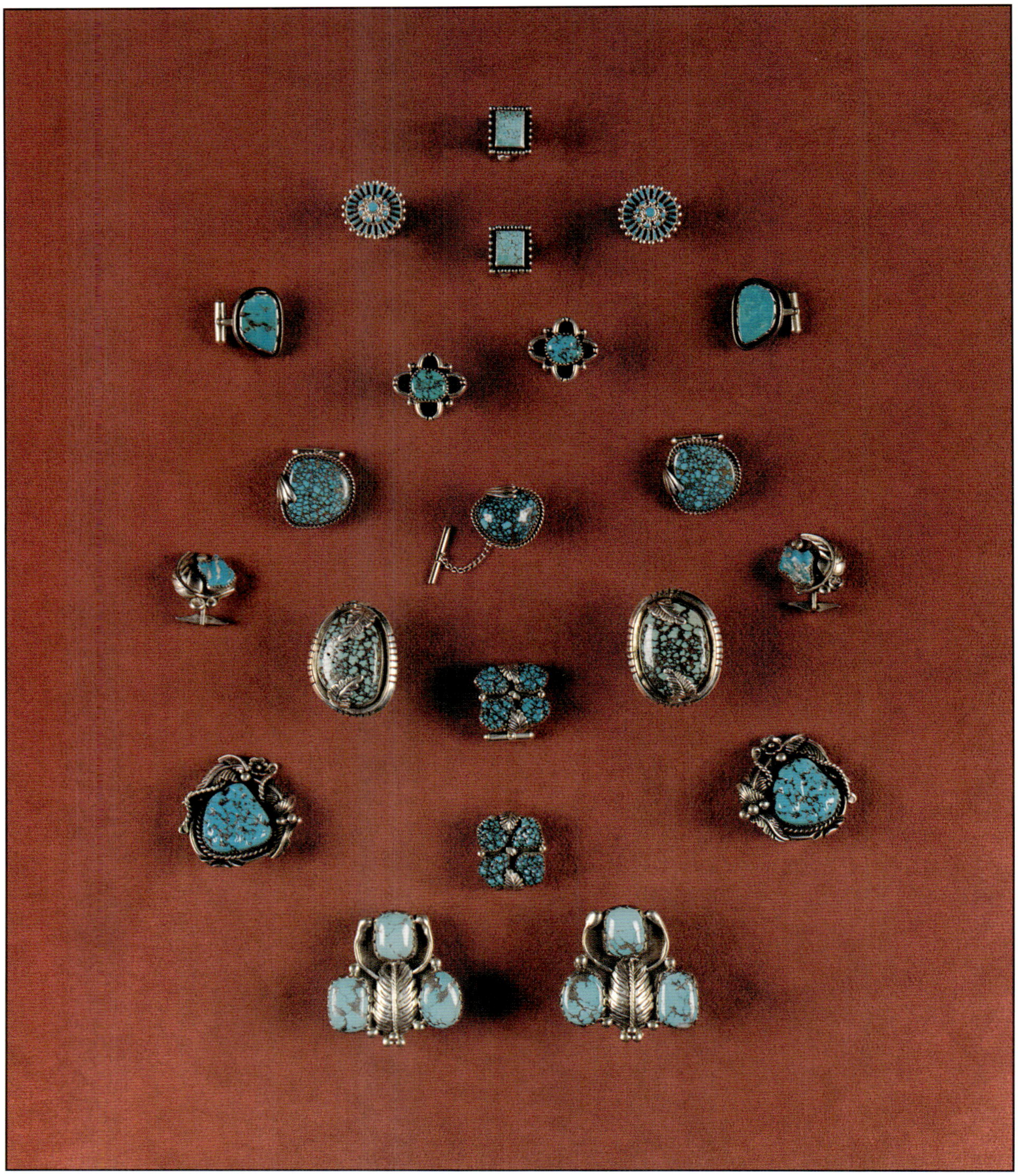

Men's jewelry featuring: From the top, Square Number 8 turquoise with beaded border. / Needlepoint cluster by Rosemary Panteah, Zuni, 1987. / Single ovoid stone in setback frame, 1963. / Silver openwork setting, 1978. / Cufflinks and tie tack of Spiderweb Indian Mountain turquoise stone side decorations by M.M., 1978. / Carved stone and one leaf by B.E. / Large oval stone and two leaves. / Four foam nuggets with two leaves, 1984. / Large nugget with leaves and flowers by J.J.M. / Large with three turquoise nuggets and leaf. *Private collection on permanent loan to Ohio University*

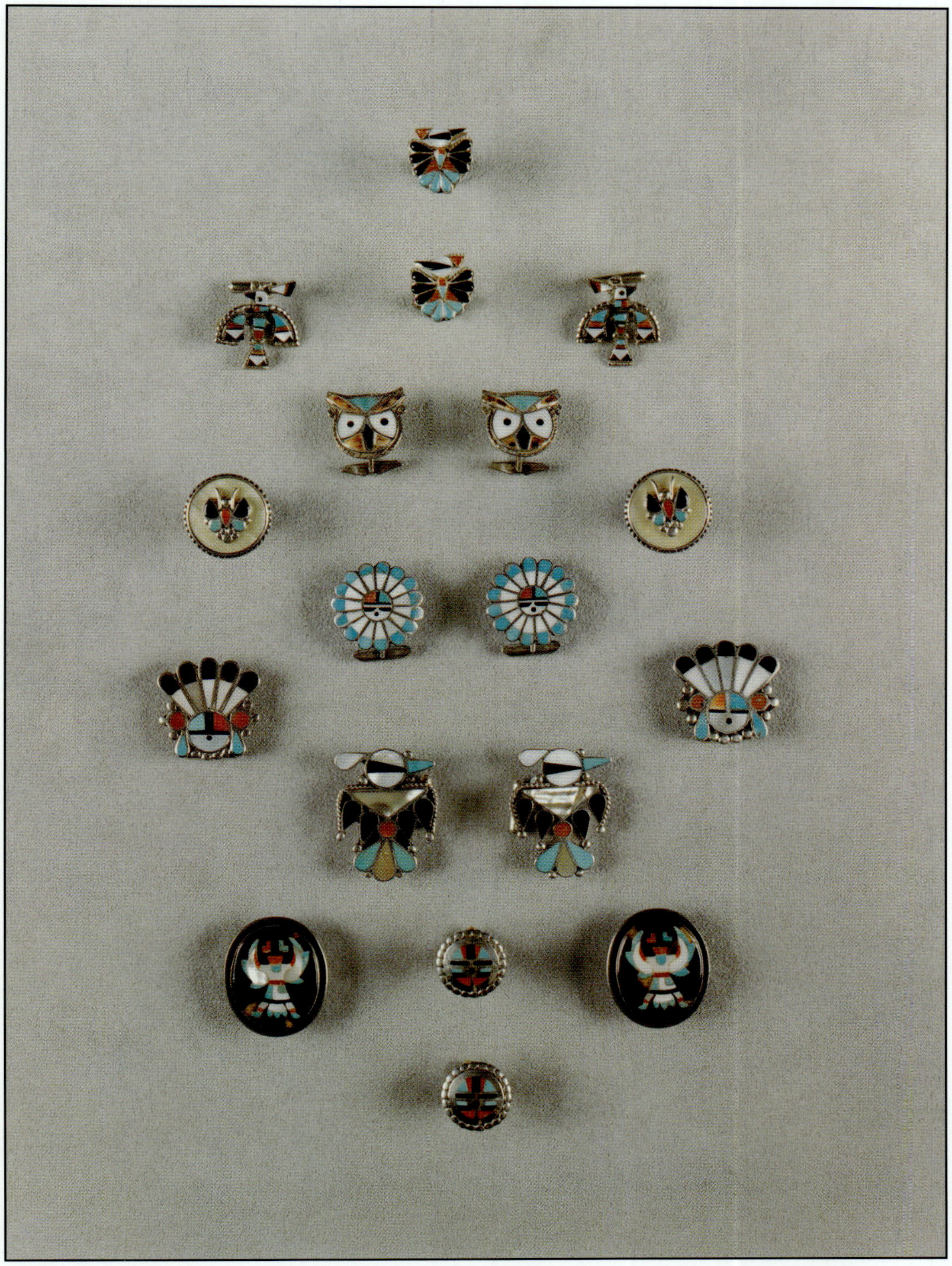

Zuni cufflinks with a variety of inlaid stone designs: From the top, Small black thunderbirds, 1984. / Pair of thunderbirds. / Owl heads. / Round with bee inlay. / Turquoise sun masks. / Sunface and feathers. / Large thunderbirds with mother of pearl. / Oval with eagle dancers. / Round with inlay face. *Private collection on permanent loan to Ohio University*

Rings

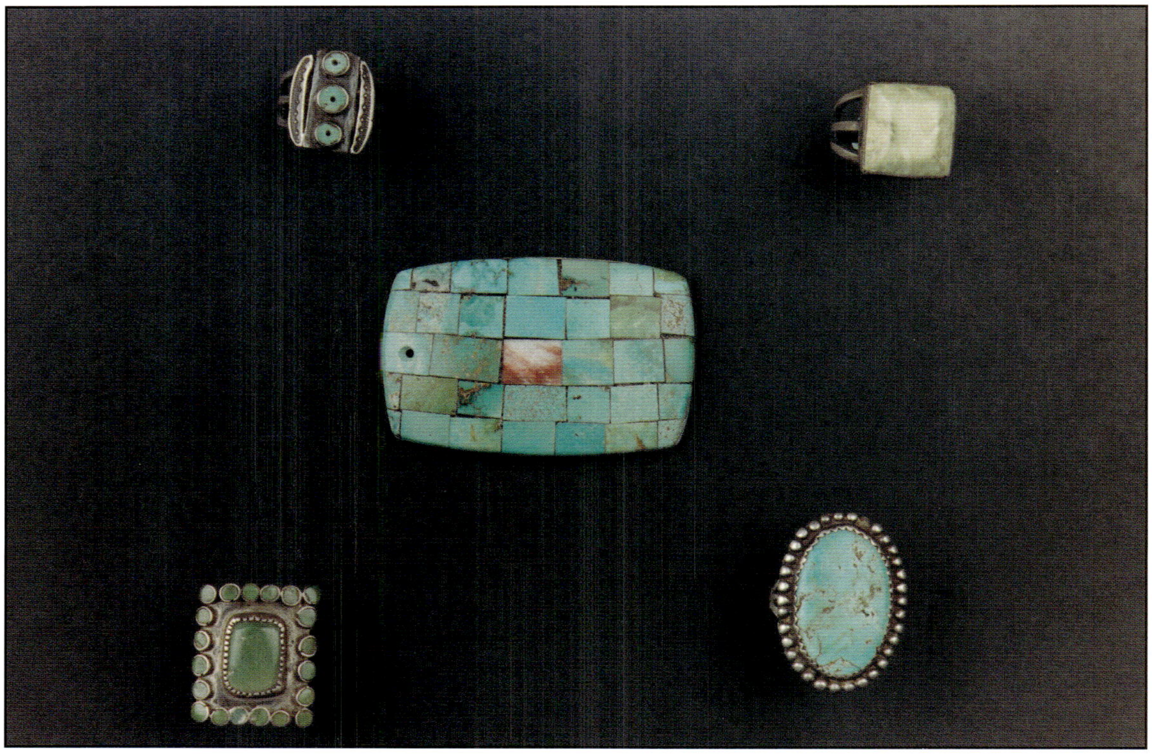

Old oval Zuni turquoise ring with beaded border, circa 1890-1910. / Rectangular ring with small green Cerillos turquoise stones around a central one. / Pendant with turquoise and shell mosaic inlay. / Ring with old turquoise on three silver bands. / Ring with three turquoise beads. *Maxwell Museum collection*

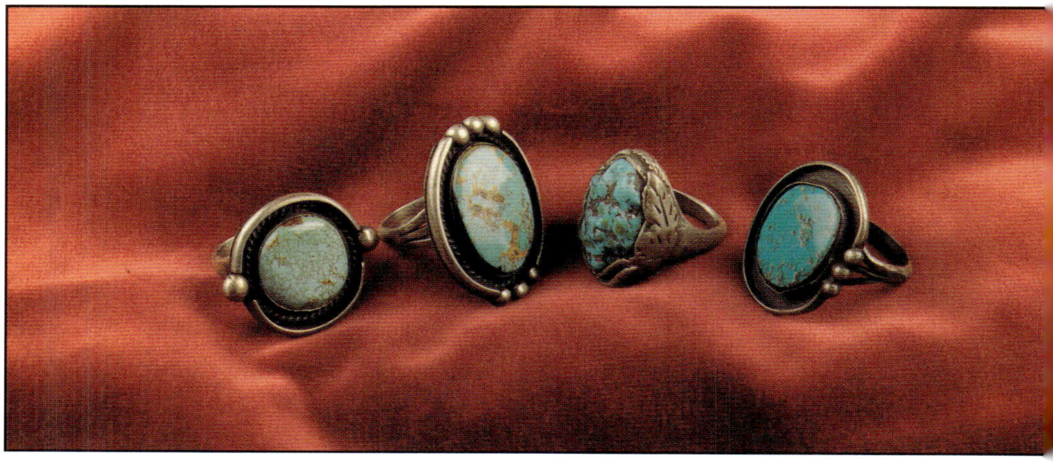

Navajo sterling silver rings, circa 1950s: From left, Sand-cast band and setting with Kingman turquoise. / Oval Royston turquoise. / Hachita turquoise nugget. / Villa Grove turquoise. *Dennehotso collection*.

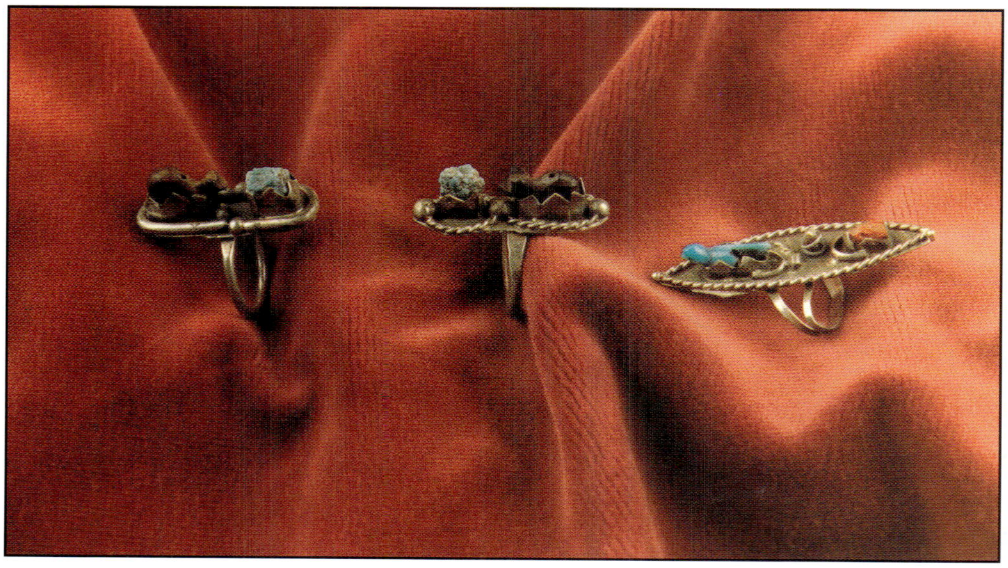

Three Zuni sterling silver rings with treated turquoise and fetish designs from the early 1970s. *Dennehotso collection*.

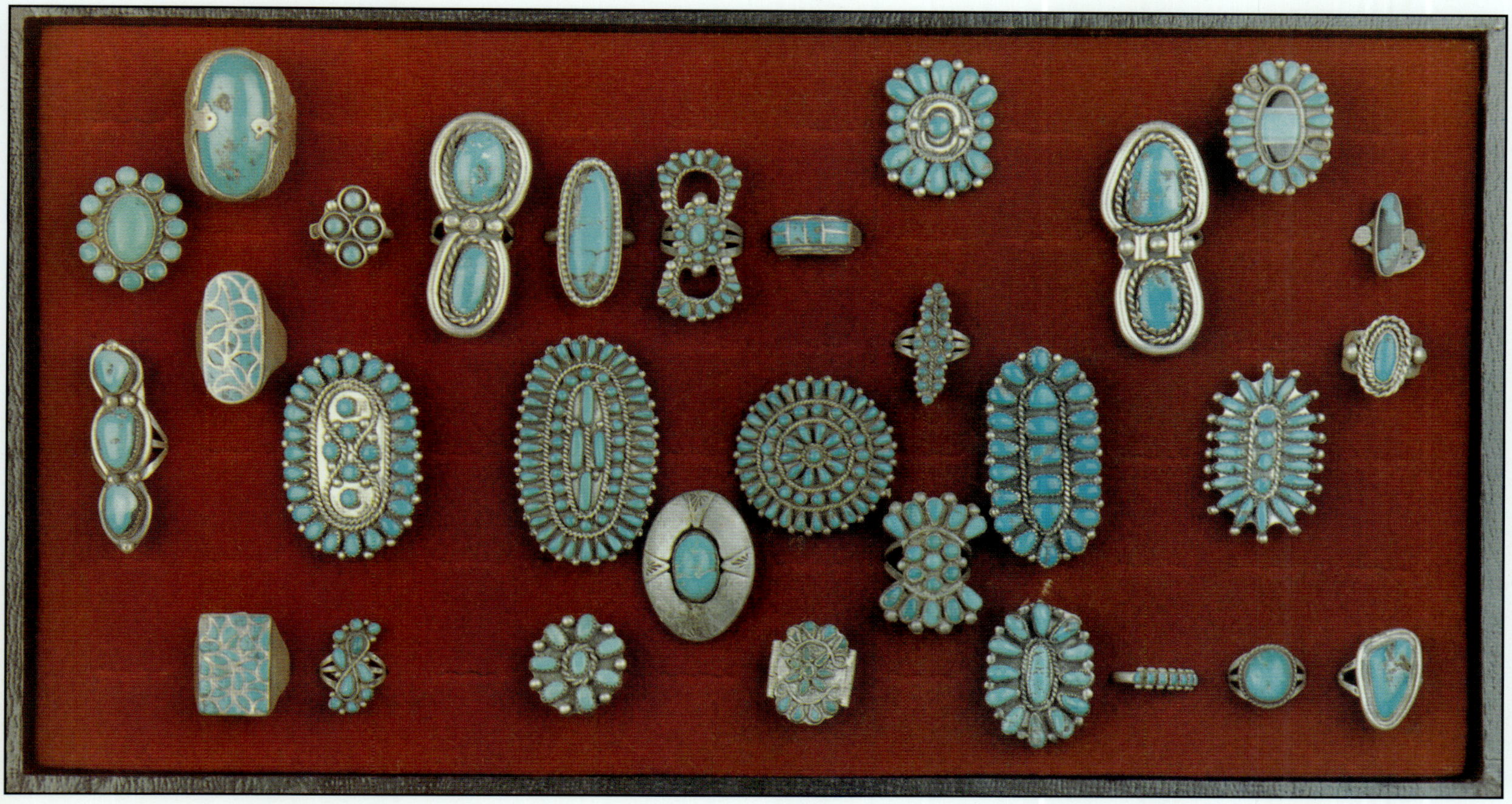

A smorgasbord of rings: Top row, from left: Man's ring with treated Morenci turquoise, appliqué eagle, and sand-cast shank, circa 1940s. / Zuni ring with Morenci turquoise, circa 1950s. / Zuni ring with Morenci turquoise and jet, circa 1940s. / Second row: Navajo cluster ring with Kingman turquoise, circa 1950. / Zuni ring with Morenci turquoise, Gaspar family, 1968. / Navajo lady's ring with two stones of Castle Dome turquoise, circa 1950s. / Navajo ring with Carlin, Nevada, turquoise, circa 1950. / Zuni lady's ring with Kingman turquoise, circa 1940s. / Zuni ring of channel band with Morenci turquoise, circa 1960s. / Navajo ring with treated Kingman turquoise, circa 1960s. / Navajo ring with turquoise chips in Devcon body compound, circa 1970s. / Third row: Zuni man's ring of cobblestone design with sand-cast shank and Kingman turquoise, circa 1950. / Zuni lady's ring with "Snake Eye" turquoise from the Lone Mountain mine, circa 1930s. / Navajo ring with Morenci turquoise, circa 1950. / Fourth row: Zuni lady's ring with treated Kingman turquoise, dye evaporating and returning to turquoise chalk, circa 1960s. / Zuni cluster ring with Kingman turquoise, circa 1960. / Zuni petite-point ring with Morenci turquoise, circa 1950s. / Zuni ring with Morenci turquoise, circa 1950s. / Zuni cluster ring of nickel and treated Morenci turquoise, circa 1970s. / Zuni-style, Navajo-made needlepoint rings with Kingman turquoise, probably Victor Moses Begay, circa 1960s. / Fifth row: Navajo shadow box ring with Persian turquoise, circa 1950. / Zuni cluster ring with Kingman turquoise and fourteen-gauge half-round wire shank, circa 1950. / Sixth row: Zuni cobblestone ring with Kingman turquoise and sand-cast shank, circa 1960. / Zuni lady's ring with Kingman turquoise, circa 1960s. / Zuni cluster ring with low-end Morenci turquoise, circa 1950. / Crude petite-point ring with Kingman turquoise and homemade repairs, circa 1940s. / Zuni cluster ring with Kingman and other turquoise, circa 1950. / Zuni square ring with Morenci turquoise and seven rows, circa 1950s. / Navajo ring with treated Kingman turquoise, circa 1960. / Navajo ring with treated Pilot Mountain turquoise, circa 1960s. *Dennehotso collection*.

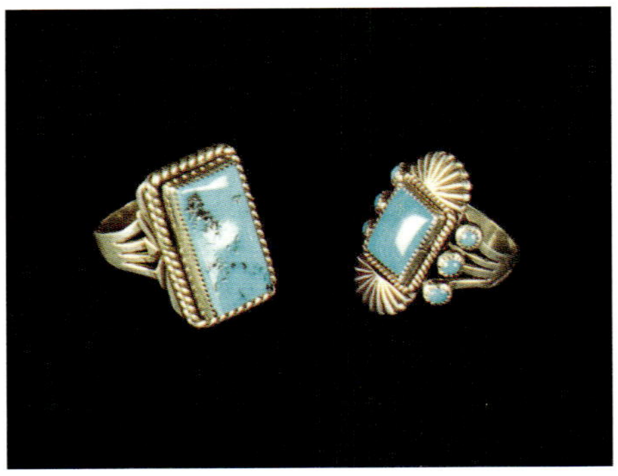

Two silver and turquoise man's rings by Joe Kiyoomia, Navajo. *Shiprock Trading Company collection*

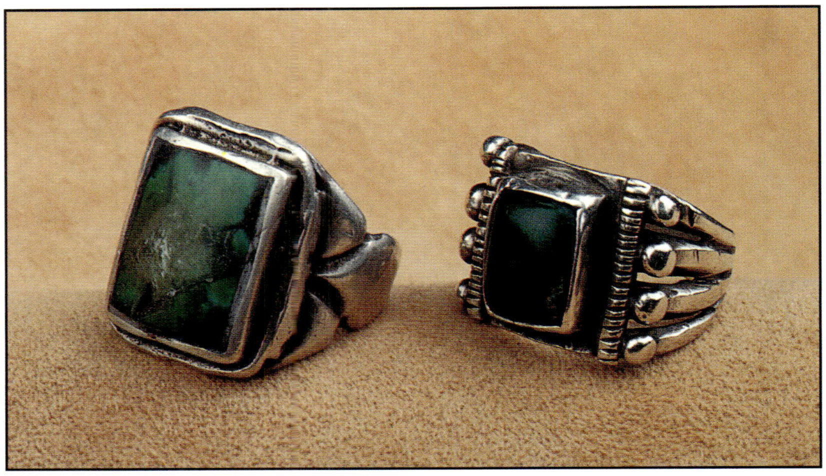

Two early 20th century Navajo finger rings with square turquoise stones: Left, with a worked and flattened band. Right, with a 4-way split shank. *Lynn D. Trusdell, Crown & Eagle Antiques*

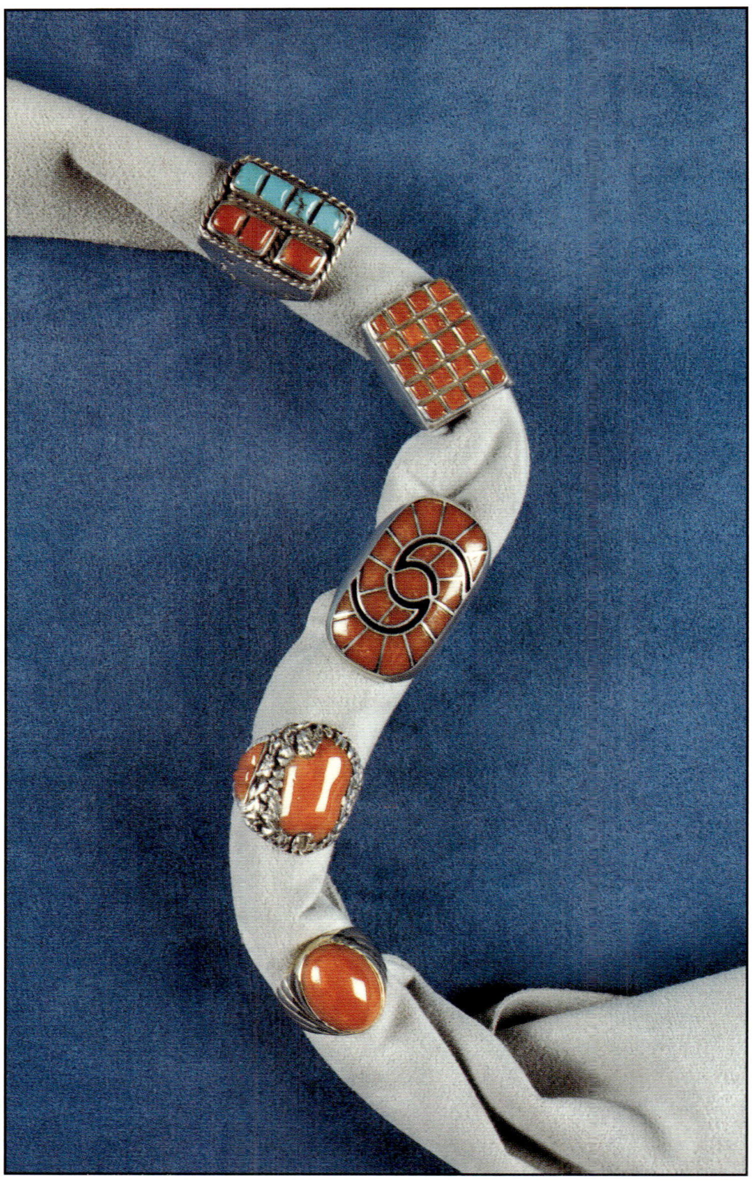

Five Zuni and Navajo silver finger rings featuring coral, 1980s. *Private collection*

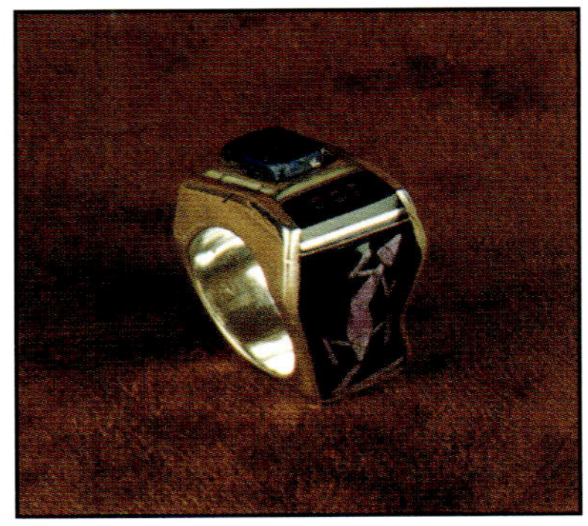

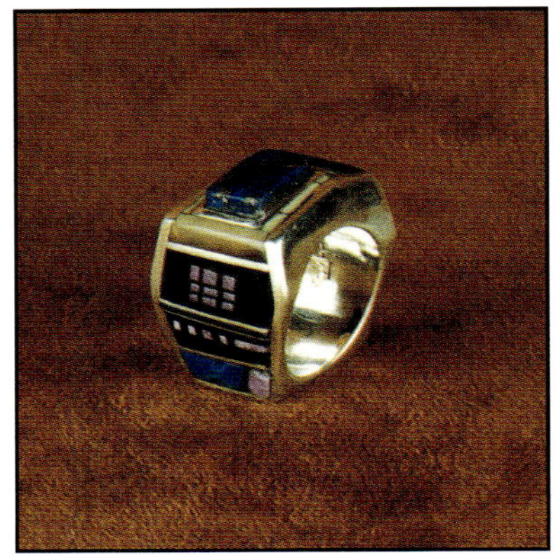

Man's gold ring with onyx, ivory, lapis lazuli, and sugalite inlay made by Danny Romero, 1988. *Brett W. Bastien collection*

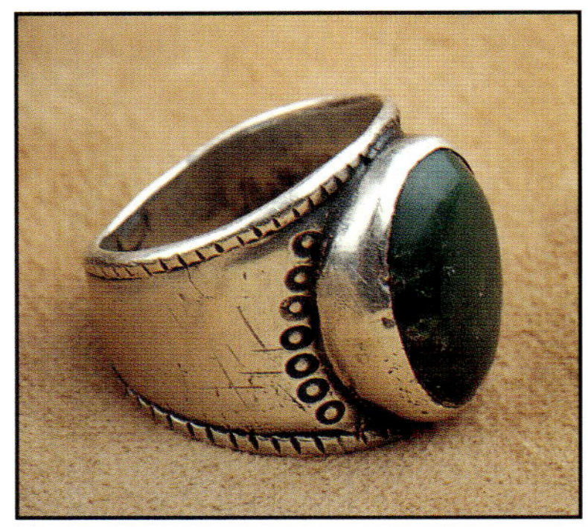

Navajo man's finger ring with oval green turquoise stone in a smooth bezel, c.1900-1910. *Lynn D. Trusdell, Crown & Eagle Antiques*

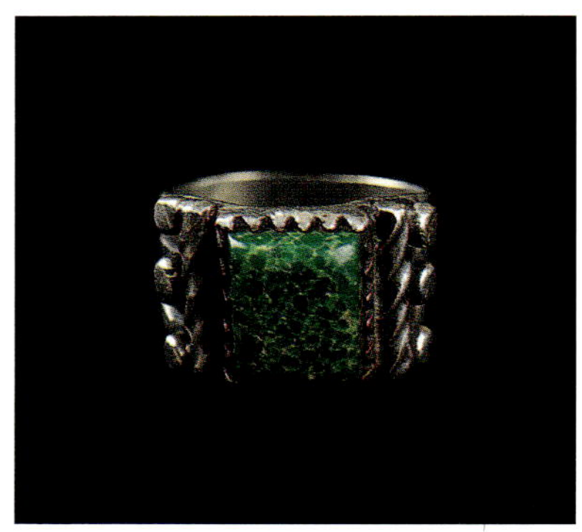

Man's Navajo silver finger ring with square Cerillos turqupise stone in a divided bezel with silver raindrops on each side, c.1910-'15. *Photograph by Freddy Perojo, Courtesy Timothy Pitt*

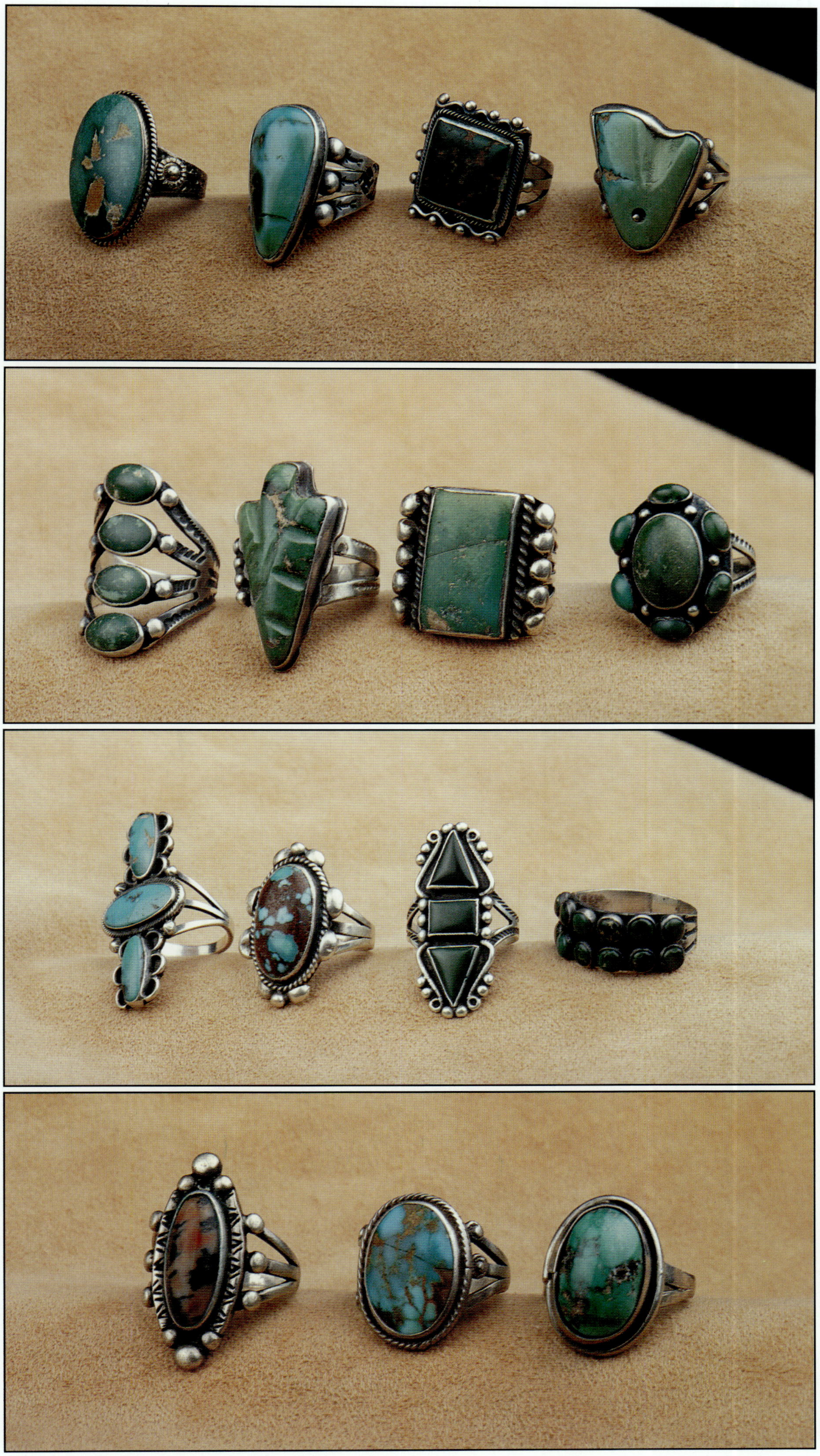

Wonderful tourist-trade finger rings from the 1920s and 1930s. *Lynn D. Trusdell, Crown & Eagle Antiques*

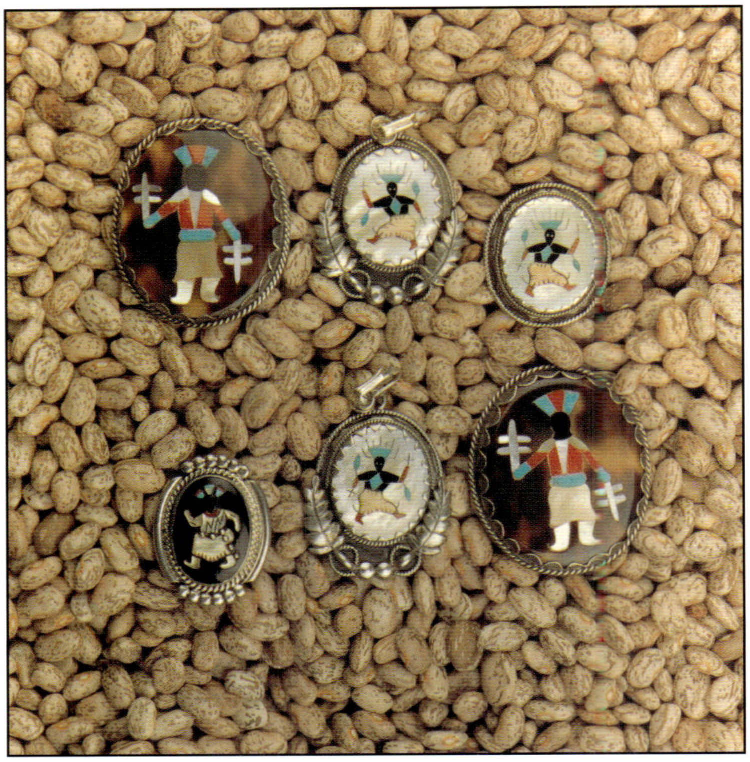

A group of Zuni inlaid silver jewelry featuring human figures in the decoration: Two brown tortoiseshell pins with inlaid Kachina dancers design. / A pair of earrings and a ring with white shell background and matching Apache crown dancers. / Black background to silver ring with dancer of inlaid stones, circa 1960s. *Enchanted Mesa collection* .

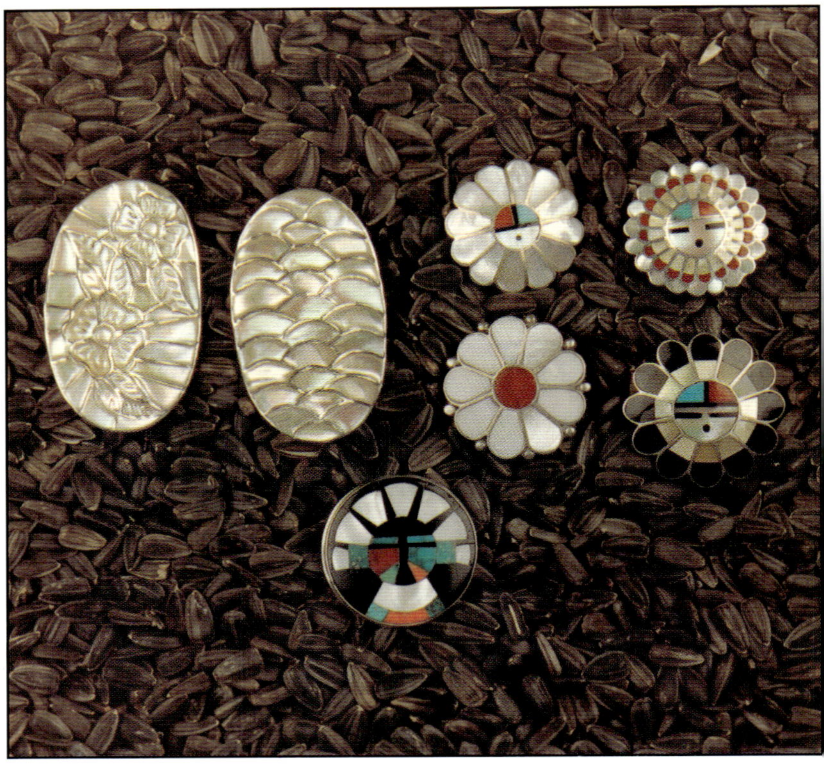

Zuni rings with intricate shell and stone inlaid decorations: Two ovals of white shell inlay by Nicholas and Theresa Lehela. / A group of sunface and floral round inlays, unmarked, 1980s. *Enchanted Mesa collection* .

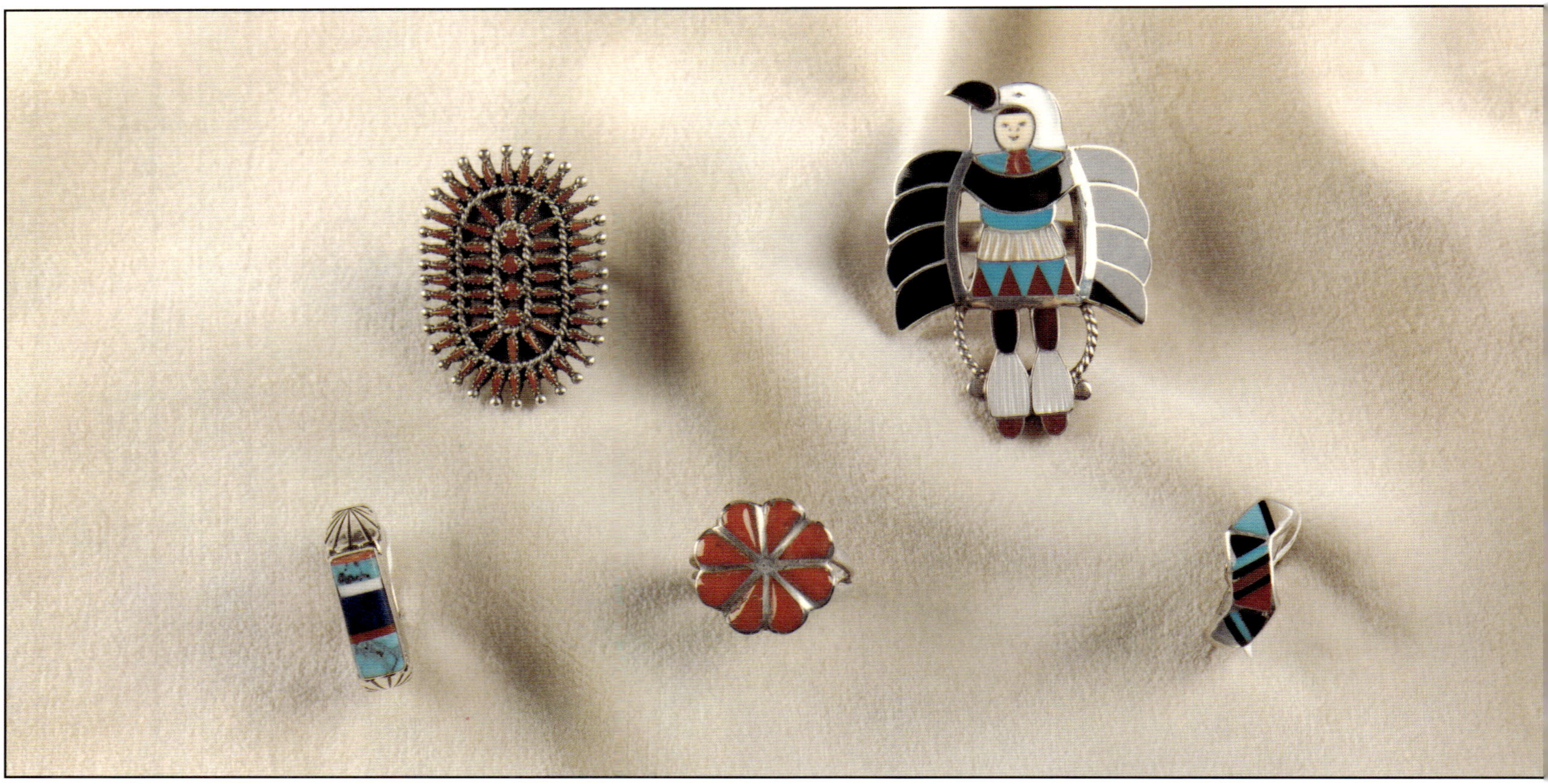

Zuni lady's rings, from top left: Red petite point ring by Bonnie Quam, Zuni. / Eagle man inlay ring by M.B. / Bar mosaic inlay ring. / Coral ring with eight petals. / Zigzag design inlaid ring by R.L. Kellestura. *Indian Post collection*.

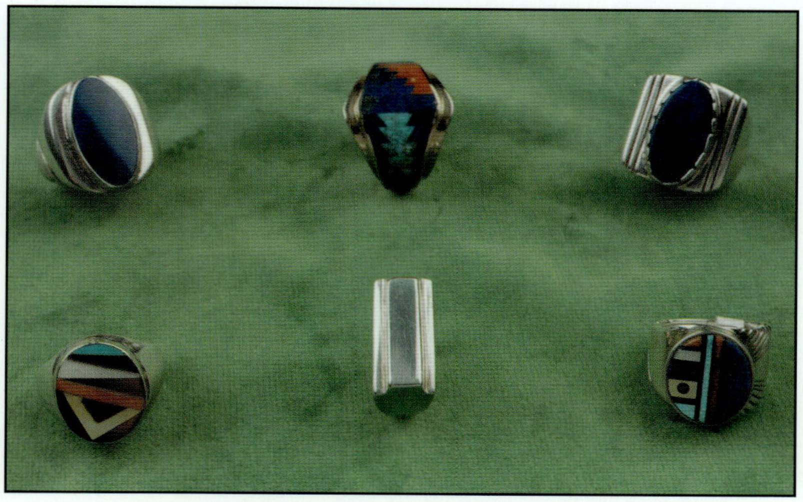

Man's silver rings, Top row: Two lapis lazuli and silver oval rings by Cipi Crazyhorse, Cochiti. Gold band with lapis lazuli, turquoise, and coral stepped inlay by Don Johnson, Navajo.
Bottom row: Two inlaid "Zuni-style" rings in silver by Jesse Monongye, Hopi. / Plain silver raised ring by Joe Quintana, Cochiti. *Leonard D. Prins collection*

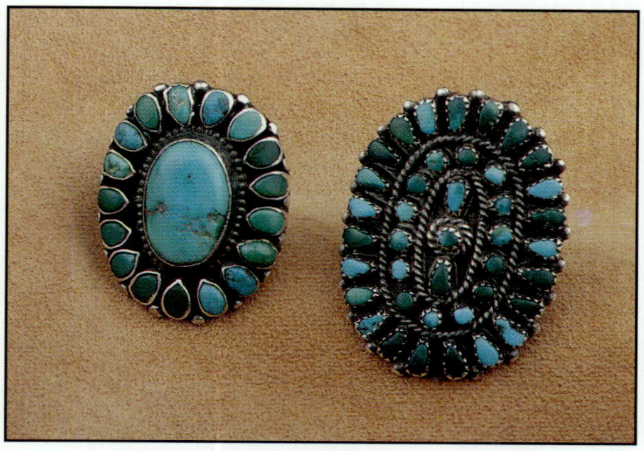

Two Zuni finger rings with clustered turquoise stones, 1920s-1930s. *Lynn D. Trusdell, Crown & Eagle Antiques*

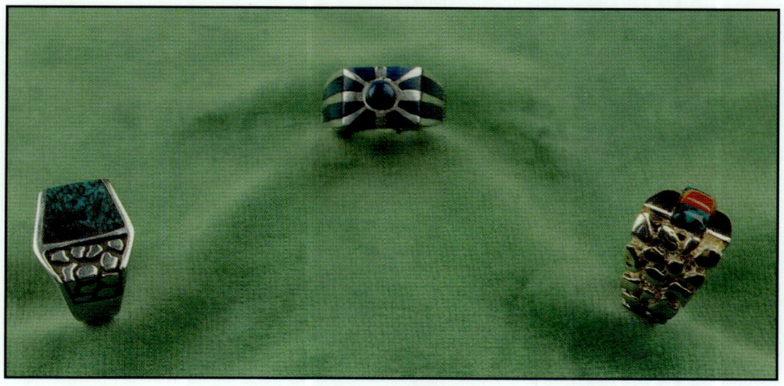

Man's rings by Andy Kirk, Navajo, 1980s: Turquoise and silver ring. / Geometric designed ring with flat lapis lazuli inlay. / Gold ring with raised coral and turquoise stones. *Leonard D. Prins collection*

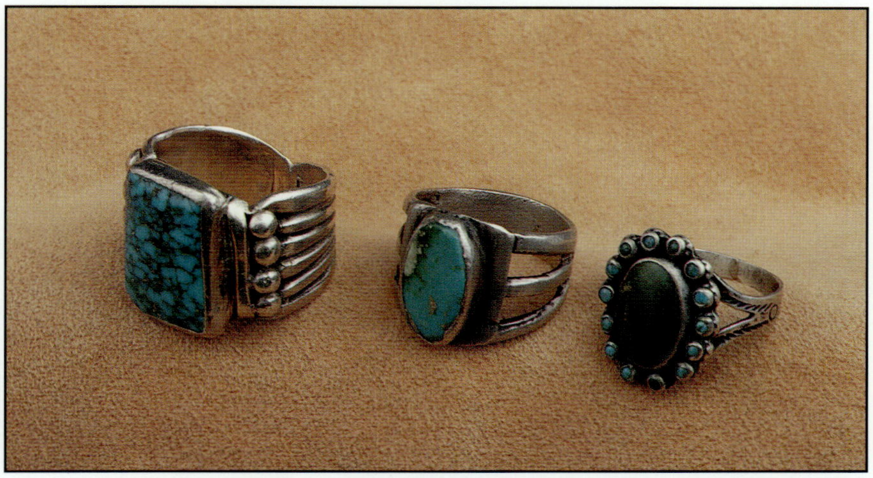

Left: Navajo finger ring with a chiseled shank, Spiderweb turquoise stone, and silver raindrop accents. / Navajo silver ring with a split shank and a small silver snake ornament overlapping the oval turquoise stone. / Early Zuni finger ring made for the tourist trade. *Lynn D. Trusdell, Crown & Eagle Antiques*

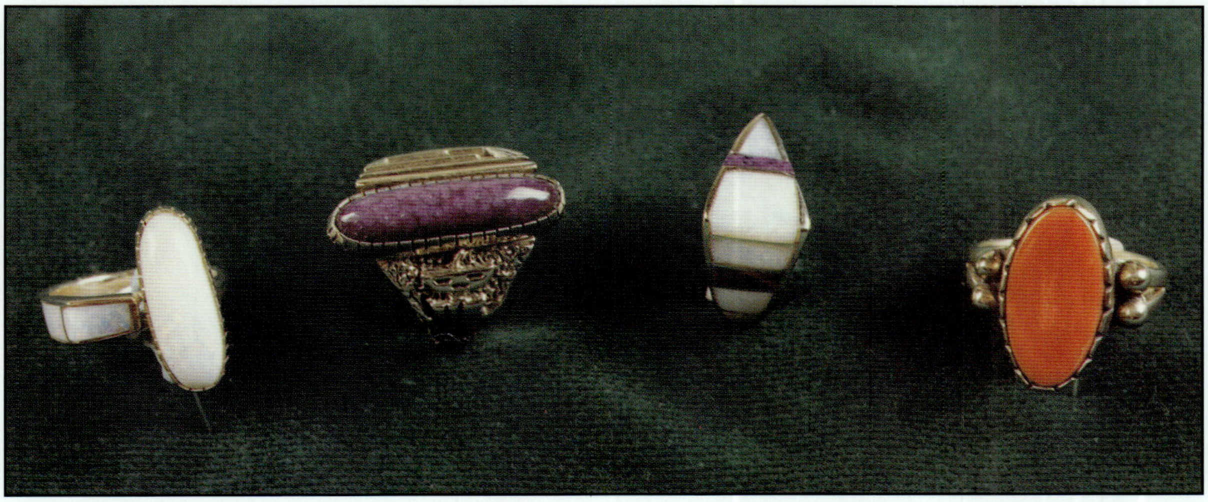

Lady's finger rings from the 1980s: Three by Andy Kirk, Navajo, with opal and lavulite set in gold. / Oval coral and gold ring by Joe Quintana, Cochiti. *Indian Post collection*

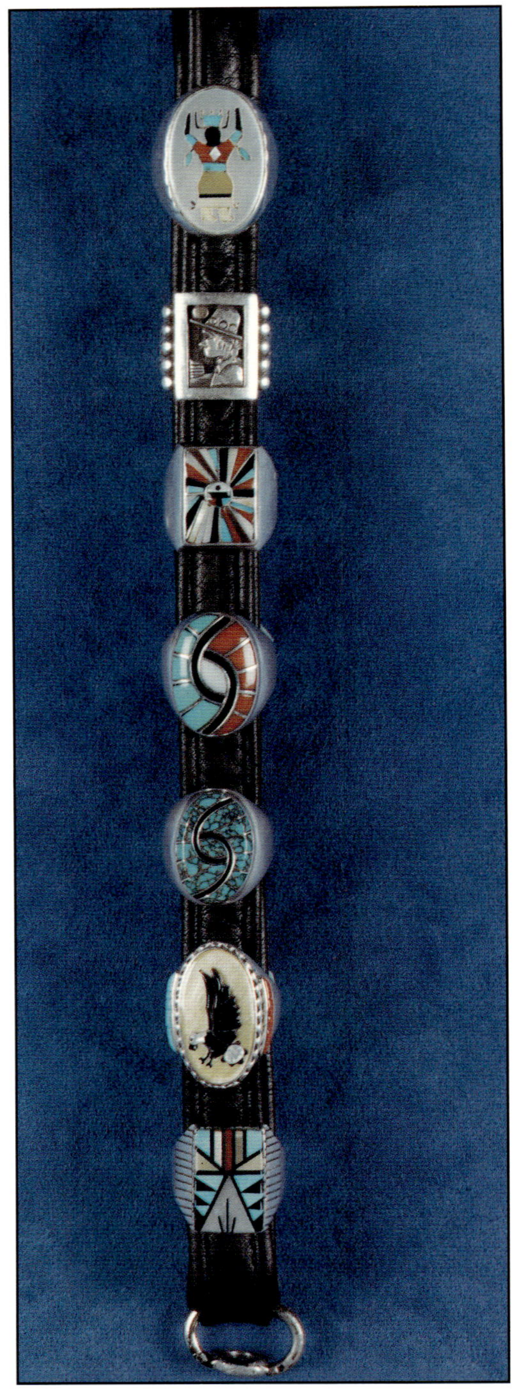

A group of man's rings shown from the top: Zuni inlaid lady with pot on head. / Navajo silver cutout ring of a man in a hat with a gold moon by Paul Arviso, 1986. / Zuni sunburst around sunface with inlay. / Turquoise and coral inlay ring by D. and A. Quandelacy, Zuni, 1976. / Turquoise inlay ring by D. Quandelacy, Zuni. / Eagle inlay ring by Don C.Dewa, Zuni. / Geometric inlay ring by B. Jack. *Private collection on permanent loan to Ohio University*

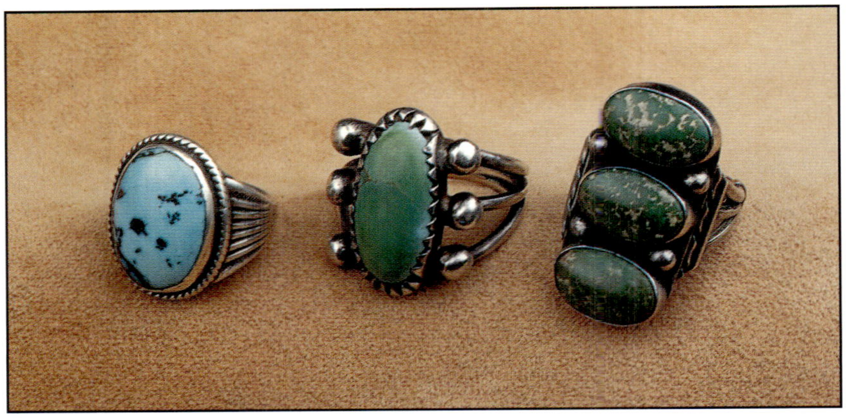

Left: Navajo silver finger ring with a single Lone mountain turquoise stone and flattened silver work on each side, c.1940s. / Navajo split-band silver finger ring with a single oval turquoise stone and silver raindrops decorations, c.1900-1910. / Navajo silver finger ring with a split band and three oval turquoise stones, 1920s. *Lynn D. Trusdell, Crown & Eagle Antiques*

Four Navajo silver finger rings set with Coral nugget or turquoise single stones and one Zuni ring set with channel inlay.

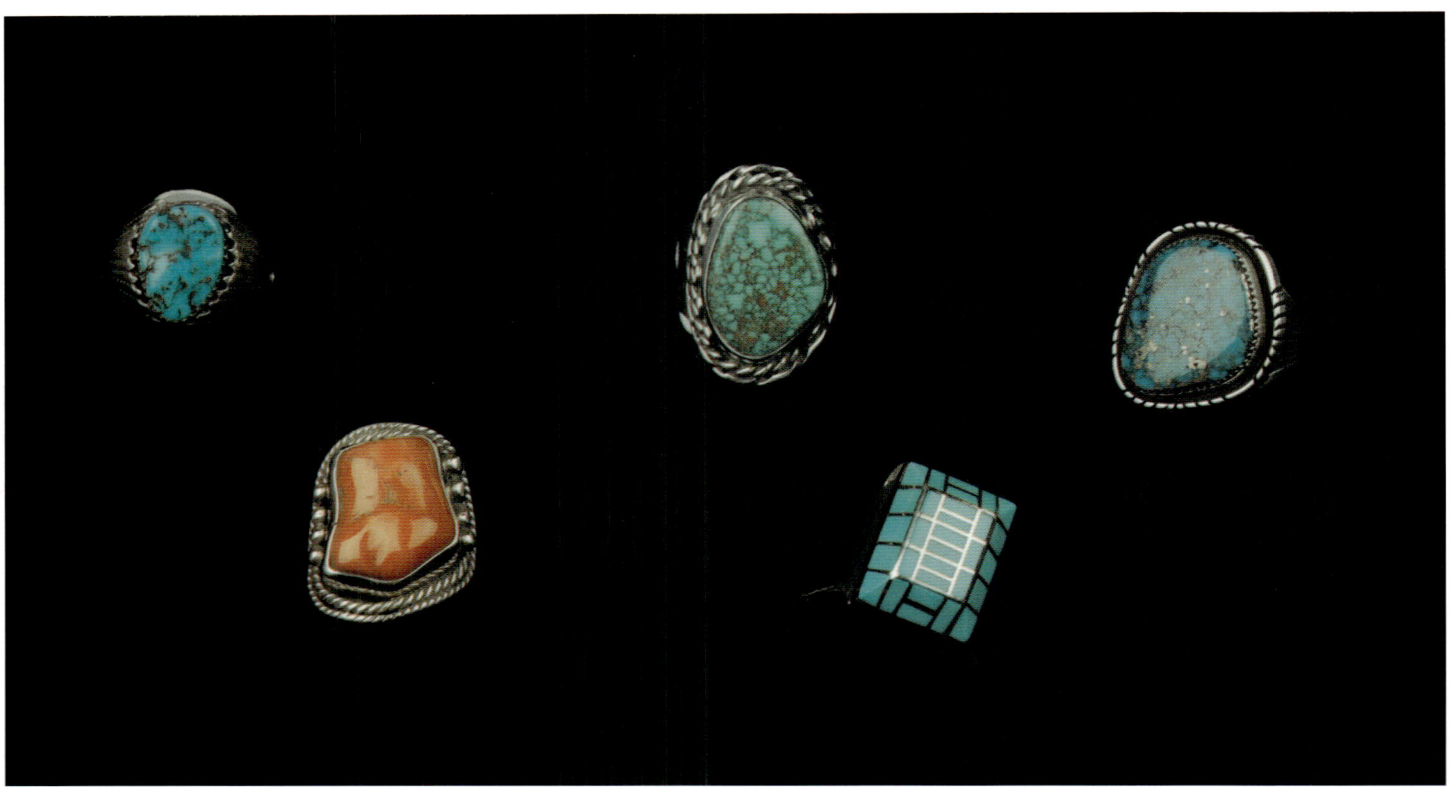

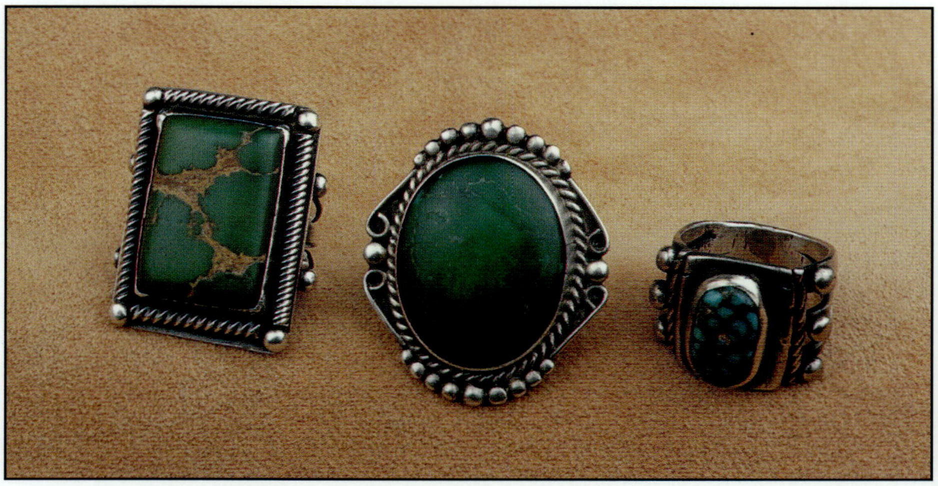

Three early Navajo finger rings. Left and center with single Cerillos turquoise stones and right with Spiderweb turquoise stone. *Lynn D. Trusdell, Crown & Eagle Antiques*

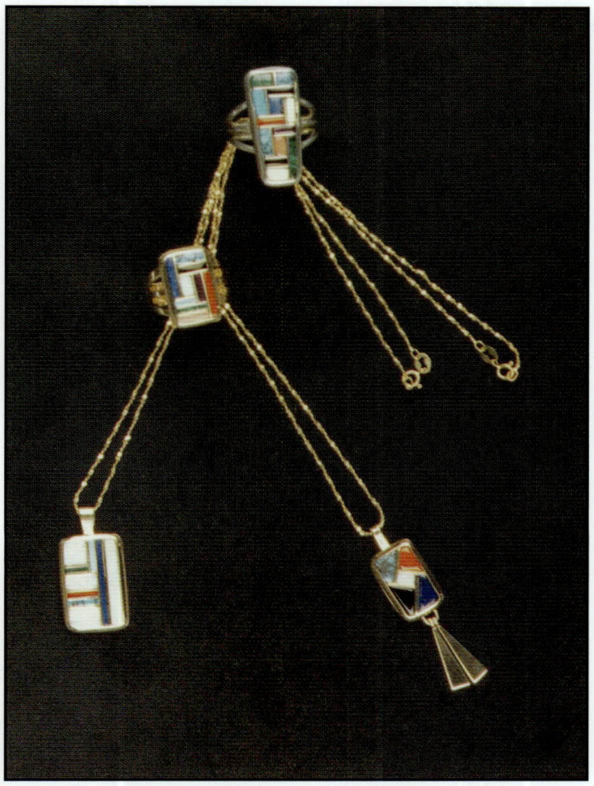

Two gold and silver matching pendant and ring sets with stone inlay by Bitsui and Russell (Philip and Fannie [Bitsui] Russell). *Keams Canyon Arts and Crafts collection*

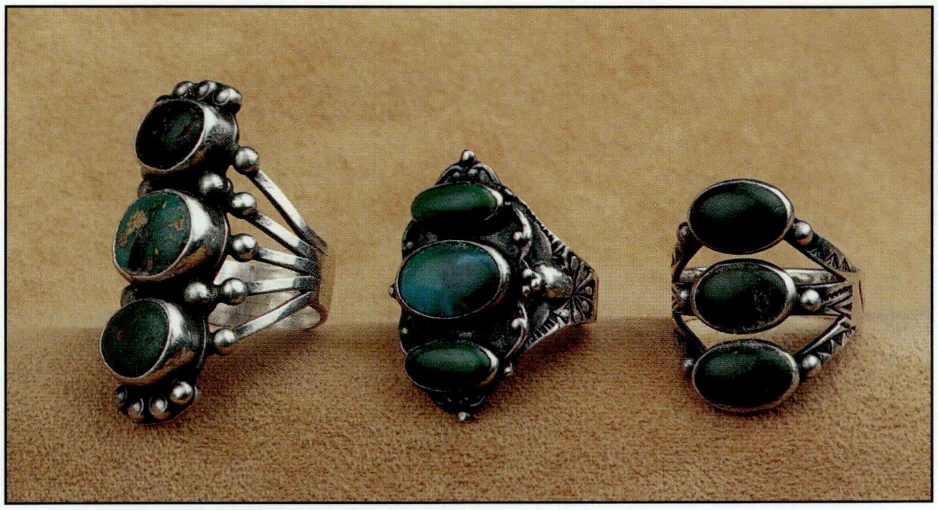

Three Navajo silver finger rings with split shanks and each set with three turquoise stones, 1920s. *Lynn D. Trusdell, Crown & Eagle Antiques*

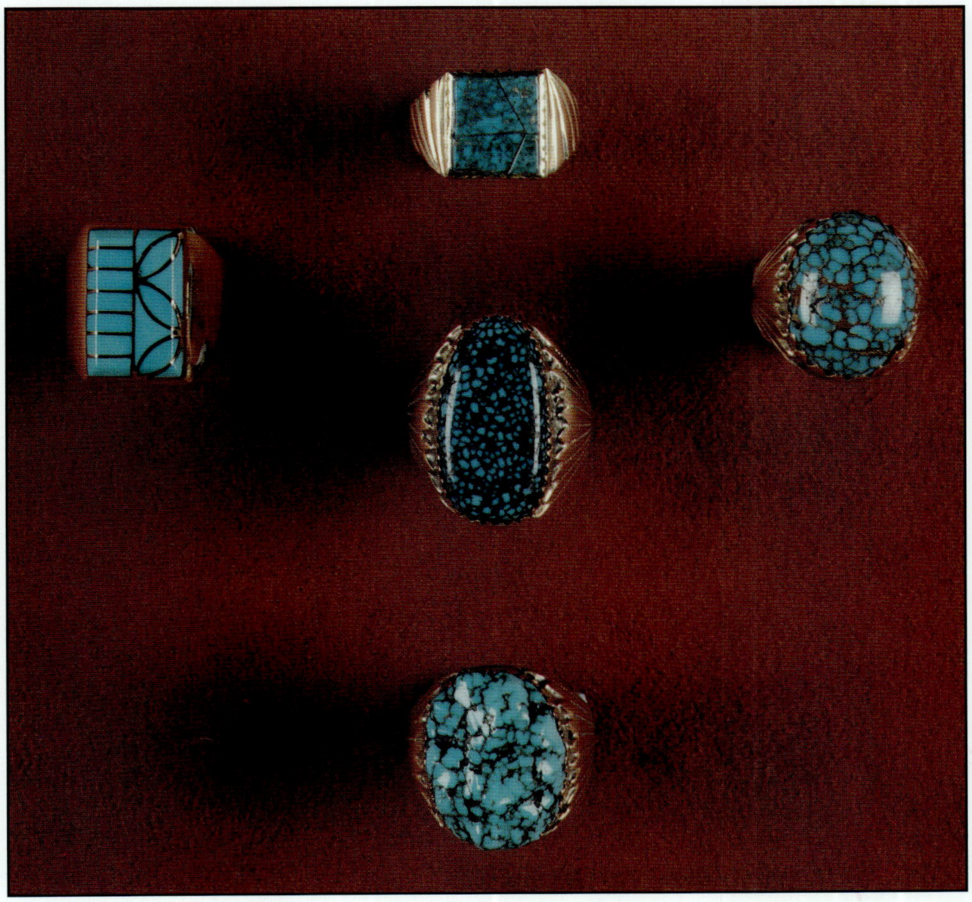

Man's rings of cast gold and turquoise: From the left, Channel inlay by D. and A. Quandelacy, Zuni, 1979. / Square mosaic ring by B.K.M., 1979. / Oval Lander's blue turquoise ring by Robert Leekya, Zuni, 1977. / / Carioca Lake turquoise nugget by Robert Leekya, Zuni. / Oval Nevada Blue Spiderweb turquoise ring by Bernice Leekya, Zuni, 1970s. *Private collection*

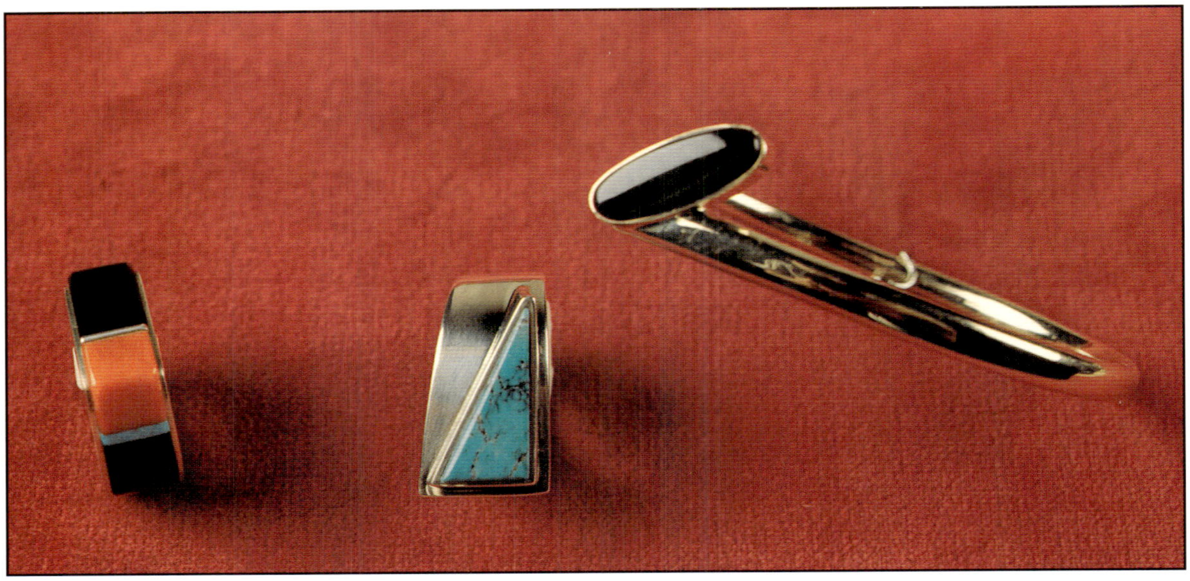

Two lady's gold rings and one gold bracelet by Richard Chavez, San Felipe: Bracelet with oval lavulite stone. / Triangular turquoise set in a gold band. / Coral, onyx, and turquoise inlaid in a gold band. *Indian Post collection*

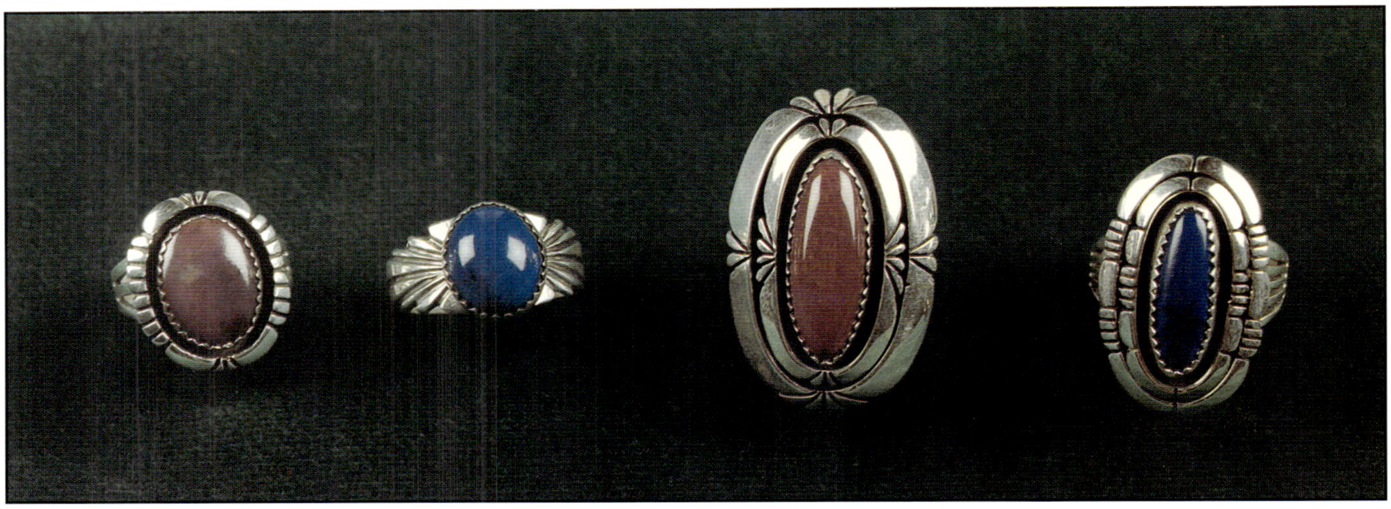

Four Navajo wrought silver lady's rings featuring lavulite and lapis lazuli. *Leonard D. Prins collection*

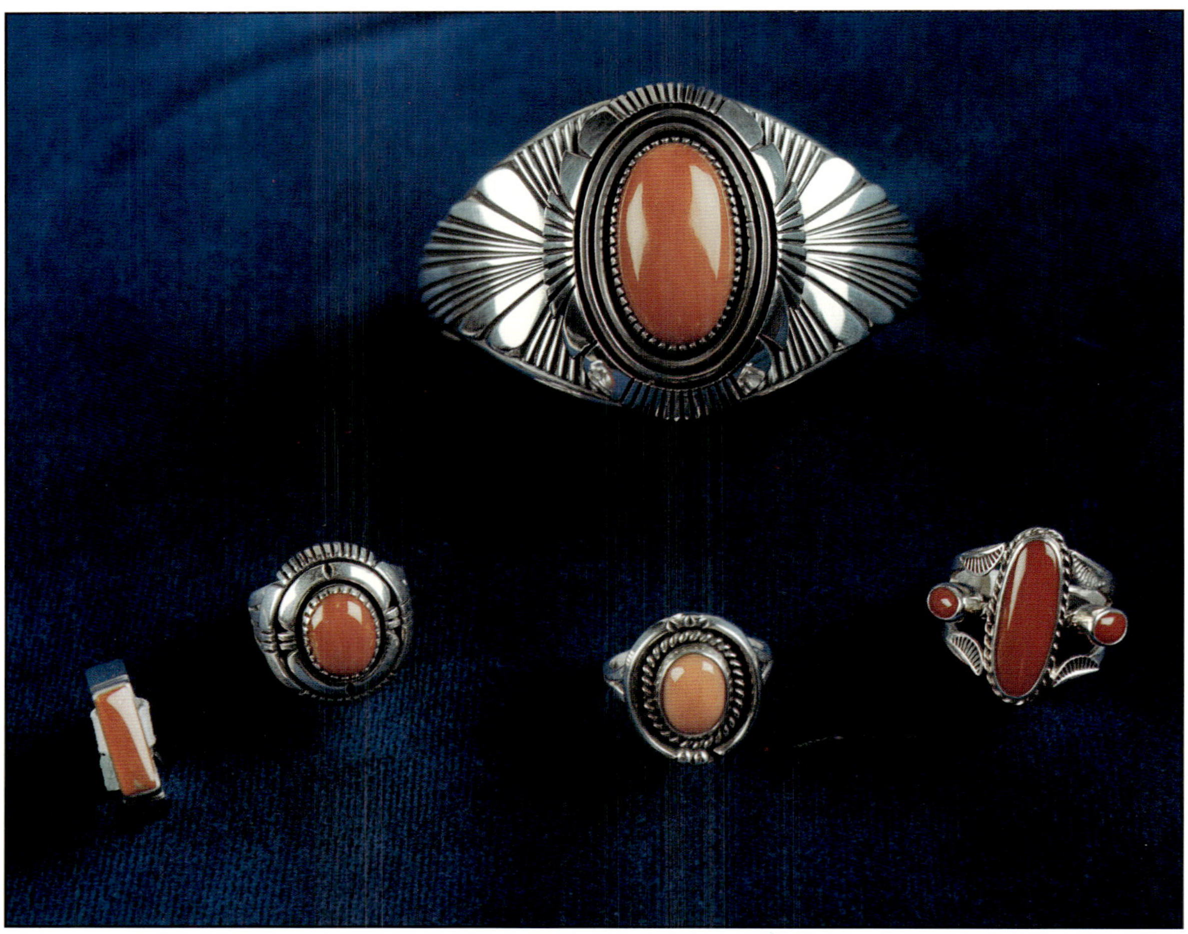

Four dynamic Navajo lady's rings and one bracelet made with wrought sterling silver and coral from the late 1980s: Bracelet by G. Nelson / Rectangular inlaid ring in a silver band./ Dark red oval coral in a heavy silver bezel. / Oval light red stones in silver band with rope wire bezel. / Three dark stones in stamped silverwork band. *Indian Post collection*

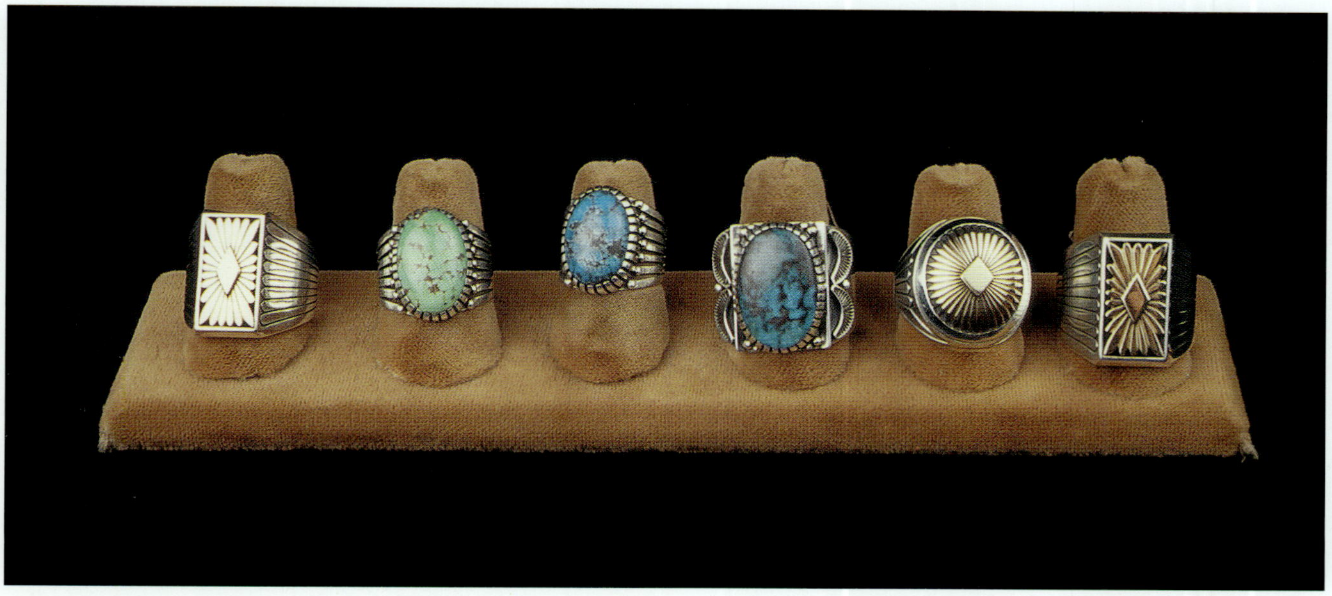

Six silver finger rings by Howard Nelson, Navajo, 2002. *Courtesy McGee's, Keams Canyon*

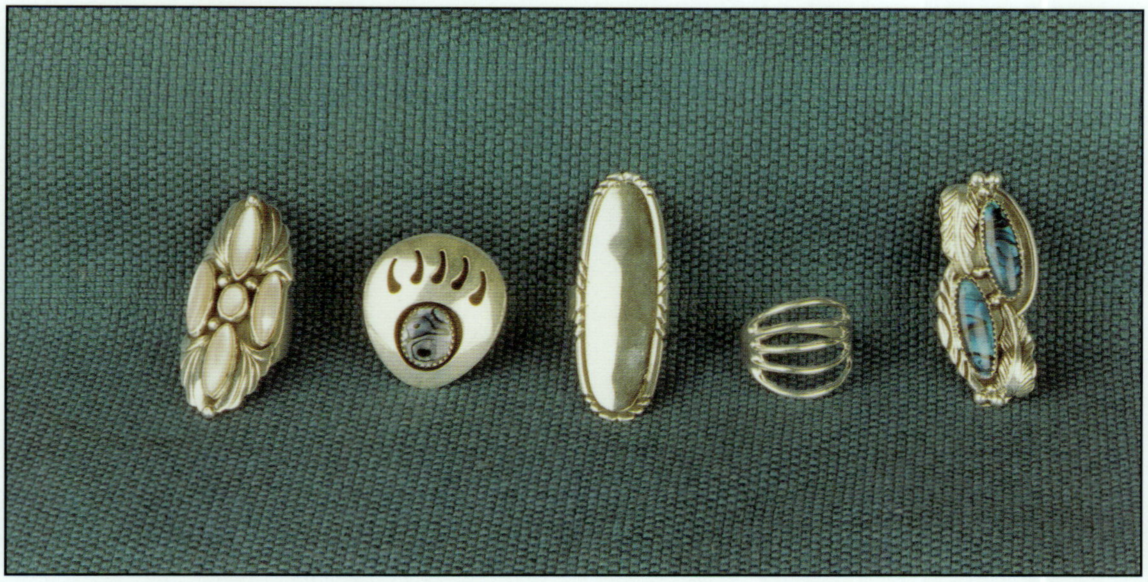

Five Navajo sterling silver lady's rings made in 1989. *Bing Crosby collection*

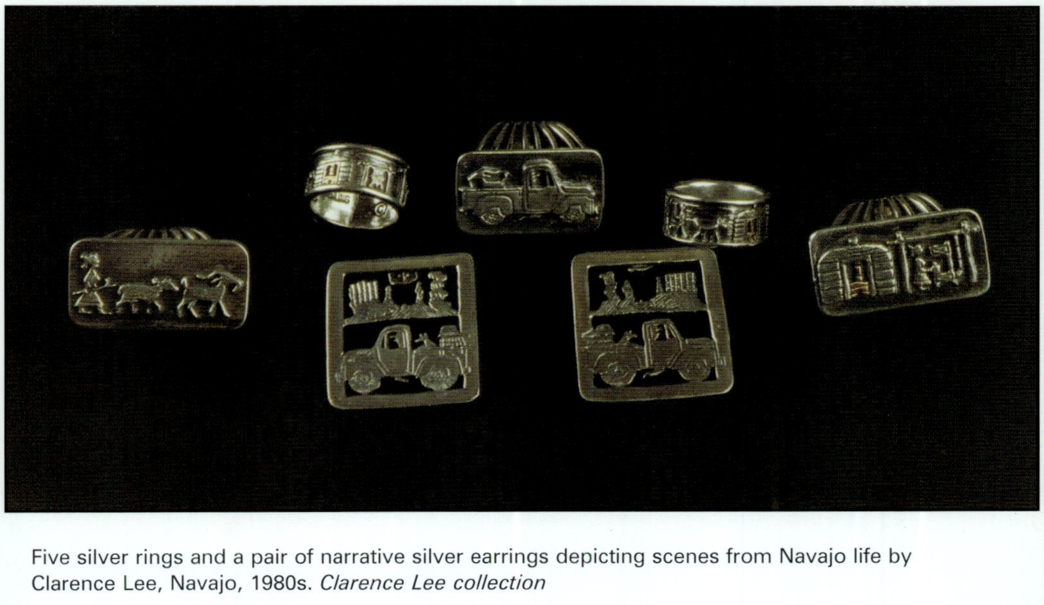

Five silver rings and a pair of narrative silver earrings depicting scenes from Navajo life by Clarence Lee, Navajo, 1980s. *Clarence Lee collection*

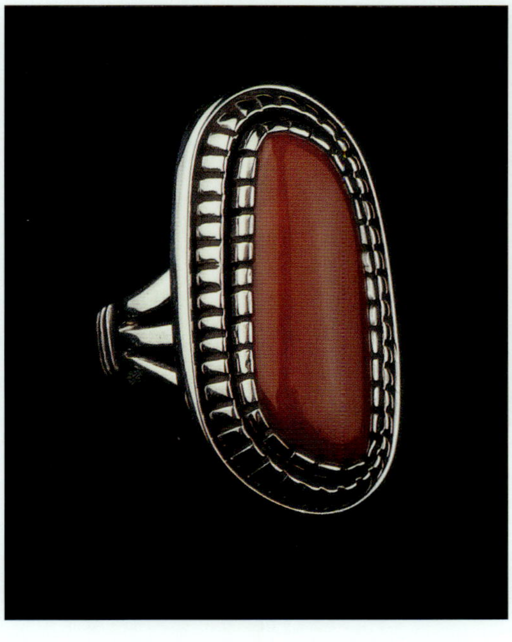

Silver and coral finger ring by Fannie Bitsui and Philip Russell, Navajo, 2002. *Courtesy McGee's, Keams Canyon*

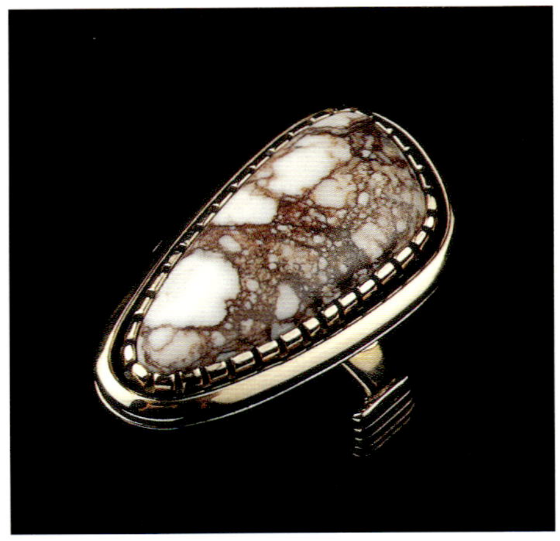

Silver and stonel finger ring by Fannie Bitsui and Philip Russell, Navajo, 2002. *Courtesy McGee's, Keams Canyon*

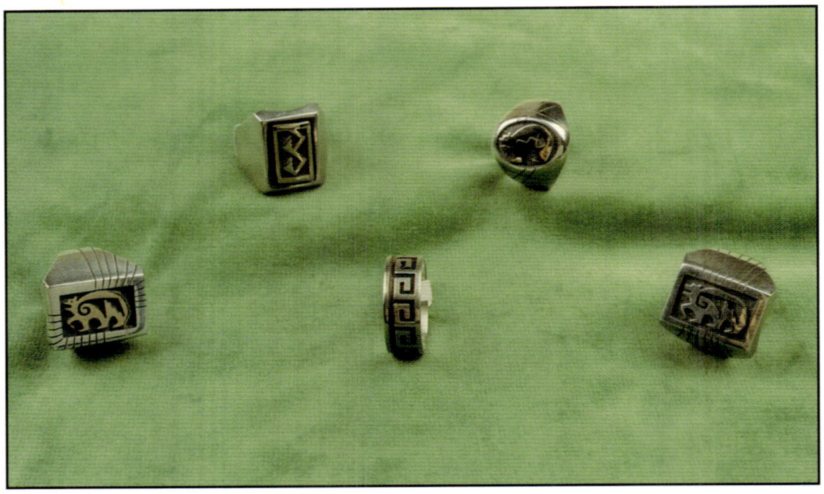

Silver Hopi man's rings, including four with gold overlay designs by Mitchell Sockyma. / One silver band with gold overlay "Greek key" design by Te'*ma. *Leonard D. Prins collection*

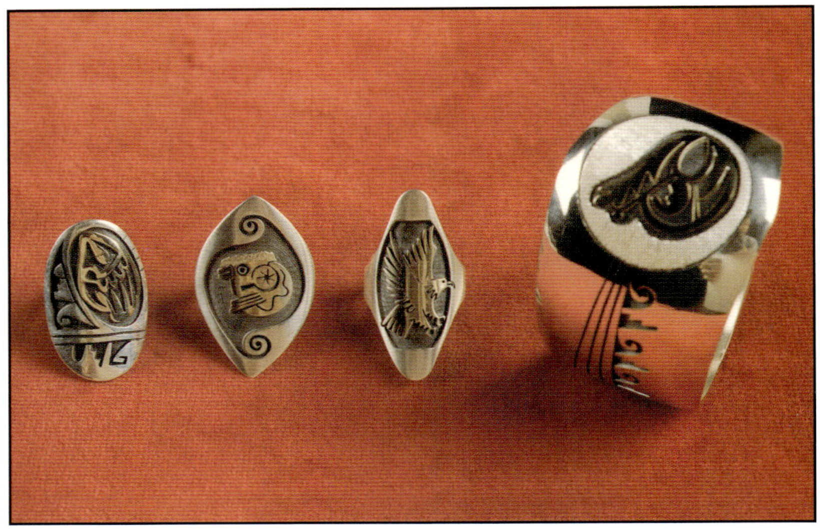

Hopi lady's rings and bracelet of gold overlay and silver, late 1980s: Bear paw designed ring by Mitchell Sockyma. / Two rings with geometric bird and eagle designs by Yoyokie. / Beautiful cuff bracelet by Poseyesva. *Indian Post collection*.

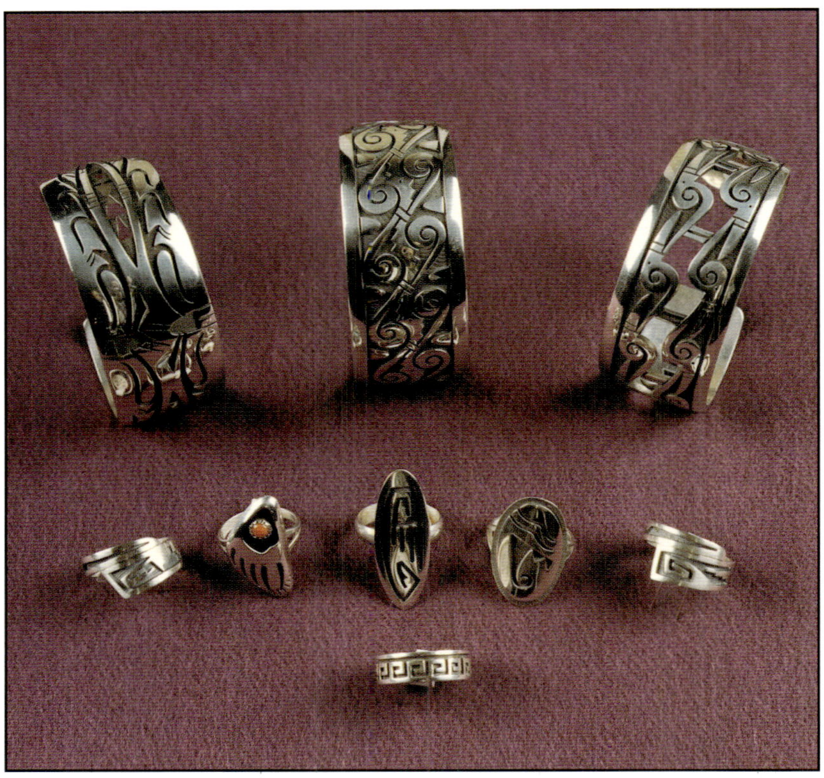

Three bold silver bracelets and six silver lady's rings, all in Hopi overlay work, late 1980s. *Leonard D. Prins collection*

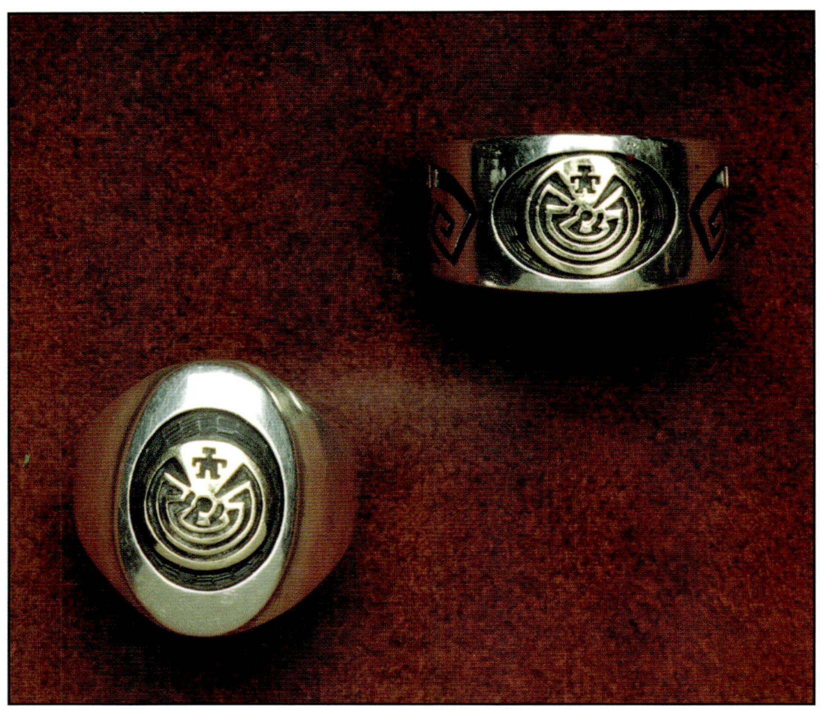

Man in the Maze silver overlay rings of gold and silver by Jason Takala. *Keams Canyon Arts and Crafts collection*

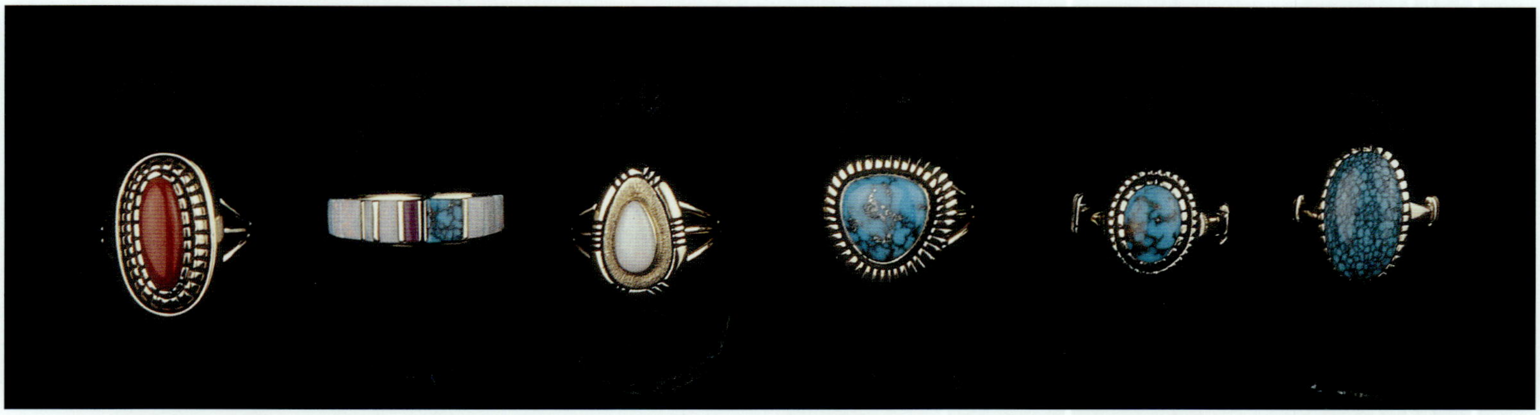

Silver finger rings with coral, shell, and turquoise by Fannie Bitsui and Philip Russell, Navajo, 2002. *Courtesy McGee's, Keams Canyon*

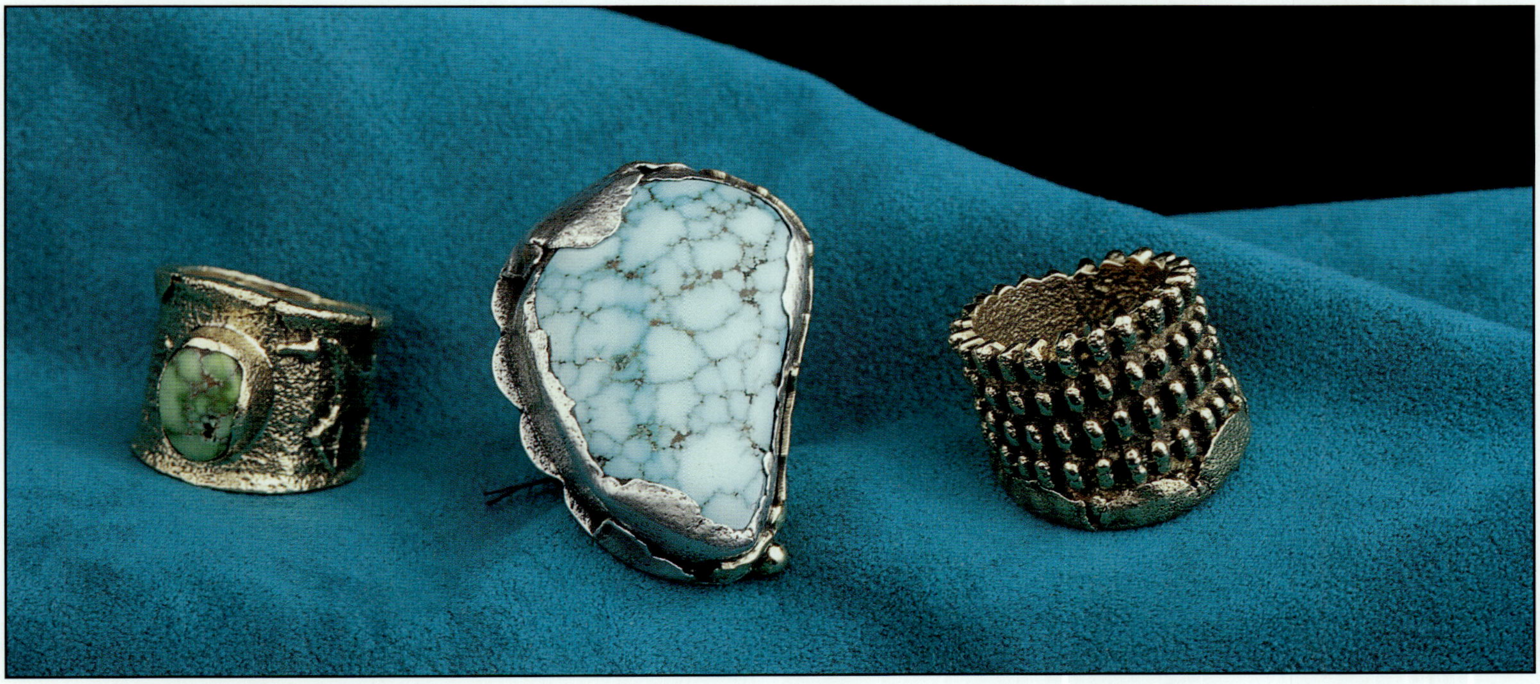

18k gold ring with horse design and Carico Lake turquoise. (1200) / Silver, 18k gold, and old Kingman turquoise ring, "Blue Sky Over Santa Fe." (800) / 18k gold rim in corn design. (900) All by Anthony Lovato, Santo Domingo, 2002. *Courtesy of Gerald Peters Gallery, Santa Fe, New Mexico*

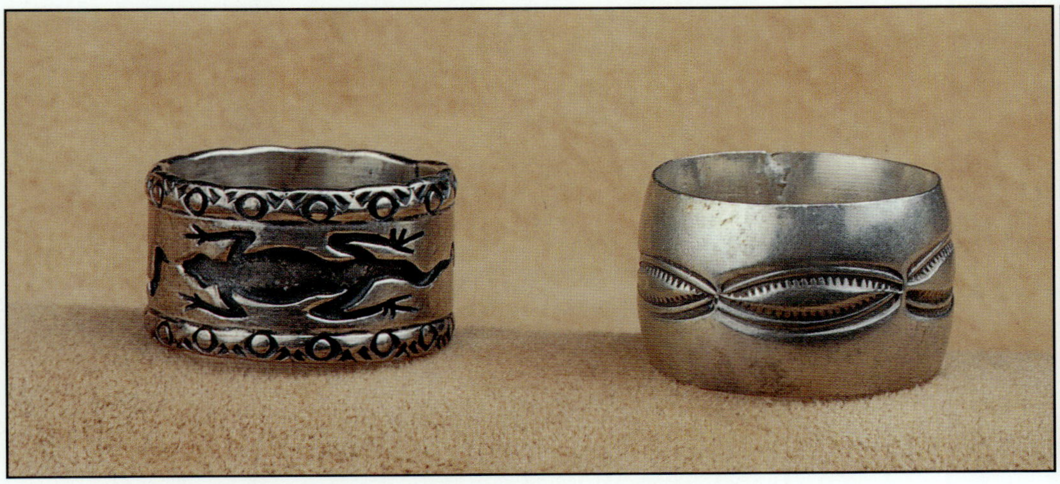

Wedding band style rings: Left, Hopi. Right, Navajo. *Lynn D. Trusdell, Crown & Eagle Antiques*

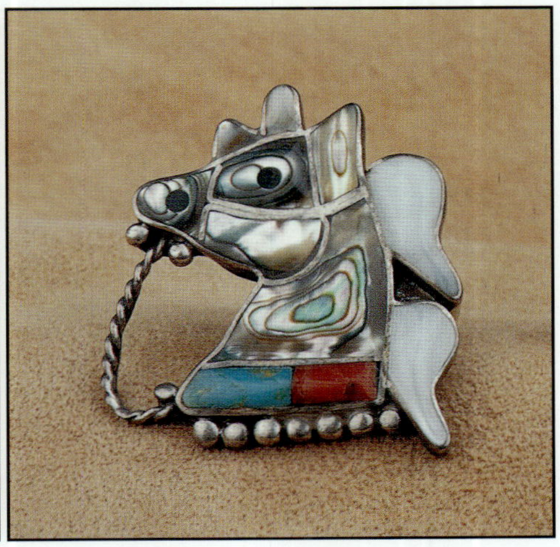

Zuni finger ring in a horse's head design with shell, coral and turquoise stones, and with the unique use of abalone shell to make the horse's hide. 1950-60s. *Lynn D. Trusdell, Crown & Eagle Antiques*

Matching Sets

Women's sets

By the 1970s the public was interested in acquiring matching pieces: necklaces and bracelets, or bolo ties and buckles, or earrings and rings. Silversmiths complied, and then the public wanted larger matching sets. Eventually the craftsmen designed pieces that could be mixed to the customer's taste.

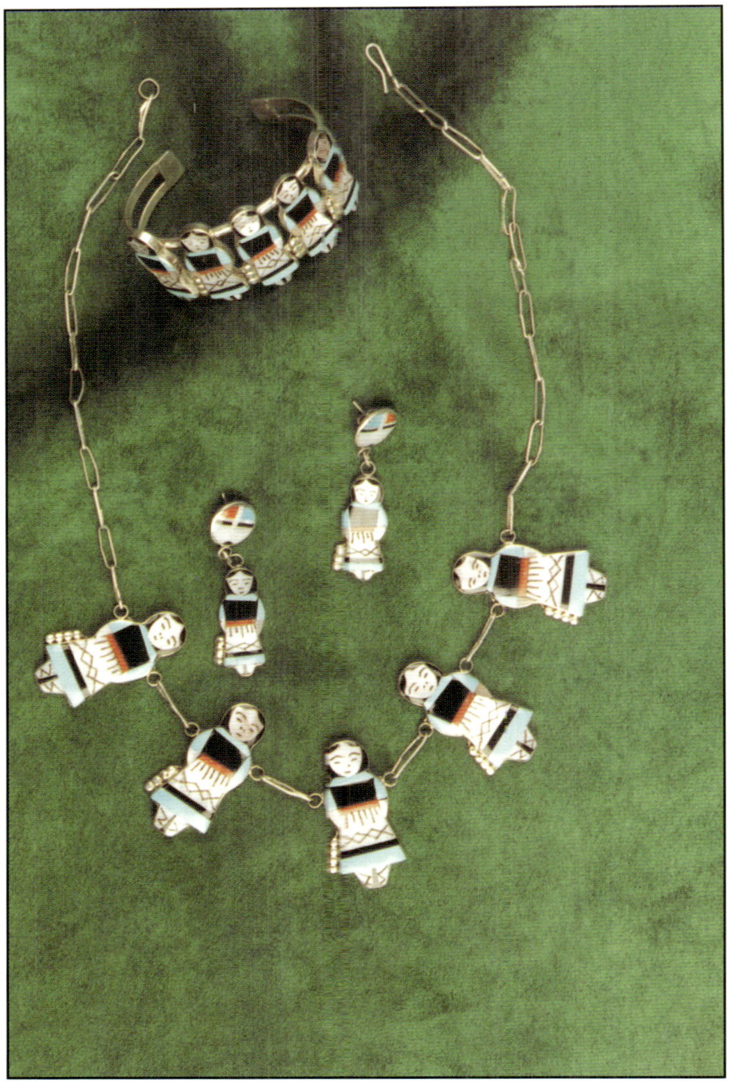

Zuni lady's matching set including earrings, necklace, and bracelet with inlaid figural design of young Indian girls by Theresa Waseta. *Turquoise Lady collection.*

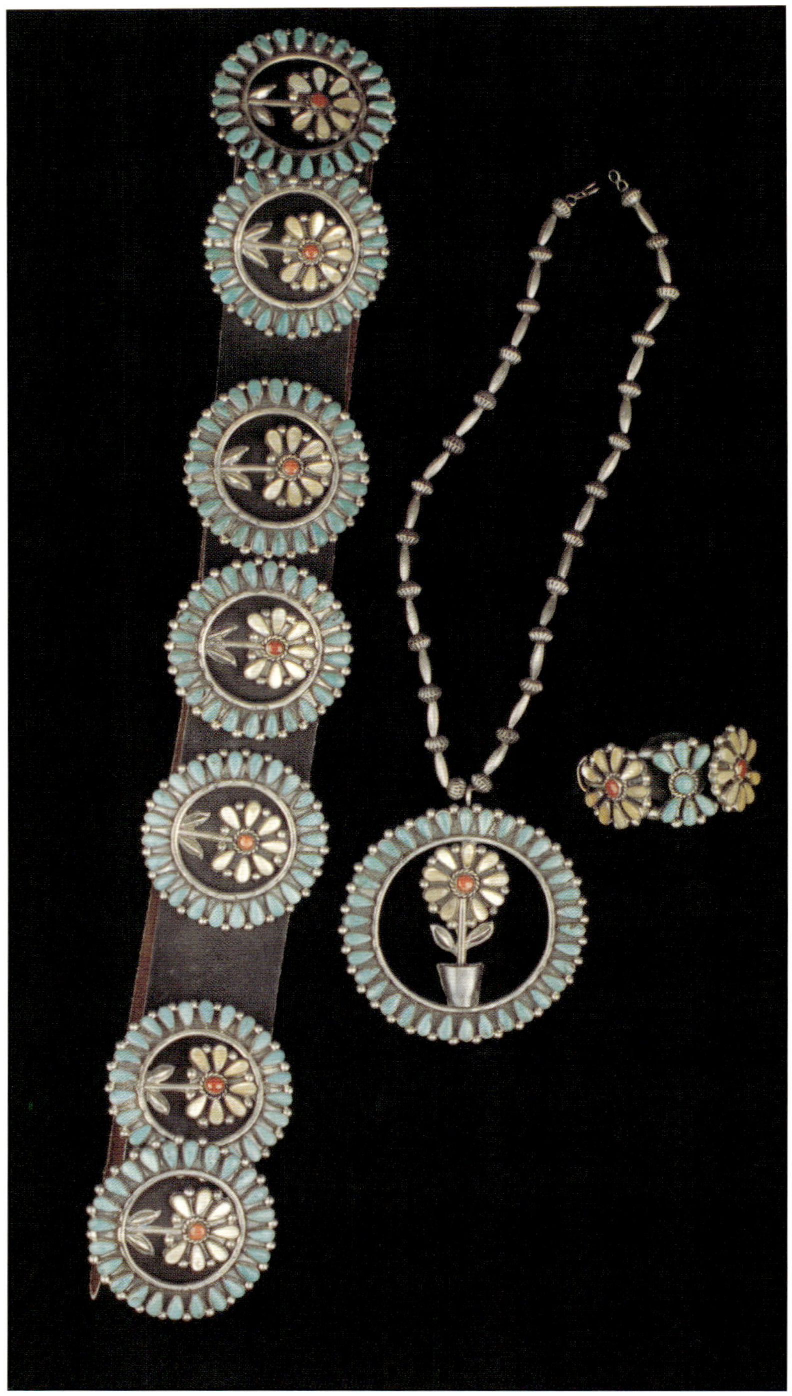

Zuni inlay lady's concho style belt, pendant necklace, and bracelet set of round floral inlay design from the 1970s. *Private collection*

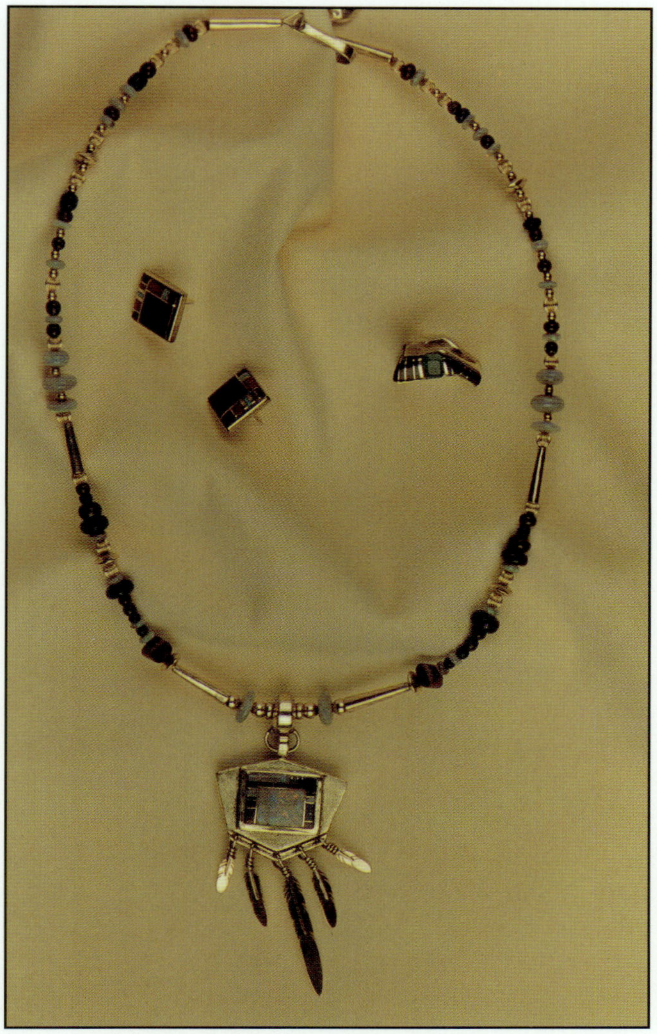

Gold necklace, ring and earrings set featuring opal and other stones by Romero. *Turquoise Lady collection*.

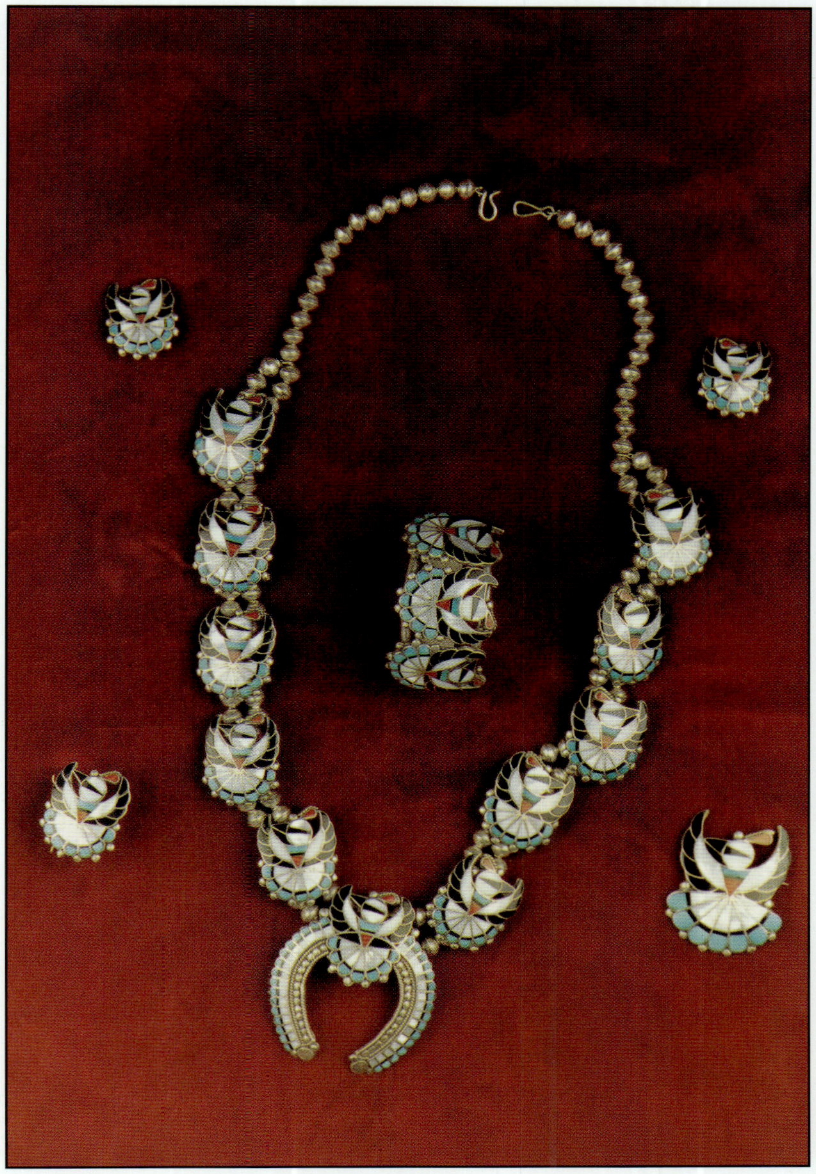

Elaborate Zuni bird-design inlaid matching set including a necklace, bracelet, pin, ring, and earrings made in the 1970s. *Private collection*

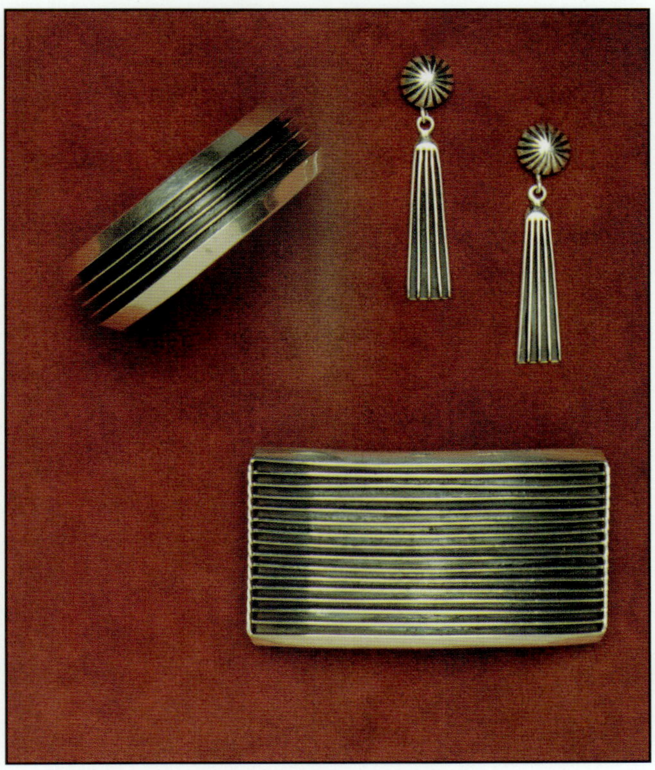

Silver "railroad ties" design buckle and bracelet by Ronald Yazzie, Navajo, and earrings by L.T., 1980s.

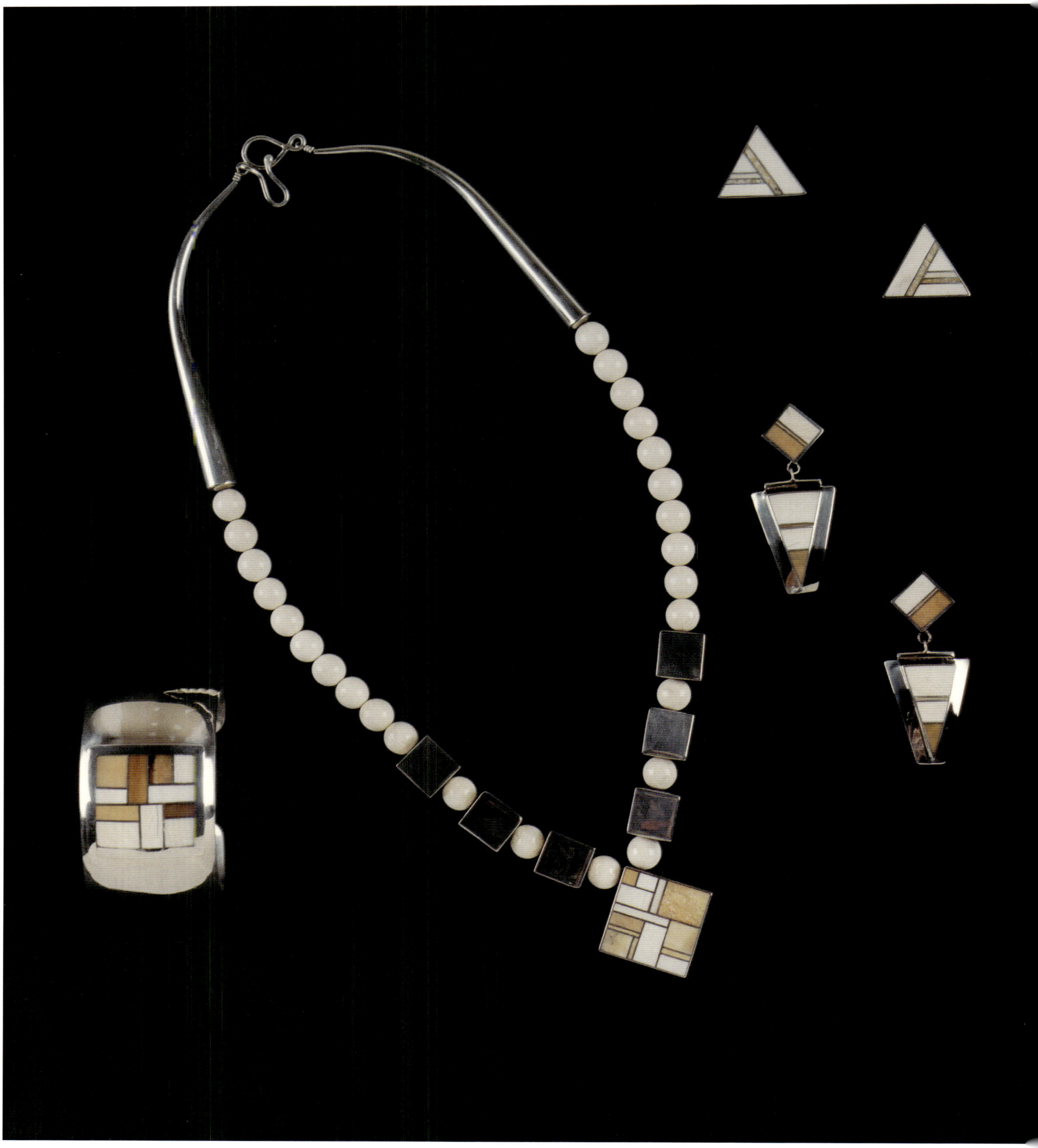

Bead necklace, cuff bracelet, and two pair of earrings all featuring fossilized ivory and sterling silver inlay made by Knifewing (Ray Tracey), late 1970s. *Indian Post collection*.

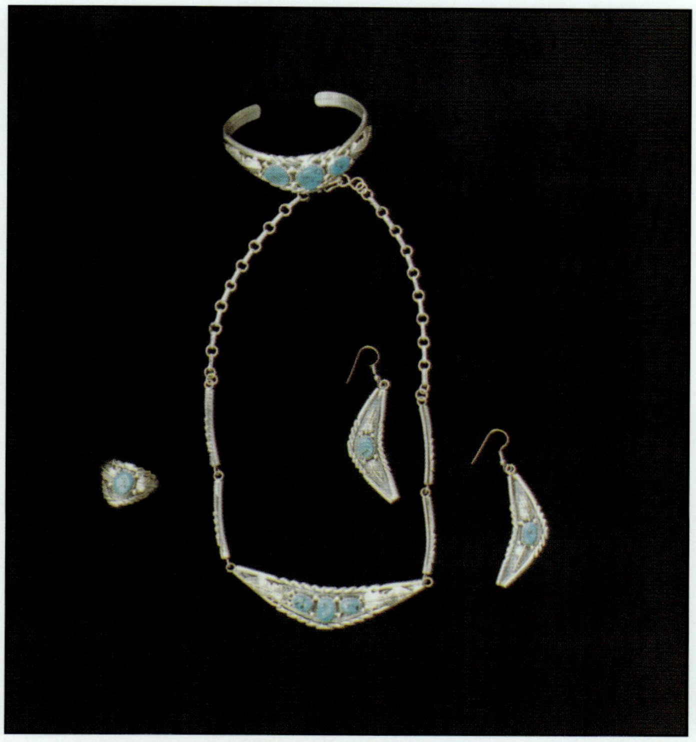

Sterling silver and turquoise set of a link necklace, bracelet, earrings, and ring by L. Bennett, 1989. *Bing Crosby collection*

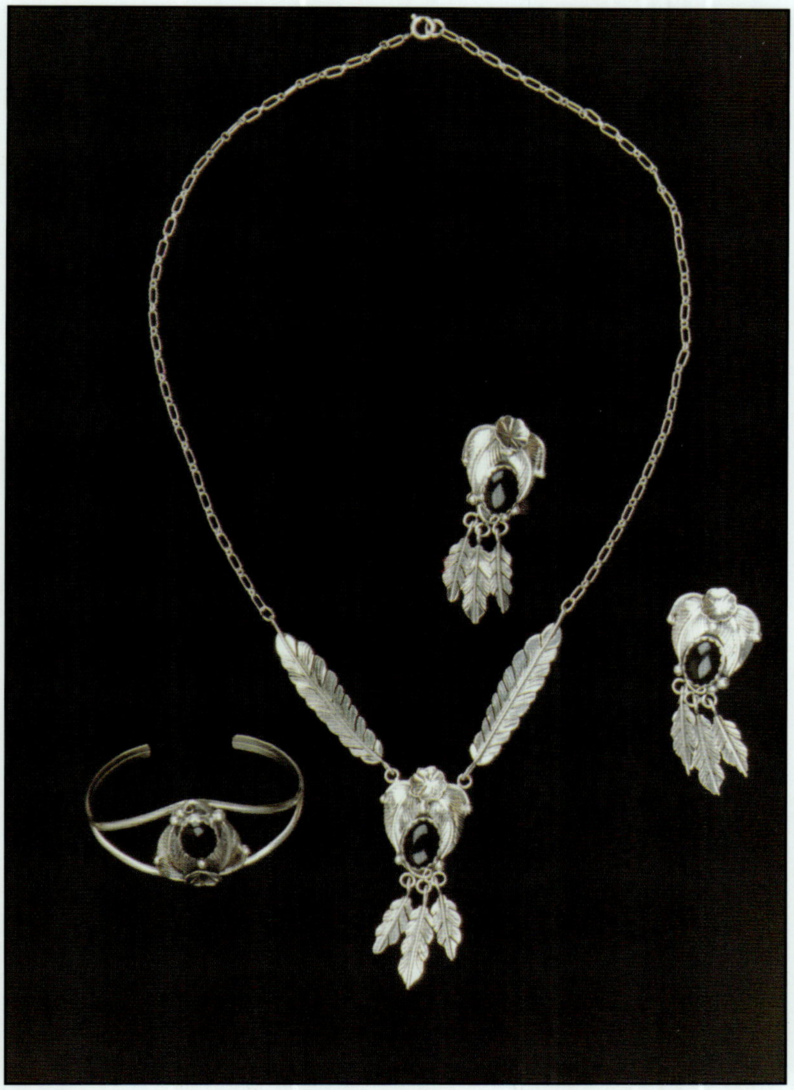

Necklace, bracelet, and earrings with onyx set in silver feather design, 1989. Necklace and earrings feature dangling feathers. *Bing Crosby collection*

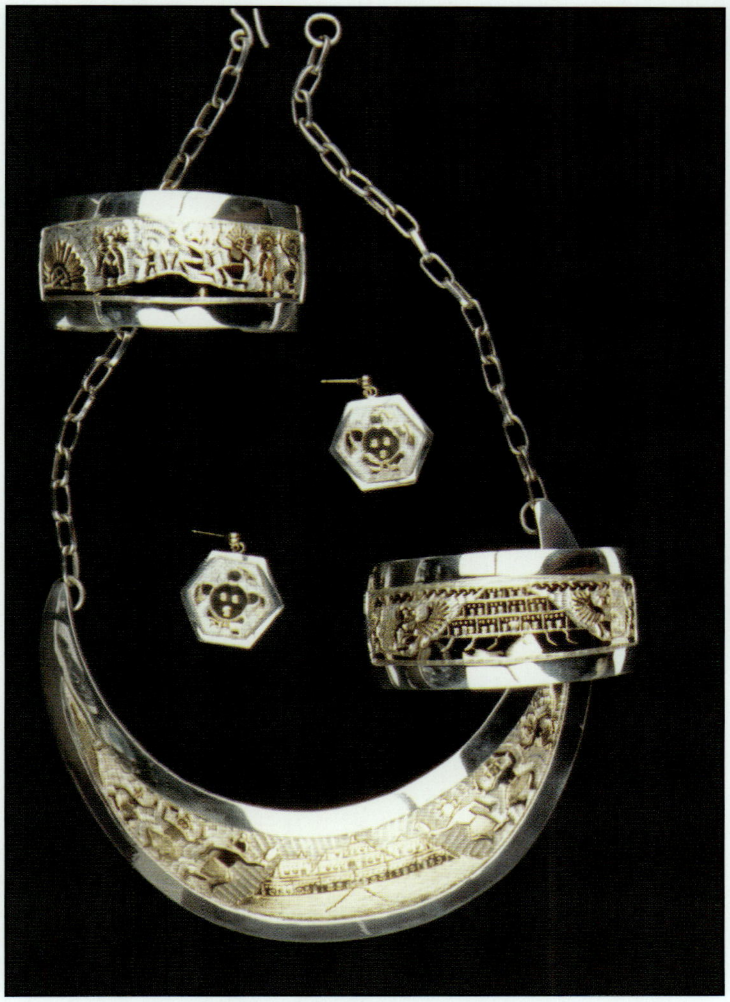

Gold and silver narrative overlay group that includes a necklace, two bracelets, and earrings made by Watson Honanie, Hopi. *Keams Canyon Arts and Crafts collection.*

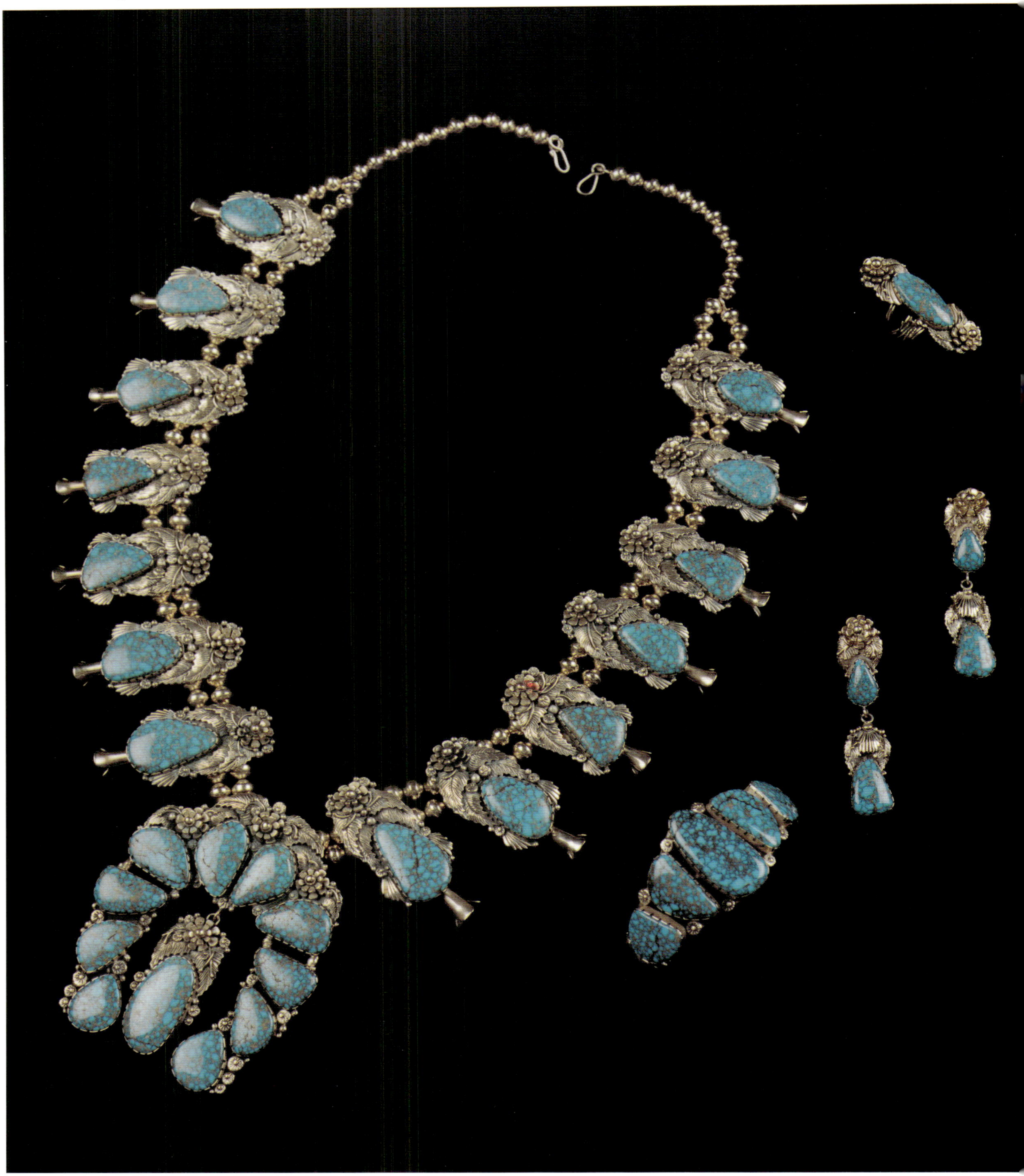

Important and elaborate squash blossom necklace with matching bracelet, ring, and dangle earrings made of gold appliqué and Spiderweb turquoise by Boyd Richard Tsosie, Navajo, 1977. *Private collection on permanent loan to Ohio University*

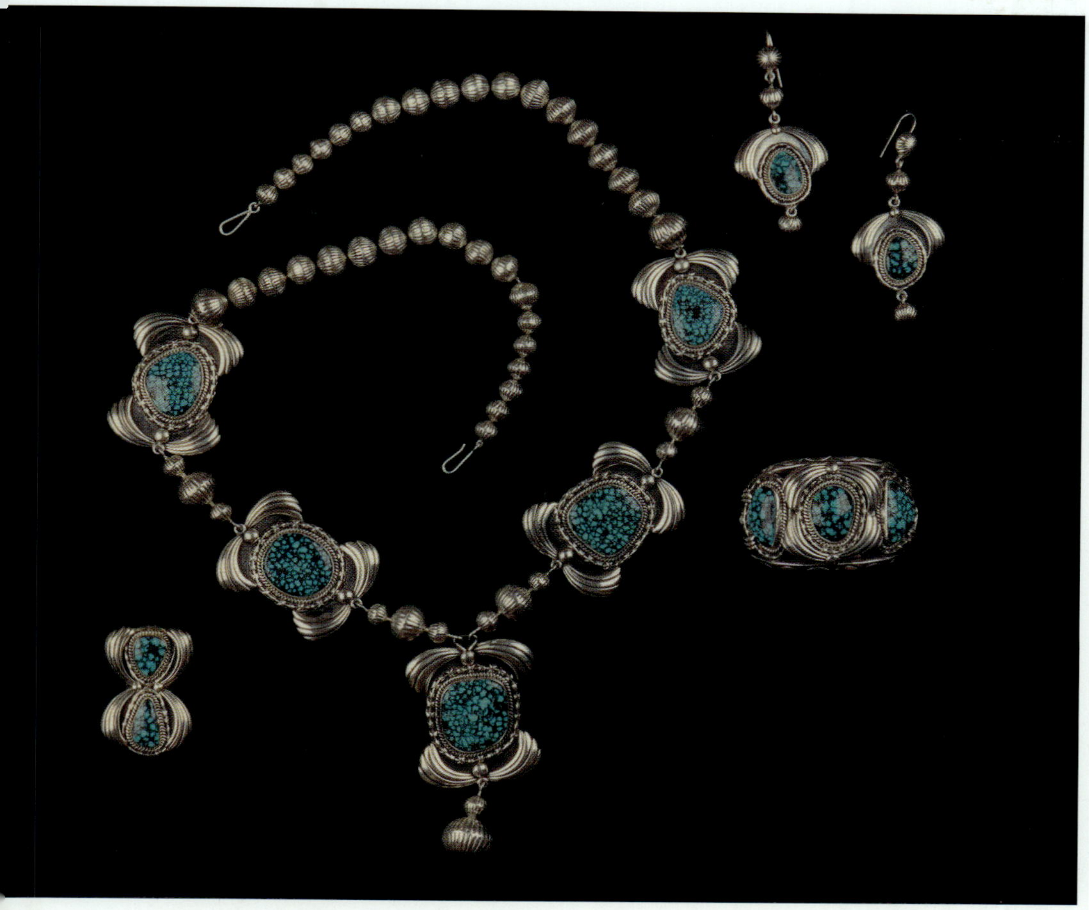

Matching bead necklace, cuff bracelet, dangle earrings, and ring of sterling silver and Kingman Spiderweb turquoise from Tobe Turpen (shop mark), circa 1978. *Private collection on permanent loan to Ohio University*

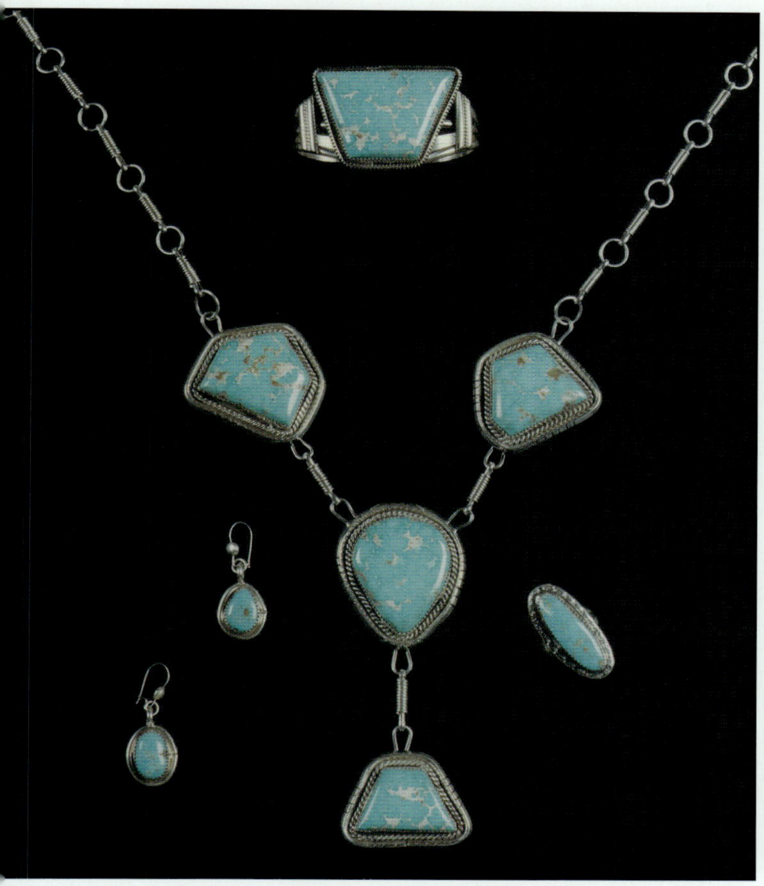

A bold Navajo set including a link necklace, cuff bracelet, ring, and dangle earrings with beautiful turquoise made in the late 1980s. *Leonard D. Prins collection*

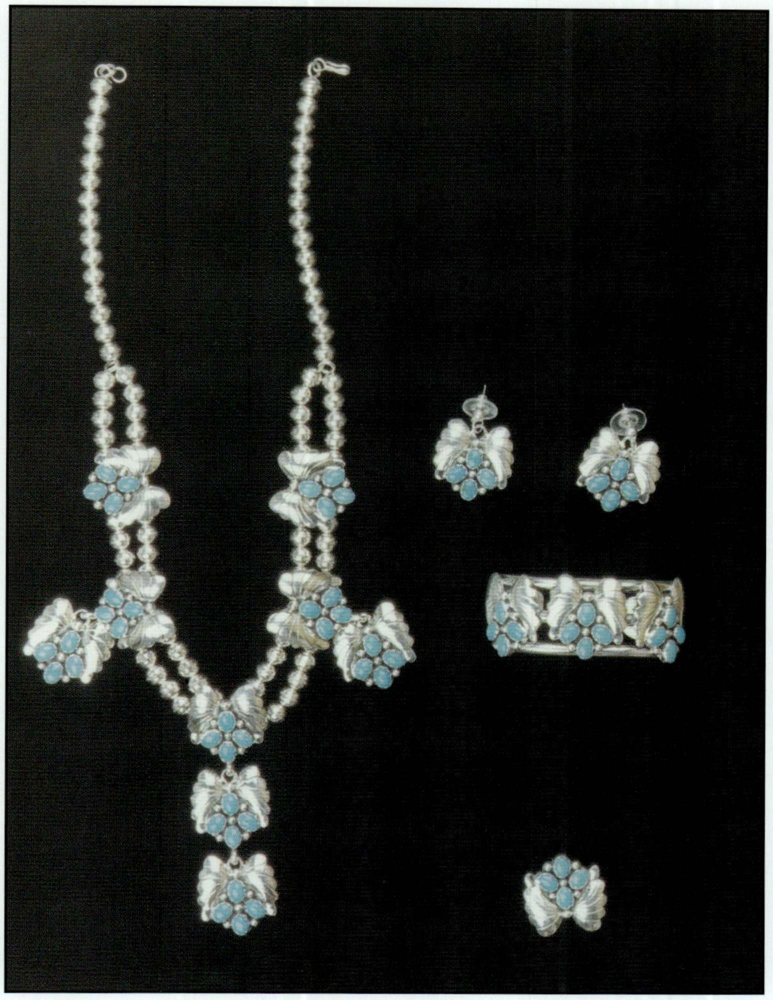

Designed to be worn together, this set of necklace, bracelet, earrings, and ring of silver appliqué has groupings of four turquoise stones, 1989. *Bing Crosby collection*

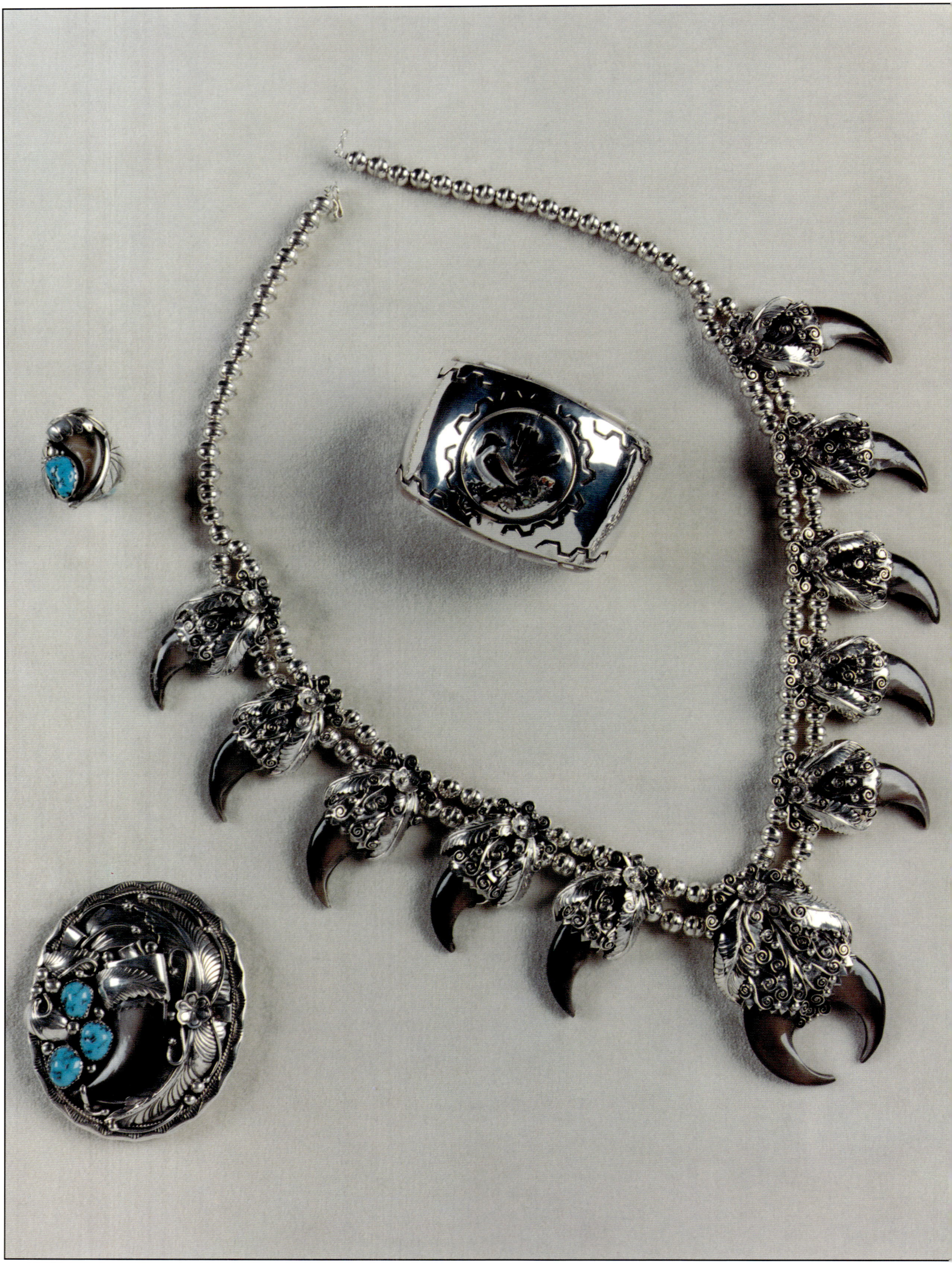

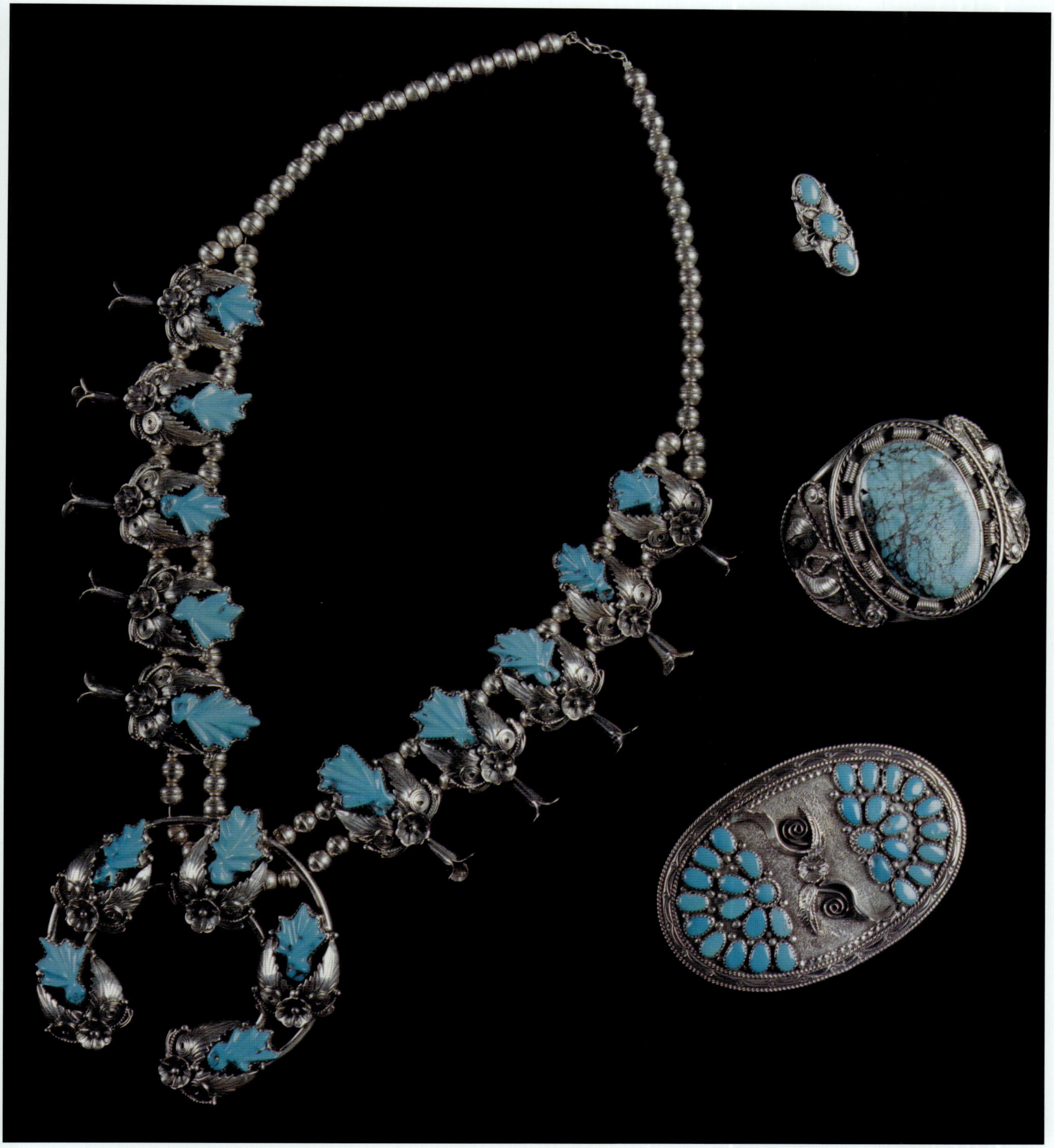

Another assembled set, this group includes an unusual carved turquoise and silver squash blossom necklace by Who G. / The cuff bracelet of silver appliqué work is by Eddie Burns / The oval buckle of symmetrical design has thirty turquoise stones and was made by N.E.F. / A ring by L.W. has three turquoise stones. *Leonard D. Prins collection*

Opposite page: This group is an assembled set of forms by different makers with common features: here bear claws predominate the designs. The necklace of sterling silver has elaborate appliqué and scrollwork and bear claws. / The bracelet has bird and cactus design by F. / an oval buckle has a bear claw, three turquoise stones, and appliqué silverwork by H. Spencer, Navajo. / The ring has a bear claw and turquoise set in silver. *Leonard D. Prins collection*

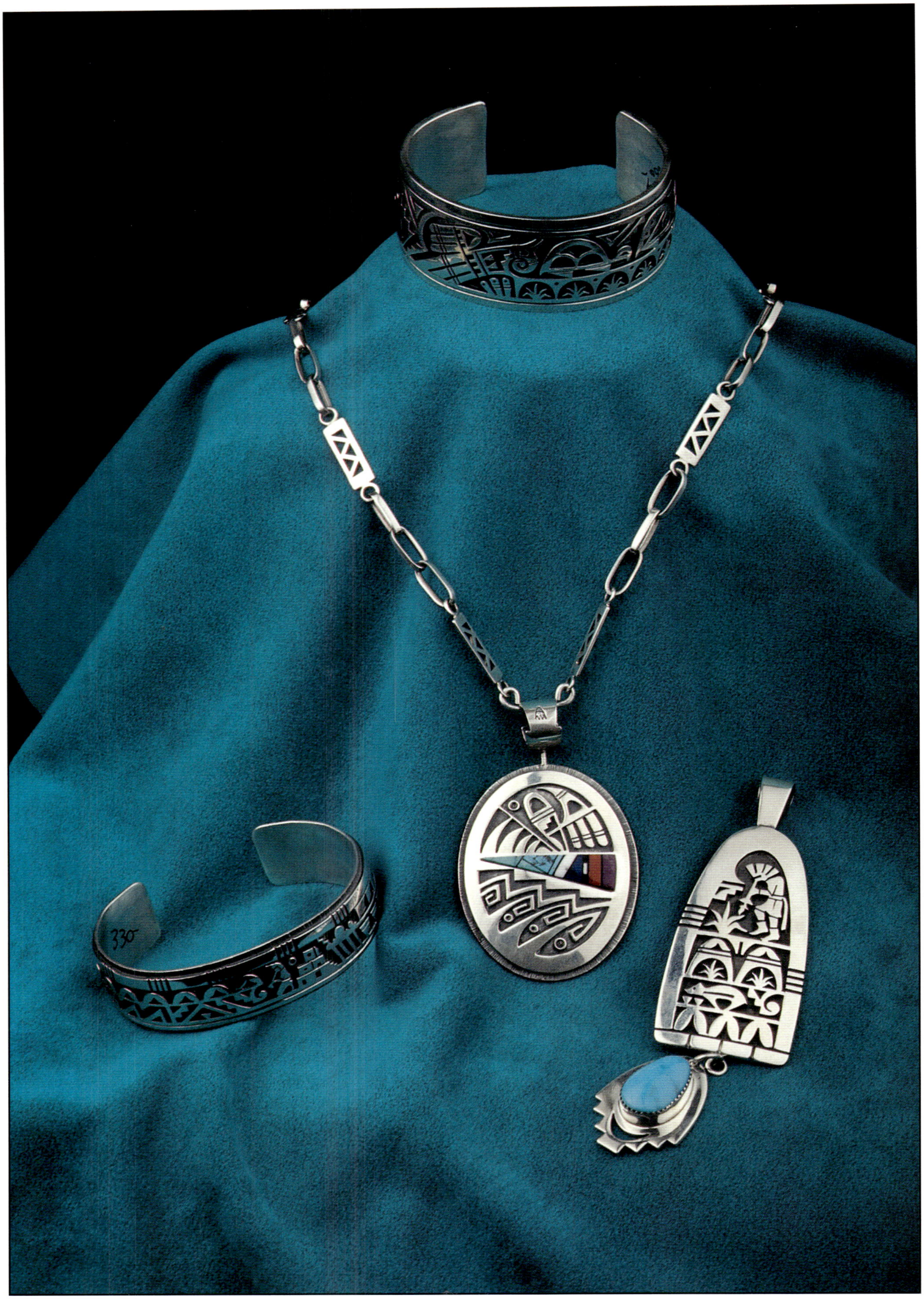

Group of silver jewelry by Chalmers Day, Hopi: Reversible pendant necklace ($750). Long pendant with hinged turquoise ($420). Two cuff bracelets ($330 and $600) *Courtesy of Palms Trading Company*

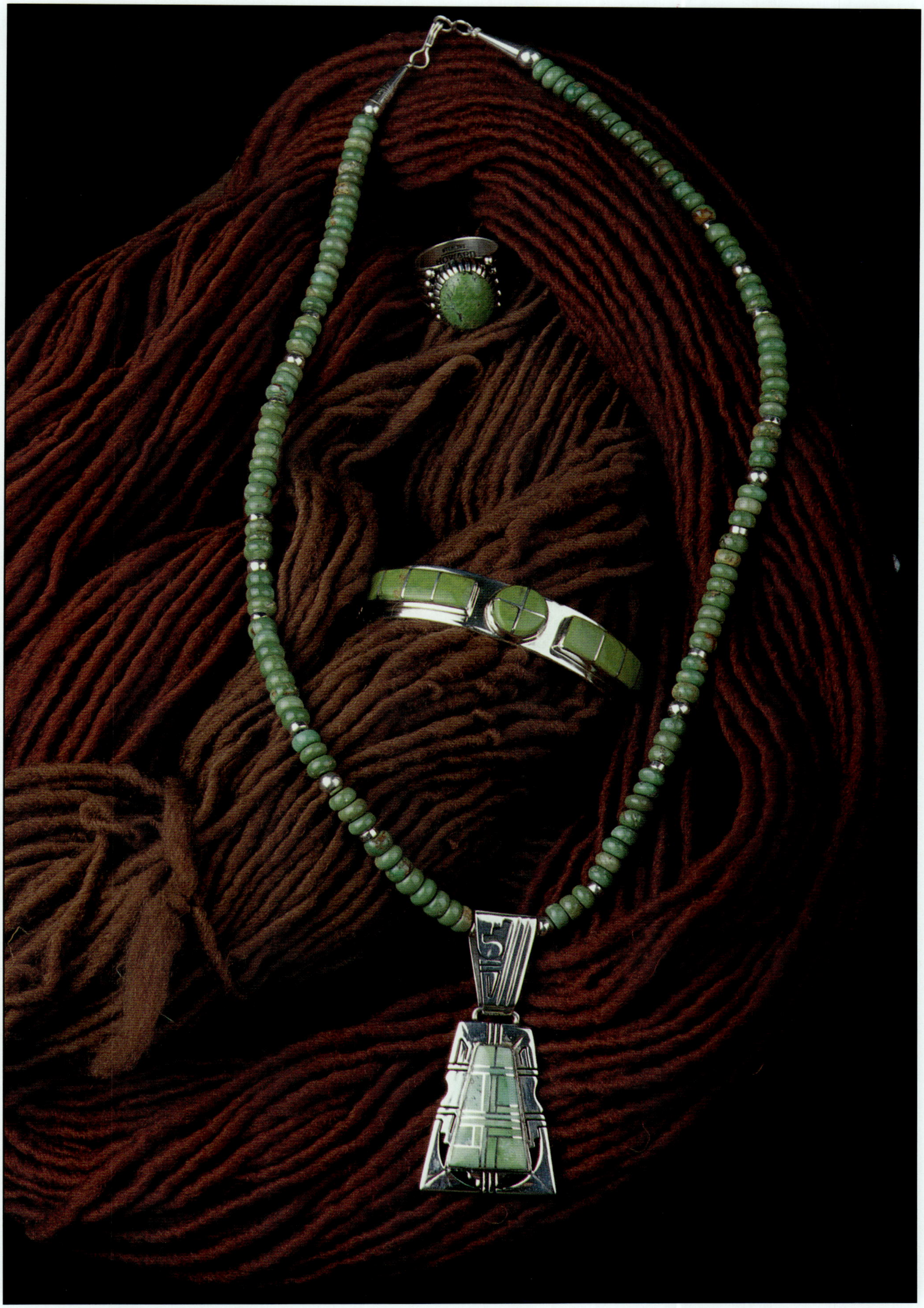

Group of Navajo silver jewelry with green stones including a bead necklace and pendant by Jerry T. Nelson ($648); bracelet by Cathy A. B. ($395); and ring by Howard Nelson ($180). *Courtesy McGee's, Holbrook*

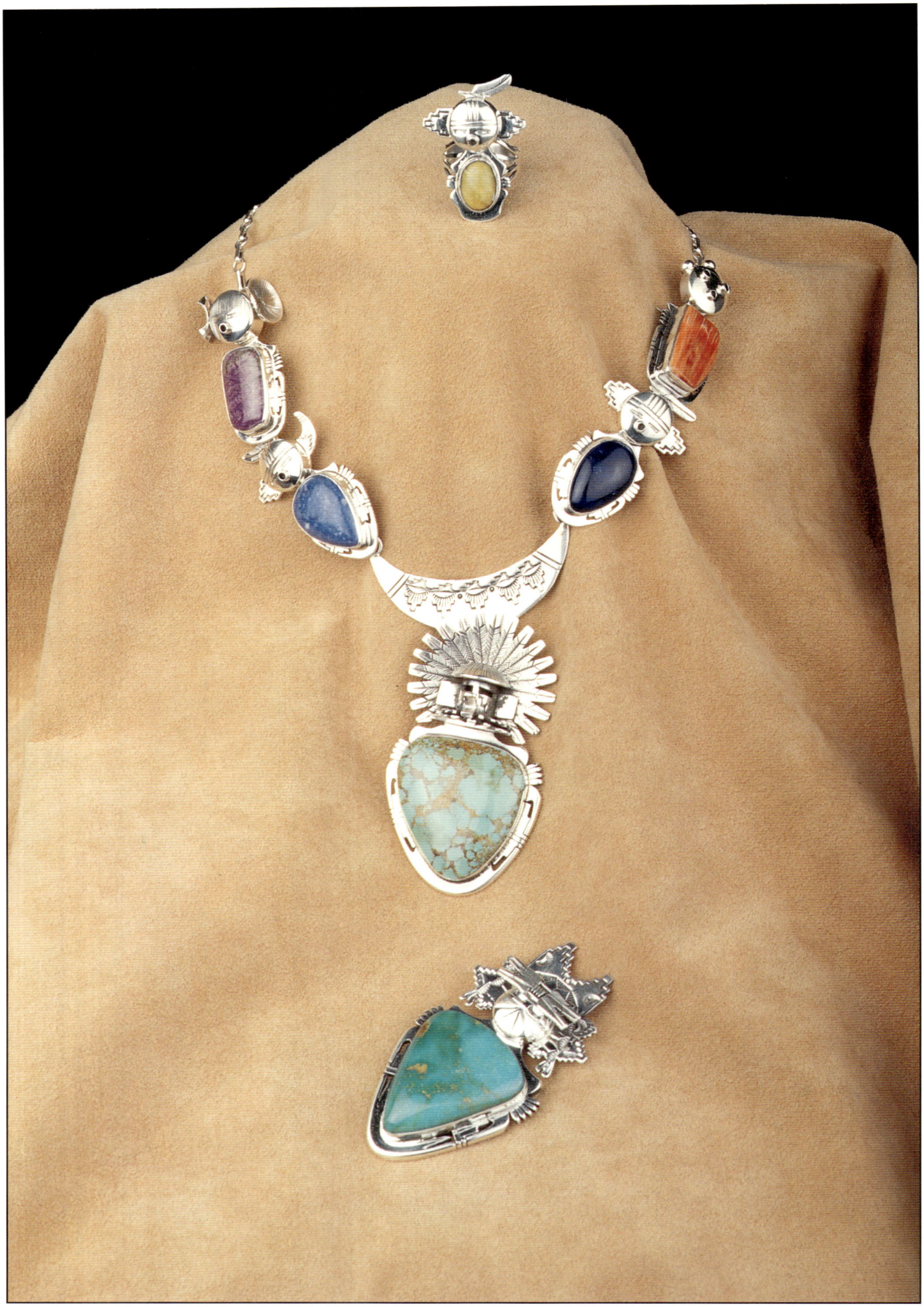

These elements separate for versatile wearing: pins and pendant with chain and large assorted stones, by Benny Ration, Navajo. Ring ($105), pin/pendant ($270), and a necklace ($900) *Courtesy of Palms Trading Company*

Men's sets

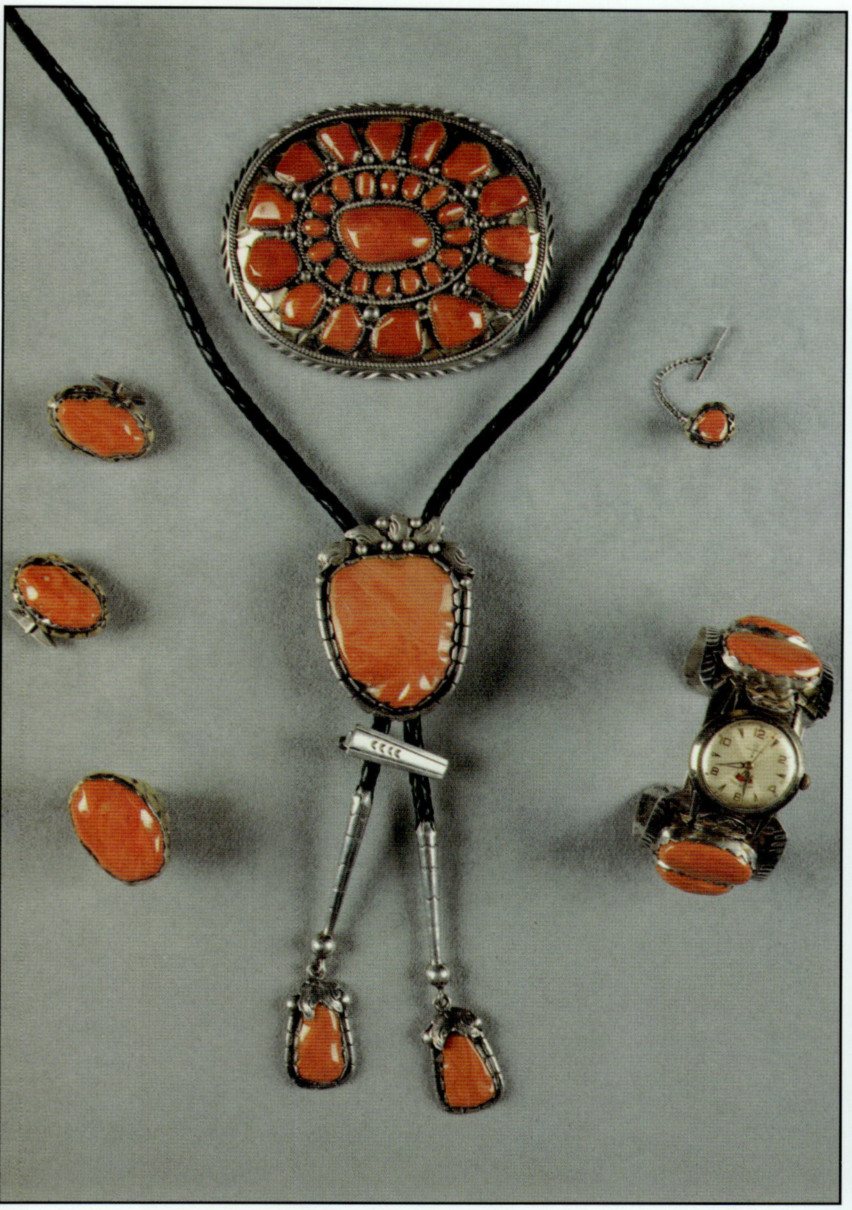

The oval silver buckle with coral of irregular shapes is marked M, circa 1980. / The matching set of light coral and beautifully made gold and silverwork includes a bolo tie, watch bracelet, tie tack, cufflinks, and ring made by Dan Simplicio, Zuni. *Private collection*

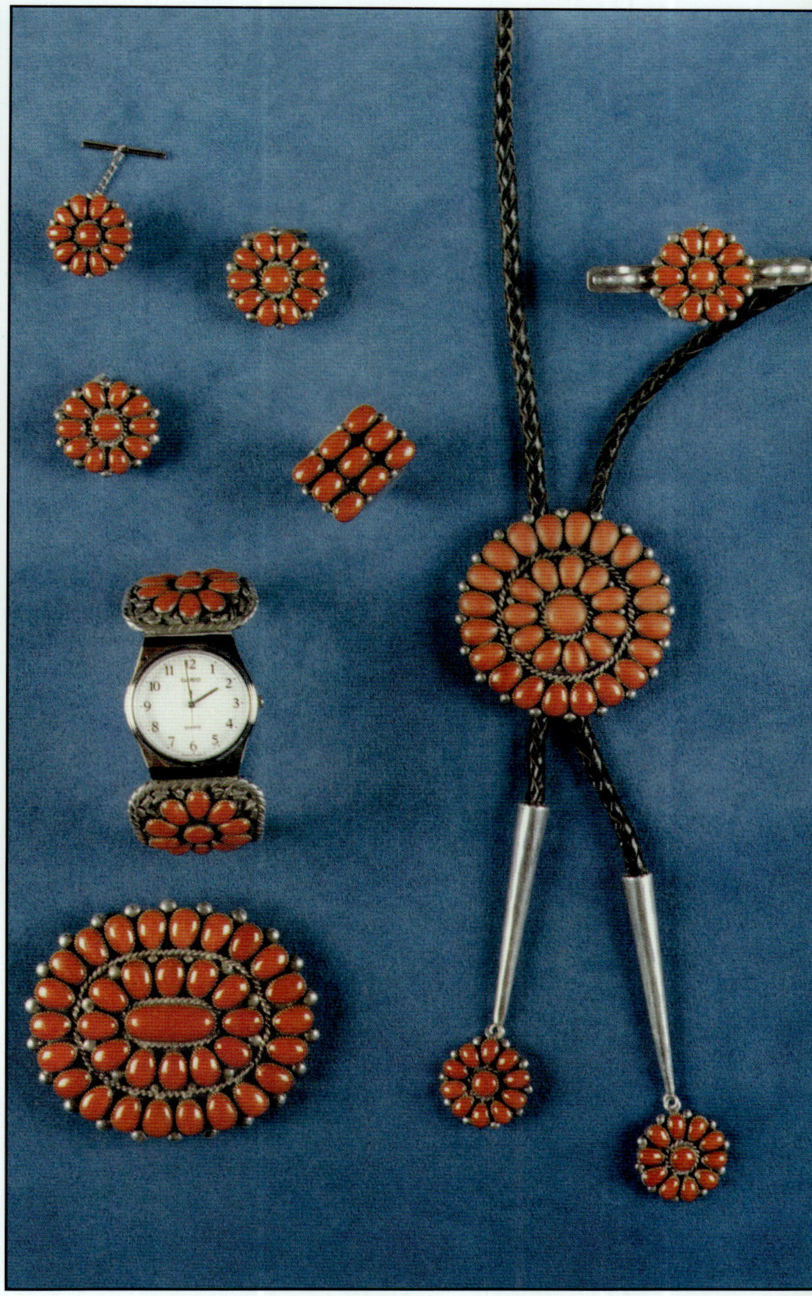

This is a magnificent Zuni set of men's jewelry that is unusually complete. It is comprised of a bolo tie, tie clip, ring, pair of cufflinks, tie tack, buckle, and watch bracelet with coral and silver made by Lee and Mary Weebothee, Zuni, 1980. *Private collection*

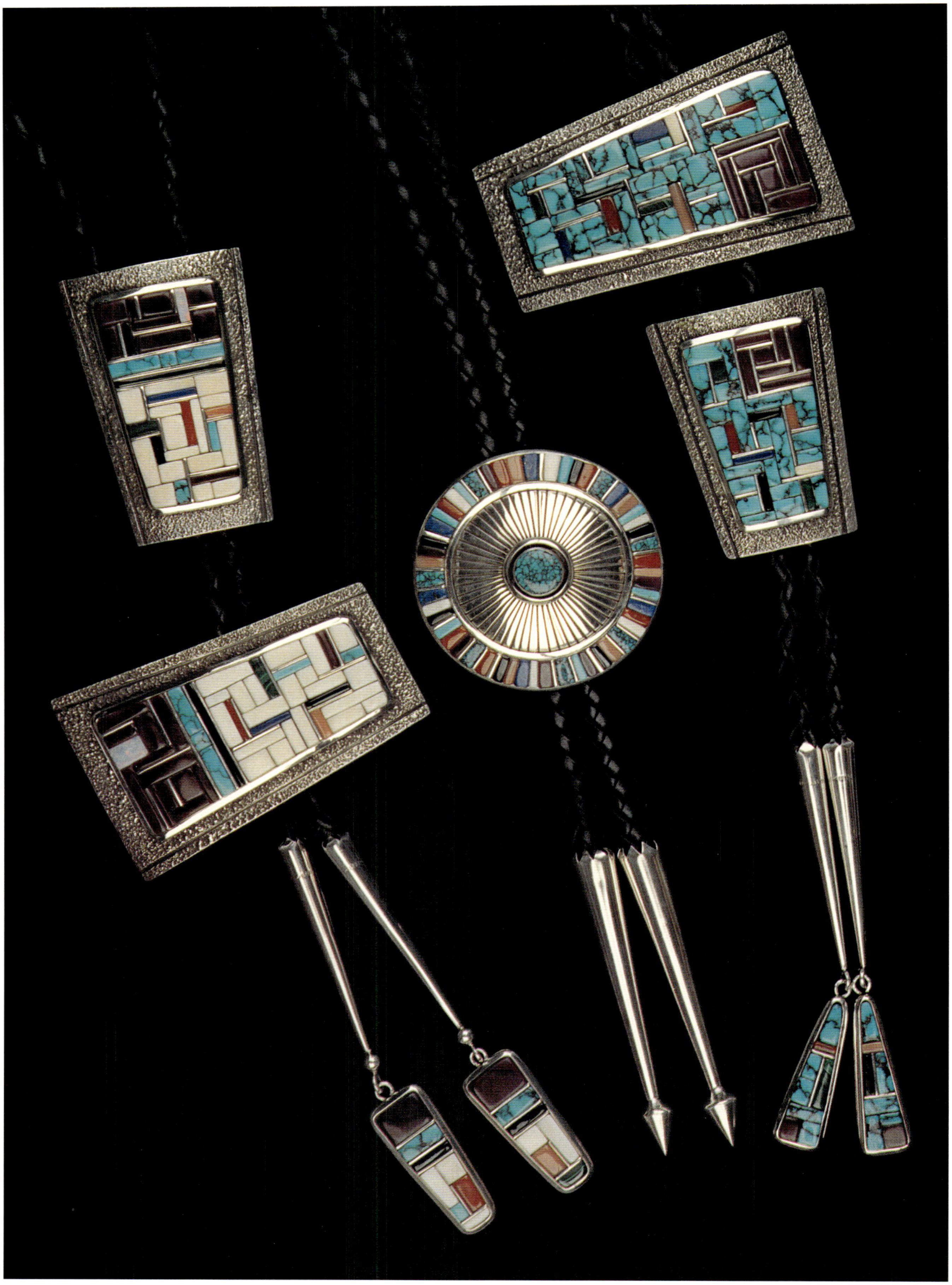

Two magnificent bolo slide and buckle sets and a single bolo slide of cast silver with inlaid turquoise and other colored stones by Bitsui and Russell. Fannie Bitsui cuts the stone while Philip Russell creates the silverwork. *Keams Canyon Arts and Crafts collectio.*

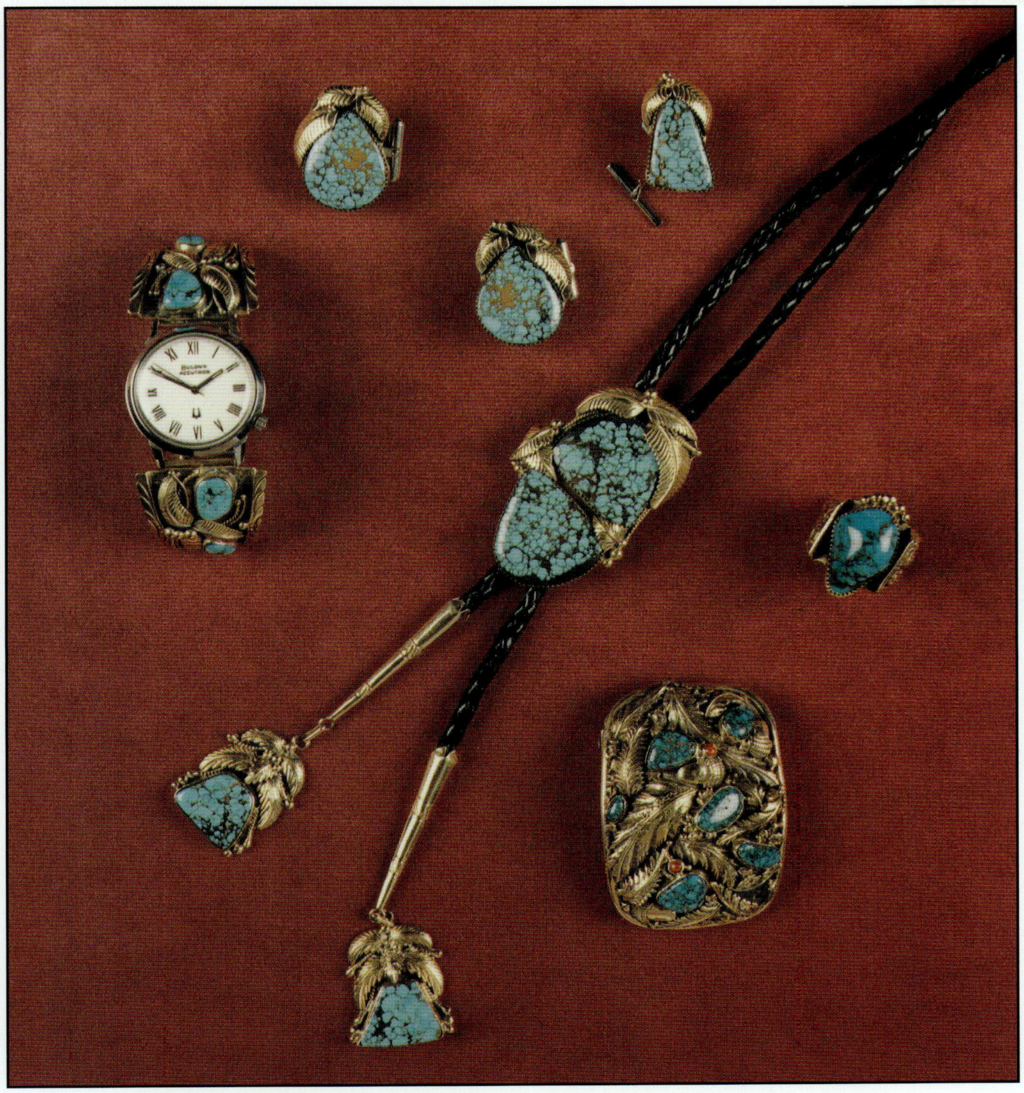

Gold appliqué leaf work and fine turquoise unify this assembled set of magnificent man's jewelry. The bolo tie, cufflinks, and tie tack are unmarked. / The watchband was made by Ivan Valencia. / A beautiful ring has Bisbee turquoise and gold. / David Zachary made a buckle of gold and turquoise. *Private collection on permanent loan to Ohio University*

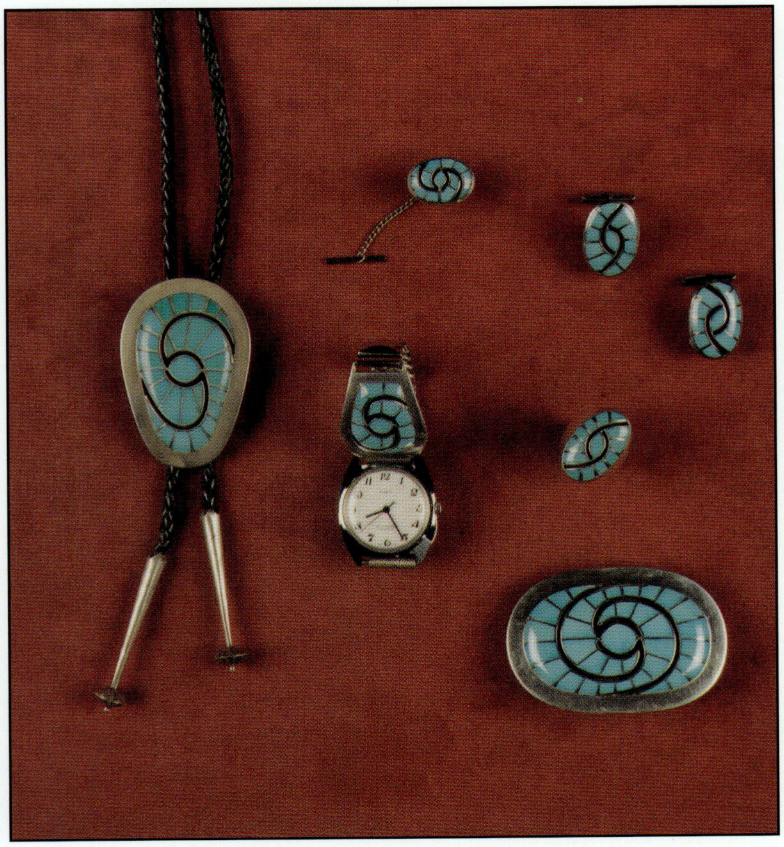

The now-familiar spiral turquoise channel inlay design by D. and A. Quandelacy, Zuni, 1977-1978, includes a belt buckle, bolo tie, cufflinks, tie tack, ring, and bracelet. *Private collection*

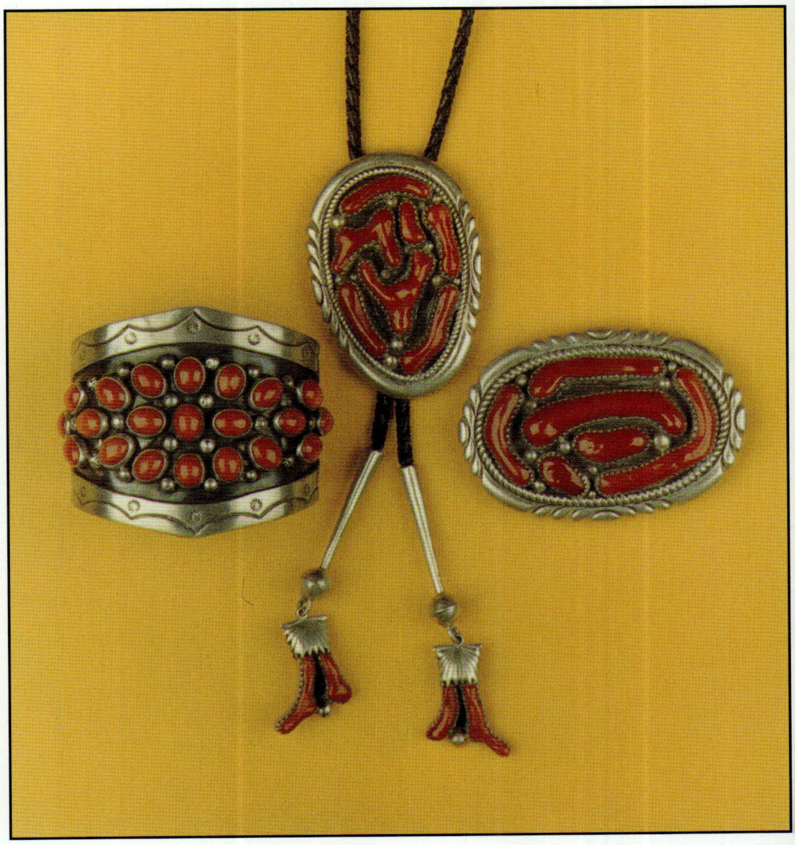

This bolo tie and buckle of branch coral and silver was made by Leonard Begay, Navajo / the coral and silver bracelet was made by T.K.W. *Private collection*

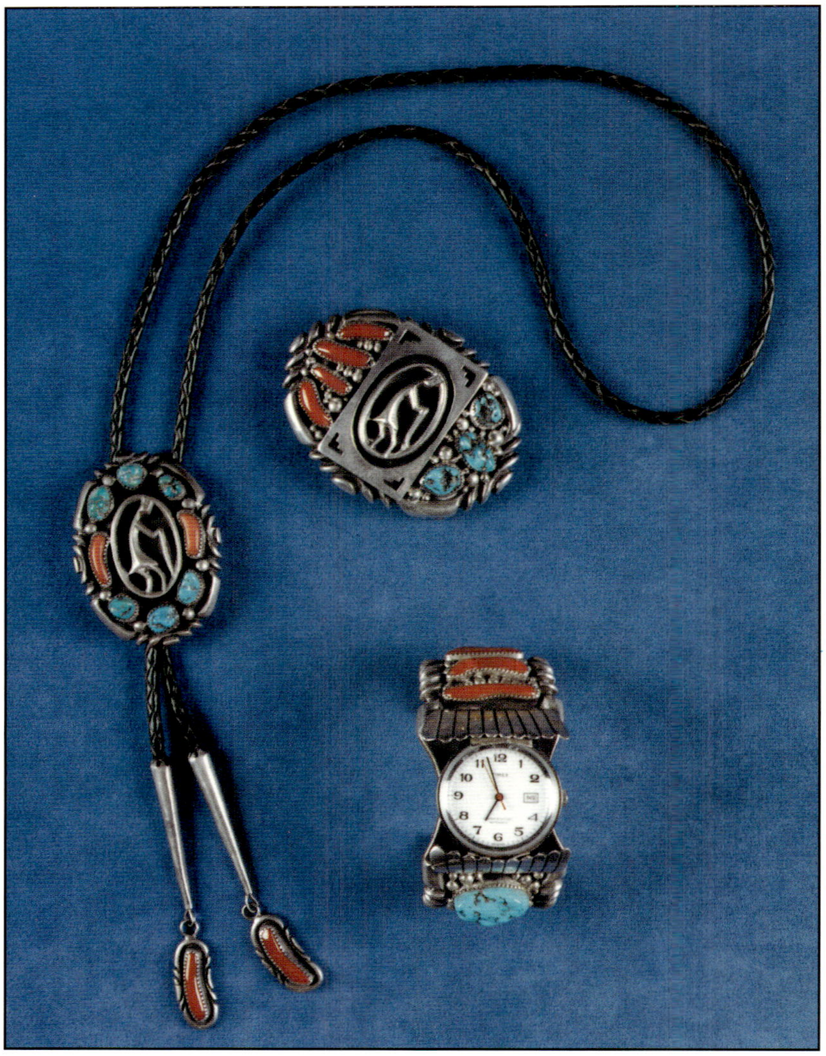

This set includes a sand-cast oval medallion with wrought silver in a bolo tie and buckle with coral, turquoise, and "old man with cane" design and a watch bracelet all by Wilson Begay, Navajo. *Private collection on permanent loan to Ohio University*

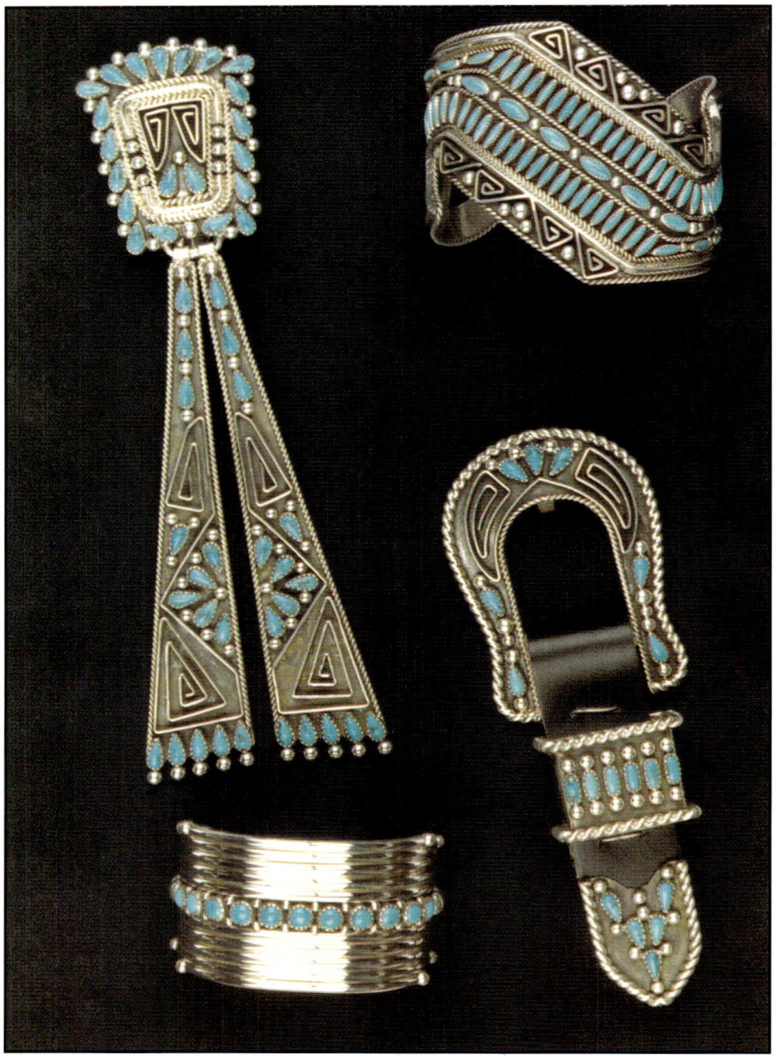

Very interesting silverwork and turquoise are combined in this set with bolo tie, two bracelets, and western buckle made by silversmith Billie Betoney and Betty Betoney who does the stonecutting. *Keams Canyon Arts and Crafts collection.*

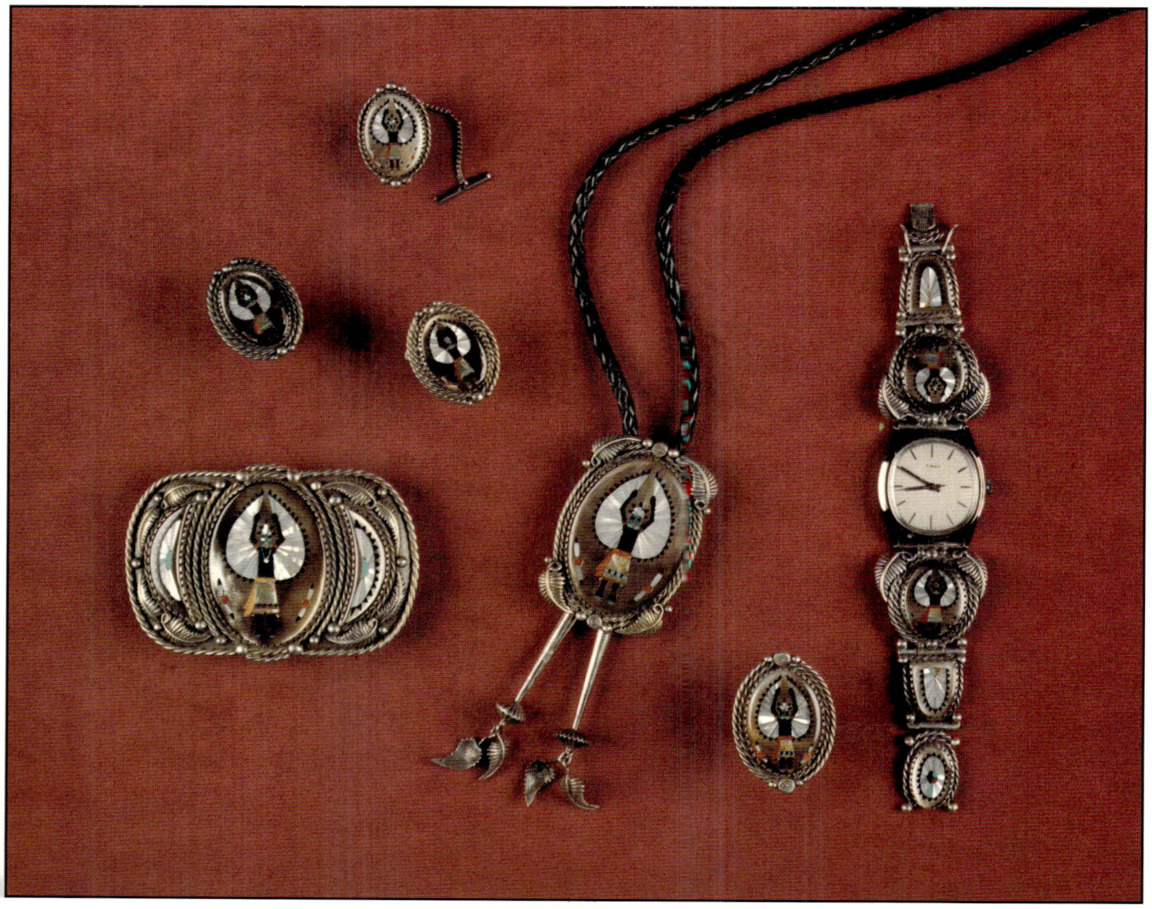

This six-piece silver and shell inlaid set is comprised of a bolo tie, buckle, watch bracelet, tie tack, cufflinks, and ring with an extensive inlay design featuring an eagle dancer by Tom Z. *Private collection*

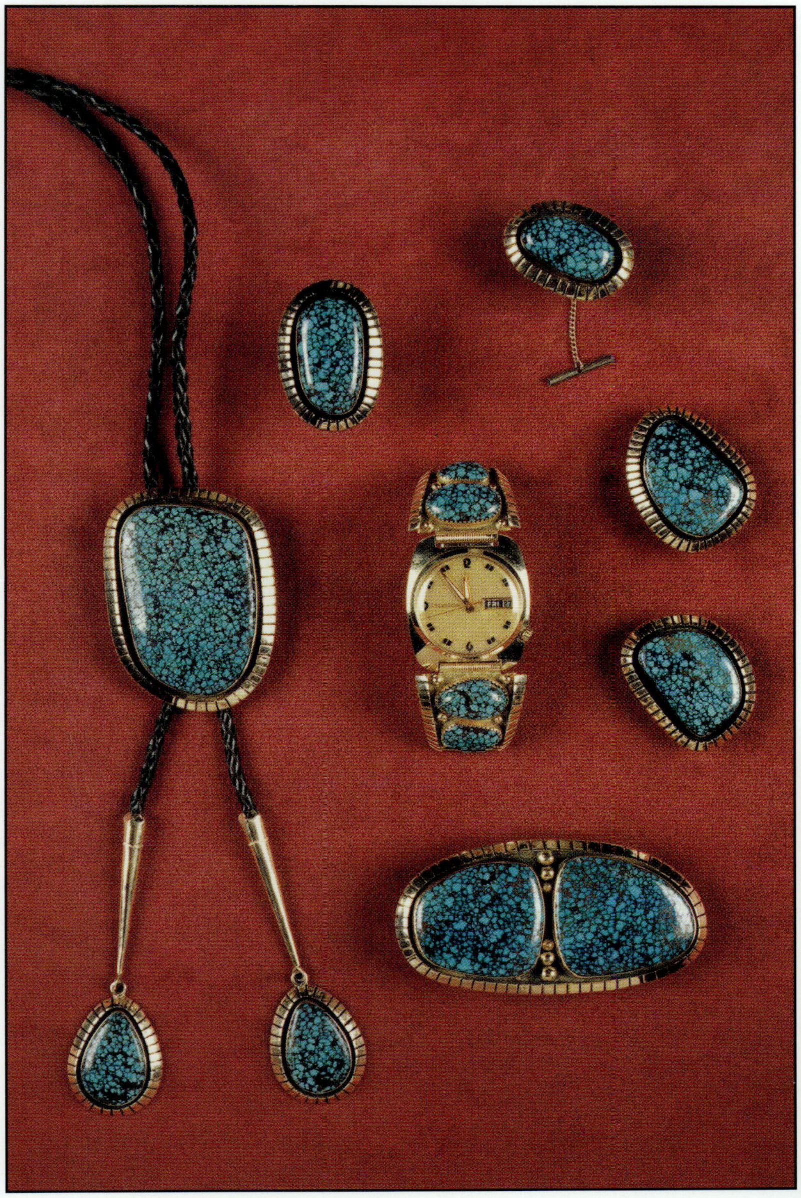

This is a very refined man's matching set of a bolo tie, cufflinks, ring, watch bracelet, tie tack, and buckle made in fourteen-carat gold with Indian Mountain turquoise by Mary Morgan, Navajo. *Private collection on permanent loan to Ohio University*

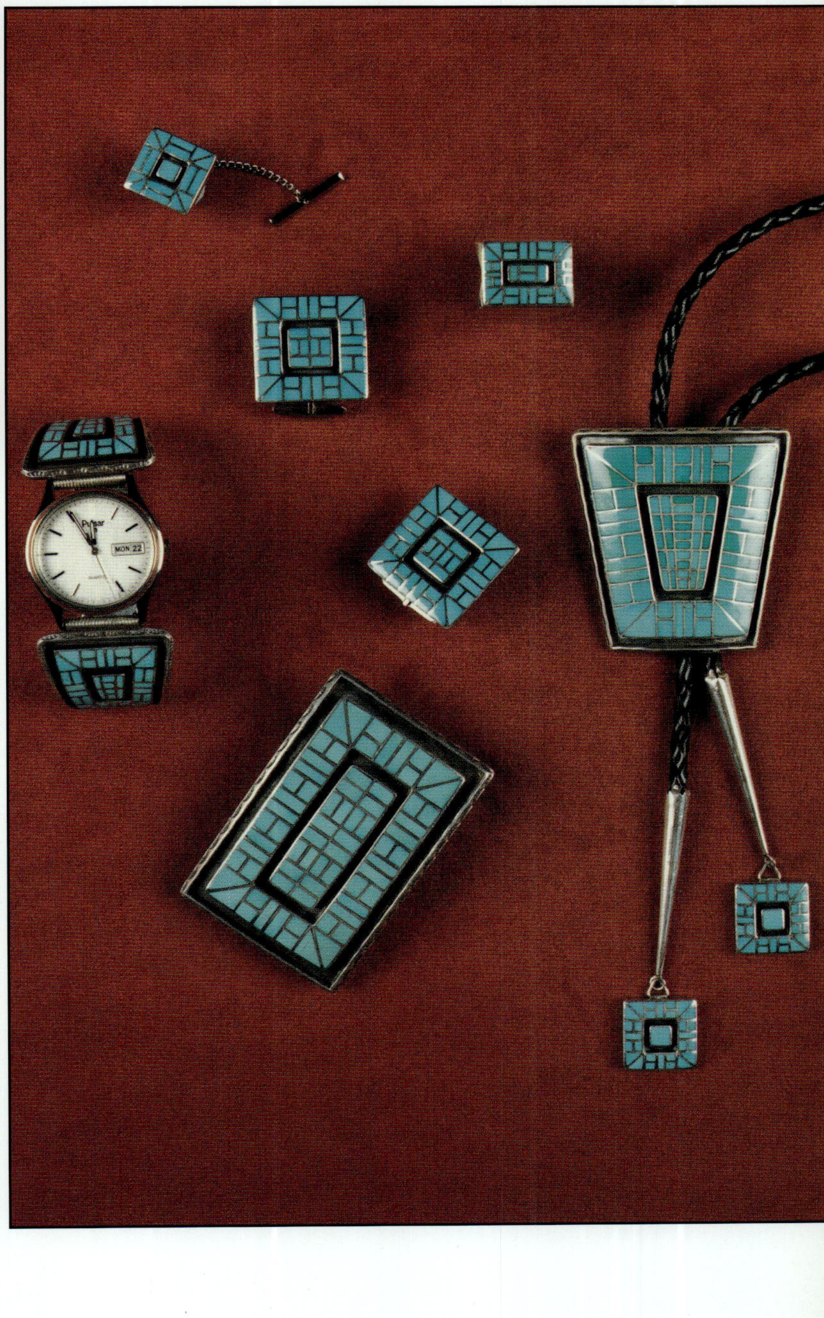

A highly unusual and very beautiful turquoise geometric shadow box and channel inlay set includes a bolo tie, buckle, ring, cufflinks, tie tack, and watch bracelet by Sheldon and Nancy Westika, Zuni, 1988. *Private collection on permanent loan to Ohio University*

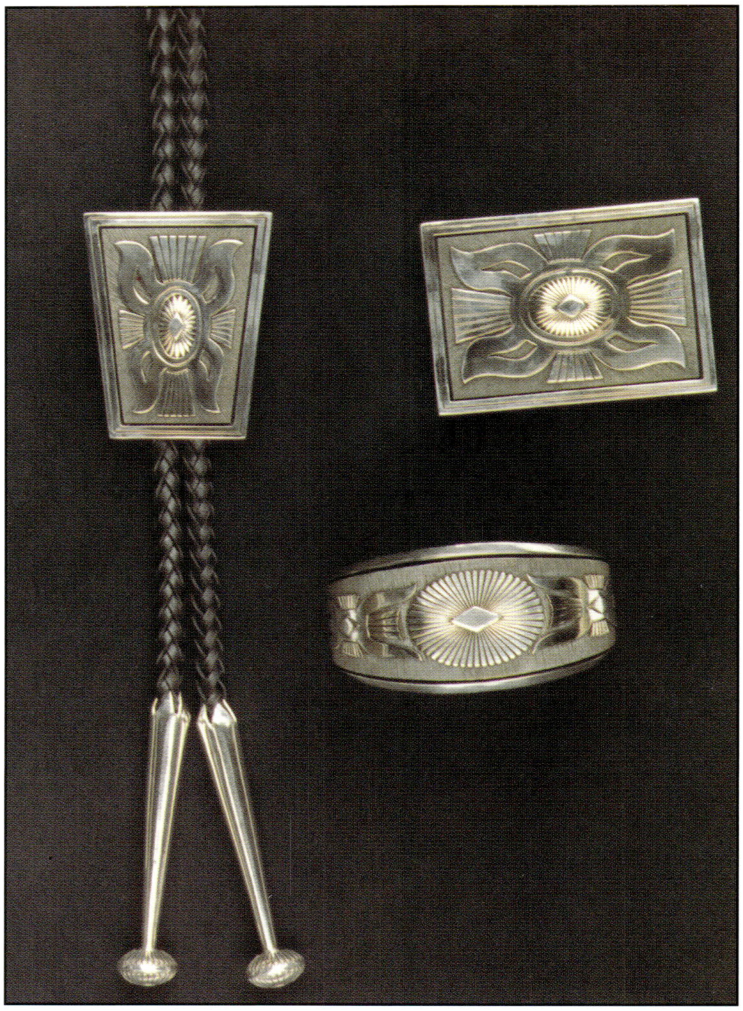

Silver bolo tie, bracelet, and buckle set with a design often associated with wrist guards including corn leaves, made by Howard Nelson. *Keams Canyon Arts and Crafts collection.*

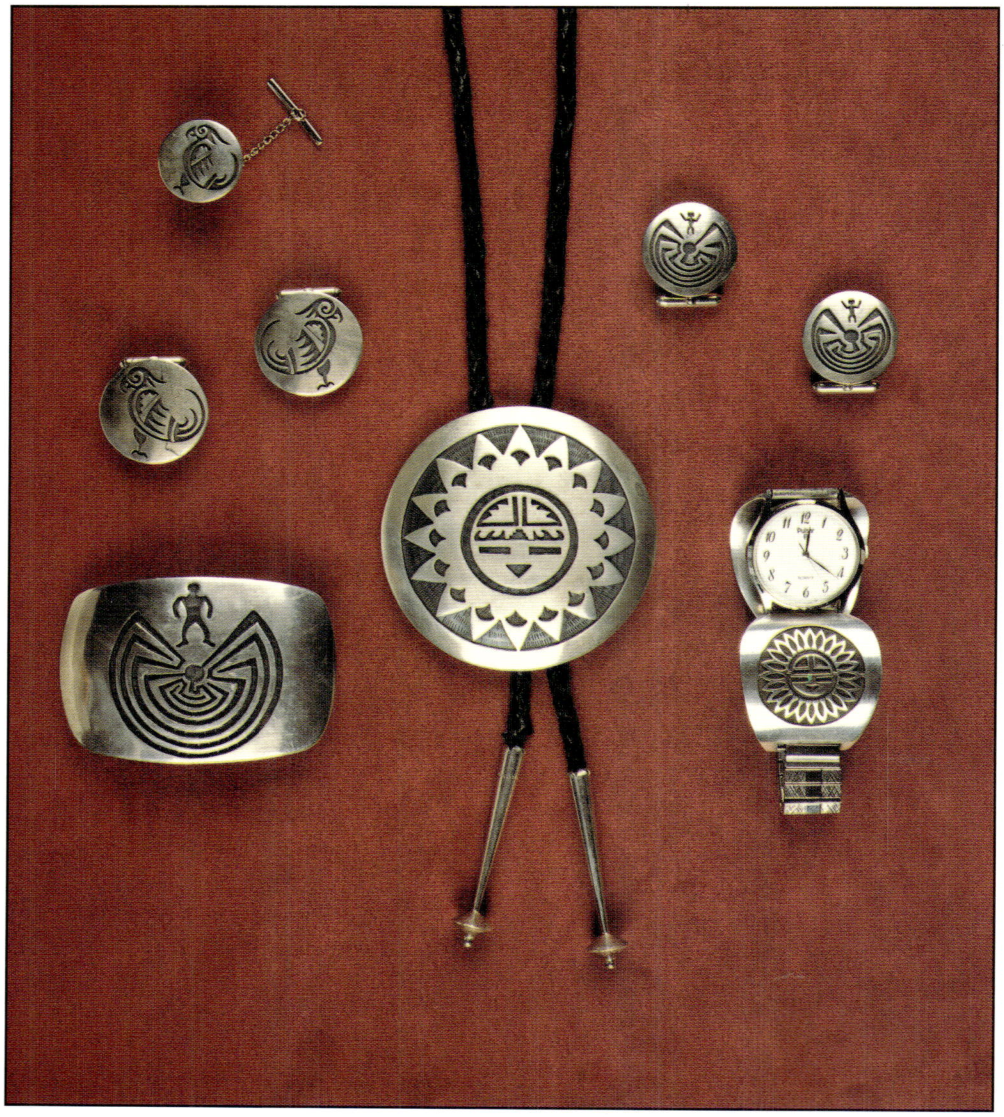

These silver Hopi overlay pieces made about 1980 form an assembled set of quite harmonious pieces. Larry Polivenna made the bolo slide with the sunface design. / The watch bracelet and buckle with Man in the Maze design are unsigned. / The two pair of cufflinks and tie tack with bird design were made by E. and J. *Private collection*

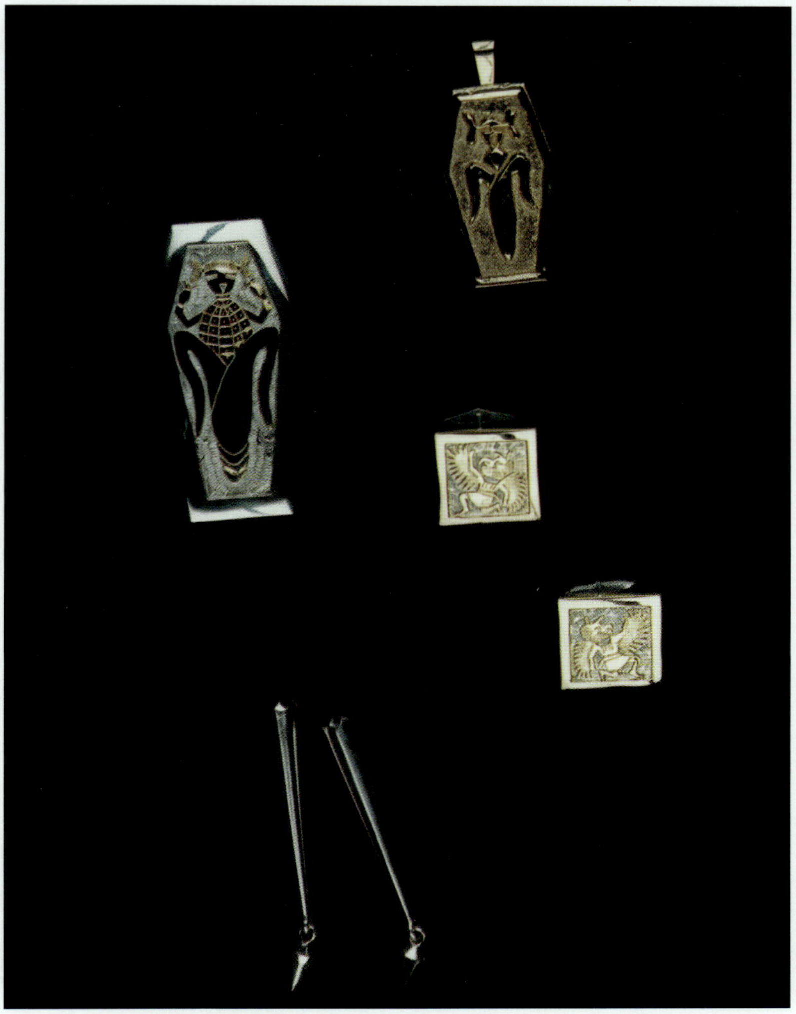

Gold and silver sand-cast pendant and bolo tie with corn maiden design, and a pair of cufflinks with an eagle dancer design made by Watson Honanie, Hopi. *Keams Canyon Arts and Crafts collection.*

This is an unusual and beautifully designed lady's set including a watchband, pair of large oval earrings, and two finger rings of gold and silver overlay design with corn plant by Phil Puo, 1989. *Indian Post collection*.

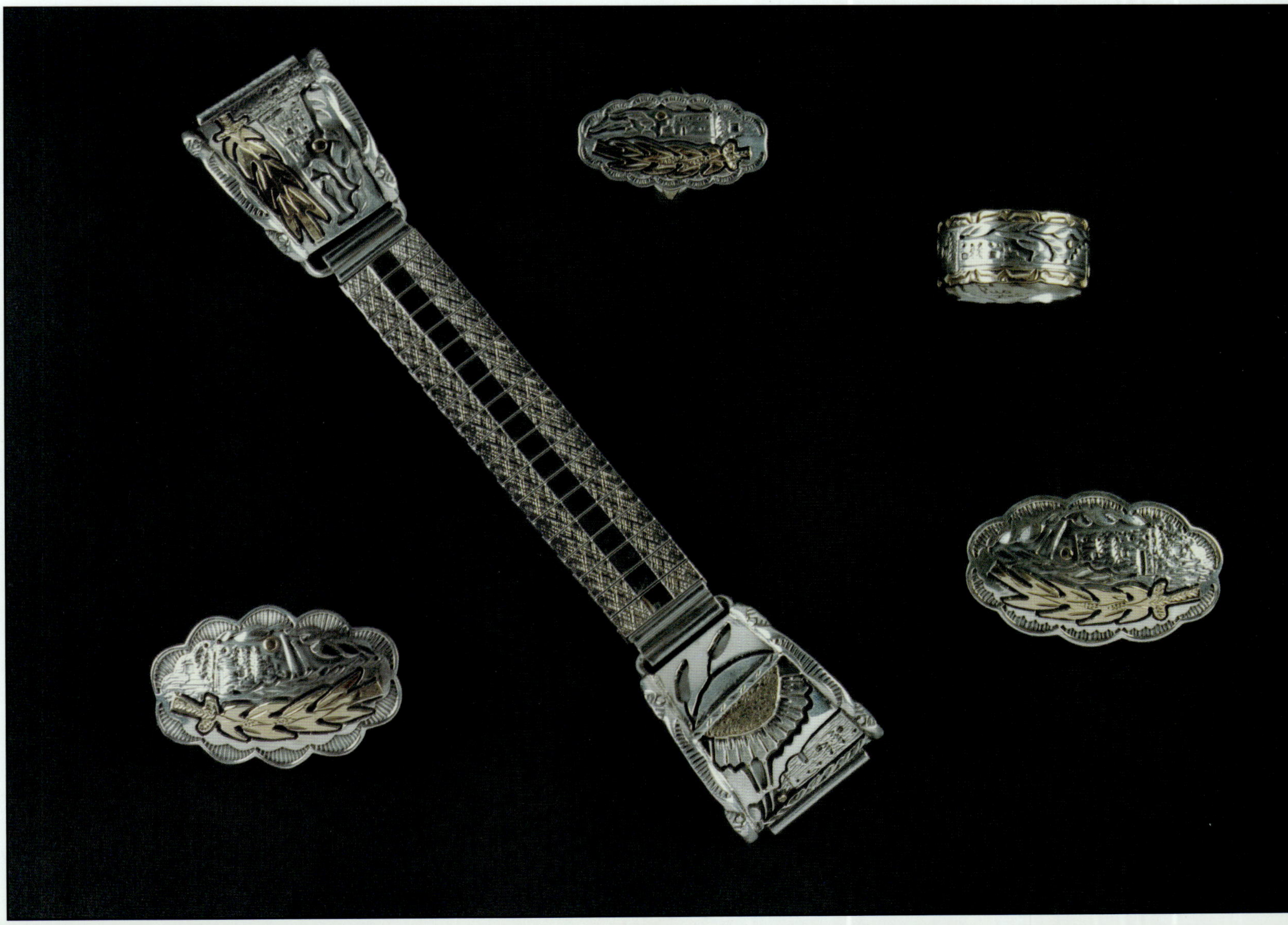

Bibliography

Adair, John. *The Navajo and Pueblo Silversmiths*, Norman, Okla.: University of Oklahoma Press, 1975.

Arizona Highways, January 1974; August 1974; April 1979; Phoenix: Arizona Department of Transportation.

Arizona Highways Turquoise Blue Book, Indian Jewelry Digest, Phoenix: Arizona Department of Transportation, 1975.

Bedinger, Margery. *Indian Silver, Navajo and Pueblo Jewelers*, Albuquerque; University of New Mexico Pres, 1974.

Bell, Barbara and Ed. *Zuni, The Art and the People*, volumes 1,2,3, Grants, N.M.: Squaw Bell Traders, 1975, 1976, 1977.

Bennett, Edna Mae and John F. Bennett. *Turquoise Jewelry of the Indians of the Southwest*, Colorado Springs, Colo.: Turquoise Books, 1973.

Branson, Oscar T. *Fetishes and Carvings of the Southwest*, Tucson: Treasure Chest Publications, Inc., 1976.

———. *Turquoise, The Gem of the Centuries*, Santa Fe: Treasure Chest Publications, Inc., 1975.

Cushing, Frank Hamilton. *Zuni Fetishes, 1880-81*, Las Vegas: Facsimile Editions by KC Publications, 1988.

Davis, Mary L. and Greta Pack. *Mexican Jewelry*, Austin: University of Texas Press, 1963.

Dockstader, Frederick J. *Indian Art of the Americas*, New York: Museum of the American Indian, Heye Foundation, 1973.

Frank, Larry and Millard J. Holbrook II. *Indian Silver Jewelry of the Southwest, 1868-1930*, West Chester, Pa.: Schiffer Publishing Ltd., 1990.

Gillmor, Frances and Louisa Wade Wetherill. *Traders to the Navajos, The Story of the Wetherills of Kayenta*, Albuquerque: University of New Mexico Press, 1983.

Harvey, Byron III, E. W. Jernigan, and Gary Witherspoon. *White Metal Universe: Navajo Silver from the Fred Harvey Collection*, Phoenix: The Heard Museum, 1981.

———. *et al., Fred Harvey Fine Arts Collection, An Exhibition*, Phoenix: The Heard Museum, 1976.

Jacka, Lois Essary and Jerry Jacka, photographer. *Beyond Tradition*, Flagstaff, Ariz.: Northland Publishing Company, 1988.

James, H.L. *Rugs and Posts, The Story of Navajo Weaving and Indian Trading*, West Chester, Pa.: Schiffer Publishing, Ltd. 1988.

King, Dale Stuart. *Indian Silverwork of the Southwest, Illustrated—Volume Two*, Tucson: Dale Stuart King, 1976.

Levy, Gordon. *Who's Who in Zuni Jewelry*, Denver: Western Arts Publishing Company, 1980.

Lincoln, Louise, ed. *Southwest Indian Silver from the Doneghy Collection*, Minneapolis Institute of Arts, Austin: University of Texas Press, 1982.

Matthews, Washington. *Navajo Weavers, Navajo Silversmiths*, Palmer Lake, Colo.: Filter Press, 1968.

McNitt, Frank. *The Indian Traders*, Norman, Okla.: University of Oklahoma Press, 1972.

Mera, Harry P. *Indian Silverwork of the Southwest, Illustrated—Volume One*, Tucson: Dale Stuart King, 1974.

Moore, J. B. *The Catalogues of Fine Navajo Blankets, Rugs, Ceremonial Baskets, Silverware, Jewelry and Curios Originally Published Between 1903 and 1911*, Albuquerque: Avanyu Publishing Inc., 1987.

Ortiz, Alfonso, ed. "Southwest" vols. 9 and 10, *Handbook of North American Indians*, William C. Sturtevant, gen. ed., Washington: Smithsonian Institution, 1979, 1983.

Pogue, Joseph E. *Turquoise, Memoirs of the National Academy of Sciences*, vol. XII, part II, 1915, as reprinted by the Rio Grande Press, Inc., Glorietta, N.M., 1975.

Rodee, Marian. *Weaving of the Southwest*, West Chester, Pa.: Schiffer Publishing Ltd., 1987.

Rosnek, Carl and Joseph Stacey. *Skystone and Silver, The Collector's Book of Southwest Indian Jewelry*, Englewood Cliff, N.J.: Prentice-Hall, Inc., 1976.

Tanner, Clara Lee and Clay Lockett, John F. Tanner, Jerold R. Collings, Richard M. Howard. *Ray Manley's Collecting Southwestern Indian Arts and Crafts*, Tucson: Ray Manley Publishing, no date.

Turnbaugh, William A and Sarah Peabody Turnbaugh. *Indian Jewelry of the American Southwest*, West Chester, Pa.: Schiffer Publishing Ltd., 1988.

Williams, Lester, L., M.D. *C. N. Cotton and His Navajo Blankets*, Albuquerque: Avanyu Publishing Inc., 1989.

Woodward, Arthur, *Navajo Silver: A Brief History of Navajo Silversmithing*, Flagstaff, Ariz.: Northland Press, 1971.

Wright, Barton. *Hallmarks of the Southwest*, West Chester, Pa.: Schiffer Publishing Ltd., 1989.

Wright, Margaret Nickleson, *Hopi Silver, The History and Hallmarks of Hopi Silversmithing*, Flagstaff, Ariz.: Northland Press, 1989.

Index of Artists